A CULTURAL HISTORY OF INDIA

Śiva Dakṣiṇāmūrti (Śiva as Teacher). South side of East Gopura, Cidambaram, Tamilnadu. *c.* A.D. 1200. Ht. approx. 2 m

A Cultural History of India

Edited by

A. L. BASHAM

CLARENDON PRESS · OXFORD
1975

Oxford University Press, Ely House, London W. 1
GLASGOW NEW YORK TORONTO MELBOURNE WELLINGTON
CAPE TOWN IBADAN NAIROBI DAR ES SALAAM LUSAKA ADDIS ABABA
DELHI BOMBAY CALCUTTA MADRAS KARACHI LAHORE DACCA
KUALA LUMPUR SINGAPORE HONG KONG TOKYO

ISBN 0 19 821914 8

Printed in Great Britain by
William Clowes & Sons, Limited, London, Beccles and Colchester

PREFACE

THE *Legacy of India*, edited by G. T. Garratt, appeared in 1937. Its contributors included some of the ablest specialists of the time and several of its fifteen chapters are as valid today as they were at the time of writing. Nevertheless, the Second World War, the independence of India, and the change of attitudes since those two momentous events, have rendered some of the chapters quite out of date. Others have become obsolete as the result of the many discoveries made and new theories put forward since the war.

The need for a new edition was clear and Dr. Raghavan Iyer first drafted out a plan and approached a number of contributors some fifteen years ago. In 1968 the Clarendon Press asked me to assume responsibility for bringing the work to a conclusion, on the basis of the material collected by Dr. Iyer. I agreed to do so, and was given authority to commission authors and recast the plan of the volume in whatever way I might think fit. As is almost inevitably the case with large collaborative works, composed by contributors scattered across the world, the task took longer and proved more arduous than I had expected. But it is completed at last, and the result is offered to the reader, not without some misgiving, in the hope that he will accept it as a sincere attempt on the part of the contributors and the editor to explain India's heritage from the past, and the world's heritage from India. The original *Legacy*, for all its merits, contained several lacunae. In the attempt to fill these and to produce an even more comprehensive survey, it became increasingly clear that what was emerging could not be contained under the original title. It was no longer a 'Legacy', and so, not too immodestly I hope, it was decided to call the book *A Cultural History of India*[1].

While many of the chapters are the work of senior scholars with well-established international reputations I have not hesitated to enlist the help of younger and less well-known specialists, where this has seemed advisable. The very fact that contributions have been received from four of the five continents (and one contributor now works in the fifth, Africa) is surely evidence in itself of the importance of India in the world today.

Four of the contributions to Garratt's original *Legacy* have been retained. The venerable Professor Radhakrishnan's sincere and well-written chapter on Hinduism survives, with some editorial additions. Similarly, with editorial changes, I have retained the chapter by the late Professor S. N. Das Gupta, whose monumental survey of Indian Philosophy is still the most authoritative and comprehensive study of the subject. The late Professor H. G. Rawlinson's sympathetic chapter on India's cultural influence on the western world remains, but it is now divided into two and is brought up to date by a German

[1] Even as it stands, this book contains lacunae. I should have liked to include a chapter on the Gypsies, who are also part of the history of India; and the much-debated question of trans-Pacific contacts, of which there were certainly some in Pre-Columbian times, though very slight and indirect, might also have been considered. More serious is the absence of a chapter on the Indian dance, one of her greatest contributions to the world's culture.

scholar who has made a special study of the subject. The contribution of Martin Briggs on Indian Islamic Architecture is also kept, purged of several pages of discussion of matters which were once controversial, but are now no longer so. Other than these chapters, all the material is new.

In my editorial capacity I have made no attempt to force my numerous helpers to fit their contributions to a particular pattern, beyond explaining to them at the outset that I hoped that the book would emphasize the inheritance of modern India from the past, and her many bequests to the world of the present. My main task, except in respect of the chapters inherited from the Garratt *Legacy*, has been in trying to impose a uniform system of transliteration, orthography, and typographical conventions, in occasionally adding brief explanatory remarks, and in abridging a few contributions which were definitely over length.

It was part of my original plan to include chapters on 'India since Independence' and 'Pakistan since Independence', which would survey the main trends in the two countries over the last twenty-five years. But I finally decided against this in view of the size of the volume, and of the fact that many aspects of the contemporary situation were covered in other chapters. In the place of these two unwritten chapters a brief conclusion tries to draw the many and diverse threads of this book together. If in this I have allowed myself to make value judgements, some of which may be in disagreement with the statements of certain contributors, I put my views forward with all deference, as those of one who has had close contacts with the region of South Asia for many years, and has deep affection for the people of that region and for their culture.

Some readers may be irritated by the numerous diacritic marks to be found over the letters even of well-known Indian names. I take full responsibility for any annoyance this may cause. It has long been one of my minor tasks in life to encourage the English-speaking public to pronounce Indian names and terms with at least an approximation to accuracy, and the attention of readers is drawn to the notes on pronunciation which immediately follow this preface.

One of the most difficult problems facing the editor of a work such as this, in the present-day context, rests in its title. When the original *Legacy* was published the whole of the region of South Asia, with the exception of Nepal, the foreign affairs of which were controlled by India, and of Ceylon (now officially Śrī Lankā), which like India was part of the British Empire, was clearly and unequivocally India. The region now consists of five completely independent states, of which the Republic of India is unquestionably the largest in size and population. This fact, perhaps understandably, sometimes leads to expressions of protest when the word 'India' is used, in certain contexts, to cover regions beyond India's present-day frontiers. As an extreme example I remember a student from Kāthmandū indignantly declaring that his country had not received the credit that was its due because Gautama Buddha was invariably referred to as an Indian when in fact he had been a Nepalese. The endemic tension between India and Pakistan leads to similar protests, on grounds too numerous to mention. I recognize the force of national feeling, and I do not wish to give offence to citizens of the other countries of South Asia, but here inevitably 'India' must be understood at times in its broadest historical sense.

Let it be remembered in any case that the word *India* itself owes its derivation, not to India, but to Greece. Until the Muslims came to South Asia none of the inhabitants of that region ever thought of calling their country by such a name. The river Indus is known in Sanskrit as *Sindhu.* The Indus region, most of it now Pakistan, became a satrapy of the Achaemenian Empire of Iran under the name *Hindush*, the Indian *s* becoming Persian *h* by a regular sound-shift between the two languages. The Greeks, borrowing the word from the Iranians, called the river *Indos* and the country through which it flowed *India.* It would appear that for Herodotus the Indus basin was the whole of India.

At least from the time of Alexander of Macedon, and probably before him, the Greeks realized that beyond the Indus valley lay the valley of another even greater river which they called Ganges, from the Sanskrit *Gangā.* This latter name, incidentally, is now officially used in India, not only in Indian languages but also in English. Since it is the name by which those who dwell on its banks have known the sacred river for some 3,000 years, there seems no point in retaining the classical modification of the Indian word, and we have therefore adopted Gangā regularly in this book.

Later classical writers, though their geographical knowledge was very inaccurate, regularly applied the term India to the large land mass which extended from the Himālayas to the sea. The Arabic *Hind* and the Persian *Hindūstān* had the same connotation at a later date. Thus Europe and western Asia have applied the word India to the whole of mainland South Asia, irrespective of political boundaries, for over 2,000 years. In contexts such as this one, circumlocutions like 'the Indo-Pakistan subcontinent' are quite impossible. We are compelled to retain 'India', even if we go beyond the bounds of the present Indian Republic.

It remains for me to express my acknowledgements for much help and advice received in the course of my task. First I must thank Dr. Rāghavan Iyer, for collecting the first drafts of several chapters before he relinquished his editorship. I am very grateful to Professor J. Duncan M. Derrett for first suggesting that I take up the task, as well as for acting as my contact in London and for contributing an excellent chapter to the volume. I have to thank all the contributors for their generous co-operation and (in many cases) for their patience; I am especially grateful to a few of them who came to my help at the last minute, and produced chapters at very short notice. A number of colleagues gave me very helpful advice on the selection of contributors and other matters of importance—I think specially of Mr. W. G. Archer, Professor J. W. de Jong, Dr. H. H. E. Loofs, and Dr. S. A. A. Rizvi. To bring this complex editorial task to a successful conclusion I have been greatly helped by the very competent professional assistance of Mrs. Jocelyn Bergin, Secretary of the Department of Asian Civilizations, of Miss Mary Hutchinson, Departmental Research Assistant, and of the ladies of the typing pool of the Faculty of Asian Studies of the Australian National University. Dr J. C. Harle, of the Ashmolean Museum, Oxford, has given invaluable help with the illustrations. I must also thank the staff of the Clarendon Press for exemplary patience and for trusting my judgement.

Canberra, 1972 A. L. BASHAM

POSTSCRIPT. While this book has been in the press, several important political changes have taken place. The secession of East Pakistan, to become the independent state of Bangladesh, occurred shortly before the final typescript was submitted, and note of this has been taken in the text. The change of the familiar name Ceylon to Śrī Lankā came later, and I have not attempted to alter the text of this book accordingly. More recently the Indian state of Mysore has become Kārnātaka, and several small hill-states have been detached from the former Assam. It would delay the appearance of the book still further if I attempted to bring every reference to these regions of South Asia up to date, and I crave the reader's indulgence for inconsistencies in this respect.

A. L. B. (1974).

CONTENTS

LIST OF PLATES

LIST OF MAPS

AT END

CHRONOLOGY

B.C.		POLITICAL-ECONOMIC: NORTH		POLITICAL-ECONOMIC: SOUTH	CULTURAL AND RELIGIOUS	EVENTS ABROAD	B.C.
	PREHISTORY	Stone Age—Soan Industries		Stone Age—Madras Industries			
2500		*c.* 2400–1700 Indus Valley Civilization					2500
	INDUS VALLEY					*c.* 2300 Sargonid period of Sumer-Akkad Civilization	
2000					*c.* 2000–1500 Development of Indo-Āryan as distinct language	Āryans (Indo-Iranians) detached from other Indo-Europeans	2000
						c. 1750 Hammurabi	
1500	VEDIC PERIOD	*c.* 1500 Āryans invade India Cemetery H Harappā people				Āryans in Mitanni-Hurrian state	1500
					c. 1300–1000 Composition of *Rig Veda*		
1000		Āryans in Gangā Valley—states of Kosala, Kāśī, Videha–			*c.* 1000–800 Composition of *Brāhmanas*	Āryans (Iranians) occupy Iran	1000
900		Mahābhārata War				975 Phoenician trade in Indian goods	900
800		*c.* 800–550 Third stage—Āryan colonization reaches Bengal			Beginning of composition of *Mahābhārata*		800
700					*c.* 700 Pārśva Āruni Gautama *c.* 700–500 development of doctrine of trans-migration	7th–6th cent. Composition of *Iliad*	700
600					*c.* 563/6–483/6 Gautama Buddha	*c.* 600 Pythagoras and Orphism	600
500	BUDDHIST PERIOD			5th cent. Āryans in South Āryan colonization of Ceylon Irrigation in Ceylon	*c.* 500 Mahāvīra Composition of *Upanishads*	510 Darius of Persia sends Scylax down Indus Herodotus	500
					Composition of *Tripitaka*	428/7–348/7 Plato	
400							400
		326 Alexander in Panjāb 321 Chandragupta founds Mauryan Dynasty 305 defeats Seleucus Nicator			*c.* 350 Pānini Kautilya's *Arthaśāstra* in original form Gangā Valley terracottas	323 Death of Alexander of Macedon	
300							300
	Mauryas	*c.* 272/3–232 Aśoka		King Tissa, Ceylon Mauryans in Deccan Tamil kingdoms: Cholas, Pāndyas. Keralāputras, Satiyaputras	Sarnāth *stūpa* in original form *c.* 3rd cent. B.C. First Ajantā caves Earliest Tamil (Brāhmī) inscriptions *bhakti* in early form	Egypt, Greek Bactrian kingdoms and South-East Asia in contact with India 285–247 Ptolemy Philadelphus	
200							200
	AGE OF INVASIONS	*c.* 185 End of Mauryan Dynasty *c.* 183 Foundation of Śunga kingdom *c.* 150 Menander rules Indo-Greek Bactrian kingdom in Panjāb			Patanjali		
100							100
		Kānva kingdom comes to end Khāravela, King of Kalinga	SĀTAVĀHANA KINGDOM	Sīmuka founds Sātavāhana (Andhra) kingdom in Deccan	*c.* 1st cent. B.C. Final composition of *Rāmāyana*	Discovery of monsoon winds	
B.C. A.D.							B.C. A.D.
				c. 20–50 Arikamedu—South Indian site of trade with Rome	*c.* A.D. 10 Kārlī cave temple Aśvaghosha St. Thomas brings Syrian Christianity to South India 1st–3rd cents. Tamil *Ettuttogai*	Indianization of South-East Asia under way A.D. 68 Buddhism reaches China	
100		78 A.D. Foundation of Śaka Era			*c.* 100 Begram ivories	A.D. 99 Trajan receives Indian Mission in Rome	100

A.D.	POLITICAL-ECONOMIC				CULTURAL AND RELIGIOUS		EVENTS ABROAD	A.D.
		NORTH		SOUTH				
100	AGE OF INVASIONS	Kushānas in North-West Kanishka, Kushāna king Sakas (Scythians) in Kutch and Kathiāwar	SĀTAVĀHANAS		c. 100–200 Lawbook of Manu in final form 2nd cent.? Bhāsa Caraka, physician Fourth Buddhist Council—split between Mahāyāna and Hīnayāna c. 150 Nāgārjuna Gandhāra Art	30 B.C.–A.D. 550 Intercourse between India and Roman world	Growth of Gnosticism	100
200				c. 250 Decline of Sātavāhanas				200
300	CLASSICAL (GUPTA) PERIOD	319/20–335 Chandra Gupta I founds Gupta Dynasty c. 335–375 Samudra Gupta c. 375–414 Chandra Gupta II Vikramāditya	PALLAVAS OF KANCI (Madras State) MEDIAEVAL DYNASTIES OF SOUTH INDIA	c. 300 Rise of the Pallavas c. 4th cent. Mayūraśarman founds Kadamba kingdom	*Purānas* *Panchatantra*			300
400		400–411 Fa-hsien visits India c. 415–454 Kumāra Gupta Hūnas in North-West 454–467 Skanda Gupta			c. 400 Asanga Hindu temple, Sānchī Kālidāsa		476 End of Roman Empire	400
500		Toramāna and Mihirakula (Hūna rulers in Panjāb and Kashmīr) temporarily conquer N. India c. 540 End of Imperial Guptas c. 550 Gurjara dynasties first appear	FIRST CHĀLUKYA DYNASTY (West and Central Deccan)	c. 550 First Chālukya Dynasty	499 Āryabhata I, mathematician and astronomer		Development of Amitābha Buddhism in China	500
600	MEDIAEVAL DYNASTIES OF NORTHERN INDIA	606–47 Harsha(vardhana), king of Kānyakubja 629–45 Hsüan Tsang visits India 647 Gurjara ruling dynasties			c. 578 Bādāmi cave temple Last Ajantā paintings *Bhakti* movement in South India Bāna 628 Brahmagupta, mathematician and astronomer c. 660–710 Dandin c. 670 Māmallapuram temples 680–730 Bhavabhūti		632 Death of Muhammad Chinese sculpture shows Indian influence	600
700		712 Arabs in Sind c. 760 Rise of Pālas	PALAS OF BENGAL AND BIHAR GURJARA-PRATIHĀRAS	c. 757 Rāshtrakūtas overthrow Chālukyas	c. 775 Kailāsanātha Temple, Ellora		750–1258 'Abbāsid Caliphate in Baghdād Sanskrit works translated into Arabic	700
800		c. 800 Dharmapāla takes Kānyakubja Govinda III drives him out c. 806 Nāgabhata II takes Kānyakubja c. 836–890 Mihira Bhoja		Govinda III, Rāshtrakūta king c. 850 Rise of Cholas c. 888 Fall of Pallavas	9th cent. Śankarāchārya		c. 800 Borobudur temple, Java 845 Buddhism persecuted in China	800
900		890–910 Mahendrapāla 916 Indra III, Rāshtrakūta king, occupies Kānyakubja	CHOLAS OF THANJĀVŪR (Madras State) SECOND CHĀLUKYA DYNASTY (East Deccan)	c. 973 Chālukyas regain supremacy	c. 950–1050 building of Khajurāho temples			900
1000		1001 Mahmūd of Ghaznī begins raids on India 1024/5 destroys Somnath 1031 occupies Panjāb		985–1014 Rājarāja I, Chola ruler 1012–1044 Rājendra I increases Chola conquests	Chola bronzes c. 1000 Chola temple at Tanjore c. 1000 Abhinavagupta c. 1000–1070 Kshemendra 1031 Jain temple at Mt. Ābū		999–1030 Mahmūd of Ghaznī Albīrūnī Rājendra sends Chola naval exdedition to South-East Asia	1000

A.D.		POLITICAL-ECONOMIC				CULTURAL AND RELIGIOUS	EVENTS ABROAD	A.D.
		NORTH			SOUTH			
1050	MEDIAEVAL DYNASTIES	RĀJPUT dynasties	PALAS / SENAS, Bengal	HOYSALAS of C. & S. Deccan / CHĀLUKYAS | PĀNDYAS of Madurai | BAHMANI KINGDOM | AHMADNAGAR / CHOLAS OF THANJĀVŪR | VIJAYANAGARA EMPIRE / MEDIAEVAL DYNASTIES OF SOUTH INDIA			1038–1157 Saljūq Dynasty in Iran	1050
						Sūfism in India		
		c. 1118–99 Senas of Bengal			*c.* 1110 Rise of Hoysalas			
1100		1142–73 Kumārapala, king of Chaulukyas in Gujarāt				1137 Death of Rāmānuja		1100
		1173–1206 Muhammad bin Sām (Mu'izzu'd-Dīn Muhammad) of Ghūr				1150 Bhāskara II, mathematician and astronomer Hemachandra Hoysala-style architecture		
		1192 defeats Prithvīrāja at Tarāin			*c.* 1189 Fall of Chālukyas	?1197–1276 Madhva		
1200	DELHI SULTANATE PERIOD	Turkish Sultanate in Delhi				1198 First mosque built in Delhi		1200
		1229 Iltutmish recognized as Sultan of Delhi			*c.* 1216 Rise of Pāndyas	1225 Building of Qutb Mīnār *c.* 1230 Konārak sun-temple	*c.* 1200 Jayavarman VII builds Angkor Thom	
		1266–87 Balban				1253–1325 Amīr Khusrau		
					c. 1267 Fall of Cholas	1271–96 Jnāneśvara, *bhakti* writer		
		c. 1290 Rise of Khaljīs					1258 Baghdād destroyed by Mongols	
1300		1296–1316 'Alā'u'd-Dīn Khaljī 1300–1307 Three Mongol Invasions 1320 Khusrau Khān			*c.* 1310 Khaljī general Malik Kāfūr obtains Deccan for Muslims			1300
		1325–51 Muhammad bin Tughluq 1338 Bengal independent of Delhi			1336 Rise of Vijayanagara 1347 Deccan independent of Delhi with rise of Bahmanīs			
		1351–88 Fīrūz Shāh 1398 Tīmūr sacks Delhi				*c.* 1400–1470 Rāmānanda		
1400		1412 End of Tughluq Dynasty 1414–51 Saiyid Dynasty			1422–1526 Bīdar period of Bahman Dynasty	1440–1518 Kabīr		1400
		1451–89 Bahlol Lodī (founder of Afghan Lodī Dynasty)				1469–1539 Gurū Nānak 1473–1531 Vallabhāchārya 1485–1533 Chaitanya		
					1482 Fall of Bahmanīs			
					1498 Vasco da Gama reaches India		European and Chinese influence in South-East Asia increases	
1500		1506 Sultan Sikandar Lōdī founds Āgrā			Sultans of Ahmadnagar, Bijāpūr and Golconda become Shī'ī	1532–1623 Tulsīdās	1501–24 Shāh Ismā'īl, founder of Safavid Dynasty in Iran	1500
	MUGHALS	1526 Bābur in Delhi 1538–45 Shēr Shāh (Afghan) 1555 Humāyūn reconquers Delhi 1556–1605 Akbar			1565 Vijayanagara defeated by Deccan sultans	1542–1545 St. Francis Xavier in India Mughal school of painting		
		1583 Akbar receives merchants sent by Elizabeth I of England				1566 First printing press in India Building of Fatehpur-Sikrī 1579 Father Thomas Stevens		
		1605–1627 Jahāngīr				1598–1650 Tukārām	1581–1629 Shāh 'Abbās I	
1600		1608 East India Company at Surat 1628–58 Shāh Jahān			1633 End of Ahmadnagar	1603–4 Compilation of *Gurū Granth Sāhib* 1631–53 Building of Tāj Mahal	1598 Death of 'Abdullāh Khān Uzbeg of Transoxiana	1600
		1658–1707 Aurangzeb					1642–66 Shāh 'Abbas II	
					1677–80 Śivājī builds up Marātha state 1681–1707 Aurangzeb in Deccan	1699 Gurū Gobind Singh forms Sikh Khālsā	1662 Qushāshī takes Shattārī order to Malay archipelago 1683 Turks defeated at Vienna	
1700		Death of Aurangzeb						1700
		1739 Invasion of Nādir Shāh of Iran				'Kāngrā' Pahāri style of painting		
		1761 Third battle of Pānipat						
						1784 Sir William Jones founds Asiatic Society of Bengal 1772–1833 Rām Mohan Roy	1788–1860 Schopenhauer	
1800		1793 Permanent Settlement of Bengal				1800 Foundation of Fort William College		1800
	BRITISH INDIA	1835 Bentinck's Resolution on education				1817–98 Sayyid Ahmad Khān 1828 Foundation of Brāhmo (later Sabhā) Samāj	1808 F. von Schlegel publishes *On the Language and Wisdom of the Indians*	
		1857/8 Sepoy Mutiny and risings 1858 British Crown takes over from East India Company				1834–86 Rāmakrishna Bengal literary renaissance 1869–1948 Mahātma Gāndhī	1838 Opening of overland route to India	
		1876 Victoria becomes Empress of India				1872–1950 Srī Aurobindo 1875 Foundation of Ārya Samāj by Dayānanda Saraswatī	1869 Opening of Suez Canal	
		1878 Indian Association formed 1885 Foundation of Indian National Congress				1891 Foundation of Mahā Bodhī Society		
1900		1906 Foundation of Muslim League						1900
1910		1909 Morley–Minto Reforms 1914 Nationalist activity revives with Home Rule Movement				1913 Tāgore wins Nobel Prize for Literature	1914–18 First World War	1910
		1919–24 Khilāfat Conference 1919–42 Gāndhī's non-violent non-co-operation campaigns						
1920		1921 Montague–Chelmsford Reforms 1929–31 Round Table Conference						1920
1930		1930 Iqbāl suggests 'Pakistan' 1935 Government of India Act						1930
1940		1940 Pakistan Resolution 1947 Independence and partition					1939–45 Second World War	1940
1950								1950
1960		1961 Portuguese leave India						
1970		1971 Creation of Bānglādesh						1970

NOTES ON THE PRONUNCIATION OF INDIAN WORDS

EVERY Indian language has a complex phonetic system and contains phonemes which to the average speaker of English seem almost exactly the same, but to the Indian ear are completely different. Only after long practice can the hearing be trained to recognize these differences, or the vocal organs to pronounce them accurately. The scripts of Indian languages reproduce these sounds, but they can only be expressed in roman script by means of numerous diacritic marks below or above the letters. It is assumed that most of the readers of this book will not be students of Indian languages, and therefore a simplified system of transliteration has been used, which will give some idea of the approximate sound.

Words in classical languages are transliterated according to the simplified system mentioned above. Place-names in general follow the present-day official spellings of the governments of the countries of South Asia, as given in Bartholomew's Word Travel Map, *India, Pakistan and Ceylon*, 1970. Proper names of nineteenth- and twentieth-century Indians are given in the spelling which they themselves favoured, including the thoroughly inaccurate 'Tāgore', which should be Thākur, with the stress on the first syllable. Diacritic marks have been placed over the long vowels in such names, in order to give some idea of the correct pronunciation. Exceptions are made only in the case of a very few Anglicized words, like *Calcutta* and *Bombay*. In quotations from Sanskrit the full system of diacritics has been used, for the benefit of those who know something of the language.

Only four letters with diacritic marks are normally used—*ā*, *ī*, *ū* and *ś*. The first three distinguish long from short vowels. In most Indian languages *e* and *o* are always long, and therefore do not need diacritics.

VOWELS

a short is pronounced like *u* in 'hut', never like *a* in 'hat'. Bengālī speakers usually pronounce it like a short *o* as in 'hot'.

ā long, as in 'calm'.

e approximately as the vowel in 'same', but closer to the long *e* in French or German.

i as in 'pin'. The word *Sikh*, incidentally, should sound approximately like English 'sick'. The pronunciation like 'seek' seems to have been adopted by some Englishmen in India for this very reason, in order to avoid depressing overtones in the name of a tough, vigorous people.

ī as in 'machine'.

o, approximately as in 'so'. Closer to long *o* in French or German.

u as in 'bull', never as in 'but'. ('Punjāb', however, is an Anglicized spelling, and is more accurately written 'Panjāb'. In the case of this word we have deviated from our rule about using the accepted spelling, in order to avoid the pronunciation 'Poonjab', which one sometimes hears from speakers who are doing their best to be correct. The first syllable is like the English 'pun'.)

ū as in 'rule'.

ai as *y* in 'my'.

au as *ow* in 'how'.

CONSONANTS

Most of the consonants are pronounced roughly as in English, but special care should be taken of the aspirated consonants *kh*, *gh*, *chh*, *jh*, *th*, *dh*, *ph*, and *bh*. These are exactly like their unaspirated counterparts, *k*, *g*, *ch*, *j*, *t*, *d*, *p*, and *b*, but with a stronger emission of breath. English speakers often aspirate these letters when they begin a word or syllable. Thus the English 'cake', according to Indian phonetics, might appear as *kheik*. The distinction between the two sounds is immediately obvious to the Indian (except perhaps if his mother tongue is Tamil), but to the English speaker they are virtually alike. In a native Indian word, *th* is never pronounced as in 'thing', *ph* never as in 'phial' (except by some Bengālī speakers). The letter *j* is pronounced as in the English 'joke', never as in French or German.

The letter *ś* is pronounced approximately as *sh* in 'sheet'. The reader will find both *ś* and *sh* used in spelling Indian words in this book; this is not due to carelessness. The two represent two separate letters in Indian scripts, which are nowadays pronounced alike, or almost alike, by most Indians, though once the distinction was much more definite.

The letter *v* varies from region to region between the sounds of English 'v' and 'w'. Bengālīs and some other Indians regularly pronounce it as 'b'. The biggest difficulty of the Indian phonetic system—the distinction between the retroflex consonants, *ṭ*, *ṭh*, *ḍ*, *ḍh*, and *ṇ*, and the dentals, *t*, *th*, *d*, *dh*, and *n*—is too specialized for the ordinary reader who does not intend to learn an Indian language, and is not indicated in the system used here.

Urdū has imported several sounds from Arabic and Persian. Many speakers are inclined to pronounce words in these languages according to the Indian phonetic system, but educated Muslims attempt to pronounce them correctly. For example *q* is a very deep *k* sound pronounced with the throat in the position of swallowing. The 'rough breathing' indicated by '' is a similar deep swallow associated with a vowel, rather like the 'glottal stop' which replaces *t* in the broad Cockney pronunciation of 'bottle'. In Persian and Arabic loanwords *kh* is pronounced as *ch* in Scots or German 'loch'; *gh* is the same, but voiced, like the French *r*. The English sounds of *th* in 'worth' and 'worthy' occur in Arabic, and some speakers attempt them, but in India and Pakistan they are usually pronounced as English *s* and *z*, even by the educated.

STRESS

The amount of stress placed on any one syllable of a word varies with different speakers. With some, especially in the south, every syllable of a word has almost the same value, while others make a definite stress.

In classical Indian languages (Sanskrit, Pāli, and the Prākrits) the stress is on the last prosodically long syllable of a word, other than the final syllable. A prosodically long syllable is one containing a long vowel or diphthong (*ā*, *e*, *ī*, *o*, *ū*, *ai*, *au*) or a short vowel followed by two consonants. Thus *Himālaya* is stressed on the second syllable, not on the third.

The situation is more complicated in the modern languages because the short final *-a*, with which many Sanskrit words terminate, is no longer pronounced in most contexts, and is not usually written in transliteration. Thus Sanskrit *vihāra* 'monastery', with the stress on the second syllable, becomes the modern state of Bihār, with the stress on the last. Hence no simple rule can be given for the stress of words in modern languages, including Persian and Arabic loan-words, but in nearly all cases it is on a prosodically long syllable if the word contains one.

LIST OF CONTRIBUTORS

Ahmad, Aziz, D.Lit.(Lond.). Professor of Islamic Studies, University of Toronto, Canada.

Basham, A. L., D.Lit.(Lond.), Hon.D.Lit.(Kurukshetra), F.S.A., F.A.H.A. Professor of Asian Civilizations, Australian National University, Canberra, Australia.

Briggs, Martin S. (1882–), F.R.I.B.A. Formerly Lecturer, London University School of Architecture.

Burrow, T., M. A., Ph.D.(Cantab.), F.B.A. Boden Professor of Sanskrit and Fellow of Balliol College, Oxford, U.K.

Chandra, Pramod, Ph.D. Professor in the Departments of Art and of South Asian Languages and Civilization, University of Chicago, U.S.A.

Das Gupta, S. N. (1885–1952), M.A., D.Litt.(Cantab.), Hon.D.Litt.(Rome). Formerly Lecturer in Philosophy, University of Cambridge, and Professor of Mental and Moral Science, University of Calcutta, India.

Davidson, J. LeRoy, Ph.D.(Yale). Professor (and Chairman) of the Department of Art, University of California, Los Angeles, U.S.A.

Derrett, J. Duncan M., D.C.L.(Oxon.), LL.D., Ph.D.(Lond.). Professor of Oriental Laws in the University of London, Lecturer in Hindu Law in the Inns of Court School of Law, London.

Harrison, J. B., M.A.(Cantab.). Reader in the History of South Asia in the University of London.

Jairazbhoy, N., B.A.(Wash.). Associate Professor of Asian Studies, University of Windsor, Ontario, Canada.

Jordens, J. T. F., Lic.Philos., Ph.D.(Louvain). Reader in South Asian Civilization, Australian National University, Canberra, Australia.

Kripalani, Krishna, B.A.(Bombay), Bar-at-Law (Lincoln's Inn, London). Formerly Secretary, Sāhitya Akademi (National Academy of Letters), New Delhi, India.

Lal, B. B., M.A. Professor of Ancient Indian History, Culture and Archaeology, Jīvajī University, Gwalior, M.P., India. Formerly Director-General, Archaeological Department, Government of India, New Delhi, India.

Lamb, Alastair, Ph.D.(Cantab.). Formerly Professor of History, University of Ghana.

McLeod, Hew, M.A.(N.Z.), Ph.D.(Lond.). Associate Professor of History, University of Otago, Dunedin, New Zealand.

Marr, John, Ph.D.(Lond.). Lecturer in Tamil and Indian Music, School of Oriental and African Studies, University of London.

Owen, Hugh, Ph.D.(ANU). Lecturer in History, University of Western Australia, Perth, Australia.

Radhakrishnan, Sarvepalli (1888–), O.M., F.B.A., D.Litt., LL.D., D.C.L. Numerous honours and honorary degrees. Formerly Professor of

Philosophy, University of Calcutta, Professor of Eastern Religions, University of Oxford, Vice-Chancellor, Banares Hindu University. 1962–1967, President of the Republic of India.

Rawlinson, H. G. (1880–1957), C.I.E., M.A.(Cantab.). Formerly Principal, Deccan College, Poona.

Rawson, Philip, M.A.(Lond.). Curator, Gulbenkian Museum of Oriental Art, University of Durham, U.K.

Rizvi, S. A. A., M.A., Ph.D., D.Litt.(Agra), F.A.H.A. Reader in South Asian Civilization, Australian National University, Canberra, Australia.

Sangharakshita, Bhikshu

Spear, T. G. Percival, O.B.E., M.A., Ph.D.(Cantab.). Fellow of Selwyn College, Cambridge. Formerly Hon. Reader in History, Delhi University, and University Lecturer in History, University of Cambridge, U.K.

Thapar, Romila, Ph.D.(Lond.). Professor of Historical Studies and Chairman of the Centre for Historical Studies, Jawaharlal Nehru University, New Delhi, India.

Upadhye, A. N., M.A., D.Litt. Professor of Jainology and Prakrit, University of Mysore, India.

Warder, A. K., Ph.D.(Lond.). Professor of Sanskrit and Indian Studies, University of Toronto, Canada.

Wilhelm, Friedrich, Dr.Phil. Professor of Indology and Tibetology at the University of Munich, West Germany.

Winter, H. J. J., Ph.D., D.Sc.(Lond.). Senior Lecturer in Education at the University of Exeter, U.K.

CHAPTER I

Introduction

by A. L. BASHAM

THERE are four main cradles of civilization, from which elements of culture have spread to other parts of the world. These are, moving from east to west, China, the Indian subcontinent, the 'Fertile Crescent', and the Mediterranean, especially Greece and Italy. Of these four areas India deserves a larger share of the credit than she is usually given, because, on a minimal assessment, she has deeply affected the religious life of most of Asia and has provided very important elements in the culture of the whole of South-East Asia, as well as extending her influence, directly and indirectly, to other parts of the world.

It has been commonly believed in the West that before the impact of European learning, science, and technology 'the East' changed little if at all over many centuries. The 'wisdom of the East', unchanging over the millennia, it was thought, preserved eternal verities which Western civilization had almost forgotten. On the other hand 'the East' was not ready to enter into the rough and tumble of the modern world without the guidance for an indefinite period of more developed Western countries.

These ideas were no doubt held in good faith by many well-informed people of earlier generations, and there may have been a grain of truth in them from the point of view of the nineteenth century. But there is no reason to believe that the rate of change in India in earlier times was any slower than that of other parts of the world. It was only from the sixteenth century onwards, when a combination of many factors led to increasingly rapid technological and scientific advances in Europe, that the myth of the changelessness of Asia began to appear.

In fact India has always been steadily changing. The civilization of the Guptas was different from that of the Mauryas, and that of medieval times was different again. The Muslims altered conditions considerably, and the high flowering of Indian Muslim civilization under the four great Mughals brought yet more changes. The religious life of India, for all her 'ancient wisdom', has changed greatly over the centuries. Between the time of the early Greek philosophers and that of St. Thomas Aquinas, Buddhism developed into a great religious movement in India, changed its outlook almost completely, declined, and finally sank back into the Hinduism from which it had emerged, but only after Buddhist missionaries had spread their message throughout half of Asia. The Athenian Acropolis was at least 500 years old before the first surviving stone Hindu temple was built. Some of the most popular gods of Hinduism, for instance, Ganeśa and Hanumān, are not attested until well after the time of Christ. Certain other features of Hinduism also, for instance the cult of the divine Rāma and the complex and difficult system of physical training known as *hatha yoga*, are centuries later than Christianity.

Yet the older strata of India's cultural life go back far beyond anything we have in the West. The whole of the *Rig Veda* had been composed long before the *Iliad*, and there is hardly anything in the Old Testament in its present form which is as old even as the latest Rig Vedic hymns. Some practices and beliefs of popular Hinduism, for instance the cults of the sacred bull and the *pīpal* tree, are as old as the prehistoric Harappā culture, and probably even older. In fact every generation in India, for over 4,000 years, has bequeathed something, if only a very little, to posterity.

No land on earth has such a long cultural continuity as India, since, though there were more ancient civilizations, notably in Egypt and Iraq, these were virtually forgotten by the inhabitants of those lands, and were overlaid by new intrusive cultures, until nobody remembered the *Book of the Dead* or the *Epic of Gilgamesh*, and great kings such as Ramesses II or Hammurabi were not recorded in any living tradition. Only nineteenth-century scholarship resurrected them from oblivion, and if they are now national heroes, remembered by every school-child in their respective lands, this is not thanks either to the historical genius or to the retentive folk-memory of the countries concerned.

On the other hand in India the brāhman still repeats in his daily worship Vedic hymns composed over 3,000 years ago, and tradition recalls heroic chieftains and the great battles fought by them at about the same time. In respect of the length of continuous tradition China comes second to India and Greece makes a poor third.

The pre-Vedic Harappā culture bequeathed to later times sacred animals and trees, the Mother Goddess, the preoccupation with personal cleanliness, and, less certainly, other aspects of Indian culture. From the Vedic Āryans came many of the gods, the Vedic hymns, some of the most important personal rituals of Hinduism, the patriarchal and patrilineal family system, and the horse. Later Vedic times (*c.* 1000–600 B.C.) brought the passion for speculation on ultimate causes, the quest for the Absolute, the doctrine of transmigration, the search for release from the round of rebirth, and mystical gnosis. In social life and material culture the same period saw the crystallization of the four classes (*varnas*) of Hindu society, the introduction of iron from western Asia, the domestication of the elephant, the development of kingdoms out of tribal chieftainships.

In the 300 following years coined money became common, and writing, known in the time of the Harappā culture and later apparently forgotten, became widespread. Heterodox teachers, chief of whom was the Buddha, spread new doctrines which bypassed the gods, the Vedas, and the brāhmans, and the area of civilization steadily expanded into the remoter parts of the subcontinent.

Political developments over the preceding period led to the first great empire of India, that of the Mauryas, when for the first time most of the subcontinent was united under a single government. This period (*c.* 320–185 B.C.) produced the Machiavellian system of statecraft associated with the name of the minister Kautilya, the reputed author of the famous *Arthaśāstra*. From the Mauryas also come the earliest surviving stone sculpture of India, the oldest artificial caves, and the most ancient Buddhist *stūpas*. Under Aśoka (*c.* 272–232 B.C.) Buddhism increased its influence, and was taken to Ceylon.

The 500 years between the Mauryas and the Guptas (*c.* 184 B.C.–A.D. 320) saw tremendous developments in Indian civilization, partly due to fresh influences brought in by various invaders and traders, and partly the result of internal developments. New forms of devotional religion emerged, centring round the gods Vishnu and Śiva, and these led to the composition of the *Bhagavad Gītā*, now the most influential text of Hinduism. Buddhism developed a theology, the Mahāyāna, which was carried to China. Schools of law appeared, codifying in written form earlier traditions. The two great epics of India, the *Mahābhārata* and the *Rāmāyana*, were edited in something like their present form. Courtly literature began developing out of vanished prototypes: drama, ranging from the heroic to the sentimental, and verse, wonderful in its polish and ingenuity yet often filled with deep and sincere feeling. Logically reasoned philosophical schools emerged, as distinct from the older religious teachers, most of whose arguments were analogical. Contact with South-East Asia became closer with the spread of trade, and that region began to adopt many features of the religion and culture of India. These are only a few of the many innovations of this, perhaps the most formative period of Indian history before the nineteenth century.

The period from the rise of the Guptas to the death of Harshavardhana (320–647) can truly be called the classical period of Indian civilization. In this age the greatest sculpture of ancient India was produced, and the finest literature written, in the poems and plays of Kālidāsa. This was the time of the best surviving ancient Indian mural painting, typified by Ajantā. Knowledge grew also in this period. India's most important practical contribution to the world, the system of place notation of numerals, with nine digits and a zero, was known by A.D. 500, and led to the great development of Indian mathematics and astronomy. The recording of ancient legends and traditions in the *Purānas* began. The Mother Goddess, after centuries of neglect, became an important object of worship again. Stone-built temples appeared throughout the land.

Between the death of Harshavardhana and the coming of Islam (647–*c.* 1200) the ecstatic devotional religion (*bhakti*), associated with the singing of hymns in the common tongue, appeared in Tamilnādu, later to spread all over the subcontinent. Temples became larger and grander, with spiring towers. The system of *hatha yoga* was developed, and tantrism, with its sacramentalization of sex, spread in both Hinduism and Buddhism. In Śankara and Rāmānuja Hindu religious philosophy saw its greatest teachers. Some of the finest schools of bronze-casting in the world appeared in Bengal and Tamilnādu. The former region also developed a fine school of miniature painting.

With the coming of Islam fresh cultural influences made themselves felt. The sultanate period (1192–1526) saw the introduction of new styles of architecture, bringing the dome and arch. New schools of miniature painting, both Muslim and Hindu, emerged. Sūfī teachers disseminated the doctrines of Islam and helped to make the religious climate of northern India favourable to the spread of popular devotional Hinduism from the south. Paper was introduced, slowly replacing the traditional Indian writing materials—palm-leaf and birch-bark. The Urdū language began to appear as the lingua franca of northern India, and poets began to compose in the everyday languages instead of classical Sanskrit.

The great days of the Mughal Empire (1526–1707) witnessed the perfection of the schools of Muslim architecture and miniature painting, with the production of such splendid buildings as the Tāj Mahal at Āgrā. Cannon and smaller fire-arms began to be used in warfare. Europeans established trading stations at various ports, and through them, especially the Portuguese, new crops were introduced into India, among them the potato, tobacco, the pineapple, and, surprisingly, the spice which nowadays is commonly thought typical of India, the chilli pepper. The Sikh religion was born just as this period began, as a small devotional sect, and at about the time when the period concluded it was reborn as a martial brotherhood, to play an important part in the confused political life of the following century.

The eighteenth century saw the break-up of the Mughal Empire and the steady expansion of the power of the British East India Company. It was a time of general cultural decline in India, but the genius of the land was still at work. The Urdū language, little used hitherto as a medium of literary expression, became the vehicle of great poetry at the decadent courts of Delhi and Lucknow; while in the Himālayan foot-hills, at the end of the century at the petty courts of local mahārājas, by some unexplainable miracle, there worked painters who produced works of unprecedented beauty and sensitivity. With the nineteenth century the subcontinent was exposed to the full force of Western influence, and innovations are too numerous to list.

This cursory survey of the history of cultural change in India is sufficient in itself to show that, as long as civilization has existed there, the country has never been stagnant, but has steadily developed through the ages. India has enjoyed over 4,000 years of civilization, and every period of her history has left something to the present day.

As well as this great legacy of the human past, the people of the subcontinent have another inheritance from Nature itself—the land and its climate. We cannot understand South Asia without knowing something about what its people have received from the primeval forces which shaped the surface of the earth millions of years before man existed. In this sense perhaps India's most important inheritance is the great chain of the Himālayas, without which the land would be little more than a desert.

As the plateau of Central Asia grows warmer in the spring, the warm air rises and winds bearing heavy masses of cloud are attracted towards the high tableland from the Indian Ocean. The movement of the clouds is interrupted by the mountains, and they shed their burden of rain upon the parched, overheated land. The monsoon, beginning in June, lasts for about three months, and brings water for the whole year. Except along the coast and in a few other specially favoured areas, there is little or no rain in other seasons, and thus the life of almost the whole subcontinent depends on the monsoon.

The conservation and just sharing out of the available water among the cultivators is a very important factor in the life of India. It has been one of the main concerns of Indian governments for over 2,500 years and indeed the high civilization which is discussed in the pages of this book has depended, and still largely depends, on irrigation, promoted and supervised by government, for its very existence. In the past, whenever the rains have been inadequate, there has been famine; whenever a local government has lost grip and become ineffective, irrigation has been neglected, dams have broken, canals have been choked with mud and weed, and great hardship has resulted. Thus villagers have learnt to co-operate independently of their rulers, by forming their own village government, under a committee of locally respected leaders, the *panchāyat*, to care for matters of common concern such as irrigation, and to settle disputes as far as possible outside the royal courts. On a large scale the climate has perhaps encouraged autocracy, but at the local level it has necessitated government by discussion.

Let it not be thought that the South Asian climate is one which encourages idleness or quietism. There are certainly periods in the agricultural year when little work can be done in the fields, but in a different way, in most parts of the subcontinent, the challenge of nature is just as serious as it is in northern Europe or America. The driest part of the year is also the hottest, in April and May, and it is perhaps just as difficult to sustain life in such conditions as it is in the cold northern winter. The rainy season brings problems of another kind—almost constant heavy rain, floods destroying thousands of lives, rivers changing their courses, epidemics, and stinging insects, some of which carry the germs of such diseases as malaria and elephantiasis. In the winter season, moreover, though the days are mild and sunny, the nights may be very cold, especially in Pakistan and the western part of the Gangā basin. In such times, when the midnight temperature may be below freezing-point or only a little above it, deaths from exposure still occur. Only in the tropical coastal areas of the peninsula would climatic conditions permit the survival of a considerable population without much hard work and foresight, sustained by coconuts, bananas, and the abundant fish of the Indian Ocean; and in these favoured areas the population passed the limit at which such a way of life was possible over 2,000 years ago.

The abundant bounty of tropical and sub-tropical nature has been qualified by extreme heat, extreme rainfall, and extreme dryness in different parts of the year. In fact the climate of the subcontinent tends to extremes, and possibly this too has influenced the Indian character and attitude to life, because, though one of the greatest of India's teachers counselled 'the Middle Way', succeeding generations have not always taken this course, and the extremes of rigorous asceticism and abandoned luxury have often gone hand in hand.

South of the Himālayas lie the great plains of the subcontinent, the centres from which civilization expanded in ancient times. Composed of deep silt carried down by the rivers Indus (Sind, Sindhu) and Gangā (Ganges) these plains are naturally very fertile, but for centuries they have supported a dense population, whose peasants used the most easily available form of manure, cow-dung, as fuel. Hence the fertility of the plains declined, until by the end of the last century many areas had reached a rock bottom of productivity, from which they have begun to emerge only recently, with the introduction of artificial fertilizers and the spread of knowledge of better agricultural methods. In ancient days, however, the fertility and the healthy well-fed peasantry of India were noticed by foreign travellers from the Greek Megasthenes (*c*. 300 B.C.) onwards.

South of the Gangā are the Vindhya Mountains and the long and beautiful River Narmadā, dividing the north from the plateau region of Mahārāshtra, generally called the Deccan (from Sanskrit *dakshina*, 'south'). The region, less naturally fertile than the great plains, has been for at least 2,000 years the home of tough martial peasants who, whenever energetic leadership appeared to consolidate their clans, would take advantage of the political weakness of their neighbours to raid the wealthier lands to the north, south-east, and south.

The Deccan plateau becomes steadily less rugged and more fertile as one proceeds south and south-east. Along the eastern littoral of the peninsula are fertile riverine plains, the most important historically being that of Tamilnādu, reaching from Madras to Cape Comorin (Kanyākumārī, the extreme southern tip of India). Here, over 2,000 years ago, the Tamil people developed a fairly advanced civilization independently of the Āryan north; this region has throughout its history maintained a consciousness of its differences from the north, and has cherished its own language, while remaining part of the whole Indian cultural area; there may be an analogy between the Tamil attitude to the northern Āryans and that of the Welsh to the English, with the difference that, while many Welshmen have English as their mother tongue, few if any Tamils have a mother tongue other than Tamil.

Yet another inheritance of India from the distant past is her people. Despite the difficult mountain passes and the wide seas barring access to India, people have been finding their way there from the days of the Old Stone Age, when small hordes of primitive men drifted into the subcontinent. These are probably the ancestors of one of India's three main racial types—the Proto-Australoid, so called because of the resemblance to the Australian Aborigines. In India the most pure Proto-Australoid type is to be found among the tribal peoples of the wilder parts of the peninsula, but Proto-Australoid features can be traced almost everywhere in the subcontinent, especially among people of low caste. The ideal type is short, dark-skinned, broad-nosed, and large-mouthed.

The next main stratum in the population of India is the Palaeo-Mediterranean, often loosely called Dravidian, a word not now favoured by anthropologists. These people seem to have come to south Asia from the west, not very long before the dawn of civilization in the Indus valley, and they may have contributed to the foundation of the Harappā culture. Graceful and slender, with well-chiselled features and aquiline noses, the ideal type is particularly to be found among the better-class speakers of Dravidian languages, but it also occurs everywhere in the subcontinent.

Then, in the second millennium B.C., came the Āryans, speakers of an Indo-European language which was the cousin of those of classical Europe. Some have suggested that these people came in two or more waves, the earlier invaders being round-headed (brachycephalic) people of the type called Alpine or Armenoid, and the later long-headed folk, typical Caucasoids, similar in build to northern Europeans. Long before they entered India the people who called themselves Āryans had intermixed with other peoples, and their advent meant a severe cultural decline, which lasted for many centuries. Only when

Āryan culture was fertilized by the indigenous culture did it begin to advance, to form the classical civilization of India. There are good arguments for the view that in the finished product non-Āryan elements are more numerous than Āryan. Nowadays the Caucasoid type is chiefly to be found in Pakistan, Kashmīr, and the Panjāb, but even here one rarely meets pure or nearly pure specimens. As one proceeds east and south the type becomes progressively rarer.

These three, the Proto-Australoid, the Palaeo-Mediterranean, and the Caucasoid or Indo-European, are the most strongly represented racial types among the inhabitants of India; but they are by no means the only ones. Almost every race of Central Asia found its way to India. Turks provided the ruling families in much of what is now Pakistan long before the coming of the Muslims, who were also Turks. Mongolians of various races have been entering India over the Himālayan and north-eastern passes since long before history. The Muslim ruling classes imported numerous African slaves, who have long since merged with the general population. Persian and Arab traders settled along the west coast from before the Christian era. Some married Indian women, and the descendants have become indistinguishable from the rest of the population. Others, such as the small but vigorous Pārsī community, have kept their stock pure. The various European traders and conquerors have left their mark also. Along the west coast of India and Ceylon an appreciable quantity of Portuguese blood circulates in the veins of the general population, while elsewhere in India the so-called Anglo-Indian community is the result of many marriages and liaisons between European (not only British) soldiers and traders and Indian women.

Thus, in reading these chapters, we must remember also India's enduring inheritance of climate, land, and people, the basis on which her high civilization has been built, and which will remain, more or less unchanging, to condition the lives of her people in all their triumphs and vicissitudes in future centuries.

PART ONE

THE ANCIENT HERITAGE

CHAPTER II

The Indus Civilization

by B. B. LAL

MORE than 4,000 years ago there flourished in the north-western parts of the Indo-Pakistan subcontinent a civilization which, deriving its name from the main river of the region, is known as the Indus civilization. In fact, however, it extended far beyond the limits of that valley—from Sutkagen-dor, on the sea-board of south Balūchistān, in the west to Alamgīrpur, in the upper Gangā-Yamunā *doāb* in Uttar Pradesh, in the east; and from Ropar, almost impinging upon the sub-Himālayan foot-hills, in the north to Bhagatrāv, on the estuary of the Kim, a small river between the Narmadā and Tāptī, in the south. In other words from west to east the Indus civilization covered an area of 1,600 kilometres, and from north to south of 1,100 kilometres, and it will not be surprising if future discoveries widen the horizons still further. This is an area much greater than that occupied jointly by the contemporary civilizations of Egypt and Mesopotamia. And throughout the region a notably high standard of living was reached which is reflected in almost every walk of life.

The first thing that strikes a visitor to an Indus site—be it Harappā or Mohenjo-dāro in Pakistan or Kālibangan, Lothal, or Surkotadā in India—is the town-planning. One finds the streets and lanes laid out according to a set plan: the main streets running from north to south and the cross-streets and lanes running at right angles to them. At Kālibangan, among the north–south streets there was a principal one, 7·20 metres wide, while the other north–south streets were three-quarters of its width. The cross-streets and lanes were, once again, half or a quarter of the width of the narrower streets from north to south. Such typical and minutely planned residential areas, often called the 'lower towns', were themselves only a part of the entire settlement complex. For at Harappā, Mohenjo-dāro, Kālibangan, and Surkotadā, there was a 'citadel', smaller in area than the 'lower town' and invariably located to the west of it. At Lothal, although no 'citadel' as such has been found, a similar conception seems to have existed, for the more important structures rested in a group on a high mud-brick platform. In marked contrast might be cited the contemporary example of Ur in Mesopotamia, where there was no rigorous planning of this kind, the main street wandering and curving as it wished.

Both at Harappā and Mohenjo-dāro the houses were made of kiln-burnt bricks. At Kālibangan and Lothal too, although mud bricks were used for most of the residential houses, kiln-burnt bricks in large quantities were used for drains, wells, and bathing-platforms, and in particular for the dockyard at the latter site (below, p. 14). Such bricks were rare in contemporary Mesopotamia or Egypt. At Mohenjo-dāro and Kālibangan, where large areas have been excavated, an average house consisted of a courtyard around which were situated four to six living-rooms, besides a bathroom and a kitchen. Larger houses, however, might have up to thirty rooms, and the presence of staircases in many of them indicates a second storey. For the supply of fresh water, most of the houses had their own wells, and in addition, there were public wells. Sullage-water was discharged through well-covered street-drains made of kiln-burnt bricks. At intervals they were provided with man-holes for clearance.

The citadel at Mohenjo-dāro contained many imposing buildings, all made of kiln-burnt bricks: for example, the great bath, the college, the granary, and the assembly hall. In the bath the actual tank measured 12 metres in length (north to south), 7 metres in width, and 2·5 metres in depth. It was approached by two staircases, one each on the northern and southern sides. The floor and side-walls of the tank were rendered watertight by the use of gypsum in the mortar, while the side-walls were further backed by a damp-proof course of bitumen. Around the tank ran a pillared veranda from which there was access to a series of what might be called 'dressing-rooms'. The tank was fed with water from a large well situated in the complex, while, for the discharge of used water, there was a corbelled drain in the south-west corner.

Whether the bath had a purely secular use or had a religious function as well is very difficult to say. However, it has been surmised that beneath the *stūpa* of the Kushāna period, situated hardly fifty metres to the east of the bath, there may be the remains of a temple. And this is not improbable, for a kind of worship-place has indeed been identified within the citadel at Kālibangan, closely associated with a well and bathing-platforms (below, p. 14).

Between the bath and the *stūpa* lie the remains of a building 83 metres long and 24 metres wide, with a large number of rooms on three sides of a 10-metre square courtyard. The presence of staircases suggests the possibility of there having been some more rooms, besides terraces, on the first floor. From the general disposition of the building, the excavator was inclined to regard it as the residence of 'the high priest' or of a 'college of priests'.

Juxtaposed to the south-western wall of the bath was a granary covering an over-all area of 55 by 37 metres. It consisted of a podium formed by 27 blocks of solid brickwork, arranged in three rows of nine each, and separated one from the other by passages about a metre wide. The latter were evidently provided for the circulation of air underneath the timbered floor of the storage hall that stood above the podium. Built on to the northern side of the podium was a platform, with a ramp going down to ground level outside. To this, one can imagine, were brought wagons full of wheat and barley (below, p. 13) for unloading.

There are many other buildings within the citadel, but one is particularly striking. Though not completely excavated, it covers an area of over 750 square metres. It has twenty massive piers of kiln-burnt bricks arranged in four rows of five each, with traces of corresponding pilasters at the ends. Thus there are six aisles from north to south and at least five from west to east, the further plan on the east being incomplete. The building was very probably an assembly hall, which would fit the general context of other specialized buildings in the citadel.

Harappā was regarded as another 'capital' of the 'Indus Empire'.[1] Here hardly any excavation has been done in the 'lower city' to the east of the 'citadel'. In fact, even within the citadel, the sporadic diggings have not helped very much to produce a coherent picture. Of the enclosing wall, however, many details are available. A section cut across it at about the middle of the western side showed that it was built of mud bricks, externally revetted with kiln-burnt bricks. The mud-brick wall measured over 13 metres in width at the base and tapered inwards on both the exterior and interior. At places it was found to rise to a height of about 15 metres above the surrounding plain. Behind it was a 7-metre-high mud-brick platform upon which stood the buildings inside the citadel. Externally, the citadel wall was punctuated at places by rectangular towers, and the one at the north-west corner shows that it was substantially rebuilt on three occasions.

The lack of data regarding the buildings inside the citadel is more than compensated for by what has been excavated to the north. In its shadow, there lay the workmen's quarters, their working-platforms, and a granary, the entire complex suggesting a high degree of regimentation of the working population. Enclosed by a boundary wall, of which only odd bits are now to be seen, the workmen's quarters stood in two rows running from east to west. Each dwelling, covering an area of about 17 by 7 metres, comprised two rooms and was entered through an oblique passage, evidently so arranged for privacy. The remarkable uniformity of these quarters reminds one of modern barracks and all that they imply.

Immediately to the north of these quarters have been identified five east–west rows of working-platforms, and, although six is the maximum number excavated in any row, there were doubtless many more. Made of kiln-burnt bricks set on edge in circular rings, each platform measured about 3·5 metres in diameter. Excavation has revealed a central hole about 60 centimetres in diameter into which, it is surmised, was inserted a wooden mortar for pounding grain. Such a guess is supported, on the one hand, by the presence of straw or husk and wheat and barley in the hole and on the platform and, on the other, by the location of a granary barely 100 metres to the north.

Why the granary at Harappā, unlike that at Mohenjo-dāro, was located outside the citadel is a matter for debate. The proximity of the river Rāvī may be the answer, enabling the harvest from the neighbouring countryside to be transported by water direct to the granary. As to its safe control, which its location within the fortified citadel would have otherwise guaranteed, it may be assumed that an ever-vigilant eye was kept over the entire area, right from the coolie quarters through the workshops up to the granary. Comprising two blocks, the granary complex occupied an over-all area of 55 by 43 metres. Each of the blocks contained six storage halls, each hall measuring 15 by 6 metres externally. As in the case of the Mohenjo-dāro example, here also air-ducts were provided underneath the floor.

Situated on the left bank of the now-dry river Ghaggar in Rājasthān, Kālibangan reveals the same pattern of planning as do Mohenjo-dāro and

[1] This expression is rather loosely used, for there is no concrete evidence to prove that the system of government was that of an empire. The possibility of there having been city states, as in Mesopotamia, should not be overlooked.

Harappā, with a 'citadel' on the west side and a 'lower town' on the east, and also it tells us rather more. Thus the citadel complex, fortified with a 7-metre-thick mud-brick wall with towers at intervals, consisted of two equal and well-defined parts, one to the south containing several large mud-brick platforms meant for specific purposes and the other to the north containing residential houses, perhaps of those concerned with the affairs in the southern part. The platforms were separate one from the other as also from the fortification wall, there thus being regular passages around them. Access to the top of the platforms was by steps leading from the passages. On top of one of the platforms were located a well, lined with kiln-burnt bricks, several bathing-pavements of the same material, and a series of juxtaposed clay-lined pits running in a north–south alignment, of which at least eight have been identified. Each pit measured about 60 by 45 centimetres and contained, besides ash and charcoal, a prominent stump of burnt clay in the middle, measuring about 25 centimetres in height and 10 centimetres in diameter. In other similar pits, usually found singly in the houses in the lower city, have been discovered biconvex terracotta 'cakes', placed around the clay stump. Thus it would appear that the entire complex on this platform—the well, the bathing-pavements, and the clay-lined 'fire-altars'—had a ritualistic purpose. A similar indication is given by another platform on the top of which were located a well, a 'fire-altar', and a rectangular pit (1 × 1·25 metres) lined with kiln-burnt bricks and containing antlers and bones of cattle, which seem to suggest a sacrifice.

The lower town at Kālibangan, while showing the usual grid pattern of main thoroughfares, subsidiary streets, cross-streets, and lanes, revealed that it too was fortified. Piercing the fortification wall, which was made of mud bricks, were at least two gateways, one on the northern side leading to the river and another on the west providing access to the citadel. (It would not be surprising if further excavations on the periphery of the lower town at Mohenjo-dāro brought to light the remains of a similar town wall. At any rate, an attempt is worth making.) In width the Kālibangan lanes and streets followed a set ratio: thus, while the lanes were 1·8 metres wide, the streets, in multiples of the former, were 3·6, 5·4, and 7·2 metres wide.

Lothal, situated not far from the Gulf of Cambay, an inlet of the Arabian Sea, is the only site with a dockyard; this is 216 metres in length (north to south) and 37 metres in width, situated immediately to the east of the township. It is lined with a wall 1·2 metres thick of kiln-burnt bricks, now rising to a maximum height of 4·3 metres. In the southern part of the eastern wall is a 7-metre-wide gap, and excavation further to the east, in continuation of this opening, has revealed the bed of a channel of identical width. It is surmised that it was through this channel that the dockyard was connected with the Bhogavo river, which, though now located about 2 kilometres away, flowed much nearer in ancient times. It is thought that boats entered the dockyard through this channel at high tide, when the water swelled up and pushed upstream. For the discharge of excess water a sizeable spill-channel was provided in the southern wall. The boats, it would appear, returned to the river when the tide was falling.

In this context, reference may also be made to a structure located not far from the dockyard to the south-west. It consisted of twelve rectangular blocks made of mud bricks, arranged in four rows of three each and covering an over-all area of 17 by 14 metres. Between the blocks ran criss-cross channels, evidently air-ducts, over a metre in width. It is surmised that overlying these blocks was a spacious hall of timber, some slight evidence of the latter being the debris of charcoal and fragments of charred wood found in the air-ducts. In these ducts were also found over 100 lumps of clay, now partly or wholly baked, bearing impressions of typical Harappan seals (below, p. 16) on one side and of reeds on the other. These were evidently sealings on packages made of reed. What the packages contained we can only guess. In the context of the dockyard, however, it seems likely, though not proved, that this building was a warehouse where commodities ready for export or received from abroad were temporarily stored.

About 270 kilometres north-west of Ahmadābād in Gujarāt is Surkotadā. The settlement pattern of Harappā, Mohenjo-dāro, and Kālibangan is repeated here, but with a difference. The citadel and the lower town were joined, although their relative directional position remained the same, the former to the west and the latter to the east. As at Kālibangan, both the citadel and the lower town were fortified. Each had its independent entrance, located on the southern side; there was also an intercommunicating gate between the two. In addition to mud bricks, stone rubble which is easily available in the neighbourhood was liberally used for construction. The massive wall of the citadel can still be seen to a height of 4·5 metres (Pl. 3). No less impressive is the gateway complex of the citadel, with its ramps and staircases (Pl. 4).

So much for the structural remains which, apart from revealing the architecture and town-planning of the time, have also thrown valuable light on organizational, religious, and commercial aspects of the life of the people. Now we shall consider the finds—the pottery, terracottas, sculptures, seals, weights, etc.

Pottery is found in very large quantities at all ancient sites and may well be regarded as the index to the economic and artistic standards of the population—standards which may also be reflected in the few sculptural or other artistic pieces that survive. The Indus people used a very characteristic sturdy red ware, made of well-levigated and very well-fired clay. Often it had a red slip and was painted over in black pigment with a variety of pleasing designs, floral as well as geometric. Sometimes birds, animals, and human figures were depicted. In one case there is a she-goat suckling her kid, while a hen loiters nearby. In another, a man carries across his left shoulder an equipoise with two large nets. Judging from the portrayal of the fish and tortoise in the scene, the person may well have been a fisherman. On a painted pot from Lothal there occurs a scene in which are depicted a bird perched on a tree holding a fish, and a fox-like animal below. The scene is very reminiscent of the story of 'the clever fox' narrated in the *Panchatantra*, wherein the fox praised the crow seated on the tree-top for its sweet voice and thus made it open its mouth and drop the morsel which the fox ran off with.

The terracotta figurines, human as well as animal, show vigour, variety, and ingenuity. The often illustrated short-horned bull from Mohenjo-dāro and a similar one from Kālibangan are among the most powerful portrayals of the animal from any ancient civilization. The human head from Kālibangan, though only an inch in height, is a keen competitor, from the point of view of expression and art, with the head of the famous steatite figure from Mohenjo-dāro (below). The female figurines, with their pannier head-dresses and bedecked bodies, though hand-modelled, are indeed pleasing little things. And then there are the terracotta toys, some of which are to be noted for their ingenuity: for example, a bull with a mobile head or a monkey going up and down a string.

The Indus people had a highly developed art of making stone sculptures in the round. There is a striking steatite figure of a bearded man, supposed to be a priest, from Mohenjo-dāro. The inward-looking eyes and the serene expression induce a reflective, meditative mood. Likewise the two sandstone statuettes from Harappā, one representing a youth with muscular body and another a dancer with one leg entwined round the other, are of a really high order. These could well have been the envy even of Greek sculptors some 2,000 years later.

In the art of metal sculpture too, great heights were achieved. The famous bronze female figure from Mohenjo-dāro, supposed to represent a dancing girl, with her right hand poised on the hip, her bracelet-covered left arm swung to rest on a bent left leg, a necklace dangling between her breasts, and, above all, her well-braided head haughtily thrown back, is a perfect piece of art. In this case the feet are missing, but one is tempted to imagine that she wore anklets as shown in another fragmentary bronze sculpture, of which only the lower portion is preserved. As well as the human figures there are fine specimens of bronze animals, the buffalo from Mohenjo-dāro with its massive head upraised, for example, or the dog attacking a deer depicted on the top of a pin from Harappā.

But the Indus artist was at his best when he dealt with his seals (Pl. 1). Cut out of steatite, the seals are usually 20 to 30 millimetres square. On the obverse is an inscription, generally accompanied by an animal figure; on the reverse, a perforated knob, evidently for suspension. It is in the engraving of these seals that the great gifts of the Indus valley artists are especially reflected. Indeed, there can be no two opinions about the superb depiction on the seals of the brāhmanī bull, with its swinging dewlap, pronounced hump, and muscular body.

That the Indus people were literate is fully borne out by the inscriptions on the seals. The occurrence of inscriptions even on pottery and other household objects further shows that literacy was not confined to a select few. The script, seemingly pictographic and having nearly 400 signs, has not yet been deciphered. The various attempts so far have not been based on the strictest scientific principles and little agreement has been reached. However, overlaps of the signs inscribed on some potsherds discovered at Kālibangan clearly show that the direction of writing was from right to left. Wherever the inscription ran into a second line, the style seems to have been *boustrophedon*.

While reading and writing are duly attested to by these inscriptions, proficency in the third R, arithmetic, is clearly shown by the cleverly organized system of weights and measures. Made usually of chert and cubical in shape, the weights fall in the progression of 1, 2, 8/3, 8, 16, 32, etc. up to 12,800. The scales, of ivory or shell, indicate a 'foot' of about 13·0 to 13·2 in. and a 'cubit' of 20·3 to 20·8 in. Mention in this context may also be made of plumb-bobs and 'angle-measures' of shell.

The Indus civilization represented a perfect Bronze Age, though chert blades continued to be used for certain specific purposes. Bronze objects for domestic use included knife-blades, saws, sickles, chisels, celts, razors, pins, tweezers, fish-hooks, and the like. Those for defence or offence comprised spears, arrow-heads, and short swords. That bronze was used in plenty is shown by its employment for non-essential items like vessels.

However, as in most other contemporary civilizations of the world, agriculture was the backbone of the Indus economy. The extensive use of kiln-burnt bricks, for the firing of which plenty of wood was needed, and the frequent depiction of jungle fauna such as the tiger, bison, and rhinoceros on the seals, suggest the possibility of there having been more rainfall during the Indus period than there is now. Today it is news if Mohenjo-dāro gets even 10 centimetres of rain during the whole year. Moreover, dry channels occurring close to the sites show that in ancient times the Indus, Rāvī, Ghaggar, Satluj, and Bhogavo flowed respectively on the outskirts of Mohenjo-dāro, Harappā, Kālibangan, Ropar, and Lothal. Thus there was an adequate water-supply which, coupled with a rich alluvial soil, produced crops of wheat and barley, besides bananas, melons, and peas. However, perhaps the most remarkable agricultural achievement was the cultivation of cotton. Even Egypt did not produce it until several centuries after it was grown in the Indus valley.

There is evidence to show that the people ate, besides cereals, vegetables and fruits, fish, fowl, mutton, beef, and pork. The relevant animals were evidently domesticated. There is also evidence of the domestication of the cat, the dog, and perhaps the elephant. The data about the camel and horse are less conclusive.

Not much evidence is available regarding the dress of the Indus people. The portrayal of a man on a potsherd from Harappā shows the use of the *dhotī*, while the shawl as an upper garment is indicated by the famous figure of a priest from Mohenjo-dāro (above, p. 16). The two—the *dhotī* and shawl—bring to mind the picture of an average Hindu of the modern Indian village. The occurrence of needles and buttons shows that at least some of the clothes were stitched.

The variety of ways in which the women-folk did their hair and bedecked their persons suggests that life was not all toil. The ornaments included, from head to foot, the *bīja*, ear-rings, necklaces, bracelets, girdles, and anklets. The *bīja*, a hollow conical object, is typical even today of the maids of Rājasthān. There were pastimes too, like the playing of dice or, for the more daring, the hunting of wild animals. The youngsters played hopscotch and marbles, while the small children played with rattles and toys, some being noteworthy for their clever methods of manipulation (above, p. 16).

The Indus population, particularly of the cities, was a cosmopolitan one. It included Mediterraneans, Proto-Australoids, Alpines, and Mongoloids. In keeping with such a mixed population, there was a wide variety of religious practices. The portrayal on several seals of a horned, three-faced figure, surrounded by various animals, wild and domesticated, brings to mind the conception of Śiva in the form of *Paśupati*, the Lord of Animals. The presence of a prototype of the later Śaivite cult is also suggested by the occurrence of what may have been *lingas* and *yonis*. A kind of ritual associated with fire-places has already been referred to. There was also the worship of the Mother Goddess. The adoration of trees and streams, or perhaps of the spirits supposed to be residing in them, is also suggested by the relevant data. A belief in life hereafter is evident from the burial practice according to which along with the dead person were placed objects like mirrors, antimony rods, mother-of-pearl shells, and a large number of pots, some of which in life seem to have been used for eating and drinking. In one case a fowl was also placed in the grave-pit. For some reason now unknown, the body is invariably to be found lying from north to south, the head being towards the north. Among the graves excavated at Harappā, of unusual interest was one in which the body was placed in a wooden coffin. Coffin burials were common in Sargonid Iraq and it is not unlikely that a westerner was buried here.

This probable presence of a westerner at Harappā need not surprise us. Contacts with western Asia are suggested on the one hand by the occurrence at the Indus sites of articles of known western origin, for example spiral- and animal-headed pins, mace-heads, socketed adze-axes of copper or bronze, and vases of chlorite schist with typical 'hut-and-window' decoration; and, on the other, by the find of seals and sealings of the Indus style at west Asian sites such as Ur, Susa, Umma, Lagash, and Tell Asmar. Incidentally, a sealing at Umma is reported to have been associated with a bale of cloth—evidently an export from India. In more recent years, a seal (Pl. 2) has been found at Lothal, which is more or less of the same type as those found at contemporary sites on the Persian Gulf such as Barbar, Ras-al-Qala, and Failaka. This discovery, combined with that of the dockyard at the same site (above, p. 14), proves beyond doubt that the trade with western Asia was, at least in part, maritime. Overland trade, perhaps in the fashion of the caravan trade of historical times, also seems to have taken place. For the presence in the Indus sites of articles of lapis lazuli, jade, turquoise, etc., not indigenous to the soil, cannot be explained except by trade with Iraq, Iran, Afghanistan, and Central Asia, the last two of which are connected with the Indus valley by land alone.

Until recently, the main evidence for fixing the chronological horizon of the Indus civilization was the aforesaid seals of Indian origin found in western Asia. Of these, a dozen were found in a datable context, seven in the Sargonid period (*c.* 2300 B.C.), one in pre-Sargonid, three in Larsa (*c.* 1800 B.C.), and one in Kassite (*c.* 1500 B.C.). To add to this was the evidence of segmented beads of faience from late Indus levels, the composition of which has spectrographically been found to be similar to that of beads of the same material from Knossos, ascribable to *c.* 1600 B.C. On these bases, a rough millennium, 2500–1500 B.C., was regarded as the period of this great civilization. During the past decade, however, Carbon-14 measurements have been carried out on materials from Kālibangan, Lothal, Surkotadā, and Mohenjo-dāro. While broadly upholding the above dating, the Carbon-14 determinations indicate a somewhat shorter duration of the civilization, from *c.* 2400 to 1700 B.C. At the same time it must be added that scientists working on the subject have observed that Carbon-14 activity has not been constant in the past and that there is a likelihood of the C-14 dates between 200 B.C. and 4000 B.C. being pushed back slightly. Again, at Mohenjo-dāro there still remain the unfathomed lower levels. Thus, it may well be that the beginning of this civilization was earlier than that indicated at present by the Carbon-14 dates.

What brought the Indus cities to an end has for long been a matter of debate. The occurrence in the habitation area at Mohenjo-dāro of some human skeletons, including one of which the skull bears the mark of a cut, has been interpreted as evidence of a massacre at the hands of the invading Āryans. This view, however, now seems untenable. In the first place, the skeletons do not all belong to one and the same occupation-level, which should also be the latest, marking the end of the Indus settlement. Secondly at the site there is no evidence of an alien culture immediately overlying the Indus one. To save the situation, the post-Indus Cemetery H at Harappā has been brought into the picture. It has, however, been demonstrated elsewhere by the present writer that there was an appreciable time-lag between the end of the Indus civilization and the beginning of Cemetery H. Thus the Cemetery H people can hardly be regarded as the invaders if those invaded had ceased to exist at the time. And to regard the Cemetery H people as Āryans is fraught with still greater difficulties. In the present state of our knowledge, such people are conspicuously absent from the Ghaggar (ancient Sarasvatī), Satluj, and upper Gangā valleys—regions where the early Āryans are known from their own literature to have resided.

Another theory ascribes the end of the Indus civilization to heavy flooding. This may, however, be only partly true. For, while some evidence of devastation by floods is to be found at Mohenjo-dāro and Lothal, there is no such evidence in respect of other sites, for example Kālibangan. At this site, neither the invader nor the flood can be invoked. Here perhaps the drying up of the Ghaggar—gradual or sudden, owing either to climatic changes or to the diversion of the waters resulting from factors at or near their source—may have been the cause of the desertion of the site. Pestilence and the erosion of the surrounding landscape owing to over-exploitation may also be reasons for the end of certain settlements.

Be that as it may, there is enough evidence to show that the great Indus civilization did not come to a sudden dead end. For example, at Lothal, from its Period A (Indus) to B (post-Indus), there is a gradual change in the pottery and the disappearance or replacement by others of certain kinds of antiquities. This devolution is further continued at the neighbouring site of Rangpur. Likewise a change of face is also indicated by the evidence from sites in eastern Panjāb and north-western Uttar Pradesh. The Indus civilization no doubt fell; all the same it left many indelible imprints on the latter-day cultures of the subcontinent.

CHAPTER III

The Early Āryans[1]

by T. Burrow

The classical civilization of India developed from the earlier Vedic civilization, and the Vedic civilization was the creation of the Āryans, an invading people, whose first arrival in the subcontinent is probably to be dated about 1500 B.C. Perhaps some 200 years after this estimated date there began to come into being a collection of religious hymns which were eventually organized as the *Ṛgveda*, the final redaction of which probably antedates 1000 B.C. Our knowledge of the Āryans in India during this earliest period is based primarily on this work. From the *Ṛgveda* emerges a fairly clear picture of the situation at that time. A series of related tribes, settled mainly in the Panjāb and adjacent regions, speaking a common language, sharing a common religion, and designating themselves by the name *ārya-*, are represented as being in a state of permanent conflict with a hostile group of peoples known variously as Dāsa or Dasyu. From the frequent references to these conflicts it emerges that their result was the complete victory of the Āryans. During the period represented by the later *Saṃhitās* and the *Brāhmaṇa* texts the Āryans are seen to have extended their territory, principally in the direction of the east, down the Gangā valley, and references to conflicts with the Dāsa are rare. Other terms, e.g. *mleccha-* and *niṣāda-* are used as designations of non-Āryan tribes, while the word *dāsa* becomes the usual word for 'slave'. On the other hand the term *ārya-* is opposed not only to the external barbarian, but also to the lowest of the four castes, the *śūdra*. In the latter context the word *ārya-* naturally acquires the meaning 'noble, honourable', and the word continues in use in both senses down to the classical period. North India is referred to as Āryāvarta, 'the country where the Āryans live', or, in Pāli, as *ariyaṃ āyatanaṃ*. The Jaina texts have frequent references to the distinction between Ārya and Mleccha. In Tamil literature the kings of north India are referred to as Āryan kings. On the other hand the ethical use of the word is illustrated by the Buddhist 'Noble Eightfold Path' (*ariyaṃ aṭṭhaṅgikam maggaṃ*) where the word has no ethnic significance.

The Āryans, whose presence in north-western India is documented by the *Ṛgveda*, had reached the territory they then occupied through a migration, or rather, a succession of migrations, from outside the Indian subcontinent. The final stage of this migration cannot have been very far removed from the beginning of the composition of the *Ṛgveda*, but, at the same time, a sufficient period of time must have elapsed for any clear recollection of it to have dis-

[1] This chapter, in view of the many Sanskrit terms and quotations which it contains, employs the full apparatus of diacritic signs used in the scholarly transliteration of Indian languages. The reader should remember that *ṛ* is elsewhere transliterated as *ri* and *ṣ* as *sh*. *C* is here sounded as English *ch*. The Iranian *š* is also pronounced as *sh*, Iranian *θ* sounds like English *th* in 'thing'. Iranian *x* is like *ch* in Scottish or German *Loch*.

appeared, since the hymns contain no certain references to such an event. The Āryan invasion of India is recorded in no written document, and it cannot yet be traced archaeologically, but it is nevertheless firmly established as a historical fact on the basis of comparative philology. The Indo-European languages, of which Sanskrit in its Vedic form is one of the oldest members, originated in Europe, and the only possible way by which a language belonging to this family could be carried all the way to India was a migration of the people speaking it. The general outline of this process can be elucidated to some extent on the basis of the mutual relationship of the languages concerned.

Apart from its belonging to the Indo-European family in general, Sanskrit, or Old Indo-Āryan, is more closely and specifically related to the Iranian group of languages, of which the oldest representatives are Old Persian and Avestan. The relationship is in fact so close that these two peoples, who both designated themselves as Āryans, must, at some earlier time, have constituted a single nation or people, speaking, with due allowance for dialectal divergence, the same language. This earlier Āryan language, commonly referred to as Primitive Indo-Iranian, is the source from which the later Iranian and Indo-Āryan languages are derived. In the period preceding the Āryan invasion of India, they were settled, in all probability, in the Central Asian regions bordering the Oxus and the Jaxartes, and the Aral and Caspian seas. From this base, sections of them may be presumed to have pushed up into the highlands of Afghanistan, and then to have descended from this base into the plains of the Panjāb. In the opposite direction other Āryan tribes from the same region moved westwards into Iran, where they first appear in Assyrian records in the middle of the ninth century B.C. The beginning of their occupation of Iran is commonly put not earlier than 1000 B.C., which is considerably later than the Āryan migrations into India if the above-mentioned estimated dates are correct. The Iranians retained a memory of their original home, under the name of *airyanam vaējō* (*Ērān Vēj*), and the region continued to be occupied by them down to the time of the Turkish invasions.

The common culture and religion developed by the Āryans in their earlier home is still reflected in the earliest texts of the Iranians and Indo-Āryans respectively. In the case of the latter the religious reforms of Zarathuštra led to some remarkable alterations, which resulted, for instance, in the old word for 'god' (Skt. *deva-*) acquiring the meaning of 'demon' (Av. *daēva-*), while certain prominent gods in the Veda (e.g. Indra) have been reduced to the latter status in the Avesta. In spite of this, a considerable amount of the common heritage remained. Although the name Indra came to be applied to a demon, his title *Vṛtrahan-*, in its Iranian form *Vṛθragna-*, designates an important deity. The Iranian Mithra, corresponding to the Vedic Mitra, remained one of their most important gods, later to have a remarkable career in the Roman Empire. Fire-worship and the cult of Soma are a common inheritance in both India and Iran. A common mythology is illustrated by such figures as Vedic Yama the son of Vivasvant and Avestan Yima the son of Vīvahvant. A basic religious terminology is shared, e.g. Vedic *hotar-* 'priest', *yajña* 'sacrifice', *ṛta-* 'truth, divine order': Av. *zaotar-*, *yasna-*, *aša-* (O. Pers. *arta-*). Common terms occur likewise in the political (Skt. *kṣatra-* 'sovereignty': Av. *xšaθra*), military (Skt. *senā* 'army': Av. *haēnā*, O. Pers. *hainā*), and economic spheres (Skt. *kṣetra-* 'field', *urvarā* 'arable land': Av. *šōiθra-* 'homestead', *urvarā* 'crop'). A division of society into classes which in India crystallized into the four-caste system is closely paralleled in Iran.

The evolution of this common inherited culture may be held to have taken place, in its later stages, in the Central Asian homeland of the Āryans, and their residence there, prior to the Indian migration, may have lasted for a considerable period. At a still earlier period the evidence points to a localization of the Āryans much further to the west. In the first place the Indo-European connections of the Āryan languages, which indicate that they originated in Europe, make it necessary to assume a still earlier migration which took them from Europe to Central Asia. In the second place interesting confirmation of an earlier Āryan homeland further to the west is provided by the evidence of Āryan loan-words in the Finno-Ugrian languages. An example is the Finnish word *sata* 'hundred', which can be shown to represent phonetically *śata-* (i.e. the Indo-Āryan and Primitive Indo-Iranian form of the word, and not the later Iranian *sata-*). There is a considerable body of loans like this which cannot be derived from Iranian, and which must therefore have been taken over in the Primitive Indo-Iranian period. At the time of these borrowings, therefore, the Āryans and the ancestors of the Finno-Ugrians must have been in close contact. In view of the present distribution of the Finno-Ugrian languages, and of their probable ancient situation, it is concluded that, when these words were borrowed, the primitive Āryans from whose language they were taken must have been situated not further east than the Volga and the Urals. It was only after the period of their influence on Finno-Ugrian that the main centre of the Āryans shifted towards Central Asia.

At this stage, which may be provisionally fixed towards the beginning of the second millennium B.C., we are already dealing with the Āryans as a separate community, already detached from the other branches of the Indo-Europeans. At a still earlier stage, say the middle of the third millennium B.C., a situation must be assumed in which the speakers of the language from which the later Āryan tongues were derived were still members of the original Indo-European community, and their language was a dialect of Indo-European, not having developed into a separate language of the group, as it had done during the stage previously referred to (2000–1500 B.C.). This assumption implies an original location still further to the west, and for this also linguistic evidence can be produced. Out of all the languages of the Indo-European family, the Balto-Slavonic group shows signs of having had the closest relationship with Indo-Iranian. Since these languages are not likely to have moved far from the region where they are first historically attested, this connection is a useful pointer to the earliest place of origin of the Indo-Iranian family.

In addition to many other special similarities the two groups are characterized by an early palatalization (illustrated by Skt. *śatam*, Av. *satam* 'hundred', as opposed to Lat. *centum*), which is also found in Albanian and Armenian. On the strength of this common innovation, these languages are usually considered to form a special group among the Indo-European languages, and are termed the *satəm* languages, after the Avestan word for 'hundred'. It does in fact seem likely that this change took place at such an early period that the ancestors of all these languages were still in contact. In addition to these special relationships Indo-Iranian also shows evidence of a special relationship with Greek, which is particularly noticeable in the morphology of the verb.

With other Indo-European languages Indo-Iranian shows no sign of special connection. This is not to be expected in the case of the western Indo-European languages (Italic, Celtic, Germanic) in view of their geographical situation. Hittite and the kindred languages of Asia Minor are in a special position, since they show such profound differences from the more familiar type of Indo-European that it is necessary to assume their very early separation. These peoples must have passed over from the Balkans into Asia Minor at a period long preceding their earliest appearances in the written historical record. More problematical is the case of the two closely related languages, conventionally styled Tochārian A and B, of which manuscript remains were discovered in Chinese Turkestan at the beginning of the present century. In view of their situation it might have been expected that they would have shown some signs of closer contact with Indo-Iranian, but of this there is no indication whatever. They further show no sign of any particular connection with any other section of Indo-European, and these facts are best explained by the assumption of an early separation of this group (though not as early as the separation of Hittite, etc.). The later eastward expansion of the Āryan tribes outlined above must have been responsible for pushing them further and further to the east, until they finally settled in Chinese Turkestan. There are no linguistic traces of early contacts between the two groups, and it is only much later that the influence of Iranian on Tochārian can be noted.

So far we have had to rely entirely on linguistic relationships to account for the origin and early movements of the Āryans. After about 1500 B.C. documentary evidence becomes available, not from India and Iran, the countries of their permanent settlement, but from the Near East, where a section of Āryans established a temporary domination which was to have no lasting effects. The documentary evidence from this quarter consists of a number of proper names, some names of gods, and some words, from which the presence of Āryans in this region during the period 1500–1300 B.C. can be deduced. They appear always in connection with the Hurrians, a non-Indo-European people of local origin, who were also engaged in considerable expansion at the time. In particular the Hurrian state of Mitanni, to judge by the names of its kings, was, during its most influential period, under the domination of Āryan kings backed up by an Āryan aristocracy. Other minor states in Syria had rulers with similar Āryan names.

These Āryans did not come in sufficient numbers to impose their own language and civilization on the country in which they had settled; they seem always to have used Hurrian as their official language, and after the end of this period they were absorbed into the native population without leaving any further trace. The most important document is a treaty between the Hittite and Mitanni kings, in which appear four divine names familiar from the Veda, namely, Indra, Varuna, Mitra, and Nāsatya. In addition Šuriaš, meaning the sun-god, appears in a document of the Kassites (who otherwise show little trace of Āryan connections), and Agni the fire-god, attested in Hittite documents, seems to have been borrowed by them from the Āryans. A treatise on horse-training, composed by the Mitannian Kikkuli in the Hittite language, contains some Āryan technical terms and a series of Āryan numerals. Other Āryan words occur sporadically in documents connected with the Hurrians.

The question as to whether the Āryans of the Near East were more closely connected with the Indo-Āryan or Iranian branch of the Āryans, or whether they represent the undivided Proto-Āryans, has been much discussed. At present the prevailing opinion is that they are to be connected with the Indo-Āryan branch. This conclusion is based partly on linguistic considerations (e.g. the word *aika-* 'one' corresponds to Skt. *eka-*, and not to Iranian *aiva-*), but also on the fact that the above-mentioned gods are specifically Vedic gods, whereas in Iranian only Mitra among them appears as a god, and, as regards the Proto-Āryans, it is doubtful whether any of them except Mitra can be assumed for this stage.[2]

If the Āryans of the Near East are to be connected specifically with the Indo-Āryans, some interesting conclusions emerge. In the first place we must conclude that the division of the Āryans into two branches was already in being before the Indo-Āryans invaded India or the Iranians came to occupy Iran. Secondly we must conclude that the Proto-Indo-Āryans were in occupation of north-eastern Iran before the migrations to India took place. Since the date of the appearance of the Āryans in the Near East corresponds roughly with that commonly assumed for the Āryan migration into India, it follows they both proceeded from the same base, i.e. north-eastern Iran, territory which was later to be taken over by the Iranians.

At the time of their greatest expansion the Āryans occupied a territory much greater than that of all other Indo-European peoples put together. Even before their major migrations which led to the occupation of India and Iran, while they were still confined to the Eurasian steppes, the territory involved was much greater than that of any other Indo-European people. To account for the later vast expansion we must assume that favourable climatic and other conditions had led to a continuous increase of population. Only on this basis can we account for their ability to colonize such extensive areas in Iran and north India. As already observed, it was during this period, in the centuries preceding 1500 B.C., that the characteristic features of Āryan civilization were evolved. It is this culture which we find in the earliest Indian and Iranian literature, and which, on account of the great similarities between the two traditions, must be regarded as a common inheritance. The culture which we find in the *Ṛgveda* was not developed in India, but, in most essentials, imported, already formed, from outside.

A frequent misconception which should be mentioned arises from the misuse of the term Āryan. This name can be applied properly only to the Indo-Iranians, since it was the name they used to designate themselves. Its use should not be extended to apply to the Indo-Europeans in general, as has too frequently been done. The result of this extension of usage has been a confusion, which is often encountered, between the early Āryans and the primitive

[2] On the Āryan gods of the Mitanni see the article by P. Thieme, 'The Aryan Gods of the Mitanni Treaties', in *JAOS*, 80 (1960), 301–17.

Indo-Europeans. As a result the Russian and Central Asian steppes, which were the habitat of the Āryans, i.e. the Indo-Iranians, in the period preceding the migrations to India, etc., that is to say for an unspecified, but no doubt considerable period before about 1500 B.C., have often been regarded as the home of the original Indo-Europeans. The result has been that Greeks, Hittites, etc. are represented as migrating from this region at a time when only the Āryan branch of the Indo-Europeans was in occupation of it. On the contrary the evidence is that the European branches of the Indo-European family are native to Europe, and that after separating from them the Āryans extended to the east. As already observed, during this period, between their separation from the other Indo-Europeans and the later migration beginning about 1500 B.C., the characteristic features of their civilization were evolved.

It has been observed that the Āryan invasion of India seems to have taken place some considerable time before the composition of the Vedic hymns, since no clear recollection of this migration is to be found in them. On the other hand references are frequent to the struggle with the previous inhabitants, the Dāsas or Dasyus, and to the occupation of their land and the capture of their possessions. As to the identity of these people who were displaced or subjugated, the predominant and the most likely view is that they were the authors of the Indus civilization. This civilization, which was quite unexpected when it was first discovered, was certainly earlier than the Vedic period, but there has been some argument as to whether its fall was brought about by the invading Āryans, or whether some period of time elapsed between the end of the Indus civilization and the appearance of the Āryans. The evidence of the Vedic texts themselves is decidedly in favour of the former view, notably on account of the frequent references to the destruction of cities, the war-god Indra being known as *puraṃdara*, 'destroyer of cities'. Agni, the fire-god is also prominently mentioned in this capacity, understandably, since many of the Indus cities appear to have been destroyed by fire. In view of these repeated references the conclusion seems inescapable that the destruction of the Indus cities was the work of the Āryans.[3]

It is clear from the material remains that the Indus civilization was in certain respects superior to that of the Āryans. In particular it was a city civilization of a highly developed type, while by contrast city life was unfamiliar to the Āryans. The superiority of the Āryans lay in the military field, in which their use of the light horse-chariot played a prominent part. Their victory resulted in the almost complete abandonment of the cities, in much the same way as the Anglo-Saxon invasion of Britain put an end to Romano-British city life. Not only had the Āryans no interest in using the cities they conquered, but also they lacked the technical ability to keep them going. The Āryans built their settlements of wood and they were distributed in small units, villages rather than towns, during most of the Vedic period. Since their houses and furniture were made mainly of wood and other perishable materials, not much has remained for the archaeologists to record, and until very recently

[3] This statement may not apply to Mohenjo-dāro in Sind, where strong evidence has been produced to show that the city decayed owing to frequent disastrous floods. Mohenjo-dāro, however, was not in the main line of the Āryan advance. [Ed.]

the Vedic period in India remained archaeologically almost a complete blank. Even now the position has not advanced far beyond this. It was only towards the end of the Vedic period that the development of cities was resumed. Whereas for the Indus civilization archaeology is the only source of our knowledge, information concerning the Vedic Āryans depends entirely on literary texts which were handed down by oral tradition. These do not provide any proper historical account, since that is not their concern, but a good deal of incidental information of a historical or semi-historical character emerges, and also a fairly clear and consistent picture of the life and civilization of the period.

It is a much-discussed question to what extent the Indus civilization influenced that of the Āryans, and opinions on this matter have considerably diverged. On the whole the Vedic texts themselves give the impression that such influence, if it existed, was not of great importance. In the first place, the attitude of the Vedic poets towards the Dāsas and their civilization was one of uncompromising hostility, and was distinctly unreceptive to any influences in the religious field, which might otherwise have had some effect. Furthermore the physical destruction and depopulation of most of the Indus cities, which is attested by archaeology, must have effectively removed most of the bases from which such influence could spread. Later, of course, as Āryan civilization developed into Hindu civilization, many non-Āryan influences appeared, but they are not prominent in the Vedic period, and they do not seem to have had any direct connection with the prehistoric civilization of the Indus cities.

The territory occupied by the Āryans at the time of the *Ṛgveda* can be defined with reference to the river names mentioned in the text. These are, in the first place the Indus (Sindhu) and its main tributaries, the five rivers of the Panjāb. To the west of this there is mention of the Krumu, Gomatī, and Kubhā (the Kurram, Gomal, and Kābul rivers) and of Suvāstu (Swāt), showing that the Āryans extended to within the boundaries of present Afghanistan. To the east the Sarasvatī, Dṛṣadvatī, and Yamunā are in Āryan territory, and the Gangā is mentioned in one late hymn. Most of this territory had lain within the sphere of the Indus civilization. On the other hand little is heard of the regions of the lower Indus where that civilization had equally flourished.

The Āryans were divided into a large number of independent tribes, normally ruled by kings, who, when not fighting the Dāsas or Dasyus, were frequently engaged in fighting each other. Nevertheless, the Āryans were highly conscious of their ethnic unity, based on a common language, a common religion, and a common way of life, and of the contrast between themselves and earlier inhabitants. The latter were partly absorbed into the Āryan community in the capacity of śūdras, and partly they withdrew to regions temporarily out of the reach of the Āryans. The fact that the Āryans were able to retain their identity and maintain their culture so completely, in a country which had previously been both well populated and highly civilized, implies that they must have come in great numbers, not in one campaign of conquest, but in a series of waves lasting over a long period, sufficient to provide a numerous population which in turn could form the basis of further expansion. The situation was just the opposite of that which prevailed in the Near East, where conquests effected by small bands of warriors resulted in temporary domination, but where their numbers were too small to prevent their absorption after a few generations into the native population.

The area occupied by the Āryans continued to expand in the period represented by the later Vedic texts, and there was a shift eastwards in the centre of gravity. By the time of the *Brāhmaṇas* the centre of Āryan civilization had become the country of the Kurus and Pañcālas, corresponding roughly to modern Uttar Pradesh, while the western settlements in the Panjāb were less important. Further expansion to the east had taken place and the most important states in this region were Kosala, Kāśī, and Videha. The main Āryan advance at this period was down the Gaṅgā valley, keeping primarily to the north of the river. It is likely that the main route of migration followed the foot-hills of the Himālaya, avoiding in the first instance the densely forested country surrounding the river itself. By far the greater number of tribes and kingdoms mentioned in the texts of this period lay to the north of the Gaṅgā. Those lying to the south, e.g. the Cedis, the Satvants, and the kingdom of Vidarbha, were much fewer, and more rarely mentioned. The Āryans were at this time surrounded by a variety of non-Āryan tribes, of which a list is provided by the *Aitareya Brāhmaṇa*: Andhras, Puṇḍras, Mūtibas, Pulindas, and Śabaras. The countries of Aṅga and Magadha appear from the sources to have been only partially Āryanized.

In the *Ṛgveda* the conflict between Ārya and Dasyu figured prominently, reflecting, as we have seen, a prolonged armed struggle in which the Āryans finally emerged as the undisputed victors. Such references cease in the later Vedic literature, and the term Dasyu, as applied to non-Āryan peoples, is comparatively rare. On the other hand the term *Niṣāda*, applied to primitive forest-dwellers, is comparatively frequent. The explanation is that the nature of the Āryan advance and settlement had changed. Once the Indus civilization had been overthrown, and the greater part of its territory occupied, there remained no advanced civilized states to contend with. The Gaṅgā valley seems at this time to have been thinly populated by forest tribes, possessing no advanced civilization and unable to offer any coherent resistance to the Āryans. The colonization that took place down the valley, at first principally to the north of the river, was mainly a matter of clearing forests and founding agricultural settlements, a continuous and prolonged process extending over centuries. In the uncleared forest regions the primitive tribes of *Niṣādas* continued to reside in the midst of Āryan territory, and relations between the two seem to have been established on a basis of mutual toleration. Naturally as the activity of forest-clearing proceeded the scope for the independent existence of the forest-tribes became more limited, and sections of them, under such names as Pukkasa and Cāṇḍāla, attached themselves to the fringe of Āryan society, forming the nucleus of what were to become eventually the depressed classes.

The third stage in the Āryan occupation of India falls within the period 800–550 B.C. It has been observed that at the beginning of this period, according to the evidence of the *Brāhmaṇas*, the portion of India occupied by the Āryans was still comparatively limited, and that they were surrounded by a ring of non-Āryan peoples, some of whose names are mentioned. A very much wider extension of Āryan language and culture can be observed at the time of the rise of Buddhism and Jainism, towards the end of the sixth century B.C. Obviously the intervening period had been one of extensive migration and colonization. The result was that the boundaries of Āryāvarta, the country of the Āryans, were defined as the Himālaya and Vindhya mountains to the north and south, and the eastern and western oceans. One of the main lines of expansion at this time lay to the south-west, embracing Avanti and adjacent regions, and extending as far as Aśmaka and Mūlaka in the region of the upper Godāvarī. The advance to the east continued with the occupation of the greater part of Bengal (Puṇḍra, Suhma, Vaṅga, etc.) and Orissā (Kaliṅga). The areas to the south of the Gaṅgā connecting these two lines of advance were also progressively brought within the Āryan fold. References to these events can be found scattered throughout the epics and *Purāṇas*, of which it will be sufficient to mention the foundation of Dvārakā on the west coast ascribed to Kṛṣṇa, and the activities of the Haihayas and allied tribes in Avanti. The over-all result was that by the end of the sixth century B.C. the portion of India occupied by Āryans was vastly increased, and the currency of the Indo-Āryan language was correspondingly extended. A map representing the extent of the Āryan occupation at the end of this period would probably show a general correspondence with the boundaries of Indo-Āryan in a modern linguistic map. After this, Āryan influence further south, in Dravidian India, was a matter of cultural penetration, not, as previously, of conquest and settlement.

During the *Brāhmaṇa* period the Āryans maintained in essentials their ethnic identity and their Vedic culture. There was considerable internal development, and, in particular, the brāhmans increased their status and strengthened their organization. The ritual was enormously developed, and the texts on which we depend for a picture of the period are mainly concerned with this. This state organization was stabilized and developed, and a variety of offices are recorded, even though their precise functions are not always clear. The political units became larger and the state began to replace the tribe. There were considerable advances in material culture, as attested by both literature and archaeology. City life began again in a small way, since a number of places mentioned, e.g. Kāmpilya, Paricakrā, Āsandīvant, appear to have been towns rather than villages.

The rapid expansion during the period 800–550 B.C. had the result that in the new territories the Āryans were much more thinly spread than in the old, and they were to a greater extent mixed with the pre-existing population. This fact is noted in some ancient texts. For instance the *Baudhāyana Dharmasūtra* says that the peoples of Avanti, Aṅga, Magadha, Surāṣṭra, Dakṣināpatha, Upāvṛt, Sindhu, and Sauvīra are of mixed origin (*saṅkīrṇa-yoni-*), and further lays down an offering of atonement for those who visit the countries of the Āraṭṭas, the Kāraskaras, the Puṇḍras, the Sauvīras, the Vaṅgas, the Kaliṅgas, and the Prānūnas. These lists cover a large part of the territories colonized during the period 800–550 B.C., and attest to the fact that these territories were only imperfectly Āryanized in contrast to what had happened in the earlier periods. The lists also contain the names of a number of non-Āryan tribes, many of which still no doubt retained their identity and language.

The influence of the pre-Āryans on Āryan culture should probably be regarded as having begun to take effect during this period, and it is associated with the transition from the Vedic civilization to the later Hindu civilization. This was probably also the time when the epic traditions, later to culminate in the *Mahābhārata* and the *Rāmāyaṇa*, began to take shape. New developments in religion which eventually evolved into the later Hinduism, which contrasts in many ways with the Vedic religion, also had their first beginnings in this period. The great increase in the complexity of the caste system which characterizes later Hindu civilization was also stimulated at this time by the necessity of somehow fitting into the framework of Āryan society a large variety of previously independent tribes, who in many parts of the newly conquered area must have formed the majority of the population. The Āryan culture, based on the Vedic culture, remained the centralizing factor, but from now on it was more subject to non-Āryan influences. The influence of Āryan civilization was felt latest in the Dravidian south. The first Āryan colonization of Ceylon is supposed to have taken place about the time of Buddha, and the earliest Āryan penetration in south India is likely to have occurred about the same time. Later the Maurya Empire was in control of most of the Deccan, only the Tamil princes of the extreme south remaining independent. The Sātavāhana Empire which followed also represented Āryan domination and penetration in this region, as can be seen from the fact that the official language of this dynasty and of some of its immediate successors was Middle Indo-Āryan. This political influence was associated with the spread of religions from north India, both Brahmanical and Buddhist or Jaina. In contrast, however, to the previous stages of expansion, the Āryan language was not permanently imposed on this region, and after about A.D. 500 Kannada, and later Telugu, began to be used in inscriptions. Gradually the native Dravidian element gained the upper hand, and the boundaries between Āryan and Dravidian India were restored to a line representing the limit of Āryan conquests about 500 B.C. At the same time the whole subcontinent was united by a common culture, of which the Āryans were the original founders, but to which Dravidians and others also made their contributions.

CHAPTER IV

The Early Dravidians[1]

by JOHN R. MARR

THE word that has come down to us as 'Dravidian' has had a very long history as a referential term for the southern portion of India. Greek geographers knew the area as *Damirica* or *Limyrikê*: 'Then come Naura and Tyndis, the first marts of Damirica.'[2] '8. Limyrikê: Tyndis, a city . . .'[3]

The latter reference reminds one of course of the legendary Atlantis of the Indian Ocean, Lemuria, supposedly inhabited by lemurs. It will be noticed that both Greek forms, *Damirica* and *Limyrikê*, have an *r* at the beginning of the third syllable. They too had difficulty with a Dravidian sound in the source-word, as will be seen shortly.

Sanskrit sources have *Dravidi* and *Damili*, and later *Dramida* and *Drāvida*, the immediate sources of our 'Dravidian'. It seems likely that all these words are to be connected ultimately with a non-Indo-Āryan word, possibly in the form in which we have it today, namely, *Tamil*. The last sound of this word, a retroflex affricate, is one peculiar to one or two languages in the south of India, and has been dispensed with in two of the main ones, Telugu and Kannada. Clearly, Greek and Sanskrit had difficulties with it, and did their best, as shown above. There is, however, no justification for assuming that, at the period of the classical geographers, the word meant the Tamil language as at present differentiated from other south Indian tongues. It seems more likely that there was at that time a relatively undifferentiated non-Indo-Āryan speech in the south to which the term *Proto-Dravidian* is usually applied. Such a situation must have obtained long before the earliest surviving literary or other records in what is now the Tamil-speaking area of south-east India. Such records can be with some assurance assigned to a period around the third century B.C. for inscriptions, and to one about the commencement of the Christian era for literature. Both are recognizable as Tamil, and we have no evidence of any sort for any other distinct Dravidian speech from so early a date. Indeed there is some evidence that points the other way; at the level of court-poetry at least, Tamil was still used in the area where Malayālam is now spoken at the time of the earliest extant Tamil literature. This region was known in Tamil as *Śeranādu*, and in Sanskrit as *Kerala*.[4]

[1] The author's original transliteration of Tamil words, following the system of the Madras University *Tamil Lexicon*, which is standard nowadays among specialists, has been simplified and adapted for the benefit of the general reader, except in the case of a few words discussed in their linguistic context. The letter transliterated here as *ś* will be found in other chapters expressed as *ch*, according to its usual pronunciation in Indo-Āryan languages. [Ed.]

[2] *Periplus* 53; see K. A. Nilakanta Sastri, *Foreign Notices of South India*, p. 57.

[3] Ptolemy, *Geography*, vii. 1. See J. W. McCrindle, *Ancient India*, pp. 48–9.

[4] *Kerala* probably preserves a Proto-Dravidian velarized *Keral*. See T. Burrow in *BSOAS*, 11 (1943), 126. In the Tamil anthology-poems the kings of this region were called *Śeral*, pl. *Śeralar*.

Proto-Dravidian, then, was a non-Indo-Āryan speech, and it follows from this that the languages we know as Dravidian languages are distinct too. It lies beyond the scope of this essay to enter into a detailed linguistic discussion as to the differences. One of the characteristics of the Dravidian, as of the Turkic languages, is what is known as *agglutination*, whereby suffixes, themselves often recognizable as connected with meaningful roots, are added to nouns and verbs to inflect their meaning, providing case-endings, for example. For instance, the locative case-suffix in Tamil, *-il*, would seem to be connected with the word for 'house' in various Dravidian languages; Tamil has *il*, Telugu *illu*, etc. Number and case are indicated by two distinct suffixes, in that order, e.g. Tam. *mīṉ* 'fish', *mīṉai* 'fish' (accusative), *mīṉgaḷ* 'fishes', *mīṉgaḷai* 'fishes' (acc.). Notice that the case-suffix in the plural is the same as in the singular. It will be recalled that quite a different situation obtains in Indo-European or Indo-Āryan languages, where one set of single suffixes is used in the singular and a different set in the plural, wherein such suffixes denote both case and number.

Following from the readily analysable nature of agglutinative languages, at least in a primitive or theoretical stage, it can be seen that to write such languages in a pictographic or ideographic script is an attractive possibility. Of recent years, Dravidian has been the strongest contender for the language of the as yet undeciphered Mohenjo-dāro seal characters. These appear on about 2,000 seals as short inscriptions accompanying rather conventionalized pictures of animals, the bull figuring prominently among them.[5]

It will at once be clear that we are speaking of an area very distinct geographically from that of present-day Dravidian languages which is that of peninsular India south of a line from, say, Goa on the west coast to Ganjām on the east. The area of the Mohenjo-dāro and Harappā city-cultures is that of the Indus valley, in Sind and the Panjāb. But, just as in Britain and western Europe the Celtic languages, once widely prevalent, were pushed westwards to the Atlantic coast, extending from north-west Spain to the Hebrides, by intrusive languages from the east, it has been argued that Dravidian languages were once prevalent throughout India, being pushed southwards by the invasions of Indo-Āryan speakers from the north-west, a movement that, it is pretty clear, took place between about 2500 and 1500 B.C. That there were Dravidian languages in the north would be mere speculation were it not for the fact that, to this day, there remains a pocket of Dravidian speech, the language Brāhūī, spoken by about 250,000 people in the highlands of Balūchistān, on the Pakistan-Afghanistan border. Notwithstanding the meagre nature of the historical evidence,[6] it seems more reasonable to assume a relict status for Brāhūī, rather than an improbable migration from the plains of Dravidian speakers some 800 miles away, and the exchange of a settled agricultural regime for a harsh, nomadic, and pastoral one.

On the assumption then that Dravidian languages were once widely prevalent in the subcontinent and that they were displaced by Indo-Āryan in the north, the attractiveness of them as the language of the city-cultures of Pakistan becomes clear. The most important and recent statement of this

[5] For a recent account of these cultures see S. Piggott, *Prehistoric India*, pp. 132–289.

[6] See M. B. Emeneau, *Brahui and Dravidian Comparative Grammar*, p. 1.

position is that of Asko Parpola and others, in three special publications of the Scandinavian Institute of Asian Studies.[7] While the authors have indeed amassed much evidence in support of their view, it is the case that the second and third publications contain some corrections of their original position, together with speculative matter connected with Indus valley culture, religion, and iconography, all of which detracts from the acceptability of the purely linguistic argument out of which their theories originated. The authors do not, for instance, advance really convincing reasons for reading the ideographs from right to left.[8] Moreover, we are of course still none the wiser about the sound of the words or syllables 'depicted' and the best the authors can do is to read them as reconstructed Proto-Dravidian. It should be added that similar conclusions have been reached by Russian scholars, led by Yu. Knorozov, also using computers.

If we accept the view of Parpola, Knorozov, and others that speakers of Dravidian languages were productive of cultures as far back as the third millennium B.C., a central date for the Indus valley culture, we are still faced with a gap of 1,500 years during which no certain records of Dravidian were produced, a period when, we may assume, the Dravidians were overthrown from their culture-centres in north India and pushed into the centre and south of the peninsula by the Indo-Āryans. Such a gap takes us up to the earliest known Tamil inscriptions, which are in the Brāhmī script and belong to the third century B.C. These will be discussed shortly.

Whether Dravidian languages or the speakers thereof existed in India from the beginning of man in the subcontinent, or were themselves incursors like the Indo-Āryans and their languages later, is likely to remain unresolved in the present state of knowledge. Because of their agglutinative structure, these languages have been associated with Caucasian languages, and even with Basque.[9] Better established is the longest-held view as to the external affiliations of Dravidian. It is that of Caldwell[10] and Rask, that Dravidian is affiliated to what they termed Scythian languages, now usually called Turkic and Finno-Ugrian.

Similarly there remains ignorance of what languages were spoken by the various Stone Age cultures in India, there being the added difficulty of the co-existence of a number of these with cultures of an altogether higher order synchronically. We know nothing, for instance, of the languages of the *Soan Industry* in the Himālaya foot-hills or of the *Madras Industry* in south-east India. The most promising archaeological link with the admittedly tenuous theory of the Mediterranean affinities of the Dravidians is provided by the south Indian megalithic culture. This, however, may not itself be older than about 200 B.C.[11] Gordon Childe has seen possible links with Mediterranean

[7] Publications Nos. 1 and 2, Copenhagen, 1969, No. 3, Copenhagen, 1970. The theory was previously advanced, somewhat romantically perhaps, by such writers as H. Heras, *Studies in Proto-Indo-Mediterranean Culture*, Vol. 1, Bombay, 1953.

[8] See Parpola *et al.* in Publication No. 1, pp. 18–19.

[9] See N. Lahovary, *Dravidian Origins and the West*, Bombay, 1964.

[10] See R. Caldwell, *A Comparative Grammar of the Dravidian or South-Indian Family of Languages*, 3rd edn., pp. 61 ff. The original edition of this work, in 1856, effectively marked the commencement of the study of Dravidian linguistics, and a good deal of Bishop Caldwell's work has yet to be surpassed. [11] Piggott, op. cit., p. 38

and Caucasian megaliths of sites such as Brahmagiri via the Sialk B graves in Iran; the connection may have been by sea.[12] It may be speculative to assign Dravidian speech to any one particular racial type but it has been suggested that brachycephalic Armenoid types in India, having affinities in Armenia, Anatolia, and Iran, brought Dravidian into India. While there are, then, reasonable hypotheses on linguistic, cultural, and anthropological grounds for suggesting that Dravidian languages originated outside India, specifically in western Asia, there is as yet no direct evidence for the existence of Dravidian outside the subcontinent,[13] nor for its currency in the north other than that afforded by Brāhūī. The Mohenjo-dāro seals are not yet read, nor is their language or its structures identified for certain.

However, we can look back a little further than 200 B.C., a possible date for south Indian megalithic culture, for definite record of Dravidian; this is provided by the south Indian Brāhmī inscriptions mentioned earlier, and these date from the third century B.C. The first of the seventy-six known inscriptions was discovered by Venkoba Rao in 1903 some 23 miles north-east of Madurai. There are in addition twenty short graffiti in the same script on pottery from Arikkamedu, an important site on the east coast of Tamilnādu, excavated by Wheeler in 1945 and by others since. The first certain identification of their language as being Old Tamil was made by K. V. Subrahmanya Ayyar and presented by him at the Third All-India Oriental Conference, held in Madras in 1924.[14] The most important and recent work on these inscriptions is that of I. Mahadevan and R. Panneerselvam.[15] They show that the inscriptions confirm certain kings and place-names mentioned in the earliest extant Tamil literature, of roughly the same date.

Mahadevan's brilliant work demonstrates that, as early as the third to second centuries B.C., the main modifications to the 'All-India' syllabary of 36 consonants and 10 vowels plus diphthongs had been made to equip the script suitably for writing Tamil: the consonants had been reduced to 18, by the removal of letters for the voiced plosives, aspirated plosives, and sibilants, and by the addition of characters to represent Tamil retroflex *ḻ* and *ḷ* and alveolar *ṟ* and *ṉ*. As for vowels, these were reduced to 9 by the omission of the diphthong *au*, the existence in Tamil of separate short *ĕ* and *ŏ* not being recognized in this script (or until the time of Beschi in the eighteenth century). Mahadevan established an important phenomenon in these inscriptions, the use of the character for medial *ā* to represent medial *a* also, the vowel considered inherent in all consonants in all other Indian scripts and in those in South-East Asia developed from them. Thus there was no need for a 'killer' symbol to remove this inherent vowel, such as the *virāma* in Sanskrit, and

[12] V. Gordon Childe, 'Megaliths' in *Ancient India*, 4 (1947–8). The antiquity and importance of the sea link between southern peninsular India and the Middle East (and later, via the Middle East, with the Roman Empire) cannot be exaggerated.

[13] Comparable, for example, with the close affinities with Vedic Sanskrit of Old Iranian, both linguistically and in subject-matter of hymns.

[14] See *Proceedings* thereof, pp. 275–300.

[15] See R. Panneerselvam, 'An Important Brahmi Tamil Inscription' in *Proceedings of the First International Conference-Seminar of Tamil Studies*, Kuala Lumpur, IIATR 1968, and I. Mahadevan, 'Tamil Brahmi Inscriptions of the Sangam Age' in *Proceedings of the Second International Conference-Seminar of Tamil Studies*, Madras, IIATR 1971.

Mahadevan is able in consequence to read the hitherto-baffling *kāla* (inscr. 29), *mākāna* (inscr. 13), and *maṇiya* (inscr. 72) as correct Tamil *kal, makaṉ*, and *maṇiy*. In effect, the early Tamil Brāhmī inscriptions show a letter system comparable to our own alphabet, rather than a syllabary; thus the other 'All-India' development of conjunct consonants for such sounds as *kṣa, tra*, or *ktva* was rendered unnecessary. Mahadevan convincingly suggests that the absence of the (available) voiced plosive characters from this script means that Tamil at this stage did not have the voiced intervocalic plosive phonemes that are one of its principal modern features (though one still uncatered for in the script).[16]

In addition to their linguistic interest, these inscriptions have helped corroborate some of the royal names occurring in early Tamil praise-poetry, as just noted. One king mentioned is *Ko Ātaṉ Ce(ra)l Irumpŏṟai* (inscr. 56 and 57), and from one of the earliest collections of Tamil poems, *Padiṟṟuppattu*, an anthology of praise-poems on the Śeral kings, we know of two with the title of 'He of the great mountain', *Irumpŏṟai*.[17] More important perhaps is the fact that Pugalūr, where these two inscriptions were found, is about ten miles from the modern *Kārūr*, mentioned in the form *Karuūr* in the same cavern (inscr. 66). We know from Ptolemy that Karoura was 'the royal seat of Kerobothros'[18] and several references in the colophons to early Tamil poems indicate that Karuvūr was a Śeral royal town.[19]

Consideration of these inscriptions has led us, then, to a discussion of the earliest Tamil literature, with which much of the remainder of this essay will be concerned, as it represents probably the most important single contribution of Dravidian language and culture to the Indian heritage. The bulk of it is contained in *Eight Anthologies* (*Ettuttogai*) two being of bardic poetry, and six of courtly love-poems (though one, *Paripādal*, includes religious praise-poetry and descriptive verse also). On the basis of internal evidence most of these anthology-poems have been assigned to the first three centuries of our era, and it looks as if the epigraphical evidence now to hand confirms this.

While it is clear that a good deal of synthesis with Indo-Āryan, especially Brāhmanical, cultural and linguistic elements from the north had already taken place, these poems yet present a distinct culture, one in which attitudes and values come across to us in a very vivid and fresh manner. For its part, the literature is simple and direct in appeal, and relatively free of the obscurity and sophistication of much later Indian literature, including that of Tamil itself. Unlike the near-totality of medieval literatures in the south, these poems are secular. The praise-poetry is quite unlike anything else extant in the south. At the same time, a 'grammar', *Tolkāppiyam*, parts of which are probably contemporaneous, sets out an elaborate rhetoric for bardic and love-poetry that is quite unlike other Indian literary theories which have their origins in Sanskrit rhetoric, in which the needs of drama played a large part. While it is true that, in Tamil courtly love-poetry, there are 'dramatis personae', stock characters such as the hero, heroine, foster-mother, and so on

[16] The contrast is comparable to that between Spanish intervocalic *s* (always unvoiced) on the one hand and that of Portuguese or Italian on the other.

[17] See Panneerselvam, op. cit., pp. 422–4.

[18] McCrindle, *Ancient India*, Vol. 4, p. 180.

[19] See further, Mahadevan, op. cit., pp. 94–5.

(it being a convention that personal names are never mentioned),[20] the rhetoric of this poetry, and even more that of the heroic, arises in the context of 'Natural Tamil' (*Iyarramil*), the name given to poetry, as opposed to 'Drama Tamil' and 'Musical Tamil' (*Nāṭakattamil* and *Icaittamil*). For this purpose, love is considered as interior or subjective, *Agam*, and the heroic as exterior, *Puram*. Both topics are classified under seven heads, five plus two in each case, the sets of five being the kernel, as it were, of both *Agam* and *Puram*. For *Agam*, five aspects of love are involved: union, separation, awaiting (the return of the lover), anguish, and love-quarrel. For *Puram*, five stages of warfare are envisaged: the cattle-raid, the fight of two kings over disputed territory, the attack on the fort, open warfare, and praise of the king. The five aspects of love are suggested by associations with regions of the Tamil country by means of the names of five plants that grew therein; the literature is, then, one of allusion. For example, union is suggested by *Kurinji*, the Strobilanthes that grew in the mountains, which were considered suitable for elopement. It sufficed to mention the Strobilanthes to set the tone of the whole poem: 'My love for the lord of this land, where delicious honey is won from the black-stemmed Strobilanthes on the mountain-slopes, is greater than the earth, vaster than the sky, and deeper than the ocean.'[21]

The two other aspects of love were unrequited and forced love; they were considered to lie outside the realm of usual love-poetry; indeed some of these poems are not in the *Agam* anthologies at all, but in *Puram* collections. An example of unrequited love is: 'My bangles are slipping off, for I waste away with love for the young stalwart with the dark beard and closely fitting anklets. I have my mother to fear; I have to fear the assembly because I caressed his death-dealing shoulders. May this city of confusion be stricken with great distress like me, ever smitten not from one side but from two.'[22]

In the same anthology, the poet Paranar addresses the chieftain Pegan on behalf of Kannagi, whom he had deserted:

> Not to have pity is cruel. While in the evening I sang of your rain-drenched forest to the strains of the *rāga* Śevvali, she whose kohl-bedecked eyes resemble blue water-lilies was so distraught that the tear-drops were as dew upon her breast. Piteous was she. 'Young lady, tell me whether you are related to him who desires my friendship', said I as I greeted her. She wiped away the tears with fingers slender as the flame-lily's petals as she replied: 'I am nothing to him! Listen. Even now he is savouring the beauty of another girl like me. Every day they gossip about how the famous Pegan goes in his noisy chariot to that fair place surrounded with wild jasmine'.[23]

A good description of a very human situation appears in poem 7 of *Paripadal*. This is a rather later anthology; its poetry is more sophisticated and much of it is religious verse in praise of Tirumāl (Vishnu) and Śevvel (Skanda). However, there are some fine poems describing the river Vaiyai that flows through Madurai, the capital of the Pāndiyar, another Tamil 'dynasty'. Poem 7 is one of these, and, after a description of the bathing of girls in the river, the following incident occurs:

> Wet from the river she had sought, and wishing to avoid a chill, she whose eyes resembled water-lilies took some strong toddy around which hummed bees. As she

[20] Compare the medieval practice in Europe of alluding to the beloved merely as *S.A.*, *Son Altesse*. [21] *Kuruntogai* 3 (by Tevakulattār). [22] *Puram* 83 (Nakkaṇṇaiyār).

drank a great draught of the liquor that bestows joy, her eyes shone like honey-sweet flowers. Seeing the loveliness of her eyes, he praised them; he sang her praises as if he were a bard. Not realizing the direction in which his interest lay, another girl thought he was singing about her, and was rather surprised. He whose chest was broad grew nervous at this and, sorrowfully wondering what would happen to him, went up to his beloved. Because of the ridiculous misunderstanding, her eyes, already inflamed through drinking the toddy, grew still redder. The pretty girls who had gone bathing began squabbling among themselves; she became very cross and snatched the chaplets from their heads. Her lover, who had seen how beautiful she was while she bathed, prostrated on the ground his body smeared with sandalwood-paste. But she would not stop scolding him, and even trod on his head! Meanwhile, the others went on bathing in the bright river.[24]

One example of the bardic poetry must suffice.[25] The five stages of warfare were likewise suggested by flowers; garlands of them were worn by warriors to indicate what stage of warfare they were engaged upon, recalling American Indian war-paint. *Tumbai*, the white Indian dead-nettle,[26] was worn in open combat, and we have a poem upon this theme in *Puram*: 'Whoever you are, do not talk about collecting your scouts and flanking-troops before you have seen my lord of the drum-like shoulders. His warfare is good, and is celebrated with festivals. On his beautiful and mighty chest he wears finely wrought ornaments that flash in the sun. He is a renowned scion of the vigorous Malavar clan whose glittering, scintillating spears are long.'[27]

All the literature so far considered, and another extensive collection called the Ten Songs, *Pattuppāttu*, consists of discontinuous poetry. Until the epic *Śilappadigāram*, composed some time between the second and the fifth centuries A.D., we do not find in Tamil a continuous narrative of the type present in other early literatures, such as heroic poetry from outside India. Space forbids a detailed examination of *Śilappadigāram*, but it must be mentioned as being a distinctly Tamil story contributed to Indian literature. The portion of it relating to the Śeralar kings clearly shares the traditions embodied in the early anthology of praise-poetry about them, *Padirruppāttu*. The story is the popular theme extolling the virtuous wife. Kovalan, the chief male character, hardly a hero, is a merchant in the Śola city of Pugār. He neglects his wife Kannagi, throwing away his fortune upon a courtesan well versed in music and dancing called Mādavi. After quarrelling with her, however, Kovalan returns to his faithful wife Kannagi and they both migrate to the Pāndiya city of Madurai. They attempt to start life afresh, and raise capital by selling Kannagi's anklets (*śilambu*).[28] But an evil-minded goldsmith brings a false charge of theft of the queen's anklet, that had been reported lost; Kovalan is apprehended, accused, and killed. Kannagi goes to the king and proves that the charge was baseless; the king dies of grief, but the enraged widow curses the city to destruction by fire, plucking off her breast and hurling it over the town.[29] She then goes to Vanji, another Śeral city, and is received into heaven as the Lady, Pattini, together with her husband.[30]

[23] *Puram* 144 (Paranar). [24] *Pari.* 7, lines 61–76 (Maiyota Kkovanār).

[25] The subject of *Puram* has been thoroughly surveyed by K. Kailasapathy in *Tamil Heroic Poetry*, Oxford, 1968. [26] *Leucas aspera Spreng.* [27] *Puram* 88 (Avvaiyar).

[28] The title *Śilappadigāram* means 'Tale of the Anklet'.

[29] One is left wondering if there is any connection between this story and the androgynous Śiva-Pārvatī image Ardhanārīśvara. [30] A recent translation is by Alain Daniélou.

The sequel to this story, *Manimegalai*, need not detain us. It is largely a Buddhist work, inspired by the logical system of the philosopher Dinnāga, and demonstrates the extent to which, by the time of its composition, Tamil had become influenced by external factors. Much of its later literature, and all of the extant literatures of Kannada, Telugu, and Malayālam, the other three main Dravidian languages, consists of the reworking of themes originally presented in Sanskrit. They are none the less important for this, but it becomes less easy to quantify the purely Dravidian element in them.

By reason of the fact that these four were, and are, spoken as well as written languages, there is an element of the popular and spontaneous in their literatures that may seem to be absent from some Sanskrit writing. But this feature they of course share with Indo-Āryan vernaculars such as Marāthī and Hindī. Thus the Tamil version of the epic *Rāmāyana* presents the hero Rāma as a god, and to that extent is a religious poem, unlike its Sanskrit prototype. But this feature is common to all the vernacular Rāma stories, in India and in South-East Asia.

One must in conclusion note that the great medieval *bhakti* movement, expressing itself in hymns and mystical utterances in all the spoken languages of India, had its real beginnings in the Tamil Śaivite hymns composed from the sixth century onwards, and collectively known as the *Tirumurai*. The most famous portion is the Garland of God, *Tevāram*, but the mystical poems by Manikkavāśagar, *Tiruvāśagam* and *Tirukkovaiyār*, should be mentioned. The figure of the divine lover and his beloved, the soul, becomes common enough in medieval India, especially in the worship of Krishna. But Mānikkavāsagar's *Tirukkovaiyār* antedates this to a considerable extent. The Vīraśaiva *Vacanakāvyas* of Basava were, in Kannada, an extension of this genre.

Similarly, the medieval philosophical texts of the *Śaiva Siddhānta* were popularized through Tamil and, with the digest of moralistic treatises known as *Tirukkural*, were hailed by early European missionary-scholars as the finest literary work produced in the south. But it is difficult to avoid the conclusion that, in this roseate view, they were influenced by the apparent closeness of many of the concepts in *Tirukkural* and in, say, *Śivanānabodam*[31] to those of Christianity. The Tamils brought to these subjects an original and fresh approach, but in their anthology-poems they were themselves the originators.

[31] By Meykandadevar. The principal Śaiva Siddhānta work in Tamil.

CHAPTER V

Aśokan India and the Gupta Age

by ROMILA THAPAR

AŚOKAN India and the Gupta age are the terminal points of a span of one thousand years, from the fourth century B.C. to the sixth century A.D. The span extends over a period of considerable historical change; yet it is possible to perceive an underlying continuity. The origin of institutions which were to mould Indian culture is frequently traceable to this period. The Aśokan age saw the establishment of a centralized imperial structure which embraced almost the entire subcontinent and rested on a methodically organized and efficient bureaucracy. This was the first time that the imperial idea found expression in India. In the subsequent period the personality of India acquired new contours and delineations which were both the result of an imperial system and the foreshadowing of other patterns. The Gupta age, for a brief period, came close in spirit to the government of the Mauryas, but it carried the seeds of a new political system—the early stages of a feudal-type organization—which was not conducive to empire building. The Gupta age is better remembered as the age which saw the triumph of Sanskritic culture in many parts of the subcontinent.

Chandragupta Maurya conquered Magadha (south Bihar) and in 321 B.C. founded the Mauryan Dynasty with his capital at Pāṭaliputra (in the vicinity of modern Patnā). He proceeded to annex various parts of northern India and campaigned against the Greek, Seleucus Nicator, the former general of Alexander. The successful outcome of this campaign brought him the trans-Indus region and areas of Afghanistan. His son, Bindusāra, continued the campaign into peninsular India. But it was his grandson Aśoka who, inheriting the subcontinent, established an all-India empire and discovered both the advantages and problems inherent in such a political structure.

The mechanics of a centralized empire came into existence after a lengthy germination involving the life and death of numerous kingdoms and republics in northern India from the sixth century B.C. onwards. Perhaps the earliest glimmerings of empire were visible to the Nandas, the dynasty which immediately preceded the Mauryas, though the actual birth of empire had to wait until the arrival of the latter. Aśoka inherited an efficiently running machine dominated by a central administration. The imperial structure was provided with a base through the spread and establishment of an agrarian economy. In later centuries, in spite of the contribution of other types of economic activity such as internal and overseas trade, agriculture remained the dominant factor in the economy, with these other activities providing substantial but subsidiary incomes.

Land revenue had been recognized as a major source of state income before the Mauryas. The proverbial wealth of the Nandas was doubtless due to their efficient collection of revenue from the fertile middle Gangā plain. That the legitimacy of taxation had been established by the time of the Mauryas and its potentiality in terms of income recognized, is evident from the references to land revenue and taxes in Kauṭalya's *Arthaśāstra* and a significant reference in the inscriptions of Aśoka.[1] According to the *Arthaśāstra* every activity, from agriculture to gambling and prostitution, might be subjected to taxation by the state. No waste land should be occupied nor a single tree cut down in the forest without permission from the state, since these were all ultimately sources of revenue. It was conceded that the main item of income was land revenue and this was dependent on correct assessment and proper collection. But other activities had also to be controlled and supervised by the state so that they would yield the maximum revenue.

All this necessitated a carefully worked out bureaucratic system, and from descriptions of administration in Mauryan sources this seems to have been achieved. Practically every professional and skilled person was registered and was under the ultimate control of a superintendent. The officers were very well paid, in the belief that a well-paid bureaucracy was likely to be more efficient. High salaries could be maintained only if taxes were rigorously collected. Thus the two factors of taxation and administration were interlinked.

These two factors had a bearing on yet another factor: the army and its role in the politics and economy of the Mauryan period. A large army was not only essential to vast conquests, it was equally important as a means of holding the empire together. Mauryan rulers were aware of this. The estimated strength of Chandragupta's army, according to near-contemporary classical sources, was 9,000 elephants, 30,000 cavalry, and 600,000 infantry. Even allowing for a margin of exaggeration in these figures the Mauryan army was a large one by any standards. To maintain such an army would require a large state income, and this in turn would depend on taxation and the size of the kingdom. Thus it was the interdependence of taxation, administration, and armed strength which went into the making of a centralized empire.

Control over these factors lay with the king, who was regarded as the supreme source of power and authority. This enabled the king to adopt a paternalistic attitude towards his subjects, as is evident from Aśoka's edicts, where he says, 'All men are my children and just as I desire for my children that they should obtain welfare and happiness both in this world and the next, the same do I desire for all men . . .'[2] Or as, when referring to his officers in the rural areas, he writes, 'Just as one entrusts one's child to an experienced nurse, and is confident that the experienced nurse is able to care for the child satisfactorily, so my *rajukas* have been appointed for the welfare and happiness of the country people . . .'[3]

Paternalism demands a continued contact between king and subjects. The

[1] Kauṭalya, alternatively known as Kauṭilya and Chānakya, was the chief minister of Chandragupta Maurya and a work on political economy, the *Arthaśāstra*, is attributed to him. In its present form the work has been dated by scholars to the second and third centuries A.D. But parts of it appear to reflect notions which were current in the administrative system of the Mauryas. With regard to land revenue, it is significant that, on visiting Lumbinī, Aśoka ordered a reduction in land revenue as a favour to the birth-place of the Buddha. This is a clear indication of the importance of such revenue to the Mauryan political and economic system.

[2] Second Separate Rock Edict.

[3] Fourth Pillar Edict.

Mauryan kings, we are told, were always available for consultation. Megasthenes, who visited India as the ambassador of Seleucus Nicator and stayed at the Mauryan Court during the reign of Chandragupta, describes the king receiving complaints and discussing matters of state even when being massaged. Aśoka emphatically declares in one of his edicts that, no matter where he may be, no member of the ministerial council should be debarred from seeing him.

But the availability of the king was not sufficient. In a system as centralized as that of the Mauryas it was essential that communication be maintained with all parts of the subcontinent and with every level of society. This was done in part by building a network of roads linking the entire empire with Pāṭaliputra. Aśoka's justified pride in the excellence of the roads which he had constructed is corroborated by Pliny the Elder's enthusiasm in describing the Royal Highway which ran from Taxila to Pāṭaliputra, a distance of over a thousand miles.

At another level, contact with the populace was maintained through the use of agents and informants. These were used both to propagate the ideas of the king and to bring him reports on public opinion.[4] Frequent tours and the appointment of specially trusted inspectors were other means of communication with the people.

Although agriculture provided the most substantial part of the state income it was not the sole source of revenue. An indirect source of income for the Mauryan state was the use of the śūdras, the lowest of the four orders of Hindu society, as free labour when so required. The settlement of new areas, the opening of waste land to agriculture, the working of the state-owned mines such as the salt mines of the Panjāb and the iron ore deposits in Magadha, were some of the activities for which śūdras, in addition to prisoners of war and criminals, provided labour power.

Among the more significant changes which had taken place by the middle of the first millennium B.C. was the development of towns and urban culture. The coming of Āryan culture, based on pastoralism and agrarian village communities, resulted in the entire process of development from village cultures to urban cultures being re-experienced in northern India. Towns evolved from trade centres and craft villages, and consequently the dominant institution of urban life was the guild. By the end of the fourth century B.C. artisan and merchant guilds were an established part of the urban pattern.

The manufacture of goods and trade formed additional sources of income in a tax-oriented system. Not surprisingly the *Arthaśāstra* lists a number of taxes on goods at various stages of production and distribution. The existence of an all-India empire under a single political authority and the excellent communications developed within the subcontinent led to an expansion in internal trade which added to the growing profits of the guilds. Ventures in overseas trade were doubtless encouraged by the protection of diplomatic missions sent by the Mauryan emperors. The exchange of envoys between the Greek kings of western Asia and Egypt and the Mauryas is on record, as also

[4] A similar system was adopted by the Achaemenid kings of Persia, where the inspectors were called 'the king's eye' and 'the king's ear', and also by Charlemagne, in whose kingdom they were known as the *missi*.

the curious request for gifts such as sophists, singing boys, and wine. The close and friendly ties between Aśoka and Tissa, the king of Ceylon, must have resulted in greater communication between the two countries.

The improved economic status of the guilds introduced complications in the existing social pattern. Guild leaders became powerful citizens controlling large economic assets. But, in the caste-based society of this period, the trader or the artisan was not included among the most socially privileged citizens. The challenge which the mercantile community presented to the more established sections of society was yet to come, but the germinal tensions came into being at this stage. That there was an element of fear on the part of the authorities of the growing power of the guilds seems evident from the *Arthaśāstra*, which favours a rigid control of guild activities. For instance every guild had to be registered with the local administration and no guild was allowed to move from its location without prior permission.

There was yet another factor which possibly aggravated social tensions. The two new religions, Buddhism and Jainism, had won the sympathy of the artisans and the merchants; and these religions were heterodox sects which challenged the established order. The association of the emergent urban groups with dissident thinking and practice would make them suspect in the eyes of the orthodox.

These new religions sprang from a considerable intellectual ferment which had begun earlier in the period, around 600 B.C. A healthy rivalry was apparent among a number of sects, such as the Chārvākas, Jainas, and Ājīvikas, whose doctrines ranged from pure materialism to determinism. This intellectual liveliness was reflected in the eclectic interests of the Mauryan rulers, since it was claimed by the Jainas that Chandragupta was a supporter and there is evidence that Bindusāra favoured the Ājīvikas. Close contacts with western Asia must have provided yet another stream of unorthodox ideas.

This then was the empire which Aśoka inherited. In area a subcontinent, inhabited by peoples of many cultures and at many levels of development; a society with a wide range of customs, beliefs, affinities, antagonisms, tensions, and harmonies. Magadha and the western Gangā valley were culturally Āryanized but the fringes of this area were less so. The north was in close contact with the Hellenized culture of Afghanistan and Iran; the far south was on the threshold of the creative efflorescence of Tamil culture. To rule such an empire successfully would have required the perception and the imagination of an exceptionally gifted man. This was the challenge which Aśoka attempted to meet.

For many centuries Aśoka remained almost unknown to the Indian historical tradition. He was mentioned in the genealogies of the Mauryan kings but nothing more than the length of his reign was stated about him. A vast amount of semi-historical, largely legendary, material on his life had been collected in Buddhist sources but this material practically disappeared from the Indian tradition with the decline of Buddhism in India by the end of the thirteenth century. It was preserved in Buddhist centres outside India—in Ceylon, Central Asia, and China. The proclamations issued by Aśoka were engraved on rocks and pillars throughout the subcontinent and these remained visible, but unfortunately the Brāhmī script in which they had been engraved had become archaic and the inscriptions could not be read.[5] However, in 1837 the Orientalist James Prinsep deciphered the script. Although the text was now known, the author of the inscriptions could not be identified, since he was generally referred to only by his titles—*Devānampiya Piyadassi*—The Beloved of the Gods, of Gracious Mien—and these were unknown to the Indian king-lists. A tentative identification with Aśoka was made in the late nineteenth century on the evidence from the Buddhist chronicles of Ceylon. It was not until 1915 that this identification was confirmed, however, with the discovery of an inscription which referred to the author as *Devānampiya Asoka*.[6]

The association of this name with Buddhist sources led to his edicts being interpreted almost as Buddhist documents. Undoubtedly Aśoka was a Buddhist and much of the ideology of *Dhamma*[7] which he enunciated was inspired by Buddhism. But to equate it totally with Buddhism and to suggest that Aśoka was propagating Buddhism as the state religion is to read more into the edicts than was intended by the monarch. A careful analysis of the inscriptions reveals that they were of two categories. Some were addressed specifically to the Buddhist Church or *Sangha* and were concerned entirely with matters relating to the *Sangha*. The majority of the inscriptions are, however, addressed to the public at large and deal with questions of wider interest. It is significant that it is in this second category of inscriptions that the king expounds his ideas on *Dhamma*.

It would appear that Aśoka aimed at creating an attitude of mind among his subjects in which social behaviour had the highest relevance. In the context of conditions during the Mauryan period, this ideology of *Dhamma* may have been viewed as a focus of loyalty and as a point of convergence for the existing diversities of people and activities. *Dhamma* stressed toleration, non-violence (where the emperor himself forswore violence and force as means to an end), respect for those in positions of authority, including both the brāhmans and the Buddhist monks, consideration and kindness towards inferiors, and the general acceptance of ideals conducive to human dignity. The king instituted a special class of officers—the officers of *Dhamma*—who were responsible for the propagation of this ideology and who worked for the general welfare of the people.

Yet the ideology of *Dhamma* died with the death of the emperor. As an attempt to solve the problems of the time it was perhaps too idealistic. At the same time it can hardly be described as a revolutionary doctrine, since it was largely an emphatic reiteration of certain existing principles of ethics. But credit must be given to the man who had the vision to seek such a solution and the courage to attempt it.

Fifty years after the death of Aśoka the Mauryan Empire had declined.

[5] One of the sultans of Delhi in the fourteenth century, Fīroz Shāh Tughluq, was both intrigued and impressed by an Aśokan pillar which he found near Delhi, and he had it removed to his capital. But no one could read the inscription on the pillar or explain its purpose.

[6] Minor Rock Edict at Maski: *devānampiyassa Asokassa*.

[7] The word *dhamma* is the Pāli form of the Sanskrit *dharma* and is almost impossible to translate adequately into English. Generally accepted renderings are 'morality, piety, virtue, the social order'.

Some historians have traced this decline to the policies of Aśoka, claiming that his pro-Buddhist sympathies led to a brāhmanical revolt against the Mauryan rulers; others have suggested that his adherence to non-violence led to a weakening of the military strength of the empire and laid it open to attacks, particularly from the north-west. But evidence in support of these theories is far too slight. Other possibilities must also be considered, not least among them being that the later Mauryan kings may well have been weak and ineffectual rulers, unable to hold together such a vast empire. Furthermore the pressure of a highly paid bureaucracy and a large army could not have been sustained over a period of almost 150 years without a strain on an agricultural economy. Either these two money-consuming items would have had to be whittled down and readjusted or in periods of depression fresh sources of income would have had to be found. Finally, the strongest bond in uniting people into a political entity—the desire on the part of the people to become a nation—was lacking. The divergencies in the various parts of the subcontinent were too great to allow the formation of a national unit. The doctrine of *Dhamma*, which might have created a common factor of loyalty, failed to do so.

The subsequent fragmentation of the subcontinent was not entirely arbitrary, for it led to the identification of geographical areas as political entities. These (with some modification) were to remain the nuclei of political units in the Indian subcontinent for many centuries.

In 185 B.C. the Mauryan Empire ceased to exist. The immediate inheritors of the Mauryas in the Gangā heart-land, Magadha, were the Śungas, a brāhman family which had usurped the throne at Pātaliputra. The Śungas were to give way to the Kānvas, to be followed by a series of minor dynasties until the rise of the Guptas in the fourth century A.D. During these centuries Magadha tended to remain somewhat isolated, and few attempts were made by its rulers to participate in events elsewhere.

Kalinga (a part of modern Orissā) came to the forefront with the meteoric rise of King Khāravela, and then subsided into quietude. A biographical sketch of Khāravela is available from an inscription, where he asserts his dominion over the entire Mahānadī delta and claims many victories over south Indian kings. Such maritime kingdoms rose sporadically, their prosperity being due to sea trade and the fertility of their hinterland, generally a delta region.

Meanwhile the north-western part of the subcontinent—the Panjāb and the Indus valley—was once again being sucked into the vortex of Iranian and Central Asian politics. Alexander, after his rapid campaign through Persia and north-western India, left behind a number of governors, who on his death in 323 B.C. declared themselves kings of the respective provinces which they governed. The house of Seleucus in western Asia and its erstwhile satraps, the Greek rulers of Bactria, came into conflict, and gradually the conflict spilled over into north-western India, involving the small and politically isolated Indian kingdoms which were unable to hold back the Bactrian Greeks. The latter established themselves in the north-west during the second century B.C. Fortunately for us, these kings were enthusiastic minters of coins and their history has been partially reconstructed, largely on numismatic evidence.

Further south the Parthians made a brief thrust in the region of Sind, but could not maintain their power there for long. Events in Central Asia were now to influence north Indian politics. A nomadic movement originating on the borders of China made the Yüeh-chih tribe migrate westwards to the neighbourhood of the Caspian Sea, dislodging the existing inhabitants of this region, the Śakas (Scythians). Further migrations brought both the Śakas and the Yüeh-chih to India. The early decades of the first century A.D. saw the Yüeh-chih settled in northern India and the Śakas concentrated in the region of Kutch and Kathiawar in western India. The Śakas were now neighbours of the Sātavāhana or Āndhra kings, who had established a kingdom centred around the north-western area of the Deccan plateau. In time the Śakas found themselves sandwiched between two important powers, for in the north the Yüeh-chih or Kushāna kingdom had been consolidated by Kanishka, who not only extended its southern and eastern boundaries as far as Mathurā and Vārānaṣī, but also participated in campaigns in Central Asia.[8] To the south of the Śakas, the Sātavāhanas drew their strength from the fact that they were a bridge between the northern and southern parts of the subcontinent. This characteristic of the Deccan kingdoms, deriving their power from their location, was to remain an important geo-political factor in Indian history for many centuries.

The history of south India emerges in clearer perspective during the period between 200 B.C. and A.D. 300, the evidence being that of archaeology, epigraphy, and the *Sangam* literature of the early Tamils. The extreme south of the peninsula, Mysore and beyond, had not been under actual Mauryan control, though the relationship between the imperial power and the southern kingdoms was a close and friendly one. This is revealed by Aśoka's references to his neighbours in the south, the kingdoms of the Cholas, Pāndyas, Keralaputras, and Satiyaputras, some of which are also mentioned in the Sangam literature. Archaeology provides evidence of a well-organized megalithic culture in this region during the Mauryan period. Possibly it was in contact with a similar culture in western Asia, a contact which had its antecedents and which continued in later centuries.

The anthologies of Tamil poetry contain among other things descriptive narrations of events, both actual and imagined, in the context of early tribal society in south India. Conflicts among the kingdoms were perpetual, because each had two objectives—to control the fertile deltas, the only regions where agriculture was possible on a large scale, and to have access to the important trading stations along the coasts which were lucrative sources of revenue, since many of them traded with the Yavanas, the peoples of western Asia.[9]

The fragmentation of the subcontinent which took place during this period may have been politically emasculating, but it was at this time that a new and vital interest came to be introduced into economic development. It was the age when India discovered the potential wealth inherent in trade. Despite the

[8] In fact the prestige of Kanishka is such that the inauguration of the much-used Śaka era of A.D. 78 is frequently attributed to him. His date is very uncertain, however, and recent estimates vary between this date and the third century A.D.

[9] *Yavana*, a back formation from the Prakrit word *Yona*, is believed to refer originally to Ionian Greeks and came to be used for any of the trading peoples of western Asia—the Greeks, the Romans, and in later centuries the Arabs.

many political frontiers, internal trade increased very considerably. The woollen blankets of Gandhāra and the linen of Bengal were familiar to all parts of the country, as were the precious stones from south India. But even more relevant to the economic prosperity of India was the overseas trade. Indian traders ventured out in all directions: to Central Asia and China, to western Asia, and in South-East Asia as far as the kingdom of Funan in modern Vietnam. Indian merchants became the middlemen in the commerce between South-East Asia and the Mediterranean. They were the entrepreneurs in the trade supplying the needs and luxuries of the Graeco-Roman world, a topic which is dealt with elsewhere (ch. xxx) in this book.

This increase in trade resulted quite naturally in the greater prosperity of the guilds. Guilds became not only the basis for the production and distribution of merchandise but also the financial centres of trade. The Sātavāhana rulers, for instance, often gave to religious charities donations which came from money invested with guilds. The intensification of the guild system influenced sub-caste relations within caste society, for each guild tended to become a sub-caste drawing on its own resources for manpower. Thus even in urban areas the economic basis of the organization of caste society became firmer. With the accumulation of wealth in the hands of guilds and merchants, patronage of learning and the arts was no longer limited to royalty. Not surprisingly, some of the most magnificent Buddhist monuments are of this period and many of them owe their existence to the donations of wealthy guilds and merchants. The *stūpas* at Sānchī, Bhārhut, and Amarāvatī stand witness to this.

Together with Indian traders went the brāhmans and the Buddhist missionaries. Western Asia came into contact with them in the centuries before Christ. China received its first Buddhist mission in A.D. 68 at Loyang. In the early centuries after Christ, Buddhists were active in Funan and Champā. Meanwhile Buddhism itself had undergone a considerable change, with doctrinal differences creating a split which was formally recognized at the Fourth Buddhist Council, held according to tradition during the reign of Kanishka; and two groups of Buddhists were established, the *Mahāyāna* and the *Hīnayāna*. Missionaries of Mahāyāna sects established themselves in Central Asia, China, and Japan. Hīnayāna Buddhism was more popular in Ceylon, and later it ousted the Mahāyāna in South-East Asia.

With increasing contact through commerce between the various parts of the known world, the communication of ideas between these regions improved. For instance, Indian astronomers discovered the existence of Graeco-Roman astronomy. Graeco-Roman art, particularly of the Alexandrian variety, not only found admirers in north-western India and Afghanistan but became the model for a hybrid local school which art-historians have subsequently called Gandhāra art. Yet another result was the arrival of Christian teaching in India, which according to the legends came in the mid-first century A.D., brought by St. Thomas.

The political fragmentation of the subcontinent did not put an end to the dream of an empire as vast as that of the Mauryas. An attempt was made by kings of the Gupta family to establish such an empire in the early part of the fourth century A.D.

The Guptas were in origin probably a family of wealthy landowners who gradually attained both economic power and political status. Unlike the founder of the Mauryan Dynasty, who is described as an adventurous young man with no significant antecedents, the founder of the Gupta Dynasty, also called Chandra Gupta, belonged to a family which had established its power at a local level in Magadha. A judicious marriage with a Licchavi princess gave him additional prestige, the Licchavis claiming a long-established respectability. Following his coronation as king of Magadha in A.D. 319–20 Chandra Gupta took the title of *mahārājādhirāja*—Great King of Kings.

In about A.D. 335 his son, Samudra Gupta, inherited the kingdom of Magadha. He issued a series of beautifully executed gold coins in which he is depicted both as a conqueror and as a musician, a strange combination of interests. Fortunately for later historians a lengthy panegyric on him was composed by one of his high officials and engraved on an Aśokan pillar which has since been brought to Allahābād. The inscription refers among other things to the martial exploits of Samudra Gupta; to the kings uprooted and the territory annexed in the northern part of the subcontinent. It mentions also the long march which Samudra Gupta undertook in the south, reaching as far as Kānchīpuram. Nor are the tributes from foreign kingdoms omitted. Mention is made of the Śakas, Ceylon, various Iranian rulers of the north-west and the inhabitants of all the islands. The latter may refer to Indian trading stations on the islands of South-East Asia and in the Indian ocean.

The nucleus of the Gupta kingdom, as of the Mauryan Empire, was the Gangā heartland. This and the adjoining territory to the west were the only regions over which Samudra Gupta had absolute and unchallenged control. Gupta control of the Deccan was uncertain and had to be propped up with a matrimonial alliance, a Gupta princess marrying a prince of the Vākātaka Dynasty of the Deccan, the successors to the Sātavāhana power. This secured a friendly southern frontier for the Guptas, which was necessary to Samudra Gupta's successor, Chandra Gupta II, when he led a campaign against the Śakas in western India.

It was during the reign of Chandra Gupta II that Gupta ascendancy was at its peak. His successful campaign against the Śakas, resulting in the annexation of western India, was, however, not his only achievement. Like his predecessor, he was a patron of poets, philosophers, scientists, musicians, and sculptors. This period saw the crystallization of what came to be the classical norm in ancient India on both the political and the cultural levels.

The Gupta kings took exalted titles such as *mahārājādhirāja paramabhattāraka*—Great King of Kings, the Supreme Lord. This was in striking contrast to the Mauryas who, though politically far more powerful, never used such exalted titles. Superficially Gupta administration was similar to that of the Mauryas. The king was the highest authority and the kingdom was divided into a hierarchy of administrative units—provinces, districts, and groups of villages—each with its own range of officers responsible to the most senior officer in the unit. Yet there was a significant difference between Gupta and Mauryan administration: during the Gupta period there was far greater stress on local administration and far less direct control from the centre. Even in urban administration, the City Boards consisted of representatives of local opinion and interest (such as the heads of guilds and artisan and merchant bodies) rather than officers of state.

A parallel tendency was developing in the agrarian system, particularly in the sphere of land revenue. The revenue was still collected by the king's officers, but they retained a certain predetermined percentage in lieu of a regular cash salary. This procedure of payment to officers came to be adopted with increasing frequency. On occasion the king would even grant the revenue from an area of land or a village to non-officials, such as brāhmans renowned for their learning. Inscriptions recording such grants are known from the early centuries A.D. onwards. Since a major part of the state revenue came from the land, grants of revenue were gradually to cause a radical change in the agrarian system. Although it was the revenue alone which was granted, it became customary to treat the land itself as part of the grant. Technically the king could resume the grant, but in fact he seldom did so. The lessening of central control in any case weakened the authority of the king and emphasized local independence, an emphasis which increased in times of political trouble. The recipient of the grant came to be regarded as the lord of the land and the local patron, and he attracted local loyalty towards himself. The more obvious shift in emphasis from central to local power took place later, but its origin can be traced to the Gupta period. However, the more forceful of the Gupta kings still kept authority in their hands and continued to be regarded as the lords of the land *par excellence*.

Patronage requires the easy availability of money, and the Gupta kings had the financial wherewithal to be patrons on a lavish scale. The steady stream of revenue from the land was augmented by income from commercial activity. Indian trading stations were dotted throughout the islands of South-East Asia, Malaysia, Cambodia, and Thailand. The gradual acceptance of many features of Indian culture in these areas must doubtless have been facilitated by activities such as commerce. Indian merchants carried spices from Java to Socotra or were busy participating in the trade between China and the Mediterranean lands via the Central Asian 'Silk Route', not to mention the increasing trade within the subcontinent itself. Goods were transported by pack animals and ox-drawn carts, and by water when rivers were navigable. The literature of the period is replete with descriptions of the marvels and wonders witnessed by sailors and merchants in distant lands. There are frequent references to rich financiers and wealthy guilds. The textile guilds had a vast market, both domestic and foreign. Ivory-workers, stone-workers, metal-workers, and jewellers all prospered in the economic boom. Spices, pepper, sandalwood, pearls, precious stones, perfume, indigo, herbs, and textiles were exported in large quantities. Amongst the more lucrative imports were silk from China and horses from Central Asia and Arabia.

Some of the wealth of merchants and princes was donated to religious causes. Large endowments had made the Buddhist Church extremely powerful, and provided comfortable if not luxurious living for many Buddhist monks in the more important monasteries. These endowments enabled the monasteries to own land and to employ labour to work it. The surplus income from such sources was invested in commercial enterprises which at times were so successful that monasteries could even act as bankers. Monastic establishments built in splendid isolation, like the one at Ajantā, were embellished with some of the most magnificent murals known to the ancient world. The growth of centres of Buddhist teaching led to devoted scholars spending many hours on theology and philosophical speculation, thus sharpening the intellectual challenge which the Buddhists presented to the brāhmans.

Hindu institutions and personalities were also the recipients of enviably lavish patronage. There are references to donations of land or revenue from villages to learned brāhmans and renowned priests, enabling them and their families to live in comfort for many generations. This was the age which saw attempts at building small stone temples to Hindu deities, temples which within half a millennium were to become the dominant focuses of society in many parts of the subcontinent. Together with the temples came the carving of images and the depiction of popular legends in stone.

Hinduism had by this time evolved from the beliefs of the Vedic period into a humane and sophisticated religion. Perhaps the most fundamental changes were the two features which arose partially out of the heterodox challenge to early Hinduism. The first of these was the tendency towards monotheism, which was stressed by the increasing worship of either of the two deities Vishnu and Śiva. In addition the ritual of worship was also changing in favour of personal devotion (*bhakti*) rather than sacrifice. Thus Hinduism revitalized itself and was able slowly to supplant the heterodox religions. The brāhmans, who regarded themselves as the interpreters of Hinduism, were able to rewrite the older texts to conform to their own vision of society, as is evident from Purānic literature, and were able to convert popular secular material, such as the two epics, the *Mahābhārata* and the *Rāmāyana*, into sacred literature.

It was from these cultural roots that the classical norm evolved. The language of brāhmanism, Sanskrit, became the language of erudition and court literature. The works of Kālidāsa exemplify the inspired literary craftsmanship of the period. The brāhman genius for classification was given full vent, as is apparent from the careful categorizing of the divergent philosophical schools. Compendia of scientific writings were produced and the classification of scientific knowledge led to many exciting results. Medical knowledge began to travel west and aroused the interest of west Asian physicians. Experienced metallurgists displayed their skill in minting beautiful coins, in the use of iron of such excellence that it defies reproduction (as in the famous Iron Pillar of Mehraulī), in metal sculpture, and in copper-plate charters. Indian mathematical knowledge was probably the most advanced of its time, with the use of place notation of numerals and familiarity with the concept of the cipher. Astronomy saw even more spectacular progress. In A.D. 499 Āryabhata calculated π as 3·1416 and the length of the solar year as 365·358 days. He also postulated that the earth was a sphere rotating on its own axis and revolving round the sun, and that the shadow of the earth falling on the moon caused eclipses. The works on astronomy written by Varāhamihira show knowledge of Greek and Roman systems.

The advancement of knowledge lay in the hands of the brāhmans. This had the advantage of intensifying the intellectual tradition within a small group of society. Unfortunately however, owing to the evolution of the social pattern in ancient India, this also led to intellectual constriction. Brāhman superiority was in part sustained by the maintenance of caste in Indian society. With the rewriting of early literature, especially legal literature, the division of society into castes was reiterated and the pre-eminent status of the brāhman was emphasized. The result was a fairly rigid ordering of society, in theory at least. In addition, the educational function was appropriated by the brāhmans, who, with the decline of the Buddhist monasteries in the post-Gupta period, became the major purveyors of formal education in many parts of the subcontinent. Technical knowledge was gradually relegated to the position of a craft tradition practised in the guilds. Formal education was to become entirely scholastic, resulting in intellectual in-growing.

Despite the theoretical rigidity of the caste system, the śūdras now had a somewhat more advantageous position than in the Mauryan period, doubtless due to the decreasing need for establishing new settlements and clearing waste land. But the position of the untouchables—those beyond the pale of caste society—had declined considerably. Even accidental contact with an untouchable by a high-caste person was a source of great pollution and required ritual ablutions, a custom which mystified the Chinese Buddhist pilgrim Hsüan Tsang when he visited India in the early seventh century. The untouchables lived on the outskirts of towns and villages and theirs were the lowlier and unclean occupations such as scavenging, keeping the cremation grounds clean, and making leather goods. The village or the town itself, generally enclosed by a wall, was divided into sectors, each occupational group living and working in a particular area. Undoubtedly the finest parts of the town were those in which the main temple or the royal palace was situated and the residential area of the wealthy merchants, landowners, and courtiers. Fa-hsien, who was in India between A.D. 400 and 411, was favourably impressed by the prosperity of the people, more particularly the town-dwellers, an impression which is borne out by archaeological evidence.

One of the most interesting of the documents throwing light on the social mores of the well-to-do citizens is the *Kāmasūtra*. Better known as a manual on the art of love, it incidentally also depicts the young dilettante in his daily routine: a life given over to a certain relaxed comfort; devoted to poetry, music, painting, and sculpture; and embellished with flowers, delicate perfumes, well-seasoned food, and other refinements of gracious living. An even more graphic documentation of life in the Gupta age is available from the vast number of terracotta figurines and models of this period, ranging from toys and representations of ladies and gentlemen of fashion, to cult images relating to the more popular manifestations of religion.

The supremacy of Gupta power in northern India did not remain unchallenged. The challenge came from the unexpected invasion of northwestern India by a distinctly barbaric people, the *Hūnas*. The name is etymologically related to the late classical *Hunni* or Huns, but they were probably only remotely connected, if at all, with the barbarian hordes of Attila. The threat was felt during the reign of Chandra Gupta's son and successor Kumāra Gupta (A.D. 415–54) when a tribe of Hūnas, branching away from the main Central Asian hordes, had settled in Bactria, and gradually moved over the mountains into north-western India. Slowly the trickles became streams as the Hūnas thrust further into India. The successor of Kumāra Gupta, Skanda Gupta (A.D. 454–67) had to bear the brunt of the Hūna attacks, which were by now regular invasions. Gupta power weakened rapidly. By the early sixth century the Hūna rulers Toramāna and Mihirakula claimed the Panjāb and Kashmīr as part of their kingdom.

Once again northern India experienced migrations of people from Central Asia and Iran, and a pattern of readjustment followed. The coming of the Hūnas not only created political disorder but also put into motion new currents whose momentum was felt for centuries to come. The migration of the Hūnas and other Central Asian tribes accompanying them and their settling in northern India resulted in displacements of population. This disturbance led in turn to changes in the caste structure, with the emergence of new sub-castes. The rise of many small kingdoms was also due to the general confusion prevalent during this period.

With the decline of the Guptas the northern half of the subcontinent splintered into warring kingdoms, each seeking to establish itself as a sovereign power. But, unlike the picture at the end of the Mauryan period, this sovereignty was to be based on a distinct regionalism which, though blurred and confused at first, achieved clarity in later centuries. The successors of the Guptas attempted to recreate an empire, but the political fabric was such that an empire was no longer feasible, a possible exception being the Pratihāra kingdom in limited periods. The ability to create large kingdoms and empires moved south to the powers of the peninsula—the kingdoms of the Deccan and the Tamil country. In the centuries that followed the Gupta period it was in the kingdoms of the Chālukyas, Rāshtrakūtas, Pallavas, and Cholas that Indian civilization showed its greatest vitality.

CHAPTER VI

Medieval Hindu India

by A. L. BASHAM

THE Gupta Empire broke up and disappeared. By the middle of the sixth century a line of rulers with the same surname, but not connected in their official genealogy with the imperial line, ruled in Bihār and parts of Uttar Pradesh. The great emperors of the fourth and fifth centuries were soon forgotten, with the exception of Chandra Gupta II, who was remembered by his title Vikramāditya (in colloquial Hindī Rājā Bikram) and the palmy days of whose reign passed into folk tradition.

In the second half of the sixth century a city on the Upper Gangā, before its confluence with the Jamunā, Kānyakubja (later known as Kanauj), rose to prominence as the capital of the Maukhari kings. The city of Sthānvīśvara, now Thānesar, in the watershed between the Gangā and the Indus, became the capital of a rising family of rulers descended from a certain Pushyabhūti. Gujarāt and Mālwā were in the power of the Maitraka Dynasty, founded by a general of the Guptas. In the Deccan the Chālukya Dynasty was gaining in strength, while in Tamilnādu the Dynasty of the Pallavas was also enlarging its boundaries.

This is the pattern of Indian politics until the Muslim invasion. There were generally five or six main focuses of power throughout the subcontinent, with numerous lesser kingdoms, sometimes independent, sometimes tributary to one of the greater rulers. Those corners of the subcontinent with well-defined natural frontiers, such as Kashmīr, Nepāl, Assam, Orissā, and Keralā, were less involved in the constant struggles for power, and their political life, though also often marked by local conflict, was rarely much affected by the constant strife in the great plains.

The usual system of government bore some resemblance to the feudal system of medieval western Europe. As the previous chapter has shown, the Mauryas established a bureaucracy, and the Guptas revived some features of Mauryan administration, though they allowed greater devolution of power. As the Guptas declined, provincial governors, whose posts were already often hereditary, took to calling themselves mahārājas, and increasingly assumed the status of kings. The typical larger kingdom of medieval times consisted of an area controlled directly from the capital city, and a number of provinces under hereditary *sāmantas*, a term loosely translated as 'vassal'. The more powerful *sāmantas* took regal titles and had subordinate chiefs who paid them homage and tribute.

These quasi-feudal conditions were encouraged by the political values of the times and given religious sanction in the epics and lawbooks. From the days of the later Vedas, when the tradition of the horse-sacrifice (*aśvamedha*) began, warfare had been looked on as good in itself, the natural occupation of the kshatriya. Aśoka's voice, raised in favour of peace, had few echoes in succeeding centuries. Yet the traditional warfare of the Hindu king was mitigated by a chivalrous and humane ethical code, which discouraged such ruthless aspects of war as the sacking of cities and the slaughter of prisoners and non-combatants. Moreover the kshatriya ethic was averse to the complete annexation of a conquered kingdom. The righteous conqueror accepted the homage of the vanquished king, received tribute, and replaced him on his throne as a vassal. If the conqueror 'violently uprooted' his enemies, as Samudra Gupta had done, it was believed that he might suffer for his ruthlessness in future lives, or even in the present one. Thus Hindu political ideology encouraged the ruler in his efforts at empire building, but did not make for stable, long-lasting imperial systems.

The political history of India between the end of the Gupta Empire and the coming of the Muslims can be traced in some detail from thousands of inscriptions which contain the genealogies and brief accounts of the reigns of kings, and in the panegyrics which form the preambles to records of land-grants, mostly to religious bodies—temples, monasteries, or groups of learned brāhmans. The piecing together of history from such sources is a fascinating intellectual exercise, and the specialist takes up his task with enthusiasm; but the general reader may find the dynastic history of early medieval India dull in the extreme, and there is no need to do more than summarize it here.

A temporarily successful effort at empire building was made by Harsha or Harshavardhana (606–47), of the Pushyabhūti line of Sthānvīśvara, who gained control of Kānyakubja and made it his capital. His reign is comparatively well documented, thanks to his court poet Bāna and the Chinese pilgrim Hsüan Tsang. The former composed an account of his rise to power, *The Career of Harsha* (*Harshacharita*), in ornate poetic prose, while the latter left a lengthy account of his travels, *Records of Western Countries* (*Hsi-yu chi*), which tells us much about Harsha and the general condition of India at the time. Harsha appears to have governed his empire according to the system which was by now traditional, through vassal kings and henchmen, resembling the barons of medieval Europe, who might hold high offices at court or act as district or provincial governors, but who were also great landowners, and were virtually kings in their own domains. Harsha succeeded in maintaining their loyalty and holding his loose empire together through the strength of his personality and his untiring energy. When he died, apparently without heirs, his empire died with him.

The succeeding period is very obscure and badly documented, but it marks the culmination of a process which had begun with the invasion of the Hūnas in the last years of the Gupta Empire. The sixth and seventh centuries saw the rise of many new dynasties, small and great, in the northern part of the subcontinent. Few of these ruling families are to be found mentioned in sources from periods before the Guptas, and many of their genealogies begin with names which do not seem Sanskritic. These people appear to have been newcomers. Some of them may have been related to the Hūnas. A new people, who began to make their presence felt towards the end of the sixth century, the Gurjaras, gave their name to the present Gujarāt and founded several important ruling dynasties. Since place-names containing a similar element can be found as far to the north-west as Pakistan and Afghanistan, it is commonly suggested that the Gurjaras entered India in the wake of the Hūnas. Their name has been linked with that of the ancient people of the south Russian steppes called Khazars, and with the Georgians (*Gruz*) of the Caucasus. Other obscure tribes of Central Asians may also have followed the Hūnas, and wilder peoples from outlying areas may have profited from the unsettled conditions to gain political control of important regions. In any case, new ruling houses arose in the post-Gupta period and many of their names survive to the present day as those of the Rājput clans.

Towards the end of the eighth century three of the recently arisen dynasties contended for Kānyakubja, by now the acknowledged metropolis of northern India. These were the Pālas of Bihār and Bengal, the Rāshtrakūtas of the Deccan, and the Gurjara-Pratihāras, who controlled parts of Mālwā and Rājasthān. The great city was for a time occupied by the Pālas, whose Buddhist king Dharmapāla drove up the Gangā valley and exacted tribute from many kings of the area. The Rāshtrakūta Govinda III, whose policy of raiding the north, continued by his successors, was to have many repercussions, drove Dharmapāla out, but was forced to return to his base owing to trouble at home. The vacuum was filled, very early in the ninth century, by Nāgabhata II of the Gurjara-Pratihāras.

For about a hundred years the Gurjara-Pratihāras of Kānyakubja restored a little of the glory of the earlier empires. Under their greatest kings, Mihira Bhoja (*c.* 836–90) and Mahendrapāla (*c.* 890–910), they received tribute from rulers from Gujarāt to the borders of Bengal, and Muslim travellers were much impressed by the peacefulness and prosperity of their quasi-feudal empire. But their old enemies, the fierce Rāshtrakūtas from the Deccan, were constantly worrying them, and in about 916 Kānyakubja was again temporarily occupied by Indra III of the Rāshtrakūtas, whose lightning raids provided a foretaste of the similar attacks of the Marāthās 800 years later.

Indra III soon returned to the south; but his effects were longer-lasting than those of previous Rāshtrakūta raiders. Though the Pratihāras returned to their capital, they were humiliated and weakened, and their vassals ceased to respect them. Within a generation or two the greater vassals had thrown aside their allegiance, and were fighting with their former masters and among themselves. It was in these circumstances that Mahmūd of Ghaznī, in the early years of the eleventh century, carried out his seventeen raids on India; but though the Turkish raiders ransacked and destroyed palaces and temples, and returned to their headquarters in Afghanistan with immense caravans of riches and slaves, India resumed her traditional political ways as if nothing had happened.

The Turks overwhelmed the Śāhī kingdom, which had controlled a large area of the north-west, from Kābul to Lāhore. The rulers of this realm had also been Turks, but Turks who had adopted Hindu traditions, and who offered no serious threat to their neighbours to the east. The Ghaznavids also conquered the Muslim kingdoms of Sind, occupied by the Arabs early in the eighth century, whose chiefs had long ceased to trouble the Hindu kingdoms on their frontiers. Thus the Hindu states of the Gangetic basin and Rājasthān now had on their borders a young aggressive kingdom with new methods of warfare and with a religious ideology which might be expected to encourage aggression.

The most remarkable feature of the situation was that, as far as surviving records show, nobody whatever in Hindu India recognized the menace of the Turks. The Ghaznavids made a few further raids, but these were far less impressive than those of Mahmūd. The Turks were soon torn by internal strife and, though they continued to hold the Panjāb, it must have seemed to the Hindu politicians of the time that, like the Arabs before them, they would be contained indefinitely. Having no real historical tradition, the Indian memory of earlier conquerors coming from the north-west—Greeks, Śakas, Kushānas, and Hūnas—was so vague that it was quite ineffectual as a warning to the rulers of the time.

In the involved situation arising from Mahmūd's raids, five larger kingdoms shared most of northern India between them, the Chāhamānas (Chauhāns) of Rājasthān, the Gāhadavālas (Gāhrwāls) of Kānyakubja (Kanauj) and Vārānasī (Banāras), the Chaulukyas or Solānkis of Gujarāt, the Paramāras (Parmārs) of Mālwā, and the Chandellas (Chandels) of Bundelkhand, to the south of the Gangā. These dynasties bore names which are among the best-known of the thirty-six Rājput clans. Their kings had already acquired something of the traditional Rājput character—gallant, extremely sensitive to points of honour, glorifying war, but war of a gentlemanly kind, intensely devoted to tradition, and quite incapable of serious co-operation one with another. The Pālas, who governed Bihār and Bengal, had been quite untouched by Mahmūd's invasions. Early in the twelfth century they were replaced by the Sena Dynasty, which reversed the Pālas' traditional support of Buddhism and encouraged Hindu orthodoxy. They seem to have played little or no part in the politics of the western part of India, where the five major kingdoms and numerous lesser tributary realms fought honourably among the themselves, basing their strategy and tactics on principles inherited from epics.

In 1173 Ghaznī was captured by Ghiyās-ud-dīn, whose headquarters were Ghūr in Afghanistan. From his new capital Ghiyās-ud-dīn turned his attention to India. His brother, Muhammad bin Sām, occupied the Panjāb and deposed the last ruler of the line of Mahmūd. Then in 1191 Muhammad bin Sām attacked Prithvīrāja, king of the Chāhamānas, the Hindu ruler on his eastern frontier. Prithvīrāja, fighting on his own ground with a larger army, defeated Muhammad at Tarāin, and he retreated. In the following year, 1192, Muhammad came again with stronger forces, and on the same field of Tarāin Prithvīrāja lost the day, and the Gangā valley was open to the invaders. Before the century was over Turkish control was established along the whole length of the sacred river.

It is easy to suggest reasons why the Hindus were unable to resist the Turks, and many such suggestions have been put forward. In dealing with the question it must be remembered that the invasion of the Turks was only one of numerous attacks through the north-western passes which took place in historical times. The Āryans, by a process not fully known to us, gained control of the Panjāb from the decadent Harappans. The Achaemenians of Iran occupied part at least of the Indus valley; Alexander's troops reached the Beās, but were compelled to retreat; in the second century B.C. the Greeks from Bactria occupied the Panjāb; they were followed in the next century by the Śakas or Scythians; in the first century A.D. came the Kushānas, and in the fifth the Hūnas. Mahmūd's raids in the early eleventh century were precursors of the even stronger Turkish attacks of Muhammad bin Sām, which led to the protracted domination of most of India by Muslim rulers.

These were not by any means the last attacks from the north-west, however. Soon after the Turkish occupation, Mongol hordes swept into India and occupied much of the territory west of the Indus. In 1398 Tīmūr, the great Mongol conqueror, sacked Delhi and raged through western India, causing tremendous carnage and destruction. In 1526 Bābur the Mughal defeated the Afghan rulers of Delhi and occupied the country. In 1555 his son, Humāyūn, reconquered it from his base in Afghanistan. During the eighteenth century Persians and Afghans raided India in turn, both sacking Delhi before returning to their homelands.

If we examine all these conquests together it becomes clear that many frequently heard explanations of the failure of the defenders of India to resist invasion are facile generalizations, based on too few instances. Indian Muslims were hardly more successful at defending themselves against invasion than Hindus, and the weakness of Indian armies in these circumstances cannot therefore be due to the fact that the pacific Hindu is essentially a less competent soldier than the Muslim. If the hillmen of Afghanistan and Iran and the nomads of Central Asia were tougher and stronger than the inhabitants of the sub-tropical riverine plains of northern India, in all the battles the hillmen were greatly outnumbered by the plainsmen and the latter should have made up in numbers for what they lacked in individual stamina. Moreover there is no evidence to show that the Hindu troops were essentially less courageous than the Muslims, though the former were perhaps more prone to take to flight when their leader was killed.

Some modern Indian historians are inclined to blame the caste system for the Hindu débâcle, which, they suggest, was brought about by the fact that most Hindus were non-combatants, who felt no real sense of national patriotism but only loyalty to their caste brotherhoods. But Hindu armies never consisted only of kshatriyas, and all classes, including brāhmans, could take part in war. Moreover to deplore the fact that the Hindus did not adopt a scorched-earth policy against their attackers is tantamount to regretting that they did not share the nationalist values of the nineteenth and twentieth centuries. The same is probably true of nearly every people of the period which we are considering.

In all the invasions which we have listed there seems to be at least one common factor. The Indian armies were less mobile and more cumbrous, archaic in their equipment and outmoded in their strategy, when compared with those of their attackers. The invaders generally had better horses and better-trained cavalry. They were not burdened by enormous bodies of camp-followers and supernumeraries, nor did they make use of the fighting elephant, the courage of which in the face of the enemy was unpredictable, but which Indian commanders, whether Hindu or Muslim, seem to have found fatally fascinating. Often the invaders had new weapons which added greatly to their effectiveness. The Āryans had the horse-drawn chariot, the Achaemenians siege engines, Alexander *ballistae*. The Central Asian nomads were equipped with small composite bows, carried by mounted archers, who could hit their mark while they were in full gallop. Bābur made effective use of a small park of field guns. In fact one of the main reasons for the repeated ineptitude of Indian armies in the defence of the natural frontiers of India was their outdated and ineffective military technique.

Another important factor in the weak defence of India was the failure of her rulers to recognize the very existence of the threat from the north-west. Where this threat was recognized, the defence was more successful. The three great empires of the Mauryas, the Guptas, and the Mughals were able to maintain their frontiers because they were united. Even the Hūnas, who invaded India towards the end of the period of the Gupta Empire, were expelled in the end, though the empire disintegrated in the process. The great Mughals were well aware of the potential danger from the north-west and tried to maintain their hold on Kābul and Kandahār, beyond the natural frontiers of India, in order to keep out invaders. Only when their empire was already disintegrating after the death of Aurangzeb did the Iranians and Afghans mount their great raids into Mughal territory. The early Turkish sultans managed to hold off the Mongols because, though their henchmen were far from united and not always loyal to their leaders, they were well aware of the common danger and took what steps they could to ward it off.

The Hindu kings at the time of the Turkish invasions were hopelessly divided. We have seen that, when Mahmūd of Ghaznī defeated the Śāhīs of the north-west and occupied the Panjāb, no Hindu king seems to have been aware of the danger to the rest of India. When, nearly 200 years later, Muhammad bin Sām threatened a further attack, the main kingdoms of northern India were in a state of constant friction, frequently erupting into warfare, but warfare of the inconclusive type traditional to Hinduism, which never pushed a victory home and thus inhibited both the building up of stable empires and the establishment of firm alliances. If Prithvīrāja had some help from his neighbours to the east, as certain Muslim accounts assert, it was half-hearted and ineffectual. The same factors assisted the establishment of the power of the East India Company in the eighteenth century, for as soon as the Company began to take a part in Indian politics it learnt to profit from the dissensions of the Indian powers, playing one off against another by a combination of bribes, promises, and threats.

Thus the Turkish conquest of most of India, like other conquests both earlier and later, must chiefly be ascribed to the Indian political system and to the intense conservatism of the rulers of India, especially in military matters. These factors were cancelled out in the internal warfare of the subcontinent, when foreign invasion was not involved, for in any such conflict both sides were equally affected by them. When an army of vigorous marauders appeared on the north-west frontier, though outnumbered, it stood a very good chance of overrunning the plains, for the rulers of India were generally at loggerheads one with another, and their military methods were technically outdated in comparison with those of the attackers.

The period from A.D. 550 to 1200 saw the rapid development of Āryanized culture in the peninsula. Two main focuses of power emerged, one in the Deccan and the other in the Tamil plain, and their rulers contended constantly and indecisively for mastery for more than 600 years. The events of this region throw an interesting light on the workings of the Hindu political system. For instance in the Deccan the Chālukya Dynasty held power from the middle of the sixth to the middle of the eighth century. A sudden revolt by an important vassal, Dantidurga of the line of the Rāshtrakūtas, brought about the overthrow of the Chālukyas. They were not completely eradicated, however, but were allowed to continue as the Rāshtrakūtas' vassals, Thus the Chālukyas persisted for 200 years, until in the tenth century the Rāshtrakūtas grew weak. Then the Chālukyas seized their chance and regained supremacy, only for their empire to be partitioned among three of their own vassals after a further 200 years.

The first great dynasty to contol the Tamil plain was that of the Pallavas, whose rulers introduced many features of northern civilization into the south. Between the Pallavas and the Chālukyas were several minor kingdoms, usually tributary to one of the greater powers, but always ready to become independent whenever they found an opportunity. Among these the Kadambas are worth mentioning because of their origin. The line was founded in the fourth century by a young brāhman, Mayūraśarman, who gave up his studies and became leader of a troop of bandits, and levied protection money from villages in the hilly western part of the Pallava kingdom. In the end the Pallava king recognized Mayūraśarman as a vassal; he established his capital at Vanavāsī in Mysore and his descendants were classed as kshatriyas, though they remembered their brāhman ancestry with pride.

In the ninth century the Pallavas gave way to the Cholas, who claimed descent from the early Tamil kings of the same surname who had disappeared from history over 500 years earlier. The Cholas are noteworthy for their patronage of art and architecture—splendid temples with majestic towers and fine sculpture, especially in bronze, were produced during their rule. To some extent they revived the tradition of bureaucracy, and developed a more centralized form of government than that of most other Indian kingdoms, finding a place in the system for village councils, usually chosen by lot, the records of whose deliberations are still to be seen engraved on the walls of village temples in various parts of Tamilnādu.

The Cholas are also noteworthy as the one dynasty of India which, if only for a while, adopted a maritime policy, expanding their power by sea. Under the great Chola emperors Rājarāja I (985–1014) and Rājendra I (1012–44), first Ceylon was conquered and then the whole eastern seaboard of India as far as the Gangā. Finally, under Rājendra, a great naval expedition sailed across the Bay of Bengal and occupied strategic points in Sumatra, Malaya, and Burma. This Chola maritime empire, the only certain instance of Indian overseas expansion by force of arms, was not an enduring one. Later Chola rulers became once more involved in the endemic wars with the Chālukyas and lost interest in their overseas possessions. Within fifty years of the expedition all the Chola troops had been withdrawn to the mainland. Later the Cholas weakened, and were replaced as the dominant power in Tamilnādu by the Pāndyas, whose capital was the sacred city of Madurai, in the extreme south.

The whole of the peninsula was shaken to its foundations by the invasions of the troops of Sultan 'Alā'u'd-Dīn Khaljī of Delhi (1296–1316), led by his general Malik Kāfur. As a result the Deccan came under Muslim domination for 400 years, but the south remained under Hindu control, after a brief interlude when a short-lived Muslim sultanate ruled from Madurai. The hegemony of the Dravidian south fell to the Empire of Vijayanagara, founded in 1336 and surviving until 1565, when its forces were defeated by a coalition of Deccan sultans. This was the last of the great empires on the old Hindu model, and by the time of its fall the Portuguese were already controlling the seas around India.

The long period whose history we have outlined above is sometimes thought of as one of decline, when compared with the stable and urbane days of the Guptas. This judgement is true in some particulars. The literature of the period, though it includes many important works, has nothing as near perfection as the main works of Kālidāsa. There is much excellent sculpture from this period, but nothing as fine as the best Gupta productions. Yet in architecture there was an immense advance over Gupta times, and, only a century or two before the Muslims occupied northern India, there arose such splendid temples as those at Khajurāho, Bhubaneswar, Kānchīpuram, and Thanjavūr, among many others.

In the religious life of India, after the Gupta period, the greatest vitality seems to have been found in the peninsula. Here certain south Indian brāhmans developed Hindu philosophy and theology as never before, and, basing their work on the *Upanishads*, the *Bhagavad Gītā*, and the *Brahma Sūtras*, produced commentaries of great length and subtlety, to defend their own systematic interpretations of the texts. Chief of these was Śankarāchārya, a Keralan brāhman of the ninth century, who has with some justification been called the St. Thomas Aquinas of Hinduism. Śankarāchārya was only one of many teachers nearly as great as he, such as Rāmānuja (died 1137) and Madhva (?1197–1276), who founded sub-sects of the Vedānta philosophical school.

Perhaps even more important was the growth of simple popular devotionalism (*bhakti*), which began among the Tamils near the beginning of this period with the production of the beautiful Tamil hymns of the *Nāyanārs* and *Ālvārs*. Other products of the same movement were the Sanskrit *Bhāgavata Purāna*, which, composed in the Tamil country, soon spread all over India and was later translated into the everyday languages, to diffuse the cult of Krishna as the divine lover. Before the Muslim conquest of the Deccan this movement had begun to spread northwards, and left its traces in the earliest important Marāthī literature, such as the *Jnāneśvarī* of Jnāneśvar.

Meanwhile Buddhism steadily lost ground, though it was still very much alive in Bengal and Bihār when the Muslims occupied these regions. Both Buddhism and Hinduism had become affected by what is generally known as Tantricism or Tantrism, emphasizing the worship of goddesses, especially the Mother Goddess, the spouse of Śiva, known by many names. With this came sexual mysticism, and the sacramentalization of the sexual act, which was performed ritually by circles of initiates. Other socio-religious practices, looked on as reprehensible by most modern Hindus, became more common in this period. Among these were the burning of widows on their husbands' funeral pyres, wrongly called *satī* (suttee), child marriage, animal sacrifice, female infanticide, and the religious prostitution of the *devadāsī*. One feels that there was a definite lowering in the value of human life in comparison with the days of the Guptas, when, according to Chinese accounts, even the death penalty was not inflicted.

When the Turkish horsemen swept through the Gangā plain, Hindu culture was tending to look inwards and backwards—inwards to the private life of the spirit and backwards to the hallowed norms of the distant past. In many respects the legacy of this period to later times was a negative one. Yet, in the spiring temples built during this period all over India, the age endowed posterity with monuments of enduring splendour and beauty. The parallel with the medieval period in western Christendom is a close one. Here too there was in some respects a cultural decline, in comparison with the days of the great empire destroyed by the barbarians. But in this time new forms of religious literature and art appeared, as well as glorious monuments to faith such as the older empire could never have built.

CHAPTER VII

Hinduism

by S. RADHAKRISHNAN

PREFACE BY THE EDITOR

THE eloquent and moving contribution which follows is the work of one of the great minds of modern India, who has been President of the Indian Republic and who now (1972) lives in honourable retirement, as one of the most venerated of India's grand old men. It was written for the original edition of *The Legacy of India* when its author was a professor of Calcutta University, and had already made a name for himself as an expositor of Indian thought to the West, a task which he was to continue as Spalding Professor of Eastern Religions at the University of Oxford.

The character of this chapter is more personal than that of most of the other contributions to our volume, but it is no less valuable for that. As the record of the faith of a sensitive, highly intelligent Hindu of the early twentieth century, it introduces the reader to those aspects of India's ancient religion which have moulded his life and thought. There are, however, a number of aspects of the subject which are still very important in the life of India, but are little touched on by the author, who would himself agree that Hinduism has something for everyone, on all levels of culture. For this reason we have added a brief postscript to the chapter.

THE SPIRIT OF HINDUISM

If we look at the various and sometimes conflicting creeds which it contains, we may wonder whether Hinduism is not just a name which covers a multitude of different faiths, but when we turn our attention to the spiritual life, devotion, and endeavour which lie behind the creeds, we realize the unity, the indefinable self-identity, which, however, is by no means static or absolute. Throughout the history of Hindu civilization there has been a certain inspiring ideal, a certain motive power, a certain way of looking at life, which cannot be identified with any stage or cross-section of the process. The whole movement and life of the institution, its entire history, is necessary in order to disclose to us this idea, and it cannot therefore be expressed in a simple formula. It requires centuries for ideas to utter themselves, and at any stage the institution has always an element that is yet to be expressed. No idea is fully expressed at any one point of its historical unfolding.

What is this Idea of Hinduism, this continuous element that runs through all its stages from the earliest to the latest, from the lowest to the highest, this fundamental spirit which is more fully and richly expressed in the highest though it is present in the very lowest? Life is present in every stage of a plant's growth and it is always the same life, though it is more fully expressed in the developed tree than in the first push of the tender blade. In the Hindu religion there must be a common element that makes every stage and every movement an expression of the religion. The different phases and stages have proper content and meaning only in so far as this common element exists. With the perception of the unity which runs through error and failure up the long ascent towards the ideal, the whole achievement of Hinduism falls into coherent perspective. It is this essential spirit that any account of Hinduism would seek to express, the spirit that its institutions imperfectly set forth, the spirit that we need to develop more adequately and richly before a better age and civilization can be achieved.

HISTORICAL OUTLINE

The spirit is not a dead abstraction but a living force. Because it is active and dynamic the Hindu civilization has endured so long and proved so capable of adaptation to the growing complexity of life. The great river of Hindu life, usually serene but not without its rapids, reaches back so far that only a long view can do justice to its nature. From prehistoric times influences have been at work moulding the faith. As a result of the excavations in Harappā and Mohenjo-dāro we have evidence of the presence in India of a highly developed culture that 'must have had a long antecedent history on the soil of India, taking us back to an age that can only be dimly surmised'.[1] In age and achievement the Indus valley civilization is comparable to that of Egypt or Sumeria. The noteworthy feature of this civilization is its continuity, not as a political power but as a cultural influence. The religion of the Indus people is hardly distinguishable, according to Sir John Marshall, from 'that aspect of Hinduism which is bound up with animism and the cults of Śiva and the Mother Goddess'.[2] These latter do not seem to be indigenous to the Vedic religion.

Though the Śakti cult was later accepted by the Vedic people, their original opposition to it is not altogether suppressed. To the sacrifice of Daksha, all the Vedic deities are said to have been invited except Śiva, who soon gained authority as the successor of the Vedic Rudra. Even so late as the *Bhāgavata Purāna* the opposition to Śiva-worship is present. 'Those who worship Śiva and those who follow them are the opponents of holy scriptures and may be ranked with *pāshandins*. Let the feeble-minded who, with matted locks, ashes, and bones, have lost their purity, be initiated into the worship of Śiva in which wine and brewage are regarded as gods.'[3]

It is a matter for conjecture whether the Indus people had any relation to the Dravidians. Nor can we say whether the Dravidians were natives of the soil or came from outside. Besides the Āryans and the Dravidians there was also a flat-nosed, black-skinned people who were commonly known as *dāsas*. The religion, in the first literary records that have come down to us, is that of the Āryans, though it was much influenced by the Indus people, the Dravidians, and the aborigines. The simple hymns of the *Rig-Veda* reveal to us an

[1] Sir John Marshall, *Mohenjo-Dāro and the Indus Civilization*, 1931, Vol. I, p. 106.

[2] Ibid. Vol. I, p. viii.

[3] *Bhāgavata Purāna*, iv. 2. In the *Padma Purāna*, *pāshandins* are said to be 'those who wear skulls, ashes, and bones, the symbols contrary to the Vedas, put on matted locks and the barks of trees, even without entering into the third order of life and engage in rites which are not sanctioned by the Vedas'. *Uttara-khanda*, Ch. 235.

age when Pan was still alive, when the trees in the forest could speak and the waters of the river could sing and man could listen and understand. The spells and the charms to be found in part of the tenth book of the *Rig-Veda* and in most of the *Atharva-Veda* suggest a type of religious practice based on fear and associated with the spirits of the dark. A religious synthesis of the different views and practices on the basis of monistic idealism is set forth in the early *Upanishads*. Soon after, a composite culture, springing from a union of Greek with Persian and Bactrian influences, dominated north-western India. Successive descents of Muslim conquerors from about A.D. 1000 affected Hindu life and thought. The Pārsī fugitives who were expelled from Persia by Muslim invaders found a welcome shelter in India. St. Thomas brought the Christian faith from Syria to south India and for over a thousand years this remained the only Christian centre of influence. In the sixteenth century St. Francis Xavier introduced Latin Christianity. The modern Christian missionary movement started over a century ago. The cultural invasion of the West has been vigorous, thanks to its political superiority and industrial efficiency.

Jainism, Buddhism, and Sikhism are creations of the Indian mind and may be interpreted as reform movements from within the fold of Hinduism put forth to meet the special demands of the various stages of the Hindu faith. Zoroastrianism, Islām, and Christianity have been so long in the country that they have become native to the soil and are deeply influenced by the atmosphere of Hinduism.

India was a thorough 'melting-pot' long before the term was invented for America. In spite of attacks, Hellenic, Muslim, and European among others, Hindu culture has maintained its tradition unbroken to the present day. The spiritual life of the Hindus at the present time has not precisely the same proportion or orientation as that of either the Indus people or the Vedic Āryans or even the great teachers, Śankara and Rāmānuja. Its changes in emphasis reflect individual temperaments, social conditions, and the changing intellectual environment, but the same persistent idea reappears in different forms. Hinduism grows in the proper sense of the word, not by accretion, but like an organism, undergoing from time to time transformation as a whole. It has carried within it much of its early possessions. It has cast aside a good deal and often it has found treasures which it has made its own. The history of Hinduism is chequered by tragic failures and wonderful victories, by opportunities missed and taken. New truth has been denied and persecuted occasionally. The unity of its body, realized at the cost of centuries of effort and labour, now and then came near being shattered by self-seeking and ignorance. Yet the religion itself is not destroyed. It is alive and vigorous and has withstood attacks from within and without. It seems to be possessed of unlimited powers of renewal. Its historic vitality, the abounding energy which it reveals, would alone be evidence of its spiritual genius.

UNIVERSALITY

In its great days Hinduism was inspired to carry its idea across the frontiers of India and impose it on the civilized world. Its memory has become a part of the Asiatic consciousness, tinging its outlook on life. Today it is a vital element in world thought and offers the necessary corrective to the predominantly rationalistic pragmatism of the West. It has therefore universal value.

The vision of India, like that of Greece, is Indian only in the sense that it was formulated by minds belonging to the Indian soil. The value of that vision does not reside in any tribal or provincial characteristics, but in those elements of universality which appeal to the whole world. What can be recognized as peculiarly Indian is not the universal truth which is present in it, but the elements of weakness and prejudice, which even some of the greatest of Indians have in common with their weaker brethren.

RELIGION AS EXPERIENCE

Hinduism represents a development from the beliefs and practices of the Indus valley civilization to the complex of changing aspirations and habits, speculations and forms which are in vogue today. There are, however, certain governing conceptions, controlling ideas, deep dynamic links which bind together the different stages and movements. The unity of Hinduism is not one of an unchanging creed or a fixed deposit of doctrine, but is the unity of a continuously changing life. In this essay we can only deal with the general drift of the current of Hindu religion as a whole, not with the many confusing cross-currents and sects.

Religion for the Hindu is experience or attitude of mind. It is not an idea but a power, not an intellectual proposition but a life conviction. Religion is consciousness of ultimate reality, not a theory about God. The religious genius is not a pedant or a pandit, not a sophist or a dialectician, but a prophet, sage, or a *rishi* who embodies in himself the spiritual vision. When the soul goes inward into itself it draws near its own divine root and becomes pervaded by the radiance of another nature. The aim of all religion is the practical realization of the highest truth. It is intuition of reality (*brahmānubhava*), insight into truth (*brahmadarśana*), contact with the supreme (*brahmasamsparśa*), direct apprehension of reality (*brahmasākshātkāra*).

In emphasizing the experiential as distinct from the dogmatic or credal character of religion, Hinduism seems to be more adequate than other religions to the history of religion as well as to the contemporary religious situation. Buddhism in its original form did not avow any theistic belief. Confucius, like Buddha, discouraged his disciples from occupying their minds with speculations about the Divine Being or the Unseen World. There are systems of Hindu thought, like the Sānkhya and the Pūrva Mīmāmsā, which, in some of their characteristic phases, cultivate a spirit and attitude to which it would be difficult to deny the name of religion, even though they may not accept any belief in God or gods superior to oneself. They adopt other methods for achieving salvation from sin and sorrow and do not look to God as the source of their saving. We cannot deny to Spinoza the religious spirit simply because he did not admit any reciprocal communion between the divine and the human spirits. We have instances of religious fervour and seriousness without a corresponding belief in any being describable as God. Again, it is possible for us to believe in God and yet be without any religious sense. We may regard the proofs for the existence of God as irrefutable and yet may not possess the feelings and attitude associated with religion. Religion is not so much a matter of theoretical knowledge as of life and practice. When Kant attacked the traditional proofs of God's existence, and asserted at the same time his faith in God as a postulate of moral consciousness, he brought out the essentially non-theoretical character of life in God. It follows that the reality of God is not based on abstract arguments or scholastic proofs, but is derived from the specifically religious experience which alone gives peculiar significance to the word 'God'. Man becomes aware of God through experience. Rational arguments establish religious faith only when they are interpreted in the light of that religious experience. The arguments do not reveal God to us but are helpful in removing obstacles to the acceptance by our minds of a revelation mediated by that capacity for the apprehension of the Divine which is a normal feature of our humanity.[4] Those who have developed this centre through which all the threads of the universe are drawn are the religious geniuses. The high vision of those who have penetrated into the depths of being, their sense of the Divine in all their exaltation of feeling and enrichment of personality, have been the source of all the noblest work in the world. From Moses to Isaiah, from Jesus and Paul on to Augustine, Luther, and Wesley, from Socrates and Plato to Plotinus and Philo, from Zoroaster to Buddha, from Confucius to Mahomet, the men who initiated new currents of life, the creative personalities, are those who have known God by acquaintance and not by hearsay.

THE VEDAS

What is final is the religious experience itself, though its expressions change if they are to be relevant to the growing content of knowledge. The experience is what is felt by the individual in his deepest being, what is seen by him (*drishti*) or heard (*śruti*) and this is valid for all time. The Veda is seen or heard, not made by its human authors. It is spiritual discovery, not creation. The way to wisdom is not through intellectual activity. From the beginning, India believed in the superiority of intuition or the method of direct perception of the super-sensible to intellectual reasoning. The Vedic *rishis* were the first who ever burst into that silent sea of ultimate being and their utterances about what they saw and heard there are found registered in the *Vedas*. Naturally they attribute the authorship of the *Vedas* to a superior spirit.

Modern psychology admits that the higher achievements of men depend in the last analysis on processes that are beyond and deeper than the limits of the normal consciousness. Socrates speaks of the 'daimōn' which acts as the censor on and speaks through him. Plato regards inspiration as an act of a goddess. Ideas are showered on Philo from above, though he is oblivious of everything around him. George Eliot tells us that she wrote her best work in a kind of frenzy almost without knowing what she was writing. According to Emerson, all poetry is first written in the heavens. It is conceived by a self deeper than appears in normal life. The prophet, when he begins his message 'Thus saith the Lord', is giving utterance to his consciousness that the message is not his own, that it comes from a wider and deeper level of life and from a source outside his limited self. Since we cannot compel these excep-

[4] See Clement Webb, *Religion and Theism*, 1934, p. 36.

tional moments to occur, all inspiration has something of revelation in it. Instead of considering creative work to be due to processes which take place unwittingly, as some psychologists imagine, the Hindu thinkers affirm that the creative deeds, the inspiration of the poets, the vision of the artist, and the genius of the man of science are in reality the utterance of the Eternal through man. In those rare moments man is in touch with a wider world and is swayed by an oversoul that is above his own. The seers feel that their experiences are unmediated direct disclosures from the wholly other and regard them as supernatural, as not discovered by man's own activity (*akartrika, apaurusheya*). They feel that they come to them from God,[5] though even God is said to be not their author but their formulator. In the last analysis the *Vedas* are without any personal author.[6] Since they are not due to personal activity they are not subject to unlimited revision and restatement but possess in a sense the character of finality (*nityatva*).

While scientific knowledge soon becomes obsolete, intuitive wisdom has a permanent value. Inspired poetry and religious scriptures have a certain timelessness or universality which intellectual works do not share. While Aristotle's biology is no longer true, the drama of Euripides is still beautiful. While Vaiśeshika atomism is obsolete, Kālidāsa's *Śakuntalā* is unsurpassed in its own line.

There is a community and continuity of life between man in his deepest self and God. In ethical creativity and religious experience man draws on this source, or rather the source of power is expressing itself through him. In Tennyson's fine figure the sluices are opened and the great ocean of power flows in. It is the spirit in man that is responding to the spirit in the universe, the deep calling unto the deep.

The *Vedas* are more a record than an interpretation of religious experience. While their authority is final, that of the expression and the interpretations of the religious experience is by no means final. The latter are said to be *smriti* or the remembered testimonies of great souls. These interpretations are bound to change if they are to be relevant to the growing content of knowledge. Facts alone stand firm, judgements waver and change. Facts can be expressed in the dialect of the age. The relation between the vision and its expression, the fact and its interpretation, is very close. It is more like the body and the skin than the body and its clothes. When the vision is to be reinterpreted, what is needed is not a mere verbal change but a readaptation to new habits of mind. We have evidence to show that the *Vedas* meant slightly different things to successive generations of believers. On the fundamental, metaphysical, and religious issues the different commentators, Śankara, Rāmānuja, and Madhva, offer different interpretations. To ascribe finality to a spiritual movement is to bring it to a standstill. To stand still is to fall back. There is not and there cannot be any finality in interpretation.

AUTHORITY, LOGIC, AND LIFE

Insight into reality, which is the goal of the religious quest, is earned by intellectual and moral discipline. Three stages are generally distinguished, a

[5] *Rig-Veda*, x. 90. 9; *Brihadāranyaka Upanishad*, ii. 4. 10.

[6] Purushābhāvāt . . . nishthā, *Mīmāmsā-nyāya-prakāśa*, 6.

tradition which we have to learn (*śravana*), an intellectual training through which we have to pass (*manana*), and an ethical discipline we have to undergo (*nididhyāsana*).[7]

To begin with, we are all learners. We take our views on the authority of a tradition which we have done nothing to create but which we have only to accept in the first instance. In every department, art or morality, science or social life, we are taught the first principles and are not encouraged to exercise our private judgement. Religion is not an exception to this rule. Religious scriptures are said to have a right to our acceptance.

The second step is logical reflection or *manana*. To understand the sacred tradition we should use our intelligence. 'Verily, when the sages or *rishis* were passing away, men inquired of the gods, "who shall be our *rishi*?" They gave them the science of reasoning for constructing the sense of the hymns.'[8] Criticism helps the discovery of truth and, if it destroys anything, it is only illusions that are bred by piety that are destroyed by it. *Śruti* and *Smriti*, experience and interpretation, scripture and logic, are the two wings given to the human soul to reach the truth. While the Hindu view permits us to criticize the tradition, we should do so only from within. It can be remoulded and improved only by those who accept it and use it in their lives. Our great reformers, our eminently original thinkers like Śankara and Rāmānuja, are rebels against tradition; but their convictions, as they themselves admit, are also revivals of tradition. While the Hindus are hostile to those who revile their tradition and repudiate it altogether, and condemn them as *avaidika* or *nāstika*, they are hospitable to all those who accept the tradition, however critical they may be of it.

The authoritativeness of the *Veda* does not preclude critical examination of matters dealt with in it. The Hindus believe that the truths of revelation are justifiable to reason. Our convictions are valuable only when they are the results of our personal efforts to understand. The accepted tradition becomes reasoned truth. If the truths ascertained by inquiry conflict with the statements found in the scriptures, the latter must be explained in a way agreeable to truth. No scriptures can compel us to believe falsehoods. 'A thousand scriptures verily cannot convert a jar into a cloth.' We have much in the *Vedas* which is a product not of man's highest wisdom but of his wayward fancy. If we remember that revelation precedes its record, we will realize that the *Veda* may not be an accurate embodiment of the former. It has in it a good deal of inference and interpretation mixed up with intuition and experience. Insistence on Vedic authority is not an encouragement of credulity or an enslaving subjection to scriptural texts. It does not justify the conditions under which degrading religious despotisms grew up later.

The Vedic testimony, the logical truth, must become for us the present fact. We must recapture something of that energy of soul of which the *Vedas* are the creation by letting the thoughts and emotions of that still living past vibrate in our spirits. By *nididhyāsana* or contemplative meditation, ethical discipline, the truth is built into the substance of our life. What we accept on authority and test by logic is now proved by its power to sustain a definite and

[7] *Vivarana-prameya-samgraha*, p. I.

[8] *Nirukta-pariśishta*, XIII. ii.

unique type of life of supreme value. Thought completes itself in life and we thrill again with the creative experience of the first days of the founders of the religion.

GOD

If religion is experience, what is it that we experience? What is the nature of reality? In our knowledge of God, contact with the ultimate reality through religious experience plays the same part which contact with nature through sense perception plays in our knowledge of nature. In both we have a sense of the other, the trans-subjective, which controls our apprehension. It is so utterly given to us and not made by us. We build the concept of reality from the data of religious experience, even as we build the order of nature from the immediate data of sense.

In the long and diversified history of man's quest for reality represented by Hinduism, the object which haunts the human soul as a presence at once all-embracing and infinite is envisaged in many different ways. The Hindus are said to adopt polytheism, monotheism, and pantheism as well as belief in demons, heroes, and ancestors. It is easy to find texts in support of each of these views. The cults of Śiva and Śakti may have come down from the Indus people. Worship of trees, animals and rivers, and other cults associated with fertility ritual, may have had the same origin, while the dark powers of the underworld, who are dreaded and propitiated, may be due to aboriginal sources. The Vedic Āryans contributed the higher gods comparable to the Olympians of the Greeks, like the Sky and the Earth, the Sun and the Fire. The Hindu religion deals with these different lines of thought and fuses them into a whole by means of its philosophical synthesis. A religion is judged by what it tends towards. Those who note the facts and miss the truth are unfair to the Hindu attempt.

The reality we experience cannot be fully expressed in terms of logic and language. It defies all description. The seer is as certain of the objective reality he apprehends as he is of the inadequacy of thought to express it. A God comprehended is no God, but an artificial construction of our minds. Individuality, whether human or divine, can only be accepted as given fact and not described. It is not wholly transparent to logic. It is inexhaustible by analysis.[9] Its inexhaustibility is the proof of objectivity. However far we may carry our logical analysis, the given object in all its uniqueness is there, constituting a limit to our analysis. Our thinking is controlled by something beyond itself which is perception in physical science and the intuition of God in the science of religion. The eternal being of God cannot be described by categories. An attitude of reticence is adopted regarding the question of the nature of the Supreme. Those who know it tell it not; those who tell it know it not. The *Kena Upanishad* says: 'The eye does not go thither, nor speech nor mind. We do not know, we do not understand how one can teach it. It is different from the known, it is also above the unknown.'[10] Śankara quotes a Vedic passage where the teacher tells the pupil the secret of the self by keeping silent about it. 'Verily, I tell you, but you understand not, the self is silence.'[11] The deeper

[9] Cf. Augustine's statement that if one knows the object of one's belief, it cannot be God one knows. [10] i. 2–4. [11] *Bhāshya on Brahma Sūtra*, iii. 2. 17.

experience is a 'wordless' doctrine. The sages declare that 'wonderful is the man that can speak of him, and wonderful is also the man that can understand him.'[12] Buddha maintained silence about the nature of ultimate reality. 'Silent are the Tathāgatas. O, Blessed one.'[13] The *Mādhyamikas* declare that the truth is free from such descriptions as 'it is', 'it is not', 'both', and 'neither'. Nāgārjuna says that Buddha did not give any definition of the ultimate reality. 'Nowhere and to nobody has ever anything been preached by the Buddha.'[14] A verse attributed to Śankara reads: 'It is wonderful that there under the banyan tree the pupil is old while the teacher is young. The explanation of the teacher is silence but the doubts of the pupil are dispersed.' This attitude is truer and nobler than that of the theologians, who construct elaborate mansions and show us round with the air of God's own estate agents.

When, however, attempts are made to give expression to the ineffable reality, negative descriptions are employed. The real is the wholly other, the utterly transcendent, the mysterious being which awakens in us a sense of awe and wonder, dread and desire. It not only fascinates us but produces a sense of abasement in us. Whatever is true of empirical being is denied of the Real. 'The Ātman can only be described by "no, no". It is incomprehensible for it cannot be comprehended.'[15] It is not in space or time; it is free from causal necessity. It is above all conceptions and conceptional differentiations. But on this account it is not to be confused with non-being.[16] It is being in a more satisfying sense than empirical being. The inadequacy of intellectual analysis is the outcome of the incomparable wealth of intrinsic reality in the supreme being. The eternal being is utterly beyond all personal limitation, is beyond all forms though the sustainer of all forms. All religious systems in which mankind has sought to confine the reality of God are inadequate. They make of God an 'idol'.

While the negative characteristics indicate the transcendent character of the real, there is a sense in which the real is also immanent. The very fact that we are able to apprehend the real means that there is something in us capable of apprehending it. The deepest part of our nature responds to the call of the reality. In spiritual life the law holds that only like can know like. We can only know what is akin to ourselves. Above and beyond our rational being lies hidden the ultimate and highest part of our nature. What the mystics call the 'basis' or 'ground' of the soul is not satisfied by the transitory or the temporal, by the sensuous or the intellectual.[17] Naturally, the power by which we acquire the knowledge of God is not logical thought, but spirit, for spirit can only be spiritually discerned. While the real is utterly transcendent to the empirical individual, it is immanent in the ultimate part of our nature. God's revelation and man's contemplation are two aspects of one and the same ex-

[12] See *Katha Up.* i. 2. 7; also *Bhagavad Gītā*, ii. 29. [13] *Lankāvatāra-sūtra*, 16.
[14] *Mādhyamika-kārikā*, xv. 24. [15] *Brihad-āranyaka Up.* iii. 9, 26.
[16] See Śankara's commentary on *Chhāndogya Upanishad*, viii.
[17] 'In us too, all that we call person and personal, indeed all that we can know or name in ourselves at all is but one element in the whole. Beneath it lies even in us, that wholly other whose profundity impenetrable to any concept can yet be grasped in the numinous self-feeling by one who has experience of the deeper life.' Rudolf Otto, *The Idea of the Holy*, E.T., p. 36.

perience. The Beyond is the Within. Brahman is Ātman. He is the *antaryāmin*, the inner controller. He is not only the incommunicable mystery standing for ever in his own perfect light, bliss, and peace, but also is here in us, upholding, sustaining us: 'Whoever worships God as other than the self, thinking he is one and I am another, knows not.'[18] Religion arises out of the experience of the human spirit which feels its kinship and continuity with the Divine other. A purely immanent deity cannot be an object of worship and adoration; a purely transcendent one does not allow of any worship or adoration.

Hindu thinkers are not content with postulating a being unrelated to humanity, who is merely the Beyond, so far as the empirical world is concerned. From the beginnings of Hindu history, attempts are made to bring God closer to the needs of man. Though it is impossible to describe the ultimate reality, it is quite possible to indicate by means of symbols aspects of it, though the symbolic description is not a substitute for the experience of God. We are helpless in this matter and therefore are obliged to substitute symbols for substances, pictures for realities. We adopt a symbolic account when we regard the ultimate reality as the highest person, as the supreme personality, as the Father of us all, ready to respond to the needs of humanity. The *Rig-Veda* has it: 'All this is the person, that which is past and that which is future.'[19] It is the matrix of the entire being. The Vaishnava thinkers and the Śaiva Siddhāntins make of the Supreme, the fulfilment of our nature. He is knowledge that will enlighten the ignorant, strength for the weak, mercy for the guilty, patience for the sufferer, comfort for the comfortless. Strictly speaking, however, the Supreme is not this or that personal form but is the being that is responsible for all that was, is, and shall be. His temple is every world, every star that spins in the firmament. No element can contain him for he is all elements. Your life and mine are enveloped by him. Worship is the acknowledgement of the magnificence of this supreme reality.

We have accounts of the ultimate Reality as both Absolute and God, Brahman, and Īśvara. Only those who accept the view of the Supreme as personality admit that the unsearchableness of God cannot be measured by our feeble conceptions. They confess that there is an overplus of reality beyond the personal concept. To the worshipper, the personal God is the highest. No one can worship what is known as imperfect. Even the idol of the idolater stands for perfection, though he may toss it aside the moment he detects its imperfection.

It is wrong to assume that the Supreme is either the Absolute or God. It is both the Absolute and God. The impersonal and the personal conceptions are not to be regarded as rival claimants to the exclusive truth. They are the different ways in which the single comprehensive pattern reveals itself to the spirit of man. One and the same Being is conceived now as the object of philosophical inquiry or *jnāna*, now as an object of devotion or *upāsana*. The conception of ultimate reality and that of a personal God are reconciled in religious experience, though the reconciliation cannot be easily effected in the region of thought. We cannot help thinking of the Supreme under the analogy

[18] *Brihad-āranyaka Upanishad*, i. 4, 10.

[19] The Supreme is 'all that which ever is, on all the world' (*Sarvam idam yatkiñca jagatyām jagat*. Īśa Up. i).

of self-consciousness and yet the Supreme is the absolutely simple, unchanging, free, spiritual reality in which the soul finds its home, its rest, and its completion.

HOSPITALITY OF THE HINDU MIND

A religion that is based on the central truth of a comprehensive universal spirit cannot support an inflexible dogmatism. It adopts an attitude of toleration not as a matter of policy or expediency but as a principle of spiritual life. Toleration is a duty, not a mere concession. In pursuance of this duty Hinduism has accepted within its fold almost all varieties of belief and doctrine and treated them as authentic expressions of the spiritual endeavour, however antithetic they may appear to be. Hinduism warns us that each of us should be modest enough to realize that we may perhaps be mistaken in our views and what others hold with equal sincerity is not a matter for ridicule. If we believe that we have the whole mind of God we are tempted to assume that any one who disagrees with us is wrong and ought to be silenced. The Hindu shared Aristotle's conviction that a view held strongly by many is not usually a pure delusion. If any view has ennobled and purified human life over a wide range of space, time, and circumstance, and is still doing the same for those who assimilate its concept, it must embody a real apprehension of the Supreme Being. For Hinduism, though God is formless, he yet informs and sustains countless forms. He is not small and partial, or remote and ineffable. He is not merely the God of Israel or of Christendom but the crown and fulfilment of you and me, of all men and all women, of life and death, of joy and sorrow. No outward form can wholly contain the inward reality, though every form brings out an aspect of it.

In all religions, from the lowest to the highest, man is in contact with an invisible environment and attempts to express his view of the Divine by means of images. The animist of the *Atharva-Veda*, who believes that nature is full of spirits, is religious to the extent that he is convinced of the Divine presence and interpenetration in the world and nature. The polytheist is right to the extent that the Divine is to be treated on the analogy of human consciousness rather than any other empirical thing. The gods of the *Vedas* resemble the Supreme no more than shadows resemble the sun, but, even as the shadows indicate where the sun is, the Vedic deities point to the direction in which the Supreme reality lies. All forms are directing their steps towards the one God, though along different paths. The real is one, though it is expressed in different names, which are determined by climate, history, and temperament. If each one follows his own path with sincerity and devotion he will surely reach God. Even inadequate views help their adherents to adapt themselves more successfully to their environment, to order their experiences more satisfactorily, and to act on their environment more creatively. In the great crises of life, our differences look petty and unworthy. All of us have the same urge towards something of permanent worth, the same sense of awe and fascination before the mystery that lies beyond and within the cosmos, the same passion for love and joy, peace and fortitude. If we judge the saving power of truth from its empirical effects we see that every form of worship and belief has a strange power which enables us to escape from our littleness and become radiant with a happiness that is not of this world, which transforms unhappy dens into beautiful homes and converts men and women of easy virtue and little knowledge into suffering servants of God. All truth is God's truth and even a little of it can save us from great troubles.

Besides, the truth of religion is, as Troeltsch declared, 'polymorphic'. The light is scattered in many broken lights and there is not anywhere any full white ray of divine revelation. Truth is found in all religions, though in different measures. The different revelations do not contradict but on many points confirm one another. For the Hindu, religions differ not in their object but in their renderings of its nature.

The Hindu attitude to religious reform is based on an understanding of the place of religion in human life. A man's religion is something integral in his nature. It is like a limb, which grows from him, grows on him, and grows out of him. If we take it away from him we mutilate his humanity and force it into an unnatural shape. We are all prejudiced in favour of what is our own. In spite of all logic we are inclined to believe that the home into which we are born is the best of all possible homes, that our parents are not as others are, and we ourselves are perhaps the most reasonable excuse for the existence of the human race on earth. If strangers are sceptical, it is because they do not know. These prejudices serve a useful purpose within limits. Mankind would never have progressed to this high estate if it had not been for this partiality for our homes and parents, our art and culture, our religion and civilization. If each pushes this prejudice to the extreme point, competition and warfare will result, but the principle that each one should accept his own tradition as the best for him requires to be adopted with due care that it is not exaggerated into contempt and hatred for other traditions. Hinduism admits this principle of historical continuity, recognizes its importance for man's advancement, and at the same time insists on equal treatment for others' views. Trying to impose one's opinions on others is neither so exciting nor so fruitful as joining hands in an endeavour to attain a result much larger than we know.

Besides, truth will prevail and does not require our propaganda. The function of a religious reacher is only to assist the soul's natural movement towards life. The longing for an ideal life may be hidden deep, overlaid, distorted, misunderstood, ill expressed, but it is there and is never wholly lacking. It is man's birthright which he cannot barter away or squander. We have to reckon with it and build on its basis. It does not matter what conception of God we adopt so long as we keep up a perpetual search after truth. The great Hindu prayers are addressed to God as eternal truth to enlighten us, to enable us to grasp the secret of the universe better and better. There is no finality in this process of understanding. Toleration in Hinduism is not equivalent to indifference to truth. Hinduism does not say that truth does not matter. It affirms that all truths are shadows except the last, though all shadows are cast by the light of truth. It is one's duty to press forward until the highest truth is reached. The Hindu method of religious reform or conversion has this for its aim.

Conversion is not always by means of argument. By the witness of personal example, vital changes are produced in thought and life. Religious conviction is the result, not the cause of religious life. Hinduism deepens the life of spirit among the adherents who belong to it, without affecting its form. All the gods included in the Hindu pantheon stand for some aspect of the Supreme. Brahma, Vishnu, and Śiva bring out the creative will, saving love and fearful judgement of the Supreme. Each of them to its worshippers becomes a name of the Supreme God. The *Harivamśa*, for example, tells us that Vishnu is the Supreme God, taught in the whole range of the Scriptures, the *Vedas*, the *Rāmāyana*, the *Purānas*, and the epics. The same description is given of Śiva, who has Rudra for his Vedic counterpart.[20] He becomes the highest God. Śakti, the Mother Goddess, in her different forms represents the dynamic side of Godhead. Whatever form of worship is taken up by the Hindu faith it is exalted into the highest.

The multiplicity of divinities is traceable historically to the acceptance of pre-existing faiths in a great religious synthesis where the different forms are interpreted as modes, emanations, or aspects of the one Supreme. In the act of worship, however, every deity is given the same metaphysical and moral perfections. The labels on the bottles may vary, but the contents are exactly the same. That is why, from the *Rig-Veda* onwards, Hindu thought has been characterized by a distinctive hospitality. As the *Bhagavad Gītā* has it: 'Howsoever men approach me, so do I welcome them, for the path men take from every side is mine.' Hinduism did not shrink from the acceptance of every aspect of God conceived by the mind of man, and, as we shall see, of every form of devotion devised by his heart. For what counts is the attitude of sincerity and devotion and not the conception, which is more or less intellectual. Kierkegaard says: 'If of two men one prays to the true God without sincerity of heart, and the other prays to an idol with all the passion of an infinite yearning, it is the first who really prays to an idol, while the second really prays to God.'[21] Dominated by such an ideal, Hinduism did not believe in either spiritual mass-production or a standardized religion for all.

The great wrong, that which we can call the sin of idolatry, is to acquiesce in anything less than the highest open to us. Religion is not so much faith in the highest as faith in the highest one can reach. At whatever level our understanding may be, we must strive to transcend it. We must perpetually strive to lift up our eyes to the highest conception of God possible for us and our generation. The greatest gift of life is the dream of a higher life. To continue to grow is the mark of a religious soul. Hinduism is bound not by a creed but by a quest, not by a common belief but by a common search for truth. Every one is a Hindu who strives for truth by study and reflection, by purity of life and conduct, by devotion and consecration to high ideals, who believes that religion rests not on authority but on experience.

PERFECTION

Whatever view of God the Hindu may adopt, he believes that the Divine is in man. Every human being, irrespective of caste or colour, can attain to the knowledge of this truth and make his whole life an expression of it. The

[20] *Atharva-śiras Up.* v. 3.

[21] Quoted in *The Tragic Sense of Life* by Unamuno (3rd imp.), p. 178.

Divinity in us is to be realized in mind and spirit and made a power in life. The intellectual apprehension must become embodied in a regenerated being. The Divine must subdue us to its purpose, subject the rebellious flesh to a new rhythm, and use the body to give voice to its own speech. Life eternal or liberation or the kingdom of heaven is nothing more than making the ego with all its thought and desires get back to its source in spirit. The self still exists, but it is no more the individual self but a radiant divine self, deeper than the individual being, a self which embraces all creation in a profound sympathy. The *Upanishad* says: 'The liberated soul enters into the All.'[22] The heart is released from its burden of care. The sorrows and errors of the past, the anxiety of unsatisfied desire, and the sullenness of resentment are no more. It is the destiny of man where there is a perfect flowering of the human being. To embody this eternal greatness in temporal fact is the aim of the world. The peace of perfection, the joy of heaven, is realizable on earth. Perfection is open to all. We are all members of the heavenly household, of the family of God. However low we may fall, we are not lost. There is no such thing as spiritual death. As long as there is a spark of spiritual life, we have hope. Even when we are on the brink of the abyss, the everlasting arms will sustain us, for there is nothing, not even an atom of reality, where God does not abide. Men of spiritual insight take upon themselves the cross of mankind. They crown themselves with thorns in order that others may be crowned with life immortal. They go about the world as vagrants despising the riches of the world to induce us to believe in the riches of their world. When they gaze into men's eyes, whatever their condition of life, they see something more than man. They see our faces not merely by the ordinary light of the world but by the transfiguring light of our divine possibilities. They therefore share our joys and sorrows.

YOGA

To gain this enlightenment, this living first-hand experience of spiritual illumination, the aspirants submit themselves to long years of protracted search, to periods of painful self-denial. To be made luminous within we have to pay a heavy price. We must reduce the vast complex of actions and reactions we call human nature to some order and harmony. The appetites which call for satisfaction, the zest for life and the animal propensities, our unreasoned likes and dislikes, pull us in different directions. This raw material requires to be subdued into the pattern of self. We must attain an integrated vision, a whole life, health and strength of body, alertness of mind, and spiritual serenity. A complete synthesis of spirit, soul, flesh, and affections requires a radical change-over, so that we think and live differently. We have to endure a violent inward convulsion. As a first step we are called upon to withdraw from all outward things, to retreat into the ground of our own soul and find in the inmost depth of the self the divine reality. The world of things in its multiplicity is revealed as a unity. The vision of the true self is at the same time vision of unity (*ekatvam anupaśyati*). He beholds all beings in himself and himself in all beings.[23] 'There one perceives no other, hears no other, recognizes

[22] *Muṇḍaka Up.* iii. 2. 15. [23] *Īśa Up.* 6.

no other, there is fullness.'[24] A life that is divided becomes a life that is unified. Yoga is the pathway to this rebirth or realization of the divine in us.

There are not only many mansions in God's house but many roads to the heavenly city. They are roughly distinguished into three—*jnāna*, *bhakti*, and *karma*. God is wisdom, holiness, and love. He is the answer for the intellectual demands for unity and coherence, the source and sustainer of values, and the object of worship and prayer. Religion is morality, doctrine as well as a feeling of dependence. It includes the development of reason, conscience, and emotion. Knowledge, love, and action, clear thinking, ardent feeling, and conscientious life, all lead us to God and are necessary for spiritual growth. A relatively greater absorption in one or the other depends on the point we have reached in our inner development. When the goal is reached there is an advance in the whole being of man. Religion then ceases to be a rite or a refuge and becomes the attainment of reality.

JNĀNA

When *jnāna* is said to lead to *moksha* or liberation, it is not intellectual knowledge that is meant but spiritual wisdom. It is that which enables us to know that the spirit is the knower and not the known. By philosophical analysis (*tattva-vichāra*) we realize that there is in us a principle of awareness by which we perceive all things, though it is itself not perceived as an object in the ordinary way. Not to know that by which we know is to cast away a treasure that is ours. Yoga in the sense of the stilling of outward activities and emotions and concentration on pure consciousness is adopted to help the process of development. When we attain this *jnāna* there is a feeling of exaltation and ecstasy and a burning rage to suffer for mankind.

BHAKTI

While Hinduism is one of the most metaphysical of religions, it is also one that can be felt and lived by the poor and the ignorant. By the pursuit of *bhakti* or devotion we reach the same goal that is attained by *jnāna*. The devotees require a concrete support to their worship and so believe in a personal God. *Bhakti* is not the love which expects to be reciprocated. Such a love is a human affection and no more. Prayer becomes meditation, the worshipful loyalty of will which identifies itself with the good of the world. If you are a true devotee of God you become a knowing and a virtuous soul as well. The *bhakta* knows how to identify himself completely with the object of devotion, by a process of self-surrender.

> My self I've rendered up to thee;
> I've cast it from me utterly.
> Now here before thee, Lord, I stand,
> Attentive to thy least command.
> The self within me now is dead,
> And thou enthroned in its stead.
> Yea, this, I, Tuka, testify,
> No longer now is 'me' or 'my'.[25]

[24] *Chhāndogya Up.* vii. 24.

[25] Nicol Macnicol, *Psalms of Marāthā Saints*, p. 79.

The distinction between God and worshipper is only relative. Love and knowledge have one and the same end. They can only be conceived as perfected when there is an identity between lover and beloved, knower and known.

KARMA

Ethical obedience is also a pathway to salvation. Hinduism desires that one's life should be regulated by the conception of duties or debts which one has to discharge. The debts are fourfold: (i) To the Supreme Being. One's whole life is to be regarded as a sacrifice to God. (ii) To the seers. By their austerities and meditations the sages discovered truth. We become members of a cultured group only by absorbing the chief elements of the cultural tradition. (iii) To our ancestors. We repay these debts by having good progeny. The Hindu social code does not ask us to impose an unnatural order on the world. We discover the intentions of nature in the constitution of men and women and it is our duty to act agreeably to them. Marriage is not merely of bodies but of minds. It makes us richer, more human, more truly living, and becomes the cause of greater love, deeper tenderness, more perfect understanding. It is an achievement which requires discipline. If it is not the expression of spirit, it is mere lust. There are innumerable shades between love, the spiritual unity expressed in physical unity, and lust which is mere physical attraction without any spiritual basis, and which has created prostitution both within and without marriage. The great love stories of the world, even when they involve a breaking of human laws, are centred, lifted up, and glorified by their fidelity, by the fact that they do not pass. (iv) To humanity. We owe a duty to humanity which we discharge by means of hospitality and goodwill. Those who adopt this view are not content with merely earning their bread or seeking their comfort, but believe that they are born not for themselves but for others.

Hinduism does not believe that the use of force is immoral in all circumstances. The *Bhagavad Gītā*, for example, lays stress on the duties of the warrior and the claims of the nation. There is a place for politics and heroism, but wisdom and love are more than politics and war. In order to remain within the bonds of a class or a nation we need not free ourselves from the bonds of humanity. Real democracy is that which gives to each man the fullness of personal life. Animals are also included under objects to be treated with compassion. All life is sacred, whether of animals or of fellow men. We shudder at cannibalism and condemn the savage who wishes to indulge in this habit of our ancestors, though the slaughtering of animals and birds for human consumption continues to be regarded as right. The Hindu custom allows meat-eating but prefers vegetarianism. On days dedicated to religious functions meat-eating is disallowed. Our right to take animal life is strictly limited by our right to self-preservation and defence. The true man is he in whom the mere pleasure of killing is killed. So long as it is there, man has no claim to call himself civilized. While Hinduism has within its fold barbarians inheriting the habits of wild ancestors who slew each other with stone axes for a piece of raw flesh, it aims at converting them into men whose hearts are charged with an eager and unconquerable love for all that lives.

In the priestly codes there is a tendency to confuse virtue with ceremonial purity. To kill a man is bad, but to touch his corpse is worse. The great scriptures, however, disregard technical morality and insist on the spirit of self-control and love of humanity. To be able to fulfil the obligations expected of man he must exercise self-control. Not only what we accept but what we renounce contributes to our making. Threefold is the gate of hell that destroys the self: lust, anger, and greed. We must make war upon them with the weapons of spirit, opposing chastity to lust, love to anger, and generosity to greed. The *Veda* says: 'Cross the bridges hard to cross. Overcome anger by love, untruth by truth.' The *Mahābhārata* says: 'The rules of *dharma* or virtuous conduct taught by the great seers, each of whom relied on his own illumination, are manifold. The highest among them all is self-control.'[26] Unfortunately, in our times, the man of self-control is regarded as a weak man.[27] It is for developing self-control that austerities and asceticism are practised, but when self-control is attained these rigorous practices are unnecessary. Insistence on discipline or self-control avoids the two extremes of self-indulgence and asceticism. Discipline does not mean either the starving of the senses or the indulgence of them.[28]

There is enough scope for repentance also. 'If he repents after he commits the sin, the sin is destroyed. If he resolves that he will never commit the sin again, he will be purified.'

The *sannyāsī* is not one who abstains from work. Meditation and action both express the same spirit. There is no conflict between wisdom and work. 'It is the children of this world and not the men of learning who think of wisdom and work as different. The peace that is won by the knower is likewise won by the worker. He sees in truth who sees that wisdom and work are one.'[29]

KARMA AND REBIRTH

The world is not only spiritual but also moral. Life is an education. In the moral sphere no less than the physical, whatsoever a man soweth that shall he also reap. Every act produces its natural result in future character. The result of the act is not something external to it imposed from without on the actor by an external judge but is in very truth a part of the act itself. We cannot confuse belief in *karma* with an easy-going fatalism. It is the very opposite of fatalism. It deletes chance, for it says that even the smallest happening has its cause in the past and its result in the future. It does not accept the theory of predetermination or the idea of an overruling providence. If we find ourselves helpless and unhappy we are not condemned to it by a deity outside of ourselves. The *Garuda Purāna* says: 'No one gives joy or sorrow. That others give us these is an erroneous conception. Our own deeds bring to us their fruits. Body of mine, repay by suffering.' God does not bestow his favours capriciously. The law of morality is fundamental to the whole cosmic drama. Salvation is not a gift of capricious gods but is to be won by earnest seeking and self-discipline. The law of *karma* holds that man can control his future by creating in the present what will produce the desired effect. Man is the sole and absolute master of his fate.

[26] *Śāntiparva*, cliv. 6. [27] Ibid. 34. [28] See *Bhagavad Gītā*, vi. 16–18.
[29] Ibid. v. 4–5.

But so long as he is a victim of his desires and allows his activities to be governed by automatic attractions and repulsions he is not exercising his freedom. If chains fetter us, they are of our own forging and we ourselves may rend them asunder. God works by persuasion rather than by force. Right and wrong are not the same thing and the choice we make is a real one.

About future life there are three alternatives possible: (i) The soul dies with the body, since it is nothing more than a function of physical life. Hindu religion does not accept this mechanical view. (ii) The soul goes either to heaven and eternal bliss, or to hell and eternal torment, and remains there. For the Hindu, the doctrine that the soul has only one life, a few brief years, in the course of which it determines for itself an eternal heaven or an eternal hell, seems unreasonable and unethical. (iii) The soul may not be fit for eternal life and yet may not deserve eternal torment, and so goes from life to life. This life is not the end of everything. We shall be provided with other chances. The soul does not begin with the body nor does it end with it. It pursues its long pilgrimage through dying bodies and decaying worlds. The great purpose of redemption is carried over without break from one life to another. All systems of Hindu thought accept the idea of the continuous existence of the individual human being as axiomatic. Our mental and emotional make-up is reborn with us in the next birth, forming what is called character. Our strivings and endeavours give us the start. We need not fear that the spiritual gains of a long and strenuous life go for nothing. This continuity will go on until all souls attain their destiny of freedom, which is the goal of human evolution. If there is not a shred of empirical evidence for it, the same is true of other theories of future life also.

CONCLUSION

From the beginnings of Hindu history the culture has been formed by new forces which it had to accept and overcome, in the light of its own solid and enduring ideas. In every stage there is an attempt to reach a harmony. Only the harmony is a dynamic one. When this dynamic harmony or organic rhythm of life is missing it means that the religion stands in need of reform. We are now in a period of social upheaval and religious unsettlement the world over, in one of those great incalculable moments in which history takes its major turns. The traditional forms are unable to express the growing sense of the divine, the more sensitive insight into the right way of life. It is wrong to confuse the technique of a religion with its central principles. We must reform the technique so as to make it embody the fertile seeds of truth. In my travels both in India and abroad I have learnt that there are thousands of men and women today who are hungry to hear the good news of the birth of a new order, eager to do and dare, ready to make sacrifices that a new society may be born, men and women who dimly understand that the principles of a true religion, of a just social order, of a great movement of generosity in human relations, domestic and industrial, economic and political, national and international, are to be found in the basic principles of the Hindu religion. Their presence in growing numbers is the pledge for the victory of the powers of light, life, and love over those of darkness, death, and discord.

POSTSCRIPT BY THE EDITOR

The most important religious heritage of India from her ancient past is no doubt the doctrine of transmigration (*samsāra*) which is characteristic of all Indian religions and sharply distinguishes them from those with a Semitic ancestry, such as Judaism, Christianity, and Islam. A few ambiguous and inconclusive references in Vedic literature suggest that vague ideas of metempsychosis were known even among the early Āryans, but thoughts of the afterlife seem then to have been mainly centred on a heaven whither the souls of the righteous went on death, to feast for ever with their ancestors. Among the first fruits of the pessimism of the later Vedic period was the gnawing doubt whether even the soul of the dead might not be liable to further death. Thus the idea emerged that Death would hound the soul from world to world (*loke-loka enam mrityur vindet*, *Śat. Brh.* xiii. 3. 5). The quest for permanence, finality, and complete psychological security is very evident throughout the later Vedic literature, where the Vedic heaven begins to seem inadequate and limited, in the light of the contemporary dissatisfaction.

A definite doctrine of transmigration appears for the first time in the *Brihadāranyaka Upanishad* (vi. 2, repeated with some amplification in *Chhāndogya Up.* v. 3–10). The teaching here enunciated, which has certain primitive features such as do not occur in the developed doctrine of *samsāra*, is ascribed to the kshatriya, Jaivali Pravāhana, a chief of the tribe of Panchālas, who taught it to the brāhman Āruni Gautama, also known as Uddālaka Āruni, apparently one of the most vigorous thinkers of the period (perhaps *c.* 700 B.C.). Another passage in the *Brihadāranyaka* (iii. 2) tells how the great sage Yājnavalkya secretly taught to a questioner as a new and secret theory the doctrine of *karma*, that the good and evil deeds of a man automatically influence his state in future lives.

The first of these passages suggests that the doctrine originally appeared in non-brāhmanic circles. The second indicates that it circulated secretly for some time before it became public knowledge. From the later *Katha Upanishad* (i. 20–9) it appears that there was widespread doubt at one time about whether the personality survived at all after death, and the doctrine of transmigration is again here put forward as a new one, revealed by the god of death to the boy Nachiketas only after much importuning. In the latest of the principal *Upanishads*, however, it seems to have become widely accepted, while in the Buddhist tradition transmigration is axiomatic. There is no discussion on whether or not the personality transmigrates, but only on the mechanics by which it does so.

The evidence for the origin of this doctrine is very faint. It may have been borrowed from non-brāhman and originally non-Āryan elements in the Gangā valley, and have gained currency only against considerable opposition from conservative elements among the priesthood. The names of historical sages—Yājnavalkya and Uddālaka Āruni Gautama—are connected with it in the traditions. How this new and secret doctrine spread in a comparatively short period of time to become universally accepted is also quite unknown. We can only suggest that it was disseminated by wandering ascetics, outside the fraternities of sacrificial priests.

Once it was universally adopted, the idea of *samsāra*, the unending, or almost unending, passage from death to rebirth and redeath, conditioned the attitudes of nearly all Indians and encouraged certain tendencies in the social life of India. The prospect of endless rebirth in a vale of tears, even when punctuated by long periods of residence in the heavens, was extremely distasteful to many of the more sensitive people of the times, as it still is, and the quest for psychological security in one changeless entity where there would no longer be fear of death and rebirth was redoubled. The proliferating religious thought of the *Upanishads*, Buddhism, Jainism, and other less-known heterodox movements owes much of its existence to the growth of this doctrine, which appears to have become universal by the time of the Buddha.

Transmigration must also have encouraged the doctrine of *ahimsā* (non-injury), which was specially supported by Buddhism and Jainism in their campaign against animal sacrifice, for this doctrine linked all living things together in a single complex system—gods, demigods, human beings, demons, ghosts, souls in torment, warm-blooded animals, even humble insects and worms, all possessed souls essentially the same. The man who tried to infringe the rights of brāhmans to whom land had been granted by the king was threatened in the title-deed with rebirth for eighty thousand years as a worm in dung.[30] On such premisses it is understandable that the wanton killing of animals should be looked on as little better than murder, and meat-eating as little better than cannibalism, for the ant which a man carelessly treads on as he walks down the road may contain the soul of his grandfather.

The great majority of Indians still believe in this doctrine, and the concomitant doctrine of *karma*, that man is reborn in happy or unhappy conditions according to his works, and these doctrines, in their Buddhist form, have affected more than half of Asia. They provide a potent sanction against evil-doing, or at least against a man's infringing the ethical norms of his society, for this leads to inevitable suffering, while righteous conduct brings happiness to the next life.

Moreover the afflicted can learn to accept suffering with the thought that it is not sent at the whim of fate or chance, and is not the visitation of a capricious god, but is the just recompense for one's own evil deeds in past lives. This doctrine is not fatalism, and does not imply that the sufferer should not try to better his lot—rigid determinism, of the type propagated by the heterodox sect of the Ājīvikas, is strongly attacked in many classical Indian texts—but it makes suffering of all kinds intelligible, and gives hope to the sufferer who bears affliction patiently. Thus, as a source of consolation, it has done much to mould the Indian character and to shape the Indian way of life.

A further potent factor in the moulding of the Indian mind, a relic from the same axial period that produced the doctrine of transmigration, is the concept of endless cyclic time in a cosmos so immense that the mind boggles at conceiving its size. The simple and comparatively small universe of Ptolemy, which provided the traditional world-view of later Judaism, Christianity, and

[30] This threat, occurring in many copper-plate grants, gives the lie to those neo-Hindu apologists who declare that it is impossible for the soul inhabiting human beings to fall to the state of an animal. Modern Hindus and their supporters may believe this, but it has no basis in any classical Hindu source.

Islam, is intelligible and homely by comparison; and the traditional Semitic and Christian doctrine of linear time—commencing at a period some 4,000 years B.C. and likely to come to an end and give way to eternity in the comparatively near future—was equally intelligible, giving an urgency to man's life which might not be felt in a society which believed that time was infinite, with an infinite number of opportunities for the individual to rise or fall in the scale of being. The Hindu universe is closer to that of modern science than the Ptolemaic one, and for this reason among others Hindus, even orthodox ones of the old school, have little difficulty in accepting scientific theories on the nature of the cosmos or of man.

The forbidding universe of science differs from that of the Hindus in one particular, however. The Hindu world, in all its immense length and breadth, is completely and fully underlain by the Divine. There is no corner of the cosmos where God, or the impersonal *Brahman* for the monistic Vedāntin, is not. Facets of the personality of the one Lord behind the many appear in all aspects of life on earth, and the immense empty spaces of the universe are full of deities, all aspects or partial manifestations of the One.

If the intellectual Hindu prefers to think of the One spirit as impersonal and to equate that One with the *Ātman*, the innermost kernel of his own being, the ordinary Indian of all times has thought of the One as personal—a High God who created for himself all the lesser gods and the whole cosmos. Complicated theogonies evolved in the period following the composition of the Vedic literature, and continued to develop throughout the pre-Muslim period and even after. New gods appeared and old gods faded away and almost vanished, in response to the needs of the times. They formed two broad groups, crystallizing round the two High Gods, Vishnu and Śiva respectively; and the fantasy and inventiveness of the whole folk, not merely of the learned brāhmans, expressed itself in the richest collection of mythology and legend in the world—ranging in quality from the sublime to the grotesque and occasionally even to the repulsive.

The universe for the simple Hindu, therefore, despite its vastness, is not cold and impersonal, and, though it is subject to rigid laws, these laws find room for the soul of man. The world is the expression of ultimate divinity; it is eternally informed by God, who can be met face to face in all things, but especially in the image in the temple or family shrine, for divine images undergo consecration ceremonies at which they are converted into channels of godhead, means whereby the god they represent can reveal himself to his worshippers. God, infinite and omnipresent, nevertheless, in his condescension, projects himself in the form of an image so that his simpler worshippers may feel nearer to him.

For the Vaishnavites, the worshippers of Vishnu, the god has in the past taken material form, in order to save the world from impending disaster. His incarnations (*avatāras*), especially those as Rāma and Krishna, have given the Hindus their most exuberant and vital mythology, legend, and folklore. Rāma and his faithful wife Sītā combine the ideals of heroism, long-suffering, righteousness, loyalty, and justice in a story so full of exciting incident that it has become part of the tradition not only of India, but also of most of South-East Asia. And Rāma's henchman, the gigantic monkey Hanumān, the archetype of the loyal helper, striding out with his mighty club, is still among the most popular of the lesser gods of Hinduism. He figures as the divinity of countless minor shrines throughout the length and breadth of India, and is the personification of the strong arm of the Lord, ever ready to help the righteous in the hour of need.

Krishna, probably even more popular than Rāma, is a divinity of a rare completeness and catholicity, meeting almost every human need. As the divine child he satisfies the warm maternal drives of Indian womanhood. As the divine lover, he provides romantic wish-fulfilment in a society still tightly controlled by ancient norms of behaviour which give little scope for freedom of expression in sexual relations. As charioteer of the hero Arjuna on the battlefield of Kurukshetra, he is the helper of all those who turn to him, even saving the sinner from evil rebirths, if he has sufficient faith in the Lord.

Śiva, the divine dancer and the divine ascetic, has a less vivid body of mythology and legend associated with him. He dwells in the heights of Mt. Kailāśa with his beautiful wife Pārvatī, his bull Nandi, and his two sons, the elephant-headed Ganeśa and the six-headed Kārttikeya. Despite its superficial forbiddingness, and its bizarre elements, this group of divinities forms a sort of paradigm of family life. Often worshipped in the *lingam*, a much-formalized phallic symbol, Śiva represents the eternal power through which the universe evolves. As the divine dancer, subject of some of the most wonderful bronze sculpture in the world, Śiva dances new steps in never-ending variety until at length, in a very fierce and wild dance (*tāndava*), he will dance the universe out of existence, later to create a new one by yet another dance.

Stories and legends like these are perhaps almost as important as the austere monism of the intellectual *Advaita* of Professor Radhakrishnan. It is they that have provided the raw material for most of India's early art and literature, and they have given courage and consolation in face of adversity to countless millions through the centuries. Moreover they have provided India with her main source of entertainment.

Hinduism has its dark side. Psychopathic self-torture has long been part of it. Evil customs such as widow-burning, animal (and sometimes even human) sacrifice, female infanticide, ritual suicide, religious prostitution, and many others like them have in the past sometimes been practised in the name of the eternal Āryan dharma. But let it not be thought that Hinduism is morbid, gloomy, or forbidding. It is fundamentally a cheerful religion. In its temple courts children play unforbidden; at its temple gates the beggar finds his most profitable place of business. And all the larger temples are places of pilgrimage on holy days, centres of jolly religious fairs, to which peasants come from many miles around, not generally with feelings of guilt, fear, and sin, though awe is certainly present, but with the intention of combining religious business with pleasure, just as did the pilgrims of Chaucer's *Canterbury Tales*. Here they are refreshed after hard weeks of labour in the fields, the burden of material care left behind in their villages. The dust and weariness of the road are washed away in the ritual bath in the sacred river or tank beside the temple. For a while they visit the shrine and pay their respects to the god who, like a mighty potentate, sits within it. As a symbol of his grace towards them they receive from an officiant the *prasāda*, in the form of holy water, sandal-wood ash, or red pigment, which they rub on their foreheads. Then, freed from earthly care, they enjoy their holiday among their fellows, secure in the knowledge of God's love, as they understand it.

We do not intend to disparage the Hinduism of the intellectual and the mystic, the Hinduism of the kind expounded by Professor Radhakrishnan. But let us remember the other Hinduism, the Hinduism of the artist and poet, with its rich mythology and legend, the Hinduism of the simple man, with its faith, its ritual, its temples, and its sacred images. Both are part of India's heritage, and it is impossible to pronounce objectively on their relative merits or importance; but there is little doubt which has the more strongly affected the majority of the inhabitants of the subcontinent for more than 2,000 years.

CHAPTER VIII

Buddhism

by BHIKSHU SANGHARAKSHITA

THE BUDDHA

FROM the traditional point of view Buddhism begins with the believer going for refuge to the Three Jewels (*triratna*), the Buddha, the Doctrine (*Dharma*) and the Community of monks (*Sangha*). As the first of these, the Buddha himself, although there is no longer any doubt about his historical existence, the exact dates of his birth and *Parinirvāna* (his physical death) are still the subject of controversy. In all probability those given by the Ceylon chronicles, the *Dīpavamsa* and the *Mahāvamsa* (excluding its continuation the *Cūlavamsa*, the dates of which are sixty years out), equivalent to 563–483 B.C., are not too far wrong.

The events of his life are too well known to be recounted in detail. Born at Lumbinī, in the territory of the Śākya republic, of wealthy patrician stock, he went forth 'from home into the homeless life' at the age of twenty-nine, attained Supreme Enlightenment at Bodh Gayā at the age of thirty-five, and passed away at Kuśinagara at the age of eighty. During his lifetime his teaching spread throughout the kingdoms of Magadha and Kośala (corresponding to the modern south Bihār and eastern Uttar Pradesh), as well as in the circumjacent principalities and republics. His disciples were recruited from all classes of society, and included both men and women. Besides instructing an extensive circle of lay adherents, he trained a smaller, more select band of monks and nuns who constituted the Sangha proper and upon whom, after the Parinirvāna, the responsibility for carrying on his mission mainly devolved.

His personality, as it emerges from the ancient records, was a unique combination of dignity and affability, wisdom and kindliness. Together with a majesty that awed and daunted kings he appears to have possessed a tenderness that could stoop to comfort the bereaved and console the afflicted. His serenity was unshakable, his self-confidence unfailing. Ever mindful and self-possessed, he faced opposition and hostility, even personal danger, with the calm and compassionate smile that has lingered down the ages. In debate he was urbane and courteous, though not without a vein of irony, and almost invariably succeeded in winning over his opponent. Such was his success in this direction, that he was accused of enticing people by means of spells.

In addition to the 'historical facts' of the Buddha's career, notice must be taken of the myths and legends from which, in the traditional biographies, these facts are inseparable. When Buddhism first came within the purview of Western learning it was generally assumed that myth and legend were synonymous with fiction and that, except as illustrations of primitive mentality, they were valueless. Since then we have begun to know better. Some incidents in the Buddha's biography, such as those in which he exercises supernormal powers, may be based on actual occurrences recorded with legendary accretions. Others apparently relate to a different order of reality and a different type of truth altogether, being poetic rather than scientific statements of psychological processes and spiritual experiences. Yet others are in the nature of illuminations caused by the tremendous impact of the Buddha's personality on the minds of his disciples, and express the greatness of that personality subjectively in terms of the feelings of rapturous adoration which it evoked.

This introduces the great question of the alleged 'deification' of the Buddha. According to some modern scholars the Buddha was a human teacher whom the devotion of his followers turned into a god, or God. Based as it is on assumptions quite different from those of Buddhism, such an interpretation of an important doctrinal development must be rejected outright. Within the context of a non-theistic religion the concept of deification has no meaning. The Buddha claimed to be a fully enlightened human being, superior even to the gods, and as such he has invariably been regarded. Since he was already the highest being in the universe there remained no higher position to which he could subsequently be exalted. What really happened was that, since Buddhists believed that the Buddha had realized the Truth, thereby becoming its embodiment and symbol, absolute Reality came to be interpreted concretely in terms of Buddhahood and its attributes, as well as abstractly in terms of *śūnyatā, tathatā,* etc. At the same time the devotion with which the Buddha was worshipped was analogous to that which, in the theistic religions, is the prerogative of the Creator.

Thus there is no question of the deification of a teacher whom his contemporary followers looked on as 'merely human'; hence we must also dismiss the several theories according to which the Buddha was in reality an ethical teacher like Socrates or Confucius, a rationalist, a humanist, a social reformer, and so on.

THE DHARMA

The word Dharma probably has more meanings than any other term in the entire vocabulary of Buddhism. As the second of the three Refuges it has been variously translated as Law, Truth, Doctrine, Gospel, Teaching, Norm, and True Idea, all of which express some aspect of its total significance. To the West the Dharma is known as Buddhism, and the question has often been asked whether it is a religion or a philosophy. The answer is that so long as religion is thought of in exclusively theistic terms and philosophy remains divorced from any kind of ethical and spiritual discipline, Buddhism is neither.

The general characteristics of the Dharma are summarized in an ancient stereotype formula which occurs repeatedly in the *sūtras* and which is still widely used for liturgical purposes. The Dharma is well taught; it belongs to the Lord, not to any other teacher; its results, when it is put into practice, are visible in this very life; it is timeless; it invites the inquirer to come and see personally what it is like; it is progressive, leading from lower to higher states of existence, and it is to be understood by the wise each one for himself.[1]

[1] 'Svākkhāto bhagavatā dhammo sanditthiko akāliko ehipassiko opanayiko paccattam veditabbho vinnūhi.'

The Dharma consists of various doctrines or teachings. These represent neither speculative opinions nor generalizations from a limited range of spiritual experience, but are, for the Buddhist, conceptual formulations of the nature of existence as seen by a fully enlightened Being who, out of compassion, makes known to humanity the truth that he has discovered. It is in this sense that Buddhism may be termed a revelation. According to the most ancient canonical accounts of a crucial episode, the truth, law, or principle which the Buddha perceived at the time of his Enlightenment—in the perception of which, indeed, that Enlightenment consisted—and which, on account of its abstruseness, he was at first reluctant to disclose to a passion-ridden generation, was that of the 'conditionally co-producedness' (*paticca-samuppanna*) of things. Conditioned Co-production is, therefore, the basic Buddhist doctrine, recognized and taught as such first by the Buddha and his immediate disciples and thereafter throughout the whole course of Buddhist history. Questioned by Śāriputra, then a non-Buddhist wanderer, only a few months after the Enlightenment, about his Master's teaching, the Arhant Aśvajit replies in a resounding verse that has echoed down the centuries as the credo of Buddhism: 'The Tathāgata has explained the origin of those things which proceed from a cause. Their cessation too he has explained. This is the doctrine of the great Śramana.'[2] Elsewhere the Buddha clearly equates Conditioned Co-production with the Dharma and both with himself, saying: 'He who sees Conditioned Co-production sees the Dharma; he who sees the Dharma sees the Buddha.'[3]

As interpreted by the gifted early Buddhist nun Dhammadinnā, whose views were fully endorsed by the Buddha with the remark that he had nothing further to add to them, the doctrine of Conditioned Co-production represents an all-inclusive reality that admits of two different trends of things in the whole of existence. In one of them the reaction takes place in a cyclical order between two opposites, such as pleasure and pain, virtue and vice, good and evil. In the other the reaction takes place in a progressive order between two counterparts or complements, or between two things of the same genus, the succeeding factor augmenting the effect of the preceding one. The *Samsāra* or Round of Conditioned Existence represents the first trend. Herein, as depicted by the 'Wheel of Life', sentient beings under the influence of craving, hatred, and bewilderment revolve as gods, men, demons (*asuras*), animals, ghosts (*pretas*), and denizens of hell in accordance with the law of karma, and experience pleasure and pain.

The process is set forth briefly in the first and second of the Four Āryan Truths, the Truth of Suffering and the Truth of the Origin of Suffering, and at length in the full list of twelve *nidānas* or links, which is often, though wrongly, regarded as exhausting the entire content of Conditioned Co-production. Conditioned by spiritual ignorance (*avidyā*) arise the karma-formations (*samskāra*); conditioned by the karma-formations arises consciousness (*vijnāna*); conditioned by consciousness arises name-and-form

[2] 'Ye dharmā hetuprabhavā hetum teshām tathāgatah hyavadat, Teshām ca yo nirodha evamvādī mahāśramanah.'

[3] 'Yah pratītyasamutpādam paśyati sa dharmam paśyati; yo dharmam paśyati so Buddham paśyati.'

(*nāma-rūpa*); conditioned by name-and-form arise the six sense-fields (*shadāy-atana*); conditioned by the six sense-fields arises contact (*sparśa*); conditioned by contact arises feeling (*vedanā*); conditioned by feeling arises thirst (*trishnā*); conditioned by thirst arises grasping (*upādāna*); conditioned by grasping arises 'becoming' (*bhāva*); conditioned by 'becoming' arises birth (*jāti*); and conditioned by birth arises decay-and-death (*jarāmarana*), with sorrow, lamentation, pain, grief, and despair. These twelve links are distributed over three lifetimes, the first two belonging to the past life, the middle eight to the present, and the last two to the future.

The Path to Deliverance and Nirvāna together represent the second trend, Nirvāna being not only a counter-process of cessation of the cyclic order of existence (i.e. the twelve links in reverse order) but the furthest discernible point of the progressive one. This process is set forth briefly in the third and fourth Āryan Truths, the Truth of the Cessation of Suffering (= Nirvāna) and the Truth of the Way Leading to the Cessation of Suffering, as well as at length in another set of twelve links which is continuous with the first one in the same way that a spiral winds out of a circle. Conditioned by suffering (*duhkha*, the 'decay-and-death' of the first list) arises faith (*śraddhā*); conditioned by faith arises delight (*pramodya*); conditioned by delight arises joy (*prīti*); conditioned by joy arises serenity (*praśrabdhi*); conditioned by serenity arises bliss (*sukha*); conditioned by bliss arises concentration (*samādhi*); conditioned by concentration arises knowledge and vision of things as they really are (*yathābhūta-jnānadarśana*); conditioned by knowledge and vision of things as they really are arises disgust (*nirvid*, *nirveda*); conditioned by disgust arises dispassion (*virāga*); conditioned by dispassion arises liberation (*vimukti*); and conditioned by liberation arises knowledge of the destruction of the intoxicants (*āsravakshaya-jnāna*). The whole process can be experienced within a single lifetime. The Path is usually formulated, however, not in terms of the twelve 'higher' links but in various other ways, such as the Three Trainings (*triśikshā*), or Morality (*śīla*), Meditation (*samādhi*), and Wisdom (*prajnā*); the Āryan Eightfold Path; and the Six or Ten Perfections (*Pāramitā*). Despite the fact that the connection of these formulations with the doctrine of Conditioned Co-production is often lost sight of, the fact that the Path is essentially a sequence of progressively higher mental and spiritual states, and that the practice of the Dharma consists above all in the cultivation of these states, is in all of them made sufficiently clear for practical purposes.

As the doctrine of Conditioned Co-production is not a theory of causation in the philosophical sense, there is no question of whether, in the case of either the Round or the Path, the succeeding link is identical with the preceding one or different from it. The Buddhist position is simply that conditioned by, or in dependence on A, there arises B. To say either that A and B are identical, or that they are different, is an extreme view, leading in one case to eternalism (*śāśvatavāda*) and in the other to nihilism (*ucchedavāda*). For Buddhism neither the category of being nor the category of non-being possesses ultimate validity. The Dharma is the Mean. As applied to the process of Conditioned Co-production this signifies that the one who is reborn and the one who died, and the one who gains Enlightenment and the one who followed the Path, are in reality neither the same nor different persons. Rebirth takes place but nobody is reborn; Nirvāna is attained, but nobody attains it. Thus the doctrine of Conditioned Co-production involves that of *anātmā* or no-self.

THE SANGHA

The last of the three Refuges is the Sangha. In its primary sense this means the *Ārya-Sangha*, or Assembly of the Elect, consisting of all those who have succeeded in traversing at least that stage of the Path whence retrogression into the Round for more than seven karma-resultant births is impossible. Such are the Stream-Entrants, the Once-Returners, the Non-Returners, the Arhants, and the Bodhisattvas.

Even as the Buddha is symbolized by the sacred icon and the Dharma by the handwritten or printed volumes of the Scriptures, so the Ārya Sangha is represented, for practical purposes, by the *Bhikshu-Sangha* or Order of Monks. This great institution, which with the possible exception of its Jain counterpart is the oldest surviving religious order in the world, came into existence within a few months of the Buddha's Enlightenment. It consisted—and ideally still consists—of those of the Buddha's followers who, having renounced the household life, devote the whole of their time and all their energies to the realization of Nirvāna. Like the Dharma, the Sangha passed through various stages of development. At first, during the early lifetime of the Founder, the *Śākyaputra śramanas*, as they were called, remained outwardly indistinguishable from the other religious fraternities of the time. What in fact set them apart was the special Dharma they professed. They, too, were of eleemosynary and eremitical habit, assembled twice a month on the days of the full moon and new moon, were of fixed residence during the rains, and so on. The second period of development may have started before the Parinirvāna. It saw the compilation of a Rule of 150 articles known as the *Prātimoksha*, the recitation of which replaced the original chanting of Dharma-stanzas at the fortnightly assemblies. Finally, the Sangha became coenobitical, whereupon the primitive undivided 'Bhikshu-Sangha of the Four Quarters' split up into a number of virtually autonomous local communities, and the *Prātimoksha* had to be supplemented by the *Skandhakas* or complete institutes of coenobitical monasticism. All these developments occurred within the space of about two centuries. Prātimoksha and Skandhakas together constitute the *Vinaya*, a term originally connoting simply the practical or disciplinary aspect of the Dharma.

Parallel with the Bhikshu-Sangha there developed the *Bhikshunī-Sangha* or Order of Nuns. But according to the tradition the Buddha was reluctant to allow women to go forth into the homeless life and, in the history of Indian Buddhism at least, the Bhikshunī-Sangha plays an insignificant part.

In a more general sense the Sangha comprises the entire Buddhist community, sanctified and unsanctified, the professed *religieux* and the lay devotees, men and women. As such it is sometimes known as the *Mahāsangha* or 'Great Assembly'. Lay devotees (*upāsakas* and *upāsikās*) are those who go for refuge to the Three Jewels, worship the relics of the Buddha, observe the Five Precepts of ethical behaviour, and support the monks.

The growth of coenobitical monasticism naturally encouraged the development within the Sangha of different regional traditions which, after being consolidated into distinct versions of the Dharma, eventually emerged as independent sects. Thus a century or more after the Parinirvāna tensions arose between the monks of the east and the monks of the west; and the *Mahāsanghikas*, who were more sympathetic to the spiritual needs of the laity, seceded from the *Sthaviravādins* (more commonly known as *Theravādins*, the Pāli form of the name) who tended to interpret the Dharma in exclusively monastic terms. This was the first formal schism within the Sangha. During the century that followed the Sthaviravādins subdivided twice. First came the schism of the *Pudgalavādins*, who believed in the existence of the person as a real absolute fact; then that of the *Sarvāstivādins*, who asserted the real existence of the ultimate elements of experience (*dharma*) throughout the three periods of time. In this way there had arisen, by the time of Aśoka, four independent monastic corporations, each with its own centres, its own ordination-lineage, its own orally transmitted version of the Dharma, its own distinctive tenets, and its own peculiarities of outward observance. Together with their respective sub-divisions, the four make up the so-called 'Eighteen Sects' (actually there were many more) of early Buddhism.

In contradistinction to the *Mahāyāna*, 'The Great Vehicle', the seeds of which were transmitted by the Mahāsanghikas and their offshoots, all the other sects, but especially the Sarvāstivādins, were retrospectively designated the Hīnayāna, 'The Inferior Vehicle'.

THE ORAL TRADITION

It is well known that the Buddha himself wrote nothing. Spiritual influence and personal example apart, his teaching was communicated entirely by oral means, through discourses to, and discussions with, his disciples and members of the public, as well as through inspired spontaneous utterance. While we do not definitely know what language he spoke, it would appear that he rejected the more 'classical' Sanskrit in favour of the vernacular, especially the dialects of Kośala and Magadha. When two monks 'of cultivated language and eloquent speech' complained that monks of various names, clan-names, and races (or castes) were corrupting the Buddha's message by repeating it in their own dialects, and asked for permission to put it into Vedic verse he firmly rejected their petition. 'Deluded men!', he exclaimed, 'How can you say this? This will not lead to the conversion of the unconverted'. And he delivered a sermon and commanded all the monks: 'You are not to put the Buddha's message into Vedic. Whoever does so shall be guilty of an offence. I authorize you, monks, to learn (and teach) the Buddha's message each in his own dialect (*sakkāya niruttiya*).'[4] In order to impress his teaching upon the minds of his auditors, as well as to facilitate its dissemination, he moreover had recourse to the repetition of key words and phrases, the drawing up of numbered lists of terms, and other mnemonic devices.

All these facts are of far-reaching consequence. In the first place, the Dharma having been orally taught, there intervened between the Parinirvāna of the Buddha and the committing of his teaching to writing a period of oral transmission lasting two or three centuries in the case of some scriptures, and

[4] *Vinaya Piṭaka*, ii.139.1 ff.

much longer in the case of others. Then the fact that the monks had been authorized to learn and teach the Buddha's message in their own dialects meant that the Dharma was from the beginning extant in a number of linguistic forms, so that, when finally it did come to be written down, this was done not in one language only but in many. Thus, it is said, the Canon of the Mahāsanghikas was in Prākrit, that of the Sthaviravādins in Paiśācī, that of the Pudgalavādins in Apabhramśa, and that of the Sarvāstivādins in Sanskrit.

Hence when Buddhism spread outside India it came about that the Scriptures were translated into the language of those countries where the message was preached, into Chinese, Tibetan, Uighur, and so on. At no time, not even when Buddhism was confined to north-eastern India, was there any one canonical language for all Buddhists. The attempts made by some writers to present Pāli as such are mistaken. The word *pāli*, meaning a line of the sacred text, is in fact not the name of a language at all, and the 'Pāli' Canon of Ceylon is probably a Middle Indic recension of a version of the *Tripitaka* originating in western India. The historical accident of its being the only Indian canon to have survived complete in the original language should not cause us to overestimate its importance, much less still to regard its excellent but selective contents as the sole criterion of what is and what is not Buddhism. Finally, when the oral tradition was reduced to writing, the mnemonic devices employed by the Buddha and his disciples for the transmission of the Dharma were responsible for giving the Scriptures as literary documents certain distinctive characteristics.

THE CANONICAL LITERATURE

With the exception of the Pāli Canon, the actual writing down of which took place in Ceylon, and certain Mahāyāna *sūtras* that may have been composed in Central Asia or even in China, the canonical literature of Buddhism is of exclusively Indian provenance. Where, when, and in what circumstances the thousands of individual texts of which it consists were first committed to writing is in most cases unknown. All that can be affirmed with certainty is that the canonical literature came into existence over a period of roughly a thousand years, from the first to the tenth century of the Christian era, as a series of deposits from the oral tradition, the tendency apparently being for the more exoteric teachings to be committed to writing before the more esoteric ones. Even during the period of oral tradition the complete words of the Buddha were referred to as the *Tripitaka*, the three 'baskets' or collections of the Buddha's words. These three are the *Vinaya Pitaka*, the *Sūtra Pitaka*, and the *Abhidharma Pitaka*. Together with the *Tantras* they make up the four chief divisions of the canonical writings.

The word *vinaya*, meaning 'that which leads away from (evil)', stands for the practical or disciplinary aspect of Buddhism, and the *Vinaya Pitaka* comprises the Collection of (Monastic) Discipline. In the form in which it is now extant it consists essentially of two parts, the *Vinaya-vibhanga* and the *Vinaya-vastu*, together with historical and catechetical supplements. The *Vinaya-vibhanga* or 'Exposition of the Vinaya' contains the *Prātimoksha-sūtra* in 150 articles and its commentary the *Sūtra-vibhanga*, one work being embedded in the other. While the former embodies the various categories of rules binding upon members of the eremitical Sangha, the latter gives a word-for-word explanation of each rule and narrates the circumstances in which it came to be promulgated. The *Vinaya-vastu* contains the *Skandhakas* or 'The Chapters', of which there are seventeen or more according to the individual recension. These comprise the complete institutes of coenobitical monasticism, and deal with such topics as ordination, the *Poshadha* or fortnightly meeting, the rains residence, medicine and food, robes, dwellings, and schism. *Inter alia* the *Vinaya Pitaka* records not only the regula of the monastic life but also, in the words of the pioneer scholar Csoma de Körös, 'the manners, customs, opinions, knowledge, ignorance, superstition, hopes, and fears of a great part of Asia especially of India in former ages'.[5] Together with the *Sūtra Pitaka* it is one of our richest sources of information on the civilization and culture, the history, geography, sociology, and religion of India at about the time of the Buddha. In the Buddhist world there are now extant seven complete recensions of this collection, one in Pāli and six from Sanskrit. These are essentially alternative arrangements of the same basic material and differ mainly in the extent to which non-monastic matter has been incorporated. The existence, however, of the *Mahāvastu Avadāna*, a bulky Vinaya work of the *Lokottaravādins* (a sub-sect of the Mahāsanghikas) which is not a disciplinary work at all but a life of the Buddha in which numerous legends have been inserted, suggests that the original nucleus of the Vinaya was a primitive biography of the Buddha in which the monastic elements themselves were a later, though still very early, interpolation.

The *sūtra*, literally a thread, and hence by extension of meaning the 'thread' of discourse connecting a number of topics, is perhaps the most important and characteristic of all Buddhist literary genres. It is essentially a religious discourse delivered by the Buddha as it were *ex cathedra* to one or more disciples, whether members of the Sangha, Bodhisattvas, lay devotees, ordinary people, or gods. The *Sūtra Pitaka* is thus the Collection of Discourses, and constitutes the principal source of our knowledge of the Dharma. Some discourses are either partly or wholly in dialogue form. Others are delivered not by the Buddha but by disciples speaking either with his approval or under his inspiration. Broadly speaking the *sūtras* belong to two groups, Hīnayāna and Mahāyāna, the latter being those discourses which were not recognized as authentic by the followers of the Hīnayāna schools, though the converse was not the case. The Hīnayāna sūtras comprise four great collections known as *Āgamas* in Sanskrit and *Nikāyas* in Pāli. The *Dīrghāgama* (*Dīgha Nikāya*) or 'Long' collection contains, as its name suggests, the lengthy discourses, thirty in number, while the *Madhyamāgama* (*Majjhima Nikāya*) or 'Middle' collection contains those of medium length, of which there are about five times as many. These collections are the most important. The *Samyuktāgama* (*Samyutta Nikāya*) or 'Grouped' collection contains some thousands of very short *sūtras* arranged according to subject, and the *Ekottarāgama* (*Aṅguttara Nikāya*) or 'Numerical' collection a similar number of texts arranged according to the progressive numerical value of the terms and topics dealt with. Both collections draw partly on the first two Āgamas and partly from original, sometimes extremely ancient, sources. The Pāli Canon also contains a *Khuddaka Nikāya*

[5] Quoted A. C. Banerjee, *Sarvāstivāda Literature*, Calcutta, 1957, p. 79.

or 'Minor' collection, consisting of works such as the *Dhammapada*, the *Thera-* and *Therī-gāthā*, and the *Jātakas*, which are found in Sanskrit, either elsewhere in the Canon, mostly in the *Vinaya Pitaka*, or outside it as independent quasi-canonical works.

The Mahāyāna sūtras are distributed into six great collections, the first five of which represent natural divisions, while the last consists of miscellaneous independent works. First comes the group of *Prajnāpāramitā* or 'Perfection of Wisdom' sūtras, of which there are more than thirty, ranging in length from some thousands of pages to a few lines. Their principal subject-matter is *Śūnyatā* or Voidness, and the Bodhisattva as the practitioner of Voidness, and they are among the profoundest spiritual documents known to mankind. The *Vajracchedikā*, popularly known as the 'Diamond Sūtra', forms one of the shorter texts in this class. The *Avatamsaka* or 'Flower-Ornament' group consists principally of three enormous and complex discourses of that name, one of which, also known as the *Gandavyūha* or 'World-Array' *Sūtra*, describes the spiritual pilgrimage of the youth Sudhana, who in his search for Enlightenment visits more than fifty teachers. In a boldly imaginative manner it expounds the mutual interpenetration of all phenomena. The *Daśabhūmika Sūtra*, dealing with the ten stages of the Bodhisattva's career, also belongs to this group. The *Ratnakūta* and *Mahāsannipāta* groups are both made up of much shorter sūtras, the former including such valuable and historically important works as the *Vimalakīrti-nirdeśa* or 'Exposition of Vimalakīrti' and the longer *Sukhāvatī-vyūha* or 'Array of the Happy Land'. As its name suggests, the Nirvāna or Parinirvāna group deals with the Buddha's last days and his final admonitions to his disciples. The sixth and last group, that of the miscellaneous independent works, includes some of the most important and influential of all Mahāyāna sūtras. Among them are the grandiose *Saddharma-pundarīka* or 'White Lotus of the Good Law', which presents in dramatic and parabolic form the main truths of the Mahāyāna, the *Lankāvatāra*, an unsystematic exposition of the doctrine of Mind-Only, and the shorter *Sukhāvatī-vyūha*, in which is taught salvation by faith in Amitābha, the Buddha of Infinite Light.

Abhidharma means 'about Dharma', though traditionally the term was often interpreted as 'higher Dharma' in the sense of a philosophically more exact exposition of the Teaching. The *Abhidharma Pitaka* is a collection of highly scholastic treatises which annotate and explain the texts of the *Sūtra Pitaka*, define technical terms, arrange numerically-classified doctrines in order, give a systematic philosophical exposition of the teaching, and establish a consistent method of spiritual practice. Above all, they interpret the Dharma in terms of strict pluralistic realism and work out an elaborate philosophy of relations. Two different *Abhidharma Pitakas* have come down to us, one compiled by the Theravādins and one by the Sarvāstivādins. Each contains seven treatises which, though covering similar ground in a similar manner, are really two independent sets of works.

Among the Theravāda treatises the most important are the *Dhamma-sanganī* or 'Enumeration of (Ultimate) Elements' and the gigantic *Patthāna* or '(Book of) Origination'. The most important Sarvāstivāda work is the encyclopedic *Jnāna-prasthāna* or 'Establishment of Knowledge', which is known as the *kāya-śāstra* or 'trunk treatise', the others being the *pada-śāstras* or 'limbs'. According to Theravāda tradition the *Abhidharma Pitaka* is canonical inasmuch as, though the details are the work of disciples, the *mātrikas* or 'matrices of discourse' were laid down in advance by the Buddha. Sarvāstivāda tradition ascribes the treatises to individual authors. The philosophical writings of the great Mahāyāna sages, such as Nāgārjuna and Asanga, which stand in the same relation to the Mahāyāna sūtras as the Abhidharma treatises do to their Hīnayāna counterparts, are sometimes referred to as the *Mahāyāna Abhidharma*; but, although immensely authoritative, they were never collected into a *Pitaka*.

The *Tantras* are the most esoteric of the canonical texts. The word itself, derived from a root meaning 'to spread', is applied to a variety of treatises, and affords no clue to the contents of these works. While resembling the sūtras in literary form, they differ from them in dealing with ritual and yoga rather than with ethics and philosophy and in being unintelligible without the traditional commentary. Moreover, the techniques they prescribe can be practised only when, through the rite of *abhiśeka* or 'aspersion', the requisite spiritual power has been transmitted to the disciple by a spiritual master in the succession. How many *Tantras* were originally published it is impossible to say. Standard editions of the Tibetan *Kanjur* contain twenty-two huge xylograph volumes of these works, to which must be added twenty-five volumes of so-called *Nyingmapa Tantras*. Some *Tantras* exist in various degrees of expansion and contraction, each set of such recensions making up a complete Tantric Cycle, the publication of which is associated with the name of a particular *Siddha* or 'Perfect One'.

The greater part of this enormous literature is now available only in translation, the principal collections being the Imperial Chinese *Tripitaka* and the Tibetan *Kanjur* or 'Translated Word [of the Buddha]'. Within the last hundred years, however, a number of Sanskrit Buddhist texts, both canonical and non-canonical, have come to light in Gilgit (Pakistan) and been recovered from the sands of Central Asia. While the value of the Buddhist canonical literature will always be primarily spiritual, much of it provides, at the same time, a useful corrective to any view of the social, cultural, and religious history of India derived exclusively from brāhmanical sources.

PHASES OF DEVELOPMENT

From the Parinirvāna of the Buddha to the sack of Nālandā (*c.* 1197) Indian Buddhism passed through three great phases of development, traditionally known as the Hīnayāna, the Mahāyāna, and the Vajrayāna, each with its own characteristics and its own spiritual ideals. These phases were not mutually exclusive. The earlier *yānas*, besides continuing to exist as independent schools, were also incorporated in the later ones and regarded as constituting, with modifications, their indispensable theoretical and practical foundation.

The Hīnayāna, 'Little Vehicle' or 'Lower Way', was so called by the Mahāyanists because it teaches the attainment of salvation for oneself alone. It is predominantly ethico-psychological in character and its spiritual ideal is embodied in the austere figure of the Arhant, a person in whom all craving is extinct, and who will no more be reborn. While mindfulness, self-control, equanimity, detachment, and the rest of the ascetic virtues are regarded as indispensable, in the final analysis emancipation (*moksha*) is attained through insight into the transitory (*anitya*) and painful (*duhkha*) nature of conditioned things, as well as into the non-selfhood (*nairātmyatā*) of all the elements of existence (*dharmas*), whether conditioned or unconditioned. This last consists in the realization that personality is illusory, and that, far from being a substantial entity, the so-called 'I' is only the conventional label for a congeries of evanescent material and mental processes. At the price of complete withdrawal from all worldly concerns emancipation, or Arhantship, is attainable in this very birth.

The Hīnayāna therefore insists upon the necessity of the monastic life, with which, indeed, it tends to identify the spiritual life altogether. The laity simply observe the more elementary precepts, worship the relics of the Buddha, and support the monks, by which means merit (*punya*) is accumulated and rebirth in heaven assured. As for the difference between Buddha and Arhant, it is only a matter of relative priority of attainment, and of relative extent of supernormal powers. The most widespread and influential Hīnayāna school in earlier times was that of the Sarvāstivādins, who were greatly devoted to the study and propagation of the Abhidharma. They were later also known as the *Vaibhāshikas*, the *Vibhāsha* being the gigantic commentary on the *Jnāna-prasthāna* which had been compiled by the leaders of the school in Kashmīr during the first or second century of the Christian era. The contents of the *Vibhāsha* are systematized and explained in Vasubandhu's *Abhidharma-kośa* or *Treasury of the Abhidharma*, a work which represents the culmination of Hīnayāna thought and has exercised enormous historical influence. The commentary incorporates Sautrāntika views, thus not only bridging the gap between the Hīnayāna and the Mahāyāna but paving the way for Vasubandhu's own conversion to the latter *yāna*.

The Mahāyāna, literally 'Great Vehicle' or 'Great Way', is so called because it teaches the salvation of all. Predominantly devotional and metaphysical in character, its ideal is the Bodhisattva, the heroic being who, practising the six or ten Perfections (*pāramitā*) throughout thousands of lives, aspires to the attainment of Buddhahood for the sake of all sentient beings. Perspectives infinitely vaster than those of the Hīnayāna are here disclosed. The earlier vehicle is regarded by the Mahāyānists not as wrong but only as inadequate, the provisional rather than the final teaching, given out by the Buddha to disciples of inferior calibre whom a sudden revelation of the transcendent glories of the Mahāyāna might have stupefied rather than enlightened.

In the Mahāyāna Arhantship, far from being the highest achievement, is only a stage of the path; the true goal is Supreme Buddhahood. This is achieved not merely by piercing the gross veil of passions (*kleśāvarana*) by insight into the non-selfhood of the person (*pudgala-nairātmya*) but, in addition, by piercing the subtle veil of cognizable objects (*jneyāvarana*) by the realization that the so-called ultimate elements of which, according to the Hīnayāna, the person consists, are only mental constructs and, therefore, themselves devoid of selfhood (*dharma-nairātmya*) and unreal. In this radical manner the

Mahāyāna reduces all possible objects of experience, whether internal or external, to the Void (*Śūnyatā*), which is not a state of non-existence or privation but rather the ineffable non-dual Reality which transcends all apparent oppositions, such as being and non-being, self and others, Samsāra and Nirvāna. Expressed in more positive terms, all things exist in a state of suchness or thusness (*tathatā*) and, since this is one suchness, also in a state of sameness (*samatā*).

On the mundane level, the polarity of the Sangha and the layfolk represents a socio-ecclesiastical rather than a spiritual division, all followers of the Buddha being united through their common devotion to the Bodhisattva ideal. Faith, as a means of attaining Enlightenment, ranks co-ordinate with Wisdom. The Buddha is regarded not only as an enlightened being but also as the embodiment of the Truth and Reality behind the universe. Besides being endowed with three Bodies (*trikāya*), the *Dharmakāya* or Body of Truth, the *Sambhogakāya* or Body of Reciprocal Enjoyment, and the *Nirmānakāya* or Created Body, corresponding to the absolute, the celestial, and the mundane planes of existence, he has various forms and attributes. These are the different Buddhas and Bodhisattvas, such as Amitābha, the Buddha of Infinite Light, and Manjuśrī, Avalokiteśvara, and Vajrapāni, the Bodhisattvas of Wisdom, Compassion, and Power respectively, around each of whom there centres a popular cult.

In the field of philosophy the Mahāyāna is represented by the two great schools of the *Mādhyamikas* and the *Yogācārins*, the first founded (or rather systematized) by Nāgārjuna (*c.* 150 A.D.) and the second by Asanga (*c.* 400 A.D.). Both are based primarily on the doctrine of *Śūnyatā* as taught in the Perfection of Wisdom sūtras; but there are important differences of approach which give to each their special character. The Mādhyamikas or followers of the Mean emphasize Wisdom, and their method is dialectical. They reduce mind and matter directly to *Śūnyatā*, the truth of which is revealed by exposing the self-contradictory nature of all statements about the Absolute. The Yogācārins or practitioners of Yoga, on the other hand, stress Meditation, and their approach is intuitive. They reduce matter to mind and then mind to *Śūnyatā*, the truth of which dawns upon the purified consciousness in the depths of meditation. In later centuries the two teachings were sometimes regarded as constituting one continuous doctrinal system, wherein the Yogācāra represented the relative and the Mādhyamika the absolute truth.

The Vajrayāna, the 'Diamond Vehicle' or 'Adamantine Way', is so called because, like the irresistible *vajra*, meaning both thunderbolt and diamond, it immediately annihilates all obstacles to the attainment of Buddhahood. It is predominantly yogic and magical in character, and its ideal is the *Siddha*, 'a man who is so much in harmony with the cosmos that he is under no constraint whatsoever, and as a free agent is able to manipulate the cosmic forces both inside and outside himself'.[6] Except that it aims at the realization of *Śūnyatā* not only mentally but also physically, the Vajrayāna differs from the Mahāyāna less in respect of doctrine than in its methods. Its goal is the transmutation of the body, speech, and mind of the initiate into the Body, Speech

[6] E. Conze, *A Short History of Buddhism*, Bombay, 1960, p. x.

and Mind of the *Tathāgata*, that is to say, into the *Nirmānakāya*, the *Sambhogakāya*, and the *Dharmakāya*. In the case of the Lower Tantra it is believed that this transmutation can take place in sixteen lives, and in that of the Higher Tantra in the space of one life. Such a tremendous acceleration of the normal rate of spiritual evolution requires not only the concentrated practice of various highly esoteric yogic exercises but also a special transmission of spiritual power from an enlightened *guru*. For this reason the *guru* occupies in the Vajrayāna an even more exalted position than in the other *yānas*, being regarded as the Buddha himself in human guise. Various forms of Vajrayāna can be distinguished. These are not doctrinal schools but lines of spiritual transmission which, so far as the human plane is concerned, originated with one or another of the eighty-four *Siddhas*, prominent among whom were Padmasambhava or Padmākara and Sarahapāda.

THE SPIRITUAL LIFE

While the experience of enlightenment is instantaneous, the approach to it is always gradual. In Buddhism, therefore, the spiritual life consists essentially in the following of a path, the successive steps and stages of which have been carefully mapped out by tradition in accordance with the spiritual experience of the Buddha and his disciples, both immediate and remote. As temperaments and methods of practice differ, this path can be formulated in various ways and the number and order of its constituent factors determined and described from various points of view. Thus it comes about that we have not only the Āryan Eightfold Path, and the Path of the Ten Perfections and Ten Stages—two of the best-known formulations—but also the Path as consisting of seven stages of purification, thirteen 'abodes' (*vihāra*), fifty-two *yānas*, and so on, the list being practically interminable. What we may call the architectonic of the Path, however, does not vary, just as different types of bridges, built in accordance with the same principles of mechanics and for the same purpose, reveal the same basic structure. This architectonic is most clearly exhibited in the formula of the Three Trainings (*triśikshā*), namely Morality (*śīla*), Meditation (*samādhi*), and Wisdom (*prajnā*), which according to one tradition was the recurrent theme of the discourses delivered by the Buddha during his last tour, and concerning which he is represented as declaring, 'Great becomes the fruit, great the advantage of *samādhi*, when it is set round with *śīla*. Great becomes the fruit, great the advantage of *prajnā* when it is set round with *samādhi*.'[7]

In its primary sense *śīla* means 'behaviour' and in its derived sense 'good behaviour'. All behaviour, good or bad, is the expression of a mental attitude. Despite the formidable lists of precepts with which, in practice, Buddhist ethics has tended to become identified, *śīla* is in the last analysis defined in purely psychological terms as those actions which are associated with wholesome mental states, productive of good karma, and dissociated from those which are unwholesome. What constitutes a wholesome mental state differs from one *yāna* to another; or rather, there is a difference of emphasis. For the Hīnayāna, good actions are those connected with the wholesome mental roots

[7] *Dīgha-Nikāya*, ii.81 ff.

of non-greed (*alobha*), non-hate (*advesha*), and non-delusion (*amoha*); for the Mahāyāna and Vajrayāna, those inspired by love (*maitrī*) and compassion (*karuṇā*) for sentient beings. Bodily and verbal actions being the extensions of mental states, these states can be induced by the performance of the actions, whether good or bad, self-regarding or altruistic, which are their natural expression. In this fact lies the importance of *śīla* as a preparation for *samādhi.*

Samādhi or Meditation (the translation is approximate only) comprises the exercises by means of which the practitioner attains mental concentration and the superconscious states, as well as these states themselves. It is the heart and centre of the Buddhist spiritual life. Broadly speaking, in the Hīnayāna the term *samādhi* generally refers to the practice of the meditation exercises, and in the Mahāyāna to the spiritual states attained by such practice. Thirty-eight or forty meditation exercises are enumerated, but in fact there are more. Among the most popular are the contemplation of the ten stages of decomposition of a corpse, by means of which craving (*lobha*) is destroyed, the cultivation of loving kindness (*maitrī*) towards all sentient beings, which destroys hate (*dvesha*), and mindfulness of the bodily movements and the process of respiration, which leads to the destruction of delusion (*moha*). The Mahāyāna makes use of the same exercises but combines them with the practice of *Śūnyatā.* In the Vajrayāna, meditation includes the repetition of the mantras of the Buddhas and Bodhisattvas and the visualization of their forms, which, after being conjured forth from the Voidness, worshipped, and meditated upon, are resolved back into it again. There are also various exercises which, by manipulating the gross energies of the physical body, aim at activating their subtle and transcendental counterparts. Whatever the type of exercise may be, the aim of it is to attain a state of purity and translucency of mind wherein the Truth can be as it were reflected.

In general *prajnā* or Wisdom is threefold, as based upon learning (literally 'hearing'), upon independent thought and reflection, and upon meditation (*bhāvanā,* that which is mentally developed, or 'made to become'). Here the third kind or Wisdom proper is to be understood. This may be described as a direct, non-conceptual apprehension of transcendental Reality. For the Hīnayāna such apprehension arises when things and persons are viewed exclusively in terms of the *dharmas,* or ultimate elements of existence; for the Mahāyāna, when the *dharmas* themselves are seen as *Śūnyatā.* In either case, the result is a permanent disruption of the web of illusion, resulting in Hīnayāna in the attainment of Arhantship and in Mahāyāna of Supreme Buddhahood. What, for want of a better word, we are compelled to term Buddhist philosophy is, in fact, essentially the conceptual formulation of the non-conceptual content of Wisdom or Enlightenment. Correctly understood, the Sarvāstivāda, the Sautrāntika, the Yogācāra or Vijnānavāda, and the Mādhyamika are not rival systems of thought, one of which must be true and the rest false, but expressions on the intellectual plane of successively more advanced degrees of spiritual insight. The technique is for a philosophy pertaining to a more advanced degree of insight to utilize the formulations of a less advanced degree in order to undermine its basic assumptions, thus impelling the practitioner to move from a more to a less limited experience of Reality.

NIRVĀNA

Although the state of perfection attained by following the Path is said to be ineffable, it is referred to in the Scriptures by a bewilderingly rich variety of names. The best known of these in the West is Nirvāna (Pāli, *Nibbāna*), from the root *vā*, meaning to blow, and the prefix *nir*, out or off. Hence the traditional explanations of Nirvāna as the 'blowing out' of the fires of greed, hatred, and delusion and as the state wherein the thirst for sensuous experience, for continued existence, and even for non-existence, is altogether absent. Notwithstanding these etymologies, however, the goal of Buddhism is far from being a purely negative state, a metaphysical and psychological zero wherein individuality disappears, as some of the older Orientalists maintained that the Buddhists believed. What does not in reality exist cannot be said to cease to exist: all that is extinguished is the false assumption of an individual being distinct from and independent of the psychophysical processes of which it is composed.

Positive descriptions of Nirvāna are in fact of no less frequent occurrence in the Scriptures than negative ones, though in both cases it must be borne in mind that these are not so much definitions in the logical sense as conceptual and verbal signposts pointing in the direction of a realization which leaves them far behind. No necessary connection exists between the word 'orange' and the fruit of that name; but one who has been told that it is a golden, nearly globose fruit belonging to the genus *Citrus* may be able, with the help of this description, to identify it and experience its unique and indefinable flavour for himself. Psychologically, Nirvāna is a state of absolute illumination, supreme bliss, infinite love and compassion, unshakable serenity, and unrestricted spiritual freedom. Ontologically, it is for the Hīnayāna an eternal, unchanging, extra-mental spiritual entity, wholly unconnected with the cosmic process, and for the Mahāyāna the Absolute Reality transcending all oppositions including that between itself and Samsāra. As the supreme object of the spiritual consciousness, or *Dharmakāya*, it is the embodiment of Great Wisdom and Great Compassion and embraces all possible virtues and perfections. It is the Infinite Light (*Amitābha*) and the Boundless Life (*Amitāyus*), which has nothing to do with personal immortality.

SOCIAL AND POLITICAL IDEALS

As a teaching aiming at the experience of Enlightenment, Buddhism has no direct concern with the collective life of man on the social and political level. It does not tell its followers how many wives they may have or what form of government they should support. At the same time, as the existence of the monastic order indicates, external conditions are not altogether irrelevant to the development of the wholesome mental attitudes on which the experience of Enlightenment depends. A minimum of social and political teachings is, therefore, scattered here and there throughout the *Tripitaka*. That, notwithstanding the example of Aśoka, they were never taken up and systematically developed in India is perhaps due to the predominantly philosophical and other-worldly tendency of the Indian Buddhist mind.

Matters of everyday social ethics apart, the social teachings of Buddhism concentrate upon two vitally important issues: caste and means of livelihood. The Buddha rejected the system of hereditary caste. A man's position in society, he maintained, is determined not by birth (*jāti*) but by worth, by conduct (*charana*), and by character (*charitra*) rather than by descent. Brāhmanical pretensions to hereditary holiness were therefore dismissed with ridicule, and membership of the Buddhist community, whether as monks or lay devotees, was thrown open to all who took refuge in the Three Jewels and were prepared to observe the *śīla* appropriate to their vocation. Means of livelihood (*ājīva*) are of two kinds, right (*samyak*) and wrong (*mithyā*). The Buddha refused to concede that a man's life could be compartmentalized, with his professional conduct governed by one set of standards and his private life by another, or that the former constituted a neutral field to which ethical considerations need not apply. He went so far, indeed, as to prohibit essentially unethical occupations, such as those of the butcher, the dealer in poisons, and the weapon-maker, and to make Right Means of Livelihood (*samyak-ājīva*) the fifth member of the Āryan Eightfold Path.

In the sphere of politics Buddhism holds that the government should promote the welfare of the people (not excluding animals) by all possible means. Religion is to be made the basis of national life. In particular, morality is to be encouraged and the Sangha supported. This simple but sublime ideal finds picturesque embodiment in the figure of the *Chakravarti-rāja* or *Dharmarāja* (the latter representing, perhaps, the most distinctly Buddhist phase of the conception) as described, for example, in the *Mahāsudassana Suttanta*.[8] Historically speaking, it receives splendid exemplification in the person of Aśoka, who in his Thirteenth Rock Edict renounces war and proclaims the ideal of *dharma-vijaya* or victory through righteousness, as well as being cultivated with varying degrees of success by some later rulers, both Indian and non-Indian, who strove to emulate the most illustrious of the Mauryas.

DECLINE AND REVIVAL

The reason for the decline and alleged disappearance of Buddhism in the land of its birth is a problem that has perplexed historians ever since it became the object of scientific study and research. The key to the solution lies in the relation of the religion to what is now popularly known as Hinduism. Both systems were tolerant to a degree which to the exclusive monotheisms of the West and the Middle East seems incredible, and neither hesitated to borrow from the other what was required for its own development. Poetic genius needs a language as its medium of expression; but by being used in this way the character of the language itself is modified. Thus Buddhism, though at the beginning it had perforce to communicate its unique message in terms of the current ethnic religious culture, at the same time charged that culture with part of its own more spiritual meaning. Or, to change the metaphor, while Buddhism put some of its new wine into the old bottles, Hinduism redesigned its bottles the better to accommodate and preserve the new wine. The result was that if Buddhism appropriated the forms of Hinduism, Hinduism assimilated something of the spirit of Buddhism.

After fifteen centuries of mutual interaction the existence of a Sangha in

[8] *Dīgha-Nikāya*, *Sutta* 17.

large centres of monastic learning remained the chief discernible difference between the two religions. When these centres—Nālandā, Vikramaśīla, Odantapurī, and others—were destroyed by the fury of the Muslim invader, and the native kings who might have sponsored their restoration were replaced by rulers with an uncompromising and alien faith, Buddhism quietly disappeared. There is no evidence whatever of a deterioration of spiritual life in the monasteries, much less still of a collapse of morality, as some have maintained. The suggestion that the disappearance of Buddhism was somehow connected with the introduction of 'Tantrism' (i.e. the Vajrayāna) not only involves the grossest misunderstanding of this form of Buddhism but also fails to explain why Hinduism, which had also developed a Tantric aspect, failed to disappear too.

Modern Buddhist revival in India began about a hundred years ago with Mahāvīr Swāmī, an Indian Mutiny veteran who, after receiving higher ordination in Burma, settled at Kuśinagara, the place of the Buddha's Parinirvāna. Only towards the end of the century, however, with the interposition of other factors, was real momentum gained. After being awakened by the pioneer work of Western Orientalists, historians, and archaeologists, interest in the cultural and religious achievements of the long-forgotten faith was stimulated by the resurgence of national feeling and reinforced by the missionary endeavours of Buddhists from other Asian countries. In 1891 Anāgārika Dharmapāla, a Sinhalese, founded the Mahā Bodhi Society of India, which ever since its inception has worked for the revival of Buddhism in the land of its birth. During the first half of the present century appreciation of the importance of Buddhism for the history of Indian religion and culture became fairly general among the educated classes, from them percolating down here and there among the masses. This appreciation was signalized when, upon the attainment of Independence in 1947, the Aśoka Chakra was inscribed upon the Indian national flag. Shortly afterwards, the relics of the Arhants Śāriputra and Maudgalyāyana, chief disciples of the Buddha, which for nearly a century had lain in the Victoria and Albert Museum, London, were at the instance of the Mahā Bodhi Society restored to India and made a triumphal progress throughout the land. In 1956–7, the 2,500th anniversary of the Buddha's Parinirvāna, according to the Theravāda tradition, was celebrated on a nation-wide scale. The year 1959 saw the flight of the Dalai Lama from Tibet to India and the influx of about 50,000 Tibetan refugees, among them more than a thousand monks. From the point of view of Buddhist revival, however, the most decisive and far-reaching event of modern times occurred when the late Dr. B. R. Ambedkar, the Untouchable leader, embraced Buddhism at Nāgpur on 14 October 1966 along with half a million followers. Despite his untimely death a few weeks later the movement of mass conversion among the Untouchables snowballed to such an extent that whereas the Census of 1951 returned 181,000 Buddhists for India, that of 1961 recorded 3,250,000, the greatest gains having been made in Mahārāshtra. With this great upheaval, Buddhism may truly be said to have revived in India and from being 'the cherished dream of a few' to have become once more 'the living hope of millions'.

CHAPTER IX

Jainism

by A. N. UPADHYE

JAINISM is essentially an Indian religion and it is still a living faith in some parts of the country. The number of its followers is just over two million. Its contribution to the Indian heritage is more significant than might be expected for its numerical strength. As an institutionalized religion, it has held its ground all along. It has sometimes enjoyed royal patronage, and it has produced worthy monks and laymen of whom any society could be proud. The Jaina contributions to Indian art and architecture, to the preservation and enrichment of Indian literature, and to the cultivation of languages, both Āryan and Dravidian, are praiseworthy. Lastly, the religious instincts inculcated by Jainism have left an abiding impression on many aspects of Indian life.

The origins of Jainism go back to prehistoric times. They are to be sought in the fertile valley of the Gangā where there throve in the past, even before the advent of the Āryans with their priestly religion, a society of recluses who laid much stress on individual exertion, on the practice of a code of morality, and on devotion to austerities, sometimes of a severe type, as a means of attaining the religious *summum bonum*. These recluses held a number of primitive views, such as a pessimistic outlook on life, a belief in man's potentiality to become god through his own exertions, the doctrine of the transmigration of the spirit, an animistic belief in the presence of souls or life in all things, and in *karma*, then conceived of as material, and its supreme force over the lives of all beings. All these ideas were later merged into the general stream of Indian thought. With the growth of Brāhmanism the practices and preachings of these recluses were often antagonistic to those of the priestly Vedic religion. These two categories of religious leaders, *śramanas* and *brāhmanas*, caught the attention of foreign travellers; Aśoka mentions both in his inscriptions; they are frequently referred to in early Jaina and Buddhist works; and Patanjali mentions the natural conflict between their interests. In the sixth century B.C. we know the names of a number of *śramana* teachers such as Makkhali Gosāla, Pūrana Kassapa, etc.; and at least two of them, Mahāvīra and Buddha, have won recognition in the religious history of India as leaders of faiths living to this day. In all likelihood even Kapila, of Sānkhya fame, showed positive śramanic tendencies in his doctrines.

According to Jainism there have flourished in this age twenty-four *Tīrthankaras*, or leaders of their religion. The first of them was Rishabha, the twenty-second Nemi or Neminātha, the twenty-third Pārśva, and the last Mahāvīra. Rishabha figures as a great saint of antiquity; and, in later Hindu literature, he is noted for his queer practices and credited with propagating heretic doctrines which are common to Jainism. He is said to have laid the foundations for orderly human society. Neminātha is associated in Jainism with Krishna of the Yādava clan, whom the Hindus adopted as an *avatāra* of

Vishnu. These and other Tīrthankaras are prehistoric in character. It is now accepted on all hands that Pārśvanātha, who according to Jaina tradition flourished two centuries before Mahāvīra, was a historical person. His followers lived in the time of Mahāvīra, with whose disciples they held discussions. The parents of Mahāvīra followed the creed of Pārśva.

Mahāvīra was a senior contemporary of Buddha. He was born at Kundagrāma near Vaiśāli to the north of Patnā in Bihār. He belonged to the Nāya (Jnāta) clan; and he is called Nātaputta in the Pāli canon. His father was Siddhārtha, a ruler of that area. His mother, Triśalā alias Priyakārinī, hailed from the royal family of the tribe of the Licchavis. Tradition is not unanimous about Mahāvīra's marriage. He left home at the age of thirty and started practising penances in search of knowledge. Unlike Buddha, he had no need to wander in search of a teacher, because he belonged already to the well-established religious order of his predecessor, Pārśvanātha. While wandering as an ascetic he endured a number of hardships. After twelve years of rigorous penance and meditation he attained enlightenment: the knowledge he is said to have attained was free from the limitations of time and space. He preached what he lived. His was a career of supreme detachment, and he was called *Nirgrantha*, one without any ties, whether internal or external.

All living beings want to live, and therefore he conceded to every being the right to live: thus the sanctity of life in all its forms constituted the basis of his moral values. Everyone is responsible for his own *karmas*; and when *karmas* are annihilated there is an end to transmigration, followed by the attainment of supreme spiritual bliss. The age Mahāvīra lived in was marked by great philosophical speculation, in which a number of eminent teachers participated, both brāhmanas and śramanas. The seeds of the *ātmā* doctrine of the *Upanishads* and the further flowering of religious systems like Ājīvikism, Jainism, and Buddhism are to be assigned to this period. Mahāvīra had family connections with the ruling dynasties of eastern India. He preached *ahimsā* or universal love; and his metaphysics was based on common-sense realism and intellectual reconciliation. His followers consisted of monks, nuns, householders and their women-folk; and a well-knit *Sangha*, or socio-religious organization, was formed in his own times. He travelled for thirty years preaching his doctrines, only halting for any length of time at one place during the rainy season. He died at the age of 72, traditionally in 527 B.C., at Pāvā in Bihār. This occasion was celebrated with a lamp-festival by the two ruling families of the region, the Mallakis and the Licchavis; and the present-day *Dīpāvalī*, one of the most widespread and popular of Hindu festivals, is said in Jaina tradition to be a continuation of this.

Unlike Buddhism, which soon spread far and wide, with numerous monasteries in India and elsewhere, the Jaina Church has shown quite a modest yet steady progress. After Mahāvīra eminent teachers such as Gautama, Jambū, and others led the Church, which received patronage from such kings as Śrenika Bimbisāra of Magadha, Chandragupta Maurya, India's first great emperor, Khāravela, the Orissan conqueror, and others. The influence of Jainism gradually spread to the western parts of India. Under the leadership of Bhadrabāhu a number of monks also went to the south owing to adverse conditions caused by famine in the north. Possibly it was the subsequent differences in ascetic practices which led to a split in the Church, dividing it into its two main sections, the Digambara and the Śvetāmbara. This division affected both the monks and laity. The basic religious principles remained the same for both, but they differed among themselves on minor dogmas, mythological details, and ascetic practices. However, the fundamental philosophical doctrines of Jainism have remained the same, unlike those of Buddhism which went on changing from school to school.

The ruling classes and the mercantile community were often attracted by the rigorous asceticism and religious life of the Jaina monks and adopted the Jaina way of life. In the south, during the early medieval period, royal dynasties such as the Gangas, Kadambas, Chālukyas, and Rāshtrakūtas patronized Jainism. Some of the Rāshtrakūta kings were zealous Jainas, and they heralded an Augustan age in the south, in literature, art, and architecture, to which the Jaina contributions have been of classical significance.

In Gujarāt patronage came from wealthy merchants rather than from the rulers. Under the Chaulukya King Kumārapāla (1142–73), however, Jainism saw glorious days in Gujarāt. A new era of literary activity started under the leadership of the Jaina scholar Hemachandra and other teachers and scholars. Ministers such as Vastupāla constructed magnificent temples in marble. Later, Akbar highly honoured the Jaina teacher, Hīravijaya; and some of the Mughal rulers issued *firmāns* prohibiting the slaughter of animals during the Jaina festival of *Pajjūsana* in all those places where the Jainas lived. Prominent Jaina families in Delhi and Ahmedābād built excellent Jaina temples and had influence in the Mughal Court. Jaina laymen also played an important part in the political activities of Rājasthān during the Mughal period. Even during the period of the East India Company Jaina families like the Jagatseths and Singhīs acted as state bankers, and naturally wielded great influence in society.

Jainism has all along instilled a religious zeal among its votaries, the concrete expression of which is seen all over the country in works of art and architecture: statues, free-standing pillars (*mānastambha*), caves, and temples. The 57-foot-high statue of Gommateśvara at Śravana Belgola in Mysore, erected in about 983 or 984 by the Ganga minister Chāmundarāya, is a marvel of its kind; and it is imitated in many places even to this day. The temples at Mount Ābū and those at Pālithānā in Gujarāt and Moodbidri and Karkal in the south make a rich contribution to the Indian heritage.

Language is just a means to an end which, according to Jainism, is one's own spiritual advancement coupled with the welfare of humanity. Obviously, therefore, Jainism has not invested any particular language with religious sanctity. Mahāvīra preached in Ardhamāgadhī, possibly a mixed contemporary Prākrit dialect: and hence the language of the Jaina canonical texts is designated by that name. Jaina authors used Sanskrit for polemic and literary works, according to the need of the times. Besides these two, Jaina contributions to the literature in Prākrit including Apabhramśa, Old Hindī, Old Gujarātī, etc. are quite striking. Jaina authors were among the pioneers in cultivating Tamil and Kannada and in enriching the early literature in these languages. Jaina literature is not only religious but also embraces many secular branches of learning including mathematics and astronomy.

Jainism starts with two principles, the living (*jīva*) and the non-living (*ajīva*). The living is already in contact with the non-living from beginningless time. This contact subjects the living being, on account of thoughts, words, and acts, to the influx (*āsrava*) of fresh energies known as *karmas*,[1] which are conceived as subtle matter. This influx can be counteracted (*samvara*) by religious discipline; and the existing stock (*bandha*) of *karmas* can be exhausted (*nirjarā*) through severe austerities. Then salvation (*moksha*) is attained; and therein the living being reaches its pristine purity, divested of all that is alien to its nature. This, in general terms, is the scheme of Jaina principles (*tattvas*).

Soul and non-soul (*jīva* and *ajīva*) are the basic principles which comprise all that exists in the universe. The soul is characterized by sentiency or consciousness; but in its embodied state it also has sense-organs, activities of mind, speech, and body, respiration, and a period of life. Souls are infinite in number; they always retain their individuality, and they cannot be destroyed or merged into any other supreme being. Living beings can exist in two states, liberated (*siddha* or *mukta*) and worldly (*samsārin*). The latter ordinarily are classified as mobile (*trasa*) and immobile (*sthāvara*); and still a third state is conceived, namely that of *nigoda* beings. Mobile beings are of five kinds according to the number of sense-organs they possess; and some of those with five senses have a discriminating faculty, seen in men and divinities, and dimly in some of the higher animals. The immobile are in the form of earth, water, fire, air, and vegetables, having only the sense of touch. The *nigoda* are host-souls with a common body and respiration; and they are present all over the world. They represent the lowest state of life, as contrasted with the highest state of the liberated ones; both are infinite, and balance the infinite sum-total of the living world. Such a close study of living beings has, besides metaphysical insight, an ethico-moral object: to show the Jaina how to practise *ahimsā* at various stages of his spiritual career.

Knowledge is inherent in the soul, being the manifestation of the consciousness which characterizes the latter; but its function is hindered by Karmic encrustment, so it is found in different degrees in different souls. Direct knowledge by the soul itself is of three types: of remote time and space (*avadhi*), of the thoughts of others (*manahparyāya*), and of everything in the universe without the limits of space and time (*kevala-jnāna*). Indirect knowledge covers our experience through our sense-organs (*mati*) and that which we obtain through scriptures etc. (*śruta*). The indirect belongs to all of us in varying degrees; the first two of the direct types are possessed by great saints; and the third is seen fully in the omniscient Teacher, who is soon to obtain liberation.

Non-living (*ajīva*) substance is devoid of sentiency and is of five kinds. Matter (*pudgala*) is possessed of sense-qualities. Earth, water, fire, and air are gross forms of matter, the indivisible ultimate unit of which is the atom or *anu*. Even sound, darkness, light, shadow, etc. are looked upon as forms of matter. The next two types of non-living substance are *dharma* and *adharma*, the principles of motion and rest. These two terms are used in Jainism in this special sense, which should be distinguished from their usual meaning. They

[1] The reader should take special note of the Jaina use of this term, which differs from its general usage in Hinduism and Buddhism, and may thus lead to confusion. [Ed.]

are imperceptible and all-pervasive. They serve as necessary conditions for, or fulcrums of, motion and rest, and facilitate all movements and static states in this physical universe. The next non-living substance is space (*ākāśa*); it is of two kinds, physical and super-physical; its function is to accommodate all substances; but the superphysical space is *only* space, real void, extending over infinity. The fifth *ajīva* substance is time or *kāla* which produces the continuity (*vartanā*) in the things of the physical world. It is constituted of minute points which never mix.

The living and the non-living (*jīva* and *ajīva*) constitute reality, which, according to Jainism, is uncreated and eternal. It is characterized by origination or appearance (*utpāda*), destruction or disappearance (*vyaya*), and permanence (*dhrauvya*). It is possessed of infinite characteristics, with respect both to what it is and to what it is not. It has its modifications (*paryāya*) and qualities (*guna*), through which persists the essential substratum, substance, at all times. This basic substance with its qualities is something that is permanent, while modes or accidental characteristics appear and disappear. Thus both change and permanence are facts of experience. The soul with its consciousness is permanent even when it is changing through various bodies in different births. Gold, likewise, with its colour and density, is something that persists, though it takes different shapes at different times.

The object of knowledge, thus, is highly complex; it consists of substances, qualities, and modifications; it is extended over three times (past, present, and future) and infinite space; and it is simultaneously subjected to origination, permanence, and destruction. It can be fully known only in omniscience (*kevala-jnāna*), which is not possessed by ordinary human beings who perceive through their organs of sense. What they know is only partial; they are like blind men who touch some part or other of an elephant and variously describe it as a fan, a pillar, a snake, etc. Thus the apprehension of an ordinary human being is partial, and therefore valid only from a particular point of view. This is what is called *nayavāda* in Jainism. For example, in describing different ornaments, if one has in view only the modifications of gold, that is the modal point of view (*paryāyārthika-naya*); but if one concentrates one's attention only on the basic substance gold with its inherent qualities, that is the substantial point of view (*dravyārthika-naya*). In other contexts, they are also known as the common-sense or practical (*vyavahāra*) point of view and the realistic (*niśchaya*) point of view. There are seven points of view or *nayas*. Some refer to the substance and others to modification; while some arise out of the nature of the subject and some out of the verbal statement.

A thing or an object of knowledge is of infinite characteristics (*anekāntātmaka*) which require to be analysed and apprehended individually, and this function is fulfilled by the *nayas*. This doctrine serves as a unique instrument of analysis. The Jaina philosopher has taken the fullest advantage of it, not only in building his system by a judicious search for, and balancing of, various viewpoints, but also in understanding sympathetically the views of others from whom he differs and in appreciating why the difference is there. This analytical approach to reality has saved him from extremism, dogmatism, and fanaticism, and has fostered in him remarkable intellectual toleration, a rare virtue indeed.

What the *nayas* divulge individually is only a part, which should not be misunderstood for the whole; and it is not enough if various problems about reality are understood merely from different points of view. What one knows one must be able to state truly and accurately. In Jainism this need is met by the theory of *syādvāda*. The object of knowledge is a huge complexity covering infinite modes and related to the three times, past, present, and future; the human mind is of limited understanding; and human speech has its imperfections in expressing the whole range of experience. In these circumstances none of our statements is more than conditionally or relatively true. So Jaina logic insists on qualifying every statement with the term *syāt*, i.e., 'somehow' or 'in a way', to emphasize its conditional or relative character. Such a qualification is to be always understood, whether a term like *syāt* is added or not. A judgement, ordinarily speaking, can assume two forms: affirmative and negative, and refers to the substance (*dravya*), place (*kshetra*), time (*kāla*), and shape or concept (*bhāva*) of an object.

An affirmative judgement predicates the characteristics possessed by a thing, while a negative one denies characteristics absent in it but belonging to others. Besides these two judgements, 'Somehow S is P' and 'Somehow S is not P', Jaina logic admits a third kind of judgement, that of indescribability: 'Somehow S is indescribable.' This is of great philosophical significance. In view of the complexity of the objective world, and of man's limited knowledge and imperfect speech, Jaina logic anticipates and admits situations which cannot be described in terms of simple 'yes' or 'no'. A thing cannot be described at all when no distinction is made as to standpoints and aspects. Some aspect can be affirmed, or denied separately from a certain point of view, or both affirmed and denied successively. But, when this predication is to be made simultaneously, one is faced with contradiction which can be wisely avoided by this third judgement of 'indescribability'.

These three are the basic predications; and when they are combined successively and simultaneously, the maximum number of combinations is seven and not more. These should be able to answer every purpose, however complex it may be. This doctrine of sevenfold predication is often misunderstood and misrepresented by idealists who have not been able to appreciate its metaphysical basis and intellectual approach. It reminds one of the realist relativists of the West, such as Whitehead and others. The Jaina logician is neither a sceptic nor an agnostic; but he is a realist working with sound common sense. He does not want to ignore the relative or conditional character of the judgement arising out of the very nature of the object of knowledge.

The soul has been in association with karmic matter from time immemorial, and the object of the Jaina religion is to free the soul from *karma*. The activities of mind, speech, and body lead to the constant influx of *karmas* which form the *kārmana-śarīra*, or karmic body, for the soul, whereby it moves in *Samsāra*. Everyone is responsible for his own *karmas*, and there is no escape from them unless one experiences their fruits, good or bad. Jainism admits no God to bestow favour or frown: the law of *karma* works automatically in shaping one's lot. There are eight basic types of *karmas* named according to their effect on the nature of the soul, which is inherently endowed with the infinite quaternity of knowledge, insight, energy, and happiness. The first two *karmas* obstruct knowledge and insight, the third infatuates the soul, the fourth gives rise to pleasure and pain, the fifth determines the period of life, the sixth shapes the body, etc., the seventh fixes family, etc., and the last brings about hindrances of various kinds. The type, duration, intensity, and quantum of each *karma* is determined when the bondage thereof takes place. These eight types are further subdivided into 148 sub-types which explain man's various experiences in life.

As the influx and destruction of *karmas* entirely depend on man's activities, Jainism lays special stress on the ethical code. This takes two forms, one intended for the householder and the other for the monk. Both are complementary; and if they differ, it is only in the degree of the rigour of practice. The basic vows are five: (1) abstention from injury to living beings (*ahimsā*); (2) speaking the truth (*satya*); (3) not stealing (*asteya*); (4) chastity (*brahmacharya*); and (5) limiting one's possessions (*aparigraha*). The principle of *ahimsā* is the logical outcome of the Jaina metaphysical theory that all souls are potentially equal. No one likes pain. Naturally, therefore, one should not do to others what one does not want others to do to oneself. The social implications of this principle of reciprocity are profoundly beneficial.

Jainism is perhaps the only Indian religion which has explained the doctrine of *ahimsā* in a systematic manner, because all other values were elaborated on this basis. Violence or injury is of three kinds: physical violence, which covers killing, wounding, and causing any physical pain; violence in words, which consists of using harsh language; and mental violence, which implies bearing ill feeling towards others. Further, violence may be committed, commissioned, or consented to. A householder is unable to avoid all these forms of violence in an absolute manner, so he is expected to cause minimal injury to others. In view of the sort of society in which we have to live, injury is classified under four heads: first, there is accidental injury in the course of digging, pounding, cooking, and other such activities essential to daily living; second, there is occupational injury, as when a soldier fights, an agriculturist tills the land, etc.; third, there is protective injury, as when one protects one's own or other people's lives and honour against wild beasts and enemies; and last, there is intentional injury when one kills beings with the full intention of killing them, as in hunting or butchery. A householder is expected to abstain completely from intentional injury and as far as possible from the rest. It is the intention or the mental attitude that matters more than the act. So one has to take the utmost care to keep one's intentions pure and pious and to abstain from intentional injury. The practice of these various vows puts some restriction on the choice of a profession and makes for a humane outlook in society.

There are seven additional vows which help one to develop qualities such as self-restraint, self-denial, and renunciation. In fact, a layman gradually prepares himself for the life of an ascetic. Practices such as these have maintained a close tie between the layman and the monk; both are actuated by the same motive and moved by the same religious ideals, with the result that this close association between them has contributed remarkably to the religious solidarity of the Jaina community.

The course of right conduct prescribed for laymen is conveniently divided into eleven steps (*pratimā*) which are included in the fifth stage of spiritual evolution (*guna-sthāna*). A layman, after shedding all superstition, adopts a right attitude and starts observing the vows given above; he practises self-contemplation thrice a day, with a view to attaining mental equipoise; he observes weekly fasts, and stops taking green vegetables etc. and meals after sunset; he observes strict celibacy, claims no property as his own, does not take interest in worldly matters, and stops taking food specially cooked for him. He can proceed stage by stage according to his ability and environment; but once he reaches the eleventh stage, he is fully prepared for practising the severe course of ascetic life.

According to Jainism, dying is as much an art as living. A layman is expected not only to live a disciplined life but also to die bravely a detached death. There are elaborate rules about voluntary death (*sallekhanā*), which has been practised not only by Jaina monks but also by pious laymen; and we have innumerable inscriptions commemorating the detached deaths of pious Jainas. This voluntary death is to be distinguished from suicide, which Jainism looks upon as a cowardly sin. When faced by calamity, famine, old age, and disease, against which there is no remedy, a pious Jaina peacefully relinquishes his body, being inspired by a higher religious ideal.

What apparently distinguishes a Jaina monk from a layman is his itinerant way of life, with no abode of his own and no possessions or paraphernalia beyond those required for his religious observances. In outward form and equipment there are different schools among the Jaina monks. The *Digambara* monk, who goes about naked if of the highest grade, has a water-pot made from a gourd (*kamandalu*) for the calls of nature and a bunch of peacock feathers to clean the place where he sits, etc. But if he belongs to the lower stage, he has a minimum of clothing to cover his private parts. A *Śvetāmbara* monk is clad in white robes, and he is equipped with a staff, a bunch of wool, and wooden pots. These sects differ somewhat in their rules of outward behaviour, which affect their mode of travelling, eating, etc. The inner religious life, however, is fundamentally the same for the various schools.

The five *anuvratas* (lesser vows) of a layman, not to kill, not to lie, not to steal, to abstain from sex, and to renounce property, are called *mahāvratas* (great vows) in the case of a monk, who has to observe them with maximum rigour and thoroughness. These sins lead to the influx of *karmas*; therefore the monk must abstain from them in thought, word, and deed, and neither commit, commission, nor consent to them. The rigidity with which he is expected to observe the rules and the elaborate details of conduct only show how minutely the whole system of ascetic morality is worked out.

The entire spiritual career of the soul is divided into fourteen stages called *gunasthānas*. The soul marches from bondage and gross ignorance to final liberation and omniscience, gradually overpowering at different stages wrong belief, unrighteousness, negligence, passions, and channels of activities. In the first four stages the soul is struggling against wrong belief, which is overcome in the fifth stage, where righteous conduct begins and is practised by a layman through the eleven *pratimās* cited above. In the sixth, he is already a monk, but still liable to negligence and lapses. In all stages up to the eleventh, regress may take place, and the soul may even fall back to the first stage. When he reaches the twelfth, however, the passions etc. are destroyed, and he begins meditation. In the thirteenth stage he is still in the world, retaining some activities of body, speech, and mind. When all his activities stop, he enters the last stage, where all *karma* is destroyed and the soul attains its fullest spiritual status.

Here we may broadly outline the disciplinary code of a monk, which he has to practise for the perfection of his *mahāvratas*. His one aim is to stop the influx of fresh *karma* and to destroy all that has already bound him. The flow of *karmas* into the *ātmā* or soul is caused by the activities of body, speech, and mind; so it is necessary for him to keep these channels under strict control (*gupti*). It is just possible that even in performing the duties of a monk the vows might be transgressed out of inadvertence. As a precautionary measure, the monk must be very cautious in walking, speaking, begging food, taking up and putting down things, and in voiding the body (*samiti*).

It is mainly due to the passions that the soul assimilates *karma*; so anger, pride, deception, and greed must be counteracted by cultivating 'the ten best virtues' (*daśadharma*), forgiveness, humility, straightforwardness, contentment, truthfulness, restraint, austerity, purity, chastity, and renunciation. To cultivate the necessary religious attitude he should constantly reflect on twelve religious topics (*anuprekshā*): (i) everything is transitory, (ii) men are helpless against death, (iii) the circuit of existence is full of misery, (iv) the soul has to struggle all alone, (v) relatives and others are quite separate from oneself, (vi) the body is impure, (vii) *karma* is constantly inflowing, (viii) *karma* should be stopped by cultivating necessary virtues, (ix) *karma* should be destroyed by penances, (x) the nature of the universe, (xi) the rarity of religious knowledge, and, lastly, (xii) the true nature of religion.

To keep himself steady on the path of liberation and to destroy *karma*, a monk has to bear cheerfully all the troubles (*parīsaha*) that might cause him distraction or pain. There are twenty-two troubles which a monk is expected to face unflinchingly, including hunger and thirst, cold and heat, trying circumstances, unpleasant feelings, illness, etc. His spiritual discipline or conduct is fivefold, and its pitch ranges from equanimity to ideal and passionless conduct (*chāritra*).

The monk has also to practise austerities, external and internal. External penances are extremely rigorous. He barely sustains the body with a minimum of food and exacts maximum work from it in attaining his spiritual ideal. Internal penances are intended for self-purification. The most important of them is *dhyāna* or meditation.

It is pure (*śukla*) meditation which ultimately leads the soul to liberation; there is a complete cessation of physical, verbal, and mental activities, and the *ātmā* or self is absorbed in it. With the entire stock of *karmas* exhausted the soul rises to the top of the universe, where it remains for ever.

It is clear from Jaina metaphysics that there is no place in Jainism for God as a creator and distributor of prizes and punishments. By God Jainism understands a liberated soul as well as the *Tīrthankaras*, who provide the highest spiritual ideals to which every soul can aspire: in this sense God is an example to inspire and to guide. Thus the Jaina conception of God is very different from that in Hinduism. Though God is not a creator, the Jaina religion lacks neither devotional fervour nor ceremonial rituals. Jainas offer prayers to him, worship him both in concept and in concrete form as an image, and meditate on him. Respectful prayers are offered to the *Tīrthankara,* the liberated soul, the preceptor, the preacher, and the monk, because these represent various stages of the soul's spiritual progress. Such a routine keeps the Jaina vigilant in pursuit of his ideal and strengthens his heart, constantly reminding him that he must depend on himself to destroy the *karmas.*

Numerous traces of Jaina influence on Indian life can be detected. The worship of idols in a refined form, the building of temples, the founding of charitable lodges for men and animals, the preservation of rich libraries of manuscripts, and the distribution of food and other necessities to the poor; these are some of the outstanding features of Jaina society, and to a large extent they have been imitated by other Indian religious groups. Jainism and Buddhism have been foremost in upholding the doctrine of *ahimsā,* and Jainism has held firm to its original ideology much more closely than Buddhism.

Jaina monks have led exemplary lives, and as living embodiments of kindness to all beings they have wandered all over India winning the sympathies even of non-Jaina peasants and princes for the doctrine of *ahimsā.* The practice of this has often been misunderstood and misrepresented. The ideal *ahimsā* was meant only for a houseless monk, but to the layman it is prescribed according to his position and stage of religious progress. This has allowed Jaina kings and heroes to fight on the battlefield for their kingdoms and for their safety and honour. Under some of the dynasties of the south and Gujarāt, there flourished many soldiers who were both heroes and pious Jainas. As a community the Jainas have been strict vegetarians, and wherever they are found in large numbers they have influenced the society around them. Throughout their literature and in the preachings of their teachers, animal sacrifice is condemned. In modern times Jaina leaders in different centres have tried to stop the sacrifice of animals to local deities, and they have been successful in many places. Jaina authors disapprove of even the sacrifice of a paste model of an animal, because this involves the intention of taking life.

Jaina literature includes myths, fairy tales, proverbs, popular stories, model behaviour patterns, and moral exhortations, all of which unanimously denounce cruelty to living beings. All these have done much to discourage animal sacrifice. Most of the Indian religions have casually preached *ahimsā,* but nowhere, except in Jainism, is the basic creed so systematically worked out to pervade the entire moral code.

Mahātmā Gāndhī was the greatest exponent of *ahimsā* in modern times. Though he gave it a fresh and up-to-date orientation, the seeds of his doctrines are to be traced in Jainism rather than in any other Indian creed. Some of the facets with which Gāndhījī invested his *ahimsā* are not found in Jaina works, because the purpose for which and the circumstances in which he preached it were different. The Jaina monks were quite aware of the power of *ahimsā* as a social factor, but their spiritual aim necessitated no application of it outside the religious life. To manage with the minimum necessities of life, to bear no ill will towards anyone, to take recourse to fasting for self-purification, to undertake long tours on foot to make contact with the people: all these aspects of Mahātmā Gāndhī's life remind us of Jaina monks and their routine. This great son of India, Mahātmā Gāndhī, has reinterpreted the doctrine of *ahimsā*, non-violence, and *satya*, truth, for the modern world; and these two principles can be looked upon as universal moral norms, by which to judge the behaviour of men and women, individually and collectively.

CHAPTER X

Philosophy

by S. N. DAS GUPTA

INTRODUCTION BY THE EDITOR

THIS chapter, somewhat abridged and otherwise edited, has been carried over from the original *Legacy of India*. It is the work of one of the greatest Indian specialists in the field, who died in 1952. From the point of view of the general reader it may be found difficult in places, for within the limits of the space permitted the author has attempted not only a mere survey of some of the more obvious basic doctrines, but also a discussion at considerable depth of more recondite aspects of the doctrines of some of the Indian philosophical schools. In doing so he seems to have been compelled by considerations of space virtually to ignore several other important schools of Indian philosophy. By drastically removing Professor Das Gupta's rather lengthy treatment of Buddhism, which is dealt with elsewhere in this volume, we have found room for a few extra paragraphs on the Nyāya, Vaiśeshika, Mīmāmsā, and Vedānta schools, which are the work of the editor.

One may divide the philosophical development of India into three stages: pre-logical up to the beginning of the Christian era, logical up to the Muhammadan domination of India, A.D. 1000 or 1100, ultra-logical, A.D. 1100–1700. The contribution of the first period is to be found in the philosophical hymns of the *Vedas*, in the more mature *Upanishads*, in the *Gītā*, which is something like a metrical commentary on the *Upanishads*, working out their ideals in their practical bearing to life; and in the rise and growth of Buddhism and the Sānkhya and the Vaiśeshika philosophy. From about the beginning of the first or second century B.C. we have the various systems of Indian philosophy, the *Yoga-sūtras*, the Sānkhya treatises, the *Mīmāmsā-sūtras*, the *Brāhma-sūtras*, and the *Nyāya-sūtras*, and their numerous commentaries and sub-commentaries. In the third period we have keen discussions and dialectics of an extremely subtle character such as had never developed in Europe at that time, and which are in part so difficult that few Occidental scholars have been able to master them.

In the philosophical hymns of the *Vedas* we come across men who were weary of seeking mere economic welfare through religious rituals of a magical character. They wished to know something greater than their ordinary religion and sought to delve into the mystery of the Universe—the highest and the greatest truth. They formed the conception of a being who is the depository and the source of all powers and forces of nature, from whom nature with its manifold living creatures has emanated and by whom it is sustained and maintained. In spite of all the diversity in the world there is one fundamental reality in which all duality ceases. The highest truth is thus the highest being, who is both immanent in the world and transcendent. He holds the world within him and yet does not exhaust himself in the world. The ordinary polytheism and henotheism of Vedic worship thus slowly pass away, sometimes into monotheism and sometimes into pantheism; and in this way some of the Vedic hymns declare the spirituality of the world and denounce the common-sense view of things.

This view is developed in the *Upanishads*, which may be regarded as a continuation of the philosophical hymns of the *Rig-Veda* and the *Atharva-Veda*. In the *Kena Upanishad* we are told the story of how all the presiding gods of the powers of nature, such as fire and wind, tried their best to compete with Brahman, as this ultimate being was called, but the fire could not burn a piece of straw and the wind could not blow it away against the wishes of Brahman, for they all derived their powers from him. We have a vivid description in the *Mundaka* of how the world has emanated from Brahman, like sparks from the fire or like the spider's web from the spider. But the *Upanishads* advance the thought a little further. They do not merely speculate on the nature of Brahman externally as both the immanent and the transcendent cause of the world, but they also try to demonstrate its reality in experience. Neither the *Upanishads*, nor the philosophical hymns of the *Vedas*, give us any reasons in demonstration of their conception of the ultimate being. They do not raise any questions, or give any premiss from which they drew their conclusions. Their opinions are only dogmatically asserted with the forceful faith of a man who is sure of his own belief. But, after all, it is only a belief, and not a reasoned statement, and there naturally arises the question as to its validity.

The *Upanishads* are driven by their inner thought to give some grounds for such assertions. Yet there is no attempt at logical speculation and demonstrative reasoning. The intuitive affirmations surge forth with the reality of the living faith of one describing an experience which he himself has had. They affirm that this ultimate reality cannot be grasped by learning or reasoning. It reveals itself only in our heart through sublime purity, absolute self-control, self-abnegation, and cessation of mundane desires. Man not only becomes moral in his relations to his fellow beings, but becomes super-moral, as it were, by an easy control of the conflicts of his lower instincts and desires, and by superior excellence of character. It becomes possible for him to merge himself in an intuitive contact with the transcendental spiritual essence with which he can immediately identify himself.

The *Upanishads* again and again reiterate the fact that this spiritual essence is incognizable by any of the sense-organs—by eye or by touch—that it is beyond the reasoning faculties of man and is therefore unattainable by logic, and that it is indescribable in speech and unthinkable by thought. The apperception of it is not of an ordinary cognitive nature, but is an apperception of the essence of our beings; and, just as external nature was regarded as being held and maintained in Brahman, so the totality of our being, our sense-functions, and thought-functions were regarded as having come out, being held and sustained in this inner being. It was also regarded as the *Antar-yāmin* or the inner controller of our personality—the spiritual entity which is its root and in which lie sustained and controlled all our vital activities and cognitive and conative functions. We can have an apperception of it only when we transcend the outer spheres of ordinary life and penetrate into the cavern on which neither the physical luminaries nor the luminaries of thought and sense shed any light. Yet it is a light in itself, from which all other lights draw their illumination. It is subtle and deep, and reveals itself only to those who attain that high spiritual perfection by which they transcend the limits of ordinary personality,

We find anticipations of doubt as to the possibility of such a subtle essence, which was our inmost being, becoming identical with the highest reality of the universe from which everything else emanated. Various parables are related, in which attempts are made to prove the existence of a subtle essence which is unperceived by the eye. In the parable of the banyan tree we are told how the big tree can reside inside a grain-like seed. In another parable it is shown that the salt which is invisible to the eye can be tasted in every drop of saline water. We have also the parable by which Prajāpati instructed Virochana and Indra how two different states of the self can be distinguished from the corporeal body, the dream self and the dreamless self, and how it is the self of the deep dreamless sleep that displays the nature of the eternal unthinkable within us. The deep dreamless sleep brings us into daily contact with the eternal self within us, which is dissociated from all changes, and which forms the essence of our whole being. In the dialogue between Yama and Nachiketas, when the latter seeks instruction regarding the fate of men at death, he is told that when inquiry is earnestly made the true self in man is discovered to be eternally abiding, and can be grasped only through spiritual contact and spiritual union. Taken in this sense, death is a mere illusion which appears to those who cannot grasp the one absolute reality.

There are other passages in which this absolute reality is regarded as one which is undetermined in itself, but from which all our faculties and experiences emanate in concrete determinations. We have thus in ourselves an epitome of the emergence of the world from Brahman. From the subtle state of indifference in deep dreamless sleep one suddenly awakes to the varied experiences of ordinary life. Similarly, concrete varieties of objects have emerged into being from the pure subtle being of Brahman, in which they existed in an undivided and undifferentiated state. Since that which emerges into manifold variety ultimately loses itself in the being of the transcendent cause, and since the transcendent cause alone remains unchanged through all the processes of emergence and dissolution, that alone is the truth. The multiplicity of things is false, for the truth in them is the one abiding essence.

The *Upanishads* are not philosophy, if we mean by the word philosophy a reasoned account or a rationalization of experiences; yet they contain suggestions of rationalization as to the nature of reality from concrete experience of dreamless sleep and from ineffable mystical experience. Though ineffable, the mystical experience is not regarded as an ecstatic communion with the divine; it is a revelation of the subtlest essence of our being, which lies far below the depth of the common animal man. It is only when we transcend the limits of the ordinary biological man that we can come in contact with the pure personality which the *Upanishads* call the *Ātman* or the self. This pure self is one in all and is identical with the highest reality of the universe. It is pure spirituality and pure experience (*Jnāna*) and, as such, the absolute concrete truth which is immanent and transcendent at the same time in all our experiences and in all objects denoted by it. It is infinite reality, limitless and illimitable. The *Upanishads* thus lay the foundation of all later Hindu philosophy. All Hindu thinkers accept in more or less modified form the fundamental tenet of the *Upanishads* that self is the ultimate reality, and all experiences are extraneous to it.

By the beginning of the Christian era six philosophical schools or systems had emerged in Hinduism. Though differing very widely, they were all looked on as orthodox, since they all accepted the inspiration of the *Vedas* and the claim of the brāhmans to ritual supremacy. They were linked together in pairs, as complementing one another or otherwise showing close relations. The three pairs were: (i) *Sānkhya* and (ii) *Yoga*; (iii) *Nyāya* and (iv) *Vaiśeshika*; and (v) *Mīmāmsā* and (vi) *Vedānta* or *Uttara-mīmāmsā*.

The *Sānkhya* is probably the earliest Indian attempt at systematic philosophy. Its foundation is attributed to Kapila, who is said to have written the original textbook of the school, the *Shashti-tantra* in sixty chapters. This work is now lost, and we know only the names of those chapters. We find elements of Sānkhya even in the earliest *Upanishads*, and we have reason to believe that the system was probably not originally written, but underwent a course of development at different stages and under different influences; though it is possible that at some particular stage Kapila may have contributed so much towards its systematization as to be generally regarded as the original expounder of the system. It is generally accepted that the Sānkhya has two principal schools, the atheistic and the theistic. The theistic Sānkhya is now associated with Patanjali and is otherwise called the Yoga system. The oldest surviving text of the atheistic or non-theistic School of Sānkhya in its generally accepted form is a compendium of Īśvara Krishna (third century A.D.). Patanjali is supposed to have flourished somewhere about the middle of the second century B.C. The Sānkhya and Yoga, in their various forms, have profoundly influenced Hindu culture and religion in all their varied aspects.

According to Sānkhya the word *prakriti* means the original substance, which consists of three classes of neutral entities called *gunas*—*Sattva*, representing truth and virtue, *Rajas*, present in all that is active, fiery, or aggressive, and *Tamas*, the principle of darkness, dullness, and inactivity. These are continually associating with one another for the fullest expression of their inner potentialities. They form themselves into groups, and not only are the inner constituents of each of the groups working in union with one another for the manifestation of the groups as wholes, but the wholes themselves are also working in union with one another for the self-expression of the individual whole and of the community of wholes for the manifestation of more and more developed forms. Causation is thus viewed as the actualization of the potentials. The order of all cosmic operations is deduced from the inherent inner order and relations of the neutral reals. Relations are conceived as the functions of these reals, with which they are metaphysically identical. *Prakriti* is regarded as the hypothetical state of the pure potential conditions of these reals. It is supposed that this pure potential state breaks up into a state which may be regarded as the stuff of cosmic mind. This partly individuates itself as individual minds, and partly develops itself into space, from that into potential matter, and later on into actual gross matter as atoms. The individuated minds evolve out of themselves the various sensory and conative functions and the synthetic and analytic functions called *manas*. They also reveal themselves in the psychical planes or personalities of individuals.

It is evident that the complexes formed from the neutral reals derive their meaning and functioning through a reference to the other or the others, for the manifestation of which they are co-operating together. This other-reference of the reals (*gunas*) is their inherent teleology. But such other-references must have a limit, if an infinite regression is to be avoided. In a general manner it may be said that the two broad groups, the psychical and the physical, are working together in mutual reference. It is therefore assumed that there is an unrelational element, called *purusha*, a pure consciousness which presides over every individuated mind. By reference to this the non-conscious psychic phenomena attain their final meaning as conscious phenomena. The whole history of conscious phenomena attains its last metaphysical purpose in self-annulment, by an ultimate retroversion of reference from *purusha* towards the ultimate principle of consciousness, by which the final other-reference to the *purusha* ceases. There must be a stage in which the positive other-references end themselves in self-reference, whereby the ultimate bond of the psychic manifestation or the personality with the *purusha* will cease. This cessation in the history of any individual psychic plane marks its culmination and is regarded as a final metaphysical liberation of the *purusha* associated with that individual psychic plane. There are as many *purushas* as there are psychic planes. The *purusha* is regarded as the principle of consciousness unrelated to its fellow *purushas* and also to any of the complexes of the neutral reals.

It has already been said that space is derived as a modification of the reals. Time is to be regarded as having a transcendental and a phenomenal aspect. Under the former, time is identical with the movement inherent in the *guna* reals and as such it is even prior to space. In the latter aspect, that is time as measurable, and as before and after, it is mental construction in which the ultimate unit of measure is regarded as the time taken by an atom to traverse its own dimension of space. Since all conceivable objects in the world are products of the *guna* reals, and since there is no other agent, the *guna* reals hold within themselves in a potential manner all things of the world, which are manifested first in the emergent categories of cosmic personality, ego, the eleven senses, five kinds of potential matter, and five kinds of actual matter. These together form the twenty-five categories from the enumeration of which the Sānkhya system is supposed to have drawn its name, meaning numeration or counting.

The *Yoga*, which is in general agreement with the entire metaphysical position of the Sānkhya, thinks that the elements leading to a positive misconception or misidentification of the *purusha* as being of the same nature as the *guna* complexes are responsible for the possibility of the *nisus* and the resulting experience. This is technically called ignorance or *avidyā*. Yoga further holds that this *avidyā* manifests itself or grows into the various cementing principles of the mind, emotional and volitional, such as ego-consciousness, attachment, antipathy, and the self-preservative tendency. As a result of the operation of these principles, as grounded in the *avidyā*, the mind behaves as a whole and acquires experience and determines itself in the objective environment. According to both Sānkhya and Yoga, the individuated mind has a beginningless history of emotional and volitional tendencies integrated or inwoven, as it were, in its very structure as it passes from one cycle of life to another. The determination of the mind in pursuance of its end as desire, will, or action is called *karma*. It is further held that all such determinations create potential energies which must fructify as diverse kinds of pleasurable or painful experiences, environments, conditions, and the periods of particular lives in which these experiences are realized.

The self-determining movement of the mind for the attainment of liberation can only start when one begins to discover that all experiences are painful. As a result thereof the young saint becomes disinclined towards all the so-called joys of the world and ceases to have any interest in the propagation of the life-cycle. Such a cessation cannot be by death. For death means further rebirth. The cessation of the life-cycles must necessarily be sought in the extinction of the conditions determining the mind-structure. For this, he adopts means by which he can invert the process of operation of the mind-structure, which consists of the integrated content of images, concepts, and their emotional and volitional associates, of various kinds, below the surface. These are immediately absorbed below the conscious level as the subconscious, semiconscious, and unconscious. The various elements of the psychic structure in the different levels are held together to a great extent by ties of emotion and volition referring to the enjoyment of worldly objects. It is these that are continually attracting our minds.

The followers of Yoga should in the first instance practise a definite system of moral and religious restraints, such as non-injury, truthfulness, purity, sincerity, sex-control, self-contentment, and the like, called *yamas* and *niyamas*, for the external purification of mind. Ordinarily all activities associated with mental life are of the nature of continual relationing and movement. The Yogin who wishes to invert the processes underlying the maintenance of psychic structure arrests his mind statically on a particular object to the exclusion of all others, so that on the focal point of consciousness there may be only one state, which does not move, and all relationing process of the mind is at complete arrest.

Yoga is defined as a partial or complete arrest or cessation of the mental states. As an accessory process the Yogin learns to steady himself in a particular posture (*āsana*) and gradually to arrest the processes of breathing (*prānāyāma*). His efforts to exclude other objects and to intensify the selected mental state which is to be kept steady on the focal point are called *dhāranā* and *dhyāna* respectively. As a result of his progressive success in arresting the mental states, there arise new types of wisdom (*prajnā*) and the subconscious potencies gradually wear out; ultimately all the subconscious and unconscious potencies of the structural relations are destroyed, and, as a result thereof, the *avidyā* which was determining the *nisus* of the mind is destroyed, and the whole fabric of the mind is disintegrated, leaving the pure *purusha* in his transcendent loneliness (*kaivalya*), which is regarded as the ultimate aspiration of the human mind.

In the Yoga process supreme ethical purity in thought, word, and deed is the first desideratum. When the mental field is so prepared the Yogin attacks the more difficult bondage of its psychological nature, consisting of the subconscious and unconscious forces which may drive him to sense-objects and sense-gratifications. At each stage of meditative concentration he has a supra-consciousness which destroys the roots of the conserved experiences and the fundamental passions, and yet does not build any psychological structure. This leads to the ultimate destruction of mind and self-illumination of the transcendent *purusha* in an utterly non-phenomenal and non-psychological manner.

The Yoga believes in the existence of God, who is associated with an absolutely pure mind. With such a mind he exerts a will such that the evolution of the *prakriti* or the *guna* reals may take the course that it has actually taken in consonance with the possible fruition of the mundane and supramundane or spiritual needs of the individual persons. The Yoga thinks that, had it not been for the will of God, the potentialities of the *gunas* might not have manifested themselves in the present order. The Sānkhya, however, thinks that the necessity inherent in the potentialities is sufficient to explain the present order, and the existence of God is both unwarrantable and unnecessary.

The Yoga School of philosophy, of which Patanjali was the traditional founder, must not be confused with what is commonly called yoga in the Western world. This, the system of training known as *hatha-yoga*, is of much later origin, as far as can be gathered from the sources, and is based on physiological theories related to the 'serpent-power' (*kundalinī*), which from its seat in the base of the spine may be raised by breathing and other exercises to rise through a vein or channel in the spine to reach 'the thousand petalled lotus' (*sahasrāra*) at the top of the skull. This is scarcely a philosophy at all, but is rather a magico-religious system of training, with its roots probably to be found in primitive Shamanism.

The *Nyāya* School was essentially a school of logic, maintaining the view that clear thinking was an essential preliminary to salvation. This school evolved, about the beginning of the Christian era, a system of syllogistic logic which seems to have been quite independent of the Aristotelian system which conditioned the thought of Europe. The usual formula of the Indian syllogism was as follows:

(i) There is a fire on the mountain,
(ii) because there is smoke on it,
(iii) and where there is smoke there is fire, as, for example, in a kitchen.
(iv) This is the case with the mountain,
(v) and therefore there is a fire on it.

We may compare this with the Aristotelian formula:

(i) Where there is smoke there is fire.
(ii) There is smoke on the mountain.
(iii) Therefore there is fire on it.

The Indian syllogism is more cumbrous than the Greek one, but it might be more effective in debate, since the point is driven home by repetition, the first proposition being virtually the same as the fifth and the second the same as the fourth. The example (here the kitchen) was looked on as an essential element of the syllogism, and also seems to derive from debating technique. It is a survival from the earliest phase of Indian philosophical thought, when listeners were often satisfied with analogical arguments. An example of such an argument is the famous parable of the salt in the *Chhāndogya Upanishad* (vi. 13), which is mentioned above (p. 113). As salt dissolves in water, so the individual is dissolved in the absolute Brahman. This, from the point of view of logic, is no argument at all, but it helps to explain a mystical theory and is very effective as a means of enforcing conviction upon one already predisposed to believe the proposition.

On this basis the Nyāya logicians developed the very subtle and difficult doctrines referred to at the beginning of this chapter as ultra-logical, which have been little studied outside circles of specially trained pandits until quite recently. They are too recondite for consideration here, but it should be noted that in some respects they prefigure the new logic of the twentieth-century West, and represent a significant element in the intellectual heritage of India.

The *Vaiśeshika* School was based on a system of atomism, explaining the cosmic process in which the soul was involved. The Vaiśeshikas, like the Sānkhyas, held that the soul was wholly different from the cosmos, and that its salvation lay in fully realizing this difference. The first stage in this process was the recognition of the world's atomic character. The universe was an infinitely complex and endlessly changing pattern of atoms (*anu*) combining and dissolving according to regular principles. At the end of the cosmic cycle the atoms reverted to a state of complete equilibrium from which they only emerged at the beginning of the next cycle, as the raw material of a new cosmos.

The Indian atomic system, in many respects anticipating the theories of modern physics, was the result not of experiment and observation but rather of logical thought. Since an endless regress was logically and psychologically unsatisfactory, it was believed that there must be a final stage in the subdivision of any piece of matter, beyond which further subdivision was impossible. Hence the universe must be atomic in structure. Further developments of the theory led to a doctrine of molecules to account for the multifarious variety of the world. The Vaiśeshika philosophers agreed thus far with modern scientific physics; they did not, however, hit on a realistic theory of elements, which would have demanded practical investigation and experiment. Like most other Indian philosophers, they maintained the existence of five atomic elements—earth, water, fire, air, and *ākāśa*, which filled all space; *ākāśa* is generally translated 'ether', in the sense in which this term was used in Western pre-relativity physics.

The *Mīmāmsā* School was primarily one of Vedic exegesis, and set out to prove the complete truth and accuracy of the sacred texts, in much the same manner as did the doctors of the medieval Catholic Church or such Protestant reformers as Calvin. The world-view of this school was not distinctive, but its teachers produced interesting and original theories of semantics, and some of them made contributions in the field of law.

Out of the Mīmāmsā School emerged the most important of the six systems, the *Uttara-Mīmāmsā* ('Later Mīmāmsā'), more commonly known as *Vedānta*,

'The End of the Vedas'. This term was apt because, unlike the Mīmāmsakas, who placed equal emphasis on all the Vedic literature, the Vedāntins stressed the significance of the *Upanishads*, which for them formed a sort of New Testament, not a mere appendix to the earlier Vedic literature. The main task, as they conceived it, was to harmonize the teachings of these texts into a consistent body of doctrine.

The basic text of the Vedānta School is the *Brahma Sūtras* of Bādarāyana, composed perhaps 2,000 years ago. These are a series of very terse aphorisms, perhaps originally intended as lecture notes, to be filled out extempore by the teacher. Since they are so elliptical and ambiguous they were commented on and differently interpreted by numerous great doctors of medieval Hinduism to produce a wide range of philosophical and theological systems.

Undoubtedly the most influential and probably the most subtle of these teachers was Śankara, a south Indian Śaivite brāhman who, early in the ninth century, composed lengthy commentaries on the *Brahma Sūtras*, the chief *Upanishads*, and the *Bhagavad Gītā*. In these he put forward his famous doctrine of *Advaita* ('No second', i.e. monism), maintaining that the phenomenal universe with all its multifariousness, and the whole hierarchy of being from the greatest of the gods downwards, were not absolutely real, but were *māyā*, the secondary emanations of the one ultimate absolute being, the impersonal neuter entity known as Brahman, characterized by the three atributes of being (*sat*), consciousness (*chit*), and bliss (*ānanda*). Brahman was unchanging and eternally stable, while everything else, being finally unreal, was subject to change, which, in the case of the individual being, manifested itself in the form of *samsāra*, the process of transmigration.

The eternal quest of the Indian mystic was to be fulfilled by the complete and final realization of the identity of his soul or inmost self (*ātmā*) with Brahman. This was to be achieved by spiritual training and meditation. Śankara did not reject the gods, but taught that they were the primary manifestations of the impersonal Absolute, sharing up to a point in the unreality of all things. Their worship might help humble souls, but the spiritual athlete strove to pass beyond them, to direct knowledge of final reality, which was to be found in his own self. Thus Śankara's system is sometimes referred to as 'The Way of Knowledge' (*jnāna-mārga*). It is wrong, however, to look on this system as fundamentally an intellectual one. The knowledge referred to is not comparable with that acquired by learning, but rather with the knowledge gained from intensely close acquaintance—the knowledge of the man who declares 'I know my wife', rather than that of the one who says 'I know the theory of prime numbers'.

The *Upanishads* contain a very wide range of doctrines and Śankara's reduction of their contents to a single consistent system was only achieved by brilliant exegesis, in no way inspired by the modern open-minded attempt to think the thoughts of the authors of the texts. Like most medieval Christian schoolmen faced with similar exegetical problems, Śankara approached his texts with the full conviction that he already knew what they meant. His task was to convince his readers and hearers that this was what they really did mean. His brilliant dialectic was on the whole successful with later generations, and his system even today is the most important one in intellectual

Hinduism. It has influenced modern scholarship, and many students of the *Upanishads* have been inclined to ignore the wide range of speculation in these texts and have followed Śankara's lead, reading almost everywhere the identity of the soul (*ātmā*) and the Absolute (Brahman).

Rāmānuja, a Tamil brāhman who flourished about A.D. 1100, gave the rising piety of the times a firm philosophical basis, with a philosophy of 'The Way of Devotion' (*bhakti-mārga*). He interpreted the same texts as Śankara had commented on in a different light, to produce the system known as *Viśishtādvaita* ('Qualified Monism'). Rāmānuja rejected Śankara's impersonal Brahman, which he interpreted as an inadequate and partial realization of 'The Supreme Person' (*Purushottama*), the god Vishnu, who was ultimate, eternal, and Absolute. Vishnu, inspired by a sort of cosmic loneliness, had diversified himself at the beginning of time, and hence had produced the cosmos, which, being the work of the wholly real creator, could not be ultimately unreal, but shared in God's reality. In the same way the individual soul, created by God who was also an individual, could never wholly lose its individuality, and even in the highest state of bliss was always conscious of itself as being part of God and the recipient of God's grace and love.

Rāmānuja may not have been as brilliant a dialectician as Śankara, but his theology has probably as much justification in the *Upanishads* as that of Śankara. It provided a philosophy for the *bhakti* movements of the medieval period, and thus ramified into many sub-schools, whose doctors debated learnedly and earnestly on problems of faith and grace. The most remarkable of these later schools was that of Madhva, a Canarese theologian of the thirteenth century. Madhva's doctrine, also theoretically based on the *Brahma Sūtras* and the *Upanishads*, was one of unqualified dualism (*Dvaita*). According to his system the individual soul was created by God, but never was and never would become one with him or part of him. In the state of highest bliss the individual soul drew infinitely close to transcendent godhead, and remained thus forever, but it was always aware of its difference from God. Several features of Madhva's system, as well as this one, suggest Christian influence, and he may have gathered some of his ideas from the Syrian Christians of Keralā.

There was a heretical school of thought which was associated with the name of Chārvāka, supposed to be its founder. It was also known by the name *Lokāyata* ('popular'). The literature of the system is now practically lost, and we have to depend on the accounts of others to learn its main contents. The system had many schools, but the fundamental tenets seem to be the same. This school denied the existence of any soul or pure consciousness, which is admitted by all schools of Hindu thought. It also denied the possibility of liberation in any form, the infallible nature of the *Vedas*, and the doctrine of *karma* and rebirth. All Hindu schools of thought assume as their fundamental postulates the above doctrines, and it is on account of their denial that this system was regarded as heretical (*nāstika*). It held that consciousness was an emergent function of matter complexes, just as the mixture of white and yellow may produce red, or fermented starch become an intoxicant. Consciousness being thus an epiphenomenon, nothing remained of the man after death. According to the Dhūrta Chārvākas, in the state of life some sort of a soul was developed which was destroyed at death; but, according to the other adherents of the Chārvāka School, no such soul was formed and the behaviour of a man was guided in responses by physico-physiological stimuli. Thus Chārvākas did not believe in the law of *karma* or of rebirth and they also had no faith in any religious creed or ritual of any sort. In the field of logic they thought that since there is no way of proving the unconditional validity of inductive propositions all inferences have only a probable value: perceptions are all that we can depend upon.

Side by side with the doctrine of the Chārvāka materialists we are reminded of the Ājīvaka School of Makkhali Gosāla, and of the sophistical school of Ajita Keśakambalī, and we read also of the doctrines of Panchaśikha, Sulabhā, and others, which were also intensely heretical. Thus Gosāla believed in a thoroughgoing determinism and denied the free will and moral responsibility of man. According to him, everything was determined by conditions and environments. Keśakambalī also denied the law of *karma* and insisted on the futility of all moral efforts. In the specific details, there is a great divergence of views in the different systems of Indian philosophy regarding the concept of the law of *karma*. Stated in a general manner, the theory supposes that the unseen potency of action generally requires some time before it becomes effective and bestows on the agent merited enjoyment or punishment. Through the beginningless series of past lives, through which everyone passes, the mysterious potency of the action accumulates and only becomes partially mature from time to time. The period of life, the nature of enjoyment and suffering in a particular life, and the environments are determined by the nature of the *karma* which has ripened for giving fruit. The unripe store of accumulated *karma* may be annulled by the destruction of ignorance, the rise of true wisdom, devotion, or the grace of God. But there is a difference of opinion as to whether the inevitable fruits of the ripened actions can be annulled. The theory of *karma* is the foundation-stone of all Indian systems of thought, except the aforesaid heresies.

The system of thought that began with the Buddha and was developed by his followers was also regarded by the Hindus as heretical, as it did not accept the infallibility of the *Vedas* and the existence of an eternal and immortal soul. This, and the system known as Jainism, are both very important products of the Indian philosophical genius, but as they are treated in other chapters of this volume they are not considered here.

ETHICAL PHILOSOPHY

The *Bhagavad Gītā* is a metrical interpretation of the instructions of the *Upanishads* in their bearing on social life. The *Gītā* accepts the four types of duties fixed for the four classes, brāhmana, kshatriya, vaiśya and śūdra, respectively, as study and sacrifice; fighting and the royal task of protecting subjects; looking after economic welfare, agriculture, and trade; and service and the menial duties. It also accepts the final instruction of the *Upanishads* regarding the nature of the self as the ultimate reality, and the means of the highest moral perfection as leading to it. But at the same time it enjoins on all persons that the moral and social duties should be strictly followed. It argues, therefore, that, having attained the highest moral perfection by cleansing himself of all impurities of passion, such as greed, antipathy, self-love, and the like, having filled the mind with a spirit of universal friendship, compassion, and charity, and having attained perfect stability of mind, so as to be entirely unaffected by pleasures and afflictions of any kind, and being attached to God through bonds of love which also unite man with his fellow beings, the true seer should continue to perform the normal duties that are allotted to his station of life in society. Even if he has no self-interest in the performance of his duties, no end to realize, no purpose to fulfil, no fruition of desire to be attained, he must yet continue to perform all normal duties, just as an ordinary man in his station of life would. The difference between the seer and the ordinary man in the sphere of performance of actions is that the former, through the attainment of wisdom, the conquest of passions, the wasting away of all inner impurities, through the bonds of love with God and fellow beings, and through the philosophical knowledge of the ultimate nature of the self, though dissociated and detached from everything else, yet takes his stand in the common place of humanity, as represented in society and continues to perform his duties from a pure sense of duty in an absolutely unflinching manner. The ordinary man, however, being engrossed with passions and bound down with ties of all kinds, cannot take a true perspective of life, and while performing his duties can only do them from motives of self-interest. His performance of duties is thus bound to be imperfect, and vitiated by self-seeking tendencies and the promptings of lower passions.

The aim of transcendent philosophy is thus not merely theoretical, but is intensely practical. However high a man may soar, to whatsoever higher perspective of things he may open his eyes, he is ultimately bound in ties of social duties to his fellow beings on earth in every station of life. A high and transcendent philosophy, which can only open itself through the attainment of the highest moral perfection and which leads one through the region beyond good and evil, again draws him down to the sharing of common duties with the other members of society. The attainment of the highest wisdom, which makes one transcend all others, is only half of the circle. The other half must be completed by his being on an equal footing with his fellow beings. The philosophy of 'beyond good and evil' does not leave a man in the air, but makes him efficient in the highest degree in the discharge of duties within 'good and evil'. The illusoriness of good and evil has to be perceived only for the purpose of more adequately obeying the demands of duties in the common social sphere. Almost all systems of Indian philosophy, excepting the followers of the Śankara School of Vedānta, agree in enjoining the perfect performance of normal duties on the part of a seer.

Though the chief emphasis of the Vaiśeshika and Nyāya systems of thought may ordinarily appear to be placed elsewhere, yet keener analysis would show that in their case also the ultimate aim is fundamentally the same—the attainment of salvation through moral perfection. A large number of sub-schools associated with various religious sects developed in India through a form of eclectic admixture of Vedānta, Sānkhya, and Yoga together with the Bhāgavata theory of love. But in all these systems the central idea is the same, the attainment of transcendent moral perfection and of the perfect social behaviour induced by it.

There is another vein of thought which runs through Indian minds, probably from pre-Buddhistic times, and which may be regarded as being in some sense a corollary and in another sense a supplement to the attitude and perspective of life described above. This attitude consists in the lowering of emphasis on one's limited self-sense as egoism or selfishness, in the consequent experience of equality with all men, and in the development of a spirit of love towards them and towards God, who manifests himself in the persons of all men. The cultivation of love of humanity was one of the dominant characteristics not only of the *Gītā* and Buddhism and Jainism, but also of Yoga and most systems of Indian theism, such as those of Rāmānuja, Madhva, Nimbārka, and others. The *Vishnu-Purāna* says that to look upon all beings as equal to one's self and to love them all as one would love one's own self is the service of God; for God has incarnated himself in the form of all living beings. The Christian principle of love and equality is anticipated in Buddhism and Bhāgavatism, which flourished in India long before Christ; but the force of innate sin is not emphasized as it is in traditional Western Christianity.

Limitations of space forbid me to enter into the various logical concepts and philosophical creeds, criticisms of thought, and dialectic developed in the semi-logical and logical epochs of the evolution of the history of philosophy in India, which could be demonstrated as anticipating similar doctrines and modes of thought in medieval and modern philosophy. Philosophy developed in India continuously for about 3,000 years over a wide tract of the country, and a large part of it still remains unexplored and unexplained in any modern language. A careful reader of Indian philosophy who is fully acquainted with Western philosophy is naturally agreeably surprised to see how philosophic minds everywhere have traversed more or less the same path and how the same philosophical concepts which developed in later times in Europe were so closely anticipated in India. But it is impossible to dilate on this here. My chief effort in this chapter has been to show the Indian conception of the bearing of philosophy to life, which has been almost uniformly the same in almost all systems of Indian philosophy and which has always inspired all philosophy and all religion. That philosophy should not remain merely a theoretic science, but should mould our entire personality and should drive us through the hard struggles of moral and spiritual strife on the onward path of self-realization and should ultimately bring us back again to the level of other men and make us share the common duties of social life in a perfected form and bind us with ties of sympathy and love to all humanity—this is the final wisdom of Indian thought.

CHAPTER XI

Social and Political Thought and Institutions

by J. DUNCAN M. DERRETT

A CIVILIZATION may be known by its ideals and the means by which these are sought to be realized. No observer of the complicated picture of ancient and medieval Indian polity can fail to note the ideals which were affirmed. He will find them voiced in adages and maxims as numerous as their companions, the witty formulae that embody the essence of statecraft. The ideals were common to all regions, and were shared by learned and illiterate alike. Our treatises on law and politics contain principles popularized through the epics and the *Purānas*. The essence of good manners and good policy reached the uneducated by such means, while the worldly wisdom of these texts fed the compilers of fables and less juvenile handbooks. The great popularity of *Cānakya-nīti*,[1] that great pool of wise sayings on 'good policy', proves that techniques of managing any social or political question were not the perquisite of courtiers.

Translation blurs the wording in which the ideals are carried, and obscures the function and purpose of the social and political organs. Our texts, too, answer questions which we should not ask, and ignore problems which we tend to think inescapable, used as we are to a non-Hindu traditional society. Western writers sought to see familiar elements in an Oriental setting; some Indian patriots again have either followed that example or idealized the material at their disposal. The relation of ideals and theory to practice cannot be ignored; but we concentrate rather on the former, since the legacy of the past, both to present-day India and to the world at large, consists rather in the peculiar balance she achieved and in her view of life as it should be lived, a view which has, in large measure, outlived experiments and survived failures. Now that Indians have migrated in such numbers to countries which might never have expected them in the heyday of classical Indology, a need has arisen to know the virtues, and also the limitations, of men and women of Indian stock, and to estimate what they can, and what they will not, contribute to their new environments.

Traditional Indian values must be viewed both from the angle of the individual and from that of the geographically delimited agglomeration of peoples or groups enjoying a common system of leadership which we call the 'state'. The Indian 'state's' special feature is the peaceful, or perhaps mostly peaceful, coexistence of social groups of various historical provenances which mutually adhere in a geographical, economic, and political sense, *without* ever assimilating to each other in social terms, in ways of thinking, or even in language.

[1] See e.g. *Cāṇakya-rāja-nīti*, ed. Ludwik Sternbach, Adyar, 1963, and the surprisingly original little handbook, *Laukikanyāyaślokāḥ*, ed. V. Krishnamacharya, Adyar, 1963.

Modern Indian law will determine certain rules, especially in relation to the regime of the family, upon the basis of how the loin-cloth is tied, or how the turban is worn, for this may identify the litigants as members of a regional group, and therefore as participants in its traditional law, though their ancestors left the region three or four centuries earlier. The use of the word 'state' above must not mislead us. There was no such thing as a conflict between the individual and the state, at least before foreign governments became established, just as there was no concept of state 'sovereignty' or of any church-and-state dichotomy. Modern Indian 'secularism' has an admittedly peculiar feature: it requires the state to make a fair distribution of attention and support amongst all religions. These blessed aspects of India's famed tolerance (Indian kings so rarely persecuted religious groups that the exceptions prove the rule) at once struck Portuguese and other European visitors to the west coast of India in the sixteenth century, and the impression made upon them in this and other ways gave rise, at one remove, to the basic constitution of Thomas More's *Utopia*.[2] There is little about modern India that strikes one at once as Utopian: but the insistence upon the inculcation of norms, and the absence of bigotry and institutionalized exploitation of human or natural resources, are two very different features which link the realities of India and her tradition with the essence of all Utopias.

Part of the explanation for India's special social quality, its manifest virtues and compensating shortcomings, lies not in any prudent decisions by any men or groups of men, but in the traditional concept of the society in which *prajā* (the subjects) and *rājā* (the ruler) were the two principal elements, one might say, polarities; and part again lies in the fact that, though the ruler was a guardian of morals, the 'cause', as it was put, 'of the age', the power of penance was immeasurably more vigorous than any service the state could perform—even granted the fact that the prerogative of corporal or capital punishment (*danda*) served also as a penance for the guilty, and granted, too, that it was in theory one of the king's tasks to see to it that penances were actually performed. Ideals were expressed in terms of ethics, and are related, some to people in general, and some, more specialized, to the principal classes, in particular the brāhmans, whose inherited religious and magical powers, and responsibility for the spiritual and even material welfare of the state, marked them out for respectful treatment, financial patronage, and, if they were suitably conscientious, cramping taboos. Special ideals were naturally developed for the *rājā*, the key figure in leadership, whether he was a head of a clan, or an emperor.

The 'twice-born', to whom we shall return, reached, according to Manu (vi. 92), supersensory bliss by obeying a tenfold 'law', which was a mixture of moral and intellectual requirements. Hārita,[3] who goes into greater detail, gives the constituents of *śīla* (good conduct) as 'piety, devotion to gods and ancestors, mildness, avoidance of giving pain, absence of envy, sweetness,

[2] J. D. M. Derrett, 'Thomas More and Josephus the Indian', *JRAS*, Apr. 1962, pp. 18–34. The topic is pursued by the same at 'More's *Utopia* and Indians in Europe', *Moreana* (Angers), 5 (1965), 17–18; 'More's *Utopia* and Gymnosophy', *Bibl. Hum. Renaiss.* (Geneva), 27 (1965), 600–3; 'The Utopian Alphabet', *Moreana*, 12 (1966), 61–4.

[3] Cited by Kullūka commenting on Manu ii. 6. Manu himself may be studied conveniently in the translation of G. Bühler, *Sacred Books of the East*, Vol. 25, 1886.

abstention from injury, friendliness, sweet speech, gratitude for kindnesses, succouring the distressed, compassion, and tranquillity'. *Dharma*, a term we shall discuss, in its wider sense of a general moral ideal (it is also used of a 'law' as such), requires of every man truthfulness, abstention from stealing, absence of anger, modesty, cleanliness, discernment, courage, tranquillity, subjugation of the senses, and (right) knowledge.[4] This attitude towards moral qualities and forms of behaviour introduces us to the fact that equilibrium rather than equality, peace rather than liberty, were the fundamental ideals. These notions can be interpreted partly as an escape from, and partly as an attempted insurance against the primeval chaos which was supposed to lurk in the background, the chaos which was believed to justify indirectly, and positively to require, the state itself.

Unseen benefits hereafter and prestige in this life were not to be attained merely by moral qualities and good behaviour. The quality of absolute 'goodness' consists also in the study of the Vedas, austerity, pursuit of knowledge, purity, control over the organs of the body, performance of meritorious acts, and meditation on the soul. These properly belong to brāhmans or brāhmanized classes, but the opposite, the state of 'darkness', is demonstrated by covetousness, sloth, cowardice, cruelty, atheism, leading an evil life, soliciting favours, and inattentiveness,[5] and these were not confined to the upper classes. A similar arrangement of ideals is found in the maxim that one falls from caste (i) by not observing what is laid down (in law or custom), (ii) by observing what is prohibited, or (iii) by not bringing the senses under control.[6] Civilized life required that all three sources of 'fall' should be eliminated—an object no individual's power could achieve. The leading themes are well evidenced in that distinctively Indian, if non-brāhmanical, sect, Jainism, which combines venerable age and longevity.

The ideal Jaina householder is characterized by spiritual virtues, namely a spiritual craving, tranquillity, aversion from the world, devotion, compassion, remorse, repentance, and loving-kindness; and by social virtues, namely non-violence, abstention from unrighteous speech (of which lies and slander are illustrations), abstention from theft or unrighteous appropriation (including embezzlement), chastity, avoidance of covetousness, and non-attachment. Since many Jainas have been commercially minded the significance of these virtues is apparent. How the social and personal intermingle is revealed in these standard characteristics of the Jaina householder: possessing honestly earned wealth, eulogistic of the virtuous, wedded to a well-guarded spouse who is of the same caste but of a different patrilineage, apprehensive of sin, following the customs of the locality, not denigrating others (particularly rulers), dwelling in a secure house (affording no temptations to in-dwellers or strangers), avoiding evil company, honouring elders, eschewing sites of calamities, eschewing occupations that are reprehensible according to family, local, or caste customs, economical and making a right use of his income, of controlled diet and balanced aims (following righteousness (*dharma*), wealth (*artha*), and physical pleasure (*kāma*), the three *purushārthas* or aims relevant to this life, in due proportion), charitable to monks and the afflicted, mindful

[4] Yājñavalkya iii. 66. Cf. the summary at Manu x. 63. [5] Manu xii. 31, 33.
[6] Yājñ. iii. 219; cf. Manu xi. 44.

of his dependants, and victorious over the organs of sense.[7] We find throughout that the most reprehensible misdeeds are theft and adultery, and a commentary on Indian ethics could be woven on these items alone. Insistence that women must not be exposed to even a nominal risk of unchastity, the requirement that marriage should subserve the family's interest and not primarily that of the spouses, and the disfavour in which anything resembling 'courting' before marriage is held, have developed an attitude towards women, and a level of expectation on the part of women themselves, which set special limits to Indian social behaviour and give a peculiar quality to Indian life. Concern for the chastity of their womenfolk has, at least in the last millennium, been at the summit of every Indian family's prime concerns, and when hatred boiled over, the females were the immediate targets. Obedience to rulers, as such, we do not find amongst the typical virtues: but it is inculcated elsewhere. Avoidance of sin and social disgrace was a primary obligation, while duty to the ruler was secondary and dependent upon the first, for the ruler's function was to facilitate such avoidance. Respect for the caste-system is implicit in the scheme outlined. 'Honestly earned wealth', 'reprehensible occupations' are terms referring to an established, if theoretical, apportionment of activities amongst the castes (*jāti*). To search for social and political ideals anterior to the caste-system would be fruitless.

No Indian ideal could be inconsistent with *dharma*, 'righteousness'. This word tends to bring cosmology down into touch with the mundane details of private law.[8] One who follows his *dharma* is in harmony, and attains bliss, though it remains doubtful how far his contemporaries' behaviour should guide him in his understanding of his *dharma*. Without *dharma*, in however etiolated a form, fertility, peace, civilized life are considered to be imperilled. *Dharma* is in one sense natural, in that it is not created or determined (though in practice in obscure cases its exponents determine what its sense is), and in another it is always to be striven for. *Dharma* is unnatural in that to achieve it one must put forth uncongenial efforts of self-control, irrespective of popular reactions. If *dharma* (as contrasted with positive legislation) only in part resembles natural law it is nevertheless a code of moral obligations to which the uninstructed nations (*mlecchas*), innocent of brāhmanical learning, cannot attain. *Dharma*, indeed, means duty (*kartavyatā*), and the study of *dharma* involves a discovery of the duties of individuals, groups, and, among them, their political leaders. For *dharma*, in the sense which predominates in political theory, is an abstraction of *sva-dharma*, the 'own *dharma*' of each caste and category of person. As D. H. H. Ingalls, the Harvard scholar, has neatly put it, the 'essentially isolationist society' recognized a religious sanction behind an infinite variety of personal laws. Perhaps the categorization and tendency to division was overdone in the writings, but they are faithful to the essential character of that society. Nominate the man, state his age, caste, and status, and one can be told what his *dharma* is. He deviates from it at his peril, his spiritual peril in any case, his physical or financial peril too if the king is as alert to deviations as he ought to be. But this is not to suggest that *dharma*

[7] R. Williams, *Jaina Yoga*, 1963. Cf. Manu xii. 2–10.

[8] The legal system based on *dharma* lives on in a spiritual sense, but its application in litigation ceased in India by virtue of the acts constituting the 'Hindu Code' (1955–6).

was a 'natural law' in the European sense: the ruler's conduct could not be tested by reference to *dharma* and invalidated thereby, and, though it justified, it could not delimit his administrative authority.

Adharma (unrighteousness) is the forerunner of chaos. Man has a natural tendency to decline into chaos. In one myth chaos required the invention of kingship and the appointment of a semi-divine king. *Dharma* and kingship are thus inseparable. *Dharma* derives linguistically from a root meaning 'to hold'. A loose hold is no hold. *Dharmas* vary according to the person's *varna* (his 'quality', class, or 'caste') and his *āśrama* (stage of life, or status). *Varna* was acquired by birth (a principle nowadays under attack), *āśrama* was optional, though the family lost prestige if the *samskāras* or sacramental ceremonies were neglected by which entry into the essential stages was prepared for and celebrated. Every *dharma* had the king as its protector; and law could not, as a set of practical requirements, effectively demand anything that was not at the same time morally and legally binding.[9] Unrighteous government, illustrated by the fall of the mythical king Vena, is understood, but the point of the myth is that miracles are needed to dissolve the obligation of obedience. Texts evidencing the theory that a wicked king could be put to death by his subjects[10] are rare and uncharacteristic. *Varnāśrama-dharma* is nominally encyclopedic, comprehensive; laying the king, noble, commoner, citizen, and peasant under an apparently equal burden of obligation to a common complex ideal. If the subjects rebelled they did so because the king's duty to protect their *dharmas* was being neglected, and because his own life, conflicting with *dharma*, prejudiced their welfare from a religious point of view. Chaos could be forestalled by rebellion, but our texts do nothing either to encourage or to justify such an attitude. The effort concentrates on making the reigning king a success.

Some illustrations of *dharma*'s 'hold' are needed or we cannot grasp what was expected of the king. The *varna* of the brāhman would limit his freedom to associate, to mate, to dine; it seeks to number the occupations he may pursue—to study, to teach, to officiate at religious ceremonies (including the *samskāras*), and to advise and, if necessary, to chide rulers. To trade (especially in certain goods) and especially to lend at interest are forbidden, except in times of distress. And the brāhman's *dharma* demands at least a minimum of classical education. The *varna* of the śūdra, at the other end of the scale of 'clean' castes, also delimits. Not being one of the twice-born, as are the brāhman and those who intervene between them, he does not study the Veda, and does not take the sacred thread which indicates initiation; nor may he teach Vedic studies or have social intercourse with the twice-born except upon

[9] Note Manu vii. 13 (where *iṣṭeṣu* means, probably, 'topics provided for in the śāstra'): an important verse, poorly (as so often) expressed. The problem of the difference between 'law' as we understand it and Law as the *dharmaśāstra* writers understood it is handled in *Festschrift für Otto Spies*, ed. W. Hoenerbach, Wiesbaden, 1967, pp. 18–41.

[10] Viśvarūpa on Yājñavalkya i. 340. The general complexion of the status of 'subject' is handled in 'Rulers and Ruled in India', *Recueils de la Société Jean Bodin*, 22 (1969), 417–45; and the effect of these concepts on principles of international law is handled in 'Hinduism and International Law: a Review of K. R. R. Sastry's Lectures at The Hague', *Indian Yearbook of International Affairs*, 15–16 (1966–7), 328–47. Both articles contain bibliographical indications. His subjects may kill a violent king: *Mahābhārata* xiii. 60, 19–20.

the footing of service, whether in the house, the workshop, or the field. Ideally his very name should suggest a humble status and the higher castes are entitled to his labour—an ideal which, needless to say, the most numerous *varna* from time to time repudiated. We hear, accordingly, of 'good śūdras' who were supposed to be degraded twice-born and generally copied the latter in their behaviour. Between brāhman and śūdra were ranked the warrior (kshatriya) and mercantile (vaiśya) classes, upon a theoretical basis explained in terms of their objective qualities and tendencies. Anomalies abounded from the first and we meet the theory of 'mixed castes', sprung from unions between the four *varnas*. Distribution of functions between the *varnas* and the mixed castes was often in debate, both historically and throughout our literature.

The brāhman's ancient hereditary function as a teacher (*guru*) of the other castes is not dead. To this day brāhmans are from time to time approached to resolve problems and act as 'confessors' by other castes; and a careful anthropological survey of a remote village in Madhya Pradesh, the abode for several centuries equally of brāhmans and non-brāhmans, both occupied in agriculture, revealed the strange fact that when the economy suddenly changed, due to improvements in communications and markets, a large number of the brāhmans, but not of the other classes, took to teaching and other intellectual pursuits. Students of Western medieval literature know of the 'gymnosophists' whom Alexander the Great and his companions found in northern India. These made an impression on the Greeks and earned a notable place for the ascetics in the Alexander romance and its many derivative contributions to Western culture. They spoke fearlessly to kings, telling them their *dharma*, and their status as teachers (they were ostentatiously naked) depended on their utter indifference to the world and contempt for death. The Jewish heroes of Masada, before committing suicide, as the Romans scaled the last wall, reminded themselves that they must not be inferior in faith to the poor Indians (whom they believed to be polytheists at that).[11]

The ideals of the *dharma-śāstra*, the 'science', or rather 'teaching' of righteousness, proceeded far beyond these classifications. Marriage was a prime concern. Marriage between *varnas* was lawful provided that it was in the hypergamous form, the husband having the higher caste. The ideal marriage for a brāhman was in the form of a gift of the bride, along with her dowry, to the bridegroom summoned for the purpose; that for the kshatriya was by capture or in the love-match which, to the minds of some moralists, masked too often a mere seduction; while marriage by purchase, deprecated as barely suited to the furtherance of *dharma*, was left to the śūdras. Ideals outlived facts, both in marriage and in occupations. Brāhmans are found functioning as money-lenders or soldiers; śūdras are actually found occupying thrones (an eventuality pathetically deplored in many texts). Intercourse with a woman other than one's wife was a sin; yet the keeping of concubines persisted (never, though, to the total exclusion of marriage) amongst well-to-do classes until very recent times.

The *dharmas* of a Vedic student (*brahmacārī*) were naturally not relevant to a śūdra youth. The principal *āśrama* of the *grihastha* (householder), the

[11] Josephus, *Bellum Judaicum*, vii. 341–57. Y. Yadin, *Masada*, London, 1966, p. 226.

āśrama upon which in practice all the others depended, was reached by all *varnas* ideally at marriage, which should be celebrated soon after the completion of a young man's academic training (if any) and would signalize his entry into full social responsibility. Marriage was the one *āśrama* which was nearly obligatory. Religious and social pressure made it virtually unavoidable. Procreation of at least one son was recommended, and better of two, so that at least one might go to Gayā and perform the efficacious *śrāddha* there which would secure perpetual bliss for deceased ancestors. If an *aurasa* (legitimate) son could not be expected, the mature male ought to provide himself and his paternal ancestors with a substitute by one of the approved methods of adoption. Spiritual responsibility towards the ancestors and the right to inherit their property were ideally inseparable.

No survey of the social order can neglect the slaves, for whom, as a social class, curiously, the *varnāśrama-dharma* (which calls them biped chattels) makes little or no room, satisfied, we note, to provide that a brāhman could not be enslaved unless he lapsed from the status of *sannyāsī*, or renunciate. This, the last *āśrama*, was in theory available to every former householder who chose to retire from the world, but in practice it became a title to live on charity, from which, naturally, only a lunatic would be likely to defect. Slaves were not, in the ideal view, a division of society, though they were a fact. In the status and fate of slaves, especially the 'born' slave, some would see a dark feature of Indian social ethics.[12] Yet even an extreme example of their situation has its dharmic aspect. A young female orphan, selling herself into slavery in return for her keep, would acknowledge that if she committed suicide as a result of her keeper's chastisement she would commit a dreadful sin.[13] On the footing that it is a charity to buy children as slaves in times of famine, the residual right to commit, or to threaten to commit, suicide seemed properly subject to limitation by contract.

The politically most significant branch of *dharma*, to which we shall devote attention, was that relating to the *rājā*. Preferably a kshatriya, his *dharma* could be summarized as 'to conquer and to protect'. To fix him with his responsibilities there must be a state. This existed (and could survive) when, according to traditional theory, there existed each of the seven constituents, the so-called *saptānga*, of that organism. These were the king himself, a minister of official class, a capital city, a rural area or inhabited tract, a treasury or revenue administration, an army, and at least one foreign ally. It was recognized that since all are constituents of the state no one could be aggrandized at the expense of others without endangering the organism. Mention of the state calls into play the two sciences of *dharma* and *artha*. The last word means politics and economics, and Kautilya's *Arthaśāstra* is in fact the sole substantial treatise on the art of public administration.[14] The passages dealing with the king's duties and powers in the *smritis* of Manu and Yājnavalkya, for example, were influenced by *artha-śāstra* learning. Wherever the

[12] Y. Bongert, 'Réflexions sur le problème de l'esclavage . . .', *BEFE-O*, 51 (1963), 143–94.

[13] *Lekhapaddhati*, p. 44.

[14] The text as well as the translation should be consulted now only in the versions of Prof. R. P. Kangle, to be modified by specialist discoveries published in the books of H. Scharfe (Wiesbaden, 1968) and (*cum grano salis*) T. R. Trautmann (Leiden, 1971).

two sciences conflicted the ruler was expected to follow righteousness rather than politics, and the cunning inculcated by the latter was supposed to be at the disposal of the former.

Politics, sarcastically called the *khattavijjā*, or 'kshatriyas' science', i.e. unrestrained opportunism, by the Buddhist writers, subsumed a minimum of righteousness in any scheme upon the basis that the end justifies the means. The ideal and the righteous king is insistently overdrawn in our sources, a fact telling its own story. It is claimed that, however kings came to exist as phenomena (a question to which we return), the function of a king is divinely predetermined. 'The kshatriya he (the Creator) commanded', says Manu,[15] 'to protect the people, to bestow gifts, to offer sacrifices, to study the Vedas, and to abstain from attaching himself to sensual pleasures.' The last has a comical sound, for to frame a negative precept as if it were a positive one betrays the historical state of affairs rather plainly.

For the king's role an education of some intensity was recommended, and no doubt required. 'Command of armies, royal authority, the office of a judge, and sovereignty over the whole world he alone deserves who knows the Veda science', says Manu elsewhere.[16] 'Let him act with justice in his own domains—Punishment (*danda*) strikes down a king who swerves from his duty—with rigour chastise his enemies, behave without duplicity towards his friends, and be lenient towards brāhmans.' The duties of a king are to protect the good like a father and to put down evil-doers with rigour. The fourteen 'faults' in a king which the epics point to are these: atheism, falsehood, hot temper, carelessness, procrastination, not seeing the wise, laziness, addiction to the five pleasures of the senses, considering state matters by himself (without consulting competent ministers), taking counsel with those who do not know politics, not commencing that which is decided upon, not keeping state secrets, not practising auspicious acts, and taking up undertakings in all directions at once.

In order to uphold *dharma* a bureaucracy was required, whose functionaries were suspected of corruption, for, as Kautilya puts it, who can tell whether fish in water are drinking? A plenitude of regal power was called for, and obedience to the king's orders was imperative, whether or not they were capricious (as the *Jātaka* tales would have us believe they frequently were). To complain even after obeying seems not to have been contemplated. 'The unrighteous man who does not obey the laws promulgated by the king, shall be punished and even put to death. . . .' 'Whatever a king does for the protection of his subjects, by right of his kingly power, and for the best of mankind, is valid. . . .' 'As a husband should always be respected by his wives . . . a monarch should always be respected by his subjects, even though he be a bad ruler.' 'It is through devotion (or austerities in previous lives) that kings have acquired their subjects; therefore the king is lord; the subjects of a king must obey his commandments, and (as if from a father) they derive their substance from him.'[17]

The king was surrounded with pomp and demonstrated conspicuous consumption. His consecration symbolized the dependence of the state for its crops and cattle upon the king's existence and attributes. Fertility, power,

[15] i. 89. [16] xii. 100. [17] These passages are taken from Nārada's *prakīrṇaka* section.

success were typified by the *rājā*, and a large share (ideally one sixth) of the produce of the lands (except those of brāhmans and deities) and of every productive occupation was not begrudged to him. Unproductive persons such as ascetics shared with their king their spiritual merit. He was like eight deities himself, and to some thinkers he appeared to have been created out of their attributes. He should shower benefits like Indra who showers rain (Indra and the king are often equated in the texts); he should extract taxes as the sun sucks up moisture; he is to penetrate everywhere with his spies like the wind; with the rod of chastisement (*danda*) he is to control all his subjects as Yama, the deity of death, subdues all in the end; he must punish the wicked as Varuna binds sinners with his rope; he is to gladden his subjects by shining upon them as the full moon gladdens men; he is to visit criminals with his anger and destroy wicked subordinates as fire burns all; and he is to support his subjects as the earth supports all creatures.[18]

Dharma upheld the king with the aid of superstitious symbolism, but its requirements from him were very practical and detailed. The *rājā* was viewed as the apex of a broad-based pyramid of authority, judicial and administrative. A family's patriarch, with recognized powers of coercion, ruled his household according to the ideals which we have reviewed. If he failed, relations would attempt to coerce him. There might be some debate whether custom permitted his acts. Social and moral misdeeds, and many crimes besides, were dealt with by a similar machinery. A father might fine his wives and servants, and, where delay in bringing the crime to the notice of an official might result in a failure of justice, a husband was authorized to slay an adulterer.[19] A fiction of delegated authority left the men on the spot with a large responsibility for keeping the peace, suppressing crime, and compensating injured persons. There can be no doubt but that the stifling atmosphere of the smaller of the extended families out of which Hindu society was made up created many personal problems which remained quite unknown, until a dramatic explosion (such as a daughter-in-law's suicide) drew public attention to latent evils.

In pre-classical times the *rājā* led in war and administered criminal justice; the *danda* was wielded to repel invaders, to acquire territory, and to execute or mutilate criminals. The notion that he was the fountain of all human justice came later, and until modern times the distinction persisted between the military and police power on the one hand and jurisprudence and the *śāstric* learning of the brāhmans (rather than professional administrators as such) on the other. Regulations, therefore, proposing to coerce an erring father would rely upon what corresponded to public opinion. If a compromise was impossible an eccentric could be brought under the ban of the village, the district, and eventually the state, which, slow to awaken and usually keen to delegate responsibility to local officials, was dreadful when aroused.

The maintenance of discipline therefore began in the home, and if that failed, higher forces, summoned *ad hoc*, could be brought to bear. The books speak of *pūga*, *śreni*, and *gana* tribunals, and these antiquated names refer, *inter alia*, to local, lay courts. The books suggest that the members should be

[18] Ghoshal, *History of Indian Political Ideas*, pp. 164, 273.
[19] Vijñāneśvara on Yājñ. ii. 286.

impartial. The notion of *ius strictum* was totally absent. The aim, even today, outside the regular courts, is to effect reconciliation.[20] Not even the king desired to blind justice, come what might. *Dharma*, as a guide to the solution of disputes, had a built-in equity. What was abhorred by the public could not be *dharma*. Rule-of-thumb decisions were avoided and mutual adjustment was favoured even at the cost of repeated adjournments, a fact which the theory of the *śāstric* tests, however, by no means brings out. These envisage an ideal court and ideal conditions for discovering the truth, and then a flexible legal system fit to cope with it. Many of the legal rules of the *dharma-śāstra* seem vague, or frankly provide the judge with alternatives; the bald prescription of harsh punishment for offenders masks a system in which much wrongdoing was accounted for by groups interacting in an extra-legal manner.

Securing property-rights, repressing deviations from caste regulations, the king and his deputies were engaged for much of their time with actual or imaginary complaints against transgressions of the social order. Blessings awaited the king who so occupied himself. Instances might be a projected marriage between *jātis* not yet regarded as socially equal; a claim that a market price had been fixed unconscionably high; a claim that a sect should have an endowment comparable with that granted to rival sects; or a complaint that a caste had in a public meeting determined to assume an arrogant title. In all hearings which were judicial an ancient maxim came into play, that the four feet of *vyavahāra* (litigation) were *dharma*, *vyavahāra* (court practice), *charitra* (custom), and *rāja-śāsana* (royal decree). The latter in order overruled the former, a principle which speaks for itself. These were originally sources of law, but the notion that the king could not overrule *dharma*, in its transcendental sense, grew as time went on, and medieval commentators and even some late *smriti* sources saw the maxim as referring to methods of proof, and twisted the words accordingly.

In keeping order at home, forestalling attacks from abroad, planning attacks upon neighbouring kings, and finding his own level within the *mandala*, or circle of rulers amongst whom the theory of statecraft found his natural allies and opponents, assistance was available to the king from various quarters. Trained personnel abounded in the corps of officials. Their titles do not much interest us. The departments of state, headed by that of the *purohita* or family priest of the *rājā*, included those responsible for war and peace, the treasury, the elephant corps, registry and archives, forts, markets, and prostitutes (an important source of royal income). There was a *mantrī-parishad*, or council of ministers, to whom the king might have recourse. Promotion to such a council was within his gift, but unfortunately removal from it was nearly impossible. The ideals of unquestioning loyalty to a righteous king and his family produced ministerial houses with hereditary ties to the sovereign. Such ministers were set up with fiefs in lieu of salary, they took no oaths of loyalty, and there were no reciprocal agreements; thus they could become troublesome subordinates, feudatories (without a true feudal system) capable of becoming kings in their turn. According to the recommendations

[20] *Report of the Study Team on Nyaya Panchayats*, Govt. of India, Ministry of Law (1962), which has a valuable historical section.

of the texts on statecraft these ministers were to be selected for their knowledge, abilities, and character, and were to be tested by *agents provocateurs*; but there was nothing but loyalty to prevent their intriguing with junior members of the royal family, and even offering their support to a foreign king. The king was obliged to consult ministers, especially those holding prestige, but he was never bound by their advice; responsibility for unpopular acts was therefore entirely his, and, as we have seen, the possibility of deposition was never entirely lost sight of.[21] The position of the hereditary minister was more comfortable than that of the king, for all the books' recommendation that he should be constantly spied upon: even a righteous king is warned by these same books to be ever on the alert and to trust no one. An unsuccessful traitor, had, however, a great deal to lose, for the king's revenge would destroy him, family, dependants, and all.

The administration of justice, to which we have already alluded, was ideally the task of kshatriya judges advised by brāhman assessors; the books lay down the qualifications of the *sabhāsad* (judicial assessor), which are admirable by any standard. But in the villages all decisions would be taken by village councils; the villager would be bound by them because *dharma* required compliance with an agreement to which he was theoretically a party,[22] even if (as in the case of an untouchable) he had no right of speech at the meeting, and even if his opinion failed to win the general acceptance which always did duty for majority vote. The villager was theoretically present in his village parliament, and the *rājā*, his far-away 'father', was related by less tangible if definite religious ties. The *rājā*, not surprisingly, was required by the *śāstras* to take the local decisions seriously, and if they affected custom to inquire into and register them. The king's own orders, the *śāsanas* referred to above, were likewise recorded and put up in archives for future reference.

If the village could enact by-laws and the king promulgate regulations by decree it would seem to follow that the society was progressive, moulding its laws and constitution to meet developments. On the contrary some observers emphasize the static nature of both. It was at one time supposed that *dharma* could disallow positive legislation, but this view has no foundation. Decrees emanating from the palace are actually contemplated by the *dharma-śāstra* itself. 'These goods shall not be exported' and 'Animals shall not be slaughtered on these days' are examples. The *artha-śāstra* actually authorizes the aggressor to combine tactics, noble and ignoble, and the conflict between the transcendental and the expedient ends, with a distinct advantage to enlightened expediency. From successful treachery the king can purify himself by penance; by a failure in diplomacy he may lose his kingdom and inflict chaos upon his former subjects. In a war, or with reference to a projected war, the *dharma-śāstra* itself did not purport to chart the king's fiscal and administrative powers.

Dharma had thus an isolated existence of its own. It was not adjustable to suit opinions and occasions. We should look into its origins and relations with secular law more closely. In matters of detail, where the established ideals

[21] Manu vii. 111–12.
[22] Manu viii. 219. See Derrett, *Religion, Law and the State in India*, London, 1968, Ch. 6.

were not clear guides, the *śāstra* must needs follow custom.[23] As customs so recorded became antiquated the *śāstrīs*, or teachers, felt authorized to pass over many of the *smritis*, i.e. the immemorial maxims or oracular statements, which had accompanied the inspired philosophical and ethical material that made the greater *dharma-śāstras*, in particular that attributed to Manu, such splendid vehicles for law. Alternatively, they would interpret them if they retained them, in ways which would save their validity whilst insinuating a more contemporary meaning.[24] What was *dharma* was enunciated by the teachers, not the books, a jealously and successfully guarded privilege. Manu tells us that a committee of ten, of three, or, if need be, only one brāhman, properly qualified in point of character and learning, can give an authoritative and binding decision on a point of law, whether ritual or spiritual, or on judicial matters.[25] No appeal from such a decision is contemplated, though evidently the royal court acted as a supreme court of revision, where the best-qualified pandits could give a 'final' reading of the *śāstra* to meet the case. The state as such could not redefine *dharma* in any context. A custom, properly established, or a genuine *śāsana* might authorize a departure from *dharma* in a particular class of cases or a particular litigation, but then only if the court's attention was drawn to the former, and then without any bearing on the spiritual aspects of the question, in respect of which what was both 'right' and 'law' was immutable. Legislation by consent of the people did not exist, and the provision, which we have seen, that what the public abhorred could not be law, was of merely temporary and conditional effect. The *dharma-śāstra* from its very beginnings must have presupposed professional interpreters and a governmental machinery lacking jurisdiction to make more than *ad hoc* inroads upon it. This in turn presupposes a multiple, if 'isolationist' society, far from the tribe or clan. What was best had been discovered by ancestors long ago, who had obtained it evidently from revelation; their insight and experience sufficed for their descendants; and it was thought that scholarship should be devoted to collating, systematizing, and rationalizing what had survived from the supposed corpus of injunctions. Debate was confined to the question whether current versions correctly appraised what the past had achieved.

Such a theory of society and its government left no room for progress in any modern sense. On the contrary the contemporary state of society was attributed to an inevitable decline, by stages, from a golden age. Apparently 'progressive' rules, such as that a girl could obtain an annulment of her marriage with an impotent man, preserved in ancient *smritis*, were held by the time of the *Smriti-chandrikā*, a thirteenth-century encyclopedia of law, to belong to previous ages, and to be unavailable for the author's own period. The seemingly socialistic Directive Principles of the current Constitution of India would have astonished men of that age. Kautilya himself nowhere suggests that the resources of a region should be exploited to their utmost in

[23] N. C. Sen-Gupta, *Evolution of Ancient Indian Law*, 1953, esp. pp. 329–35. See also R. Lingat, *The Classical Law of India*, Berkeley, Cal., 1972, pt. 2, ch. 2.

[24] On the role of the jurist see *Études . . . Jean Macqueron*, Aix-en-Provence, 1970, pp. 215–24; Derrett, *Dharmaśāstra and Juridical Literature*, Wiesbaden, 1973, pp. 3, 52, 53.

[25] xii. 110, 113.

the national interest, or that individuals should employ their earning power or their talents to their utmost limits. That the king should squeeze the peasantry to the limits of their capacity for regular payment was indeed recommended, but that was another matter. The principles of royal monopoly in numerous objects of production, and the regulation of market prices to avoid undue competition, indicate that the attainment of a balance was much more the object of policy than any adventure into the unknown. Individuals carried weight according to their membership of a group, and no group was independent. Hoarding, for example, was the function of merchant groups, who might live very economically, and to appropriate their hoards at his discretion, and so put the coins back into circulation, was a right of the *rājā*. In turn the *rājā* admitted responsibility for the occasional unfortunate (provided he was not an outcaste) who found himself or herself without support, and the *rājā* was the channel through which groups maintained their balance and those without groups to defend them were themselves protected.

Unduly successful claims upon the *rājā* for increasing the power or privileges of one group would drive the others into the hands of a rival for the throne. Since stability justified the state, the king was, as the *śāstras* interminably insist, bound to practise restraint, not least in forwarding those whom he favoured, for it was all too simple to exchange one *rājā* for another. We hear of puppet *rājās* whose seals authenticated their hereditary ministers' acts, and of conspiracies between notables which terminated in their favourite's being offered the crown.[26] Ultimately the system aimed at maximizing the spiritual capacity of the individual as a member of a *contented* household, unambitious, protected from envy and unduly efficient competition, content with lawful acquisition, and relying upon the state for opportunities to put the good things of this world to the service of candidature for higher things in the next. The entire responsibility for this prospect lay upon the king, a figure who has obtained less sympathy than he deserved.

The machinery of government was well suited to its limited aim. The *rājā* rested immune from unseen harm and his enemies' attacks if his subjects' welfare was secure, if castes kept to their functions, sages practised austerities, sacrifices were properly performed, nobles and leisured people roamed about gaily clad, merchants accumulated infinite wealth, and the toiling multitudes abstained from protest at the inequalities of life.[27] An army of spies informed him of maladjustments and plots. Which of the three conventional 'powers' of the king was the most essential, his strength of counsel, his material resources, or his personal energy? We have seen what were his conventional 'faults'. He needed each of these powers to perform his functions. The petty *rājā* needed neither elaborate espionage nor bureaucracy. He had his *parishad* or council, as later more extensive kingdoms relied on their *sabhā* or *samiti*, the assembly that represented local populations. In Vedic times the clan assembly advised the king on peace or war. Then women might actually

[26] Gopāla, the founder of the Pāla Dynasty, and the Pallava Parameśvaravarman II are illustrations. Derrett, 'Hindu Empires', *Recueils de la Société Jean Bodin*, 31 (1973), 565–96.

[27] There is a telling quotation to a similar effect from *Mahābhārata* xii. 78. 9–17 by D. H. H. Ingalls, in 'Authority and Law in Ancient India', in *Authority and Law in the Ancient Orient*, suppl. No. 17, *JAOS* (1954).

be heard as counsellors, a possibility scarcely contemplated in classical times, when women had their own rights to property but only anomalously took upon themselves public responsibility.

In later times the king's deputy used to attend local gatherings and gave the royal assent to proceedings which often originated in the secretariat. The peace of small units was managed by the delicate interrelations between locally prestige-worthy families and the royal officials, from the village headmen to the district governors and tax-collectors, who were often the ministers to whom we have alluded already. These latter assisted in but did not necessarily take responsibility for local self-government. Checks and balances, threats of force, and more than anything the appearance of strength, kept people in their places. Officials were regulated by custom, and by *dharma* (if they were uncorrupt), under the ruler's oral or written instructions. The village assemblies were ruled by *dharma* in its most elemental sense, the conscience of the people understood through its customs.

Upon what did this obedience to the king rest? We have seen that in most ancient times his powers were circumscribed. Though a human fertility 'deity', he was, in his political aspects, more of an expedient than a necessity, so long as the tribe had not acquired for itself dominion over strangers. But that people by that time puzzled over the king's powers is evident from the variety of explanations offered for their existence. According to Kautilya, when the king is making an eve-of-battle speech he should point out that he shares the fruits of the earth with his troops, and that he is, like them, an employee. But did anyone really believe that the king was appointed by his subjects or that he owed any of his powers to an agreement with or between them?

The *Mahābhārata*, rich in material on this subject, tells of a primeval king who took an oath to gods and sages that he would rule justly. But this was not a case of subjects electing their leader, nor of his making promises exclusively to them. What would be the outcome of a breach of such a promise is not hinted at. It is true that at the consecration of each king a suggestion appears that he should be acclaimed, but elements of free choice are missing. The Vedic *ratnins*, who seem in very ancient times to have been kingmakers, may have had no more than symbolic or ritual functions, and in any case indicate the humble suites of kings of a period too remote to serve any purpose in the discussion. Undoubtedly the ancient preference for prestige and natural leadership, when coupled with the later hereditary principle, must have enabled the most worthy member of the royal stock to obtain the approval necessary for consecration, but an uneasy balance between the supreme power of the king and the goodwill of his most powerful supporters is visible in the torrents of advice poured on him by the *śāstras*.

That a king secure on his throne bears divinely sanctioned powers is evident. Constant reiteration of the theory that the king is the subject's servant, taking revenue as his wages, is coupled with the identifications with Indra of which we have made mention, and with the legendary origin of kingship from the intervention of the gods in a crisis. Prithu is said to have been created king by the gods, upon complaints by the sages, and he took an oath only to the gods. The people, in another legend, making compacts with each other, ask the god

Brahmā to supply them with a king. Both these theories are found in the *Mahābhārata*. True, in Buddhist writings we have reference to the mythical king Mahāsammata, whose very name suggests compact, who, in keeping with the then fashion to place kshatriyas above brāhmans, was appointed by consent of a public whose growing lawlessness required the kshatriya *varna* for their protection. But there is no suggestion, even in the Buddhist tradition, that the king's duties are fixed by the public, that it can interfere with his day-to-day business, or that any part of the public, such as the nobles, has a right to preferential treatment from him. The amalgamation of the ideas that a king must 'please' (*ranjayati*), and that his function exists by divine provision, ideas hardly reconcilable, shows that the themes were available for use as occasion demanded.

Yet no king could have functioned without the agreement of the people, ill organized as they were for expression of disagreement with him. Similarly, the religious aspect of kingship, admitted by all shades of opinion, was so pervasive that any state must have had someone able to contain it, and unlike some ancient societies India kept the religious and the political headship in the same person. In protecting *dharma*, and relieving or forestalling distress, the *rājā* lived out a role which gave rise to both these explanations.

This leaves open the questions where power resided, and what was its justification. Self-conscious in regard to aberrant customs, fruitful in expression of individual opinions and outlooks, tolerant of curiosities of faith or ethic, Indian literature provides no evidence that these problems were ever probed, and exemplifies at present (there may always be a dramatic discovery!) no specimen of a profound penetration into political philosophy. Perhaps the failure is to be explained by the lack of conflicts to which we referred at the head of this chapter. The kingly power was a trust, as it were, from the people; his religious status depended from his kingship. The trust was unconditional, and would have been meaningless without unbounded discretion. The divergent images suggesting that the king had rights against his subjects and they against him are misleading, and the concept that *dharma* reigned over all is merely uninformative. Power in fact stemmed from a state of affairs produced in a caste society; the state was a symptom or function of such a state of affairs. To maintain equilibrium, which caste cannot dispense with, detailed interventions in the nature of adjustment were required. An inherent characteristic was assumed to have an eternal meaning and purpose, and on this basis restraints were rationalized. No school of thought could doubt the transcendental expediency of kingship or the utter necessity of a state, the leader of which had the widest possible discretion subject only to revolution if the ultimate goals were prejudiced.

The goals themselves were a product of the rationalizing of that caste society. We have seen them in connection with the ideals, conventionally phrased as *dharma*, *artha*, *kāma*, and, ultimately, *moksha*, 'release from rebirth', 'salvation'. The possibility of pursuing one's *sva-dharma* was the test of the state; the vast authority of the *rājā* was justified by this narrow requirement alone. In modern terms this seems a high price to pay for a rather flimsy and speculative security. But we must remember that throughout Indian history until relatively recently the stoical patience of a people expecting nothing beyond subsistence and regarding prosperity as a temporary and delusory windfall moulded their goals and their requirements. By contrast, foreign ideals, still looked down upon in many quarters, make room for comfort, liberty, planning a career, and personality in this-worldly terms as an individual. The discovery in the *Arthaśāstra* of recommendations which are unethical by Indian standards is thus to be reconciled, for without *artha* (material advantage) *dharma* cannot be practised, nor *kāma* obtained, without which sons cannot be born to worship gods and ancestors, and thus *moksha* itself is in jeopardy. The need, psychologically, for *moksha* explained all aspects of the ancient Indian polity, in theory and in history; and with the decline of the desire for *moksha* we now find a redefinition of values, and a different conception of the state.

The background we have now surveyed may throw a welcome light on features of the Indian civilization noticed elsewhere. A combination of *rājās* against foreign enemies or ideological opponents was hardly contemplated. Only an emperor could organize defence against such a foe. The advent of a new *rājā* was not feared as such, since even a foreign ruler was still a *rājā*,[28] and only the notion that he would convert the subjects to a different religion dissolved this recognition. Intrigue or competition between groups was innocuous in a society whose institutions were designed to prevent aggrandizement by groups, let alone individuals. The supreme social category was not the individual propelled by competitive self-interest.[29] Under the umbrella of the *rājā*'s gift of *abhaya* (security) tolerance caused no strain, bigotry could develop no inhuman aspects, enthusiasms were confined to individuals and leant towards personal immortality. Opinions which did not deny the fundamental requirements of *dharma* could flourish. Good behaviour or stereotyped attitudes were more important than opinions. Hypocrisy, self-deception, morals confined to the groups in which they were significant, an articulant rather than an integrated concept of society, these fitted a state in which dogmas had no absolute value, and there was no machinery to repress any but those who flouted the established order.

Similarly the system bred the notion that breaches of caste discipline, lapses from virtue, were not so much the fault of individuals as of the state, and that just as the king must restore the value of a cow which was stolen and not recovered, so he must punish adulterers; otherwise part of the guilt attaches to his own person. Underlying this concept is the fear (perhaps not unsupported by experience) that the removal of political authority turns every other man into a thief and a fornicator. India had a respect for order, custom, institutions, unaccompanied by any belief that these must be justified, without questioning the very assumption that there must be institutions. One could argue, and people did argue, that fraternal polyandry was congruent with *dharma*, but no one was so eccentric as to doubt for a moment that marriage and property were possible only in civilized political life, namely the state.

On the other hand India admitted the individual's right to try to leaven the lump in which fate had placed him. Hence the great importance of religious

[28] Pandits refer to the East India Company as *rājā* in their report referred to in (1817) *Morton's Montriou* 547, 548.

[29] Varma, *Studies in Hindu Political Thought*. . ., p. 189.

movements. These took the place occupied in the West by liberal movements in which political reforms and scientific advances came together. Another explanation, however, for the non-emergence in India of a popular striving for reform, even in the face of gross exploitation, may be the theory, itself part of the system, that those who denied that the king was entitled to his revenue (on account of his ignoring their petitions) might properly decamp and live elsewhere. If grumbling could not keep revenue demands within practicable limits there was always this remedy. True, the migrants would soon be subject to a state like that which they had abandoned, but this possibility of migration, which remained well into the nineteenth century, excused an investigation of inherent weaknesses in the system.

Freedom of speech, provided the speech was not to the king's face, and freedom of movement were accepted; likewise freedom to agitate and propagate theories of an intellectual character, whether or not these had practical implications. Freedom of property, in the modern sense of the term freedom, or of choice of occupation and of way of life in a chosen environment, no one seems ever to have desired. Freedom to choose one's own direction seemed synonymous with insecurity,[30] with disorder and the dreaded state of affairs when the large fish swallow smaller fish, or, according to another explanation of the celebrated *mātsya-nyāya* (the maxim of the fish),[31] when people are roasted as fish are roasted on a spit. The ideals of the Indian peoples presupposed insecurity, from which political power rescued them. Against this background one sought one's soul's comfort by practising personal and social virtues; apart from that background, virtues were hardly to be aspired to. It is of interest that as soon as the fear of primeval chaos was actually removed, a taste for reform, for fundamental rights, and civil liberties actually made an entrance into the Indian mind, and, so far as recent history indicates, their continuance in India seems not unconnected with a firm intention not to relapse into it.

[30] Spellman, *Political Theory of Ancient India*, p. 99.

[31] This maxim migrated, like other scraps of Indian wisdom, and recurs in Talmudic literature (G. F. Moore, *Judaism*, Vol. 2, pp. 114–15) whence, via Spinoza at the latest, it finds a place in European political thought (S. von Pufendorf, *De Iure Naturae et Gentium*, II. ii. 3.5).

CHAPTER XII

Science

by H. J. J. WINTER

FOR the study of the history of science in Asia the present position is one of hope and anticipation. Not many decades ago European historians, content to regard Islamic science as merely a Greek legacy, tended to look no further east, whilst in respect of India H. T. Colebrooke as an interpreter of her science had stood almost alone since 1817. China remained an enigma. Now critical evaluations of ancient astronomical methods by O. Neugebauer have supplied a new background to our studies. Islamic scientific manuscripts, though rich in examples of the Greek geometrical and deductive approach, also reveal new discoveries beyond those of Hellenism. Further light has been shed in recent years on the complex nature of the sciences in India through archaeological research and the collection and examination of additional manuscripts. Above all, for the first time, we have a full and systematic account of the history of science in China, the monumental work of Joseph Needham.[1]

Looking at the development of science through the centuries we see an accumulating body of knowledge to which the races of Asia have made their own particular contributions by their own methods of investigation, but we are also confronted by a jigsaw of transmissions which render our interpretation of these discoveries all the more difficult and uncertain. In studying the science of India[2] these transmissions can only be examined at present against a chronology sometimes open to dispute. Yet in spite of this a fascinating story emerges which indeed gains in interest because of its mystery.

I

The earliest indigenous cultures which interest the historian of science are those centred upon Harappā in the Panjāb and Mohenjo-dāro in Sind, the so-called Indus valley civilization. In technology the prominent characteristic is that of standardization: cities built to a uniform plan resembling the layout of a chess-board and of well-fired bricks of a controlled size,[3] and domestic pottery turned from the wheel in specification form and capacity. These suggest in turn a methodical system in weights and measures. Indeed, a very large number of weights consisting of accurately cut cubes of blended grey chert, which are found to follow the ratios 1 : 2 : 8/3 : 4 : 8 : 16 : 32 : 64 : 160 : 200 : 320 : 640, have been collected at various sites in the Panjāb, Sind, and south Balūchistān, and probably the Makrān.[4]

This system of weights is unique in the ancient world. It is unfortunate that

[1] J. Needham, *Science and Civilization in China*, Vols. 1–3, and Vols. 4 (1), (2), (3) so far, Cambridge, 1954–72.

[2] See also J. Filliozat, *La Doctrine classique de la médecine indienne*, Imprimerie Nationale, Paris, 1949, Introd. p. 1.

[3] Usually 11 by 5·5 by 2·5 inches.

[4] S. Piggott, *Prehistoric India to 1000 B.C.*, Harmondsworth, 1961, pp. 181–3.

no numerals appear on any of these weights—as in the case of the Harappā script, which is pictographic and has yet to be deciphered, the mathematical achievements of the people remain largely a mystery. Clearly there was a considerable merchant class, through whom a commercial arithmetic developed, but academic achievements, like those of contemporary Egypt, were no doubt both channelled and circumscribed. However, it will be seen that the above system of ratios may be based upon 16, an important number[5] in ancient Indian numerology, and that certain others may be successively obtained by doubling or halving; also of interest is the use of fractional thirds and the development of a decimal form in the higher numbers. Further study of the metrology of the Indus valley civilization does, in fact, reveal decimal divisions of length, e.g. the use of a 'foot' of 13·2 inches divided into tenths. It is clear from the planning and architecture of the cities that there was a competent knowledge of simple geometry and surveying based upon two units of length, a 'foot' of about 13·2 inches and a 'cubit' of about 20·6 inches.

Some interesting suggestions might be made from all this, but it would be unwise to resort to idle speculation in the face of such incomplete evidence. Let us be content to add three further practical achievements—the construction of main drains having brick 'manhole-covers', the cultivation of cotton and the manufacture of cotton-cloth, and the working of copper, bronze, and copper-arsenic alloy. The over-all picture is of a technology standardized through several centuries by an inflexible and authoritarian regime.

II

The Āryan invasions of northern India (*c.* 1500 B.C.) may be said to mark the end of the Indus valley civilization. From henceforth the growth of Indian science is to be influenced by the speculative and philosophical mind, to become richer in generalization, to transcend the limited technology of Harappā, Mohenjo-dāro, and Chanhu-dāro. In the hymns of the *Rig Veda* is to be found the first account of the way of life of the Indo-European conquerors, their recognition of and devotion to one supreme cause, their realization that behind the phenomena of the natural world, which appear shifting and changeable, there is a constant principle (*rita*) or order in events. Piggott[6] has shown that the war-chariot (*ratha*) of the *Rig Veda* had a central pole and yoke harness, the so-called throat-and-girth harness, not only unpleasant for the horse but most inefficient mechanically, yet nevertheless common to the regions of Indo-European colonization, for example Homeric Greece and Celtic Britain. Despite the gradual development of philosophy the personification of the primal forces of nature in, for instance, the god of the sun, Sūrya, or the god of fire, Agni, continued. Sacrificial altars, at first mere heaps of turf, evolved into elaborate designs demanding arithmetical and geometrical calculations.

Vedic literature, broadly considered, tells us only fragmentary information concerning the early stages of Hindu science. The wisest procedure is to examine the whole evaluation in the light of certain terminal writings such as the

[5] This has been found equivalent to 13·64 grammes in the series of weights.

[6] S. Piggott, op. cit., pp. 276–81. An excellent plan and side elevation are drawn to scale on p. 280. See also S. D. Singh, *Ancient Indian Warfare with Special Reference to the Vedic Period*, Leiden, 1965.

Kautilīya Arthaśāstra, the *Śulva Sūtras*, the *Caraka Samhitā*, and ultimately the *Sūrya Siddhānta*, which present us with an established body of knowledge or doctrine. Assuming tentatively a date of 1500–1400 B.C. for the *Rig Veda* we are confronted by a vast ocean of time from which small 'islands' appear at irregular intervals to provide a few bearings, and firm ground is denied us until after the dawn of the Christian era in Europe.

Perhaps the earliest source dealing exclusively with astronomy is the *Jyotisha Vedānga*; from this work, the text of which is corrupt and condensed in form, and may date from 500 B.C., one learns the rules for calculating the position of the new and full moon amongst the 27 *nakshatras*, and of the *ayanas* which fall in cycles of 5 years each of 366 days. In 5 solar years were 67 lunar months, so that if these are taken as equivalent to 62 synodic months, then a year of 12 months may be retained if the 31st and 62nd months are omitted from each cycle. This ancient system of lunar-solar reckoning was widely used in India and occurs also in Jaina literature. An earlier statement on the *nakshatras* in the *Taittirīya Samhitā*[7] (of the same period as the *Brāhmanas* or priests' books of ritual) gives a complete list of their names, which must have been well established by the eighth or seventh centuries B.C.,[8] and certainly existed in the sixth century at the very latest. Of the three independent systems of astronomical reference used in antiquity, the decans of Egypt, the zodiac of Mesopotamia, and the lunar mansions, i.e. the 27 or 28 positions occupied by the moon in one sidereal rotation, the last seems to have appeared in India as *nakshatras* and in China as *hsiu* at about the same time.[9] There is no evidence to show that at this early period the development could have been anything but independent: but if one is looking for a common origin there is just the possibility that moon-stations could have arisen from the old Babylonian astronomy of *c.* 1000 B.C. and the conception been diffused through Iran: their reappearance as *al-manāzil* among the Arabs, the heirs of Sassānian Iran, in pre-Qur'ānic times is suggestive.

Early Indian cosmology is generally based upon the square and cube—a quotation from C. P. S. Menon[10] summarizes the basic concept adequately:

> There is first of all the earth based on a square, with a corner towards the south, and shaped like a pyramid, with a number of successive homocentric square terraces rising up to a point (or rather, to a small square): on the top of this is the mount Meru, a pyramid widening out as it rises, at a small angle to the vertical; round this lie the orbits of the sun forming homologous squares on a horizontal plane; above the sun's plane is that of the moon with similar orbits. We may imagine above this were the planes of the different planets at increasing heights, as described in the Vishnu-Purāna (of the Hindus); if these were also originally square orbits, we should have the original conception of the orbits of the planets as forming the successive terraces of a pyramid representing the heavens.

Associated with this early Meru cosmology were a series of numbers, such as 4, 12, 28, 60, obtained through sub-division of the square, or rectangle. The

[7] *Taittirīya Samhitā*, iv. 4. 10.

[8] This is supported by another list of 27 in the *Kāthaka Samhitā* (xxxix. 13) and lists of 28 in the *Maitrāyanī Samhitā* (ii. 13, 20) and the *Atharva-Veda* (xix. 7).

[9] For Uighur and Tibetan versions see W. Petri, *Indian Journal of History of Science*, Vol. 1, pt. 2, New Delhi, 1966, pp. 83–90.

[10] C. P. S. Menon, *Ancient Astronomy and Cosmology*, London, 1931, p. 94.

system was dictated by mathematical rather than by astronomical requirements. Thus a 'square' orbit of 28 could be represented by placing unit squares around the periphery of an original square of side 6 (containing 36 unit squares) and adding in the unit square at each corner, i.e. $(4 \times 6)+4$, giving a geometrical picture of the alighting stations of the moon.

Later Meru cosmology, which is to be found in the Jaina texts, adopts the circle as the basic form. This radical departure occurs in the *Sūrya Prajnapti* (perhaps 200 B.C.) where the earth is represented as a circular disc with Mount Meru as its centre and the pole-star directly above. Surrounding the earth are seven concentric oceans and continents, whilst coplanar rotations of the planets are from east to west around Mount Meru. In the *Jambudvīpaprajnapti* a further step is taken when the detailed geometry and associated calculations of this circle are made on the basis of the ratio circumference: diameter $= \sqrt{10}$. Numerical results are obtained for lengths of arcs, sagittae, and segments of chords, and in certain cases quadratic solutions are required. Though the history of Jaina canonical literature is such that it is difficult to date, some useful papers have already appeared on the mathematical and astronomical aspects.[11]

Mahā Meru, or Sineru, also occupies the central position in the Buddhist universe as described in the Pāli Books[12] *Sāra Sangaha, Visuddhi Magga, Satta Suryuggamana Suttanta*, and *Jinālankāra*. Only one half of it is visible above the level of the ocean, whilst between Meru and the outermost circle of the system, the ridge of rock called Sakvala, there are seven circles of rock, and seven oceans the 'waters' of which are so attenuated that the feather of a peafowl could not float in them. This picture has been much elaborated, so that to proceed further would only involve us in vast numbers and fanciful speculations having no relation to fact, curious and interesting though these may be. The most important achievement of Buddhist thought from our present standpoint is the law of causation, which was initially concerned mainly with human conduct but has since interested philosophers of science.[13]

Whilst dealing with Jaina and Buddhist cosmology we must mention the doctrine of *paramānus*, better known as the atomic theory. Atoms could be grouped together to form molecules, and whilst the atoms envisaged by the Jains and Vaiśeshikas were eternal, those of the Buddhists, being included in a phenomenalist view of nature, appear and disappear by cycles. In the *Kevaddha Sutta* appended to the *Dīgha Nikāya*[14] we also find that all matter is ultimately formed from the four elements, fire, air, water, and earth. To these is added, in the *Maitrī Upanishad*, a fifth 'element', non-material and all-

[11] e.g. G. Thibaut. 'On the Surya-Prajñapti', *JASB*, 49 (1880), 107–27, 181–206. B. Datta. 'The Jaina School of Mathematics', *Bulletin of the Calcutta Mathematical Society*, 21 (1929), 114.

[12] See G. P. Malalasekera, *The Pali Literature of Ceylon*, R.A.S. London, 1928. M. H. Bode, *The Pali Literature of Burma*, R.A.S. London, 1909. Also issues of the Pali Text Society, Dawson Place, London.

[13] W. McGovern, *A Manual of Buddhist Philosophy*, Vol. 1, *Cosmology*, London, 1923.

[14] G. S. P. Misra, 'Logical and Scientific Method in Early Buddhist Texts', *Journal R.A.S. London* (1968), Pts. 1–2, pp. 54–64. T. W. Rhys Davids and J. E. Carpenter, *Dīgha Nikāya*, 3 vols., Pali Text Society, London, 1889–1910, reprinted 1947–1960.

pervading. The fully developed atomic theory in the *Abhidharma Hridaya*, which was translated into Chinese in the third century A.D., represents the refinement of a doctrine which had existed for several centuries, but McGovern is inclined to the view that both the Jaina and Buddhist versions are not original, but probably derived from the Vaiśeshikas. Whatever the source, it is Indian and seems independent of the Greek theories of Leucippus and Democritus.[15]

To learn more of the worldly activities of the Indian peoples in the last few centuries B.C. one must seek information other than that supplied by the many religious and metaphysical writings, and it is fortunate that a text of the *Kautilīya Arthaśāstra*,[16] a unique work on statecraft attributed to Kautilya, prime minister of the Mauryan emperor Chandragupta who ruled from about 321 to 300 B.C., was discovered in 1909. Probably elaborated from the Mauryan original and containing references to the economics and technology of a mean date *c.* 100 B.C., it is a store of information on land and sea communications, agriculture and irrigation, ores and mining, plants and medicine, and especially mechanical contrivances or *yantras*.[17] Engines of war and *yantras* of architecture are mentioned, with emphasis mainly on the former; a whole chapter is devoted to armoury, and the *yantras* are classified as stationary or mobile; and even though their detailed operation can often only be inferred it is clear that the main descriptions refer to siege warfare, the role of elephants in war, catapult devices for hurling projectiles, and incendiary missiles, the composition of the inflammable materials used indicating the absence of gunpowder. In the furtherance of cultivation, irrigation canals and large artificial reservoirs such as the lake of Girnar in Saurāshtra (Kāthiāwār) were constructed, and these had their counterpart in the massive 'tanks' of Ceylon, first seen in the Abayawewa of King Panduwasa built near the capital Anurādhapura as early as 504 B.C.[18] A successor, King Pandukābhaya, had constructed in the latter half of the fifth century B.C. two further 'tanks', the Jayawewa and the Gāmini, in the same region, and such stupendous activity in irrigation works went on, as in India, into the medieval period. One cannot but marvel at these splendid monuments, some of which were 40 miles in perimeter, and the phenomenal agricultural progress achieved during half a millennium from the accession of Vijaya, the first of the Great Dynasty, nor fail to record the scholar's indebtedness to George Turnour, who sought out the 'tika' with the help of the Buddhist priest Gallé and through inconceivable difficulties produced an English version of a third of the *Mahāvamsa* in 1836, which rendered our historical knowledge of these early public undertakings possible.

The machines of the period of the *Arthaśāstra* and of the early centuries

[15] Olufsen noted that the Vakhans believe in fire, air, water, and wind, and refers back to the Mazdak sect of the old Iranian religion. We come to the Hindu theory of wind later. O. Olufsen, *Through the Unknown Pamirs*, London, 1904, p. 199. See also P. Rāy, *Indian Journal of History of Science*, Vol. 1, No. 1 (1966), 1–14.

[16] R. Shāmasastry, *Kautilya's Arthaśāstra*, 3rd edn., Mysore, 1929. R. P. Kangle, *Kautilīya Arthaśāstra*, Pt. 1, Bombay, 1960.

[17] V. Raghavan, *Yantras or Mechanical Contrivances in Ancient India*, Indian Institute of Culture, Bangalore, 2nd edn., 1956.

[18] R. L. Brohier, *Ancient Irrigation Works in Ceylon*, 3 pts., Colombo, 1934–5.

A.D. were either useful devices of everyday life such as the *vāriyantra*, probably a revolving water-spray for cooling the air, mentioned by the poet Kālidāsa in his *Mālavikāgnimitra;* or automata and toys such as those described by Hero of Alexandria, Philo of Byzantium, and Vitruvius.[19] References to *Yavanas*, who were often engineers, in early Tamil literature, and commercial intercourse between southern India and the West, especially in Augustan times, suggest acquaintance with Greek and Roman ideas. Though Bhoja in his treatise *Samarānganasūtradhāra* gives many technical properties of machines neatly classified, refers to the use of toothed wheels in the operation of types of merry-go-round, and has a general statement concerning the magnitudes of effort and load in a machine, we do not find scientific laws as in Greek mechanics. Perhaps most remarkable is the absence from the Jaina physics of a concept of force, action and change arising out of time, but, as in the case of the atomic theory, this must be considered in terms of the contemporary philosophy; there is error in reading too much into early texts.

Ancient Hindu mathematics shows an early interest in large numbers expressed in powers of ten, in the nature of numbers and their factors, and in the division of time into its smallest units. These large powers occur in the Vedic *Samhitās*, *Brāhmanas*, and *Sūtras*, in the epics *Mahābhārata* and *Rāmāyana*, and in the *Lalitavistara* (where 10^{53} is given). Of particular interest is the *Śatapatha Brāhmana*, which lists all the factors of 720 as far as 24, and after stating that 360 nights and days contain 10,800 *muhūrttas* proceeds by four successive multiplications by 15 to reach the ultimate *prānas* or breathings. The occurrence of the word *rāśi* (a heap) in the *Chāndogya Upanishad* recalls the use of the same concept by the Ancient Egyptians, and is clearly the humble origin of what was later to become the burden of many a schoolboy, standing for the unknown quantity x.

Of the greatest importance to the historian of mathematics are the *Śulva Sūtras*,[20] which form part of the *Kalpa Sūtras* and deal with the construction of sacrificial altars used in Vedic ritual. As terminal writings they summarize the knowledge of several preceding centuries and provide an excellent picture of the achievements of Hindu geometry prior to the mathematics of the Jaina sect; furthermore, when temple worship replaced the old rites of the *agnicayana*, this geometrical tradition lapsed[21] and was subsequently superseded by the growth of analysis for which Hindu mathematicians are justly renowned. From the mass of literature which must have been the prerogative of the priesthood seven *Śulva Sūtras* have survived and of these three are especially valuable—those of Baudhāyana, Āpastamba, and Kātyāyana.[22] They deal with such matters as the construction of squares and rectangles, the relations of the sides to the diagonals, the construction of equivalent squares and rectangles, the construction of equivalent squares and circles, the construction of

[19] See e.g. H. J. J. Winter, 'Muslim Mechanics and Mechanical Appliances', *Endeavour*, 15 (1956), 25–8.

[20] Bibhutibhushan Datta, *The Science of the Śulba*, University of Calcutta, 1932.

[21] Bibhutibhushan Datta, 'Geometry in the Jaina Cosmography', *Quellen und Studien zur Geschichte der Mathematik*, Abt. B. Bd. 1 (1930), 245–54.

[22] See e.g. V. Sharma, *Kātyāyana Śulva Sūtra*, Benares, 1928. D. Srinivasachar and V. S. Narasimhachar, *Āpastamba Śulva Sūtra*, with the commentaries of Kapardisvāmī, Karavindasvāmī, and Sundararāja, University of Mysore, 1931.

triangles equivalent to squares and rectangles, and the construction of squares equal to two or more given squares or equal to the difference between two given squares. In this connection we may note two interesting formulae, those giving the diagonal of a square and the squaring of the circle. Thus, according to Baudhāyana and Āpastamba, to obtain the *dvi-karanī* or diagonal[23] 'Increase the measure by its third part, and again by the fourth part (of this third part) less the thirty-fourth part of itself (i.e. of the fourth part).' This gives a value for $\sqrt{2}$ of

$$1+\frac{1}{3}+\frac{1}{3\cdot 4}-\frac{1}{3\cdot 4\cdot 34} \qquad \text{or } 1{\cdot}4142156\ldots$$

diverging from modern calculation only in the sixth place of decimals.

Baudhāyana says: 'If you wish to square a circle, divide its diameter into eight parts; then divide one of these parts into twenty-nine parts and leave out twenty-eight of them; and also the sixth part (of the previous division) less the eighth part of this (last).'[24] A relation between the radius of the circle (r) and the side ($2a$) of the equivalent square is finally obtained in the form:

$$a = r-\frac{r}{8}+\frac{r}{8.29}-\frac{r}{8.29.6}+\frac{r}{8.29.6.8}$$

In the construction of altars (*vedi*) requiring numbers of bricks of differing sizes in various layers, e.g. in the falcon-shaped fire altar, we see the origin of those indeterminate problems which form a notable part of later Hindu algebra. Bibhutibhusan Datta, after examining Jaina canonical literature and the commentaries of Kapardisvāmī and Karavindasvāmī, inclines also to the view that the irrationality of $\sqrt{2}$ was understood in the time of the Śulvas.

Archaic Hindu medicine in its earliest context is to be found mostly in the hymns of the *Atharva Veda*, and the Vedic term *bheshaja*, used to denote medicinal charms, which occurs also in the *Avesta* as *baesaza* or *baesazya*, suggests a common Āryan origin. It is a 'psychosomatic' approach to healing, part of a philosophical system, a scheme in which the lay physician and the priest perform their respective roles in controlling the ills of the body and of the soul. Native pre-Āryan lore and practice were absorbed. Mohenjo-dāro, which had the finest public health facilities in the ancient East, could boast bathrooms and a drainage system, and no doubt influenced personal hygiene. The deity Dhanvantari, custodian of the elixir of immortality, became the fount of wisdom for virility and duration in life (*āyurveda*) and the remedies (*bhaishajya*) to ensure these. He figures in Suśruta as the divine authority in medicine. We cannot, therefore, compare such a system with contemporary medical education, drawing as it does upon several of the exact sciences, but we can perceive the beginnings of certain features in general practice and in surgery which are still with us; thus, we find the practitioner teaching his pupil by personal example, a blend of experience and tradition with fresh observation and speculation, whilst specialized surgical equipment in common use by the first century A.D. consisted of twenty types of knives and

[23] Being the side of a square of area twice that of the original square. Numerically this was usually a surd; thus *dvi-karanī* meant $\sqrt{2}$, *tri-karanī* meant $\sqrt{3}$ (B. Datta, *The Science of the Śulba*, p. 188).

[24] *Baudhāyana Śulva Sūtra*, i. 59.

needles (*śastra*), thirty probes (*śalākā*), twenty tubular instruments, and twenty-six articles of dressing (*upayantra*).[25]

Its theoretical basis being metaphysical, Hindu medicine was restricted by tradition and by isolation from other sciences. Life originated in the primal waters, man the microcosm was inevitably moulded by the forces of the macrocosm;[26] the types of physiognomy are the result of specific incarnations. In the *Purānas* fever is a demon, offspring of indigestion—the commonest cause of illness. Since illness in general could be attributed either to a disturbance in the organism or to the entry of super-human forces, then, should the physician fail, prayers must be recited and offerings made to propitiate the intruder. The human body was maintained in a state of health by the three humours, phlegm, gall, and wind (or breath) in their correct proportions.[27] These proportions could be achieved by proper diet, an important consideration in a trying climate. The humours were forms of the life-energy and corresponded to divine forces or agents in the macrocosm, i.e. outside the body; thus phlegm, cool and heavy, which resided in the chest and lungs, was associated with the moon. Hindu interpretation gave wind prime significance among the humours, since it appeared to govern the dynamics of the body; from the pre-Āryan Yoga to the Vedānta philosophy there developed a theory of winds (*vāyu*) or manifestations of the life-breath.[28] *This is a theory of breathing which ignores the lungs.* In fact, the lungs (*kloman*) and the palate were regarded by Caraka[29] as the source of the vessels which carry water through the body. Existing alongside Caraka's description of the vascular system was that of Suśruta, postulating the navel as the source; of the tubular vessels (*śirā*) radiating therefrom, each of the humours (now four in number) occupied 175. So in all: 'There are seven hundred tubular vessels. As a garden or a rice field is irrigated by a system of canals carrying water, the body, by means of these vessels, is moistened and maintained; . . . the root from which they spring is the navel . . . the navel is surrounded by the tubular vessels, as the hub of a wheel is surrounded by spokes.'[30]

Disregard of proper diet leads to a disturbance of the balance of the humours; these become incensed, and overflowing their normal channels invade the domain of others, thereby causing disease. The basis of dietetics and pharmacology was the Hindu theory of the six essences (*rasa*), which appear to correspond to the Greek *glyky*, *liparon*, *stryphnon*, *halmyron*, *pikron*, and

[25] H. R. Zimmer, *Hindu Medicine* (Hideyo Noguchi Lectures), Johns Hopkins Press, Baltimore, Md., 1948, p. 82.

[26] P. J. Deshpande, K. R. Sharma, and G. C. Prasad, 'Contribution of Suśruta to the Fundamentals of Orthopaedic Surgery', *Indian Journal of the History of Science*, Vol. 5, No. 1 (1970), 13–35. L. M. Singh, K. K. Thakral, and P. J. Deshpande, 'Suśruta's Contributions to the Fundamentals of Surgery', ibid., pp. 36–50. See J. Filliozat, *La Doctrine classique de la médecine indienne*; *ses origines et ses parallèles grecs*, Imp. Nat., Paris, 1949, Ch. VIII.

[27] A fourth humour, blood, was later added and is mentioned in the writings of Caraka and Suśruta.

[28] As many as ten are listed in the Yoga treatise *Gorakshaśataka*.

[29] Caraka, vi.5. A. C. Kaviratna and P. S. Kavibhushana, *Charaka-Saṁhitā*, Calcutta, 1890–1911.

[30] Suśruta, iii. 7. Kaviraj K. L. Bhishagratna, *Suśruta*, Calcutta, 1907–18. *Sushruta Samhitā*, Chowkhamba Sanskrit Studies, 30. 4 vols., 1963–4.

drimy.[31] Tradition had established an elaborate doctrine of correspondence between the essences (qualities or flavours) in certain foods and the specific substances in the humours. A vast pharmacopoeia enshrined traditional remedies. In the treatment of the patient an all-powerful arcanum was blended from various herbs, each contributing specific healing properties, and these material properties were reinforced by supernatural powers invoked by the brāhman practitioner who claimed a special relationship with the twin horsemen and divine physicians, the Aśvins. Honey possessed unusual healing virtues, being associated with *amrita*, the elixir of immortality.

Another significant feature of Hindu medicine was *the absence of any attempt to recognize diseases of the brain*. One would not have expected much progress in this study in ancient times in any case, but the reason for such neglect is to be found in the assumption that the centre of consciousness, thought, and feeling is the heart, a generalization which is implicit also in the writings of Homer.[32] Caraka[33] certainly mentions insanity, but it is covered by the general explanation of the overflowing of 'incensed elements', in this instance into the special vessels carrying the 'mind-stuff', or by the entry of demons.

Among the diseases mentioned in Vedic medical texts are diarrhoea (*āsrāva*), fever (*takman*), dropsy (*jalodara*), consumption (*balāsa*, *yakshma*), tumour (*akshata*), abscess (*vidradha*), leprosy and certain skin diseases (*kilāsa*), and congenital diseases (*kshetriya*). Dropsy was sent by Varuna, the god of the primal waters. Jaundice, for which Caraka later records diagnosis and treatment,[34] is characterized by the presence of the demon who causes yellowness (*hariman*).

On pursuing inquiry to the borders of the realm of legend the historian gleans one indisputable fact, namely, that the fount of ancient Hindu medical wisdom was the oral teaching of Punarvasu Ātreya. According to the Buddhist *Jātakas* a physician Ātreya taught at Takshaśilā (Taxila) in the age of Buddha. It appears that six pupils of Ātreya first set down this wisdom in encyclopedic form, but of these versions only two, those of Bhela and Agniveśa, have survived. A defective manuscript of *Bhela Samhitā*,[35] discovered in south India, reveals the same tradition as is to be found more fully expounded in the *Caraka Samhitā*, which is the final form of the compilation of Agniveśa and is our best source of Hindu medical knowledge as it existed in the last few centuries B.C. Caraka is generally believed to have been the court physician to King Kanishka at Peshāwar in the first or second century A.D.

H. R. Zimmer, on the evidence of the Bower manuscript,[36] suggests a possible third school parallel with Bhela and Agniveśa. This oldest extant medical manuscript, discovered by Lieut. A. Bower in 1890 in a Buddhist monument at Kuchā, Chinese Turkestān, has been dated on the basis of palaeography in the second half of the fourth century A.D. but contains

[31] H. Zimmer, op. cit., p. xlix. J. Filliozat, op. cit., Ch. VIII.

[32] See J. Filliozat, op. cit., Ch. IX. [33] Caraka, vi. 9. [34] Caraka, vi. 16.

[35] The *Bhela Samhitā*, Sanskrit text, University of Calcutta, 1921. See also P. Rāy, 'Medicine—as it evolved in Ancient and Mediaeval India', *Indian Journal of History of Science*, Vol. 5. No. 1 (1970), 86–100.

[36] A. F. R. Hoernle, *The Bower Manuscript*, Pts. 1, 2, Arch. Survey of India, New Imp. Ser. 22, Calcutta, 1893–1912.

material deriving from several centuries earlier, and not only has certain chapters corresponding to those of Caraka but almost identical pharmaceutical formulae. The work is interesting in that no reference is made to Caraka; it is also significant in showing the penetration of Hindu medicine into Central Asia.

Āyurveda (the science of longevity) as set forth in Caraka makes no mention of surgery, being solely the province of the physician. The development of surgery is initially attributed to the genius Suśruta who may have taught and practised in Kāśī (Vārānasī, Banaras). He incorporated surgery into the general field of medicine, advised a wide training and experience gained under several teachers, stressed the importance of surgery in the study of anatomy (which was the major weakness in Hindu medical knowledge), and attempted a stricter classification of existing data[37] which still resided in separate monographs marred by confusion and repetition. With Suśruta also there ended the specialized tradition of elephant medicine.[38]

Hindu tradition made an eight-part division of the field of study, broadly in respect of (a) diseases, their diagnosis and treatment, and (b) the means of healing in relation to the whole man, the philosophical and ethical approach. Thus under (a) we find illnesses requiring surgery (*śalya*) and the science of obstetrics; diseases of the eye, ear, nose, and throat (*śālākya*); diseases due to the disturbance of the humours which involve the therapy of the whole organism; mental and other disturbances of demoniacal origin; pediatrics, i.e. children's diseases, caused by demons; and finally, three aspects of *āyurveda* —medicinal drugs (*agada*) and antidotes, elixirs of life (*rasāyana*), and virility (*vājīkarana*). More widely (b), we consider the organism (*śarīra*), its moral and physical health (*vritti*), the origins of disease, and the nature of pain and illness in terms of the balance of the humours, treatment or action (*karman*), the consequences of treatment, the influence of time (*kāla*) in respect of the age of the patient or perhaps the seasons, and lastly, the professional conduct of the agent or physician, his diagnosis, his methods and instruments (*karana*). Emphasis was laid upon the preventative aspect and early treatment.

There is no reference to hospitals in the ancient Hindu medical literature, but they evolve with the spread of Buddhism. The second Rock Edict (*c.* 256 B.C.) of the Mauryan Emperor Aśoka celebrates the beginnings of social medicine, whilst Ceylon, by the fourth century A.D., could boast some hospitals, and a medical service; by royal command each physician served the villages, and veterinary officers tended the king's elephants and horses. Ample evidence of the treatment of out-patients in dispensaries occurs in the *Sangam* literature of southern India.[39]

[37] The present text of the *Suśruta Samhitā* probably dates from the fourth century A.D.

[38] *Hastyāyurveda*, ed. Mahādeva Cimanājī Apte (Ānandāśrama Sanskrit Ser. No. XXVI), 1894. H. Zimmer, *Spiel an der Elefanten*, München, 1929. Franklin Edgerton, *The Elephant-Lore of the Hindus, the Matanga-Lila of Nilakantha*, New Haven, Conn., 1931. On horse medicine see *Aśvavaidyaka* by Jayadatta, and *Aśvacitiksitā* by Nakula, ed. Umeśacandra, Bibliotheca Indica, Calcutta, 1887.

[39] S. Gurumurthy, 'Medical Science and Dispensaries in Ancient South India as gleaned from Epigraphy', *Indian Journal of History of Science*, Vol. 5. No. 1 (1970), 76–9.

III

We conveniently leave the ancient world via the *Siddhāntas*, the astronomical treatises which in themselves exhibit a transition from the *Paitāmaha Siddhānta*, which retains the Vedānga astronomy, to the *Sūrya Siddhānta* of A.D. 400,[40] which largely establishes the form of native astronomy for the duration of the Middle Ages.[41] Varāhamihira, *c.* A.D. 505 summarized in his *Panchasiddhāntikā* the five *Siddhāntas* entitled *Paitāmaha, Vāsishtha, Pauliśa Romaka*, and *Sūrya*, though his version of the last-named indicates that gradual changes in the text of this, the most important Siddhānta, must have occurred subsequently. K. S. Shukla lists as a minimum twenty-eight commentaries on it by known authors, mostly in Sanskrit but two in Telugu, reaching to the early eighteenth century, together with at least seventeen works based essentially upon its theory; his recent edition[42] includes the commentary of Parameśvara (A.D. 1432) written in Keralā in south India.

Much discussion has centred around the transmission of Greek astronomical ideas to India during the first four centuries of the Christian era.[43] This period coincides with that of the growth of the Siddhānta literature, and the *Romaka Siddhānta* especially shows signs of Greek influence, an influence which is notably present in the terminology of astrological writings such as the *Brihajjātaka* and *Laghujātaka* of Varāhamihira. It is also the period of close commercial intercourse between imperial Rome and the coasts of Keralā and Tamilnādu, embracing both the Augustan age and the Sangam age.[44] Tamil poems of the latter make frequent references to *yavanas*,[45] who were Westerners familiar with Hellenistic science and Roman technology, and who assisted in the design and construction of *yantras*, especially engines of war. More or less contemporary influences of Greek and Roman craftsmanship are evident in coinage and in sculpture in northern India.[46] Nor should one overlook the intellectual contacts of the Gupta Empire with Sāsānian Persia, where there was some study of astronomy.[47]

The Tamil tradition in respect of astronomy is especially significant. By the study of two Greek papyri of the Roman period, which seem to have been written *c.* A.D. 100 and *c.* 250 respectively,[48] and of the Tamil methods of

[40] The earlier limit. It may still have been developing as late as A.D. 1000.

[41] For further sources, see D. Pingree, 'Sanskrit Astronomical Tables in the United States', *Trans. Amer. Philos. Soc.*, Vol. 58, No. 3 (1968), 77.

[42] K. S. Shukla, *The Sūrya-Siddhānta, with the Commentary of Parameśvara*, Dept. of Mathematics and Astronomy, Lucknow University, 1957.

[43] H. J. J. Winter, *Eastern Science*, London, 1952, Ch. III.

[44] R. E. M. Wheeler, *Rome beyond the Imperial Frontiers*, London, 1954.

[45] V. R. Ramachandra Dikshitar, Translation of the *Śilappadikāram*, Oxford, 1939. A. Danielou, Translation of the *Śilappadikāram*, New York, 1965. P. T. Srinivas Iyengar, *History of the Tamils from the Earliest Times to 600 A.D.*, Madras, 1929.

[46] W. W. Tarn, *The Greeks in Bactria and India*, Cambridge, 1951. J. Marshall, *Taxila*, 3 vols., Cambridge, 1951. R. E. M. Wheeler, 'Roman Contact with India, Pakistan and Afghanistan', in *Aspects of Archaeology, Essays Presented to O. G. S. Crawford*, London, 1951.

[47] S. H. Taqizadeh, *Bull. School of Oriental Studies*, 9 (1939), 133–9. D. Pingree, 'Astronomy and Astrology in India and Iran', *Isis*, Vol. 54, No. 2 (1963), 229–46.

[48] O. Neugebauer, *The Astronomical Treatise P. Ryl. 27*, Kgl. Danske Vidensk. Selsk. hist.-filol. Meddelelser, XXXII, 2, 1949. Knudtzen-Neugebauer, 'Zwei astronomische Texte', *Bull. de la Soc. Royale de Lettres de Lund* (1946–7), pp. 77–8.

reckoning time,[49] O. Neugebauer has revealed the persistence of the Babylonian methods of the Hellenistic period up till recent times in southern India. Starting from the work of Lt. Col. John Warren of 1825, entitled *Kala Sankalita: a Collection of Memoirs on the various modes according to which the natives of the southern parts of India divide time*, he has found exact numerical parallels between the planetary theory of Varāhamihira's *Panchasiddhāntikā* and that of Seleucid cuneiform tablets of *c.* 200 B.C., the intermediary phase being the Roman transmission of the earlier form of Greek astronomy, which owed much to Babylonia, into southern India, probably mainly through the medium of the astrological literature. Calculations were made directly for the prediction of astronomical phenomena through certain numerical schemes, and we may call this tradition 'arithmetical'.

With the *Almagest* of Ptolemy we reach a new and more highly developed process of mathematical deduction from geometrical models, which represent in themselves the complicated motions of the planets in terms of epicycles or eccentrics. The *Sūrya Siddhānta*, in addition to the use of terminology and units of Greek origin, employs epicyclic models in its planetary theory. But it is significant that it does not include Ptolemy's refinement of the lunar theory or the 'punctum aequans' of Ptolemaic planetary theory.[50] Neugebauer has now succeeded in reducing the essential features of the planetary theory of the fully developed *Sūrya Siddhānta* to modern terms; thus he says: 'The leading idea is the following. The planet moves on an epicycle of radius r which is carried on a circle of radius R and eccentricity e, the 'deferent' around the observer. Thus we are dealing with two variables, the 'mean distance' α of the centre of the epicycle from the apogee of the deferent, and the 'anomaly' γ which determines the position of the planet on the epicycle. The problem now arises to tabulate this rather complicated function of α and γ.'[51] Into this Greek geometrical system the Hindus injected the important concept of the sine of an angle, thus initiating a second tradition which we may call 'trigonometrical'. Both the *Pauliśa* and *Sūrya Siddhāntas* contain a table of sines (*jyā*).

By remembering that there is a Dravidian component as well as an Āryan one, that there are, in fact, two traditions, the arithmetical and trigonometrical, a proper perspective on the development of Indian astronomy may be obtained in terms of the data furnished by both Tamil and Sanskrit sources.

The chapters of the *Sūrya Siddhānta*[52] deal with (I) the mean motions of the planets, (II) the true positions of the planets, (III) direction, place, and time, (IV–VI) the nature of eclipses, (VII) planetary conjunctions, (VIII) asterisms, (IX) heliacal risings and settings, (X) the rising and setting of the moon, (XI) 'certain malignant aspects of the sun and moon' treated in part astro-

[49] O. Neugebauer, 'Tamil Astronomy', *Osiris*, 10 (1952), 252–76; *The Exact Sciences in Antiquity*, Copenhagen, 1951, Ch. VI. See also: *Arch. Internat. d'Hist. des Sciences*, No. 31, Paris, 1955, pp. 166–73.

[50] O. Neugebauer, 'The Transmission of Planetary Theories in Ancient and Mediaeval Astronomy', *Scripta Mathematica*, Yeshiva University, New York, 1955, p. 7.

[51] O. Neugebauer, op. cit., p. 8 and Appendix.

[52] Revd. E. Burgess, Translation of the *Sūrya-Siddhānta*, ed. P. Gangooly and P. Sengupta, University of Calcutta, 1935.

logically, (XII) cosmogony, geography, and the 'dimensions of the Creation', (XIII) measuring instruments, such as the armillary sphere, clepsydra, and gnomon, and (XIV) different ways of reckoning time. The geocentric system of the universe is assumed, and longitudes reckoned from the prime meridian through the ancient city of Ujjayinī. In spite of the imported Greek ideas, the *Sūrya Siddhānta* is characteristically Indian in its reaction to this alien knowledge; it absorbs what seems to be fitting and treats it in accordance with its own way of thinking, retaining at the same time certain elements of tradition, e.g. the established feature in time-reckoning, the *tithis*, which are constant and equal to thirtieths of a mean synodic month,[53] a division which has also been traced in Babylonian lunar and planetary texts; and the explanation of the irregularities of planetary motion in terms of the winds, which were a significant feature in ancient Hindu philosophy concerning the natural world. Thus, in the *Śatapatha Brāhmana* the smallest units of time were the *prānas* or breathings, whilst in the *Sūrya Siddhānta*[54] we find that 'Forms of Time', of invisible shape, stationed in the zodiac (*bhagana*), called the conjunction (*śīghroccha*), apsis (*mandoccha*), and node (*pāta*), are causes of the motion of the planets.

The planets, attached to these beings by cords of air, are drawn away by them, with the right hand and left hand, forward or backward, according to nearness, toward their own place.

A wind moreover, called provector (*pravaha*) impels them toward their own apices (*uccha*); being drawn away forward and backward they proceed by a varying motion.

The so-called apex (*uccha*), when in the half-orbit in front of the planet, draws the planet forward; in like manner, when in the half-orbit behind the planet, it draws it backward.

When the planets, drawn away by their apices (*uccha*), move forward in their orbits, the amount of the motion so caused is called their excess (*dhana*); when they move backward, it is called their deficiency (*rina*).

Highly regarded and widely disseminated, the *Sūrya Siddhānta* had a profound influence on the course of medieval Hindu astronomy. According to Sumati (*c.* A.D. 800), whose work was known both in Nepal and in Keralā, and who wrote his *Sumati Tantra* and *Sumati Karana* on the basis of the earlier version of the *Sūrya Siddhānta*, it provided the essential elements used by Nepalese astronomers in their construction of the Hindu calendar. Evolving during the period between A.D. 628 and 966, the later version gained greatly in popularity, especially in the twelfth century, when Bhāskara II quoted from it and Mallikārjuna Sūri wrote commentaries on it, first in Telugu then in Sanskrit.

The more important Hindu astronomers, with the approximate dates at which they flourished, were Āryabhata I (A.D. 499), his pupil Lātadeva (A.D. 505), Varāhamihira (A.D. 550), Brahmagupta (A.D. 628), Bhāskara I[55] (a contemporary of Brahmagupta and a disciple of Āryabhata I), Lalla[56]

[53] O. Schmidt, 'On the Computation of the Ahargaṇa', *Centaurus*, 2 (1952), 140–80.

[54] Ch. II, vv. 1–11. Revd. E. Burgess, op. cit., p. 53.

[55] K. S. Shukla, *Mahā-Bhāskarīya* (Bhāskara I and his works Pt. 2), Department of Mathematics and Astronomy, Lucknow University, 1960.

[56] Sudhakara Dvivedi, *Śiṣya-dhī-vṛddhida of Lalla*, Benares, 1886.

(A.D. 748), Mañjula (A.D. 932), Āryabhata II[57] (A.D. 950), Śrīpati[58] (A.D. 1039; author of the *Siddhānta Śekhara* and *Ganita Tilaka*), and Bhāskara II (A.D. 1150), who wrote the important treatise *Siddhānta Siromani*. Since most of them also made significant contributions to mathematics we shall meet them again in the ensuing pages.

Hindu mathematics is undoubtedly the finest intellectual achievement of the subcontinent in medieval times.[59] It brought alongside the Greek geometrical legacy a powerful method in the form of analysis, not a *deductive* process building upon accepted axioms, postulates, and common notions, but an intuitive insight into the behaviour of numbers, and their arrangement into patterns and series, from which may be perceived *inductive* generalizations, in a word, algebra rather than geometry. This native power has, fortunately, survived to modern times; Srinivasa Ramanujan (1887–1920), in whom resided a phenomenal memory allied with great facility in calculation, knew the positive integers 'as personal friends'. The quest for wider generalization beyond the limitations of pure geometry led the Hindus to abandon Ptolemy's method of reckoning in terms of chords of a circle and to substitute reckoning in sines, thereby initiating the study of trigonometry. It is to the philosophical mind of the brāhman mathematician engrossed in the mystique of number that we owe the origin of analytical methods. In this process of abstraction two particularly interesting features emerged, at the lower level of achievement the perfection of the decimal system, and at the higher the solution of certain indeterminate equations.

The first Hindu algebraist was Āryabhata I, of whose mathematical work we have only thirty-three *ślokas* which form a section of the astronomical writing *Āryabhatīya*.[60] He had a prolonged influence in both astronomy and mathematics, a commentary, *Bhatadīpikā*, upon the *Āryabhatīya* being written by Parameśvara as late as 1430. The condensed form in which the mathematical knowledge of Āryabhata appears serves mainly as a criterion of the state of the subject at the end of the fifth century A.D., but certain topics clearly emerge, e.g. square and cube roots, simple areas and volumes, the simpler properties of circles, sines, gnomon problems, arithmetical progressions, factors, and simple algebraic identities; whilst π is stated as $3\frac{177}{1250}$ (i.e. 3·1416). Algebra is now defined as a separate study (*bīja*) and there is given a general solution in whole numbers of the indeterminate equation of the first degree. Sections 3 and 4 of the *Āryabhatīya* deal respectively with time reckoning (*kālakriyāpāda*) and spherical astronomy (*golapāda*), the latter treatment ultimately bearing its full fruition in the spherical trigonometry of

[57] Id., *Maha-Siddhānta of Āryabhaṭa II*, Benares, 1910.

[58] Babuaji Misra, *The Siddhānta-Śekhara of Śrīpati, with the Commentary of Makkibhaṭṭa* (A.D. 1377), University of Calcutta, Pt. 1, 1932, Pt. 2, 1947. H. R. Kapadia, *Gaṇitatilaka by Śrīpati, with the Commentary of Siṃhatilaka Sūri* (*c. A.D. 1275*) (Gaekwad's Oriental Ser. 78), Oriental Institute, Baroda, 1937.

[59] For source materials see S. N. Sen, *A Bibliography of Sanskrit Works in Astronomy and Mathematics*, National Institute of Sciences of India, Calcutta, 1966.

[60] P. C. Sengupta, 'The Āryabhaṭīyam', *Journ. Dept. of Letters, University of Calcutta*, 16 (1927). W. E. Clark, *The Āryabhaṭiya of Āryabhaṭa*, Chicago, 1930. K. S. Sastri, *Āryabhaṭīya of Aryabhaṭa I, with the Commentary Mahābhaṣya of Nīlakaṇṭha* (A.D. 1500) 3 parts, Trivandrum, 1930–6.

the Muslim astronomers Abū Raihān al-Bīrūnī[61] and Nāsir al-Dīn al-Tūsī.[62]

Whilst Āryabhata I excelled as an observer and in the classification of astronomical data, Brahmagupta was stronger as a mathematician. Brahmagupta is noted for his *Brāhmasphuta Siddhānta* (A.D. 628),[63] where in the twelfth and eighteenth chapters may be found important mathematical developments, and his *Khandakhādyaka*[64] (665), with its supplement *Uttara Khandakhādyaka.* The work on cyclic quadrilaterals (i.e. four-sided figures with their angles on the circumference of a circle) is an interesting example of the achievement of the Hindus in the geometry of lines or boundaries, in terms of which they tended to think rather than in terms of angles. Brahmagupta showed that:

(1) If the sides of a cyclic quadrilateral are of lengths $a, b, c, d,$ and its semi-perimeter is s, then its area[65] is

$$A = \sqrt{(s-a)(s-b)(s-c)(s-d)}$$

(2) If the diagonals of the same quadrilateral are of lengths x and y, then the relations between these diagonals and the sides of the quadrilateral are expressed by 'Brahmagupta's Theorem'.

$$x^2 = (ad+bc)(ac+bd) \div (ab+cd)$$
$$y^2 = (ab+cd)(ac+bd) \div (ad+bc)$$

(3) If a, b, c and p, q, r are the sides of two separate right-angled triangles, such that $a^2+b^2=c^2$, $p^2+q^2=r^2$, then if we make a quadrilateral of which the sides are the products ar, cq, br, and cp, this quadrilateral, called 'Brahmagupta's Trapezium', will be cyclic and its diagonals will intersect at right angles.[66]

Using the newer concept of sines of angles, not angles, Brahmagupta, in the first stanza of his chapter in the *Khandakhādyaka* on the rising and setting of planets, gives the formula which is now expressed as

$$\frac{a}{\text{Sin } \angle A} = \frac{b}{\text{Sin } \angle B} = \frac{c}{\text{Sin } \angle C}$$

where a, b, c are the sides of the triangle ABC.

The astronomical writings of Brahmagupta were known in western India at the time of the Muslim invasion of Sind (A.D. 712) and also to Abū Raihān al-Bīrūnī on his Indian journey some three centuries later, and there is little

[61] Islāmic astronomers were indebted to Greek and Hindu mathematics and in some respects improved on both. See e.g. Al-Bīrūnī, *Al-Qānūn Al-Mas'ūdī*, 3 vols., Osmania Publications Bureau, Hyderabad-Deccan, 1954–6. E. S. Kennedy and Ahmad Muruwwa, 'Bīrūnī on the Solar Equation', *Journ. Near Eastern Studies*, Vol. 17, No. 2 (1958). H. J. J. Winter, 'Formative Influences in Islamic Science', *Arch. Int. d'Histoire des Sciences*, 23–4 (1953), 171–92.

[62] A. Carathéodory, *Traité du quadilatère*, Constantinople, 1891.

[63] Sudhākara Dvivedi, *Brāhmāsphuṭa Siddhānta and Dhyāna-Grahopadeṣādhyāya by Brahmagupta*, reprint from *The Pandit*, N.S. 24 (1902), Sanskrit text.

[64] P. C. Sengupta, *The Khaṇḍakhādyaka, with the Commentary of Pṛthūdaka*, 2 vols., University of Calcutta, 1934, 1941. 'A short treatise in astronomy which is as pleasant as food prepared with sugar-candy.'

[65] This formula, though arising from the general treatment in the *Brāhmasphuta-Siddhānta*, is first explicitly stated in the *Ganitasāra Samgraha* of Mahāvīra (A.D. 850).

[66] H. J. J. Winter, *Eastern Science*, London, 1952, p. 47.

doubt that they were one of the media through which Hindu astronomy and mathematics passed to the Arabs during the 'Abbāsid caliphate.[67] Of a practical nature, the Arabs transmitted to the West the so-called Hindu numerals and decimal system and the simpler algebraic and trigonometrical processes, but ignored the use of negative quantities and the higher algebra of indeterminate equations which they do not appear to have understood.

Medieval Hindu mathematics may be conveniently divided into two provinces of study, *pātīganita*[68] and *bījaganita*. The former comprised mainly arithmetic and mensuration; geometry, which had earlier been a distinct discipline in the *Śulva Sūtras*, was now widened in scope and assimilated into mensuration. Perhaps the earliest example of this kind of presentation is to be found in the Bakhshālī manuscript,[69] which is written in old *Śāradā* characters on seventy folios of birch-bark, and was unearthed from a mound in the Peshāwar district of north-west India in May 1881. Uncertainty surrounds its age; the *mathematics* has been dated as early as the third century A.D. and the manuscript itself as late as the twelfth. *Bījaganita*, which was concerned mainly with the solution of algebraic equations, embraced problems in which there were more unknown quantities than there were equations with which to find them. This study of indeterminate equations was a notable feature of both Hindu and Chinese mathematics during the medieval period.

In India indeterminate analysis reached its zenith in Bhāskara II. He described the solution of the first-degree equation in terms of the pulverizer (*kuttaka*),[70] a quantity such that, when it is multiplied by a given number, and the product added algebraically to a given quantity, the sum or difference is divisible without remainder by a given diviser; that is, he obtained whole-number values of x and y which satisfy the equation $ax \pm by = c$. Indeterminate equations of the second degree in the forms

$$ax + by + c = xy$$

and

$$ax^2 + c = y^2$$

had already been investigated by Brahmagupta, but the solution of the general equation

$$ax^2 + bx + c = y^2$$

by the *chakravāla* or cyclic method, was effected by Bhaskāra II in a manner which has perpetuated his name for all time in the history of the theory of numbers.[71] It is salutary to remember that Bhaskāra II made these advances

[67] The so-called Sindhind has not been precisely identified.

[68] See the *Pātīgaṇita of Śrīdharācārya*, ed. K. S. Shukla, Lucknow University, 1959, pp. vi, xv.

[69] G. R. Kaye, *The Bakhshālī Manuscript*, Archaeological Survey of India, New Imperial Series, Vol. 43, Pts. 1, 2, Calcutta, 1927; Pt. 3, Delhi, 1933.

[70] H. T. Colebrooke, *Algebra, with Arithmetic and Mensuration from the Sanscrit of Brahmagupta and Bhāscara*, London, 1817, p. 156.

[71] See H. J. J. Winter, *Eastern Science*, Ch. III. D. Apte, *Bījagaṇita of Bhāskara II, with the Commentary of Navāṅkura of Kṛṣṇa* (c. A.D. 1600), Anandāśrama Sanskrit Series, Poona, 1930. H. C. Banerji, *Līlāvatī of Bhāskara II*, Calcutta, 1893. G. P. Dvivedi, *Siddhānta-Śiromaṇi by Bhāskara II*, Sanskrit and Hindi, Vols. 1 and 2, Lucknow, 1911, 1926. M. Jha, *Siddhanta-Śiromaṇi by Bhāskara II with the Commentaries of Vasanāvārtika of Nṛsiṃha* (1621) *and Marīci of Muniśvara* (1635), Vol. I, Benares, 1917. H. T. Colebrooke, op. cit., pp. 172–8.

around the middle of the twelfth century; independent European investigations of the seventeenth and eighteenth centuries did not reach completion until about 1770, with the work of Euler and Lagrange.

The delightful *Līlavatī* and *Bījaganita*, which form part of the *Siddhānta Śiromani* of Bhāskara II, have been widely used since their composition. A Persian version of *Līlavatī*[72] appeared in 1587 on the orders of Akbar and one of *Bīja ganita* in 1635 for Shāh Jahān. *Bījaganita* is interesting in that it contains a demonstration of the theorem of Pythagoras which is distinct from that of Euclid I, 47. The deductive proof in Euclid represents the squares drawn externally upon the three sides of a right-angled triangle, whereas the figure in Bhāskara, which may well derive ultimately from the Chinese *Chou Pei Suan Ching* of the Han period, is not part of a deductive system but is simply a practical demonstration which shows how two given squares may be so cut that the parts fit together again to form a third square.[73] *Līlāvatī* was later rivalled by the *Ganita Kaumudī*, composed in 1356 by Nārāyana, a work notable for its treatment of magic squares.[74] Indian interest in magic squares is reflected in Siamese mathematics of the seventeenth century.[75]

A vast literature surrounds the history of the so-called Hindu-Arabic numerals. Whereas the first epigraphic evidence for zero occurs in India in the Bhojadeva inscriptions at Gwalior, around A.D. 870, much earlier records illustrating the use of place value come from Cambodia (604), Champa (609), and Java (732). Again, a Cambodian inscription of 683 uses the dot or *bindu* to represent zero, whilst an inscription on Banka Island of 686 shows the closed ring. These are no doubt the result of the Hindu influence in South-East Asia, just as in the case of the Po-lo-men (brāhman) books transmitted to China during the great period of Buddhist interchange (say 350–1050), or the calendrical texts of eastern Turkestān which derive from Sanskrit, or the earlier dissemination of Indian ideas amongst the Greeks, Iranians, and Chinese in Khotan in the days of Kanishka. Confining ourselves, through the limitations of space, to questions of origin only, we may quote a happy suggestion of Joseph Needham: 'It may be very significant that the older literary Indian references simply use the word 'śūnya'—emptiness, just as if they are describing the empty spaces on Chinese counting boards.'[76]

During the medieval period the medical tradition of Caraka and Suśruta was continued by the Buddhist Vāgbhaṭa (perhaps eighth century) who summarized the eight divisions of medicine in his *Ashtāngahridaya Samhitā*.[77] Im-

[72] H. J. J. Winter and A. Mirza, *Journ. Asiatic Society, Bengal, Science*, Vol. 18, No. 1 (1952), 1–10.

[73] See Euclid, *Elements*, ed. I. Todhunter, intro. Sir T. L. Heath, Everyman Reprint, London, 1955, p. 266. J. Needham. *Science and Civilization in China*, Vol. 3, Cambridge, 1959, p. 22. H. T. Colebrooke, op. cit., p. 222.

[74] Nārāyaṇa Paṇḍita, *Gaṇita Kaumudī*, Princess of Wales Bhavāna Texts, Government Sanskrit College, Benares, Vol. 1, 1936; Vol. 2, 1942.

[75] De La Loubère, *Description du royaume de Siam*, Vol. 2, pp. 235–88; *Le Problème des quarrés magiques selon les Indiens*, Amsterdam, 1714.

[76] J. Needham, op. cit., Vol. 3, p. 11 n.

[77] L. Hilgenberg and W. Kirfel, *Vāgbhaṭa's Aṣṭāngahṛdayasaṁhitā, ein altindisches Lehrbuch der Heilkunde*, Leiden, 1937–40. K. Vogel, *Vāgbhaṭa's Astāngahṛdaya Saṁhitā. The First Five Chapters of its Tibetan Version*, Berlin, 1965. *But* see also A. B. Keith, *A History of Sanskrit Literature*, Oxford, 1920, p. 510.

portance was attached to the use of minerals and natural salts in prescriptions, and books of such prescriptions appeared in popular medicine.[78] Medicine and chemistry were closely allied. Alchemy was an integral part of Tantric mysticism. Throughout the Tantric period (*c.* 700–*c.* 1300) and the ensuing Iatrochemical period (1300–*c.* 1550) the philosophy of mercury, which in the *Rasaratnākara* of the alchemist Nāgārjuna and the Śaiva tantra *Rasārnava* was concerned essentially with the elixir of life, gradually developed, as exemplified in the *Rasaratna Samucchaya* and many other similar treatises, into the more realistic study of mercurial remedies and the chemical behaviour of the metals.[79] Indian alchemy reached Tibet[80] in the early eighth century with the spread of Buddhism, and is to be found in the great scriptures *Kanjur* and *Tanjur*. In the field of metallurgy remarkable technological competence was attained as early as the fourth and fifth centuries; the casting of the pure-copper Buddha at Sultanganj in Bihār and the welding of wrought-iron shapes to complete the Iron Pillar near Delhi cannot fail to inspire the highest respect.[81]

IV

In astronomy the Muslim tradition of instrumental technology survived in India until the middle of the eighteenth century.[82] The astrolabe, which had been lovingly perfected by generations of Persian and Arab craftsmen and was again executed in fine workmanship by the family of 'Īsā b. Allāhdād in Lahore[83] in the reign of the Mughal Emperor Jahāngīr (1605–27), was used by the astronomers in the service of the Mahārāja Sawāī Jai Singh II (1686–1743) at his observatories in Delhi, Jaipur, Ujjain, Vārānasī (Benares), and Mathurā.[84] Though Jai Singh's principal astronomer was the Hindu Jagannāth he made full use of European and Islamic ideas. In particular his massive masonry quadrants and dials, constructed to attain maximum accuracy, in the absence of the telescope in India, closely follow the precedent set by the Samarkand observatory of Ulugh Beg. On a much simpler level the gnomon, which in Borneo[85] consists of a vertical staff placed in the ground (the co-tangent form), appeared with a short horizontal piece inserted near the top of the staff (the tangent form). A shepherd's timestick of the latter type, inscribed in *nāgarī* script and from Nepal, has been described elsewhere by the present writer.[86]

During the late eighteenth and most of the nineteenth centuries Europeans resident in India and South-East Asia, excited by the new world of natural

[78] See e.g. Elizabeth Sharpe, *An Eight-Hundred Year Old Book of Indian Medicine and Formulas, from Old Hindi*, London, 1937.

[79] Acharya Prafulla Chandra Rāy, *History of Chemistry in Ancient and Mediaeval India*, now edited by P. Rāy, Indian Chemical Society, Calcutta, 1956.

[80] Rāy, op. cit., Tibetan texts, pp. 449–56.

[81] See further, *Indian Journal of History of Science*, Vol. 5, No. 2 (1970), Sections X-XII.

[82] H. J. J. Winter, 'The Muslim Tradition in Astronomy', *Endeavour* 10 (1951).

[83] J. Frank and M. Meyerhof, *Ein Astrolab aus dem indisches Mogulreiche*, Heidelberg, 1925.

[84] G. R. Kaye, *The Astronomical Observatories of Jai Singh*, Archaeol. Survey of India, New Imperial Series, Vol. 40, Calcutta, 1918.

[85] J. Needham, op. cit., Vol. 3, p. 286.

[86] H. J. J. Winter, *Physis*, Vol. 4, Pt. 4 (1964), 377–84.

history around them, began the process of describing and classifying the native flora and fauna. Thus the remarkable realism of the Mughal court painters,[87] especially of Ustād Mansūr under the patronage of Jahāngīr, himself an ardent naturalist, was followed by a still more accurate art form dictated by the requirement of scientific recording. Beautiful drawings by Indian, Chinese, and European artists survive from this period.[88]

India has not failed in this century to produce her Fellows of the Royal Society. We conclude with the three names of Sir C. V. Raman, Sir J. C. Bose, and S. Ramanujan. Raman investigated both experimentally and theoretically the general problem of the molecular scattering of light,[89] which includes an explanation of the colours of the sky and the sea. In the course of these investigations he discovered in 1928 that when a transparent liquid is irradiated by a strong source of light of frequency n the spectrum lines as seen through the spectrometer used to examine the scattered light contain not only the exciting line n but several weaker lines of frequencies $n \pm \Delta n$ on either side. The small values Δn depend not upon n but only upon the nature of the irradiated liquids. This phenomenon has been named the Raman Effect and explained in terms of the quantum theory of Einstein and Planck. Bose crossed the boundaries dividing physics and biology.[90] In a remarkable series of researches during the period 1895–1927, in which the traditional Hindu sensitivity to the living world of plants and animals attained a new understanding, he made a unique contribution to our knowledge of physiological response. In the course of this work he devised delicate apparatus to measure extremely short intervals of time and rates of reaction. Of his high magnification crescograph, which could detect a rate of growth in plants of the order of one millionth of a millimetre per second, he wrote: 'So sensitive is the recorder that it shews a change of growth-rate due to slight increase of illumination by the opening of an additional window.'[91] Bose reached the ultimate in the study of the inertia of mechanical systems prior to the development of the cathode-ray oscillograph and the new methods of electronic engineering. In Srinivasa Ramanujan (1887–1920) we see once again the brāhman mathematician inspired by the theory of numbers, leaping intuitively to generalizations whilst the less gifted ponder on the intermediate steps.[92] The 'quiet, meditative child who used to ask questions about the distances of the stars', who later said that the goddess of Namakkal fed him with formulae in his dreams, and who helped to create the beautiful expressions in the Rogers–Ramanujan identities,[93] developed, as

[87] S. M. Hasan, 'The Mughal School of Zoological Portraiture', *Arts and Letters, Journal Roy. India, Pakistan and Ceylon Society*, Vol. 37, No. 1 (1963), 3–13.

[88] Mildred Archer, *Natural History Drawings in the India Office Library*, H.M.S.O., London, 1962.

[89] C. V. Raman, *The Molecular Diffraction of Light*, University of Calcutta, 1922. Raman and Krishnan, *Proc. Roy. Soc.* 122 (1929), 23.

[90] P. Geddes, *The Life and Work of Sir Jagadis C. Bose*, London, 1927. Sir Jagadis Chunder Bose, *Collected Physical Papers*, Trans. Bose Inst. Calcutta, and Longmans Green, London, 1927. [91] Ibid., p. 350.

[92] G. H. Hardy, P. V. Seshu Aiyar, and B. M. Wilson, *The Collected Papers of Srinivasa Ramanujan*, Cambridge, 1927.

[93] 'Proof of certain identities in combinatory analysis', *Proc. Camb. Philos. Society*, 19 (1919).

G. H. Hardy has recorded, an 'insight into algebraical formulae, transformation of infinite series, and so forth, that was most amazing. On this side most certainly I have never met his equal, and I can compare him only with Euler and Jacobi.'[94]

In this survey emphasis has been laid upon the more recent investigations; the older works, important though some of them, such as those of Colebrooke and Thibaut, still are, have been only briefly mentioned, but any further information relating to them may be found by studying the material listed in the select references at the foot of each page;[95] with the rapid development of researches into the history of science in Asia in the last few years priority of space must be given to the results of these researches, especially those obtained by native scholars. Thus, the pioneer writings of Sudhakara Dvivedi of Vārānasī (Benares) on Hindu mathematics have now been supplemented by the publications on ancient astronomy and mathematics to the memory of Sir Asutosh Mookerjee by the University of Calcutta and by the current series of texts being issued by the Department of Astronomy and Mathematics of Lucknow University. Islamic science is represented by Dr. Nizamuddin through the impressive series of publications of the Osmania Bureau of Hyderabad in the Deccan.[96] Two conferences in 1952 and 1961 have helped to clarify ideas,[97] and research papers are now appearing in the newly established *Indian Journal of the History of Science*.[98] (See also Addenda.)

It is in Sanskrit that the soul of India lies; the problem is one of interpretation of the *ślokas* or stanzas which enshrine the ancient wisdom, a process often rendered more difficult in astronomy and mathematics by the condensed nature of the original presentation. Moreover, many manuscripts have been lost, for example the eighth-century writings *Pātiganita* and *Siddhānata Tilaka* of Lalla and the ninth-century *Govindakriti* of Govinda; though there are others being discovered and examined. It is desirable that the significant birch-bark and palm-leaf manuscripts should be dated by the Carbon-14 process.[99]

Ancient Hindu science, though conservative, is strong in classification. This is immediately evident not only in medicine but in the world's earliest scientific grammar, that of Pānini, established by the fourth century B.C. It is associative, drawing by intuition from an accumulated background of experience; the direct path of deduction so beloved of the Greeks is alien to it. It lies outside the European tradition. In both ancient and medieval times the native master–pupil relationship had its triumphs and its failures; on the one hand 'schools' would merely perpetuate traditional methods or simply die away, on the other the torch of learning would be kindled anew by the genius of some isolated *guru*. We may study Hindu science only within the framework of

[94] *The Collected Papers of Ramanujan*, p. xxxv.

[95] Or W. E. Clark in the *Legacy of India*, pp. 335–68.

[96] See current catalogue of the Arabic publications of the Dairat ul-Ma'arif'il-Osmania, Hyderabad, Deccan.

[97] See e.g. 'Symposium on the History of Sciences in South Asia', *Proc. Nat. Inst. of Sciences of India*, Vol. 18, No. 4 (1952), 323–62.

[98] One volume has appeared annually since 1966. *A Concise History of Science in India* by D. M. Bose, S. N. Sen, and B. V. Subbarayappa has just been published by the Indian National Sciences Academy (Calcutta, 1973).

[99] W. F. Libby, *Radiocarbon Dating*, University of Chicago Press, 2nd edn., 1955.

philosophy and religion. To the *guru* intuition meant illumination from the infinite ocean of knowledge, and might, like a final cadence in Indian music, at any moment fade imperceptibly away.

ADDENDA

A recent attempt by Finnish philologists to read the Indus Valley script using a computer method seems to indicate that the *nakshatras* are of Harappan origin, as also are the later Dravidian names of the five planets related to their colours (e.g. Mars, the 'red star'). Should this be substantiated, it would locate the origin of the *nakshatras*, traditionally associated with the Hindus, within the earlier Indus Valley culture.

(See e.g. Asko Parpola, *Annales Academiae Scientiarum Fennicae*, XL, ser. B. tom. 185. Helsinki, 1973.)

An Institute of History of Medicine and Medical Research was inaugurated at Tuqluqabad, New Delhi, early in 1970, and incorporates the library of Dr. Cyril L. Elgood.

CHAPTER XIII

Ancient and Modern Languages

by T. BURROW

THE literary tradition of India goes back more than 3,000 years, and during the greater part of this time it was dominated by Sanskrit, first in its Vedic, and later in its classical form. The early Āryan invaders of India brought with them, along with other elements of a developed culture, a language of great richness and precision, and a highly cultivated poetic tradition. The chief custodians and exponents of this poetic art were the families of priests, eventually to develop into the brāhman caste, who were also the guardians and practitioners of the Vedic religion. The hymns to various deities composed by members of these families were orally preserved, first among the several families concerned, and were eventually united into one great collection known as the *Rig Veda*. This text not only served the purposes of religion, but it provided a common literary standard for the Āryan tribes of India. The compilation of the later Vedas followed after no great interval, and the corpus of Vedic poetry, whose beginnings may be fixed somewhere round 1300 B.C., was probably complete in the main by about 1000 B.C. After this date hymns were no longer composed in the old poetic tradition, and instead there developed an extensive prose literature devoted to ritual matters, in a form of language notably younger than that of the hymns, and showing some signs of being based on a dialect situated somewhat further to the east. This prose literature was also entirely oral, and its language is remarkably uniform. The period of the older *Brāhmanas*, as these prose texts are called, may be put roughly at 1000–800 B.C., but the language continued to be used without noticeable change for two or three centuries more. The next milestone in the history of Sanskrit is the Grammar of Pānini, which describes in complete detail a form of the language younger than that of the *Brāhmanas*, and based on the spoken usage of the educated brāhmans of the time. Pānini's exact date is unknown, but the fourth century B.C. may be given as a rough estimate. His grammar quickly gained universal acceptance, and as a result the form of the Sanskrit language as described by him was fixed for all time.

The reason why Sanskrit as a language evolved no further after Pānini was not only his authority, but also the fact that by this time the Āryan language had become divided into two, on the one hand Sanskrit, the language of learning, and in particular the language of the brāhman caste and of its religion, and on the other hand Prākrit, the language of the masses. These terms did not in fact come into use until some centuries later, but the dichotomy was already established by the time of Buddha and Mahāvīra. From this time on normal linguistic evolution affected only the vernacular language, Prākrit or Middle Indo-Āryan; Sanskrit remained fixed in the final form given to it by Pānini, and continued to be used as the language of the educated classes, although, as time went on, the difference between it and the ordinary spoken language increased.

Although the gap between Sanskrit and the ordinary spoken language grew progressively, this did not have an adverse effect on the use of Sanskrit, but rather its importance grew with time. For instance the language of administration in Mauryan times, as attested by the inscriptions of Aśoka, was Prākrit, and this continued for some centuries; but gradually Prākrit was replaced by Sanskrit until finally Sanskrit was almost exclusively used for this purpose. A similar development took place among the Buddhists. Originally, according to the directions of Buddha himself, their texts were composed in Middle Indo-Āryan, and the scriptures of the Theravāda School are preserved in one form of this, namely Pāli, but later, shortly after the Christian era, the northern Buddhists turned to Sanskrit. The old scriptures were translated into Sanskrit, and new works were composed in that language. As an intermediate stage some schools developed a mixed or hybrid language which continued in use for some time. The Jainas, though at a much later date, followed the example of the Buddhists, and also began to compose in Sanskrit instead of Prākrit. On the whole it can be said that during the last 600 years of pre-Muslim India Sanskrit was more extensively and exclusively used than at any time since the close of the Vedic period.

The Vedic literature, both verse and prose, was composed and handed down orally. This was a remarkable achievement, and it was only possible because there existed a class of people, the brāhmans, the major effort of whose lives was devoted to this end. At the same time it had a limiting effect, inasmuch as such literature as remains is confined mainly to the religious sphere. The introduction of writing took place probably about the same time as Pānini was codifying the rules of the Sanskrit language, and it rendered possible a vast extension of the uses to which the recently codified language could be put. Nevertheless the process was at first slow, due partly to the above-mentioned competition of Middle Indo-Āryan. The Sanskrit literature preserved from the time of Pānini and the centuries immediately following is still mainly religious, consisting of various *sūtras* attached to the Vedic schools. Their language corresponds mainly to that of Pānini, but tolerates a number of irregularities which would not later be allowed.

In the field of secular literature Sanskrit epic poetry was the next most important development, but the oral tradition in this field seems to have continued for some time, so that it was not until considerably later that the written epics in the form that we have them took shape. The epic language also, though following Pānini as a rule, admits a considerable number of irregularities. The use of Sanskrit prose for scientific, technical, and philosophical purposes is first exemplified on a large scale by the *Mahābhāshya*, Patanjali's commentary on Kātyāyana's *Vārttikas* to Pānini's grammar, which can be dated with some certainty to the second century B.C. After this time, and particularly during the early centuries of the Christian era, a great corpus of technical scientific literature, covering the fields of philosophy, medicine, politics, and administration, etc., came into existence. In the same period the rules of Pānini were more strictly applied, and deviations from them were disapproved. Classical poetry, in so far as it is preserved, is rather late, beginning with Kālidāsa, who is probably to be placed in the fifth century A.D., but its earlier cultivation is attested in inscriptions, in Buddhist literature (Aśvaghosha), and by occasional references in Patanjali. The drama also was probably established in the period immediately preceding the Christian era, and it continued to flourish in the early centuries A.D., but here again the examples that are preserved are much later.

Even allowing for the loss of a considerable amount of early literature, it still remains a fact that Sanskrit was enjoying its maximum use during the period A.D. 500–1200. It was current almost as widely in the Dravidian south as in the Āryan north, and it was also extensively used in the areas of Indian cultural expansion in South-East Asia, Indonesia, etc. At the end of the period, in spite of the fact that the difference between it and the spoken vernaculars had now become very great, it was flourishing as strongly as ever. Its preeminence was first seriously threatened by the Muslim invasions, which began seriously shortly before A.D. 1200 and quickly overran the greater part of the country. The new rulers preferred to use Persian as their official language, and they were unfavourably disposed to all branches of Hindu culture. Nevertheless the tradition of Sanskrit literature continued strongly and the number of Sanskrit works preserved, which were composed during the Muslim period, is very considerable indeed. The period of British rule exercised a further unfavourable influence on Sanskrit, since a new language of civilization appeared in the field, while the increasing use of the modern Indo-Āryan languages was a further limitation to its use. In spite of this, literary composition in Sanskrit has continued on a modest scale down to the present time, and an interesting development has been the successful adaptation of the language to the expression of modern ideas. From the practical point of view the main use to which the Sanskrit language is put at present is as a source of vocabulary for the modern languages. Sanskrit is able to provide on a large scale the new technical terms which are continually needed, and which the modern languages cannot supply from their own resources.

The Middle Indo-Āryan languages first came into use as vehicles for the teachings of Buddha and Mahāvīra, but the first examples recorded in writing are the inscriptions of Aśoka. Particular interest attaches to these, since they are recorded in various local dialects, of which there are three main varieties, the eastern or Māgadhī, the western, and the north-western. The Buddhist and Jaina scriptures were at first circulated in Māgadhī, and, of course, orally, but this dialect seems to have been of somewhat limited extension, and, in comparison with the more average type of Prākrit current in the central and western regions, rather aberrant. Consequently when these religions spread over all north India a change in linguistic practice became necessary. The Theravāda School adopted a straightforward western type of dialect, which came to be known as Pāli, into which the scriptures were transcribed, not without considerable traces remaining of the original Māgadhī. Other local languages were also used, but the only example still remaining is a version of the *Dhammapada* in the Gāndhārī dialect of the north-west. This is largely due to the substitution, mentioned above, of Sanskrit for Middle Indo-Āryan among the northern Buddhists, and, in the case of some schools, of a peculiar mixed language known as Buddhist Hybrid Sanskrit. The Jainas also modified their original Māgadhī dialect, though retaining certain Māgadhī characteristics, and this modified language is appropriately known as Ardhamāgadhī or Half-Māgadhī. It also represents a considerably later stage in the development of Middle Indo-Āryan than Pāli, and the texts composed in it are mainly of later origin.

Middle Indo-Āryan is divided into three stages, and it covers a period ranging from 500 B.C. to A.D. 1000. The first stage is represented by Pāli and the inscriptions of Aśoka and later rulers, and comprises the period up to shortly after the Christian era. The term Prākrit, when used in the narrow sense, applies to the second stage. It consists of the dialects described by the Prākrit grammarians, and it is exemplified in the drama, and in certain lyric and epic poems in the Mahārāshtrī dialect, but principally in the canonical and post-canonical writings of the Jains. The drama is governed by an interesting convention, according to which kings, ministers, and learned men speak Sanskrit, while men of lower status and women speak Prākrit, a practice reflecting, no doubt, the current usage of the time. Various Prākrit dialects are used in drama, according to the prescriptions of the grammarians. The language of ordinary dialogue is Śaurasenī, which would strictly be the dialect of the Mathurā region, but which no doubt represents the language of the wider area now known as Uttar Pradesh. The Mahārāshtrī dialect, based on what is now the Marāthā territory, is used for the lyrics that occur from time to time in the drama, and outside the drama it was the recognized medium for the composition of Prākrit poetry. The Māgadhī dialect, by a partly artificial convention, is used for the speech of the lower characters in drama, and other minor dialects are supposed to be used for specific purpose. The use of these various dialects is best exemplified by the *Mricchakatikā*, which is perhaps the earliest of the surviving dramas. As already observed, Ardhamāgadhī is the language of the Śvetāmbara Jaina canon; the non-canonical Prākrit literature of the Jainas is composed in either Jaina-Mahārāshtrī (Śvetāmbaras) or Jaina-Śaurasenī (Digambaras). Finally there is the curiously named Paiśācī (language of the goblins), in which the *Brihatkathā* of Gunādhya was composed, but which is unfortunately no longer preserved. The north-western Prākrit ('Gāndhārī') lies outside the scope of the Prākrit grammarians and of classical literature; the *Dhammapada*, translated into this language, has already been mentioned. In addition there is an extensive series of documents from Central Asia testifying to its use as an administrative language even outside the boundaries of India.

The third and final stage of Middle Indo-Aryan is represented by what is known as Apabhramśa. This represents a stage of linguistic development roughly half-way between Prākrit and the modern Indo-Āryan languages, and its period is roughly A.D. 600–1000. The earliest specimen would be the Apabhramśa verses appearing in the fourth act of Kālidāsa's *Vikramorvaśīya*, but there is doubt as to their authenticity. This form of language is described by some of the Prākrit grammarians, and an extensive Jaina literature in Apabhramśa, mostly dated round about the end of the period, has been published in recent years.

The emergence of the modern Indo-Āryan languages dates from the period after A.D. 1000, when already the division of the regional languages was assuming the shape that is familiar today. The main block of Indo-Āryan stretches as a solid mass across north and central India. In addition there are certain minor and eccentric languages outside the main block, which are of no literary importance but are often of great interest for linguistic history. Such are the Dardic languages of the north-west, which are both extraordinarily numerous and remarkably archaic. The gypsy languages were taken to the Near East and Europe by itinerant tribes who probably left India about A.D. 500 or shortly after. The only literary language outside the main block is Sinhalese, which was introduced into the island by settlers from north India about the time of Buddha. It is of great interest both on account of its independent growth, and because of the fact that, with the help of inscriptions, an almost continuous picture of its development can be formed. Its literature is extensive and the earliest portions of it considerably antedate the earliest literature produced in the modern languages of north India.

The modern languages of the main block of Indo-Āryan developed very much on parallel lines, since there were no major geographical obstacles inhibiting mutual contact. Eventually the following literary languages emerged:

south-west: Gujarātī and Marāthī
west : Sindhī and Panjābī
north-west: Kashmīrī
north-east : Nepālī
east : Assamese, Bengālī, Oriyā
central : Hindī, Western and Eastern, with which we may enumerate Rājasthānī to the west, and Bihārī to the east.

The literary development of these languages took place at various times, Marāthī and Gujarātī being among the earliest. Linguistic difference was often associated with differences of alphabet, e.g. in the case of Oriyā, Bengālī, Panjābī (Gurmukhī), and Gujarātī, which have alphabets of their own differing from the usual Devanāgarī (Hindī and Marāthī, and, according to modern practice, Sanskrit). Of greater importance was the introduction of the Arabic script by the Muslims for certain languages. In the case of Hindī this led to the development of two different literary languages, Urdū and Hindī, based originally on the same spoken dialect.

Apart from the Muslim influence the development of the modern Indo-Āryan languages followed the same lines. The early literature was predominantly religious and almost exclusively poetic. In form and subject-matter it was based on Sanskrit models. An important new feature in the modern languages, as opposed to the earlier Middle Indo-Āryan, was the introduction, on an extensive scale, of Sanskrit loanwords. In Prākrit, even at the Apabhramśa stage, words might in fact be derived from Sanskrit, but they always appeared disguised as Prākrit by the operation of phonetic rules. At the stage of Modern Indo-Āryan this practice was no longer feasible and the Sanskrit words had to be introduced as such. Another consideration was the poverty of the vernacular languages, due to the continued use of Sanskrit at the expense of the spoken languages down to a late date. This was a situation which could only be dealt with by drawing extensively on the vocabulary of Sanskrit. In the Muslim-dominated literary languages, a similar position was held by Arabic and Persian.

The development of the modern Indo-Āryan languages continued on these lines until the end of the eighteenth century, after which the full effect of British rule and European civilization began to be felt. The introduction of printing, which took place in north India about this time, had a profound effect on the development of language and literature. Works in prose, as well as poetry, began to be produced, the range of subjects for literature was extended and modernized, and literary output progressively increased. The processes initiated at this period have continued with increasing tempo till the present day.

Among the modern Indo-Āryan languages, the position of Hindī is of outstanding importance, since it has been officially accepted as the national language of India. Its history is also more complicated than that of the others. Taking Western and Eastern Hindī together, along with their various dialects, Hindī occupies the most central position and also covers a much larger area than any other language. On the other hand the modern form of literary Hindī was developed very late, in fact not until the end of the eighteenth century. The reason for this was that earlier writers had used other dialects of Hindī (e.g. Braj Bhāshā or the Eastern Hindī of Tulsī Dās), whereas the *Kharī bolī*, originally the dialect of the Delhi-Meerut area, on which both Hindī and Urdū are based, was developed in the first place under the influence of the Muslims. The first literary language to emerge from it was therefore Urdū, written in the Arabic script, and borrowing an extensive vocabulary from Arabic and Persian. At the same time, in a somewhat simplified form, it gained extensive currency as a non-literary colloquial, and this is still very widely used. On the other hand literary Hindī, written in the Devanāgarī alphabet and drawing for vocabulary on Sanskrit, hardly appears at all until the beginning of the nineteenth century.

The partition of the subcontinent between India and Pakistan had naturally considerable effects on language. The principle result was that Hindī was adopted as the official language of India, while Urdū occupies a similar position in Pakistan. Bengal was divided into two, with consequent differences developing between the Bengālī of East Pakistan (now Bānglādesh) and that of West Bengal. A similar division took place in the case of Panjābī.

The pre-Āryan languages of India are grouped into two families, Dravidian and Mundā (or Kolarian), but languages of literary status are found only among the former group. These are the Tamil, Malayālam, Telugu, and Kannada languages, occupying respectively the states of Madras, Keralā, Āndhra, and Karnātaka. In addition there are a number of unwritten, tribal languages in central India, and the family is represented even as far away as Balūchistān by Brāhūī, which has also remained a non-literary language. It is quite likely that the extension of Dravidian was originally much wider than at present, and that it has receded before the advance of Indo-Āryan. It is also possible that other families existed which have been displaced by Indo-Āryan, leaving no trace. The Indus civilization possessed a written language, but it is undeciphered and nothing can be said about its nature and affiliation.

The earliest Dravidian language to be developed for literary purposes was

Tamil, in which there is an extensive corpus of lyric poetry dating to the early centuries of the Christian era, as well as an important grammatical work, the *Tolkāppiyam*. The reason for this priority was the fact that the Tamil country was the furthest removed from the centre of Āryan expansion, and the development of the native language was not inhibited by the competition of Sanskrit or Prākrit. From this period on there is a continuous and extensive literature in Tamil, and three language periods, Old, Middle, and Modern Tamil, are distinguished. The Middle Tamil period begins with the lyrics of the Śaiva and Vaishnava religious teachers who flourished under the Pallavas, and continued until late medieval times. The modern period of the language begins, as elsewhere, round about A.D. 1800, when the influence of English and European models began to be felt. Although considerably modernized, the written Tamil language differs considerably from the spoken language, which has evolved a good deal further. A movement to bring it more in line with the spoken language has not, however, made much progress, since the latter is divided into various kinds according to both locality and class.

The Tamil language was less influenced by Sanskrit than the other three Dravidian languages, and the number of Sanskrit and other Indo-Āryan loan-words in it is considerably smaller. At the Old Tamil stage they are very few indeed, and there was perhaps a deliberate attempt to avoid them. The Sanskrit influence is a good deal more extensive in the writings of the Śaiva and Vaishnava saints, and greater still in some later works, but it never attained the same degree as it did in Malayālam, Kannada, and Telugu. Recently there has been a movement to purify the Tamil language of extraneous elements, but in view of the continual need for fresh technical vocabulary this is hardly likely to be completely effective.

The Malayālam language existed in the early period only as a dialect of Tamil, and it was not until about A.D. 1000 that it achieved the status of an independent language. It has its own alphabet with the full complement of Sanskrit letters (unlike Tamil, which manages with far fewer), and it makes liberal use of Sanskrit loan-words. A very highly Sanskritized style was at one time current under the name of *Mani-pravāla*. Its literary development in modern times has been considerable.

The literary development of Kannada and Telugu was inhibited at first by the fact that these territories were under the dominion of the Āndhra Empire, whose administrative language was Prākrit. In this respect they were followed by their immediate successors, and it is not until about A.D. 500 that we begin to have evidence of the use of the native languages. Kannada inscriptions begin to occur about A.D. 450, and Telugu inscriptions from about A.D. 650.

The earliest Kannada literary text dates from the latter part of the ninth century, but the names of a number of earlier works are known. There is a considerable body of work from the tenth century, mainly the work of Jainas. All this is written in Old Kannada, which gave place later to Middle Kannada, which was itself, by a continuing process of evolution, replaced by Modern Kannada. In the case of Kannada there is no marked difference between the spoken and written language, such as was noted in the case of Tamil.

Literary Telugu begins about the end of the first millennium with Nannaya's translation of the *Mahābhārata*. This is followed during the succeeding centuries by a considerable number of works based mainly on Sanskrit originals, as elsewhere, mainly in verse. The Vijayanagara Empire coincided with the most flourishing period of classical Telugu literature. The development of the modern language and literature followed the usual lines, and, as in Tamil, there was during most of the modern period a considerable difference between the spoken and written languages. Since about 1940, however, there has been a strong movement to bring the written language more into line with the spoken, and, by and large, this movement has been successful.

CHAPTER XIV

Classical Literature*

by A. K. WARDER

THE classical tradition in Indian literature is essentially secular. Religious scripture (*āgama*) and scholarly treatises (*śāstra*) are usually distinguished from 'literature' (*kāvya*), the latter being both human and an art. 'Tradition' (*itihāsa*), including 'antiquity' (*purāṇa*) and 'epic' (*ākhyāna*), is distinguished from all three as the inspired words of ancient sages. In fact its simple heroic verse, lacking the style and figurativeness of *kāvya*, represents the narrative poetry of an age before the institutionalization of literature as an art according to the conscious principles of criticism elaborated in the *Nāṭyaśāstra* (Treatise on Drama) and elsewhere. Tradition as extant is mostly not as antique as it purports to be, but it follows the archaic narrative style and continues to be a source of classical themes for 'literature'. On account of its aesthetic power, some critics allowed the great epic *Mahābhārata* to be 'literature' as well as 'tradition'. For our present purpose we too are interested in this 'true' epic derived from the bards (*sūtas*) of antiquity as well as in the 'artificial' epics of individual authors.

In Vedic scripture we find relics, preserved for the liturgy, of a still earlier phase (second millennium B.C.) of epic poetry, celebrating especially the deeds of Indra but sometimes of human warriors, and of lyric in which, characteristically for India, natural phenomena are personified, such as the goddesses Dawn and Night and the gods Sun and Thunderstorm. A few dialogues suggest dramatic action, e.g. Purūravas and the nymph. In prose (mainly the somewhat later *Brāhmaṇas*) there are examples of story telling, terse and abrupt in style, such as Manu and the Fish and the various wars of the gods and demons. The story of Hariścandra and Śunaḥśepa is in mixed prose and verse.

The lay of the *Jaya* ('Victory') was handed down orally for at least a thousand years after the battle it celebrates (*c.* 900 B.C.) before becoming relatively fixed in writing as the *Mahābhārata*, 'Great Bhārata (Battle)'. A shadowy Dvaipāyana or Vyāsa is recorded first to have sung of this terrible struggle of his own time. Vaiśampāyana later elaborated the epic in 24,000 verses and *c.* 750 B.C. Lomaharṣaṇa and Ugraśravas are supposed to have recited the complete *Mahābhārata* in 100,000 verses. On metrical and other grounds, however, the text constituted in the Critical (Poona) Edition, which may approximate to the manuscripts of the fourth century A.D., includes additions down to that century, with a balancing nucleus of archaic verses producing an average date of composition not earlier than *c.* 100 B.C.

The theme of the *Mahābhārata* has been well summed up, by Rājaśekhara, as the anger of the Pāṇḍavas, sons of Pāṇḍu. Pāṇḍu had been consecrated

* At the special request of the author, the full apparatus of diacritics is used in this chapter in the transliteration of Indian words.

Emperor, in the Bhārata Dynasty, because his elder brother Dhṛtarāṣṭra was blind and so legally disqualified from ruling. But Pāṇḍu died first and Dhṛtarāṣṭra seized power, though claiming to act as regent for Pāṇḍu's son Yudhiṣṭhira, who was made crown prince and later given a fief to rule. Yudhiṣṭhira formed a marriage alliance with Kṛṣṇa, leader of the Satvants, and then assumed imperial prerogatives. Dhṛtarāṣṭra's son Duryodhana, ambitious and envying Yudhiṣṭhira's prosperity, challenged him to a gambling match, sure of victory through the trickery of an uncle. Yudhiṣṭhira loses everything, his kingdom, and finally his Queen Draupadī, who is publicly stripped as a slave by Duryodhana's brother, a humiliation she will never forgive. The elders intervene and arrange terms: Draupadī is restored but Yudhiṣṭhira and his brothers are condemned to twelve years' exile and a further year incognito. After enduring this, they enter the service of King Virāṭa of Matsya. From this base, Yudhiṣṭhira sends Kṛṣṇa as envoy to negotiate the restoration of a kingdom, but Duryodhana will not give up even one village and war becomes inevitable. Yudhiṣṭhira marshals his allies against a huge enemy army and the battle lasts eighteen days. The main events are single combats: finally, through the stratagems of Kṛṣṇa (deceit and foul blows contrary to the warriors' code), the Pāṇḍavas destroy their enemies and Yudhiṣṭhira becomes Emperor.

We should note the ethical questions raised by this story of a fratricidal war of succession, with its bitter passions and terrible slaughter. Yudhiṣṭhira's claim was legally sound, but Duryodhana stood for the time-honoured right of the first born and his descendants. Yudhiṣṭhira lost his kingdom through deceit and regained it through deceit. The loss was accompanied by humiliating insult, generating an anger that only the blood of the enemy could quench. The *Mahābhārata* fascinated Indian historians, who took it as a kind of model for their work, whilst critics argued about its aesthetic significance and dramatists and other authors reinterpreted it. Many held that the ultimate aesthetic experience produced by it was the calmed state arising from the renunciation of destructive worldly ambitions. Indeed in the extant *Mahābhārata* Yudhiṣṭhira finally abdicates, after hearing of the tragic death of Kṛṣṇa, and retires to the Himālaya, leaving the Empire to his brother Arjuna's grandson.

In contrast to the simple style of the *Mahābhārata*, with its refrains and repetitions and verse-filling epithets, *kāvya*, or literature as it developed gradually from about the fifth century B.C., becomes highly organized in form, richly adorned with figures of speech, taut in style, profuse in metres, and above all aimed at producing methodically a defined aesthetic experience in an audience, hearer, or reader. This trend, especially in metres, can be traced back to some of the lyrics of the Buddhist *āgama*, the *Tripiṭaka*, available in Pāli, which appear to reflect secular lyrics in the Māgadhī language of the Buddha's time. The *Tripiṭaka* was enriched by the art of certain poets and actors who, becoming Buddhist monks, applied it in praise of the Buddha (notably Vāgīśa), in describing mountains suitable for meditation (notably Kāśyapa), and in other unworldly themes. From about 400 B.C. onwards we find also dramatic dialogues in the *Tripiṭaka*, in verse with prose stage directions, showing the same new metrical art apparently extended to the stage.

Apart from some incidental discussions on genres, figures of speech, etc., in the *Tripiṭaka* and in grammatical and other works, the *Nāṭyaśāstra* of 'Bharata' (the mythical first 'Actor') is the oldest work of Indian literary criticism now available. It is the outcome of several centuries of theatrical practice by hereditary actors, from the fifth century B.C. or earlier down to about the second century A.D., no doubt at first handed down by oral tradition like the *Mahābhārata*. The purpose of drama is the amusement of the audience, but the 'joy' (*harṣa*) and solace given them is not left to chance by the actors but induced through a special technique or method of acting. The drama is an imitation of all the actions of the world, but the essential part of this is the emotions (*bhāvas*) which the characters are represented as experiencing during their actions. There are eight basic emotions: love, humour, energy, anger, fear, grief, disgust, and astonishment. These are not conveyed directly but by playing their causes and effects, the latter including other, transient, emotions. The audience, imagining the basic emotions in the characters through this acting, enjoys eight corresponding tastes (*rasas*), in other words the perception of them, the aesthetic experience (not the emotional experience itself) correspondingly divided into sensitive (perception of love), comic, heroic, furious, apprehensive, compassionate, horrific, and marvellous. Besides being essentially enjoyable, the drama is incidentally instructive because it represents all kinds of actions, good and bad, and the ends or motives which inspire them.

According to the *Nāṭyaśāstra*, drama originated because of the conflicts which arose in society when the world declined from the Golden Age (Kṛta Yuga) of harmony. Thus a drama always presents a conflict and its resolution, and in construction, the conversion of a story into a 'plot', with its elements and conjunctions, is based on the single main action which ends the conflict. Each of the five 'conjunctions' (opening, re-opening, embryo, obstacle, and conclusion) of a full-scale play is bodied out with up to a dozen dramatic incidents and situations (its 'limbs' or parts), showing the characters in action; and a large number of other dramatic devices were available to express the causes and effects of emotion through incidents related to the ultimate action. Among these devices, the discussion of the 'characteristics' of dramatic expression leads into the figures of speech and qualities of style in the language of drama. The *Nāṭyaśāstra* describes ten types of play, distinguished as history or fiction if full scale (five or more acts, implying as many nights' performance since the Indian theatre, though highly organized, is not rapid in movement). The remaining eight types, with from one to four acts only, are heroic, tragic, or comic plays, together with the satirical monologue, the street play, and three kinds of archaic play about the gods and demons. Secondary to all these is the four-act 'light play' as a fictitious sensitive comedy about a real character, whilst the solo *tāṇḍava* dance of Śiva and the delicate *lāsya* invented by Pārvatī, as well as group dances (*piṇḍībandhas*), may be introduced in drama where appropriate. The *lāsya* represents a story, or part of a story, and is regarded as the prototype of the profusion of independent popular ballets which has always accompanied the more serious and classical theatre of India.

Bhāmaha (fifth century A.D.?), the earliest individual critic whose work is available, extended the *Nāṭyaśāstra* analysis (*rasa* aesthetics, construction) to literature as a whole, setting out the genres as drama, epic, lyric, prose biography, and the (usually prose) novel. Then he takes up as his main problem literary expression and what makes it beautiful, which the Treatise on Drama barely touched on. The 'ornament' (*alaṅkāra*) or beauty, which distinguishes literature from ordinary communication, consists in a kind of 'curvature' (*vakratā*), i.e. artistic distortion, indirectness, figurativeness. Both the meaning and the language (derivation of words) must be 'ornament' and hence the definition of literature is '(beautiful) language and meaning combined' (this is urged against earlier writers who advocated one or the other only). The beauty of meaning is analysed into some three dozen 'figures' (*alaṅkāras*), simile, metaphor, etc., taken up from earlier writers but accepted by Bhāmaha only to the extent that each embodies 'curvature'. Bhāmaha, however, favours realism and rationalism in literature, though transmuted into art in this 'curved' way, and he devotes a chapter to epistemology and logic as applied to literature.

Daṇḍin (seventh century) adds to the genres *campū* or narration in mixed prose and verse, which became extremely popular later (like the biography it is intended for live recital before an audience). His main contention is that ten qualities of style (developed from the *Nāṭyaśāstra*) are the essential in literature, the combination of the ten giving the excellent *vaidarbha* or 'southern' style. The 'figures' are secondary. Vāmana defined style as 'a special arrangement of words' and carried this stylistics much further, analysing the qualities into language and meaning. Rudraṭa, on, the other hand, greatly increased the number of figures, classifying them as 'objective' (e.g. 'contrast'), 'comparative', 'exaggerative', and 'double-meaning'. He described the genres further, adding the 'short story' under the novel, and put forward a principle of 'harmony' (*aucitya*) between form and content.

His contemporary Ānandavardhana (ninth century) redefined the essential indirectness of literature as a kind of implication or suggestion, 'revealed' (*vyaṅgya*) as opposed to 'expressed' meaning, where the revealed might even be the opposite of the expressed (like an invitation hidden in a warning). As the *Nāṭyaśāstra* method already made clear, *rasa*, which it is the main object of literature to produce, is always the result of such implication, since the emotions are portrayed indirectly through their causes and effects.

Kuntaka (eleventh century) instead revived 'curvature' but reworked Bhāmaha's doctrine, reducing the figures to eighteen, mainly on the ground that whatever belongs to the subject-matter, rather than the expression, should be excluded and treated instead under *rasa*. Though literature is really 'indivisible', it may be theoretically analysed into six levels of expression, all of which have 'curvature', the phonetic, lexical, grammatical, sentential, contextual, and the work as a whole. The figures are found at the sentential level. The subject-matter is discussed in relation to the three higher levels, the underlying principle being the effective production of *rasa*, for which the source material is selected and modified. On stylistics, Kuntaka offers a new theory of 'natural' versus 'cultivated' (studied) style, either of which may be beautiful though the second is more difficult to succeed in, as Bāṇa, Bhavabhūti, and Rājaśekhara did. Throughout, Kuntaka gives quotations and references from the literature and is in the best empiricist tradition of criticism: he is analysing literature, not setting up an abstract speculative theory. Mahiman (later eleventh century) on the other hand explained indirectness as 'inference' and sought 'middle terms' in the expressions studied by Ānandavardhana and Kuntaka, through which further meanings were inferred by readers.

Meanwhile, Udbhaṭa (eighth century) is the first critic known to us (certainly not the first in fact) to develop the *rasa* aesthetics by adding a ninth *rasa*, the 'calmed', with 'calm' as its basic emotion. Rudraṭa added a tenth, the 'affectionate', and held that all the transient emotions might give rise to as many *rasas*, apparently following Lollaṭa who believed that *rasas* were innumerable.

Lollaṭa (early ninth century) and Daṇḍin thought that *rasas* were simply emotions 'increased'. Śaṅkuka maintained they were something quite different, but imitations of basic emotions (which again did not exist, but were inferred from their causes and effects being shown). Nāyaka (late ninth century) argued for a process of 'development' which replaced the often unpleasant emotions of individual people by an experience in the highest degree enjoyable and also socially generalized and enlightened (stopping the delusion of worldly emotions). Abhinavagupta (A.D. 1000) propounded the most widely accepted theory as to how the production of *rasas* actually works. Like Nāyaka, he makes *rasa* a transcendent, non-worldly, experience, which is even identical with the highest religious experience, transcending individual involvement and emotion as well as space, time, and particular circumstances. In an act of pure contemplation the spectator in the theatre forgets himself and attains a universality of outlook which is also the highest happiness. The 'calmed', consequently, appears as the supreme *rasa*.

Dhanañjaya (A.D. 1000, partly following Nāyaka) instead described *rasa* as a single continuum, with four zones of thought corresponding to phases of a favourable or hostile environment in which the flower of beauty bloomed. These occur in the sensitive, heroic, horrific, and furious, which may be followed by the comic, marvellous, apprehensive, and compassionate as secondary *rasas* giving rise to the same zones of thought.

Bhoja (eleventh century), in the wake of these discussions on the nature of *rasa*, maintained that ultimately there was only one *rasa*, the 'sensitive', since love, the 'queen' of the emotions, absorbs all the others into herself in the form of love of these: each is in fact a kind of love, love of its own special passion. In place of Abhinavagupta's universalization, Bhoja finds in this sensitive *rasa* a supreme form of self-assertion, an aesthetic development of the primeval instinct of egoism in the individual soul. In his extensive works, treating all aspects of literature in relation to the sensitive aesthetic experience, Bhoja is the greatest Indian critic available to us, giving us the largest number of quotations and references and showing a very fine taste in selection and comment.

Later critics are too often pedants, sometimes manufacturing their own examples to suit an abstract theory, but empiricism did not die out completely, whilst some of the new explanations of *rasa* are interesting. Nārāyaṇa, Dharmadatta, and Viśvanātha held, for example, that the 'marvellous' is the only *rasa*. In the age of religious revivals, Rūpa (sixteenth century) initiated a devotional theory of drama and wrote religious plays to exemplify it. On the other hand the anonymous *Naṭāṅkuśa* (fifteenth century) defended the old practice of the theatre against innovations in Keralā which slowed down the performance to the point of disintegration in order to allow greater scope for the virtuosity of individual actors. We must at least mention a number of other critics between the tenth and the fourteenth centuries, to whose analysis of classical works we owe so much of our enjoyment of them: Rājaśekhara, Sāgaranandin, Rāmacandra, Guṇacandra, Śāradātanaya, and Śiṅgabhūpāla.

In the evolution of the very numerous and ever-changing popular theatrical genres of India, finally, Kohala (second century?—known only from quotations) early noticed various musical plays, ballets, and *rāgakāvyas*, from the last of which such modern forms as *kathakali* eventually developed. Abhinavagupta noted a series of solo performances probably evolved from the *lāsya*, among which the *ḍombikā* was most characteristic. The modern so-called *bharatanāṭyam* is evidently descended from this, in which the dancer does not wear costume but impersonates in mime various characters in a story. Meanwhile the street play gave rise to *yakṣagāna* with its eastern (Āndhra) and western (Karṇāṭaka) variants as well as the Tamil street play. We may recall here the social milieu of *kāvya* as described in the *Nāṭyaśāstra* and the *Kāmasūtra*, for 'classical' literature is not opposed to 'popular' and has usually sought a mass audience. The drama was contrasted with the *Veda* as being for the whole of society, *śūdras* (helots) included, and wealthy amateurs were responsible for patronizing regular public festivals in the villages as well as the cities, with plays and other performances (modern *yakṣagāna* in the villages has substituted the box office and sale of tickets for the vanished patrons).

Of all the characteristics of *kāvya* discussed by the critics, the easiest to identify in the earliest period is the large number of new metres, organized on different principles from Vedic metres. These appear in the Buddhist lyrics noted above and increase in number in the later parts of the Pāli Canon, where we begin to find them used for epic narrations as well. An important result of this use of originally lyric metres in epic is that an epic narration becomes a series of self-contained quatrains instead of a continuous series of running on lines.

The *Rāmāyaṇa*, in Sanskrit, is traditionally ascribed to Vālmīki, whom Bhavabhūti and others call the 'First Kavi' (*kavi* meaning the 'author' of a *kāvya*). Although this epic, as we have it, is not as old as the first Pāli *kāvyas*, it is formally on the border line between *itihāsa* (such as the *Mahābhārata*) and *kāvya*. Metrically it is certainly later than the *Mahābhārata* on the average and it shows a few of the new lyric metres just noted (though only at the ends of cantos). It is also more homogeneous, lacking completely the archaic rhythms of the earlier parts of the old Epic but also having far less apocryphal matter added after the first century A.D. The average date of composition seems to fall in the first century B.C.

If *kāvya* is defined by its power to produce aesthetic experience (*rasa*), however, the *Rāmāyaṇa*, with its unforgettable story of the conflicts of human passions, is certainly a *kāvya*. This story was reworked by 'Vālmīki' (if we apply the name to the author of the present text) from old traditions containing two or three probably separate legends in several versions (one is found in the Pāli Canon). In the *Rāmāyaṇa* we thus find: (1) the palace intrigue at Ayodhyā by Queen Kaikeyī resulting in her stepson Rāma's exclusion from the succession to his father's throne and sentence to twelve years' exile and (2) Rāma, exiled in the south, finds its inhabitants oppressed by the raids of demons (*rākṣasas*) from Laṅkā (Ceylon), the island fortress of the demon king Rāvaṇa, and himself suffers the abduction of his wife Sītā by Rāvaṇa; he raises an army (mostly of 'monkeys'), gaining allies, invades Laṅkā, kills Rāvaṇa, frees Sītā, and returns home in triumph, the period of exile having elapsed and his noble stepbrother Bharata generously surrendering the throne to him. The legend or myth of Rāvaṇa itself, with his victorious wars against the gods, may have been a separate source, as perhaps was that of the great 'monkey' hero Hanumant, son of the Wind God. Vālmīki's finest cantos are surely those of the palace intrigue, with the psychological study of the characters of Kaikeyī and her confidante. The apocryphal last book of the *Rāmāyaṇa* adds a tragic ending: Sītā's new exile on suspicion of unchastity, when a captive, and final disappearance. This changes the main *rasa* to the 'compassionate', whereas originally the poem would be 'heroic', though with a considerable compassionate element resulting from Rāma's sufferings.

Prose story-telling in the Buddhist Canon is a little less heavy and abrupt than in the *Veda* but still full of repetitions and rarely ornamented except by the occasional insertion of a verse to emphasize a point. Humour and satire, however, abound. The novel, as an extensive prose fiction (running to hundreds of pages), seems to us to begin with Guṇāḍhya's *Bṛhatkathā* ('Great Story') about 100 B.C. (the lost *Cārumatī* of Vararuci may have been an earlier novel). Guṇāḍhya's language was Paiśācī, closely related to the Pāli of the Buddhists, and both the milieu and the matter of the *Bṛhatkathā* were akin to those of the old Buddhist story telling. Unhappily Guṇāḍhya's text seems to be lost save for a few quotations, so that we have to reconstruct the narrative from the excessively free paraphrases in Sanskrit, Māhārāṣṭrī, and Tamil which superseded the archaic and forgotten language of the original. Though a fiction, the *Bṛhatkathā* is made to seem historical by giving its imaginary hero Naravāhanadatta a historical father, Udayana, one of the last descendants of the Pāṇḍavas (fifth century B.C.). His adventures take place mostly in the real cities of that time and the characterization is realistic. On the other hand, superhuman 'wizards' (*vidyādharas*) intervene, one of whom, Mānasavega, abducts the hero's greatest love, Madanamañcukā. This leads ultimately to a victorious war against the wizards beyond the Himālaya, after Naravāhanadatta has acquired the power of flight from one of them who becomes his friend. More important than this incidental acquisition of wealth and power, however, are the hero's twenty-six conquests of love. The novel moves between the intrigues and struggles of the real world and the realization of wild dreams largely in the realm of 'science fiction' (strange sciences and the construction of 'space machines'). The *rasa* is thus the 'marvellous' (Daṇḍin) rather than the 'sensitive'.

Aśvaghoṣa's (first century A.D.) are the earliest epics now available (Pāṇini's *Jāmbavatījaya* is known only from quotations) to show the fully fledged *kāvya* technique: concentration of the matter in about twenty cantos only (about 1,500 quatrains) in many metres; perception of discrete moments through the separate quatrains instead of a continuity of flowing narrative; numerous figures of speech. Each 'moment' may suggest the theme of the whole story, but we are to dwell on its significance before pressing on to know what happens next. Aśvaghoṣa was an earnest Buddhist, so that the ultimate significance he wishes to convey, through the delights of poetry, is the shallowness of the world and the true happiness of renunciation and peace of mind. Yet he appears far from indifferent to the pleasures of the world, describing most realistically just what he holds to be most ephemeral. This ambiguity and tension, which seems to reflect personal experience, inspires all the elaborate art, or 'ornament' of language and meaning, carrying Aśvaghoṣa's philosophy. Two epics are available, the Life of the Buddha (*Buddhacarita*) and the Handsome Nanda (*Saundarananda*, who was most unwilling to become a monk). It is a heavy loss that only fragments are now available of a series of dramas by Aśvaghoṣa, whose powers of characterization are so well displayed in the epics. The *Śāriputra* and *Rāṣṭrapāla* are again well-known stories of renunciation. A play with a fictitious hero, Somadatta (apparently the son of a merchant), takes us to the milieu of the wealthy amateurs (*nāgarakas*) of the *Kāmasūtra*, with a festival on a hill top and such stock characters as the jester (or 'fool'), rogue, geisha girl (who is the heroine), and maid. Another play had some allegorical characters.

In lyric *kāvya* the classic model is the *Saptaśatī*, a Prākrit (Māhārāṣṭrī) anthology collected, we are told, by a 'Sātavāhana' emperor (more rarely called 'Hāla', a dialect form), perhaps Puḷumāyi II Vāsiṣṭhīputra (second century A.D.). This seems to represent folk songs (in a dialect of the peasants, not of the imperial administration), each a single verse in a musical metre. They are miniatures of situations in life, mostly village life on the banks of the Godāvarī and in the valleys of the Vindhya. Love is the theme (always, according to the critics, though sometimes hidden) and the singers almost always women. Their joys and sorrows, invitations and complaints, or the comments of gossips, are set in the village with its cattle, buffaloes, ploughing, milling, cooking, weaving, working in rice, sesame, or millet fields, or cotton and hemp gardens. Sometimes the changing seasons and their effects on love form the background. The villages are likely to be poor and affection may either compensate for everything or be severely reprimanded by a more worldly friend. There is plenty of humour, often in the ambiguous language used by the heroines to hide their improper suggestions, Ānandavardhana quoting them for 'revealed' meanings.

Pādalipta's novel *Taraṅgavatī*, also in Māhārāṣṭrī, seems now to be available only in an abridged paraphrase in the same language by one Yaśas. The action depends on the memory of former lives, particularly of a strange incident in which a hunter accidentally shot one of a pair of ruddy sheldrakes. Killing breeding birds was against the hunters' code, so he remorsefully cremated it, whereupon its mate in despair threw herself into the fire. The pair were reborn in merchants' families in Kauśāmbī. The girl Taraṅgavatī suddenly recollects her tragic past on seeing some sheldrakes in a park. Sadly she paints the scenes of her past life on a long scroll, which a maid displays on a balcony for a festival. Her lover happens to pass and is reminded of his own past life. The girl's rich father opposes the match with a mere caravan merchant so the two elope, but are seized by robbers. A young robber frees them and Taraṅgavatī's father relents when they reach home. After a happy married life they meet a Jaina monk, who tells them he was the young robber, who was the hunter reborn, and had freed them because he remembered his past when the girl told their story. Convinced of the truth of the Jaina teaching about transmigration the two determine to escape it by joining the Jaina ascetic communities.

The Jaina Pādalipta and the Buddhist philosopher Nāgārjuna are both traditionally connected with the Sātavāhana anthologist. Nāgārjuna wrote an 'epistle' to Sātavāhana and an ethical 'tract' (*Ratnāvalī*) to the same ruler, as well as 'hymns' (lyric *stotras*) praising the Buddha, representing a flourishing Buddhist tradition in these minor *kāvya* genres. Their most celebrated practitioner was Mātṛceṭa, who wrote an 'Epistle to the Great King Kanika' (Kaniṣka III?), probably soon after A.D. 176, and some tracts. His greatest works are his hymns, describing the qualities and actions of the Buddha, especially in his former lives as *bodhisattva*, whose self-sacrificing nature is directly opposed to the worldly nature. The style is in appearance simple, unpretentious, but conceals all the art of *kāvya*, especially of originality in expression despite the well-worn subject. The figures are handled with a certain restraint, suggesting the infinite scope of the subject by contrast with the little the poet feels able to say. Mātṛceṭa's reticence implies a detachment remote from Aśvaghoṣa's involvement.

Possibly a contemporary was Śūra, who used a somewhat similar terse style in tracts but whose masterpiece is the *campū Jātakamālā*, a collection of *bodhisattva* stories (some of them illustrated in Ajantā). The prose is as elegant and fastidious, as compact and elliptical as the verse.

Bhāsa (second century A.D.?), perhaps the greatest Indian dramatist, brings us at last a comprehensive view of the classical theatre. His masterpiece is the 'Dream Vāsavadattā', a full-scale history (*nāṭaka*) in which the heroine sacrifices all her happiness in order to save her husband's (Udayana) kingdom from a powerful enemy. Her courageous action, part of a subtle plan of a minister, bears fruit after great mental suffering, which Bhāsa finely depicts, and she is reunited with Udayana restored to his throne. The 'Consecrations' deals with Rāma's victory over Rāvaṇa, the most interesting character being perhaps the demon king, vainly courting the captive Sītā and then suffering increasing anguish as his armies are defeated and his son killed. The 'Statue' treats the Rāma story more comprehensively and from the different point of view of Bharata. From such *nāṭakas* we discover the aims of classical dramatists, using a familiar story but reinterpreting it and developing new insights into the characters. Another presents the young Kṛṣṇa killing Kaṃsa. The 'Five Nights' deals very freely with an episode from the *Mahābhārata* in three acts (belonging, if not to the archaic *samavakāra* type, to that known later as a *sallāpa*, 'contention'). Further scenes from the great epic are presented in a series of one-act heroic plays (*vyāyogas*) and the death of Duryodhana, or rather his ascent to heaven because he died heroically, in a one-act tragic play (*utsṛṣṭikāṅka*). 'Yaugandharāyaṇa's Vows' is a 'light play' (*nāṭikā*) on the minister who frees Udayana from captivity. The full-scale 'fictions' (*prakaraṇas*) *Avimāraka* and *Daridracārudatta* take us to the world of Naravāhanadatta and Somadatta. The merchant Cārudatta is impoverished and consequently almost friendless, then crosses a parasitic scoundrel on the fringes of a corrupt court and narrowly escapes death.

Of Bhāsa's time or a little earlier are two 'satirical monologues' (*bhāṇas*), by Vararuci and Īśvaradatta. In this type of play the solo actor represents a 'parasite' (*viṭa*), a professional go-between for temporary relationships. He proceeds about his business through the streets and public places of some metropolis, meeting (in mime) characteristic inhabitants of the geisha quarter. 'Both Go to Meet' (*Ubhayābhisārikā*) thus gives interesting pictures of the follies and vices of Pāṭaliputra, with its cultural life (music and drama), to which the 'Dialogue of the Rogue and the Parasite' adds a discussion on the philosophy of love, the drift of which is that it is an excellent thing to spend money on women, especially if they are beautiful but best of all if they are 'amiable'.

To complete the cross-section of the theatre of Bhāsa's day we have a 'street play' of doubtful date (*Traivikrama*, in dialogue form narrating a story illustrated by a painting) and the one-act comedy (*prahasana*) 'Master-Mistress' (*Bhagavadajjukīya*) by Bodhāyana. The Master, a saintly teacher of *yoga*, disastrously shows off his powers before a student by projecting his soul into the supposedly dead body of the Mistress (a geisha), whose soul brought back from the Underworld is then lodged in his body. Meanwhile the girl's mother and lover arrive. . . .

Another *nāṭaka* of roughly Bhāsa's period is Dhīranāga's *Kundamālā* from the apocryphal last book of the *Rāmāyaṇa*, which changes the conclusion to a happy final reunion in accordance with the convention of an auspicious ending.

In this period of reinterpretation of the Rāma story the Jaina poet Vimala (*c*. A.D. 200?) produced an epic *Padmacarita* in Māhārāṣṭrī harmonizing with his own religious background. He criticized the *Rāmāyaṇa* for such falsifications as making Rāvaṇa a demon and monster, when he was really a wizard, and presenting other wizards, Rāma's allies, as monkeys when they merely lived in Monkey Island. Rāma, who in Jaina literature is often called Padma, finally attains enlightenment and *nirvāṇa*. This epic marks an important stage in the development of the Jaina version of universal history out of the brief sketches in their *āgama*. Vimala's view is rational and understands events in the light of the Jaina doctrine of moral action, which rules the universe. It is a universe in which everything is alive and assault on life is the greatest evil.

Three plays are attributed to King Śūdraka, supposed to have ruled in the third century. The *Vīṇāvāsavadatta* has the same story as Bhāsa's 'Yaugandharāyaṇa's Vows', but as a full-scale *nāṭaka* and with entirely different scenes: Udayana and Vāsavadattā dominate the stage whereas in Bhāsa's light play they do not appear at all. The 'Toy Cart' (*Mṛcchakaṭika*) stands in a peculiar relationship to Bhāsa's *Daridracārudatta*: it is the same play with a new sub-plot, a political revolution which brings fortune to the hero, and with numerous inserted verses elaborating the effects of emotion on the characters.

Henceforth all Indian dramas are on this enlarged scale. Śūdraka is the equal of Bhāsa in characterization and in filling his plays with well-arranged action, whilst putting more of the incidents on stage instead of reporting. His third play is the satirical monologue 'Lotus Gift', in which a parasite proceeds through Ujjayinī, describing the rascals he meets, in order to sound out a new mistress for Mūladeva (a historical character subsequently transformed into a legendary prince of thieves).

The anonymous 'Review of the Seasons' (often misattributed to Kālidāsa), a lyric in which the poet describes to his beloved the effects of the six seasons of the Indian year on lovers, is probably of this period.

From the fourth century little survives except famous names and some quotations, which reminds us that the greater part of the old literature of India has been lost. Sarvasena's Māhārāṣṭrī epic 'Victory of Hari', on Kṛṣṇa carrying off the Pārijāta flower from Heaven for Satyabhāmā, defeating Indra, seems to have set a new style, with a stronger focus on the emotions and also longer descriptive digressions. We get a very good idea of this lost epic from Bhoja's discussions and quotations, to which Kuntaka adds that Sarvasena was, with Kālidāsa, the greatest exponent of the delicate and natural style in *kāvya*. For the emotional content, Sarvasena made much of Satyabhāmā's jealousy of Rukmiṇī.

The dramas of Rāmila and Somila are lost, but Candragomin's 'Joy of the World', a Buddhist play on the *bodhisattva* Maṇicūḍa giving away all his possessions, survives in a Tibetan translation. Of uncertain date are a group of once-famous 'fictions', especially the *Puṣpadūṣitaka* of Brahmayaśas and the *Anaṅgasenāharinandin* of Śuktivāsa. The first is a story of unfair suspicion of the behaviour of the heroine by her father-in-law; the second has its hero in the perilous situation of a rival (in love?) of a prince and falsely accused of theft. These and the anonymous *Taraṅgadatta*, *Padmāvatīpariṇaya* ('Padmāvatī's Marriage', which a rival tries to prevent), and *Prayogābhyudaya* are all known to us from the critics, who by discussing these and many other lost plays completely change the impression of Indian theatre we might have from those available.

The *Pañcatantra* seems to have been written in the fourth century. The author was perhaps the narrator Viṣṇuśarman and his country the Vākāṭaka Empire of the south (Deccan). Its popularity was such that new versions were made, with additions from which it has been difficult to recover the original work (Edgerton's reconstruction seems a good approximation.) The genre is the 'illustrating novel' (*nidarśanakathā*), which is satirical and aims to teach by example. Here the subject is 'policy' (*nīti*), public and private. The frame story is the instruction of three young princes averse to formal education. Within this, five stories present five 'systems' (*tantras*) of policy: (1) splitting an alliance (or friendship) which obstructs one's interests, (2) forming an alliance oneself, (3) making war, (4) outwitting a strong but foolish enemy, and (5) a warning on the folly of action without reflection. Four of these are beast fables, which enhances the sharpness of the satire. Some further stories are emboxed, narrated by the characters to illustrate their own discussions of policy.

The other prose literature of this period has suffered badly. The 'Story of

Simpletons' is known indirectly from paraphrases. Haricandra, so much admired by Bāṇa, is only a name. Lost novels include the *Ratnaprabhā* (Paiśācī, therefore presumably much earlier), *Magadhasenā*, *Malayavatī*, and *Manovatī* (all named after their heroines). A classical 'biography' was the *Mādhavikā*. The story of Śūdraka, written jointly by Rāmila and Somila, was classed as a novel, therefore apparently fictitious. To widen our view of Sanskrit prose we have inscriptions in *kāvya* style, especially Hariṣeṇa's on Samudra Gupta, and the vast Buddhist religious novel *Gaṇḍavyūha*. A novice *bodhisattva* wanders all over India in search of 'good friends' who guide him. The sometimes formidable prose style harmonizes with the view of the universe as infinite, inconceivable, and ambiguous (worldly as usually experienced, beautiful as the *bodhisattva* sees it).

The Gupta Emperor Candra II or 'Vikramāditya', called also Sāhasāṅka and Harṣa, appears as a poet through quotations and references, his *Gandhamādana* seeming to be an epic. He is more celebrated as a patron, making the poet and critic Mātṛgupta king of Kaśmīra *c.* A.D. 410. Like his patron, Mātṛgupta is now known only from quotations of his beautiful and powerful verses, but Kuntaka ranks him first among masters of the 'intermediate' style combining 'natural' and 'cultivated' beauty. Mātṛgupta also wrote on dramaturgy, but here too he is known only from quotations. Probably he was a dramatist, but it is a matter of conjecture which anonymous plays discussed later were his (the 'Illusion Madālasā' constructed according to his principles, the 'Joy of Rāma', both with verses in his style?).

Meṇṭha was patronized by both these and is frequently praised later as a great, or the greatest (Padmagupta), poet, perfecting the *vaidarbha* style after Śūra and Sarvasena. His famous epic *Hayagrīvavadha*, on Viṣṇu as the Fish *avatāra* slaying the demon Hayagrīva, is imperfectly known to us from quotations, but an incomplete manuscript exists and perhaps others can be found in Keralā. Meṇṭha's style is truly epic, a forceful narrative but with many touches of humour. The story belongs to the wars of the gods and demons. At the end of the last cycle, when the Earth was overwhelmed by the Flood and Brahmā slept in the universal night, Hayagrīva conquered Heaven and carried off the *Veda* from Brahmā's mouth. The rout of Indra and the gods is described with subtle humour and Meṇṭha provoked controversy over his portrayal of Hayagrīva as a noble hero, which, however, reflected greater glory on Viṣṇu who alone could overcome him.

Since Rājaśekhara calls Meṇṭha a reincarnation of Vālmīki, suggesting that he retold the Rāma story, we should search among the *kāvyas* discussed by the critics for a work worthy of such a tribute. By way of conjecture we may draw attention to two remarkable plays which can be reconstructed in outline from the critics. The *Kṛtyārāvaṇa*, 'Rāvaṇa and the Witch', presented the main story from Sītā's abduction to her rescue, in the 'violent' mode of stage business, the *rasa* being the 'furious' but with the 'compassionate' prominent too on account of Rāma's extreme sufferings. 'Rāma Deceived', *Chalitarāma*, shows Rāma misled by surviving enemies, in the apocryphal sequel, into suspecting Sītā's virtue and banishing her. Twin sons are born to her in exile. When they grow up, Lava tries to capture Rāma's sacrificial horse released for a Vedic *aśvamedha*, but is taken prisoner by Lakṣmaṇa, Rāma's brother. At court, Lava recognizes a golden statue of his mother, her substitute at the rite. Explanations follow, Rāma is convinced that Lava is his own son and discovers that the innocent Sītā is still living. In both plays the *Rāmāyaṇa* is treated with great freedom. The style of the quotations seems consistent with Meṇṭha's, including the humour and the absence of lyricism.

Kālidāsa is associated with 'Vikramāditya' in tradition, but this may refer to Skanda Gupta, who used that title, whilst the poet is also supposed to have met the Vākāṭaka Pravarasena II (*c.* 410–40). Essentially a lyric poet, he wrote epics and dramas too, taking advantage of the lyric tendency which had always pervaded *kāvya*. He is appreciated for the *vaidarbha* style and especially for 'sweetness', whilst his waywardness sometimes puzzled the critics, sometimes pleased them (Kuntaka found in it the natural play of genius). Kālidāsa's most quoted work is the lyric poem *Meghasandeśa*, 'Cloud Message', in which a distracted lover far from his beloved attempts to send her a message by a passing cloud at the beginning of the rains. The description of the route to be taken affords opportunity for the utmost fancy in that the landmarks are such as would be thought to appeal to a cloud: beautiful rivers who will return his love, high palaces, mountains. The short epic *Kumārasambhava*, 'Origin of Kumāra', includes Indra's humorous plot to make a father of Śiva, the gods having been defeated (as usual) by a demon, whom only a son of Śiva can kill. The longer epic *Raghuvaṃśa* is a portrait gallery of the kings of Rāma's line, illustrating the four ends, virtue, wealth, pleasure, and release, pursued by the different rulers. Only in relation to this discussion of ends can we see any thematic unity and development in the poem, which otherwise is a series of detached episodes. At the conclusion the dissolute Agnivarṇa carries pleasure to a ruinous extreme, but dies leaving his pregnant queen with 'royal fortune' and hope for the future of the dynasty under the guidance of the ministers.

Of Kālidāsa's three plays, the *Mālavikāgnimitra* is dramatically the best and the least lyrical; it is probably the earliest. The story is a love intrigue at the Śuṅga court, the comic *rasa* perhaps predominating. The *Vikramorvaśīya* is a musical play (*toṭaka*, a variety of *nāṭaka*) on the Vedic story of Purūravas and the nymph Urvaśī. The main interest is the character study of Urvaśī, who is purely human. Lyric and *lāsya* elements appear, especially in the pathetic scene where the hero has lost her. The *Abhijñānaśākuntala*, 'Token Śakuntalā', is admired for its lyricism, but its hero does nothing, things happen to him through fate, a curse or divine intervention, his character is a blank. The heroine is better characterized but also the helpless plaything of supernatural powers. Thus there is no real action but only a certain depth of helpless feeling. The story is changed from the more realistic history in the *Mahābhārata* of an ancestor of the Bhāratas. Kālidāsa is a poet of love, of women sharply portrayed, and for Ānandavardhana one of the great exponents of suggestion.

The *Setubandha*, 'Building of the Causeway', by Pravarasena II, is a Māhārāṣṭrī epic on Rāma's invasion of Laṅkā, the main theme being loyalty, especially in the character of Rāma's ally Sugrīva. On the march, Rāma subdues the Ocean God so that his army of monkeys can build a causeway of mountains across to Laṅkā. At the critical moment of the battle, when Rāma is wounded, Sugrīva's heroism saves the day.

'The Kick' is a satirical monologue by Śyāmilaka (fifth century) set in 'Imperial City', evidently Ujjayinī, with a collection of 'rogues' or parasites at least partly historical and contemporary. The Producer requests informers and hypocrites to leave the theatre, since the play is only for enjoyment. The parasite, Śyāmilaka himself, then convenes the assembly of parasites to try a harlot for the sin of kicking a foolish brāhman. But they find the fault is the brāhman's and prescribe a suitable expiation for him.

Saṃghadāsa's *Vasudevahiṇḍi*, 'Wanderings of Vasudeva', shows the enrichment of Jaina universal history by the incorporation of some of the adventures of Naravāhanadatta from the *Bṛhatkathā*, but narrated of Kṛṣṇa's father Vasudeva instead. Saṃghadāsa knew he was writing fiction in this prose novel in Māhārāṣṭrī, though he illustrates Jaina doctrine by making the adventures the result of action in a former life, but later writers, such as Hemacandra, accepted it all as sober history.

Amaruka perfectly exemplifies the technique of producing *rasa* by presenting emotional situations, in this case a 'Hundred' (*Śataka*) situations between lovers, each described in miniature in a single verse. Though the form is similar, we are far from the village life of Sātavāhana, for the heroes here are aristocrats or gentry, like the wealthy amateurs of the *Kāmasūtra*. Using long metres, Amaruka concentrates an extraordinary amount of action or talk in each verse, hinting at still more in the past. He writes with tenderness; nothing is higher than love.

Bhāravi's (sixth century) *Kirātārjunīya* is the best epic now available, presenting, as Kuntaka points out, a short episode from the *Mahābhārata* as a complete whole. The narrative style is truly epic and heroic, sweeping vigorously upward from the tense opening scene, the disturbing report of a spy, to the sudden climax when Śiva, the supposed Kirāta fighting Arjuna over a hunting incident, reveals himself and grants the decisive weapons which will enable the Pāṇḍavas to win the Bhārata battle (thus the outcome of the entire *Mahābhārata* is here determined, the story is ended). The rich burden of description customary for an epic is brought in naturally by such scenes as Indra's army of nymphs attacking the ascetic Arjuna in the mountains. The characterization is brilliant.

Subandhu's novel *Vāsavadattā* is a highly romantic and improbable story treasured by the paṇḍits for the double meanings in almost every sentence.

Viśākhadatta's *Mudrārākṣasa*, 'Signet Rākṣasa', is a play of political intrigue and secret agents, in which the famous minister Cāṇakya (Kauṭalya) destroys the remaining enemies of Candragupta Maurya after the death of Nanda, winning over the best man among them, Nanda's minister Rākṣasa, to the new king's cause. This is one of the rare works in which anything like a 'national' or 'Indian' sentiment is suggested in place of the usual universalistic outlook, most of the enemies being 'barbarians' (*mlecchas*). Only fragments are now available of Viśākhadatta's other plays: the *Devīcandragupta* on Candra 'Vikramāditya' killing the last Śaka, the *Abhisārikāvañcitaka* which is a sequel to Bhāsa's 'Dream Vāsavadattā', and the *Rāghavānanda* bringing out the heroic character of Rāma in the war against Rāvaṇa. All these plays were popular with the old critics and their author was one who excelled at portraying character on the stage.

We may well remember here the rich repertory of the classical theatre in this period by naming a few apparently lost plays important in the discussions of the critics: *Nalavijaya* in which the loss of Nala's kingdom was reported, not shown, in accordance with a convention; 'Rambhā and Nalakūbara'; *Uṣāharaṇa* on Uṣā and Aniruddha; 'Menakā and Nahuṣa', a *toṭaka* on the union of a king and a nymph; 'Śarmiṣṭhā's Marriage' (with Yayāti); 'Joy of the Pāṇḍavas'; *Rāghavābhyudaya*, with Kaikeyī as the root of all Rāma's misfortunes; *Jānakīrāghava* featuring Sītā and deviating greatly from the *Rāmāyaṇa* by bringing Rāvaṇa in at the outset as Rāma's rival for her hand. The last seems the best of these 'histories'. In contrast we have six famous comedies: *Śaśivilāsa*, *Śaśikalā*, *Kalikeli*, *Sairandhrikā*, *Bṛhatsubhadraka* and *Vikaṭanitambā*, all named after their heroes or heroines; the last, 'Broad Buttocks', a learned lady who suffered from her husband's ignorance.

From the Emperor Harṣa (seventh century) we have three plays which have stood the test of time in the theatre, as well as two Buddhist hymns. The *Nāgānanda*, a *bodhisattva* play like Candragomin's, has held the stage down to the present day in Keralā, though the audiences there are not Buddhist. The *rasa* has always been a matter of philosophical controversy and practical interpretation; the excellent commentator Śivarāma concludes that it may be either the calmed or the heroic, besides which all the others are developed too in a harmonious whole. The other two are 'light plays' on invented stories about Udayana, *Ratnāvalī* and *Priyadarśikā*. Harṣa's contemporary, the Pallava King Mahendravarman I, wrote a comedy *Mattavilāsa* satirizing the quarrels among ascetics. The *Veṇīsaṃhāra* of Nārāyaṇa (in Orissa?) has been accepted as the best play on the Bhārata Battle. Yudhiṣṭhira's brother Bhīma is the hero, because he kills Duryodhana and binds up Draupadī's braid of hair (*veṇī*) which she had kept dishevelled until her humiliation was avenged. The play opens with his impatience to fight, whilst Yudhiṣṭhira is still trying for a peaceful settlement.

Bāṇa at Harṣa's court is universally regarded as the greatest master of Sanskrit prose. His style varies according to the content and the genre (biography bold and studied, novel delicate and flowing), but with more of what Kuntaka calls 'cultivated' ('beautiful' through art). The *Harṣacarita* is a biography of the young Harṣa, explaining how he found royal fortune. *Kādambarī* is a psychological novel of the timidities and missed opportunities of youth, leading to tragedy; but no tragedy is final in Indian literature, since transmigration may bring the lovers together again. Unluckily Bāṇa died leaving the novel unfinished just before the expected culminating tragedy of Kādambarī herself. His son wrote an ending, we do not know how close to his father's intentions, and others also tried their hands at the enigma. Bāṇa's dramas, of which the best-known was on the Bhārata Battle, seem to be lost, but we have his hymn in praise of the Great Goddess (Caṇḍī, Pārvatī), full of verbal fireworks such as alliteration. Mayūra, said to be Bāṇa's father-in-law, goes much further in this word play in his hymn to the Sun God.

Of epics in the seventh century we may note first two 'grammatical' poems, in which the narrative is devised in such a way as to provide systematic illustration of Sanskrit derivations. Bhaṭṭi's *Rāvaṇavadha* thus retells the story of Rāma, often with humorous effect, incorporating as a break four cantos illustrating Bhāmaha's poetics. It proved popular with students and was even translated into Javanese. Bhosa (Bhaumaka, Bhīma, Vyoṣa, seem corruptions) in his *Rāvaṇārjunīya* performed the more difficult feat of illustrating the whole of Pāṇini's grammar (except Vedic forms) in the exact order of the original. The story is the defeat of Rāvaṇa by Arjuna Kārtavīrya.

It is possible that the mysterious Bhartṛhari, author of the 'Three Hundred' lyrics on policy, the sensitive, and renunciation, was Bhaṭṭi (=Bhartṛ). Bhartṛhari is the philosopher, bitter and ironical; his vacillation between love and detachment sometimes baffled critics seeking to determine the *rasa*.

Dharmakīrti, the Buddhist philosopher, may be compared with Bhartṛhari, though with a different individual turn, in his lyrics of despair at seeing how anything good excites only envy in others, beauty likewise being wasted.

Māgha's epic 'Slaying of Śiśupāla' is outwardly regular, but in content he is essentially a lyric poet, so that half the poem is like an anthology of descriptive verses, much appreciated by critics, relating to places the hero happened to pass on his expedition. The story is Kṛṣṇa's killing of Śiśupāla at Yudhiṣṭhira's *rājasūya* consecration, but changing the original narrative in the *Mahābhārata* completely to create more *rasa*, as Kuntaka points out.

Daṇḍin, the critic, was also famous, says Rājaśekhara, for two other works, an epic telling two stories simultaneously (those of Rāma and Yudhiṣṭhira) and the novel *Avantisundarī*. The poetic *tour de force* seems lost; of the novel we have 400 pages supplemented by a summary, but the conclusion is still missing. Deliberately confounding history and fiction, or biography and novel, according to his own critical doctrine, Daṇḍin sets his imaginary story of Rājahaṃsa and his two sons against a detailed panorama of Purāṇic history. The latter having in part the form of prophecy by ancient sages, Daṇḍin uses the humorous device of having King Ṛpuñjaya of Magadha (sixth century B.C.) read his own history, with dismay at learning he is to be the last of his line. The King takes evasive action, retiring to a forest and consulting a sage, who enables him to survive more than a millennium until all the prophesied dynasties of Magadha have petered out. Ṛpuñjaya then returns and consecrates his son Rājahaṃsa, but he is defeated by the King of Avanti and driven into hiding in the forest. Here his sons Haṃsavāhana and Rājavāhana, reincarnations of Kṛṣṇa's sons Pradyumna and Sāmba, are born, and the elder is mysteriously abducted by a wild goose. Rājavāhana grows up to restore the family fortune by conquering the world. The critical point in his career is his clandestine marriage with Avantisundarī, daughter of his father's enemy, which almost proves fatal to him and further embroils him with the wizard Vīraśekhara, son of Mānasavega of the *Bṛhatkathā*, who was about to abduct her for himself. Rājavāhana is taken captive and carried along with the Avanti army, to be released in a battle which follows and reunited with seven boyhood friends who have meanwhile made their fortunes. The favourite episode of this reunion, each telling his own adventures, has been circulated separately under the misleading title 'Ten Boys' (or 'Ten Princes'). The continuation beyond this is missing, but it is clear that the story will culminate with the conquest of the wizards, rescue of Avantisundarī, and reunion with Haṃsavāhana (who is perhaps Naravāhanadatta temporarily ejected from his empire).

Daṇḍin is fond of fantastic incidents and coincidences, explained by his philosophy of fatalism, but in contrast he has many episodes of extreme realism demonstrating the attainment of power and wealth through unscrupulous cunning. His outlook is completely amoral.

Kumāradāsa from Ceylon may have studied with Daṇḍin in Kāñcī. His epic *Jānakīharaṇa* retells the *Rāmāyaṇa* from the incarnation of Viṣṇu as Rāma, preceded by the curse on his father which is supposed to have caused his exile, to the victory over Rāvaṇa. The style is more epic than Māgha and the narrative rapid and with much briefer descriptions; there is much play of sounds.

Mātrarāja is one of the masters of Kuntaka's 'intermediate' style. His *Tāpasavatsarāja* is a play on the same story as Bhāsa's 'Dream Vāsavadattā', but with Udayana as the central character instead of Vāsavadattā. The *Udāttarāghava*, 'Exalted Rāghavas' (Rāma and Bharata), like Bhāsa's 'Statue', starts with Rāma's interrupted consecration and exile and ends with the triumphant reunion of the two brothers. Mātrarāja made serious changes in the story in order to enhance the characters morally, thereby provoking controversy. The Emperor Yaśovarman (eighth century) objected to such changes, in the Prologue of his own Rāma play *Rāmābhyudaya*. This, though not now available, is extensively known as a classic of dramatic construction much discussed and quoted by the old critics. Adhering closely to the *Rāmāyaṇa*, Yaśovarman produces unity of action by starting only with Rāma's first clash with the demons, in exile. The action and characterization are powerful (e.g. Rāvaṇa's anger).

Bhavabhūti, the favourite poet and dramatist of some connoisseurs, from Mahārāṣṭra settled at Yaśovarman's court in Kānyakubja. His *Mālatīmādhava* is a 'fiction' of the triumph of love over obstacles, especially over political convenience. A king proposes to have the daughter of one of his ministers offered to a court favourite, as part of a political alliance. The girl loves another and the lovers resist the plan, aided by sympathetic Buddhist nuns in the role of go-betweens. In an unsuccessful attempt at elopement the hero shows his mettle, attracts popular support, and thus so impresses the king that he changes his plans, preferring to have a brave young man under his patronage. The *Uttararāmacarita* takes up the apocryphal last book of the *Rāmāyaṇa*, the grievous renewed exile of Sītā. Public opinion held her unfit to be queen after being the prisoner of Rāvaṇa. Here Bhavabhūti brings out most fully the pathos of human experience, bitter yet touched by the sweetness of association with happy moments in the past, the contrast intensifying both the pain and the sweetness. The minds of sublime heroes are as hard as diamonds yet as soft as flowers, says Bhavabhūti, since Rāma has unflinchingly done his public duty whilst privately suffering mental agony. A second Rāma 'history', which is incomplete as now available, the *Mahāvīracarita*, unified the action by introducing Rāvaṇa at the beginning as Rāma's rival (cf. the *Jānakīrāghava*, in which, however, Sītā is the central character instead of Rāma). Disappointed when Rāma wins Sītā, it is Rāvaṇa who brings about the intrigue and Rāma's exile, placing Sītā within his reach. Bhavabhūti's plays are in the best dramatic tradition of conflict and passion, but on a scale giving the fullest scope to lyrics evoking the feelings of his characters, in relation to society and even more to nature. His lyrics are perhaps unequalled in expressiveness and in the beauty of their sound.

Vākpatirāja, also at Yaśovarman's court, wrote an enigmatic epic in Māhārāṣṭrī, 'Slaying of the Gauḍa', on his king. The expected history of the victory over a king of Magadha (= Gauḍa) is merely alluded to and the body of the narrative describes a pleasure excursion, rather than a military expedition, to the four quarters of India. The nostalgic atmosphere and bitter verses on good and evil, on the vanity of the present age when success is reserved for mediocrity and jealously withheld from excellence, suggest that Yaśovarman had already met his tragic end in battle with the King of Kaśmīra. The ephemeral military victories of a generous poet-emperor, dear to the assembly to whom Vākpatirāja reads his epic, are superseded by a more durable poetic conquest.

The eighth century is rich in extant novels. Kutūhala's *Līlāvatī*, sometimes bracketed with Bāṇa's *Kādambarī* as typical novels, is unlike it in being in Prākrit (Māhārāṣṭrī) and in verse. The critics found verse acceptable for Prākrit novels (including Apabhraṃśa and in due course Hindī), the form being otherwise unaffected. Kutūhala like Daṇḍin blends history and fiction, for his hero is Sātavāhana and is guided by Nāgārjuna, but marries a princess from Ceylon after an adventure in the 'Underworld' (Pātāla) and other fanciful episodes; in fact he claims to have invented the story in order to amuse his wife.

Haribhadra's immense *Samarāditya*, in Māhārāṣṭrī prose, is a Jaina 'virtue' (*dharma*) novel, being written from the standpoint of ethics instead of pleasure or worldly success. It is also an 'entire' (*sakala*) novel, in that it follows the heroes' experiences through a series of lives, from the origin of a subconscious disposition (the 'cause', *nidāna*) which torments them until its secret is revealed to them. Samarāditya in a former life was negligent towards an intended guest, an ascetic; the latter misunderstood this as deliberate injury and conceived an inveterate hatred, pursuing and injuring his imagined enemy through nine lives. Thus in one they are husband and wife and the wife repeatedly tries to kill her husband through this irrational hatred. The *Dhūrtākhyāna*, 'Rogues' History', is an 'illustrating novel' satirizing Brahmanism and especially Purāṇic history and mythology. A group of rogues temporarily immobilized by the rains pass the time by holding a contest in telling lies about themselves, the loser to stand dinner for the party. Each lie must be confirmed as credible by adducing a parallel from the *Purāṇas*. In the end a female rogue confounds the others with a tale to the effect that they are all her runaway slaves. Haribhadra makes it clear that his aim in debunking myths is not sectarian but rationalist (*yuktimant*): his satire is directed at the growth of fantasy which has concealed the truth hidden in all the Indian religions.

Haribhadra's pupil Uddyotana wrote another long Māhārāṣṭrī 'entire novel', in *campū* form, illustrating the driving force of five passions, anger, pride, deceit, greed, and delusion, in five souls through several lives. He calls it a 'mixed' novel, depicting pleasure and success as well as the dominant virtue theme. It does indeed contain interesting episodes such as meeting a group of alchemists in the mountains smelting metals and trying to obtain gold.

Dāmodaragupta's 'illustrating novel' *Kuṭṭanīmata*, 'Theory of the Bawd', is in verse though in Sanskrit. The heroine goes to a marvellously ugly old bawd for instruction in making money from wealthy citizens and receives it with stories illustrating the science of harlotry and such pitfalls as falling in love and trouble with fathers. The reader of this satire, its author claims, will never be deceived by parasites, hetairas, rogues, and bawds.

Murāri, 'disregarding Bhavabhūti', again dramatized the main Rāma story. His *Anargharāghava* includes so many lyrics, admittedly beautiful but often hardly relevant, as to make his drama too tenuous.

Yogeśvara in the Pāla Empire of Magadha is known through anthologies for his vivid descriptions of the hard but usually cheerful life of the villages.

In the ninth century Abhinanda retold part of the Rāma story as a Sanskrit epic, beginning about the same point as Pravarasena. He begins in a simple style not unlike Vālmīki's, but with numerous figures, and elaborates the speeches in a leisurely manner. This *Rāmacarita* keeps close to the original and is very long, though its descriptions are strictly subordinate to the narrative. Abhinanda's sweet, melodious language, imagery, and occasional theological reflections made him a favourite of some critics. He also wrote dramas, among which the heroic play *Bhīmaparākrama* on an episode from the *Mahābhārata* is available.

Ratnākara's *Haravijaya* brought almost equal acclaim from the critics, though it is an epic opposite to Abhinanda's in every way except great length. There was little to narrate, for Śiva's victory over the demon Andhaka is a very simple story, so the epic is instead filled with descriptions, exceeding even Māgha in these and in linguistic difficulty. The description of Śiva's *tāṇḍava* dance is an appropriate and attractive opening, establishing a transcendental setting.

Śivasvāmin's epic *Kapphiṇābhyudaya* returns to the scale, and partly the style, of Māgha, whilst the poet claims to follow Meṇṭha and his style varies greatly according to the topic. The story is from Buddhist legend: a war in which the Buddha intervenes as peacemaker and sends the invader home to rule justly. Buddhaghoṣa's *Padyacūḍāmaṇi* on the life of the Buddha is an expression of devotion rather than an epic.

Apabhraṃśa epic, its conventions established by Caturmukha whose works have not yet been found, comes into its own with two examples by Svayambhū, the *Padmacarita* on Rāma and the *Ariṣṭanemicarita* on the twenty-second *jina* and the Jaina version of the events of the *Mahābhārata* with the life of Kṛṣṇa. Svayambhū takes his narratives from earlier Jaina works; he is praised for the beauty of his language and figurative expressions and is remarkable for his tolerant and syncretistic outlook.

Śaktibhadra's *Āścaryacūḍāmaṇi* has proved one of the most popular plays, partly because it makes so much of the transformations of the demons, particularly Rāvaṇa and his sister, going beyond Mātrarāja, who already had several such disguises. The play begins with Rāma's encounter with Rāvaṇa's sister disguised and Sītā's abduction by the disguised Rāvaṇa, and ends with Rāma's triumph. The transformations are counteracted (but too late) by a magic ring and the magic crest jewel which gives the play its title.

The philosopher Jayanta wrote a play on the religious situation in Kaśmīra, the *Āgamaḍambara*, 'Pomp of Scriptures'. His aim is to show the superior knowledge and humanity of the brāhmans and satirize the Buddhists, Jainas, Lokāyatikas, and Kāpālikas. Though some unworthy sects should be proscribed, the better schools share the high moral purpose of the Vedic tradition and among these there should be toleration; their scriptures are different entrances to the same house.

King Kulaśekhara (*c.* A.D. 900) wrote two plays, which have remained popular, to inaugurate new techniques of production on the Keralā stage, claiming to apply Ānandavardhana's doctrine of 'revealed' meaning. It is supposed that all the reforms of the Keralā actors stem from him, including the repetition of the speeches in gesture language and the extemporized 'Tamil' (now Malayālam) patter of the 'fool', equivocally making fun of present-day personalities along with other characters in the play, but this seems unlikely. The *Subhadrādhanañjaya* has the story of Arjuna eloping with Kṛṣṇa's sister, after numerous misunderstandings and the opposition of Kṛṣṇa's brother. The *Tapatīsaṃvaraṇa* is the love of Saṃvaraṇa, one of the Bhārata emperors, and the daughter of the Sun God. Kulaśekhara's novel *Āścaryamañjarī*, praised by Rājaśekhara, seems to be lost. A popular heroic play *Kalyāṇasaugandhika*, on Bhīma fetching the Saugandhika Flower for Draupadī but being challenged by his unknown brother Hanumant on the way, was written by Nīlakaṇṭha, perhaps at Kulaśekhara's court. Vāsudeva there composed a series of rhymed epics in Sanskrit, on Yudhiṣṭhira, Kṛṣṇa, Śiva, and Nala. Though a regular feature of Apabhraṃśa and modern Indo-Aryan poetry, rhyme in Sanskrit is a special effect like alliteration or punning. Vāsudeva's rhymes are complicated, but seem natural and effortless, which explains the widespread appreciation of his works. Līlāśuka probably at Kulaśekhara's court wrote the very popular lyric *Kṛṣṇakarṇāmṛta*, on Kṛṣṇa as the sexually precocious infant loved by all women, but interpreted as symbolizing God attracting all souls, thus an early example of Vaiṣṇava devotional *kāvya*. Another classic rhyming poem, partly double-meaning also, is Nītivarman's *Kīcakavadha* on Bhīma slaying Kīcaka, of unknown date. Dhanañjaya's *Dvisandhāna* (*c.* A.D. 800) is the earliest double-meaning epic available, simultaneously narrating the *Rāmāyaṇa* and *Mahābhārata*.

Rājaśekhara was a junior contemporary of Kulaśekhara. Though primarily a dramatist, he is appreciated rather for the innumerable brilliant lyric verses scattered through his works, being perhaps the most popular poet with the anthologists. His epic *Haravilāsa* seems to be lost. His *Bālarāmāyaṇa* is perhaps the longest play ever written, exceeding even Murāri's on the same subject, and he even remarks that it is designed to be read, expecting that it would not often be performed. Yet, unlike Murāri, Rājaśekhara has some very effective scenes, such as the confrontation of Rāvaṇa and Sītā in Act I on the occasion of Sītā's *svayaṃvara* ('self-choice' wedding). Of a similar play on the *Mahābhārata* we have only the first two acts. A 'light play' *Viddhaśālabhañjikā* is a comedy of palace intrigue, as is the *Karpūramañjarī*, a *saṭṭaka* or light play in Māhārāṣṭrī. The vivid expressions which charmed the anthologists bring a strong sense of Rājaśekhara's lively personality to the reader. This is perhaps strongest of all in his critical work *Kāvyamīmāṃsā*, where he sets up in pseudo-pedantic style as the model professional writer and legislates a life of palatial comfort, but strenuous well-organized work, for authors.

Kṣemīśvara (tenth century) follows Rājaśekhara with two plays on stories not new to the theatre but not available to us in earlier dramas. The *Naiṣadhānanda* on Nala is particularly effective, with its opening scene of the hero stopped by Indra, then his exiling and the doubly portrayed incident of Nala's separation from Damayantī, presented by both of them in turn. The *Caṇḍakauśika* on Hariścandra opens ominously but with touches of irony through the presence of the 'fool' and the queen's groundless suspicion of her husband's night vigil; after this the compassionate and horrific *rasas* are developed to the utmost in the slave market and cemetery scenes. This play has the atmosphere of a Buddhist *bodhisattva* drama such as Candragomin's, presented in Brāhmanical terms. In both plays Kṣemīśvara is faithful to his *itihāsa* sources. The style is simple and the action relatively rapid: unlike Rājaśekhara's, these are primarily plays for the stage and not for readers and anthologists. It is remarkable that both deal with utter disaster, the loss of kingdoms followed by terrible trials but eventual restoration, and possible that the stories were chosen as comment on contemporary events (Mahīpāla's struggles).

Bhallaṭa's (*fl.* 880–900) collection of *anyāpadeśas*, 'citations of something else', is the classic in a lyric form much appreciated later, which criticizes social abuses through the imagery of natural phenomena. His target is the worthless and crooked people who successfully push their way into positions of authority and wealth.

In Siddha's great allegorical novel of transmigration, *Upamitibhavaprapañcā* (A.D. 906), 'release' is the only escape from the tyranny of King Action and Queen Time. Jainism is thus shown as a subversive political movement. The hero struggles upwards from life to life, this being an 'entire' novel, against evil passions. Whereas Haribhadra, his model, studied senseless evil in human relationships, Siddha is concerned with internal struggles.

Dhanapāla's *Tilakamañjarī* (*c.* 970), though formally similar, is an interesting contrast to Bāṇa's *Kādambarī*. Since the author completed it, it offers a model of construction of a novel, beginning about the middle and bringing in other segments of the story in the wrong order narrated by characters, maintaining suspense to the end. Though the author was a Jaina, this is purely a 'pleasure' novel like those of Guṇāḍhya and Bāṇa. The more than ninety characters are quite different from Bāṇa's: youth is less diffident and tragic, especially in the person of the impetuous Malayasundarī, and the heroes are resourceful, though scrupulous (unlike Daṇḍin's).

A different Dhanapāla about the same time wrote the novel *Bhaviṣyadatta* in Apabhraṃśa verse, a story of merchant life and sea voyages in which a second wife tries to destroy her stepson.

The *campū* now seems to increase in popularity. Trivikrama's *Nala* (*c.* 915) is renowned as a marvellous exercise in double meanings; his simpler *Madālasā* is neglected. Somadeva's *Yaśastilaka* (959) on the Jaina legend of Yaśodhara, a king poisoned by his unfaithful wife, and his subsequent rebirths, resembles an 'entire novel'. His didactic intentions are evident throughout.

Puṣpadanta's *Mahāpurāṇa* is generally acclaimed as the best Apabhraṃśa epic. A modest and disillusioned wanderer who finally accepted patronage with reluctance, his poetry is deeply felt and his wit pungent. The subject is the vast universal history of the Jainas, dominated by the 'sixty-three great men' (including Rāma, Rāvaṇa, Kṛṣṇa, and the *jinas*). A short *Yaśodhara-carita* retells the legend just mentioned. The *Nāgakumāracarita* might be classed as a verse novel, or rather a romance, of an infant prince who falls down a well and is adopted by a dragon, but the story is a traditional one of one of the twenty-four Kāmadevas, the most handsome men.

Three eleventh-century epics are based on contemporary history. Padmagupta's *Navasāhasāṅkacarita* on a Paramāra king of Avanti (Mālava) romanticizes his marriage with a Karṇāṭaka princess into a war with 'demons' and union with a 'dragon' girl after descending into the underworld. But the Paramāra Rājputs themselves are of supernatural origin and their poet relates the creation of their ancestor in Vasiṣṭha's sacrificial fire. Regardless of the history, this epic has been enjoyed by critics for its descriptions and other poetic qualities. The same is true of Bilhaṇa's *Vikramāṅkadevacarita* on a Cālukya emperor, which is close to actual facts yet has been more admired as a purely literary classic. Bilhaṇa also wrote a 'light play' on another patron and the beautiful elegy *Caurapañcāśikā*, supposedly autobiographical, of a liaison with a princess which almost cost him his life. Atula's *Mūṣakavaṃśa* is the history of a dynasty in north Keralā from its legendary origin in the time of Paraśurāma. Though very useful as history, this epic too has been preserved for its poetry.

Lakṣmīdhara's *Cakrapāṇivijaya* is an epic on the traditional story of Kṛṣṇa's defeat of the demon Bāṇa, son of Bali, after the clandestine marriage of his grandson Aniruddha with Bāṇa's daughter Uṣā. There are no long descriptive digressions here, the story of love and war itself giving plenty of scope for the poet's powers. Mahāsena's epic *Pradyumnacarita* gives a Jaina version of the story of Aniruddha's father. Kanakāmara's Apabhraṃśa epic *Karakaṇḍacarita* narrates an old legend of a 'saint' recognized by both Jainas and Buddhists. Jaina epics in several languages, mostly on one or other of the twenty-four *jinas*, are too numerous from the tenth century onwards to be discussed here, despite the literary value of many of them.

Soḍḍhala's *Udayasundarī* (*c*. 1025) is a Sanskrit *campū* novel more romantic and less realistic than most, with metamorphoses and adventures in the underworld and little characterization, but beautifully and imaginatively written. The critic King Bhoja's *Śṛṅgāramañjarī* is an entertaining 'illustrating novel' on the various types of love. These are shown in cautionary tales instructing a geisha on which kinds of lover to accept or avoid, and the heroines generally have a bad time. Bhoja's simple and elegant *campū* version of the *Rāmāyaṇa* has been much more widely appreciated in recent centuries. Vādībhasiṃha's *Gadyacintāmaṇi* is one of the rare prose 'biographies' extant, but on the old Jaina legend of Jīvandhara. This legend owes much to the *Bṛhatkathā* and the work is almost a novel. It is noteworthy for its fine prose style, perhaps second only to Bāṇa's. A more regular biography is Someśvara's *Vikramāṅkābhyudaya*, on his father who was also Bilhaṇa's subject.

Some anonymous popular collections of short stories, of unknown date and in multiple recensions, may be noted here. The *Śukasaptati* has as theme faithless wives and crafty harlots. The *Vetālapañcaviṃśatī* and *Siṃhāsanadvātriṃśika* both concern the legendary Vikramāditya in most versions but originally it seems Sātavāhana was the hero (with Nāgārjuna). In the first, the king has to answer riddles with which the stories end, in the second the stories are about him. We may add that Somadeva II (*c.* 1050) used a sketch of the *Bṛhatkathā* as a frame for a huge collection of stories skilfully narrated, the *Kathāsaritsāgara*. The romance of Mādhavānala and Kāmakandalā is a popular tale of illicit love, ending happily through the intervention of the chivalrous Vikramāditya. The *Malayasundarī* likewise exists in several paraphrases, but the original is attributed to Keśin (seventh century B.C.). In fact it is a romance of magic and a wicked stepmother, a fairy story not likely to be earlier than the ninth century A.D.

Kṣemendra's illustrating novels are bitter satires on corrupt bureaucracy and successful deceit and vice. The *Kalāvilāsa* introduces Mūladeva ('Whose God is Capital') in his School of Theft, instructing a student in the science of deception and the various professions through which greed is satisfied: bureaucracy, harlotry, itinerant music and acting, jewellery, medicine, astrology, drug peddling, trade, begging, imposture, etc. Under bureaucracy the different types of arrogance are treated. These are further displayed as weaknesses in the *Darpadalana*. The *Narmamālā* satirizes the private lives of the bureaucrats and their wives. The *Deśopadeśa* displays scoundrels and cheats, including the miser, parasite, and undisciplined students. The *Samayamātṛkā* is the life of the bawd Kaṅkālī, who outlives her many husbands.

Kṣemendra's plays seem to be lost, but *Prabodhacandrodaya*, a very different allegorical play on Vedānta by his contemporary Kṛṣṇamiśra, has been a model for similar plays advocating various schools of thought.

The best twelfth-century epic is Harṣa's *Naiṣadhacarita* on Nala. The sensitive *rasa* predominates, with much of the comic also. The author was a philosopher and displays his learning, but the descriptive effusions are relevant to the story and the style full of charm. The scale is grand and Harṣa did not finish the work. Sukumāra's *Kṛṣṇavilāsa*, on the young Kṛṣṇa up to his carrying off the Pārijāta, in very simple style, is the most popular epic in Keralā. Maṅkha's *Śrīkaṇṭhacarita* on Śiva burning the three citadels of the demons is among the most beautiful epics, particularly for its descriptions of mountain scenery by the Kāśmīrī author, but its action is brief. Jayānaka's *Pṛthvīrājavijaya* prematurely celebrated the ill-fated Cāhamāna king. Kalhaṇa's *Rājataraṅgiṇī*, a detailed *vaṃśāvalī* or history of Kaśmīra, under the influence of the *Mahābhārata* aims to produce the calmed *rasa* through the contemplation of futile ambitions (the *vaṃśāvalīs* continue the history of the *Purāṇas* and are rarely literary).

The Jaina theatre flourished with eleven plays by the critic Rāmacandra, on Nala, Rāma, Kṛṣṇa, Hariścandra, etc., and three fictions. Rāmabhadra and Hastimalla dramatized Jaina legends. Heroic plays are now numerous, by Vijayapāla, Prahlādanadeva, Kāñcana, and Vatsarāja as well as Rāmacandra. The same Vatsarāja (*c.* 1200) wrote examples of the three types of archaic play on the gods and demons, a comedy, and a satirical monologue; his gods and demons are as humorous as his bogus ascetic and gambler. Śaṅkhadhara's *Laṭakamelaka* is a two-act comedy in which a ninety-nine-year-old bawd finds herself a husband among a crowd of charlatans. Jayadeva's *Gītagovinda*, a *rāgakāvya* drama in songs linked by narrative, is a most popular classic which has often been imitated. Its Sanskrit lyrics use the metres of vernacular Apabhraṃśa to express Rādhā's love for Kṛṣṇa.

The Jaina novel continued to flourish (relatively few non-Jaina novels have been preserved, though many titles are known from the critics). Dhaneśvara's *Surasundarī*, in Māhārāṣṭrī verse, is a regular novel in the manner of the *Tilakamañjarī*, except that at the end the hero and heroine leave the world and attain enlightenment. Sādhāraṇa's *Vilāsavatī* is in Apabhraṃśa and Mahendrasūri's *Narmadāsundarī* is a *dharma* novel in Māhārāṣṭrī verse and prose.

The Turkish conquests of more than half India between 900 and 1300 were perhaps the most destructive in human history. As Muslims, the conquerors aimed not only to destroy all other religions but also to abolish secular culture. Their burning of libraries explains the large gaps in our knowledge of earlier literature. Our view now depends mainly on what has been preserved in the far south, in Keralā, supplemented by some Jaina libraries which miraculously escaped and by such outlying collections as those of Nepal. Though the Indian tradition was thus cut off over wide areas, it developed vigorously where Indian rule continued, including Rājasthān, Orissā, etc., as well as the south. In fact about 90 per cent of the extant Sanskrit literature, even, belongs to the period since A.D. 1200 and was written in the regions remaining under Indian rule. If we now devote little space to it, compared with the classics above, that should not be regarded as an adverse judgement (we reject the prejudiced opinion about 'decadence') but as due partly to lack of space and partly to the general neglect and lack of printed editions. What follows is a small selection among the noteworthy *kāvyas*.

Amaracandra's *Bālabhārata* has been popular in Rājasthān as distilling the essence of the whole *Mahābhārata* in a *kāvya* epic. The author belonged to the literary circle of the minister Vastupāla of Gujarāt in the thirteenth century, from which more than ten epics and six dramas survive to show the work of such a group. Among these, the works of Someśvara and Bālacandra are outstanding and the play 'Crushing of the Arrogance of the Amīr' by Jayasiṃha is remarkable as presenting the contemporary history of Vastupāla's victory over the Turks. In this age of perpetual Turkish wars there is a strong turn towards heroic themes. In Orissā, Jayadeva's *Prasannarāghava*, though widely studied for its difficulty and word music, is a variation on Murāri's Rāma play. Sakalavidyācakravartin's *Gadyakarṇāmṛta* is a biography of a Hoysala emperor of Karṇāṭaka. The lyrics of Utprekṣāvallabha and Lakṣmīdāsa are admired. Of dramas in the south, we may note Kavivallabha's fiction and Ravivarman's *Pradyumnābhyudaya*.

Among many interesting playwrights in the fourteenth century are: Pratāparudra, for plays on Yayāti and on Uṣā; Narasiṃha who made a well-constructed drama out of the novel *Kādambarī*; Pūrṇasarasvatī who staged a delightful fable of a wild goose marrying a lotus amid dangers from an elephant, a thundercloud, and a storm; Sukumāra for a Rāma play; and Jyotirīśvara in whose comedy two 'ascetics' quarrel over a woman and call in a brāhman arbitrator who decides to keep her for himself. A satirical monologue popular in Keralā since the reign of Rāmavarman seems inappropriately entitled *Viṭanidrā* in one manuscript and is therefore nameless as well as anonymous. The intrigue is quite different from earlier plays of the type. Agastya's epic *Bālabhārata* has been more popular in the south than Amaracandra's in the north. It is perhaps superior in narrative power, whilst shorter and more independent. Agastya, a great master of Sanskrit expression, wrote also a prose *Kṛṣṇacarita* based on the *Bhāgavata Purāṇa*, in a sweet and flowing style and producing the atmosphere of a novel rather than a biography. The *Purāṇa* source was a relatively modern one, itself almost a *kāvya*, which replaced the *Harivaṃśa* supplement to the *Mahābhārata* and became extraordinarily popular as the Kṛṣṇa cult spread. Among other *kāvyas* based on it, the *campū* of the 'New' Kālidāsa (date uncertain) is very famous. Vidyācakravartin's fine but rather alliterative epic *Rukmiṇīkalyāṇa* follows the same source. In this century the three rival systems of Vedānta blossomed in the shelter of Vijayanagara with poetic as well as philosophical champions. The Advaitin Vidyāraṇya wrote an epic on the founder of his school, the Dvaitin Nārāyaṇa one on his and many other poetic works. Other Dvaitins wrote epics on different episodes of the Kṛṣṇa cycle. The Viśiṣṭādvaitin Veṅkaṭanātha perhaps deserves his greater literary fame than any of these with his epic *Yādavābhyudaya* on the birth and rise of Kṛṣṇa, a lyric poem and an allegorical play. More interesting and original than any of these is the Princess Gaṅgā's epic *Madhurāvijaya* on her husband's victory over the Turks in south India, with circumstantial descriptions such as the horrors of the Turkish atrocities in the places they had occupied. It was not new for a woman to write a major *kāvya*, for the critics mention several in earlier centuries, such as Śīlā who emulated Bāṇa as a novelist, but nothing seems to survive except the mysterious Vijayā's play *Kaumudīmahotsava* of uncertain date. Dāmodara's epic *Śivavilāsa* on the marriage of Rāmavarman of Keralā is interesting for social history. Kṛṣṇānanda took the Nala story and wrote an epic contrasting with Harṣa's in being short, complete, flowing easily in *vaidarbha* style, and free from digressions. Ahobala's *Virūpākṣavasantotsava* is a most entertaining *campū* describing the crowds at a popular festival. Guṇasamṛddhi's *Añjanāsundarī* continues the series of Jaina *dharma* novels.

The greatest fifteenth-century writer was probably Ḍiṇḍima (Kavisārvabhauma), praised by later authors, but his works, including an epic *Rāmābhyudaya* and a comedy, are not yet printed. Kāmākṣī, apparently his daughter-in-law, modestly praises him in her own 'New' *Rāmābhyudaya*, called 'exquisite' by a modern critic. Other members of the Ḍiṇḍima family wrote historical epics on the Vijayanagara emperors. The circle of the Eighteen and a Half in Keralā is famous and marks a peak of activity in the theatre and in poetry (Uddaṇḍa, Dāmodarabhaṭṭa, etc.). Gopāla's comic *campū* describes the eleventh *avatāra* of Viṣṇu—as a mango. Śaṅkara's epic *Kṛṣṇavijaya* with its delightful word music is second only to Sukumāra's in popularity in Keralā. In Rājasthān Nayacandra's tragic historical epic *Hammīra* on a Cāhamāna king introduced a new spirit into heroic poetry. In Orissā and Āndhra a historical *campū* by Vāsudevaratha and a biography by Vāmana are more traditional in outlook. Ananta's *Bhārata* is recognized as one of the best *campūs*, mainly for its elaborate style. The tradition of the drama in Mithilā was continued by Vidyāpati, using a mixture of Sanskrit and Maithilī (instead of Prākrit). His modernizing ideas appear also in his Sanskrit illustrating novel *Puruṣaparīkṣā*, introducing recent heroes in place of Purāṇic ones.

The 'classical' literature in fact everywhere developed in the closest interaction with the 'modern', i.e. with the vernacular. In the north it is arbitrary to draw a line between 'Hindī' (Braj, Rājasthānī, Maithilī, etc.) and Apabhraṃśa, for they are the same language, using the same genres and metres. Tulsīdās's epic has the same form as Puṣpadanta's. In the south, Sanskrit and Dravidian writers share ideas. The Oriyā *Mahābhārata*, *Rāmāyaṇa*, and *Bhāgavata*, assimilating antiquity into the life of the fifteenth and sixteenth centuries, influenced the Sanskrit epics of Divākara, Mārkaṇḍeya, and Jīvadeva. The last also wrote plays and belongs to the Vaiṣṇava movement of the sixteenth century, for which Rūpa produced his theory of devotional drama on Kṛṣṇa and plays exemplifying it. Many such plays were written and performed in Orissā, then circulated elsewhere, and popular forms such as the *rāgakāvya* and one-act *goṣṭhī* (e.g. Jayadeva's *Vaiṣṇavāmṛta*) were revived for the purpose. The Keralā variety of Vaiṣṇavism is expressed in Nārāyaṇa's lyric *Nārāyaṇīya* on the whole life of Kṛṣṇa, probably the finest devotional poem in Sanskrit. This Nārāyaṇa is among the greatest and most prolific Sanskrit writers of recent centuries. He wrote a long series of *campūs* on Purāṇic and Vedic themes for performance as *kūttu* monologues by comic actors. The Emperor Kṛṣṇadevarāya of Vijayanagara wrote a Kṛṣṇa play. Queen Tirumalā's *Varadāmbikāpariṇaya* is a beautiful biographical *campū* of her husband Acyutarāya, concluding remarkably with his marriage to another queen and consecration of the latter's son as heir apparent. Equal in style and much richer in content is the long biography *Vyāsayogicarita* of a contemporary logician by Somanātha.

In the seventeenth century Jagannātha, moving between Āndhra, Assam, and the Mughal Empire, reflects the brief flickering of Indian culture within that Empire in the wake of Akbar. His Sanskrit lyrics are popular with the paṇḍits. Jagadīśvara's *Hāsyārṇava* is a comedy satirizing King River of Bad Policy and his depraved administration and probably aimed at the Mughal government after it had reversed Akbar's policy in 1632. The Keralā king Mānaveda, after his *Pūrvabhārata campū* which complements Ananta's and is even more difficult, achieved a unique success with his play *Kṛṣṇagīti* which today is still performed nightly at Guruvayur (with one night a week rest). In form it is a *rāgakāvya* and the prototype of *kathakali*, but with songs in Sanskrit. It covers the entire life of Kṛṣṇa, following especially Śaṅkara's epic. The great upsurge of religion in this period was partly balanced by an output of satirical monologues and comedies too numerous to list and presenting every conceivable subject. A more elaborate satire is Veṅkaṭādhvarin's *campū Viśvaguṇādarśa*, a dialogue between an optimist and a pessimist; it contains one of the earliest references to the British (at Madras). Bracketed with this among the best *campūs* is Nīlakaṇṭha's *Nīlakaṇṭhavijaya*, on the churning of the ocean by the gods and demons and how Śiva got his blue throat, which is full of humour. Among his many other works the satire *Kaliviḍambana* is familiar to students for its verses on the evils of the present age. Among dramas we may note Mahādeva's play on Rāma, a tangle of spying, suspicion, and impersonation as the demons try to deceive him. With the rise of the Marāṭhās we have Paramānanda's epic *Sūryavaṃśa* on Śāha, Śivājī, and Śambhu. Classical literature flourished at all the Marāṭha courts. In Orissā among epic poems Govindamiśra's 'Origin of Pradyumna' and Gaṅgādhara's historical *Kośalānanda* are noteworthy.

Rāmapāṇivāda with a wide variety of works in Sanskrit and Māhārāṣṭrī is the greatest eighteenth-century writer. An epic on Rāma seems his most admired work; a play on the same hero shows the ultimate stage of unification of the elements of the legend, from the killing of Tāṭakā. Two street plays, dialogues between a king and his fool, and the two-act comedy *Madanaketucarita* are more immediately entertaining. A *campū* and two Māhārāṣṭrī poems belong to the Kṛṣṇa cycle. Rāmapāṇivāda is an elaborate stylist on the models of Bāṇa and Rājaśekhara. Ghanaśyāma is an innovator in the theatre with plays in new forms instead of the traditional act arrangement. The *Navagrahacarita* is a war among the planets; the *Ḍamaruka* a series of satirical and philosophical dialogues. The *Ānandasundarī* is a regular Māhārāṣṭrī *saṭṭaka*, introducing a telescope in a naval battle. The theatre of this period is extremely rich, including plays on contemporary events. Veṅkayāmātya wrote plays of all the ten types described in the *Nāṭyaśāstra*. Durgeśvara's *Dharmoddharaṇa* is an allegorical play on the restoration of religion and learning under the Marāṭhas, at Vārāṇasī, Ujjayinī, etc. Rājasthān and Orissā naturally shared in the Indian revival (Kṛṣṇakavi, Candraśekhara, etc.), which is marked in Vārāṇasī by the brief career of the scholar–novelist Viśveśvara.

Under the British, the Indian tradition was submerged by the imposition of English as medium of administration and education, except in the 'Native States' such as Travancore and Cochin. The modern vernaculars under this domination partly copied European models and developed a hybrid literature which is neither European nor Indian. With political independence the cultural scene has hardly changed as yet and the unity of India is threatened by the centrifugal force of the vernaculars. Vernacular writers often seek European orbits, considered 'modern', lacking the national character and relationship among themselves which only the common Indian tradition could give them. Sanskrit is the only truly national language India has ever had, linking all regions and all classes with the immortal springs of Indian thought. If it disappears, with its cultural heritage, India will never be a nation and will surely break up into a series of European-type states. The decision still lies in the future; meanwhile the semi-underground classical tradition conserves its vigour and the twentieth century has produced several hundred Sanskrit plays, whilst the theatre of Bhāsa is being revived in Keralā. India's cultural unity may yet be saved and through it her political unity.

CHAPTER XV

Early Art and Architecture

by P. S. RAWSON

VERY few people yet realize how great a debt the art of the world—especially that of the Eastern world—already owes to India. It is true to say that without the example of Indian forms and ideas the arts of the whole of South-East Asia, of China, Korea, Mongolia, Tibet, and Japan would all have been radically different, and would have lost by that difference. So, too, would modern Western art, especially architecture and painting. Buddhism, a merchants' religion *par excellence*, was the chief vehicle for this artistic influence, though Hinduism did penetrate South-East Asia and the islands; and Buddhist art, at home in India, owed a good deal to the Hindu art that flourished alongside it.

The earliest art of India, that produced in the great cities of the Indus valley civilization (*c.* 2000 B.C.), could not have had much direct impact on the art of the rest of the world. There can, however, be little doubt that this art shared a common heritage of ideas with other regions of the ancient Middle East.

Most important of all is the fact that certain symbols and images which appear in later historical art first showed themselves in the miniature sculptures, in the seals and the sealings of the Indus valley. Examples are the ithyphallic deity seated with knees akimbo as 'lord of the beasts', the naked girl, the dancing figure with one leg lifted diagonally across the other, the sacred bull, the stout masculine torso, the 'tree of life', and innumerable modest types of monkeys, females, cattle, and carts modelled in terracotta.

After the end of the Indus valley civilization there is the first of many gaps in our knowledge of Indian art history. We have always to remember that what has come down to us of early Indian art consists only of scattered fragments of what must have been a widespread and flourishing artistic activity in many media. Almost everything made from ivory or wood—including an advanced architecture—everything painted on palm-leaf or cloth, of which huge quantities must once have existed, has been destroyed by India's devastating climate. A few ivories have survived by chance, and on the walls of a handful of caves some scraps of painting. Even the stone carvings and larger modelled terracottas represent only a tiny proportion of the art produced by each successive period in these durable materials. Such items were, however, often important ones, meant to decorate major dynastic shrines; that is why they were made, say, in stone rather than something more perishable. But it is impossible to write an art history for India in the same terms as one can for medieval Europe, or even for ancient Greece.

Our knowledge of historical Indian art begins with the ceramic wares and figurative terracottas made in the cities of the broad Gangā basin during the last centuries B.C. We also know something of the building techniques and fortification of these cities. For example at Rājgir, south of Patnā, there are some superb Cyclopean fortification walls (sixth century B.C.), and at Kauśāmbī there was a palace with a substantial tunnel-vault (*c.* third century B.C.). But the representational terracottas give the best insight into the visual imagery with which the inhabitants brightened their lives. From about 200 B.C. onwards large numbers of miniature reliefs, mostly either hand-modelled or pressed in moulds, illustrate all sorts of aspects of good fortune, including women loaded with jewels, pleasure parties, and animals. In the Gangā delta at Chandraketugarh, for example, there was a factory for such works; and at Patnā have been excavated some superb terracottas of dancing girls, modelled in the full round.

These miniature works set the key for what comes after. They are imbued with an atmosphere of human sensuous pleasure which later art develops into the typically Indian imagery of sensual paradise. A flowery and jewelled opulence, combined with erotic charm, appears full fledged in the earliest known ivories, representing gorgeous girls and fantastic animals, those from Pompeii (before A.D. 79) and those excavated at Begram (*c.* A.D. 100). Such purely secular works illustrate the Indian notion of what are at once the natural prerogatives of kings and the typical accessories of the hero's heaven as it is described in the Sanskrit epics.

During the third century B.C. the first major works of architecture and stone-carving which we know were made. There are reminiscences in them of the dynastic works of Iranian Achaemenid Persepolis, and they thus reflect the dynastic pretensions of the conquering Mauryan emperors, chief of whom was Aśoka (*c.* 272–232 B.C.). Among them are tall footless pillars of polished sandstone, whose capitals are carved with symbolic animal figures. Some bear inscriptions by Aśoka, enjoining on his subjects a morality with a Buddhist flavour. Similar inscriptions appear elsewhere on rocks, one of which, at Dhaulī, is carved with the three-dimensional forepart of an elephant. Sarnāth, site of the Buddha's first preaching, was adopted as dynastic shrine by the Mauryas, who commissioned a polished sandstone railing and dedicatory figures. Buddhist *stūpas*, which may have been constructed a century or so earlier in the kingdoms of northern India to contain and honour the bodily relics of the Buddha, were enlarged and refurbished—a process often repeated later. A dynastic guild of sculptors seems to have grown up, able to carve colossal polished stone dedicatory figures, of which several survive, sometimes miscalled '*yakshas* and *yakshīs*'. The two best known are the male from Parkham and the female from Dīdārganj, the latter dating from *c.* A.D. 50. A number of caves in the Barābar hills were also cut to accommodate members of religious orders in the rainy season, and some were decorated with simple sculpture of guardian figures and inscriptions.

It was, in fact, in the decoration of major religious monuments that the next developments in Indian art showed themselves. At a number of sites, notably Bhārhut, Sānchī, Mathurā, and Bodh Gayā in the north, and Amarāvatī in the Kistnā delta, decorative and figural relief-carving was evolved to ornament Buddhist *stūpas* and their railings. At first the style was in low and flat relief, the figures being carefully outlined and isolated against their backgrounds; often they were angular and primitive, a fresh start seeming to owe nothing to the Mauryan dynastic style. But this low-relief style was capable of its own kind of sophistication, as at Bhārhut, where the pillars of the railing carried half-life-size figures of country godlings, pressed into service at the Buddhist shrine; its coping carries a continuous creeper-design, framing small reliefs, which suggests that the whole structure was interpreted as an image of the mythical 'wish-granting tree'. Then, by the early years of the Christian era, at Sānchī, on the gateways of Stūpa I the sculptural style evolved a characteristic softly rounded deep relief, which could also be developed to present virtually three-dimensional figures, as on the brackets and capitals. These works succeed in converting into stone what must have been a strongly developing style of two-dimensional narrative expression. The scrolled ends to the Sānchī lintels suggest that the Buddhist stories the lintels bear are transcriptions into a more permanent medium of the illustrations to the pictorial story-scrolls so popular in India throughout the ages. We know that there was indeed a related pictorial style; for much-damaged fragments of wall-painting survive in Caves IX and X at Ajantā in the Deccan, contemporary with the earlier of the Sānchī gates. They, too, illustrate Buddhist legend and piety, perhaps more freely than the stone-cut reliefs could, in their own softly stereotyped convention. But it is abundantly clear that these, along with all the later and more famous Buddhist paintings at Ajantā, were instances of a widespread tradition of Indian painting, now vanished, which was essentially secular but was readily adapted to religious needs.

The art first evolved in these early *stūpa* decorations lies at the root of all the later Buddhist styles of South-East Asia and the Far East. Its choice of legends for illustration, its method of presenting them through groups of principal figures, even certain of its characteristic types of costume, became canonical in all Buddhist countries, providing the basis for local developments.

In India itself, during the later first, the second, and the third centuries A.D. the Buddhist (and Jaina) *stūpa* became the focus of artistic attention, its decoration being much expanded and elaborated. The *stūpa* itself, originally a domed mound near the crest of which relics of the Buddha and his saints were enshrined, developed, by the addition of ever higher plinths and crowning umbrella-spires, into a tall tower. Each *stūpa* came to be metaphysically identified as 'the axis of the world', and ornamented with elaborate carvings which, for all their cosmic and sometimes dynastic symbolism, retained a fundamental humanity of scale. The skill of the sculptors in representing figures with a powerful plastic 'presence', and in composing complex narrative scenes full of overlaps, advanced rapidly. Especially in south-east India, at the Buddhist sites around Amarāvatī (e.g. Jaggayapeta, Nāgārjunakonda), the *stūpas*, with their railings and gateways, came to be almost totally clad in panels of white limestone carved with rich ornamental designs or sensuous figural relief. The style of these works is closely related to contemporary fragments of painting in the caves at Ajantā on the other side of the peninsula. At the vanished *stūpas* of the most important site of all, Mathurā in west-central India, what was to become the first classic style of Indian sculpture gradually evolved.

During the same period, it seems that the custom of Buddhist monks settling down to live in monasteries became widespread. Previously the old Buddhist regulations had demanded that monks live an entirely wandering life, detached from any people or places affection for which might impede their religious aim. The spirit of these regulations, however, was gradually altered by the practicalities of Indian life. From at least the third century B.C. all the great *stūpa*-sites have one constant feature: a large hall, aligned with the *stūpa*, with an internal colonnade separating a nave from two aisles, linking them across the closed end by an ambulatory. This basic plan is still preserved at many sites in Burma and Thailand. Such halls were meant for the preaching of Buddhist doctrine and the reciting of the by then numerous canonical texts. It is probable that only in the last century B.C. were these texts being written down, and the Buddhist order of begging monks depended on the support of a laity, most of whom would be unable to read anyway.

The early halls were certainly built of wood. We know more or less what they look like from representations carved in the decorative reliefs. But in the western Deccan, among the volcanic ridges and gorges of the western Ghāts, a large number of man-made caves were excavated from about 200 B.C. onwards, which were virtually sculptures in stone of these wooden preaching halls. The earlier ones (e.g. Bhājā) were meant to be completed with actual wooden features—roof-ribs, window lattices, and portico. But by about 50 B.C. they were being cut entirely in stone, each containing a symbolic *stūpa*, the carvers faithfully repeating the old wooden architectural patterns down to the rows of joist-ends. In addition, even the earliest were sculpted with 'ornamental' figures in relief, including attractive women sitting on balconies. At Kārlī (*c*. A.D. 10) and Kanherī (*c*. A.D. 100) there are opulently conceived over-life-size couples on the façade. The intention was almost certainly that they should convert the structure into a metaphor of the 'palaces of the gods', which the Buddha is supposed to have visited to preach—a metaphor which becomes a constant feature of all later Indian and South-East Asian shrines, Hindu as well as Buddhist.

It is clear that, in the course of time, the monks who preached the doctrine at these cave-halls were gradually settling down actually to live on the sites. Even at Bhājā there are a few very early living-caves cut in the rock adjacent to the hall, and decorated with legendary reliefs. Ajantā, though, is the site which illustrates the process most clearly. For here, over about eight centuries from the third century B.C., twenty-six caves were cut, four being preaching halls, the others all being progressively larger living-caves, so that in the end there was accommodation for 600 or 700 monks. All save one were painted throughout on plaster, not once, but several times over, with scenes of Buddhist legend, most of the work being in a style so sensual that it can only have been executed by artists whose normal vein was the characteristic Indian secular eroticism. Only in some of the latest paintings before A.D. 600 do more schematic and austere doctrinal representations appear. We may legitimately assume that at all the great Buddhist *stūpa*-sites, where most of the building was of wood and has vanished, large monasteries, based on courtyards surrounded by living cells, normally had similar thoroughgoing painted and carved decorative schemes. It was in such monasteries that the triumphs of Buddhist speculative philosophy, psychology, and logic were achieved.

There is one regional style of Buddhist decoration which has attracted a great deal of attention in the West, that of Gandhāra, comprising the Afghan Kābul valley with adjacent areas, in the north-west of the subcontinent. Apart from the sea routes, this valley has been the main artery along which have passed innumerable invading armies, as well as the incoming and outgoing land trade which has linked India with the rest of mainland Asia. One group of invaders, the Central Asian Kushānas, took command of this region from about the end of the first century B.C. until well into the fifth century A.D. Under their auspices, during the second century A.D., a land trade-route was opened to the eastern Mediterranean. Along this route, eastwards, came direct influence from Romano-Hellenistic art. The features assimilated into the Buddhist schist and stucco sculptures which encrusted the wealthy Gandhāran monasteries are semi-classical. The Buddha wears something resembling a draped toga; deities develop classical muscular torsos; there are swags and *putti*, and even illustrations of Greek legend.

The great importance of this regional style lies in the effect it had on the Buddhist art of Central Asia, China, Korea, and Japan, an effect only modified, not replaced, by later waves of influence. Since Buddhism was very much a merchants' religion, wherever India's merchants went during these centuries Buddhism and its art followed. Gandhāra was also a region where Buddhism underwent profoundly important philosophical developments, and the local art, with its cosmopolitan outlook, elaborated new doctrinal imagery. Under the Kushānas the eastward land routes over the Pamīr, through the kingdom of Khotan, and around the northern and southern fringes of the desert Tarīm basin, were also opened up. At the oasis staging-posts along these routes Buddhist monasteries were constructed, and decorated with sculpture and painting; some lasted until well into the thirteenth century. Monks from Gandhāra and Khotan travelled east; converts from inner China travelled back towards India. Texts were transmitted from India and translated into Far Eastern languages. The art styles which became canonical, first in China, then in Korea and Japan, were closely based, for doctrinal reasons, upon types established first in Khotan and Gandhāra, and transmitted, probably, by pattern works. Even today Buddhist artists in Japan create images which contain echoes of Gandhāra.

Also under the Kushānas the city of Mathurā took on a special importance. It lies at a focal point of several trade-routes; and by the first century A.D. it had become a centre for the manufacture of works of art. Towards the end of that century the first representation of the Buddha himself may have been made there; for all earlier Buddhist illustration had avoided representing the person of the being whose essential quality was that he had passed into Nirvāna, and suggested his presence in a narrative through symbols only. At Mathurā it seems that vestiges of the skill of the old Mauryan dynastic school of sculptors may also have survived, and have been applied to the development of massive three-dimensional sculpture, first for Buddhist subjects, and then in the second century A.D. to represent the Hindu gods Śiva and Vishnu who were adopted as patron dynastic deities by Kushāna kings. This skill also influenced the development of decorative relief styles. The local pinkish sandstone is unmistakable; and images made at Mathurā have been found at other sites in northern India, for example at Sānchī.

By the fifth century a smoothly finished, cool, and subdued type of Buddhist sculpture had evolved there, which provided one of the principal elements in the Gupta style of art (fourth to seventh centuries). The fine echoing series of raised string-like folds of garments and their curling lower hems, both influenced by Gandhāran ideas, remained, until the decline of Buddhism in India, features of many images, being either suggested by incised lines or painted on to the surface. There may well have been some stylistic relationship between such images and the life-size standing Buddhas made during the later third century in the monasteries of south-east India such as Amarāvatī, carved in the local white limestone or cast in bronze. The bronzes especially were exported to become the pattern for innumerable Buddha icons in the contemporary Indian maritime settlements around the coasts of South-East Asia.

Between the fifth and seventh centuries we find a unified Gupta style of Buddhist art established in northern India, which we know especially from the images excavated at Sarnāth, again a dynastic site. But the accounts left by Chinese pilgrims describe numerous monastery-shrines throughout Bihār, Bengal, and Orissā, many of which have long disappeared, though a few have been located and excavated. There were 100-foot-high *stūpas* and multi-storied monasteries built of wood, brick, and stone; and each site was filled with images, large and small, cut in stone, modelled in terracotta or stucco, and cast in bronze. Many of them were, no doubt, intended as costly testimonials to personal piety, since 'multiplying images of the Buddha' was considered an act meritorious in itself. Among the excavated sites is the earliest of the great Buddhist universities, Nālandā in Bihār, which expanded later in a rather haphazard way. It consists of clustered courtyards and buildings of different patterns, including, of course, *stūpas*, many of which were decorated with particularly fine stucco sculptures of Buddhas and Bodhisattvas.

Although the Chinese visitors recorded many flourishing Buddhist centres, they also recorded their dismay at the decline of Buddhism relative to Hinduism, the reasons for which are explained elsewhere. Even the Bodhi tree at Bodh Gayā was cut down in about A.D. 600 by a Hindu king and the shrine converted to Hindu uses. Buddhism was fighting, so to speak, its last rear-guard battle in most regions of India. In the ninth century the great Hindu monist philosopher Śankarāchārya hastened the doctrinal defeat of Buddhism everywhere. But in one region of India, the north-east, including parts of Orissā, Buddhism flourished greatly under the patronage of the Pāla Dynasty (*c.* 750–1150) and took on a new and fascinating lease of artistic life, partly in direct response to the Hindu challenge. Other Buddhist universities were founded, notably at Vikramaśīla, and enormous effort was devoted to the elaboration of schools of philosophy, logic, ritual, medicine, and magic—to which, incidentally, Hindus were also admitted. The scholars gathered together all the available branches of learning into a monumental synthesis based upon certain medical and yogic symbolisms usually called Tantric. The art was a direct reflection of this syncretic activity. It developed systematic groupings of ideal figures to symbolize the various elements and processes in

'Reality' and Enlightenment, all focused around a set of five differentiated Buddha-principles.

In India most of this art has disappeared. We know its character best from the still-surviving traditions based upon it which were transplanted directly into Nepal and Tibet (seventh century) and sustained by direct contact with the Pāla universities. Altars were probably furnished with small bronzes, which could be arranged in symbolic patterns. There may well have been symbolic wall-paintings and hangings, prototypes of those which are still found in Tibet, Bhūtan, and Sikkim, and were also painted on the walls in twelfth-century Burmese Pagan. We have the testimony of the great eighth-century brick temple of Somapura (Pahārpur) that architecture was used likewise to develop the symbolism of the Tantric cosmos. This joint imagery of man and world was transported during the eighth century into the Indianized kingdom of central Java, where its chief monument is Borobudur (*c.* 800). It is also virtually certain that continuously through this Pāla period beautifully illuminated long palm-leaf manuscripts of Buddhist texts were made, the pages being bound between painted boards, both covers and pages being illuminated with figures from the Buddhist pantheon. It is probable that such sumptuous works were made actually as objects of reverence rather than mere reading-matter. The earliest surviving example is dated just before A.D. 1000; but many similar manuscripts of later date survive, especially in Nepal.

An alliance of Muslim invaders and Hindu sectarian interests eliminated even this Buddhism with its art from India by the early years of the thirteenth century, leaving only strong traces of its presence in later Bengālī folk-styles.

Hindu art developed later than Buddhist art in India as a whole. The oldest, strictly brāhmanical form of Hinduism demanded no permanent installation for its various sacrificial rituals. There is an enclosure at Besnagar in Madhya Pradesh, dated perhaps in the mid-second century B.C., where a named deity, Vāsudeva, was worshipped. But the natural tendency of the Indian population has always been, since the remotest past, to adore and make offerings at any place in the countryside where the Divine seems to show its presence. Every village has a hallows-tree, a sacred ant-hill, or a holy spot marked by boulders; its inhabitants are aware of spiritual, often humanoid, beings haunting sacred places. Buddhism managed permanently to focus this sense of numen on the person of the Buddha, and extend it to the physical relics of himself and his saints enshrined in *stūpas*. From these it was eventually transferred to images of the 'essential Buddha nature' indicated by such basically human examples.

Hinduism, however, seems to have made during the second century A.D. a successful alliance with the Indian theory of kingship, whereby the metaphysical principal to which kings might appeal for supernatural patronage was awarded name and form as a deity. Only one of the major ancient Vedic gods, Sūrya, retained a central place for himself in later Hindu art as a dynastic deity. The overwhelmingly important gods of later art, to whom nearly all the major temples are dedicated, are Śiva, Vishnu, and the Mother Goddess under her various names (e.g. Durgā), of all of whom there are only traces in Vedic literature. The numerous much later medieval representations of Vedic deities appear as the consequence of self-conscious attempts to brāhmanize the iconography of religious art. It is thus natural that the evolution of Hindu stone architecture and temple carving—which is all that remains to us from the centuries earlier than *c.* A.D. 1200—took place at scattered single sites which were each for a time the capital cities of royal dynasties, large and small, and which had probably long been sacred localities. All over the subcontinent there are these sites, many certainly having vanished without trace, at each of which some tens of temples were built and decorated over a century or two, dedicated by members of a royal family and their chief subjects. With the growth of the brāhmans' encyclopedias of collected legend, the *Purānas*, places especially sacred—those perhaps where major episodes in legend were supposed to have taken place—were also dignified with successive temple foundations, attracting pilgrims over a long period of time.

The fundamental pattern behind the beautiful complexities of the Hindu temple is very simple, evolving naturally from the primitive hallows or sacred place. The sacred numinous object stands within an enclosure and a cell. The object is often a Śiva *lingam* (phallic emblem); it can also be a sculptural image, either replacing an older more primitive hallows, or ceremonially carved or cast, and dedicated as a new dwelling for the sacred. The cell is raised on a plinth and to it may be appended extra features, the commonest being a porch or portico, and a decorated door-frame. Then came an ambulatory, a crowning tower, one or more aligned approach-halls, one of which may be especially for dancing, and perhaps an encircling layout of lesser cells or even miniature temples. This last feature, in south India, might become a fantastically elaborate sequence of concentric enclosures with towering gateways. Each temple is conceived, as the Buddhist *stūpa* was, as 'the axis of the world', symbolically transformed into the mythical Mount Meru, around which are slung like garlands the heavens and the earth. The heavens are represented on the exterior of developed temples by bands of sculpture containing icons of gods and other lesser superhuman creatures which popular legend ascribes to its heaven. Among these are the famous erotic carvings, which are images of the post-mortem delights awarded by celestial girls called *apsarases* to the spirits of heroes and sages. These heaven-bands are at the level of the raised interior floor, thus converting it into an analogue of the 'courts of heaven', which are naturally adorned with ornamental designs reflecting all that the heart can desire. The principal image in its cell—called 'womb-house' —occupies at this level the place of the enthroned king in his court, to whom only the officiating brāhman has direct access. It is 'dressed', 'fed', and 'entertained', just as a king might be. From it the 'originating energy' of the cosmos is felt to flow out through the fabric of the temple into the everyday world around its foot.

The earliest certain examples of the basic form of the temple are of the early fifth century A.D., on top of Sānchī hill. But scattered stone and brick instances of comparable date occur at such places as Tigowā; at Bhūmarā is an early shrine with an ambulatory. No doubt there were yet earlier examples which have perished, especially those at Mathurā which housed the icons of Vishnu and Śiva produced there during the second and third centuries A.D. At Kundā, near Jabalpur, was also a very simple cell, restored in Gupta times. Caves, which were also developed as Hindu shrines, were being used by the fifth century; a dynastic rock-cut sanctuary at Udayagiri bears the date of 401, and among its main features is a colossal sculpture of the boar 'incarnation' of Vishnu, the patron deity of the site.

Although there are regional styles in which the temple is conceived more as a constructed shelter (e.g. Keralā, Kashmīr), the process of stone sculpture was one of the principal factors in the evolution of the fully stone-built Hindu temple. By about A.D. 750 the temple had come to offer columns and surfaces expressly meant to be cut with legendary images. Even the volumes of the building were thought of as sculptured masses of stone, rather than as engineered support, wall, and canopy.

The principal regional centres where Hindu architecture evolved are very numerous. Many remain to be properly investigated. But after about A.D. 650 it is possible to distinguish two broad types, the northern and the southern, both of which evolved as distinctive patterns out of a previous mixed experimental phase. This phase is represented first by the many ruinous and rebuilt shrines of fifth- to seventh-century date in northern India (e.g. Eran, Shankargarh, Mukundarra), whose original design can be scarcely made out; and second by the numerous groups at the successive Chālukya capital cities in northern Mysore, notably Aivalli (Aihole) and Bādāmi (sixth to seventh centuries). At Aivalli, in particular, it is possible to discern among the seventy-odd ruined shrines successive phases of invention, when different layouts and decorative schemes were apparently being tried. Some shrines built of large slabs with flat slabbed roofs (e.g. Mahūā, Parsorā) are reminiscent of the megalithic graves which were still being constructed in this part of the Deccan during historical times. Two, the Lādh Khān and Kont Gudi, even lack separate shrine-cells, the image being set on the back wall. Nearby, at Ter, another temple, once Buddhist, clearly shows how such forms result from the direct take-over of Buddhist preaching halls.

The fully characteristic northern temple stands on a plinth adorned with elaborately profiled and rhythmical horizontal mouldings. It is distinguished by its tall square-planned tower over the main cubical cell; this has a convex curve to its contour and may have, around its root, complex re-entrant angles, imitative pilasters, small duplicates of its own profiles, or ogival hood-mouldings based on the end windows of old wooden palaces. This tower is divided into horizontal bands which probably refer back to the actual reduplicated stories of earlier examples. Exactly such reduplicated stories do appear in early western Indian temples, and in the buildings of those regions in South-East Asia where early Hindu patterns of temple were adopted, notably Cambodia and Vietnam.

The variations of the basic northern Hindu temple type are many. Not all are fully documented even now. At individual sites, long lines of continuous development can be traced, leading up to immensely elaborate architectural inventions; but at all times and places small, unpretentious structures which are no more than modestly towered shrines with porticoes have been continuously built. At Osiā, in Rājasthān, for example, a surviving group of modest dynastic temples date from the eighth to the tenth century. Their porticoes and plinths exhibit several variations on the basic design. Deogarh, a hill-site where many temples once stood, is noted for its restored shrine on a cross-plan, probably built *c.* 700. Stairways run up each face of the plinth; the shrine itself has its doorway in one wall, which three magnificent large reliefs of Vishnuite mythology match on the other walls. An early and very large brick-built version of the cross-plan, with one stairway rising directly into the shrine chamber, is at Bhītargaon, near Kānpur (Cawnpore). The faces of the high plinth are tiered with flat pilasters and ogival arcading. This building, probably only one of many similar temples which have vanished, is important because it represents an early example of the type which was developed at Buddhist Somapura and transmitted to many parts of South-East Asia. At numerous other sites in the different regions local architectural schools flourished. In Rājasthān temples were built with tiers of open pillared balconies (e.g. Kiradu, *c.* 1100). In western India the temples tended to have squat towers buttressed with regular tiers of miniature repetitions of their own design, and some had superb, elaborately carved dance-pavilions aligned with the main shrine but standing free of it (e.g. Modherā, 1126). Perhaps the most famous sequences are at Khajurāho in central India and in the cities of Orissā, a Hindu state which never wholly succumbed to Islam. Both groups are distinguished by their superb figure sculpture.

At Khajurāho twenty-five temples still stand out of an original eighty-odd, all built between *c.* 950 and 1050 around a lake. One is constructed round a court on a ground-plan based upon a cosmic meditative diagram. The majority, however, follow the 'temple-mountain' design. The most beautiful individual buildings are also those which are carved with the most beautiful figure sculpture, notably the Viśvanātha and the Kandārya Mahādeva. The celestial figures carved around their heaven-bands, many of them in overtly erotic postures and groupings, all flavoured with a profound sensuality, are widely regarded as some of the greatest and most inimitable achievements of Indian art, an essential part of man's most precious heritage. The figures are all cut in what is, in fact, extremely deep relief. The depth of the cutting gives them a strong plastic presence even when they are seen from far off. The forms of the bodies are sinuous and totally convex; they seem to be bursting out of the fabric of the building itself—an intentional effect with a direct symbolic value in relation to the meaning of the temple as creative source and centre.

A number of fragments of wall-painting suggest that most of these temples, including their sculpture, were plastered and painted, as Hindu temples still are. It also seems likely that they were decorated with painted and dyed cotton hangings. We can, however, be sure that any temple of significance was elaborately decorated with precious metals and gems, just as shrines are in modern Catholic countries. The spoils gathered from Hindu temples by the early Muslim invaders are reported by the historians of Islam to have been immense. All that has now vanished, virtually without trace. However, painting and sculpture show how highly developed the arts of the Indian jeweller and worker in precious metal were; for nearly every figure represented is wearing a load of superlative necklaces, hip girdles, head ornaments, bangles, and anklets.

The second major group, in Orissā, now contains more than 200 temples, and once contained many more. At the cities of Bhubaneswar and Purī a continuous history of Hindu temple building can be traced through from the mid-eighth century almost to modern times. The sequence develops through modest stages and culminates in a handful of very large structures. The earliest typical shrine is the Mukteśvara, at Bhubaneswar. It has a tower with a curved outline and a substantial porch, both beautifully carved. Also at Bhubaneswar are the great Lingarāja, with its three aligned halls, and the Rājarānī (*c.* A.D. 1000). At Purī is the complex of temples surrounding the huge Jagannātha shrine, much restored. But perhaps the most famous Orissan building is the Black Pagoda at Konārak (*c.* 1230), an unfinished or ruined temple of the sun, conceived as a colossal stone celestial chariot. The entire sculptural scheme is dominated by erotic groups, superbly cut, once painted, and now world famous.

In Orissā today a tradition of illumination on narrow strips of palm-leaf still survives. The oldest known examples are probably fifteenth century, but there can be no doubt that this particular tradition preserves perhaps the most faithful record of what was in earlier times a widespread genre of Hindu art. Classical Hindu texts are impressed with the stylus on to the leaf-strip and colour is rubbed into the impressions; drawings to illustrate them are executed in the same way, and are painted in bright, clear colours. The figure types and conventions of design in the recent illustrations parallel very closely those which appear in the eleventh-century sculpture.

In south India, as in Orissā, artistic traditions as a whole did not suffer total eclipse at the hands of Muslim invaders, though some regions of the northern Deccan were occupied in the thirteenth century. In many parts of the far south, therefore, there are temples which have remained in worship down to the present day. Some of the oldest sites have virtually been abandoned without being systematically destroyed. At Bādāmi a number of Hindu caves, one dated *c.* 578, contain the earliest major programme of mythological sculpture, which includes many features adopted from the art represented in earlier Buddhist caves, including opulent couples on brackets and door-jambs. There are also, in Cave III, some fragments of contemporary Hindu painting, close to the later Ajantā Buddhist work in style. The most important built temples are perhaps at Pattadakal, at Kānchīpuram, and at Māmallapuram on the east coast of the Deccan. The early temples, founded at these places (late seventh to early eighth centuries) by the Śiva-worshipping Pallava Dynasty, standardize one of the experimental types evolved earlier by the Chālukyas at Bādāmi. Thereafter it becomes the pattern upon which were based both later south Indian styles and styles built in various parts of South-East Asia, notably at Angkor and in Indonesia, during the period of Tamil overseas expansion.

Its essential characteristics are these: a pyramidal tower surmounting the cell, composed of a restricted number of storeys decorated with miniature pavilions and crowned by a kind of small faceted dome; an exterior wall uniting cell and main portico, which is vertically banded with pilasters between foot and lintel, in the panels of which there may be a few relief sculptures; a surrounding wall, often lined with cells, so close to the structure that it creates the feeling of a roofless corridor; pillars supported by lion caryatids, with broad-spread capitals; and curvilinear brackets under lintels and eaves.

Pallava sculpture, descended, no doubt, from that at Buddhist Amarāvatī, is notable for its restrained elegance. Its carvers were responsible for one of the most famous monuments in India. They produced a number of mythological relief carvings in caves and on rock-faces; but the group of such carvings at Māmallapuram is one of the chief beauties of Indian art. The largest and most complete example (*c.* 670) is cut into a granite cliff facing the sea; it contains many figures of gods, sages, and animals illustrating the story of the descent of the celestial Gangā from heaven to earth.

In external architectural style—though not in sculptural—the colossal monolithic temple called the Kailāśanātha at Ellora, on the other side of the Deccan (founded *c.* 775), is related to Pallava art. It belongs to a complex of caves, some Buddhist, some Jain, but is itself sacred to Śiva. This, too, is one of the splendours of Indian architecture. It was cut in two chief stages from a volcanic hillside, carved both inside and out, so that it stands free within an enormous quarry, the walls of which are pierced with flanking cave-temples. The fundamental plan of cell with broad colonnaded hall is derived from a late type of Buddhist living-cave at the monastery of Ajantā. The sculpture, however, is unique. Enormous figures in deep relief bound, leap, and twist, their energy bursting beyond their architectural frames. They were once plastered and painted; and here and there on the fabric a few fragments of pure wall-painting survive.

Of slightly later date is the equally famous Śiva cave-temple on Elephanta island near Bombay, far more modest in scale, and architecturally not very significant. But its vast sculptures, one being the well-known triple-head (Trimūrti) of Śiva, radiate an atmosphere of powerful tranquillity.

Under the immensely powerful Chola Dynasty, the eastern coast of the peninsula became the site of yet another flowering of art. About A.D. 1000 at Thanjavūr (Tanjore) the greatest of the early Chola temples was built, a stupendous pyramidal shrine, sacred to Śiva, its tower nearly 200 feet high and crowned by an eighty-ton ornate dome-capstone. On the inner walls of the ambulatory which runs around the cell under the main tower are the remains of an original series of wall-paintings illustrating Śiva mythology and celestial female dancers—another hint at how lavish the use of colour originally was on Indian architecture. But the Cholas are perhaps more artistically remarkable for the extraordinary school of bronze sculpture which they patronized, and which has continued and evolved down to the present day. It produced icons, ranging from almost life-size to a few inches high, of Hindu deities. The largest and most important of them were sometimes dedicated as 'portraits' of members of the royal family in the guise of gods. Many were meant to be carried in procession, and so they are modelled completely in three dimensions, with slender, elegantly rounded limbs in fluid postures. There were many images of Hindu saints in adoration; but perhaps the best-known type is that which represents the god Śiva as the beautiful 'Lord of the Dance', posing with one knee cocked out, in an aureole of flame. The high period of this art was probably the eleventh and twelfth centuries. But many superb pieces were produced in later centuries, perhaps slightly coarser in feeling. Again, no doubt, there must have existed during all these centuries a far more widely diffused art of metalwork—ornamental lamps, basins, trays—of which only a few fragments have been found. This whole bronze art deeply influenced the arts of areas of South-East Asia where south Indian culture made its impact, especially Ceylon, Thailand, and the kingdom of eastern Java.

In the western Deccan the Western Chālukya Dynasty built its own temples in an extreme, mannered style, which is related to the general northern style (e.g. Ambarnāth, Bombay, eleventh century; Gadag, Palampet, twelfth century). The exteriors were elaborate and often squat; but the interiors show a proliferation of columns with deeply cut horizontal mouldings, each with a variety of sections, and with facets for sculpture. The brackets become agglomerations of fantastic animals. The figures which adorn these brackets and the pillars develop extremely sinuous postures, their limbs becoming slender, almost insect-like. In the major icons hard, clearly defined forms often betray an insensitivity of touch which suggests a hardening impersonality in social and aesthetic attitudes.

A somewhat similar effect appears in the strange flowering of a Rājasthān northern temple type in the southern state of Mysore under the Hoyśala Dynasty during the twelfth and thirteenth centuries (e.g. Somnāthpur, Belūr). The basic squat tower surfaced with repetitions of itself was multiplied and adorned with quantities of ornamental sculpture. Star-shaped ground-plans were adopted, and rows of cells were linked upon single plinths. The surface ornament was developed into a fantastic mat of curvilinear foliage-tracery, deeply undercut and so standing out against a ground of shadow. Amongst it the human figures and animals, with their somewhat ponderous, simple forms, are almost overwhelmed; their heavy jewelled ornaments are woven into the general proliferation of design.

The question of the value of this vast inheritance of early and medieval Indian art to the modern world is a most interesting one. For two centuries and more the West has been unable to come properly to terms with it. Indian society has long been, and still remains, so rigidly structured that foreigners have found it exceptionally difficult to enter sympathetically into Indian attitudes, aesthetic as well as social. Europeans are still excluded from many of the most sacred Hindu shrines. There are now clear signs that this situation is changing. Many Westerners are making their way to India not merely as tourists but as eager admirers and students of Indian culture. Many thousands of published illustrations and millions of words of text have made the reading public in the West aware that there still survive (but only just) a culture and art in India which have something unique and significant to give the modern world.

The fundamental point is that this Indian art incorporates, in its own terms, a set of ideal canons of form. The different categories of architecture were made according to strict principles of proportion, following prototypes whose patterns were considered sacred and were handed down from generation to generation of craftsmen, probably in manuals of written and diagrammatic formulae (some latish examples survive). Sculptures—and perhaps paintings too—were made according to clearly laid-down prescriptions for each type, both in iconography and in detailed proportions. These canons naturally seemed to be in violent conflict with the semi-classical idealist-realist canons of art which persisted in Europe virtually into this century. It was no accident that the first Indian art to attract widespread and serious attention in the West was the somewhat Helleno-Romanized art of Buddhist Gandhāra of *c.* A.D. 120–500. Furthermore, even when the twentieth-century Modernist and Cubist Revolution was under way, partly inspired by primitive arts, Indian art remained at something of an aesthetic disadvantage precisely because it incorporated a canon; and canons were supposedly being rejected. But in the earlier twentieth century there were discerning collectors who recognized the immense virtues of Indian sculpture; two of the most important were themselves distinguished sculptors—Rodin and Epstein. British administrators who served in the old Indian Civil Service and the Archaeological Survey of India before India became independent also admired and collected works of early Indian art. But primary obstacles to earlier Western appreciation of all this art were those of its essential qualities which were deeply at variance with puritanical Western notions—its formal exuberance, its extreme sensuality, its vivid tactile presence, and its frequent unabashed concern with sexual love. Indeed, it would be true to say that the whole of the art so far discussed is meant in one way or another to stimulate the senses. The multiplied and emphatic, but also sophisticated, rhythms of the mouldings, profiles, columns, and ornament on architecture are meant to be as vividly exciting as the subtle rhythms of Indian music. The brilliant colours of painting were intended to strike directly at human feelings. The generous, convex, smoothly strokable sculptured forms of divine and human figures, male and female alike, were meant to evoke sensuous responses which include the sexual, even when the divine person represented was an embodiment of the most awesome cosmic powers. This was all gathered by old Indian ideology under the rubric of 'heavenly splendour'. For the heavens of the Indian imagination were characterized by joys of the most direct and uninhibited kind. And art was always imbued with such attributes of the divine world, even when it was apparently dealing with exalted symbolism and solemn myth. The ornament on Indian architecture is based upon the flower-garland or flowering vase, the juicy vegetable stalk, rich pleated and embroidered cloths, swagged strings of jewels, and, of course, beautiful girls, an abundance of all of which is what gives the heavens their natural charm. For the heavens are, literally, the place where every human desire is fulfilled. So enthralling was this vision to ancient India that its artists saw no virtue in novelty at all. They aimed always to repeat and intensify the same sensuous intuition again and again. They ploughed a narrow furrow, but deep.

Even now, many people find it very hard to reconcile this exuberant art with the severely ascetic doctrines which were preached by Indian religions, whose saints tormented to the limits of endurance and immolated themselves in the interests of an absorbing and radiant vision of the Whole, the Absolute. But it has recently been recognized that, far from being at variance, these two attitudes are actually sides of the same coin, the second being inconceivable without the first. Only the vital sensuous awareness which the art stimulates can provide the fuel which is consumed in the transcendental fire. The difficulty was probably caused during the last century by the reinterpretation of Indian philosophy and religion by Western and Indian scholars alike, in the light of Western language and philosophy, for which the senses play a role of pure 'evil', and have no place in religion.

The sensual heavens of Indian art, however, *are* 'the heavens'; they do not direct the imagination towards the everyday world. Instead, they arouse desires and focus them into a state 'beyond' this world, where their fulfilment is promised. They are not incentives to appetite, but indicators of the supernatural assuaging and fulfilment of every appetite, on a scale which common life can never match, but only a life imbued with that vision of the Whole. This point was made very clearly in the great tradition of aesthetic writing produced in Sanskrit, which culminated in the monumental work of Abhinavagupta (*c.* A.D. 1000). It is probably true that the earliest art of historical India, that of the ivories and Gangā valley terracottas, was rather a reflection of the desires of a hedonistic public living in cities and towns where kings supplied their exchequers with income derived from courtesans. But by the third century A.D. there can be no doubt that the close link between heaven and the yearnings of ordinary sensuality had been well established.

The story of the Buddha's conversion of his brother Nanda, recorded in the second century by the poet Aśvaghosha, illustrates the mechanism in a crude form. The Buddha inveigled Nanda into abandoning his mistress and joining his order of monks by showing him a vision of heavenly girls. In Nanda's mind their beauty and sexual attraction completely eclipsed the appeal of his earthly lover. When he had become a monk, he gradually came to realize the emptiness and inadequacy of all his desires. But the point regarding Indian art is well made. Unless the spectator responds to the outer shell of the art, to the immediate appeal even purely secular art makes, he may not reach the meaning within, his desires will remain vagrant, constantly looking for satisfaction in the things of the outer world, and leading him into crime and cruelty in his search for self-gratification. India's world of art is a consistent whole; that is why it followed ideal forms with what may seem to us like monotonous insistence. The misunderstandings possible for modern men are that they may write off such a meaning as 'compensation'; that they may read the sensuous appeal as purely worldly, instead of as super-worldly (even well-intentioned writers still confuse the celestial images of art with the customs of the world); or that they may lose themselves in feelings that lack the true centre which Indian art always had. If it is rightly understood, the art of early historical and medieval India has something unique to offer.

CHAPTER XVI

Music

by N. A. JAIRAZBHOY

MUSIC in the Indian subcontinent is a reflection of the diverse elements—racial, linguistic, and cultural—that make up the heterogeneous population of the area. The extraordinary variety of musical types is probably unparalleled in any other equivalent part of the world. Music plays a vital role in the religious, social, and artistic lives of the people. A great deal of it could be termed functional, as it is an indispensable part of the activities of everyday life, ranging from work and agricultural songs to the music which accompanies life-cycle events, such as birth, initiation, marriage, and death. In spite of the great diversity of music in the area, it is possible to make a few general statements which would be valid for most of the music in India. For instance, apart from modern developments, Indian music is based mainly on melody and rhythm; harmony and polyphony, as known in the West, have no part in the music. Much of the music is modal in character and is often accompanied by a drone which establishes a fixed frame of reference and precludes key changes which are so characteristic of Western music. There is, however, such a great variety of melodic and rhythmic forms in India that it would be injudicious to generalize any further.

In dealing with the origins of this exceedingly complex musical culture, we are fortunate that music has been part of India's literary tradition for nearly 2,000 years, and references to music go back even further; and that there are still areas in India which have remained more or less isolated from the main cultural stream and appear to have preserved their ancient musical forms relatively unchanged. Through the literary sources, we can trace something of the history of Indian classical music, which is predominantly an art form found in the cities. These sources, however, give no indication of the nature of village music, although they often mention the music of various regions. Nor do they discuss the non-classical forms found in the cities. Classical music has an elaborate musical theory and literature, and this tends to obscure the fact that only a small minority of the population is involved with this kind of music. Even in the cities of India, classical music is by no means the most popular form of music and new forms are evolving which appear to have much more relevance to the majority of Indians. These new forms, however, derive much of their inspiration from the classical tradition and most of the musicians involved in their composition and performance have been trained in the classical idiom.

A fundamental element of Indian classical music is the use of a drone, usually provided by a wind instrument or a plucked stringed instrument, which is tuned to a pitch convenient to the singer or instrumentalist—there being no concept of fixed pitch. Classical music is performed by small ensembles usually consisting of one main melody instrument or singer, one or more secondary melody instruments which echo, but may at times carry, the main melody line, and one or more percussion instruments which mark the time measure and provide rhythmic counterpoint. The melody line is largely improvised on melodic entities called *rāgas*, each of which prescribe a set of melodic possibilities. These have been handed down as part of an oral tradition, from teacher to pupil over many generations. The bases of the rhythmic improvisations are called *tālas*, each of which prescribes the length of a time cycle in terms of time units as well as the distribution of stresses within this cycle. *Rāga* and *tāla* are the two main elements of Indian classical music. In embryonic form these two elements are also to be seen in much of the folk music of the country.

VEDIC CHANT

The literary tradition in India begins with the *Vedas*. According to Hindu tradition, these texts were imparted by the God Brahmā to sages (*rishis*) in the form of the spoken word and have been handed down from one generation of brāhmans to the next in oral form, right down to the present period.

The original Vedic language had an accent system, comparable to that of Alexandrian Greece, where a particular syllable in each word was accented. In some instances, the position of the accent had a bearing on the meaning. This applied particularly to compounds, such as *indra-śatru*, which with the accent on the first syllable, meant 'whose enemy is Indra', but with the accent on the first syllable of the second word, meant 'enemy of Indra'. In the development from Vedic to Sanskrit, the original tonic accent was replaced by a stress accent which was located automatically near or at the end of each word determined by syllable length. The original Vedic accent was expanded to involve three syllables, the *anudātta* (which can be described as a preparation for the main point of accentuation), the *udātta* (the accented syllable), and the *svarita* (a kind of return to accentlessness). In the manuscripts of the *Rig Veda* and certain other texts, which occur much later, the *anudātta* is marked with a horizontal line below, the *udātta* is unmarked, and the *svarita* is indicated by a vertical stroke above:

sahasraśīrṣā puruṣaḥ sahasrākṣaḥ sahasrapāt

a u s a u s a u a u s

There are deviations from the basic pattern indicated above, but they need not be discussed here.

The ancient phonetic and grammatical schools which followed the Vedic period paid considerable attention to matters concerning the accent and it is thus clear that the position of the accent in each word has been preserved faithfully. However, the terms *udātta*, *anudātta*, and *svarita*, and the manner of their recitation, received divergent interpretation even in these early texts. Modern scholars have put forward at least three differing views regarding the nature of the Vedic accent: that the accent was based on pitch, on stress, and on the relative height of the articulatory organ.

There is much evidence for a musical interpretation of the accent, not only in the textual sources but also among some of the traditions of *Rig* and *Yajur*

Vedic recitation which exist in India today. The most direct correlation between pitch and accent is found in the recitation style of the Tamil Aiyar brāhmans, the most widespread style of Vedic recitation in India. This is based on three tones: the *udātta* and the non-accented syllables (called *prachaya*) are recited at the middle tone, the *anudātta* at the low tone, and the *svarita* either at the high tone (when the syllable is short) or a combination of two tones, middle followed by high. This compares exactly with the manuscript notation where the *anudātta* (the low tone) is marked with a line below the syllable, and the *svarita* (the high tone) with a line above. In this style of recitation, the duration of the tones is also directly related to the length of the syllables. In the following example it should be noted that the intervals only approximate to the Western musical stave:

Musical example 1, p. 240

The Nambūdirī brāhmans of Keralā have a very individual style of chanting, characterized by shakes or oscillations (*kampa*). For the most part, however, there is a similar correlation between accent and pitch. As in the Aiyar style, there is also a correlation between the duration of tones and the length of the syllables.

Musical example 2, p. 240

The style of recitation found in Mahārāshtra, however, contrasts in principle with these two, since the *anudātta* is recited at the high tone. The relation of pitch to accent is not nearly so direct as in the two previous examples, being modified by other phonetic factors, such as length of syllable and whether it begins with a nasal, semivowel, aspirate, etc. A feature of this style is the application of stress, which falls, surprisingly, on the *anudātta*, pushing the pitch of this tone as much as a fifth higher than the *udātta*.

Musical example 3, p. 240

None of these styles of chanting compares exactly with the descriptions in any of the ancient phonetic and grammatical texts. This is surprising in view of the rigorous methods of training and preparation of brāhman initiates, which place such emphasis on exact intonation.

The close connection between the notation of the accents mentioned earlier and the Aiyar-Nambūdirī treatment of the accents, suggests that these two styles are probably more than a thousand years old and it may well be that they go back to very early times.

The chanting of the *Sāma Veda* is much more musical than that of the *Rig* and *Yajur Vedas*, and the chants use 5, 6, or 7 tones. It is clear from the phonetic texts that certain elements of musical theory were known in Vedic circles and there are references to the three octave registers (*sthāna*), each containing seven notes (*yama*). In the auxiliary *Sāma* Vedic text, the *Nāradīśikshā*, the Vedic tones are correlated with the secular tones (*svaras*) as well as the accents, suggesting that the Vedic octave was an extension of the tonal nucleus found in *Rig* and *Yajur* Vedic chant. Here two groups of notes, a descending fourth apart, are clearly implied; the *udātta* being correlated with the secular tones *ga* (F) and *ni* (C), the *anudātta* with *ri* (E) and *dha* (B), and the *svarita* with *ma* (G), *sa* (D) and *pa* (A). The two conjunct tetrachords are seen more easily below:

svarita	*ma* (G)	*sa* (D)
udātta	*ga* (F)	*ni* (C)
anudātta	*ri* (E)	*dha* (B)
svarita	*sa* (D)	*pa* (A)

As with the *Rig* and *Yajur Veda*, there are several styles of *Sāma* Vedic chant. That of the Tamil Aiyar brāhmans, who follow the *Kauthuma* branch (*śākhā*) of *Sāma Veda*, is the best-known. Their style is quite musical and appears to be an extension of the Aiyar *Rig* and *Yajur* Vedic style. The hymns seem to be based on the 'D' mode, the Ecclesiastic Dorian. However, their intonation differs quite considerably from the 'Just' and the 'Pythagorean' tuning systems. Electronic analysis of their tones shows a great deal of variation, even during the course of a single chant. However, it does show that much of their chanting seems to be based on intervals of three different sizes, a semitone of about 90 cents, a three-quarter tone of about 140 or 150 cents, and a whole tone generally just under 200 cents. The basic nucleus of the chants seems to lie in the tetrachord F–C, with D as the final (finalis). However, the interval F–C seems to be consistently smaller than a perfect fourth (498 cents). In spite of this, it is possible to see a great deal of similarity between the mode generally used in this *Sāma Veda* tradition and the ancient Indian parent scale, the *shadjagrāma*, which is discussed in the following pages.

Musical example 4, p. 241

The reciting style of the Aiyar brāhmans who follow the *Jaiminīya* branch of the *Sāma Veda* differs quite considerably from that of the Aiyar brāhmans of the *Kauthuma* branch. This chant is much less musical and there is no evidence of anything like the three-quarter tone. In addition, the upper tone is generally forced out, has very short duration, and is followed by a descending slide (portamento). This upper tone seems to be influenced by stress and varies from about a whole tone to nearly a major third.

Musical example 5, p. 241

The Nambūdirī brāhmans of Keralā, who also follow the *Jaiminīya* branch, have the most extraordinary style of *Sāma* Vedic incantation. They exhibit unusual breath control, stretching out each vowel, sometimes for as long as eight seconds, during which the voice oscillates quickly over a range of about a fourth:

Musical example 6, p. 241

There is still a considerable variety of Vedic chants which continue into the present period. Of these, the *Sāma* Vedic recitation is clearly dying out most rapidly, as it was used in the Soma sacrifices which are now seldom held. Even the *Rig* and *Yajur Veda* chants are more or less extinct in many parts of India, and south India is now the main stronghold of Vedic chant.

ANCIENT INDIAN MUSIC

The *Vedas* and their ritual are applicable to the *dvi-ja*, the 'twice born', the three upper castes of Hinduism. The fourth caste, the śūdras, were introduced to Hindu mythology and religious philosophy through the originally secular epic poems, the *Rāmāyana* and the *Mahābhārata*, and through the *Purānas*—popular stories depicting the lives of the various incarnations of the Hindu deities and other religious legends. These were probably sung and recited, perhaps even before the Christian era, by bards, in much the same way as they still are. These legends were also enacted on stage, and probably the first detailed description of music is to be found in this connection in the *Nātyaśāstra* which has been variously dated from the second century B.C. to the fifth century A.D. This work is, in many respects, a manual for the producer of stage plays and deals with all the aspects of drama, including dance and music. Much of the present-day musical terminology stems from this source, and the *Nātyaśāstra* has inspired many treatises over the centuries.

Scholars are not all agreed on the nature of this early musical system which was associated with theatrical performance. It evidently included background music, performed by an orchestra, with singers, located just off stage, in what was very much like an orchestra pit. Melodies were apparently derived from modes (*jātis*) which were taken from the heptatonic serial progressions (*mūrchhanās*) of two closely related parent scales or tone systems, *shadjagrāma* and *madhyamagrāma*. (A third parent scale, *gāndhāragrāma*, referred to in several early texts, is not mentioned in the *Nātyaśāstra*.) These two scales differed in the positioning of just one note, which was microtonally flatter in the *madhyamagrāma* than in the *shadjagrāma*. This microtonal difference was referred to as the *pramānā* ('measuring') *śruti*, which presumably served as a standard of measurement to determine that the octave consisted of 22 *śrutis*.

It would appear from the textual source that the *śrutis* were of a standard size, or at least were thought to be so. A number of modern scholars have, however, argued that the *śrutis* were in fact of three different sizes. Fox Strangways gives 22, 70, and 90 cents as the sizes of the *śrutis*. There is no doubt, however, that one *śruti* was not considered a musical interval and the seven notes of the octave were composed of tones having either two, three, or four *śrutis*. Thus, a single *śruti* is most readily seen as the highest common factor of the three different-sized tones. There has been no attempt to determine the exact size of the *śrutis* in any of the traditional Indian musical treatises.

The concept of *vādī*, *samvādī*, *vivādī*, and *anuvādī* seems to have been of primary importance in this musical system. These terms are comparable to the Western sonant, consonant, dissonant, and assonant, respectively. They expressed an abstract concept of consonance and dissonance which could be applied to specific scales or modes. As in the Greek Pythagorean system, only perfect fourths and fifths were considered consonant, while 'dissonant' seems to have referred to the semitone, and perhaps the major seventh. These relationships are expressed in *śrutis*; the consonant intervals being of either 9 or 13 *śrutis*, the dissonant of either 2 or 20. The remaining tones were considered assonant.

The difference between the two tone-systems, *shadjagrāma* and *madhyamagrāma*, is best seen in terms of consonance rather than of the microtonal deviation mentioned earlier. In the *shadjagrāma* the interval between the second degree and the fifth degree is described as 10 *śrutis*, that is one *śruti* larger than the consonant fourth. In the *madhyamagrāma* this fifth degree is lowered by one *śruti*, thus making it consonant to the second. This means, however, that the fifth degree is no longer in perfect relationship with the first degree, being 12 *śrutis* instead of the consonant 13 *śrutis*. This can be seen in the following schema. The notes of the Indian octave (*saptaka*, 'group of seven'), *shadja*, *rishabha*, *gāndhāra*, *madhyama*, *panchama*, *dhaivata*, and *nishāda*, are given in their commonly abbreviated forms, *sa*, *ri*, *ga*, *ma*, *pa*, *dha*, and *ni*:

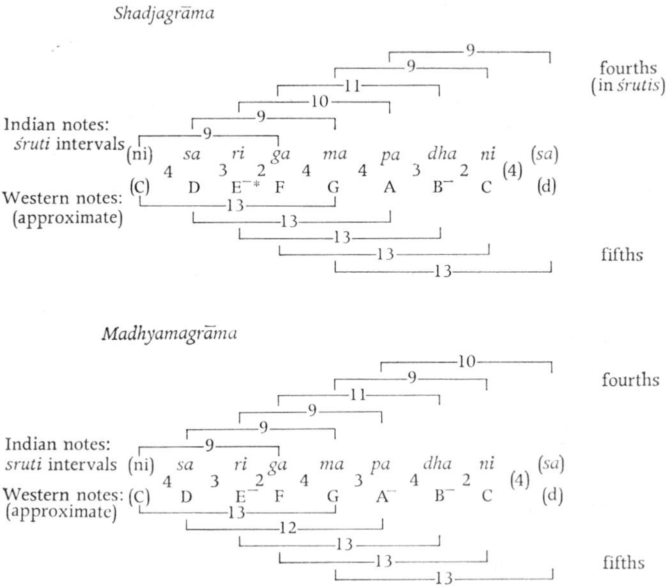

*The minus signs indicate that the Indian notes were microtonally flatter than their Western counterparts.

The *madhyamagrāma* is, however, said to begin with *ma* rather than *sa*, perhaps because the *sa* no longer has a consonant fifth. Thus, the *shadjagrāma* is similar to the 'D' mode, the Ecclesiastic Dorian, and the *madhyamagrāma* to the 'G' mode, the Ecclesiastic Mixolydian. It will be seen that, apart from the non-consonance of the *ri–pa* in the *shadjagrāma* and the *sa–pa* in the *madhyamagrāma*, both parent scales have one other non-consonance, *ga–dha*, an interval of eleven *śrutis*. This is the inevitable tritone which was described as *diabolus in musica* ('the devil in music') in Western plainsong. It was very likely that, to avoid this tritone, two altered notes were introduced into the ancient system—the *antara ga* (F#), which was two *śrutis* sharper and was thus a perfect fourth below the *dha* (B), and the *kākalī ni* (C#), a perfect fifth above the *antara ga*. These two notes may initially have been leading note accidentals, but later became scale notes which replaced the normal *ga* and *ni*.

From each of the two parent scales seven modal sequences (*mūrchhanā*) were derived, based on each of the seven notes. Thus, there were two *mūrchhanās* based on, for instance, the *ri* (E), one using the *shadjagrāma* tuning, the other the *madhyamagrāma* tuning, differing from each other only in the one *śruti* deviation of the *pa* (A). Of each of the seven pairs of *mūrchhanās*, one was chosen as the basis for a *śuddha jāti* ('pure' mode), four of which were in the *shadjagrāma* tuning, three in the *madhyamagrāma*. In addition to these seven, a further eleven *vikrita jātis* ('modified' modes) were derived by the combination of two or more of the *śuddha jātis*. Just how this was achieved, however, is not indicated in the text. The *jātis* were musical entities on which compositions and, presumably, improvisations were based and must have resembled the modern concept of *rāga*. They are described initially in terms of ten characteristics: *graha* (starting note), *amśa* (predominant notes), *tāra* (the note which forms the upper limit), *mandra* (the note which forms the lower limit), *nyāsa* (the final note), *apanyāsa* (the secondary final), *alpatva* (notes which are used only infrequently), *bahutva* (notes used frequently), *shādavita* ('hexatonic quality', i.e. the note which is omitted to make the *jāti* hexatonic), and *audavita* ('pentatonic quality', i.e. the two notes which must be omitted to make the *jāti* pentatonic).

The fact that *jātis* are often allocated more than one *amśa* and in the case of one—the *jāti shadjamadhyamā*—all the notes are given as *amśa*, suggests that these ancient *jātis* had multiple possibilities and were not quite the same as the modern *rāga*. Similarly, the use of the terms *shādavita* and *audavita* seems to indicate that a single *jāti* could be performed in either heptatonic, hexatonic, or pentatonic form. In the modern *rāga* the possibilities are generally quite limited, and although the number of notes might vary in the ascending and descending lines, a *rāga* is usually described as being just one of the three, heptatonic, hexatonic, or pentatonic.

It is not clear just when the system of *jātis* fell into disuse, since many later texts refer to them merely out of reverence for Bharata, the author of the *Nātyaśāstra*. There is, however, mention in the *Nātyaśāstra* of certain musical entities, later called *grāma-rāgas*, which are said to be performed in the formal stages of Sanskrit classical drama. The connection between these and the elaborately described system of *jātis* is not established in the *Nātyaśāstra*. The *grāma-rāgas*, seven in number, are mentioned in the seventh-century Pallava Kutumiyāmalai music inscription in Tamilnādu, in the *Brihaddeśī*, written by Matanga about the tenth century, and in the *Sangītaratnākara* by Śārngadeva, written in the thirteenth century A.D. In the *Brihaddeśī* the *grāma-rāgas* are said to have been derived from the *jātis*, but the evidence seems to suggest that they were more like the parent scales or tuning systems on which the *jātis* were based, namely the *shadjagrāma* and the *madhyamagrāma*. In fact, *shadjagrāma-rāga* and *madhyamagrāmarāga* are two of the *grāma-rāgas* listed in the music inscription. The other five seem to be variants in which either or both *antara* and *kākalī*, the altered forms of the notes *ga* and *ni*, are used. These seven *grāma-rāgas* have been reconstructed as follows:

Madhyama-grāma-rāga.

sa		ri		ga		ma		pa		dha		ni		sa
	3		2		4		3		4		2		4	
D		E^-		F		G		A^-		B^-		c		d

Shadja-grāma-rāga.

sa		ri		ga		ma		pa		dha		ni		sa
	3		2		4		4		3		2		4	
D		E^-		F		G		A		B^-		c		d

Shādava-grāma-rāga.

				(a)*										
sa		ri		ga		ma		pa		dha		ni		sa
	3		4		2		3		4		2		4	
D		E^-		$F^\sharp$		G		A^-		B^-		c		d

Panchama-grāma-rāga.

				(a)										
sa		ri		ga		ma		pa		dha		ni		sa
	3		4		2		4		3		2		4	
D		E^-		$F^\sharp$		G		A		B^-		c		d

Kaiśika-grāma-rāga.

				(a)								(k)*		
sa		ri		ga		ma		pa		dha		ni		sa
	3		4		2		3		4		4		2	
D		E^-		$F^\sharp$		G		A^-		B^-		$c^\sharp$		d

Sādhārita-grāma-rāga.

				(a)								(k)		
sa		ri		ga		ma		pa		dha		ni		sa
	3		4		2		4		3		4		2	
D		E^-		$F^\sharp$		G		A		B^-		$c^\sharp$		d

Kaiśika-madhyama-grāma-rāga.

				(a)								(k)		
sa		ri		ga		ma				dha		ni		sa
	3		4		2			7			4		2	
D		E^-		$F^\sharp$		G				B^-		$c^\sharp$		d

* (a) and (k) refer to *antara* and *kākalī*, the variant forms of the notes *ga* and *ni*.

Matanga, the author of the *Brihaddeśī*, claims to be the first to discuss the term *rāga* in any detail. It seems quite evident that during this period *rāga* was only one of several musical entities. The primary method of classification used by Matanga was in terms of musical forms called *gīti*, which appear to be related to performance styles, not to tuning systems. Five categories of *gīti* are discussed: *śuddha*, *bhinna*, *gaudī*, *rāga* (also called *vesara*), and *sādhāranī*. Matanga mentions five *śuddha* ('pure') *gītis* which are the same as five of the *grāma-rāgas* mentioned above, excluding *shadjagrāma-rāga* and *madhyama-grāma-rāga*. These two are included in the list of *śuddha gītis* given in the *Sangītaratnākara*. The *bhinna* category is apparently derived from the *śuddha* by altering one or more of the melodic characteristics, for instance, note or octave register of emphasis and variation of ornamentation. The *gaudī* category is, however, distinguished from the *śuddha* only in the style of performance; it is much more florid and is characterized by fast shakes in all three octave registers. The other two categories of *gīti*, *rāga*, and *sādhāranī* appear to be independent from the melodic point of view. Most of the *rāga-gītis* appear to have been named after the different peoples living in various parts of the country and this suggests a link with regional folk music. In terms of performance style, *rāga-gīti* is described as having 'varied and graceful ornaments, with emphasis on clear, even, and deep tones and having a charming elegance'. The difference between the *rāga-gīti* and the fifth category, *sādhār-anī-gīti*, which is said to combine the stylistic features of the other four, is not clear. There is reason to believe, however, that even in Matanga's time the *grāma-rāgas* and the *gītis* may have been slightly out of date, for Matanga mentions several other categories under the heading of *deśī* (lit. 'the vulgar dialect spoken in the provinces'). *Deśī* is contrasted with the term *mārga* (lit. 'the path'), which Matanga uses to refer to the ancient traditional musical material, whereas *deśī* refers to the music practice then current in the provinces. The title of his work, *Brihaddeśī* ('the great *deśī*'), suggests that these other categories may have been the focus of the work, but the portion of the text surviving does not support this conclusion.

In the thirteenth-century *Sangītaratnākara*, the total number of *rāgas* had increased to 264, of which just over 10 per cent were said to be no longer popular. Modern scholars have not yet been able to reconstruct these *rāgas* satisfactorily, in spite of the fact that a rudimentary form of notation, based on the Indian equivalent of the Western tonic sol-fa, was given by both Śārngadeva and Matanga. The basic difficulty lies in the interpretation of the intervals used in each of the *rāgas*. Present-day Indian classical music is normally accompanied by a drone which establishes the tonic or ground-note quite clearly. Unfortunately it is not until the modern period that texts mention the drone, and it is merely a matter of conjecture whether the drone was used in ancient Indian music, and if so which were the drone notes. In the *jāti* system, it would seem that practical considerations would preclude the use of a drone, since each of the *śuddha* (pure) *jātis* apparently had a different ground-note. On a modern drone instrument, such as the *tambūrā*, this would involve re-tuning the instrument for each *jāti* and would be extremely impractical. In modern music the ground-note remains unchanged from one *rāga* to the next and changes of scale are achieved by using *vikrita svaras* ('altered notes') i.e. flats and sharps. In the *jāti* system, however, scale changes were achieved by shifting the ground-note to different points of the two parent scales. Only two altered notes, *kākalī ni* and *antara ga*, were used, apparently serving as leading notes, and these were used only in ascent.

It may have been, at least in part, because of the proliferation of *rāgas*, and the number of overlapping categories to which they were ascribed, that new methods of classifying *rāgas* seemed to become popular during the Muslim period. These were apparently not based on musical characteristics, but rather on associations involving the ethos of the *rāgas*. From early times both *jātis* and *rāgas*, in their connection with dramatic performance, were described as having particular moods (*rasa*) and being suitable for accompanying specific dramatic events. The term *rāga* itself is derived from the Sanskrit root *ranj* 'to colour or tinge with emotion', and it was this aspect of *rāga* which seemed to gain precedence.

The most popular method of classification was in terms of *rāgas* (masculine), and their wives, called *rāginī*, which was sometimes expanded to include *putras* (their sons) and *bhāryās* (wives of sons). The number of masculine *rāgas* is usually given as either five or six, each having six wives. These *rāgas* and *rāginīs* are usually personified and are associated with particular scenes, some of which are taken from Hindu mythology, while others represent the states of feeling beginning to be expressed in the romantic-devotional literature of the period. The climax of this personification is found in the *rāga-mālā* paintings, usually in series of thirty-six, which depict the *rāgas* and *rāginīs* in their emotive settings.

The classification in terms of *rāgas* and *rāginīs* is now no longer used, and although one still occasionally hears an older musician use the word *rāginī*, only the term *rāga* (in north India usually pronounced *rāg*) is now in general use. This often leads to incongruities of gender, where the masculine word *rāga* is followed by a word with a feminine ending, for instance *rāga Bhairavī*, the wife of Bhairava, an aspect of the Hindu deity, Śiva.

MODERN NORTH AND SOUTH INDIAN CLASSICAL MUSIC

The thirteenth-century *Sangītaratnākara* was written in the Deccan, just before the Muslim conquest of this region by 'Alā'u'd-Dīn Khaljī. It is shortly after this that one notices a gradual differentiation between north and south Indian music. Although orthodox Islam frowned upon music, the acceptance of the Sūfī doctrines (in which music was often an integral part) by Islam made it possible for many Muslim rulers and noblemen to extend their patronage to this art. The attitude expressed by Amīr Khusrau, a poet and musician at the Court of 'Alā'u'd-Dīn Khaljī, who comments that the music of India was the finest in the world, was fairly representative of the Muslim attitude to Indian music. Although we know that musicians from Iran, Afghanistan, and Kashmīr were at the courts of the Mughal Emperors Akbar, Jahāngīr, and Shāh Jāhān in the sixteenth and seventeenth centuries, it is quite evident that it was Indian music which captured the imagination of the Muslim rulers. Famous Indian musicians such as Svāmī Haridās, Tānsen, and Baiju Bāvrā have left their impress on the history of north Indian music as performers and innovators. Muslim musicians took to the performance of Indian music and added to the repertoire by inventing new *rāgas*, *tālas*, and musical forms, as well as musical instruments. This Muslim influence was largely effective in the north of India and undoubtedly helped to further the differentiation between north and south Indian music, the two classical systems which are now generally referred to as *Hindustānī* and *Karnātak* (*Carnatic*) music, respectively.

The Muslim patronage of music has had two main effects on the music of north India. The first was to de-emphasize the importance of the words of classical songs, which were originally composed in Sanskrit and were, in any case, incomprehensible to anyone less than a traditional Hindu scholar. Sanskrit songs were gradually replaced by compositions in various dialects such as Bhojpurī and Dakhanī. There were also compositions in Urdū and Persian, some of which can still be heard. The textual themes of the songs were often based on Hindu mythology and were of little meaning to the Muslims, yet Muslim musicians sang these songs, with Hindu religious themes, as they do to this day. The reverse is also true, that Hindu musicians sometimes sing songs dedicated to Muslim saints. Perhaps the best example of this broad-minded attitude is to be seen in the poetry of the Muslim ruler Ibrāhīm ʿĀdil Shāh II of the Deccan, who, in his *Kitāb-i-Nauras*, composed at the beginning of the seventeenth century, wrote poems in praise of both Hindu deities and Muslim saints. These poems were sung in specified *rāgas* by both Hindu and Muslim musicians.

The second effect of court patronage on Indian music was to produce an atmosphere of competition between musicians, which placed no little emphasis on display of virtuosity and technique. A great deal of importance was also placed on the creative imagination of the performing musician and gradually the emphasis shifted from what he was performing to how he was performing it. Traditional themes remain the basis of Indian music, but, in north India particularly, it is the performer's interpretation, imagination, and skill in rendering these that provide the main substance of modern Indian music.

Beginning about the sixteenth century, we can see a direct connection between the textual literature and modern performance practice. An important feature of most of these texts is that a new system of classifying *rāgas* in terms of scales was introduced. These scales are called *mela* in south India and *thāt* in north India. While north Indian music was evolving through its contact with the Muslims, south Indian musical theory was being thoroughly revamped by its theoreticians. Here a basic difference of approach becomes evident. North Indian musicians were little influenced by the musical literature written in Sanskrit because many of them were Muslim and had no background in the language. In addition, most Hindu musicians were unable to understand Sanskrit, which had become a scholarly language in north India. South India had, however, become the centre of Hindu learning, and Sanskrit literature continued to play an important part in the development of its music. Thus north Indian music seems to have developed, for the most part, quite intuitionally during this period, and it is only in this century that musical theory has once again begun to come to grips with performance practice and to influence its development. In contrast, south Indian theoreticians had established most of the perimeters and the parameters of the system by the eighteenth century. This, unquestionably, retarded the rate of 'natural' evolution of south Indian music, but opened up a number of different avenues based on theoretical possibilities. As a result, there are now considerable differences of detail between the two systems to the point where they are, to a large extent, mutually incomprehensible.

RĀGA AND ITS CLASSIFICATION

By this time we can be sure that the old system of twenty-two *śrutis* was no longer in existence in either north or south Indian music, and in both systems the octave was composed of twelve basic semitones. In south Indian music, a great deal of emphasis was placed on heptatonic scale types, *melas*, as a means of classifying *rāgas*, and the seventeenth-century text, *Chaturdandī-prakāśikā*, lists all the possible *melas* which would fit into the south Indian musical system. This 72-*melakarta* system still provides the basis of classification in south India. In the following chart are given the modern south Indian and north Indian notes with their comparable Western notes:

South Indian	*North Indian*	*Western*
1. sa	sa	C
2. śuddha ri	komal re	D♭
3. catuśśrutī ri or śuddha ga	śuddha re	D E♭♭
4. shatśruti ri or sādhārana ga	 komal ga	D♯ E♭
5. antarā ga	śuddha ga	E
6. śuddha ma	śuddha ma	F
7. prati ma	tīvra ma	F♯
8. pa	pa	G
9. śuddha dha	komal dha	A♭
10. catuśśruti dha or śuddha ni	śuddha dha	A B♭♭
11. shatśruti dha or kaiśiki ni	 komal ni	A♯ B♭
12. kākalī ni	śuddha ni	B

In both systems, there is the underlying concept that no scale or *rāga* may use both the *śuddha* ('pure') and *vikrita* ('altered') forms of a note, but since in south Indian music there are alternate names for four of the notes, many more scales are possible than in north Indian music. The south Indian scales are described in terms of tetrachord types as follows:

1.	C	D♭	E♭♭	F	and	G	A♭	B♭♭	c
2.	C	D♭	E♭	F		G	A♭	B♭	c
3.	C	D♭	E	F		G	A♭	B	c
4.	C	D	E♭	F		G	A	B♭	c
5.	C	D	E	F		G	A	B	c
6.	C	D♯	E	F		G	A♯	B	c

Each of the lower tetrachords can combine with six of the upper tetrachords, which gives a total of 36 possible scales. These 36 scales use the F; a further 36 scales are derived by using the F♯, making a total of 72. To facilitate the memory, these scales are both numbered and named. The first two syllables of the name, when applied in a code, give the number of the scale, and from the number it is easy to reconstruct the scale if one remembers the six tetrachord types.

The *Chaturdandī-prakāśikā* states clearly that only 19 of the 72 scales were in current use. Since then, great south Indian composers have composed *rāgas* in each of these scales and they are all in the modern repertoire.

In north Indian music the first and sixth tetrachord types of south Indian music, which involve the E♭♭ and B♭♭ and the D♯ and A♯, would not be acceptable because in their system these notes would be seen as D, A and E♭, B♭. Thus, these tetrachords would be 'chromatic': C D♭ D♮ F, G A♭ A♮ c, C E♭ E♮ F, and G B♭ B♮ c. Of the 72 south Indian scales, only 32 would be acceptable in north India. The north Indian approach to scales has been quite different. The system generally adopted in north India is that advocated by the late Pandit V. N. Bhātkhande, who, after spending many years of his life notating songs in many different *rāgas* performed by a number of musicians from various parts of the country, concluded that most of the *rāgas* in north India belong to ten different scale types, which are called *thāt*. These had evolved quite naturally through performance and without the influence of musical theory. There are about ten more scales used in north Indian music, but there is reason to believe that all of these represent relatively modern innovations, some of which are clearly derived from south India. One factor which distinguishes these from Bhātkhande's ten *thāts* is the fact that, whereas there are several *rāgas* in each of Bhātkhande's *thāts*, the other scales are represented by only one *rāga*. Nine of Bhātkhande's ten *thāts* are connected to each other in the form of an incomplete circle, very much like the Western Circle of Keys. The basic difference is that in Indian music *sa* and *pa* (C and G) are not permitted modified forms, either flat or sharp. Thus, the Indian parallel of the key of D, which has F♯ and C♯, would be *Mārvā thāt* which has F♯ and D♭, the last being the enharmonic form of the C♯. The succeeding sharps, G♯ and D♯, would thus be A♭ and E♭. The equivalent of the key of 5 sharps (i.e. with F♯, D♯, A♯, E♯, and B♯) is not used in north Indian music at the present time. The diagram on page 225 shows this circle of *thāts*.

Although the circle is not complete in terms of the modern repertoire, there is evidence to show that the missing scale was in fact used until the last century. The north Indian *rāga Torī*, which had this scale, was, in the seventeenth century, described as having four flats and would thus have been classified in *Bhairavī thāt* of Bhātkhande's system. *Rāga Torī* then evolved to the scale missing in the circle, and is now classified in, and has given its name to, *Torī thāt*, with its three flats and one sharp. There have been many instances of north Indian *rāgas* evolving one or two steps around the circle over the past few centuries. There have, however, also been a few instances of *rāgas* whose scale has changed drastically, a process which cannot be explained in terms of gradual evolution. The rate of evolution of the *rāgas* in south Indian music has been slower and, as a result, the occurrence of the same *rāga* name in the two systems does not always indicate the same scale type.

Bhairav, one of Bhātkhande's ten *thāts*, is not part of this circle, but is nevertheless extremely important in both North and South Indian music. Its scale is the 'gypsy' scale: C D♭ E F G A♭ B c. The available evidence seems to suggest that this was introduced into India from Arabic music sometime before the fifteenth century. Apparently the mode was first known as *Hejāz* (*Hejujī* in south India), and the name *Bhairav* seems to have been applied later. This connects with the circle through *Pūrvī thāt*. The evidence suggests that the *Bhairav* scale was already popular by the fifteenth or sixteenth century, and some of the *rāgas* mentioned in the scale at that time, for instance in the *Rāgatarangini* of Lochana, have evolved into the circle through *Pūrvī thāt*. It may well be that the popularity of *Bhairav* may have provided the impetus which led to the completion of the circle.

CIRCLE OF THĀTS

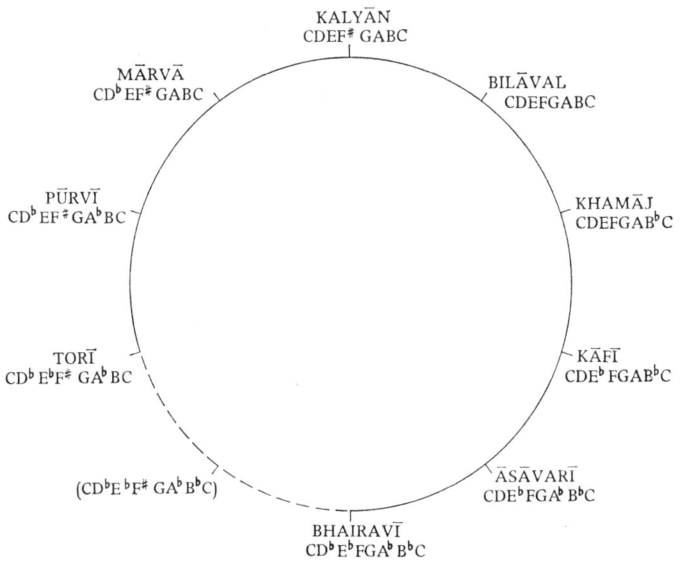

There are indications in south Indian music too, that these same ten scales may be the most important; but the fact that many new *rāgas* have been invented on purely theoretical bases in the last two hundred years tends to obscure the evidence.

Mela and *thāt* are theoretical devices for the classification of *rāgas*. They may, perhaps, be used for exercises in training students but are never heard in performance. *Rāgas* may be heptatonic (*sampūrna*), hexatonic (*shādava*), or pentatonic (*audava*). They have certain scalar elements; for example all *rāgas* have specified movements which enable the melody line of the *rāga* to be carried from one octave to another—the ascending movement being called *āroha* (*ārohana*) and the descending movement, *avaroha* (*avarohana*). In contrast to scales, however, which are step-by-step arrangements of notes, *rāgas* generally involve omissions of specific notes (*varjya svara*) and zigzag movements (*vakratva*), which are also usually specified. Nor are *rāgas* slaves to scales, since accidentals are commonly used in many *rāgas*, and in *rāgas* such as the north Indian *Bhairavī* and *Pīlū* all five accidentals are permitted. A further distinction between scale and *rāga* is found in the varying emphasis placed on the different notes, which is characteristic of each *rāga*. In this connection, the term *vādī* or *jīva-svara* refers to the most prominent note of a *rāga*, and *samvādī* to the second most prominent note. The terms *vādī* and *samvādī* were used in early Indian music to refer to the sonant and the consonant. In modern times, however, the *samvādī* is not always consonant to the *vādī*, for instance in the north Indian *rāga Mārvā*, where the *vādī* is *dha* (A) and the *samvādī re* (*komal*) ($D^{\flat}$), a descending augmented fifth.

Rāgas, however, also have melodic elements and are generally recognized by what are called 'catch' phrases (*pakar* or *rakti prayoga*). Many *rāgas* also have characteristic ornaments associated with certain notes, and these are further identifying features. In north Indian music one sees the beginnings of a different method of *rāga* classification based on these melodic elements, where a number of *rāgas* which have certain phrases in common are given generic names, such as *Kalyān*, *Malhār*, and *Kānhrā*, with specific names used to distinguish the various *rāgas* within the same genus. This is, however, a secondary means of classification and has not been fully developed.

To illustrate the difference between *rāga* and scale, a musical example gives some characteristic phrases in six north Indian *rāgas* which are traditionally described as belonging to *Khamāj thāt*, the 'G' mode:
Musical example 7, p. 242

TĀLA AND ITS CLASSIFICATION

Just as the system of classifying *rāga* is more elaborate in the south, so too is the system of classifying *tāla*, or time measure. *Tālas* are reckoned in terms of *angas* (sections) whose duration is measured either in terms of *akshara* or *mātrā*. These two terms are derived from prosody, where they refer to the syllable and the metrical unit respectively. In south Indian music, an *akshara* is the smallest time unit, the *mātrā* being composed of four *aksharas*. The main group of *tālas* in south Indian music, called the *sulādi tālas*, has three different *angas*; *laghu*, a variable unit consisting of 3, 4, 5, 7, or 9 *aksharas*; *druta*, consisting of 2 *aksharas*; and *anudruta*, which is equal to one *akshara*. By taking the different values of *laghu*, each of the seven *sulādi tālas* has five possibilities, called *jātis*. The diagram overleaf shows the *tālas* and the number of *aksharas* in their five *jātis*.

It will be seen that several of these time cycles are of the same length but are distinguished from each other by their internal subdivisions. In the course of a performance, the vocalist as well as members of the audience may mark the time by clapping, hand waving, and finger counting.

In addition to the *sulādi tālas* one may also hear one of the four *chāpu tālas*, said to have been derived from folk music and consisting of two sections of unequal length, i.e. 3 plus 4, 1 plus 2; 2 plus 3, and 4 plus 5. On rare occasions one may also hear one of the 'classical' 108 *tālas*, based on the unit of the *mātrā* (equal to four *aksharas*), which often involves a gigantic *tāla* cycle, such

TĀLA	ANGA	JĀTI tisra	caturasra	khanda	miśra	sankīrna
1. Dhruva	L D L L*	3+2+3+3 =11	4+2+4+4 =14	5+2+5+5 =17	7+2+7+7 =23	9+2+9+9 =29
2. Mathya	L D L	3+2+3 =8	4+2+4 =10	5+2+5 =12	7+2+7 =16	9+2+9 =20
3. Rūpaka	D L	2+3 =5	2+4 =6	2+5 =7	2+7 =9	2+9 =11
4. Jhampā	L A D	3+1+2 =6	4+1+2 =7	5+1+2 =8	7+1+2 =10	9+1+2 =12
5. Triputa	L D D	3+2+2 =7	4+2+2 =8	5+2+2 =9	7+2+2 =11	9+2+2 =13
6. Ata	L L D D	3+3+2+2 =10	4+4+2+2 =12	5+5+2+2 =14	7+7+2+2 =18	9+9+2+2 =22
7. Eka	L	3	4	5	7	9

* L=*laghu*, D=*druta*, A=*anudruta*.

as 64 or 72 time-units. These are sometimes to be found in the most difficult form of south Indian music, called *pallavi*, of which more will be said later.

In spite of all this sophistication of *tāla* in south Indian music, perhaps half the music is set in *āditāla*, which is technically described as *triputa tāla, chaturasra jāti*, composed of 8 beats (4+2+2). *Rūpaka tāla, chaturasra jāti* (4+2), and *miśra chāpu tāla* (3+4) are also very prominent. The difficult and long *tālas* are used primarily as a *tour de force*. Each *tāla* may be performed in one of three tempi: slow (*vilambita*), medium (*madhya*), or fast (*druta*), the medium tempo being double that of the slow, and the fast double that of the medium. There is no gradual quickening of tempi as is found in north Indian music.

In contrast to the south Indian system, the main *tālas* of north India are relatively few and are not systematized. They are usually listed in terms of an increasing number of time units, the basic north Indian unit being the *mātrā*. Three factors are of primary importance in distinguishing one *tāla* from another; the number of time units, or *mātrās*, in a cycle; the subdivisions of the cycle in terms of stress and lack of stress; and the composition of drum syllables, called *thekā*, which are used as a time-keeping pattern. Thus, two *tālas* of north Indian music might have the same number of time units and the same distribution of stresses within the cycle, but differ in the drum time-keeping pattern, and be associated with different tempi and specific musical forms. An instance of this is found in the two *tālas*, *tilvārā* and *tīntāla* (shown below). The former is only played in slow tempo and is associated with the *khyāl* form, while *tīntāla* has a more general application. This refers only to north Indian music. Another point of divergence is the idea of 'absent stress', called *khālī*, found in all the north Indian *tālas*. This is a conscious negation of stress which occurs at a point where one would normally expect a stress. Its function appears to be to create an irregularity within the cycle, usually at the half-way point, so that the repeating cycle cannot be shortened. For instance, *tīntāla*, which has 16 time units, is subdivided into four groups of four. This might be thought of as a time cycle of four beats, were it not for the fact that the third group of four begins with the empty beat—signalled by a wave of the hand—whereas the first, second and fourth groups begin with positive stresses which are indicated by claps. The beginning of the first group, called *sam* (*samam* in south Indian music) is the most important and serves as the point of reference (to some extent like *sa*, the ground-note, in the melodic system) and is the point where improvisations are often concluded. The other stresses are called *tālī* (claps). The following scheme shows the most common *tālas* in north Indian music. *Tīntāla*, like the south Indian *āditāla*, is by far the most commonly used:

NORTH INDIAN TĀLAS

TĪNTĀL (TRITĀLA)

mātrā	1	2	3	4	5	6	7	8	9	10	11	12	13	14	15	16
ṭhekā(T)	dhā	dhin	dhin	dhā	dhā	dhin	dhin	dhā	dhā	tin	tin	tā	tā	dhin	dhin	dhā
tāla	X				2				o				3			

TILVĀRĀ

mātrā	1	2	3	4	5	6	7	8	9	10	11	12	13	14	15	16
thekā(T)	dhā	tirakita	dhin	dhin	dhā	dhā	tin	tin	tā	tirakita	dhin	dhin	dhā	dhā	dhin	dhin
tāla	X				2				o				3			

ĀRĀ CHAUTĀL

mātrā	1	2	3	4	5	6	7	8	9	10	11	12	13	14
thekā(T)	dhin	tirakita	dhin	nā	tu	nā	ka	ttā	tirakita	dhin	nā	dhin	dhin	nā
tāla	X		2		o		3		o		4		o	

DĪPCHANDĪ

mātrā	1	2	3	4	5	6	7	8	9	10	11	12	13	14
thekā(T)	dhā	dhin	–	dhā	dhā	tin	–	tā	tin	–	dhā	dhā	dhin	–
tāla	X			2				o			3			

JHŪMRĀ

mātrā	1	2	3	4	5	6	7	8	9	10	11	12	13	14
thekā(T)	dhin	-dhā	tirakita	dhin	dhin	dhāge	tirakita	tin	-tā	tirakita	dhin	dhin	dhāge	tirakita
tāla	X			2				o			3			

DHAMĀR

mātrā	1	2	3	4	5	6	7	8	9	10	11	12	13	14
thekā(P)	ka	ddhi	ta	dhi	ta	dhā	–	ka	tti	ta	ti	ta	tā	–
tāla	X					2		o			3			

EKTĀL

mātrā	1	2	3	4	5	6	7	8	9	10	11	12
thekā(T)	dhin	dhin	dhāge	tirakita	tū	nā	ka	ttā	dhāge	tirakita	dhin	nā
tāla	X		o		2		o		3		4	

CHAUTĀL

mātrā	1	2	3	4	5	6	7	8	9	10	11	12
thekā(P)	dhā	dhā	din	tā	kita	dhā	din	tā	tita	kata	gadi	gina
tāla	X		o		2		o		3		4	

JHAPTĀL

mātrā	1	2	3	4	5	6	7	8	9	10
thekā(T)	dhī	nā	dhī	dhī	nā	tī	nā	dhī	dhī	nā
tāla	X		2			o		3		

ADDHĀ TĪNTĀL (SITĀRKHĀNĪ)

mātrā	1	2	3	4	5	6	7	8	9	10	11	12	13	14	15	16
thekā(T)	dhā	dhin	–	dhā	dhā	dhin	–	dhā	dhā	tin	–	tā	tā	dhin	–	dhā
tāla	X				2				o				3			

KAHARVĀ

mātrā	1	2	3	4	5	6	7	8
thekā(T)	dhā	ge	nā	tī	nā	ka	dhī	nā
tāla	X				o			

RŪPAK

mātrā	1	2	3	4	5	6	7		1	2	3	4	5	6	7
thekā(T)	dhin	dhin	tirakita	dhin	dhin	dhā	tirakita	*or*	tin	tin	nā	dhin	nā	dhin	nā
tāla	X(o)			2		3			o			2		3	

DĀDRĀ

mātrā	1	2	3	4	5	6
thekā(T)	dhā	dhin	dhā	dhā	tin	nā
tāla	X			o		

mātrā = time unit, thekā = drum syllables on tablā(T) or pakhāvaj(P), tāla = stress.

FORM AND INSTRUMENTS

Rāga and *tāla* are both independent bases for composition and improvisation and may be heard as such in a concert. *Ālāp*, with which most Indian classical music begins, presents the *rāga* without reference to *tāla*, while the reverse may be heard in the percussion instrument solo.

In general, Indian classical music is based on two movements; the first of these is in free time and is not accompanied by drums, and the second is in a fixed time-measure which is introduced by a composed piece and is accompanied by drums. It is in this second movement that *rāga* and *tāla* are both employed, since the composition involves a more or less fixed sequence of notes and a specific relationship with the *tāla* cycle. The first movement, the *ālāp* or *ālāpana*, is, from the melodic point of view, the most important of the performance. In the *ālāp*, which is completely improvised, the musician gradually unfolds the characteristic melodic features of the *rāga*, in its own natural rhythm, without the limitations of a fixed time-measure. It is sometimes described as a prelude, but may last as long as half an hour, depending on the inclination and imagination of the performer, and the nature of the audience. Within the *ālāp* there are several stages of development which may lead to a section called *jor* or *nom tom* in north India, *tānam* in south India. This is also performed without fixed time-measure, but here a distinct pulse is introduced. In north Indian instrumental music, the *jor* often culminates in a section called *jhālā* ('web'), where the fast rhythms produced on the drone strings form a kind of lattice-work through which the melody line weaves. At the conclusion of the *ālāp* there is often a short pause, when instruments are retuned before the composition is introduced and the second movement commences.

There are a number of types of compositions in north and south Indian music. Each of these types has implications, concerning not only the form of the composition, but also its stylistic treatment, such as the nature and amount of improvisation to be used, and the kind of ornaments which are considered suitable to the particular form. The form may also have the implication of over-all mood and be associated with certain *rāgas* and *tālas*. The composition is rarely an end in itself and one of its very important functions is to provide a frame of reference to which the performer returns at the end of each set of improvisations. The length of the composition and the emphasis placed upon it vary from one form to another and may also be influenced by the personal inclination of the performer. In general, however, the compositions are much shorter than in Western music, and, in extreme cases, may last only two cycles of the time-measure.

In south Indian music there are no purely instrumental compositions, whereas in the north Indian system there is a form, called *gat*, derived from plucked stringed instrumental technique, and another, called *dhun*—said to be derived from folk tunes—neither of which has text. In both systems, however, pride of place must be given to the voice, not only because it can express ideas through words, but also because of its versatility as a musical instrument. It is able to glide smoothly from one pitch to another (portamento), to produce staccato effects through the use of stop consonants, and to change timbre by using different vowels, nasalization, etc. Instrumental technique is naturally much influenced by the voice, but the exchange is not entirely one-way and certain ornaments and techniques used by the voice can be traced to the influence of instruments.

The vocal form referred to as *rāgam-tānam-pallavi* is generally the main item at a south Indian concert. The term *rāgam* refers here to an elaborately improvised *ālāpana* in completely free time. This is followed by the more rhythmic *tānam* which is still unmeasured. The final section, called *pallavi*, is a composition of words and melody set in a particular *tāla*, often a long and complex one. The composition may be either traditional or have been composed by the performer himself, and be unfamiliar to his accompanists, the violinist and the *mridangam* player. The statement of the composition is followed by elaborate rhythmic and melodic variations, still using the text of the *pallavi*. Then passages, called *svara kalpana*, using the Indian equivalent of the sol-fa syllables, are substituted for parts of the original composition and the *pallavi* serves as a point of return at the conclusion of each improvisation. It is customary for this section to be followed by a drum solo and the performance concludes with a brief restatement of the *pallavi*.

The *rāgam-tānam-pallavi* is the longest item in a recital of south Indian music and may take an hour or more to perform. It makes the greatest demands on the performer's skill and imagination, as well as on the audience, who, in order to appreciate the performance to its fullest, need to be well versed in the technicalities of south Indian music. It is not surprising, therefore, that this is not the most popular form of south Indian music. The *kīrtana* or *kriti*—a devotional song which provides a delicate blend of elements—text, melody, and rhythm, is unquestionably the most popular form. The major part of the modern repertoire of *kriti* stems from three composers, Tyāgarāja, Muttuswāmī Dīkshitar, and Śyāmaśāstrī, who lived in the late eighteenth and early nineteenth centuries. The *kriti* may be preceded by an *ālāpana*, which is generally shorter and less elaborate than that which precedes the *pallavi*. The *kriti* has three sections, called *pallavi*, *anupallavi*, and *charanam*, each of which is generally composed of more than one line of devotional poetry. Considerable importance is placed on the composition and the performer's interpretation, but there is also room for the performer to improvise new melodic variations using the song text (called *niraval*) as well as to improvise passages (called *svara kalpana*) using the Indian *sargam* (sol-fa) syllables.

Other forms, derived from the musical repertoire of *Bharata Nātyam*, the classical south Indian dance, are also heard in south Indian concerts. The *varnam*, a completely composed piece, designed to show a *rāga* in its most pure and complete form, is often performed at the beginning of a concert. *Pada* and *jāvali* are two kinds of love-song using poetic imagery characteristic of the *bhakti* movement, of which more will be said later. The form *tillānā* has a text composed of meaningless syllables, which may include the onomatopoeic syllables used to represent the different drum sounds. The *tillānā* is very rhythmic and is usually sung in fast tempo.

The ensemble used in south Indian music includes a main melody instrument or voice, a secondary melody instrument, one or more rhythmic percussion instruments, and drone instruments. Apart from the voice, the most commonly heard main melody instruments are: *vīnā*, a long-necked, fretted, plucked lute with seven strings; *venu*, the side-blown bamboo flute, usually with eight finger holes; *nāgasvaram*, a long oboe-like double-reed instrument with finger holes; *violin*, originally imported from the West, played while seated on the floor, with the scroll resting on the player's foot; and *gottuvādyam*, a long-necked lute without frets, played like the Hawaiian guitar, with a sliding stop in the left hand.

The violin is by far the most commonly heard secondary melody instrument in south Indian music, and accompanies the voice and other melody instruments, except the *nāgasvaram*. It plays in unison where the passage is composed, but imitates, with a slight time lag, the main melody instrument in the improvised passages. It is quite usual, during the course of a performance, for the main melody instrument to cease at certain points, when the violin temporarily takes its role.

Of the rhythmic percussion instruments, the double-conical two-faced drum, called *mridangam*, is the most commonly heard. The percussion group may also include the *kanjīrā*, a tambourine, the *ghatam*, an earthenware pot without skin covering, and the *morsing*, a metallic jews' harp. A special two-faced drum, called *tavil*—slightly barrel-shaped in appearance—usually accompanies the *nāgasvaram*.

The most prominent drone instrument is the four-stringed *tambūrā*, a long-necked lute without frets. The *nāgasvaram* is traditionally accompanied by the *ŏttu*, a very long version of the *nāgasvaram*, generally without finger holes. Sometimes, a hand-pumped harmonium drone, called *śruti* (or *śruti* box) replaces the *ŏttu* or the *tambūrā*.

North Indian vocal forms have many points of similarity with south Indian forms. The *dhrupad-dhamar* form, which has been out of favour for more than a hundred years, is generally preceded by *ālāp* and *nom-tom*, which are very much like the *rāgam* and *tānam* which precede the *pallavi*. The more rhythmic *nom-tom* derives its name from the use of meaningless syllables such as *te*, *re*, *nā*, *nom*, and *tom*. The *ālāp* and *nom-tom* are completely improvised and are followed by the four composed sections of the *dhrupad*, which is generally performed in slow or medium tempo. The sections are called *sthāyī*, *antarā*, *sanchārī*, and *ābhog*, each consisting of one or more lines of poetry. They are usually first sung as composed, then the performer introduces variations, the words often being distorted and serving merely as a vehicle for the melodic and rhythmic improvisations. These improvisations generally focus on the rhythmic elements, and melismatic passages are seldom employed. There are signs that the archaic *dhrupad* form is at present undergoing a period of revival.

The most popular form of vocal music in north India is the *khyāl*, a Muslim word meaning 'thought' or 'imagination'. This is in contrast to *dhrupad*, which means 'fixed words'. The *khyāl* is much less word-bound; not only is the text much shorter, having only two parts—*sthāyī* and *antarā*—but even these are not always sung in their entirety. There are two types of *khyāl*, *barā* ('big') *khyāl* and *chhotā* ('small') *khyāl*, sometimes also referred to as *vilambit* ('slow') and *drut* ('fast'), respectively. The *barā khyāl* is sometimes sung in extremely slow tempo, where each unit (*mātrā*) of the time-measure might last as long as 4 or 5 seconds, and one whole cycle of the *tāla* as long as a minute. In this slow tempo each syllable of the text of the song is sung with such extensive melisma that the words are virtually unrecognizable. It is also quite common for musicians to ignore the words, except for the short phrase, called *mukhrā* ('face'), which concludes the line and leads to the first beat of the next *tāla* cycle. The *barā khyāl* is not generally preceded by a lengthy *ālāp*; instead, freely improvised *ālāp*-type phrases may occupy the major part of each time cycle, concluding with the *mukhrā*. Three basic types of improvisations are used in the *khyāl: bol tāns*, melismatic treatment of the words of the song; *ā-kār tāns*, fast runs to the syllable *ā*; and *sargam tāns*, runs using the Indian *sargam* syllables. In the *barā khyāl* the improvisations gradually get more ornate and more rhythmic, finally concluding with the rapid *ā-kār tāns* which are limited to the *khyāl* form.

There is no set conclusion to the *barā khyāl*. At an appropriate moment the singer changes, with or without pause, to the *chhotā khyāl*, which may well begin in a tempo eight times that of the *barā khyāl*, and accelerate to a climax. The main feature of the improvisations here are the *ā-kar tāns*, so characteristic of the *khyāl* form.

Thumrī is another popular form of north Indian vocal music. Its basis is the romantic-religious literature inspired by the *bhakti* movement, and the text of songs is of primary importance. In contrast with the *khyāl*, the *thumrī* is a much more interpretative form, where the singer attempts to describe and interpret the words in terms of melody. It is usually sung in fairly slow tempo and is not preceded by a lengthy *ālāp*. The singer first sings a line of the song, more or less as composed, then repeats the line many times, each time with different melodic improvisations. When he has exhausted the melodic possibilities, he will go on to the next line. In his improvisations he generally adheres to the words of the song, but has considerable melodic freedom. It is quite usual for a singer to deviate momentarily from the *rāga* in which the composition is set by using accidentals, as well as to evoke other *rāgas* which might be suggested by the words. When the song is completed, there may be a short section in double tempo, followed by a return to the original tempo, and then the song is either repeated or concluded with a repeat of the first line.

Of the other forms used in north Indian vocal music, the *taranā*, similar to the south Indian *tillānā*, is probably the best-known. It is usually sung in fast tempo and uses meaningless syllables. The *taranā* is generally sung after the *barā khyāl* in place of the *chhotā khyāl*.

Instrumental music has gained considerable prominence in recent years. The most common instrumental form in north Indian music is the *gat*, a purely instrumental composition which seems to have derived its elements from both *dhrupad* and *khyāl*. It is usually preceded by *ālāp*, *jor*, and *jhālā*. The *gat* section usually begins in slow tempo (*vilambita lay*), like the *barā khyāl*, and is generally followed by a *gat* in fast tempo (*druta lay*), comparable to the *chhotā khyāl*. The final climax (*jhālā*) on stringed instruments is achieved by the rhythmic plucking of the drone strings at a greatly increased tempo. Other forms played on instruments are the *thumrī* and the *dhun*. The latter imposes few restrictions on the musician, and does not necessarily follow a specific *rāga*. Occasionally, one may hear a piece called *rāgamālā* (lit. 'a garland of *rāgas*'). This may be played as *ālāp* or in *tāla*. The main feature here is the gradual modulation from one *rāga* to another, finally concluding with a return to the original *rāga*.

The north Indian ensemble varies in its constitution from vocal to instrumental music. It is now becoming increasingly common to hear two main melody instruments or two singers, who generally improvise alternately. The most frequently heard main melody instruments are: *sitār*, a long-necked fretted lute; *surbahār*, a larger version of the *sitār*; *sarod*, a plucked lute, without frets and with a shorter neck than that of the *sitār*; *sārangī*, a short-necked, bowed lute; *bāmsrī*, a side-blown bamboo flute with finger holes; *shahnāī*, a double-reed wind instrument, similar to the oboe, but without keys; and the violin, played in the same manner as its south Indian counterpart. The secondary melody line is very important in vocal music, but is not generally used in instrumental music. The most common secondary instruments are the *sārangī* and the hand-pumped harmonium, a keyboard instrument which was imported from the West at the end of the last century. Another secondary melody instrument often used, especially by Muslim singers, is the *surmandal*, a plucked board zither. On occasions, all three secondary instruments may be used at the same time. The most commonly heard drone instrument is the *tambūrā*, or *tānpūrā*, which has either four or five strings. It is a plucked long-necked lute, similar to the south Indian *tambūrā* but differing slightly in appearance. The drone may also be produced on the *sur-petī*, an instrument similar to the harmonium but without a keyboard, or on drone *shahnāīs*, called *sur*, when the *shahnāī* is the main melody instrument.

The *tablā*, a pair of kettle-drums played with the fingers, is the most commonly heard percussion instrument in north Indian classical music, but the archaic *dhrupad* form is usually accompanied by the *pakhāvaj*, a two-headed double conical drum, similar to the *mridangam* of south India, while the *shahnāī* is generally accompanied by a small pair of kettle-drums, called *dukar-tikar*.

Some instruments, such as the *sitār*, are not only melody instruments, but have drone strings (*chikārī*) which are often used rhythmically, and also have sympathetic strings (*tarab*) which provide an echo effect, something like the effect produced by a secondary melody instrument.

TRIBAL, FOLK, AND DEVOTIONAL MUSIC

Classical music is the most refined and sophisticated music to be found in the subcontinent of India. There are many other forms, however, which have a specific function in the society, and these are by no means devoid of artistic expression. The great diversity of music in India is a direct manifestation of the diversity and fragmentation of the population in terms of race, religion, language, and other aspects of culture. The process of acculturation, so accelerated in modern times, is still not a very significant factor in many areas of the country. There remain remote pockets where tribal societies continue to live much as they have done for centuries. Even though some of these may show evidence of borrowing from higher cultures, they nevertheless manage to assimilate these elements into their own culture in such a way as to enhance their own identity.

There are more than a hundred different tribes in India, numbering more than 30,000,000 people, called *Ādivāsīs*. They are found mostly in the hill regions, particularly in central and eastern India, extending to the Nīlgiri Hills in the south. Racially, most of these tribes have been described as Proto-Australoid, and their religions as being animistic. Between them, they create a considerable variety of music, some of it tonally quite simple and involving only two or three notes, and some using as much as a full octave, usually pentatonic. Most of their music is monophonic, with the exception of the tribes in Manipur, Assam, where a simple form of polyphony is quite common. A variety of instruments is used: some tribes have perhaps no more than a drum, while others have quite a number, including some in each of the four major categories—chordophones, aerophones, membranophones, and idiophones.

Many of the tribes have two distinct types of music, the 'outdoor' ensemble, which is often performed by members of a different tribe or a Hindu caste, and their own characteristic tribal songs. The outdoor ensemble is used at weddings and on festive occasions. It varies in size and structure, depending to some extent on the affluence of the tribe. The main instruments are the double-reed oboe-type, a straight, curved, or S-shaped horn, a variety of drums—kettle-shaped, cylindrical, or frame drums similar to the tambourine—and cymbals. The names of these instruments sometimes vary from one tribe to another, although it seems likely that they represent a common tradition.

Songs in a tribal society are mostly functional and often have the sanctity of a ceremonial rite. Such are, for instance, the songs which accompany the events of the life-cycle—birth, initiation, marriage, and death. Similarly, the agricultural songs which accompany the burning and preparation of the fields, planting, transplanting, harvesting, etc., have an element of ritual associated with them, and there is often a real fear that the harvest may not prove fruitful unless great care is taken over the formalities. Although many of the tribes practise this 'slash and burn' method of cultivation, there are still tribes which are in the hunting and food-gathering stage. Some of these have songs to propitiate their deities, in the belief that this will ensure the success of their ventures, and songs to give thanks at the successful conclusion of the hunt. When things go wrong, in times of disease, drought, or shortage of food, the tribal shaman is often invoked, and he generally has his own repertoire of songs.

Most tribes do, however, have more or less secular songs, such as greeting songs, lullabies, love and courtship songs, ballads, and humorous songs. On the occasion of certain festivals and celebrations, members of the tribes may dance and sing for the pure joy of it. On such occasions, one may also hear songs describing their ancestry and the origin of the tribe.

Some of these songs might well be completely unaccompanied, or accompanied by just a drum. Sometimes the male musicians play one-stringed, long-necked lutes, which provide a drone. Certain tribes, however, have stringed melody instruments, either a small fiddle or a stick zither with attached resonators, and these may be used to accompany the songs. This stick zither may well have been the prototype of the *vīnā* depicted in miniature paintings during the Muslim period. The modern stick zither, *rudra vīnā*, occasionally used in north Indian classical music, still resembles the tribal instrument, but is much larger and of more elegant construction.

The folk music of non-tribal India is a vast subject which has not yet been adequately studied. There are, however, some points of similarity with tribal music, especially in the context of occurrence. Village songs, like many tribal songs, are often associated with the cycles connected with life and death, agriculture and the seasons. The songs vary in detail, not only from one region to another, but also within a region among the different strata of society. A further parallel can be found in the use of the 'outdoor' ensemble which provides festival music and is played at weddings and funerals. This ensemble is generally much like its tribal counterpart, with the oboe-like instrument (called *shahnāī* in north India, *nāgasvaram* in the south), long brass or bronze horns (usually called *turhī* or *karnā*), a variety of drums, such as kettle-drums (*nagārā*) played in pairs with sticks, and the cylindrical or slightly barrel-shaped double-headed drum (*dholak*), and one or more pairs of cymbals, generally made of bell-metal (*jhanjh*). Similar ensembles are also found in the cities.

The distinction between tribal music and folk music is not always clearly defined. Nettle proposes that folk music is an oral tradition found in those areas which are dominated by high cultures, having a body of cultivated music with which it exchanges material and by which it is profoundly influenced. This exchange is very much in evidence in the folk music of India. Hindu mythology and religious philosophy are an integral part of much of Indian folk music. Songs sung at childbirth, for example the *sohar* songs of Uttar Pradesh, often describe the birth of Krishna or Rāma, and wedding songs might well describe the wedding of Śiva and Pārvatī. A fisherman's song could begin with an invocation to a protective deity (such as Jhule Lāl in Sind) and festival songs often have a predominantly devotional character.

The *Bhāgavata Purāna*, which deals with the life and adventures of Krishna, an incarnation of Vishnu, is probably the most popular of the *Purānas* and the story of Krishna has had great influence on both north Indian folk and classical music. The ecstatic devotion of the *gopīs* (milkmaids), especially Rādhā, to Krishna, and their yearning for him, occur over and over again, in both types.

This literature, composed in Sanskrit, has been received in oral form, generally through translations, by all except the erudite. The legends have been disseminated in a number of different ways, but most often in the form of sermons or readings with commentaries (such as *Harī kathā*) at religious festivals, where they have attracted large audiences. These presentations generally include songs and music, and on occasions they may include secular, and even humorous material. A second very important source of dissemination is through religious mendicants, bards, magicians, and snake charmers, who travel from one village to another recounting the stories, often in song, and receive in exchange just enough remuneration to keep them going. A third source is through musical drama, which is found in one form or another in most parts of India, sometimes associated with the temples, as in the *kathakali* form in Keralā, sometimes produced by wandering bands of players, who travel from one village to another carrying their sets (if any), costumes, and musical instruments by bullock cart, during the festival seasons.

The role of the religious mendicant in the growth and spread of medieval Hinduism cannot be overstressed. Many of them have since then become sanctified and are now referred to as 'saint singers' or 'poet-saints'. The popular devotional movements began in Tamilnādu and gradually spread north through Mahārāshtra into north India. The songs of the poet-saints were generally composed in the vernacular languages and received immediate recognition in both the cities and the rural areas.

These songs have had a profound effect on Indian music. Modern Karnātak or south Indian classical music is said to have had its beginnings in the songs of one of the Karnātaka saints, Purandaradāsa (1480–1564), and to have reached its golden period about the beginning of the nineteenth century with the devotional and philosophical songs of the 'trinity', Tyāgarāja, Dīkshitar, and Śyāmaśāstrī. To this day, south Indian classical music maintains, for the most part, a highly devotional character. The influence of the *bhakti* saints on north Indian classical music is not quite so obvious. One of the most revered north Indian poet-saints, Jayadeva of Bengal (twelfth century), composed the *Gīta Govinda*, a series of songs in Sanskrit, describing the love of Rādhā and the milkmaids for Krishna. Each of these songs was composed in a particular *rāga* and *tāla*. Unfortunately, although the songs are still sung in Bengal at Vaishnavite festivals, the original music no longer exists; however, the themes of the songs have been carried over into north Indian classical music, particularly into the vocal form called *thumrī*. Poet-saints such as Mīrābāī and Sūrdās have also undoubtedly had some effect on north Indian music, and specific *rāgas* have been named after them (for example, *Mīrābāī kī Malhār* and *Sūrdāsī Malhār*).

The greatest impact of these saint-singers on Indian music was in the upsurge of a new type of song, variously called *bhajan*, *kīrtan*, or *abhang*. These devotional songs represent something of an intermediate stage between classical and folk music, less abstract than the classical, but more sophisticated than most folk music. While classical music placed emphasis on technique and beauty of performance, and thus became the preserve of specialists, the emphasis in the devotional songs lay in mystical and emotional experience. The sound produced was incidental to the act of singing and one did not need to be a good musician to derive spiritual benefit from the songs. The songs, however, often have 'catchy' tunes, many of which are derived from the *rāgas* of classical music. The wide appeal of these songs can also be attributed to the lively rhythms with which they are accompanied. They have provided a repertoire for congregational purposes in temple services as well as in the many informal gatherings of devotees (*bhajan mandals*) which take place during the festival seasons.

While the devotional movements were spreading through Hindu India, a parallel phenomenon was taking place among the Muslims in India. Orthodox Islam, with its strict code of ethics in which music was generally thought to be illegal, was being tempered by the mystic Sūfī movement, which emphasized a personal realization of God as its goal. One of the legitimate means of achieving this goal, according to some of the Sūfī orders, was through singing the praises of God. Accordingly, the Sūfīs had their own religious mendicants, usually attached to the shrine where they had been initiated, who wandered about the countryside visiting other shrines and singing their devotional songs, much like their Hindu counterparts. There is no doubt that both Hindu and Muslim mendicants exchanged ideas, and that they looked upon each other with respect. The famous poet-saint Kabīr (1440–1518), originally a low-caste weaver in Vārānasī (Banāras), reflects the extent of this communication, as he uses religious themes drawn from both Hindu and Muslim sources, as well as both Sanskrit and Persian vocabulary. The Indo-Muslim repertoire of religious songs, called *qawwālī*, is said to have begun with Amīr Khusrau, the famous poet-musician (*c.* 1300). This repertoire includes songs in praise of Allāh, and of the prophet Muhammad and his descendants. It also includes songs in praise of the patron saint of the singer.

Like *bhajans*, *qawwālīs* may be sung by individuals, such as the mendicants (called *darwesh* among the Muslims), or in groups, for instance at the annual festivals at shrines. *Qawwālīs* may also be sung by professional singers at the homes of patrons, and nowadays in concerts as well. The technique and sensitivity of the professional *qawwāls*, with their vast repertoire of poetry and command over music—much of which is similar to north Indian classical music—has resulted in a new form of musical expression which now seems to be spreading beyond its original Muslim religious environment. Not only may one hear *bhajans* rendered in the *qawwālī* style, but also there have been occasions when *qawwāls* have been invited to sing at Hindu religious functions. On such occasions the *qawwāl* may sing songs composed by Kabīr and others, where the basic theme is generally that there is only one God, whether he is called Rām or Rahīm ('The Merciful', an epithet of Allāh), and that all mystic paths lead to the realization of the One.

Ghazals are another form of song sung by *qawwāls*. These are derived from an Urdū poetic form of the same name, composed of independent couplets. This is essentially love or erotic poetry; underlying it, however, are the themes of the Sūfī mystics, for whom God is the beloved. The verses of the *ghazal* are open to a number of different interpretations; secular, mystical, and philosophical. Modern poets have sometimes used this form for social and political comment as well. Thus a traditional theme, such as a moth sacrificing itself in the flame of a candle, could be interpreted as depicting the intensity of human love, divine love, or even the spirit of patriotism. The *ghazal* form has achieved a great deal of popularity in the northern part of the subcontinent, and special meetings, called *musha'ara*, are held expressly to enable poets to sing or recite their poems.

MODERN DEVELOPMENTS

Modern developments in Indian music could be said to have begun with the songs of the world famous Indian poet, author and painter, Rabīndranāth Tāgore. During his lifetime he wrote more than 2,000 songs, drawing his inspiration mainly from classical, folk, and devotional music. The result was a unique individual expression in which words and melody blend together in an extraordinary way. For Tāgore, words without melody were like butterflies without wings, an attitude which captures one of the essences of Indian society. Purists in classical music have sometimes found objection to Tāgore's songs on the grounds that they are not composed in pure *rāgas*. This is indeed true, but the popularity of these songs in Bengal, especially among the intellectuals, shows that they are not without sophistication, and succeed in their intent.

The most significant factor in modern developments has been due to the influence of the mass media, particularly cinema and radio. Their influence is not limited to the cities; the travelling cinema and the temporary cinema in an open, thatched-roof structure, which has to be rebuilt each year after the monsoons, have made films available to the rural population at extremely low cost. In these cinemas the majority of the audience sits on the floor, only two or three rows of chairs being provided for the wealthier members. The influence of the radio, too, is steadily growing as relatively inexpensive transistor radios become available. In villages and small towns one may hear these radios blaring forth into the streets from the local shops.

Very early, with the introduction of sound films in the 1930s, the cinema industry in India discovered that if films were to be successful they had to include songs, and to this day nearly all successful productions are similar to the 'musicals' of the West. The songs were initially taken from traditional Indian sources, folk, devotional, and classical, as well as *ghazals* and *qawwālīs*, and were presented in a more or less traditional manner. New songs were, however, needed to suit the plot and action in the films and gradually new instrumentation and techniques were introduced. The influence of Western music was delayed, partly by the fact that India had no indigenous tradition of orchestral music, which involves lengthy compositions and accurate performance from notation—neither of which were part of the training of the traditional Indian musician. There was also the lack of experience with harmony, counterpoint, and orchestration, techniques which the West had gradually developed over a period of several hundred years.

It must also be mentioned that music based on harmony and counterpoint is, generally, not meaningful to the Indian ear, which is accustomed to listening 'horizontally' to the subtleties of melody and rhythm. Thus Western tunes based on the logic of harmony were not immediately acceptable. In its early stages, the instruments of the orchestra were used in unison, with only occasional experiments with simple polyphony. The main function of the orchestra was to provide dynamic contrasts, and, by using different instruments, to vary the timbre of the melody line. In the course of time, however, there has been increasing use of polyphony and there have been many attempts to add harmony to Indian melodies. From the Western standpoint these may sound naïve, and the chord progressions haphazard, since the melodies were not conceived harmonically. From the Indian point of view, however, the melody supplies the logic for the harmonies, and the use of harmony adds a new facet to Indian music. In film songs, the melody generally retains its Indian character and the singer often uses traditional vocal ornaments, although the accompanying orchestra shows a great deal of Western influence and may include Western instruments of all types. Recently, Western popular music, with its lively rhythms, simple harmonic structure, and emphasis on tune, has had a considerable influence on Indian film music.

Indian musicologists are generally unable to come to grips with these new trends and are apt to condemn them out of hand. This attitude is reflected in the policy of All India Radio, a government-controlled organization, which has sought to emphasize classical music. For a number of years, film music was not broadcast on All India Radio. This policy was modified when it was discovered that A.I.R. was losing many listeners to the commercially controlled Radio Ceylon, which was presenting film music virtually all day. It is true that much film music is trite, and that some of the experiments are over-indulgent, but these are necessary stages in the development of a new tradition. In the meanwhile, the popularity of film music is on the increase—sometimes to the detriment of age-old music traditions—and there is a growing audience for Indian film music in many parts of South-East Asia, the Middle East, and in Africa.

The policy of All India Radio has been to attempt to raise the cultural, artistic, and moral standards of the people of India. It is not only film music which has come under criticism, but certain aspects of classical music, for example the use of the Western-imported harmonium as an accompanying instrument for Indian music. In spite of the fact that this is one of the most widespread instruments in India, and that north Indian classical singers have been using it for at least forty years, it has been banned from the radio on the grounds that its more or less tempered tuning does not lend itself to the subtleties of Indian intonation. Since this chapter was first written, All India Radio has changed this policy.

All India Radio has not been entirely against experimentation. One of their projects, the All India Radio Orchestra, composed of seventy or more instruments—some of them being from the West—is devoted to the production of serious orchestral music, based on Indian *rāgas* and *tālas*. Some interesting ideas have emerged from these experiments, but they have not yet succeeded in creating any great impact on the Indian music scene.

Ex. 1.

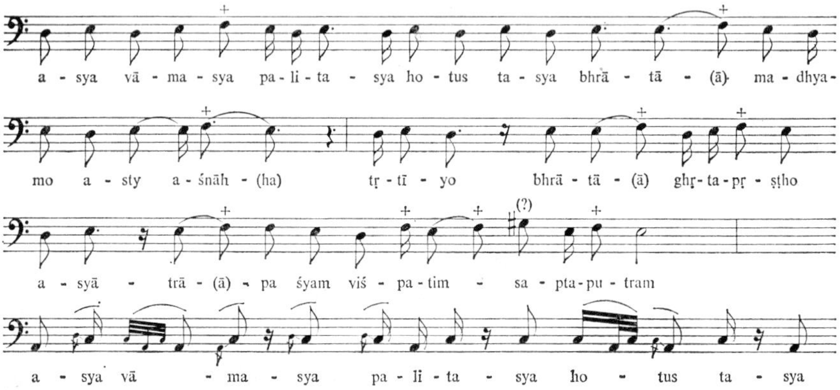

Ex. 2.

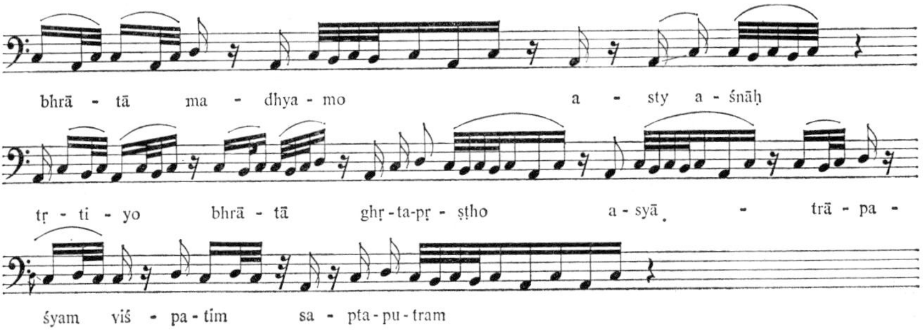

Ex. 3.

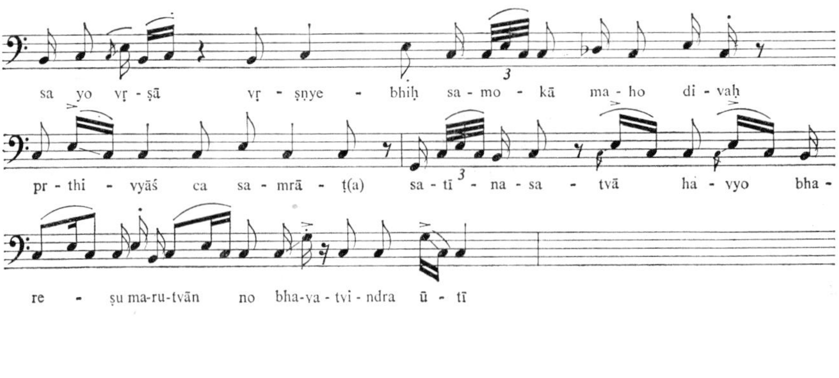

Ex. 4.

om o - gnā - i ā - yā - hī vo - i - to - yā - ā - āī
to yā - ā - āī - gṛ nā no ha - vya - dā - to yā -
ā āī to - yā - ā - ā - ī nā - i - ho - tā - tā - ā - ā
(sā ?)
tā - ā - ā i bā - ā - ā - ā au - ho - vā hi - i - i - ṣi

Ex. 5.

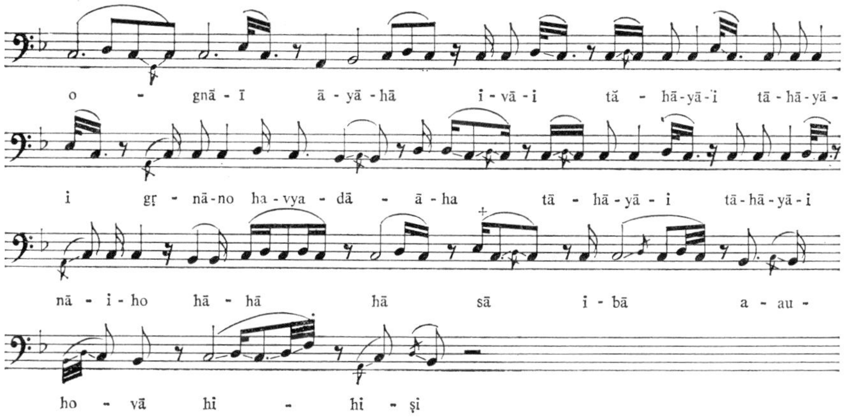
o - gnā - ī ā - yā - hā i - vā - i tā - hā - yā - i tā - hā - yā -
i gṛ - nā - no ha - vya - dā - ā - ha tā - hā - yā - i tā - hā - yā - i
nā - i - ho hā - hā hā sā i - bā a - au -
ho - vā hi - hi - ṣi

Ex. 6.

o
gnā i ā - yā
hi - vā i

Ex. 7.

rāga Khamāj
rāga Des
rāga Jhinjhotī
rāga Tilak Kāmod
rāga Rāgeśrī
rāga Gāvtī

PART TWO

THE AGE OF MUSLIM DOMINANCE

CHAPTER XVII

The Muslim Ruling Dynasties

S. A. A. Rizvi

MUSLIMS believe Muhammad (d. 632) to be the last of the prophets. He not only preached a new faith, known as Islam and based on a fresh divine revelation embodied in the Qur'ān, but also transformed the *asabīyah*, the proud narrow tribal traditions of the Arabs, into a social solidarity and military strength which conquered and colonized a large part of the world. His first four 'successors' (*Khalīfa*) are known as the *Khulafā-i-Rāshidūn* ('Pious Caliphs'). Abū Bakr (632–4) and 'Umar (634–44) seized Syria, Iraq, most of Iran, Egypt, Tripolis, and Barqah. To call this remarkable expansion an easy walk-over for the new faith is to ignore the many factors weakening the Byzantine and Sāsānian empires, and the able leadership of the victors.

The early Muslims founded several new garrison towns which became both centres of their expanded commercial activity and military bases for further incursions. Political power added a new dimension to tribal rivalries and conflicts. The reign of 'Alī (656–61), the last of the *Khulafā-i-Rāshidūn*, saw a period of bitter civil war, leading to the establishment of the hereditary caliphate of the Umaiyāds (661–750) at Damascus.

The second wave of expansion commenced under Hajjāj, appointed by the Umaiyād Caliph 'Abdu'l Malik (685–705), governor of Iraq and Khurāsān. Under Hajjāj's brilliant guidance and careful planning, his two enterprising generals Qutaybah bin Muslim and Muhammad bin Qāsim made successful dashes into Transoxiana and Sind.

Muhammad bin Qāsim marched with 15,000 men, and appeared before Debal in 711; his artillery, consisting of huge *ballistae*, was sent by sea to meet him. Sind was then ruled by a brāhman king, Rājā Dāhir, whose ancestors had snatched the throne from the Buddhist rulers. Debal, a commercial port near modern Karachi, was easily seized, but in fierce fighting at Aror north of Hyderābād, Dāhir himself fell in June 712. Aror surrendered, and early next year Multān was also conquered. In 714 Hajjāj died; and in 715 the caliph Walīd I (705–15), who had taken a keen interest in the conquests. The new government recalled Muhammad bin Qāsim, delivering a mortal blow to the progress of the Arab conquests. Many local chieftains repudiated their Arab allegiance; 'Umar II (717–20) sought to allow them to rule as tributaries on the promise of accepting Islam. This policy failed. Junaid, another enterprising governor, tried to seize both Kacch (Kutch) and Mālwā, but the Pratihāra and Gurjara kings foiled him. Sind continued to be ruled by the Umaiyād governors but the actual administration remained in the hands of the local chiefs, both Hindus and converts to Islam. In the wake of the disintegration of Umaiyād power and the establishment of the 'Abbāsid caliphate in Baghdād (750–1258), the hold of the central authority on Multān and Sind became weaker. By 985 an Ismā'ilī Fātimid dynasty had proclaimed its independence in Multān.

More lasting was the impact of the conquests of Qutaiba in Central Asia between 705 and 715, although he met an end similar to Muhammad bin Qāsim's. He established a firm foothold among the Turkic tribes beyond the Oxus by seizing Tukhāristān with its capital Balkh (Bactria of the Greeks), Bukhārā, and Samarqand in al-Sughd (Sogdiana) with the Jaxartes provinces and Farghāna.

This vast region became the breeding-ground of a new non-Arab leadership. The material and cultural glory of Baghdād, which lasted for about 150 years, was the gift of its Turkic military and Irani intellectual leadership. From the middle of the ninth century, governors in Iran and Khurāsān (Chorasmia) began to assume quasi-independent power. The Samānids (864–1005), a dynasty of Zoroastrian origin, fully subjugated Transoxiana, making Bukhārā their capital. Ever-increasing supplies of talented Turkic slaves from the steppes made them the strongest military power of the East.

Alptigīn, whom the Samānids made governor of Khurāsān in 961, was one of these men. Within one year of his appointment, he was estranged from his masters. He seized Ghaznī, the frontier fortress on the edge of the Hindu world, and an entrepôt for trade with India because of its easy access through the Kābul valley.

The real founder of the Ghaznavid Dynasty was, however, Subuktigīn (976–97), slave and son-in-law of Alptigīn. He extended his power to Peshāwar in India and to Khurāsān, leaving a rich legacy to the ambition of his son Mahmūd (998–1030), who cut all ties with the Samānids, and accepted direct allegiance to the 'Abbāsid Caliph al-Qādir (991–1031). He became a bulwark of Sunnism, which was faltering under the domination of different branches of Shī'īs in Persian Iraq and in Sind. The Caliph awarded him the title *Yamīn-ud-Daula*, 'right hand of the state'. Mahmūd and his immediate successors called themselves only *amīr* ('governor') or *saiyid* ('chief'), though posterity remembered the Ghaznavids as sultans.

Mahmūd won his first great victory against Jayapāla near Peshāwar in November 1001. The Ismā'īlī ruler of Multān was his second target. After finally crushing the Ismā'īlīs in 1008, he carried fire and sword as far as Kāngrā; he completely overthrew the Hindu Shāhī kingdom, opening the doors for repeated invasions of the Gangā and Yamunā *doāb*. The fabulously rich spoils from the temples, repositories of wealth, helped him consolidate his rule in Khurāsān and embellish Ghaznī with palaces and mosques, but he had neither the will nor the human resources to rule his Indian conquests. His dominion extended from the Panjāb to Khurāsān, and included Persian Iraq, but it was loosely held by force of arms alone. Turkic slaves were his closest confidants, but the army was composed of contingents of diverse racial groups, with commanders of their own, including Indians, whose commander was called *Sipahsālār-i-Hindūyān*. He often served as a counterweight to the Turks.

As soon as the powerful hand wielding the sword weakened, such an organization was bound to disintegrate. This happened with the Ghaznavids after Mahmūd and Mas'ūd. Their vassals the Ghūrids, styled after their native region Ghūr, around Firūzkoh and the modern Khwāja-Chisht in central Afghanistan, whom the Ghaznavids had conquered and Islamized, became their rivals. In 1151 ʿAlā'u'd-Dīn, known as *Jahān-Sōz* ('Burner of the World'), outdid Mahmūd in ruthlessness, even exhuming and burning the remains of all the Ghaznavids except Mahmūd and two of his successors. His ambitions extended only to holding Ghūr; he did not annex the Ghaznavid territory in eastern Afghanistan. This fell to the lot of two brothers, Ghiyāsu'd-Dīn Muhammad of Ghūr (1163–1203), who expanded towards Khurāsān, and Shihābu'd-Dīn (later Muʿizzu'd-Dīn) Muhammad (1173–1206), who conquered the Panjāb and Hindūstān.

Muʿizzu'd-Dīn's army comprised both Ghūrī and Afghan troops. Turkic slaves formed the strongest part of his cavalry, all on mounts from the best horse-breeding area in the East, the Sulaimān mountains west of the Indus. Marching through the Gomal pass, the Ghūrīd armies made upper Sind, which had again passed into Ismāʿīlī hands, the target of their attack. Muʿizzu'd-Dīn also tried to penetrate the kingdom of the Chaulukyas of Gujarāt, but was badly beaten in the battle of Anhilwāra in 1178. He met better luck in the Panjāb where he easily defeated Khusrau Malik, the last of the Ghaznavids, in 1186, exposing himself to direct confrontation with Prithvīrāja Chāhamāna. In their first pitched battle at Tarāin in 1191, Muʿizzu'd-Dīn was worsted, and narrowly escaped death. Prithvīrāja recovered Tabarhinda (Bhatinda), but did not garrison it effectively. Muʿizzu'd-Dīn, undaunted, marched again in 1192. Prithvīrāja, with the levies of his feudatory chiefs and other friendly *rājās*, amounting to 300,000 horses and 3,000 elephants, met the Sultan on the same field. The Sultan's army was less than half the size of the Rājput's but its strength lay in its organized mobility. His light-armed horsemen, in four divisions of 10,000, were directed to advance and harass the enemy on all sides with their arrows. When the enemy collected his force to attack, they were to support each other, and to charge at full speed. At the end of the day the Sultan's reserve swooped upon the exhausted Rājputs with lightning speed, and won the day.

Modern historians enthusiastically advance various explanations for this total Muslim victory. The religious terminology of contemporaries ascribed it to God's grace. European scholars of the nineteenth century offered such surmises as the inevitable victory of men from cold climates over the enervated inhabitants of the tropics. In Pakistan it is confidently claimed that Islam can never suffer defeat. Hindu scholars of A. L. Srīvāstava's school believe that Islam's inherent ferocity ensured the Muslim victory. K. A. Nizāmī and modernist Indian Muslims, borrowing ideas from the less unreasonable Hindu scholars, are persuaded to think that Hindu caste distinctions and the Rājput feudal system with its narrow rivalries weakened the Rājput states and brought the defeat of Hindu India. While several factors defeated the Hindu rulers, the overriding elements in the Muslim victory were their advanced military tactics and the tenacity of their Turkic leaders, who from their childhood were nurtured in the guerrilla warfare of the steppes. Prospects of limitless Indian loot united the tribes; if able leadership counted for anything, Mahmūd and Muhammad were such leaders. Mahmūd had fewer difficulties, for the Hindus were not prepared; Muhammad had to fight a formidable and expectant enemy, trained to repulse the *Turushka* raids. The Turkic irruptions followed the ancient pattern of expansion of the steppe tribes over Central Asia. Their motives were the same as those of the early Arab conquerors; Abu Tammām, in his well-known poem, *Hamāsah*, says of the Arabs:

> No, not for Paradise didst thou the nomad life forsake.
> Rather, I believe, it was thy yearning after bread and dates.

Muʿizzu'd-Dīn, unlike Mahmūd, wished to extend his rule beyond Sind and the Panjāb. Unlike Mahmūd, he had no duties in the west; Khurāsān was his brother's territory; so he had leisure to devote his exclusive attention to India. The problem of leadership and incentive was solved by the institutions of slavery and *iqtā*ʿ, which for the last 300 years had been at once a cohesive and a dissolving power for the Turkic dominion in Central Asia and Ghaznī.

The ʿAbbāsids recruited Turkic slaves as a counterpoise to their Arab and Khurāsānī contingents, but the Turkic ruling dynasties of the Iranian world, nearer the source of supply, made them the backbone of their power. The Turkic slaves of the Ghūrīds did not always co-operate with the local troops, but the slaves of Muʿizzu'd-Dīn were infinitely loyal to their master. Promising boys, seized in war or purchased by the affluent governing classes, were often trained in an atmosphere of rare intellectual and military distinction. Under the Ghaznavids and Ghūrīds, such talented slaves started their careers in the service of the Sultans in such posts as keeper of the stables, keeper of the wardrobe, keeper of the Sultan's armour or weapons, or bearer of the ceremonial parasol, and steadily rose to posts of military and administrative eminence.

*Iqtā*ʿ was the system of granting the revenue of a specified area in lieu of salary. It was prevalent in the ʿAbbāsid period, but gained a special significance in Iran, where the *dihqāns*, or village chiefs, whose power came from their hereditary possession of local administrative functions, controlled the administration of the villages. Under the Sāsānids (226–652) they had been subordinate to the feudal lords. After the conquest of Iran by the Arabs they became the link between the local subjects and the foreign government, which adopted as the system of land-tax *muqātaʿā* (assessment at a lump sum, payable according to the lunar year), in contradistinction to assessment by measurement (*misāhā*) and assessment by a share of the crop (*muqāsama*), payable according to the solar year. The areas so assessed, styled *iqtā*ʿ, began from the tenth century to be given to military leaders. Charged with the consolidation of their fiefs, they were also allowed to extend them; they were military bureaucrats, rather than feudal lords. Administration was effected by officials recruited and controlled by them, known as ʿ*āmils*.

The Ghaznavids generally paid their military in cash, food, and clothing, which spoils of Indian temples made easy. In the Panjāb, local *thākurs* and *sāmantas*, counterparts of the Irani *dihqāns*, became the link between the new rulers and their subjects, while the *iqtā*ʿ holders replaced the feudal lords and their sub-feudatories. The forts and castles of the feudatory chiefs became garrison towns of the Ghaznavids, but Lāhore remained more open, becoming a centre of Ghaznavid urban culture with a developing Muslim mercantile community which, even before the Ghūrīd conquest, had established contacts with the courts of the Rājput rulers of Gujarāt, Ajmer, and Kanauj.

The second battle of Tarāin is regarded as a landmark in the history of the Turkic expansion, for it shattered the Chāhamāna power from Panjāb to Ajmer. Some feudatory chieftains were allowed to continue ruling as tributaries. Before leaving India, Mu'izzu'd-Dīn Muhammad appointed Qutbu'd-Dīn Aibak to act as his deputy. An occupation army was stationed at Indraprastha near Delhi, which seized Baran (Bulandshahr) and Meerut and then occupied Ranthambhor and Ajmer, garrisoning all the forts there.

In 1194 Mu'izzu'd-Dīn returned to India, to crush the Gāhadavāla power; Jai Chand, the ruler of Kanauj and Banāras, fought valiantly, and lost, at Chandvār (between Kanauj and Etāwah). The Turks established garrison towns up to Banāras and Asnī. In 1195–6 Mu'izzu'd-Dīn again came to India and penetrated south to Bayāna and Gwālior. All the key points were given as *iqtā'* to Turkic slaves. Control and consolidation depended upon their ability and resourcefulness.

The expansion of Turkic power from Munēr and Bihār to Bengal was the achievement of Bakhtiyār Khaljī, who like many Turkic chiefs rose to eminence by sheer merit. He seized Nadīā in lower Bengal by an adventurous stratagem, but selected Lakhnautī, easily accessible from Bihār, as his seat of government; stations were established at Lakhanor (Nagar in Bīrbhūm district) and Devakot. The next move of Bakhtiyār Khaljī was against Tibet, to open a direct route to Turkistān, and ensure a continued supply of arms and men from that region instead of being dependent upon Delhi. This expedition failed; in 1206 he was brought back to Devakot half-dead, and was treacherously killed by his own lieutenant, 'Alī Mardān Khaljī.

Meanwhile the uprising of the Khokars in the Panjāb cut the Lāhore-Ghaznī route and brought Sultan Mu'īzzu'd-Dīn once more to India. He crushed the uprising, but on his way back to Ghaznī was slain at Damyak, on the banks of the Indus, by some unidentified assassin, either an Ismā'īlī or a Khokar.

The record of his Indian conquests was brilliant, but he was able to crush only the leading centres of Rājput power. Rājput feudatory chiefs occupying rough inaccessible areas remained a constant source of trouble to the Delhi sultans. In the thirteenth and fourteenth centuries, strategic posts from Gwālior to Rājputāna were conquered and reconquered several times, but always became independent again. In the fifteenth and sixteenth centuries, the emergence of the provincial Muslim and Hindu dynasties made Delhi only a small regional power.

Mu'izzu'd-Dīn Muhammad had no sons; even if he had, the question of succession could not have remained undisputed. The Umaiyāds and the 'Abbāsids had followed the principle of hereditary succession, but, with the rise of slaves wielding military and administrative power on their masters' behalf, the tradition changed. It was now ability to rule and qualities of leadership which decided the succession, and scholars and chroniclers soon found some legal justification for accomplished facts.

After the death of Mu'izzu'd-Dīn the battle for succession was fought by his slaves and sons-in-law. Qutbu'd-Dīn Aibak had been his deputy for his

Indian conquests, but Bakhtiyār Khaljī, after gaining power in Bihār and Bengal, had begun to consider himself independent of Aibak and directly under Muʿizzu'd-Dīn. The successor of Ghiyāsu'd-Dīn of Ghūr, who had died in 1202–3, recognized Tāju'd-Dīn Yalduz as the ruler of Ghaznī and gave him a deed of manumission. This enhanced his legal rights and he began to struggle for supremacy over Aibak. The other strong claimant was Nāsiru'd-Dīn Qabācha in Multān, but the chief contenders for the Indian possessions were Aibak and Yalduz. Aibak transferred his capital to Lāhore, gained some successes over Yalduz, but died in 1210, leaving the succession to be disputed again between his son Ārām Shāh and the slave Iltutmish. Minhāj Sirāj, the author of the *Tabāqāt-i-Nāsirī*, claims that Aibak, in accordance with his master's orders, manumitted Iltutmish, but this seems a fiction. Neither Aibak himself nor his rivals were manumitted by Muʿizzu'd-Dīn.

Ārām Shāh was soon replaced by Iltutmish, who enjoyed the support of most of the *iqtāʿdārs*, conciliated by promotion. He made Delhi his capital, and tightened his control over the areas extending from the Satlaj to Banāras. He let Yalduz and Qabācha fight for the Panjāb, and bear the brunt of fighting first with Muhammad Shāh the Khvarizm Shāhī ruler of modern Khiva, and then with the Mongol Chingiz Khān. In 1215 he defeated Yalduz, by then a fugitive in the Panjāb, and in 1228 Qabācha, already prostrated by the struggle against the Mongols. In February 1229 the ʿAbbāsid caliph recognized Iltutmish as Sultan, added the feather of legitimacy to his cap, and enhanced his prestige in the eyes of the *ʿulamā'* (Muslim theologians and scholars), the civil bureaucracy and the sūfīs, who along with the *iqtāʿdārs* formed important pressure groups.

The Sultan gave asylum to a considerable number of talented scholars, statesmen, and generals driven into exile before the onrushing Mongol hordes, and employed them to strengthen his central government, modelled on the administrative institutions of the great Saljūq sultans of Iran; however, the core of his strength was still the Turkic slaves whom he himself had purchased, trained, and promoted to offices of trust and responsibility. They held high posts at Court, and some of them controlled *iqtāʿs* of vital importance. Minhāj Sirāj gives short biographies of twenty-five of Iltutmish's nobles (*maliks*), only two of whom had been slaves of Muʿizzu'd-Dīn Muhammad. Although they included members of several tribes, such as the Khitā'ī, Qipchāq, and Ilbarī, and men from Mesopotamia and Anatolia, prudent management by Iltutmish kept racial rivalries and ambitions subdued. A class of petty military chieftains, described as *iqtāʿdārs* by the historian Baranī, the author of *Tārīkh i-Fīrūz Shāhī*, but clearly distinguishable from the governors or *wālīs* (whose extensive *iqtāʿs* approximated to the provincial sub-divisions of the present day), was also evolved by Iltutmish. They numbered about 2,000 and constituted the nucleus of the central standing army.

This gave Iltutmish better success in controlling the region to the west of Delhi as far as the Satlaj; but his hold in the east of the *Havālī-i-Dihlī* (or the region bounded on the east by the Yamunā, and on the north by the forests at the foot of the Siwāliks) was very precarious. We find the Sultan's eldest son, the energetic Prince Nāsiru'd-Dīn Mahmūd, as governor of Avadh waging incessant war against the Hindu tribes struggling for independence.

Bartū, one of these chiefs, slew about 120,000 Muslims; this number, if not exaggerated, might exceed the casualties at Tarāin.

Between 1224 and 1229, three major expeditions liquidated the Khaljī power in Bengal. Prince Nāsiru'd-Dīn Mahmūd died prematurely in Lakhnautī, and the future governors of Bengal admitted the suzerainty of Delhi only nominally. In the areas south of the river Chambal and in Rājputāna, the Parihāras, the Chāhamānas, the Yaduvamśīs, and the Guhilots repudiated their vassalage several times, and the Muslim garrison towns of Gwālior, Bayāna, Thāngir, and Ajmer were more than once cut off from one another. Even the regions round Badāūn, and Bareilly were not safe and the Katihāriya Rājputs at Aonla were formidable.

When Iltutmish died of cancer in 1235, the Rājputs were still fighting for independence in their respective regions. Yet his achievements were by no means insignificant. He gave an independent status to the Delhi sultanate, obtained legal recognition for it, and made it possible for his sons and daughters to rule until 1266. His daughter, Razīya (1236–40), was endowed with considerable tact and qualities of leadership. She tried to play dominant groups of the Turkic slaves of Iltutmish against one another, but failed, was deposed, and killed. The fourteenth-century historian, Ziyāu'd-Dīn Baranī, speaks of a group of forty (*Chihalgānī*) who dominated affairs. 'The Forty' have passed into legend, even though it is probable that the number was ascribed to them by Baranī merely because of its traditional mystical value. Their number was probably fewer. These men controlled different strategic garrisons, and concentrated as much power as possible in their own hands. Some established marital connections with the family of Iltutmish; others intrigued with ambitious ladies of the royal harem. The internecine struggle among them took a heavy toll of their ranks, and they were able neither to strengthen the royal power nor to raise one of their members to the throne.

When Balban (1266–87) seized the throne by killing his feeble son-in-law Sultan Nāsiru'd-Dīn Mahmūd (1246–66), power had been fully in his hands for over ten years. The remnants of the leaders of Iltutmish's reign were exterminated on one pretext or the other. Balban gave a new basis to his rule by rejecting the policy of co-operation with the dominant Turkic élite and proclaiming that a king is the vice-gerent of God. He buttressed this ideal by imposing strict rules of discipline in his court, calling them Sāsānid ceremonials, although he appears to have had no special knowledge of ancient Iran. He reorganized the central army, kept it active and alert, appointed loyal officers with great care, and strengthened the spy system. He retrieved the prestige of the Delhi sultanate by controlling the Mongol inroads; in 1241 the Mongols had plundered and devastated Lāhore. Balban's frequent raids in the Gangetic *doāb* subdued the turbulent Rājput chiefs and his military posts, garrisoned by Afghan troops, instead of Turks, restored order in that area. By cutting down the jungle and opening roads in the *doāb* he connected his military posts with each other. When well over seventy, in 1281, he ruthlessly crushed the rebellion of his governor Tughril in Bengal, and appointed his own son Bughrā Khān in his place.

The death of his eldest son Prince Muhammad, the warden of the marches, who fell fighting against the Mongols in 1285, was a mortal blow to his ambitions, but he retained the façade of vigour and despotism. Balban died a disappointed man, reading on the wall of time the message of the disintegration of his centralized monarchy.

His grandson Kaiqubād (1287–90) spent all his time in drinking and debauchery. Fīrūz, the aged leader of the Khaljīs, whom the proud Turks considered inferior because of their mixed origin, secured the throne in 1290 and ruled under the title of Jalālu'd-Dīn. His nephew, ʿAlā'u'd-Dīn Khaljī, both as governor of Karā under his uncle (whom he killed in cold blood in 1296) and as sultan, gave lustre to the dynasty. In 1292 he penetrated into Mālwā, and seized Bhīlsā. In 1294 he appeared before Devagiri, defeated the Yādava king, Rāmachandra Deva, and returned to Karā laden with huge wealth.

After becoming king, Sultan ʿAlā'u'd-Dīn killed all possible claimants to the throne, and extirpated a considerable number of the nobles influential under his uncle. Rebellions led by relatives and prominent men induced him to launch an entirely new policy designed to isolate potential leaders from one another, and to deprive them of power and affluence.

He resumed revenue grants to charitable institutions and the families of religious leaders into his own hands. He reorganized the intelligence system, enforced strict sumptuary laws in Delhi, and imposed harsh regulations upon the personal behaviour and social relations of the nobles, particularly prohibiting convivial gatherings.

To increase his financial resources and reduce to abject submission the village leaders, 'khūts, chaudhrīs, and muqaddams', he introduced two important reforms. First, he replaced the earlier land revenue assessments with one based on the measurement of land. Secondly, he revoked the village leaders' hereditary perquisites. To ordinary cultivators his reforms did not make much difference; the village accountant and the army of new revenue officials were corrupt, and even more cruel and oppressive than the hereditary headmen they replaced. The backbone of ʿAlā'u'd-Dīn's strength was the standing army, directly recruited by the army minister (*ʿāriz-i-mamālik*) and paid in cash from the royal treasury. A descriptive roll of the individual horsemen and a system of branding cavalry horses eliminated the fraud and deceit which had been (and were to be again) the order of the day.

The central army overawed the tributary Hindu chiefs ('rāis, rānās, and rāwats'). Almost all northern India was conquered; in 1299, Gujarāt was invaded and Rājā Karan Vāghel driven out. His beautiful queen Kamlā Devī was seized and married to the Sultan. Another army captured Sewistān, and in 1300, when a Mongol army appeared before Delhi, it was defeated with heavy loss. Next, Ranthambhor and Chitor in Rājputāna were conquered; but another Mongol invasion compelled ʿAlā'u'd-Dīn to increase his standing army, and introduce his famous price controls, reinforced with further restrictions on luxurious living. Some modern scholars believe that the reforms were introduced out of philanthropic motives. This view is based upon an anecdote narrated by the eminent sūfī, Shaikh Nasīru'd-Dīn Mahmūd Chirāgh of Delhi (*c.* 1280–1356) to a gullible sūfī audience, but Baranī's analysis of ʿAlā'u'd-Dīn's motives, followed by other medieval historians, is irrefutable.

Between 1305 and 1307, the Mongols made two more invasions, but both were easily repulsed. The Sultan's armies conquered Mālwā, penetrated into Mewār, and completely crushed the Rājā of Jālor; but the Sultan did not think Rājputāna worth the trouble of annexing. The fabulous wealth of the Deccan now attracted him; he needed money to pay his army and his swarming officials. In 1303 an expedition mounted against Wārangal, the capital of the Kākatīya kingdom of Telingāna, from Orissā had failed. Devagiri now became 'Alā'u'd Dīn's target. In 1307 he commissioned his trusted slave Malik Kāfūr to reduce Rāmachandra of Devagiri, who had paid no tribute for several years, and had given shelter to Rājā Karan of Gujarāt, who ruled in Baglāna as his vassal. The invading army was also ordered to bring to the Sultan Deval Devī, the daughter of Rājā Karan by Kamlā Devī. The unfortunate princess fell into the hands of the Sultan's army while being escorted to Devagiri, and was sent to Delhi, where she was married to the Sultan's eldest son Khizr Khān. Malik Kāfūr seized Ellichpur, and proceeded to Devagiri. The Rājā submitted, went to Delhi, and in return for enormous gifts received the title of *Rai-i-Rāyān* ('the Principal Rai'). He remained a life-long ally of the Khaljīs.

In 1308 Malik Kāfūr besieged Wārangal and inflicted a crushing defeat upon the Rājā, compelling him to accept vassalage. Two years later, he took the Hoysala ruler Vīra Ballāla III by surprise, and seized Dvārasamudra. He made a dash upon Madurai, whose Pāndya ruler abandoned it, adopting guerrilla tactics to harass the invader. Madurai was sacked, its temples plundered, and vast booty amassed. It is doubtful if Malik Kāfūr actually invaded Rāmesvaram, as many imagine; he may, however, have sent a plundering column against it.

In October 1311 Malik Kāfūr returned to Delhi and was loaded with honours. The Deccan rājās were recognized as tributary chiefs. Two years later, Kāfūr again marched against Devagiri to crush the rebellious Singhava, son and successor of Rāmachandra. Singhava fought valiantly, but was defeated and slain. Devagiri was annexed; but soon after Malik Kāfūr hastened back to Delhi, which was thrown into disorder by 'Alā'u'd-Dīn's illness. The conspiracies and intrigues of Malik Kāfūr annihilated several eminent members of 'Alā'u'd-Dīn's family. Khizr Khān was disinherited, and, after the Sultan's long-expected death in January 1316, Malik Kāfūr raised to the throne one of 'Alā'u'd-Dīn's sons, aged six, under the title of Shihābu'd-Dīn 'Umar. As regent, he blinded Khizr Khān and several others, but failed in his attempt to visit that fate upon another son of the late Sultan, Mubārak Khān, then about seventeen. The soldiers, moved by the prince's appeals, and his bribes, slew Malik Kāfūr; and Mubārak became king.

He reversed his father's harsh administrative regulations, crushed a rebellion in Gujarāt, and reconquered Devagiri; but his infatuation for an Islamized Hindu slave Hasan, whom he had entitled Khusrau Khān, cost him his life and ended Khaljī rule. Khusrau belonged to the warlike Barwār tribe of Gujarāt and commanded a considerable following of his own men.

Khusrau ruled from 15 April to 3 September 1320. Although the Muslim historians accuse him of introducing idolatrous worship to the palace and insulting Islam and the Qur'ān, a sizeable section of the important Turkic nobles, and the pious Shaikh Nizāmu'd-Dīn Auliyā', the celebrated Chishtī saint of Delhi, supported him. The Shaikh, indeed, accepted money from him. But Ghāzī Malik Tughluq, the ambitious warden of the marches in the Panjāb, and his talented son Malik Jauna rallied a party of Turkic chiefs in the name of Islam and defeated Khusrau in two hotly contested battles.

Ghāzī Malik assumed the title of Ghiyāsu'd-Dīn; his dynasty survived nominally until 1412, and is marked by two important rulers, Muhammad bin Tughluq(1325–51) and Fīrūz Shāh (1351–88).

Ghiyāsu'd-Dīn Tughluq combined the rare qualities of a general and a far-sighted statesman. He tried to recover the treasure squandered by Khusrau, thus involving himself in conflict with (among others) Shaikh Nizāmu'd-Dīn Auliyā'. He revoked 'Alā'u'd-Dīn's rules of payment of revenue by measurement of land and introduced the system of crop-sharing. He considered village headmen useful, and the *iqtā'* system best suited to the military character of his government. He maintained the descriptive rolls and the branding of horses.

Two expeditions of his son Jauna, now entitled Ulugh Khān, against Wārangal, resulted in its complete defeat and annexation; the city was renamed Sultānpur. The Sultan himself marched east and asserted his authority over West Bengal, ruled by descendants of Balban's son Bughrā Khān. Returning, he reduced Tīrhut to submission. His last halt at Afghānpur, a village six miles south-east of Delhi, proved fatal for him. After a mid-day meal in a hurriedly-built wooden pavilion, elephants were being paraded; the entire pavilion fell, crushing the Sultan and his second son. Some modern scholars argue, against medieval tradition, that Jauna Khān did not arrange this disaster; but the circumstances suggest his guilt. He proclaimed himself Sultan with the simple style of Muhammad bin Tughluq.

The Sultan was misunderstood throughout his reign. His intellectual capacity, and love for philosophy, were interpreted as hostility to Islam. His efforts to break the clique of the Delhi '*ulamā*' and sūfīs failed. His friendship with yogīs and Jains, and his participation in the Holī festival, were considered evidence of his being Hinduized. His ambition to establish political contacts with the world outside India was regarded as madness. The old political leadership dubbed him a tyrant; some of the '*ulamā*' proclaimed war against him to be lawful.

In 1326–7 he decided upon a plan to make Devagiri the second administrative capital of his empire. The policy of annexing the Deccan kingdoms made this imperative. To make it an effective seat of government, he wished a section of the élite to be permanently settled there, with the '*ulamā*' and sūfīs giving the lead. They refused to co-operate; but the Sultan was adamant. He named Devagiri Daulatābād, and forced all those whom he had selected to emigrate. What contemporary and later historians call a mass exodus was in fact the transfer of a selection of the élite. When Ibn Battūta visited Delhi in 1334, it was full of sūfīs and '*ulamā*'.

A growing shortage of silver led the Sultan to introduce a token currency of bronze in 1330. The coins were immediately and successfully forged. In 1332 he redeemed the tokens, false and genuine together, against a new debased silver currency, maintaining the prestige of the treasury to his immense personal loss.

The governor of Ma'bar in the extreme south, Saiyid Ahsan, rebelled in 1335 and became independent. That year too, Saiyid Ahsan's son Sharīf Ibrāhīm, the governor of Hansī, rebelled. The insurrection spread to Sunnām and Sāmāna, the Saiyids and other Muslim élite groups being well represented among the rebels, In 1338 'Ainu'l Mulk Multānī, governor of Avadh, led a rebellion provoked by years of famine and undiminished revenue assessments.

The rebels were predominantly non-Turkic elements whom the Sultan had endeavoured to use as a counterpoise to the intrigues of the Turks: Mongol neo-Muslims, foreign nobles, Saiyids and Afghans, and some trusted officers like 'Ainu'l Mulk. Restless ambition was as much responsible for the rebellions as fear of the Sultan and his vindictive punishments.

Harihara and Bukka, two fugitive brothers from Wārangal whom the Sultan had taken captive, Islamized, and commissioned to consolidate his rule in Kampīla, renounced Islam and founded the kingdom of Vijayanagara in 1336. In 1338 Bengal became independent, and in August 1347 Hasan Gangawī detached the whole Deccan, including Daulatābād, from the Sultan's dominions, proclaiming himself Sultan as Bahman Shāh. Never again, except briefly and insecurely for a generation after Aurangzeb's conquests, did Delhi rule the Deccan. Sultan Muhammad bin Tughluq died in Sind chasing the rebel Taghī, a leader of Turkic origin, in 1351: as a sixteenth-century historian says, the king was freed from his people and his people from the king.

The nobles, the sūfīs, and '*ulamā*' in the imperial camp raised his cousin Fīrūz to the throne. A mild man of unenterprising nature, he allowed policy to be controlled by the '*ulamā*', the sūfīs, and the strong-willed nobles. Following the path of least resistance, he overlooked corruption in the hope that such kindness would be repaid with devotion. He prohibited bloodshed and tortures and obtained deeds of forgiveness for Sultan Muhammad from the families of his victims. He assigned liberal revenue grants to religious foundations and holy men; he made hereditary the revenue assignments given as salary to soldiers and military officers. He had old monuments repaired, and founded several new towns: Hisār-Fīrūza, with a canal system, and Fīrūzābād on the Yamunā were open towns, while Jaunpur was mainly a garrison town to strengthen central control over the eastern regions. He transferred two Aśokan pillars from Toprā and Meerut to Delhi. Orchards were planted for the benefit of Muslims. Fīrūz created a special department for the recruitment of slaves, at one time maintaining 180,000 in his household. Many were hired out to the Sultan's profit; trained as artisans and craftsmen, others were assigned revenue grants. He abolished several taxes forbidden by the Islamic law which yielded little income. He imposed *jizya* (poll tax) on brāhmans, previously exempted; but Hindu agitation made him fix a concessional rate for them.

His military campaigns in Bengal, Jājnagar, and Kāngrā were ineffective; his Thatta campaign of 1365–7 was a complete disaster for the Delhi army. Fīrūz was followed by weak successors, puppets in the hands of ambitious but incompetent slave leaders. The invasion of Tīmūr (the great Mongol conqueror, known in Europe as Tamerlane) in 1398–9 was devastating both for Hindus and Muslims. Delhi was sacked and desolated. Rival representatives of the Tughluq Dynasty competed for the shadow of power; the last survived until 1412. A dynasty of Saiyids ruled Delhi and its environs from 1414 to 1451. Elsewhere, control passed to petty chieftains or to provincial dynasties. Not until 1451 did Delhi begin to revive, when Bahlol Lodī founded an Afghan dynasty. The strong central army organized by ʻAlā'u'd-Dīn maintained its hold down to the reign of Fīrūz. Restless Muslim leaders caused disturbances, but no Hindu tributary chiefs in northern India made any successful attempt to become independent. Under the successors of Fīrūz, Hindu strength surged up from the Panjāb to Bengal, and frequently attempted to overthrow the provincial dynasties.

As we have seen, Bengal was hardly ever under the effective control of the Delhi sultans. The Ilyās Shāhī Dynasty of Bengal (1339–1415 and 1437–87) unified East and West Bengal, overran Tīrhut, and then tried to annex Orissā. Many new areas, such as Khulnā, were redeemed from jungle and colonized. Sanskrit learning was revived in Bengal and Hinduism spread in Assam. The Husain Shāhī Dynasty (1493–1538) is characterized by an impressive record of military activity in Kāmrūp (Assam) and Orissā. After a brief Mughal occupation, Bengal fell to the Afghans in 1538, and until conquered by Akbar in 1576 it remained the bulwark of Afghan resistance against the Mughals.

The Sharqī ('Eastern') Dynasty of Jaunpur (1394–1479) asserted itself effectively against the rising powers of the Hindu tributary chiefs from Avadh to Bihār. The territory of Mālwā, a triangular plateau with the Vindhya mountains as its base, became independent in 1402 under Dilāwar Khān Ghūrī. As the leading independent power of central India it had to struggle on two fronts: internally against Hindu chieftains and externally against its neighbours, Mewār, Jaunpur, Gujarāt, and the Bahmanī kingdom. Sultan Mahmūd (1436–69), the first Khaljī ruler of Mālwā, consolidated and extended his state; but in the sixteenth century it decayed, being reduced in 1531 to a mere province of Gujarāt. Independent again in 1537, it was conquered by Akbar in 1561.

Rānā Kumbha (1433–68) made Mewār a very strong Rājput power, competent to contend against both Gujarāt and Mālwā in the race of expansion. Rānā Sānga (1509–28), after crushing his Rājput rivals, hoped to use Mālwā and Gujarāt as allies, and overthrow the Lodī Dynasty of Delhi. The Mughals forestalled him, and defeated him in turn in 1527.

The real founder of the independent kingdom of Gujarāt was Nāsiru'd-Dīn Muhammad Shāh, who ascended the throne in 1404. In the reigns of Ahmad Shāh (1411–43), the founder of Ahmadābād, and Mahmūd Begarh (1458–1511) Gujarāt grew great. Although Bahādur Shāh (1526–37) conquered Chitor and repulsed the Portuguese from Diu, the Mughal emperor Humāyūn defeated him in 1535, and he perished in an encounter with the Portuguese in 1537.

Sind and Multān were ruled by minor dynasties. The sultans of Kashmīr (1339–1586), independent even when the Delhi sultans were powerful, did not, on the whole, pursue an expansionist policy. There the liberal and orthodox trends in Islam ran parallel. Sultan Sikandar (1389–1413) persecuted brāhmans, and demolished and desecrated temples, but Sultan Zainu'l ʻĀbidīn

(1420–70) gave his full patronage to Sanskrit and Hinduism. He reorganized the revenue administration, fostered irrigation, and secularized the administration of justice.

In the far south the sultans of Madurai (1335–78) struggled against the new Vijayanagara Dynasty, until Harihara II (1377–1404) absorbed their shrinking domains. The independent Khāndesh Dynasty came into existence in 1382; they wrested Asīr from its Hindu chieftain and founded Burhānpur. Khāndesh maintained friendly relations with Gujarāt, Mālwā, and the Deccan sultans, thus remaining independent to 1600, when it fell to Akbar.

The Bahmanī Dynasty was the most powerful in the Deccan, ruling from Gulbarga until 1422, and then making Bīdar their capital. The founder, 'Alā'u'd-Dīn Bahman Shāh, divided the kingdom into four quarters (*taraf*) and assigned each to one trusted officer (*tarafdār*). The Raichur *doāb* was contested between the Vijayanagara and the Bahmanī rulers. In the eventful reign of Fīrūz Shāh Bahmanī (1397–1422) three major battles were fought between the two powers without disturbing the *status quo*. Fīrūz developed Chaul and Abhol as ports for trading ships from the Red Sea and Persian Gulf, carrying luxury goods not only from the Persian, Arabian, and African coasts, but also (through Egypt) from Europe. Persians, Turks, and Arabs were given a ready welcome by the Bahmanīds, producing ultimately conflicts between the sons of the soil and the foreigners (*pardesīs*).

The Bīdar period (1422–1526) was marked by wars with Gujarāt and Mālwā, continued campaigns against Vijayanagara, and expeditions against Orissā. The Irani adventurer Mahmūd Gāwān, as *wazīr* of the Bahmanī sultanate, dominant between 1466 and 1481, annexed the Karnātak region and seized Goa, which had been jealously guarded by the Vijayanagara rulers. Mahmūd Gāwān introduced several reforms in administration, but fell to the intrigues of the Deccanī élite and was put to death by Sultan Muhammad Shāh (1463–82) in 1481. The struggle between the *pardēsīs* and the Deccanīs drained the kingdom of its strength; the later sultans were puppets in the hands of the dominant Deccanī groups. By 1530 the Bahmanī realm was broken into five independent sultanates: the 'Ādil Shāhī of Bījāpur, the Qutb Shāhī of Golconda, the Nizām Shāhī of Ahmadnagar, the Barīd Shāhī of Bīdar, and the 'Imād Shāhī of Berār. Rivals, they yet co-operated in the face of external threats. Early in 1565 a confederacy of the five powers defeated the Vijayanagara Rājā at the battle of Tālikota (more precisely Banihatti). The vast Hindu kingdom fell to pieces, and Bījāpur and Golconda gathered the lion's share of the spoil.

While the provincial sultans strove to eliminate the independent power of Hindu chiefs, they were great patrons of regional culture and regional languages, and came to rely on their tributary Hindu chiefs for aid against their Muslim neighbours. With a few exceptions, even the most orthodox were tolerant of Hindus and of foreign adventurers settled in their lands. The indigenous leadership, both Hindu and Muslim, looked upon the latter with disgust; the foreigners, however, anxious to promote peaceful coexistence, enriched local administrative institutions and cultural and social life.

The story of Delhi must now be taken up once more. Sultan Bahlol (1451–89) was an Afghan of the Lodī tribe, whose home was the Sulaimān range.

Some members of this tribe had served in the Ghūrīd army; others, apparently not yet Islamized, fought under Prithvīrāja. In Balban's time, Afghans had been steadily rising as political leaders; indeed, the old nobility had reproached Jalālu'd-Dīn Fīrūz Khaljī with Afghan ancestry. Afghans, useful as soldiers, were successful also as merchants, dealing particularly in horses. Each tribe nourished traditions of independence, which sharpened distinctions and made concerted Afghan action difficult.

Bahlol Lodī, a military chief of about forty, induced Shāh 'Ālam, the last Saiyid sultan, to resign and retire to Badāūn, where he lived unmolested until his death in 1478. He gained the support of other Afghans for this *coup* with the promise that they would share equally in the fruits of power. To a large extent, he kept his promise; but he also encouraged other Afghans, and particularly Lodīs, to come down from their barren mountains to the fertile plains of Hindustān. He distributed rich *iqtā's* among them, and with the aid of their contingents, rather than by reviving a central army, he gradually built up his military strength. He was careful (like the Roman Emperor Augustus) to avoid the appearance of power; he claimed to be no more than the first among equals, and his court resembled more an Afghan tribal assembly than the council of a great king.

Most of Bahlol's energy and resources were devoted to crushing Husain Shāh Sharqī (1458–77), the last ruler of Jaunpur, who enjoyed the support of many eminent Hindu chiefs and survived in a small enclave until 1505. When Bahlol's son Sultan Sikandar (1489–1517) ascended the throne, the Rājputs of the Jaunpur district were still in the field to measure swords with the Afghans. Only Husain Shāh's death in 1505 ended this challenge to Afghan power.

In 1506 Sultan Sikandar founded Āgrā, as an advance headquarters for campaigns against Gwālior and other neighbouring Rājput lands. Abandoning his father's policy of propitiating the tribal pride of the Afghan leaders by ostentatious equality, he had spies keep him informed about the minutest details of his nobles' private lives. His son and successor Ibrāhīm Lodī (1517–26) went further, imprisoning and beheading several leading nobles. Daulat Khān Lodī, governor of the Panjāb, and his associates invited Bābur, the ruler of Kābul, to deprive Ibrāhīm Lodī of his throne and ensure them (as they hoped) predominance over a grateful king.

Bābur claimed descent from Tīmūr on his father's side, and from Chingiz on his mother's. He is commonly referred to as a Mughal, the Persian form of Mongol, but in fact his blood was very mixed. Driven out from Farghāna and Samarqand, he conquered Kābul in 1505, and began to dream of bringing the Indian territories conquered by Tīmūr under his control. Before finally defeating Ibrāhīm Lodī on the field of Pānīpat in 1526, he had four times invaded the Panjāb. His victory was the fruit of his careful planning, and of his cavalry and artillery's superior manoeuvres. His centre was protected by 700 carts connected by twisted bull-hides; between every pair of guns there were six or seven movable breastworks for the protection of matchlock men, and the flanking attacks of his cavalry transformed his carts into a formidable fort.

On 16 March 1527 at Khanuā, 37 miles west of Āgrā, Bābur met Rānā Sānga, who had seized Bhīlsā, Sārangpur, Chandērī, and Ranthambor, and his gunners made short work of the Rājputs. Bābur was now superior to any other Indian power. Emperor from Āgrā to Kābul, he marched against the Afghans in the east as far as Ghāzīpur. He shook, but did not destroy, their strength; returning to Āgrā, he died prematurely in 1530.

Humāyūn (1530–9) was no match to his energetic father. Preferring to conquer Chitor and Gujarāt rather than to consolidate Mughal power in the east, he allowed Shēr Khān Sūr, an enterprising petty Afghan chief, to become an invincible power in Jaunpur, Bihār, and Bengal. Shēr Khān proclaimed himself king in Bengal in 1538, defeating Humāyūn at Chausā in June 1539, and finally near Bilgrām in May 1540.

Shēr Shāh ruled only to 1545, dying in an explosion, when well over sixty, at his siege of Kālinjar. He had subjugated the turbulent tribes of the northern Panjāb, and conquered Mālwā, Mārwār, and Mewār. He reintroduced many healthy features of ʿAlā'u'd-Dīn's revenue system. The existing *parganās* were grouped in districts under the control of officers whose duties were carefully defined. The revenue was fixed on a measurement of land and carefully drawn schedules of rates. Shēr Shāh's road system is still remembered; he laid out the Grand Trunk Road from Peshāwar in Pakistan to Sonārgaon in Bengal. His decision to hold village headmen responsible for highway robbery and murder, and to compel them to restore losses of money and goods, restored peace in the villages and on the highways.

His son Islām Shāh (1545–52) was a competent ruler; but the tribal rivalries of the Afghan chiefs shook the fabric of the newly formed sultanate, and he failed to conciliate them, dying with potential conflicts unresolved and with no fit successor. Humāyūn, after a chequered career as a fugitive in Sind and Iran and then as ruler of Kābul, reconquered Delhi in 1555; the political power of the Sūr Sultan was in the hands of Hemū, who was not a Rājput but a pedlar by profession and a Vaiśya by caste.

Humāyūn did not rule for more than a few months, and his sudden death on 24 January 1556 made his son Akbar the ruler of Hindūstān. Even at thirteen, Akbar showed determination and promise, overthrowing Hēmū in the second battle of Pānīpat in November 1556. For more than three years his regent Bairām Khān was *de facto* ruler, but in March 1560 Akbar, with his intriguing foster-mother's help, overthrew the powerful regent and soon assumed full control of the government.

Early in 1562 he married the daughter of Rājā Bhār Mal, the Kachwāha Rājput of Amber. By 1564 he had abolished the enslavement of prisoners of war, remitted the tax on Hindu pilgrims, and ended the *jizya* (poll tax on non-Muslims). With persistent determination and dogged tenacity, he conquered northern India from Bengal to Kashmīr and Sind. By annexing Qandahār he handed down to his successors the strongest possible north-west frontier, such as was held by no ancient Indian power, nor even by the British except fleetingly in 1880–1. His unexpected death in 1605 cut short his ambition to annex the Deccan and to push the Portuguese out of their maritime strongholds.

He based his rule on the theory that kingship is a light emanating from God, a great gift 'not bestowed till many thousand grand requisites have been gathered together in one individual'. His vast conquests had convinced him that he was God's chosen, holding creation as a trust from God. It was his duty to promote universal concord (*Sulh-i-kull*). He believed that tension between ruler and subjects was not a sign of healthy government. Akbar's administrative institutions, although based on Iranian traditions, drew heavily upon the successful experiments of ancient India and the Delhi sultanate, and were immediately adapted from Shēr Shāh's practices.

He gave a new basis to the relations of the central government with the Hindu tributary chiefs. Under the sultans they were confined to the payment of tribute and offering military service whenever required. Akbar absorbed very many chieftains into his civil and military service. Rank rose in hierarchical order, with every rank (*mansab*) marked by the number of horsemen the officer was required to bring into the field. For each rank was set an appropriate *jāgīr*, an area of land whose revenue the officer had to collect through his own officials; in later years, some officers holding civilian posts were paid in cash. For a Rājput chieftain, a *jāgīr* included the assessed revenue of his hereditary dominions (*watan jāgīr*); were it insufficient for his rank, he would be granted further *jāgīrs* in the imperial dominions. As the rājās' loyal and meritorious service earned them higher and higher ranks, their share in imperial revenues steadily increased, making loyalty more profitable than rebellion.

In Mughal parlance, such chieftains were known as *zamīndār rājās*. Akbar and his successors used the term *zamīndār* for holders of all types of landed interests, except mere cultivators. To quote Nūrul Hasan's classification, primary *zamīndārs* 'were for all practical purposes the holders of proprietary rights over agricultural as well as habitational lands'. This class included both 'peasant-proprietors who carried on cultivation themselves or with the help of hired labour, and the proprietors of one or several villages'. From them, intermediary *zamīndārs* collected the revenue and paid it to the imperial treasury, to *jāgīr* holders, or to *zamīndār rājās*. In return, they enjoyed various perquisites. Their rights were hereditary, but the state reserved the right to interfere with their succession, partition their rights, and even revoke them for negligence of duty or subversive activities.

Both the intermediary and primary *zamīndārs* performed several police functions, maintained law and order in their villages, and kept roads and highways free from thieves and robbers. Like the *zamīndār rājās*, they imitated the Mughal way of life, dress, and manners. Some learned Persian; Mughal culture was grafted through them upon Indian society in the villages. The peaceable *zamīndār* impressed it upon the minds of the Indian villagers that the Mughal power was invincible and based on universal concord.

The *zamīndārs* inherited or built their own fortresses for protection alike from their rivals and arrogant officials. *Zamīndārs* whose lands were protected by hills or ravines, or screened by jungles, were often unruly. The whole of northern India was dotted with such areas; Katihar, Jalālī near Aligarh, the Panjāb hills, and the jungles of Bihār were almost inaccessible; and even close to Āgrā, there were such areas towards the north and the west, the abode of the turbulent Jāts. Such areas were usually known as *mawās*. Generally, where a large number of villages belonged to *zamīndārs* of the same caste or class, the emperor and his successors found it exceedingly difficult to assert their authority; threats, shows of force, and promises of rewards and *mansabs* were their weapons.

Other Hindu castes and classes rose to prominence upon the reorganization of the finance and revenue departments. High officers, known as *dīwāns*, were generally by caste *Khattrīs* and *Kāyasthas*, and occasionally brāhmans. The *jāgīrdārs* also employed Hindu *dīwāns*. The revenue returns of *jāgīrs*, and the rent-free land grants of Hindu and Muslim scholars, theologians, and charitable institutions, passed through the hands of Hindu *dīwāns*. Many '*ulamā*' and sūfīs, resentful yet powerless, nourished hostility to the Hindus as a class.

The administrative reforms of Akbar changed the structure of even the Muslim leadership. The state was no longer the monopoly of the Mughals, or even the Iranis; the Afghans, and Indian Muslims such as Shaikhzādas, Saiyids, and Kambōhs shared in its management. The hereditary status of a new entrant was an important consideration in assigning his first *mansab*, but promotion depended mainly upon talents and loyalty.

Akbar never ceased exploring new avenues of progress, and maintained an objective attitude. His achievements in the fields of culture, administration, diplomacy, and statesmanship would never have been so impressive without his inquiring mind and painstaking experiments. Faith in God was his guide, and his intuitive understanding of human psychology ruled his decisions. A galaxy of statesmen and scholars, both from Iran and India, transformed into reality his dreams of a great empire.

Before his death, however, he had given no clear lead in the question of succession. Two of his three sons had died, and Salīm, the only survivor, who succeeded him as Jahāngīr, was at once faced with the rebellion of his own son Khusrau. This ate into the vitality of the Mughal power, and set a precedent of factionalism and party politics. Six years after his succession. Jahāngīr married the mature but still beautiful widow of Shēr Afgan, a nobleman, and entitled her Nūr Jahān. She became his wise counsellor. Her father and brother, who already held positions of importance, obtained well-deserved promotions, raising Irani influence and disturbing other sections of the élite, particularly the Turānīs.

In Jahāngīr's reign Mewār submitted, Ahmadnagar was brought further under imperial control, and Kāngrā captured. His governor of Bengal, Islām Khān, consolidated Mughal rule by liquidating the still considerable power of the Afghan *zamīndārs*. Qandahār, negligently held, fell to Shāh 'Abbās of Iran in 1622, a serious blow to Akbar's frontier policy. The increase of the number of *mansabdārs* made the administration unwieldy. The expansion of trade with Iran and the establishment of European factories both enlarged the manufacturing resources of India and increased the extravagance and the luxury of the Imperial Court.

In the reign of Shāh Jahān, who ascended the throne in 1628, the splendour of the Great Mughals touched its height. The new Emperor, who had considerable experience in the Deccan, followed a vigorous policy of southward expansion. In 1633 Daulatābād was seized, and the Ahmadnagar Dynasty extinguished. Early in 1636 the Emperor himself marched against Bījāpur and Golconda, and forced them to accept very harsh terms of peace. Their tribute was increased; Bījāpur was required to stop Marāthā expansion, and Golconda to give up Shīʿī practices, which amounted to an admission of Iran's overlordship. Towards the end of his reign, his ambitious son and viceroy in the Deccan, Aurangzeb, arousing the cupidity of his father, made a bid to annex both Bījāpur and Golconda entirely, but the Emperor's sudden illness late in 1657, and the subsequent war of succession, put an end to the plan.

An expedition to Tibet failed; attempts to seize Balkh and Bukhāra could not be maintained; three attempts to regain Qandahār, recovered from the Persians in 1639 and lost again in 1648, ended in defeat. The Mughal army. now purely Indian, had no training in warfare in those regions, and dreaded above all else the cold. Better success was met in Assam, where after repeated attacks on the Ahoms the Mughals stabilized their boundary at the Barnadī. Imperial authority was effectively imposed upon Bundelkhand and Baghelkhand; in 1643, the Rājā of Palamau was forced into submission. The Gonds and Bhīls of Mālwā were kept subdued. Imperial orders of this period survive in large numbers. They exhibit the Emperor's deep concern for the extension of revenue-producing cultivation, and the promotion of manufactures to supply his court, particularly linen of fine quality.

In September 1657 Shāh Jahān fell dangerously ill of a strangury. All his four sons, each talented and efficient, resolved to contest the throne. Shāh Jahān had wished his eldest son Dārā, a man devoted to sūfic researches and of amiable but selfish temperament, to succeed him. The others had acquiesced, knowing full well that the sword would decide. They entered into secret alliances among themselves and with various nobles, and strengthened their power in their respective viceroyalties. Despite Shāh Jahān's help, Dārā lost the battle of Sāmūgarh at the end of May 1658 to Aurangzeb, a better general and a more effective leader. Shāh Jahān, imprisoned in Āgrā fort, died there in 1666. Through a cunning device Aurangzeb seized his brother Murād, former governor of Gujarāt, and incarcerated him in Gwālior. He pursued Dārā towards the Panjāb, but returned in January 1659 and defeated Shujāʿ, the former Viceroy of Bengal, at Khajuhā, near Allahabad; Shujāʿ was finally defeated by Mīr Jumla near Dācca in April 1660. In April 1659 Dārā, wrongly banking upon Rājput support, and entrenched in the Deorāi pass south of Ajmer, was beaten after a tenacious fight, and fled through Gujarāt, Kathiāwār, and Sind. A treacherous officer, advanced by him in the days of his glory, foiled his attempt to escape to Iran through the Bolan pass. Seized, he was brought to Delhi and executed on the frivolous charge of calling Islam and heresy twins. Some describe this war of succession as a war of ideologies, a triumph for orthodox Islam over Hinduism and the Shīʿīs. Athar ʿAlī's statistical analysis of the supporters of the contending princes has, however, strengthened the view that it was, like previous wars of succession, a war of factions, a natural event in Mughal history. All parties claimed that they were fighting to strengthen the hand of their father; Aurangzeb and his allies, after the victory of Samūgarh, added to their proclamations a claim that they took up arms to uproot the un-Islamic influence of Dārā.

Aurangzeb began his reign by remissions of revenue and other much-needed measures of economic relief. He abolished as un-Islamic many exactions which, although frequently suppressed by previous rulers, had always been levied again. He restored the department of *Ihtisāb* ('moral censorship'), which Akbar had disbanded, to enforce rigid Sunnī morality upon the Muslim masses, who were henceforth subjected to much petty irritation without any great change in their daily lives. The apparatus of 'snoopers' gave employment to many orthodox bigots, and created a vested interest among the bureaucracy, which coincided with Aurangzeb's own inclinations, in discarding Akbar's secular principles.

In 1665 Aurangzeb introduced discriminatory trade regulations; in 1668 he initiated a series of puritanical reforms; in 1669 he ordered the closing of Hindu schools and demolition of temples, and several temples were actually destroyed. By 1672 his stupendous code of Hanafī law, the *Fatāwā-i-ʿĀlamgīrī*, was completed; but it did not override customary law. In 1679, to provide the army of Islamizing officials with a source of income legal under Muslim law, as recommended by Ghazālī, he reimposed the *jizya*; 'many of the honest scholars of the time' were appointed to collect it, and it was levied with the utmost severity, the Emperor never relenting, not even in extreme old age.

Until 1681 Aurangzeb remained in northern India; from then until he died he was in the Deccan. His Irani general Mīr Jumla, after driving Shujāʿ into exile, conquered Kūch Bihār, and invaded Assam; the army was decimated by disease, Mīr Jumla himself dying in 1663, and his conquests were, piece by piece, abandoned. Palamau and Navanagar were annexed outright. In the Deccan the Emperor's maternal uncle Shāista Khān (1601–94) made little headway against the Marāthā adventurer Śivājī, who in 1663 plundered the Khān's camp, cutting off his thumb in his own harem. In 1664 Śivājī sacked the flourishing port of Surat; but in 1665 the Rājput general Mirzā Rāja Jai Singh defeated him, forced him by the treaty of Purandhar to surrender twenty-three forts, and induced him to wait upon Aurangzeb at Āgrā. This effort to bring Śivājī into the *mansabdārī* system failed; fancying himself slighted, Śivājī made a scene in court, was imprisoned, and, while the Emperor considered plans for dealing with him, escaped, and reorganized his territories.

Jai Singh meanwhile had failed to conquer Bījāpur, being unprovided with a siege train; the Emperor was displeased, and recalled him; he died on the way home in 1667. In that year the Afrīdīs and Yūsufzaīs rebelled on the north-west frontier, and these and other disturbances held Aurangzeb's attention for several years. Proclaiming himself *Chhatrapati*[1] in 1674, Śivājī assumed equality with his former master, the Sultan of Bījāpur; in 1677 he made extensive conquests in the region of Āndhra Pradesh in the name of Qutb Shāh of Golconda; but in April 1680 he died.

Śivājī united the scattered and disorganized Marāthās into a secure state, administered according to the traditions of Vijayanagara and Bījāpur, and founded upon the plunder levied from other lands by mounted guerrillas. Asserting the right to *chauth* (one fourth of the assessed revenue) and *sardeśmukhī* (a further levy of one tenth, claimed on the false ground that Śivājī's family was entitled to it as being the principal *deśmukhs*, or collectors of revenue, in Mahārāshtra), he pillaged alike the lands of the Mughals and the Deccan kings; but he raised in this way enough to pay his troops in cash, and

[1] 'Lord of the umbrella', implying a completely independent ruler.

to recruit auxiliaries, the dreaded *bargirs*, without having to depend upon a cumbrous system of *jāgīrs*.

In December 1678 Rājā Jaswant Singh Rāthor of Mārwār (Jodhpur) died on duty on the north-west frontier, with no son to succeed him. Aurangzeb resolved to annex his dominions. Ignoring Jaswant's posthumous son, he soon faced a revolt in Mārwār, aided by the Rānā of Mewār; and during the campaign, in January 1681, his son Akbar rebelled, proclaimed himself Emperor, and cut Aurangzeb to the quick by suggesting that he, like Shāh Jahān, was unfit to rule. Akbar's revolt soon failed, and he fled southwards, where he lived until 1687 under the protection of Śambhūjī, the son and successor of Śivājī, retreating finally to Iran, where he died in 1704, while waiting on the frontier for news of his father's death. Mārwār crushed but not cowed, Aurangzeb turned south with all his forces. He was never to return to the north.

The Marāthās were harassed, and Akbar prevented from breaking out; in 1686 Bījāpur was captured, in 1687 Golconda; in 1689 a daring raid brought Śambhūjī himself a prisoner to Aurangzeb. He was barbarously executed. Aurangzeb appeared totally victorious, yet stood on the verge of ruin. He was never able fully to pacify the conquered lands; Marāthā leaders, their state destroyed, rose up everywhere to harass and plunder; until the end of 1705 Aurangzeb, reluctant to leave the Deccan either to his generals or to his sons, was personally engaged in a dreary and essentially fruitless effort to secure a final victory. The very forts he snatched (or bribed) from the Marāthās often fell again into their hands, whether through attack or through bribery.

In 1707 Aurangzeb died, in his eighty-ninth year, at Ahmadnagar, conscious of his own failure, yet piously sure he had obeyed the letter of God's law. The Deccan plateau, never conspicuously productive, was ruined by twenty-five years of marching and plunder; the *mansabdārī* system was breaking up; the empire was, in fact, bankrupt. Administration, discipline, even society disintegrated.

Aurangzeb's eldest surviving son won a bloody war of succession, but in 1709 left the Deccan; senile at seventy, he died at Lāhore in February 1712. Four middle-aged brothers contested the crown; the eldest emerged victorious, called himself Jahāndār, and retired to a life of pleasure in Delhi, emerging only to confront his nephew Fārrukhsiyār near Āgrā, to lose the battle, flee ignominiously, and be as ignominiously put to death. In 1719 Fārrukhsiyār, after an ineffectual reign, was murdered at the behest of his own *wazīr*. The Emperor was now a puppet; whatever minister could dominate the dissolving administration was the true head of the state. Governors and adventurers looked to their own interests, and after the outright cession of Khāndēsh and Mālwā to the Marāthās and the destructive invasion of Nādir Shāh of Iran in 1739, the Emperor had no more authority than aspiring factions found it convenient to allow him.

As with the Delhi sultanate after Fīrūz Tughluq, independent principalities emerged under Muslim rulers: in Bengal, at Fārrukhābād, where Afghans ruled, and at Faizābād in Avadh, with many petty states elsewhere. Gujarāt fell to the Marāthās, who did not cease their raids, turning now to Rājputāna, which they ruined. In the Deccan, Nizāmu'l Mulk Āsaf Jāh created the great

Muslim state, with its capital at Hyderābād near Golconda, which was broken up in 1948. Everywhere *zamīndārs* paid no revenue unless forced at the point of the sword. They were proud to call themselves *zamīndārān-i-zor-talab* (insubordinate *zamīndārs*).

The rulers of Avadh (who in 1775 removed to Lucknow) were Shī'a; the others were Sunnīs; none followed any strong Islamic line. The Afghans in India allied themselves with Ahmad Shāh Durrānī, the new ruler of Afghanistan, in the hope of suppressing the Marāthā inroads upon northern India, and the rising power of the Jāts. Both were destroyed in 1761, at the third battle of Pānīpat; the Mughal power was entirely eclipsed, the Sikhs were definitely established in the Panjāb; and while the Marāthās retired southwards and revived, only to be destroyed by the British, the Muslim powers sank slowly and irreversibly into inanity. Bengal, indeed, had already fallen to British power.

While religious, political, and economic factors combined to weaken and finally extinguish Mughal power, the greatest single cause of the collapse was the failure of Aurangzeb to husband his resources; obstinately persisting in a false policy in the Deccan, he failed utterly to adapt the structure of the state to new stresses, while he destroyed much of the foundation upon which the imaginative skill of Akbar had raised the Mughal Empire.

CHAPTER XVIII

Medieval Hindu Devotionalism

by J. T. F. Jordens

During medieval times (thirteenth to seventeenth centuries) Hinduism underwent a transformation so great that it has been compared to that wrought in Western Christianity by the Reformation. The focus of religious attention moved from the great gods and the liturgies connected with polytheism to the one God and his avatārs, especially Krishna and Rāma. A new attitude to God, emotional, passionate *bhakti*, replaced the old approaches of sacrificial rite and monistic meditation, just as a new mysticism, practical yet ecstatic, replaced the former philosophical type. Forms of religious expression changed: love-songs to the Lord were sung, and group singing created a new popular cultural form, the *kīrtan*. Pushing aside old gods, old attitudes, old cultural forms, the new movement also drove the sacred language, Sanskrit, back into the memories of the pandits and the deepest precincts of temples and monasteries. In the first centuries of their growth all modern Indian vernacular literatures were moulded by this religious movement, and thus were essentially mass literatures. The socio-ritualistic order dominated by the brāhmans was not overthrown, but the brāhmans lost much of their spiritual authority, which passed to the saints and the *gurus*, whose songs and biographies soon became a new scripture. The new devotional religion, without destroying the Hindu social framework, fostered ideas of brotherhood and equality before the loving Lord, and its saints drawn from all levels of society proclaimed that in *bhakti* caste had no meaning.

ORIGIN AND SPREAD

Earlier theories that medieval devotionalism originated either in the north or the south under the impact of Islam are negated by the simple fact that the earliest genuine devotional *bhakti* poetry of Tamilnādu precedes the coming of Islam. Islamic, and particularly Sūfī influences, may, however, have been felt later.

The divinization of Krishna and later of Rāma emerged around the beginning of the Christian era, and connected with it was the earlier type of *bhakti*: a personal devotion, contemplative and sober, to a personal loving Lord, as we find it supremely expressed in the *Bhagavad Gītā*. In the new literature of the *Purānas*, the Krishna myth underwent a deep transformation. The epic Krishna receded into the background, and the focus of attention shifted to the marvels of his birth and infancy and to his heroic and amorous exploits as a youth among the cowherds and cowherdesses of Gokula. No doubt there is a connection between this change in the Krishna myth and the slow transformation of *bhakti* itself. But the first clear manifestation of the new *bhakti*, emotional, ardent, ecstatic, often using erotic imagery, appears in the Tamil country in the early seventh century, in the poems of the Nāyanārs, devotees of Śiva, and of the Ālvārs, devotees of Vishnu.

V. Subramaniam has proposed an interesting theory about the sociological origins of this phenomenon. Old Tamil literature was dominated by a strong tradition of romantic-erotic love. This love had two characteristics: it dealt not with the nobility, but with the people; and it was closely associated with a special nature mystique. From the second century A.D. onwards these traditions came under the strong influence of Āryan sacerdotalism and philosophy. Under pressure from the new culture, especially its reforms of marriage customs, the strong romantic urge of the Tamils was compelled to find new outlets. These were on the one hand the religious *bhakti* poetry, and, on the other, a decadent romanticism.

Whether this was so or not, the fact is that at the beginning of the seventh century we witness the eruption of the new type of passionate *bhakti* in Tamil. From the seventh to the tenth centuries a very extensive hymnal literature came to light. The collections of these hymns acquired immense importance and soon came to be considered as the 'Tamil *Veda*', the main scripture of the people, and also as the second *Veda* to many of the great theologians. These hymnodists are treated in another chapter.

How did this new *bhakti* spread from the south into Mahārāshtra, Bengal, and the northern plains? Obviously Tamil could not be the vehicle, so it happened through the Sanskritization of the new spirit. The Vaishnavite brāhman scholars infused this new spirit into the *Bhāgavata Purāna* (ninth century) which travelled the highroads of Sanskrit tradition and soon became the principal text of Vaishnavism all over India, marking a turning-point in the history of the Vaishnavite faith. Whereas the other books of this work are very much in the old purānic tradition, the tenth book erupts in a magnificent exposé of the new *bhakti*, centred on Krishna's childhood and youth. This is one of the truly great works of Hinduism, and its innumerable translations into the vernaculars (forty into Bengālī alone) testify to its great popularity and influence. The figure of Krishna holds the stage, as child or lover, hero or trickster, but always marvellous and entrancing even in his most daring exploits.

This purānic development of the new *bhakti* was paralleled by its growth in the work of the great theologians, both Śaivite and Vaishnavite. They formed religious orders, and their monks carried their message all over India. The first and greatest among them was the Vaishnava mystic Rāmānuja (died 1137) founder of the Śrīvaishnava sect. Madhva (1197–1276), a Kanarese brāhman, founded the Mādhava sect, and the Telugu brāhman Nimbārka (thirteenth century) settled near Mathurā singing the praises of Krishna and Rādhā. Vallabhāchārya (1479–1531), a Telugu born at Vārānasī (Banāras), had tremendous influence through his sect in Gujarāt and Rājputāna. Among the Śaivites, the sect of the Lingāyats was one whose influence reached several north Indian saints.

Another cluster of sects influenced *bhakti* in the later stages, especially in Bengal, the chief of which were the Buddhist Siddhas, the Sahajayāna, and the Nātha Yogīs. These all shared a basic Tantric approach in which the male–female polarity, the importance of the body, the continuous use of sexual symbolism, and also the use of sensual rites, are essential. It was mainly the Bengālī Vaishnavas and also some Hindī saints like Kabīr who came under this influence.

MAHĀRĀSHTRA

Among the Indo-Āryan vernaculars devotional *bhakti* first appeared in Marāthī. It started in the thirteenth century with Jnāneśvara (1271–96, also known as Jnānadeva), who wrote a long Marāthī commentary on the *Bhagavad Gītā*, called *Bhāvārthadīpikā*, more commonly known as the *Jnāneśvarī*, the fountain-head of Mahārāshtrian devotionalism. More than a commentary, the text constitutes a religious sermon in the form of a song composed in a rhythmic prose which should be chanted. Jnāneśvara was initiated in the Nātha sect, which explains his leaning towards monism, but his *bhakti* was due to his connection with the Vārkarī sect, which instituted the regular popular pilgrimages to the shrine of Vithobā in Pandharpur.

The *Jnāneśvarī* forms a transitional stage in the development of devotional mysticism. It is still greatly influenced by the traditional commentary style of the theologians, but breaks new ground by using the vernacular. Thus was revived that contact with the masses that the great tradition of Hinduism had lost. It innovated also by using a form meant for *kīrtan* chanting, by addressing itself to the mass of the people, and by drawing from the simple life of the village for examples and metaphors. The movement lasted till the seventeenth century, and we now describe its main personalities.

Nāmdev (1270–1350) was a contemporary of Jnāneśvara, but outlived him by over fifty years. A tailor by caste, he was surrounded by other low-caste hymnodist-saints: Gorā the potter, Samvatā the gardener, Chokhā the untouchable, Sena the barber, Janabāī the maid. The object of his devotion was Vithobā, the form of the great god Vishnu residing in the Pandharpur temple. This Vithobā was the god of the Vārkarī-Panth, a sect that has an important place in the history of Mahārāshtrian devotionalism. It differs from most other sects in several ways. Its members are householders, and have a strong aversion to asceticism. Their main cult is the twice-a-year pilgrimage to Pandharpur, when thousands of Vārkarīs walk from village to village, from town to town, singing the praises of Vithobā. The membership cuts across the whole caste structure, and their most important aid to religion is the society of saints, by which term is meant their brothers and sisters in the faith and the saints who have died but left their immortal songs behind. The spread of this intensely devotional movement over the whole of Mahārāshtra was connected with the names of Jnāneśvara and Nāmdev.

Nāmdev's songs reflect a passionate nature, completely given to the love of Vithobā and the continuous invocation of his name. Often Nāmdev is troubled by the conflict between his all-absorbing *bhakti* and his everyday duties. Either his *bhakti* bears him away from the world and its demands, or his involvement in secular life makes him lose the presence of his Lord and thus have a foretaste of that 'Dark Night of the Soul', the bitter sweetness of which Tukārām will experience to the full.

I die unless Thou succour bring,
O haste and come, my God and King!

To help me is a trifling thing,
Yet Thou must haste, my God and King!

O come (how Nāma's clamours ring)

O haste and come, my God and King![1]

After Nāmdev two centuries went by without leaving any names of great saints. The coming of the Turks and of Islam drove the movement underground as it were. The temple at Pandharpur was razed, but the spirit did not die. It was Eknāth (1533–99) who revived the inspiration and the tradition. He was a brāhman born in a family of celebrated saints. As a scholar, he published the first reliable edition of the *Jnāneśvarī*, and thus gave the Marāthī *Gītā* back to his people. By writing a commentary on the *Rāmāyana*, the *Bhāvārtha-rāmāyana*, he also presented Rāma's story to them. His mystical teachings found their supreme expression in his famous commentary on the eleventh book of the *Bhāgavata Purāna*, in which he obviously modelled himself on the great master Jnāneśvara.

But Eknāth did more. He invented, as it were, a new form of deep religious life that needed no institutions or monasteries, no resignation from the world. He was a family man, devoted, austere, whose life was regulated around his hearth and his manuscripts, and yet he was a mystic. He showed how, whatever obstacles the Muslims put in the way, the Hindu could aspire to the deepest experience of his religion within the ordinary framework of life. Every day he practised *kīrtan*, and his songs are part of the Marāthī heritage. They have a strong moral basis, are concerned with the simplest aspects of life, and yet often soar to great heights of personal mysticism.

Tukārām (1598–1650) was no doubt the greatest *bhakti* poet Mahārāshtra produced, and has high claims to be the greatest in the whole of India. He was born in a rural family of grain traders and a great tragedy set him on the path of devotion. A famine took one of his two wives and his son, and left him heartbroken and ruined. His work consists of a collection of hymns, expressing the cry of his soul.

They say that I fabricate poems
Yet words are not mine, but Another's.

It is not my art that clothes them in beauty,
It is the Cosmic Lord who makes me speak.

I am only an ignorant peasant,
How would I know those subtle words?

I am only a simple secretary, says Tukā.
On my books I print the seal of His Name.

Tukārām's hymns are the glory of devotional poetry, the favourites of the Vārkarī pilgrims, and they are woven into the very texture of the Pandharpur rites. More than any other of his fellow saints, Tukārām was a mystic overpowered by love, by the presence or the absence of his Lord. Again and again his songs describe the terrifying passage through the 'Dark Night of the Soul', where his feelings of sin and nothingness combine with the absence of the

[1] A. J. Appasamy, *Temple Bells*, Calcutta, n.d., p. 50.

Lord to crush him down in the depths of despair. Yet even there, love still possesses him. His burning desire for the Lord's vision is frequently fulfilled, and in this fulfilment an ecstasy takes hold of his mind and his senses and transports him into visions, now cosmic, now intensely personal. All this is expressed in the concise, vigorous, sometimes brutally knotted style that is all his own.

As on the bank the poor fish lies
And gasps and writhes in pain,
Or as a man with anxious eyes
Seeks hidden gold in vain,—
So is my heart distressed and cries
To come to Thee again.

Thou knowest, Lord, the agony
Of the lost infant's wail,
Yearning his mother's face to see.
(How oft I tell this tale!)
O, at Thy feet the mystery
Of the dark world unveil![2]

Yet, this poet was of the people, talking their language, using their similes, talking about their life, urging them to become pilgrims of the interior life, to disregard the pomp, deception, superstitions of official Hinduism, and to contemplate the mysteries of the love of God.

A kite careers in the sky,
Up there, so free and high,
The child holds on to the thread,
But his heart is over there.

A woman commits adultery,
She runs the house at home.
But she lives for her lover only,
And her heart is over there.

Tukā says, we are all engrossed
In our different ways and jobs,
But our heart must never be
Distracted from the Lord.

Rāmdās (1608–81), orphaned as a child, left home and, after long years of spiritual training and wandering, he settled down on the banks of the Krishnā where he built a temple to Rāma. This last of the great Mahārāshtrian hymnodists is in several ways quite different again. His main work, the *Daśabodha* is not written in the commentary form, but is rather a compilation of his writings and sermons produced over many years. The content too is new, for we have not only a theologian discussing ideas, but also a reformer concerned with the contemporary state of society, with the bad condition of the brāhmans, with the threat of Islam. There is evidence of what today we would call 'political' concern in the relationship he had with his pupil Śivājī, the founder of the new Marāthā Hindu kingdom. In him devotionalism and activism were

[2] Ibid., p. 54.

closely wedded: whereas his predecessors were householders, their concern for society was less than that of Rāmdās, the ascetic. And whereas the others centred their devotion on Krishna and the Vishnu of Pandharpur, Rāmdās, as his name proclaims, was a devotee of Rāma.

Those, then, are the main saints of Mahārāshtra. As a group they have characteristics that set them apart from those of other regions: theologically there is a strong current of monism, and although mostly devotees of Krishna their works are devoid of erotic imagery. They revitalized Hinduism, established the Marāthā literary and cultural identity, and insisted on unifying social forces: these were to become important political factors in the building of the great Hindu kingdom of the Marāthās, and later characterized the Mahārāshtrian nationalist reformist movement.

BENGAL

Medieval devotionalism in Bengal has different roots from that of Mahārāshtra, and developed in quite a different way. Two distinct streams of religiosity determined its growth. On the one hand there is the influence of the Vaishnava tradition, and on the other the non-Vaishnava influences from Buddhist and Hindu sources. The Vaishnava impetus came first of all through the *Bhāgavata Purāna* with its glorification of the Krishna-*līlā*. This came to Bengal under the Pāla kings and found its typically Bengālī literary transformation in Jayadeva's passionately lyrical *Gīta-Govinda* towards the end of the twelfth century. The *Gīta-Govinda* brings into Bengālī Vaishnavism a new aspect, derived from another source than the *Bhāgavata*, namely the prominence given to Rādhā, the favourite of Krishna. The erotic-mystical theme of the love of Krishna and Rādhā occupies here the centre of the stage, and henceforth dominates Bengālī devotionalism.

Non-Vaishnava influence came from two sources, distinct yet interrelated. Buddhism had been on the decline in India for some time, but in Bengal it survived under the Pāla Dynasty, after which it became decadent. In its decadence it produced forms that affected the development of Vaishnavism, and both these Buddhist and Vaishnava forms then influenced Bengālī devotionalism. Their emphasis was on the female principle of the universe and they exalted the religious value of sexual passion. In reaction against the rigours of the Mahāyāna discipline they preached the doctrine of naturalism, thus idealizing the sensuous and showing a new path to salvation in and through the senses. Intense emotionalism and eroticism pervaded their rites and mystical teachings. Chaitanya, the greatest of the Bengālī teachers, did not himself come under their spell, but they certainly had an impact on the erotically inspired Krishna-*bhakti* of Bengal, leading in some cases to decadent practices.

Chandīdās (fourteenth century) is the first great name in Bengālī *bhakti* literature. His poems, which include poems to the Mother Goddess and to Krishna and Rādhā, testify to his being influenced by both the *Gīta-Govinda* and the Sahajīyā doctrines. He holds that the only way to salvation is the love of God, and that this love must be based on an earthly passion for a particular person. This passion, however, needs to be sublimated, and therefore one should choose an inaccessible person, for instance a low-caste or married woman, for its object. The washerwoman Rāmī became the focus of his own desire and some of his most beautiful poems are about her. More influential than these Śākta poems was his *Krishnakīrtan*, devoted to the love of Krishna and Rādhā, imbued with great depth of feeling and transfused with profound symbolism.

Friend, what else can I tell you?
Love has captured me in my tender youth,
And You leave me no peace in my house.

I will end my life, jump in the sea,
Yearning to be reborn as Krishna,
And You as Rādhā in the next life.

Then my love will snare, then abandon You.
As You go to the well, I will gracefully
Stand under the Kadamba with my flute.

Chandīdās says, You, as a simple housewife,
Will fall under the spell of my flute.
And then it will be Your turn, O Krishna,
To suffer the burning pangs of love.

Although Vidyāpati (fourteenth to fifteenth century) did not write in Bengālī, but in Maithilī, an allied dialect, his songs on Rādhā and Krishna are part of Bengālī Vaishnavism. He wrote eight works in Sanskrit, and nearly a thousand of his love-ballads have been collected. His work is similar in content to that of Chandīdās, but his poetry is more classical, polished, and learned. In fact it mostly reads as a Maithilī version of Sanskrit courtly eroticism, and the tradition injected a religious symbolism into the poems which one sometimes suspects was absent in their making.

. . . On all my limbs
Were spells of love.
What strength I needed
To arrest desire.
My quivering breasts
I hid with trembling hands
As all my body glowed.
No longer could I check my passion
And the shut lotus bloomed in smiles.[3]

The saint who gathered together the various strands of Bengālī Vaishnavism, became a reformer, and founded a sect with enormous influence on Bengal religious life, was Viśvambhar Miśra, called Chaitanya (1485–1533). He was unique in medieval *bhakti* history in that he was the initiator of a very broad movement which covered Bengal and spilled out into the whole of east India. It was a movement which encompassed an organized sect, a strong theological school, and a broad-based popular cult. Chaitanya was probably at first a member of the Śankarite Daśnāmī sect, and he did not leave any theological writings, but only a few devotional songs. He himself was primarily a visionary ecstatic.

He sent six theologians, the 'six Gosvāmins', to the sacred Krishnaite place Vrindāvan (in Bengālī Brindāban) to work out the theology of the

[3] *Love Songs of Vidyāpati*, trans. Deben Bhattacharya, London, 1963, p. 69.

emerging sect. These were the people who codified its doctrine and formulated its rules and rites. They were learned Sanskritists, familiar with the revelation and the tradition, and primarily intent on fitting their theology into commentaries on the sacred texts, particularly the *Bhāgavata Purāna*. The main peculiarities of their theology are the following. Krishna is considered to be not a mere incarnation of Vishnu, but the highest aspect of the divine, its 'true essence'. In this aspect he is united with the highest *śakti*, which expresses the blissful power of divine life and is manifest in Rādhā. The aim of the devotee is gradually to ascend the ladder of *bhakti* till he reaches the supreme state of *mādhurya*, or sweetness, in which he emotionally identifies himself with Rādhā and achieves the blissful state of union with Krishna. This ladder of perfection is expressed in a terminology taken over from the refined science of aesthetics, describing the experience of the beautiful. The whole theological edifice is thus based on a formalization of sublimated emotional eroticism, and couched in terms derived from aesthetics. It should be stressed that this mystical theology insists strongly on virtue and on ethical training, as the necessary prerequisites for the full realization of *bhakti*.

This theology, elaborated at a physical distance from Bengal, in some way distanced itself from Chaitanya himself and the popular movement that grew around him. Chaitanya expressed himself in the *sankīrtan*, a session of hymn-singing by a group of devotees. These songs were often accompanied by ecstatic dancing to the sound of tambourines. Sessions took place in homes or temples, or erupted in the streets in the form of processions. Chaitanya, the ecstatic *par excellence*, was the centre of the cult, and a whole literature of hymns, biographies, legends, and dramas sprang up around him. In fact Chaitanya himself became the object of popular devotion, and was considered the living Krishna, or rather the incarnation of Rādhā-Krishna. The Chaitanyites were no social reformers militating against the caste structure, but within the sphere of devotional practice they completely rejected all distinction of caste and thus promoted a sense of equality that penetrated deep into Bengālī life.

For three centuries Krishna and Chaitanya remained the main inspiration of high Bengālī culture. The seventeenth century produced a new crop of hymnodists, the greatest of whom was Govinda Dās.

> The sun above is burning like fire,
> The sand beneath is burning the path,
> But Rādhā in daylight goes to the tryst,
> Butter-soft body, and lotus-soft feet.
>
> The wind blows about circles of dust,
> Screening the eyes of suspicious elders,
> The beautiful Rādhā is now on her way,
> And all her troubles are blown away.
>
> Govindadās says, O Loving Rādhā,
> You have now conquered the obstacles,
> And the mantra of love. So you must go,
> And learn from Hari the rituals of love.

Orders of *sādhus* sprang up in the Chaitanya tradition, but they came strongly under the decadent influence of the Tantric orders. The Chaitanya movement had a great impact on Bengālī life as a whole. It gave it a special identity which persisted even through periods of stagnancy, and provided time and again new inspiration to its religious reformers and poets: Keshub Chandra Sen, Bankim Chandra Chatterjee, and Rabīndranāth Tāgore cannot be properly understood without reference to that tradition.

THE LAND OF HINDĪ

In the Hindī-speaking areas the new movement started not around the figure of Krishna, but around Rāma, and found its leader and organizer in Rāmānanda (1400–70). In his early days he probably resided in south India and was at first a follower of Rāmānuja's Śrīvaishnava sect. On his return to the north he settled down in Vārānasī (Banāras) and established his own sect, the Rāmānandīs. Although the old *Vālmīki Rāmāyana* was followed over the centuries by a series of works on Rāma, we have little evidence of any Rāma cult before the advent of Rāmānanda. He looks upon Rāma as the supreme God, who is to be adored with his *śakti*, Sītā, and whose close companions like Hanumān should also be venerated. The literature of the sect is not important—only one hymn of Rāmānanda himself is extant—and its theology and ritual are largely modelled on those of Rāmānuja.

Its main influence lies in a different direction. Rāmānanda was strongly opposed to the restrictions and injustices of caste. He threw his sect open to all, and his twelve personal disciples are said to have included women, an outcaste, and even a Muslim. This frank egalitarian basis and the exclusive use of the vernacular set the sect apart from many others. Although egalitarian ideas did exist in India before, one cannot discount here the possible influence of the contemporary Muslim Sūfīs. The Rāmānandī sect has great historical importance because its followers initiated a number of other sects and movements which covered north India. The Rāmānandīs stand at the source of important later sects like the Sikhs and the Kabīrpanthīs, who inherited their social concern.

Kabīr (1440–1518) started out as a disciple of Rāmānanda, but later developed his own characteristic eclecticism. Probably a Muslim by birth, or at least brought up in a Muslim home, he was and remained a low-caste weaver. His poetry, of which a good collection has come down the ages, is essentially a poetry of the people: it is unpolished and has a rustic, colloquial quality, yet it is pervaded with a profound symbolism and often reaches great lyrical power. It is a poetry of epigrams and short verses, easily remembered, that has penetrated the life of north India nearly as much as the poetry of Tulsīdās.

For Kabīr there is only one way to God: the way of personally experienced *bhakti*, which gives one the vision of the Lord, and which is a gift of God's grace. Man must purify his soul by righteousness and humility, by renunciation and love, and by praise of God in his *kīrtan* and in his quiet meditation. Kabīr's idea of God, like his whole theology, is eclectic, with strong influences from Vaishnavism, Hatha Yoga, Vedāntic monism, and Sūfism. He called God by many names, like Rām, Hari, Allāh, Khudā, *Nirguna*, *Tat*, and even *Śūnya* (the Void) and *Śabda* (Sound). No wonder the Muslims claimed him as a Sūfī, the Hindus looked on him as a *Rāma-Bhakta*, and the Síkhs incorporated his songs in their *Ādi-Granth*.

Kabīr was at heart a reformer, and an iconoclast. Continuously he attacks the externals of religion, scriptures, pilgrimages, rituals, superstitions, idols.

> There is nothing but water at the holy bathing places;
> and I know that they are useless, for I have bathed in them.
> The images are all lifeless, they cannot speak;
> I know, for I have cried aloud to them.
> The Puranas and the Koran are mere words;
> lifting up the curtain, I have seen.[4]

To this religious iconoclasm he adds a social iconoclasm that incessantly attacks the injustices of caste, and denounces the pride of the brāhmans. Humanity to him is a brotherhood, and all varieties of human nature are but refractions of the divine.

> It is but folly to ask what the caste of a saint may be;
> The barber has sought God, the washerwoman, and the carpenter—
> Even Raidas was a seeker after God.
> The Rishi Svapacha was a tanner by caste.
> Hindus and Muslims alike have achieved that End, where
> remains no mark of distinction.[5]

Legend has it that after Kabīr's death both Hindus and Muslims claimed the body. The ghost of Kabīr appeared and told them to raise the shroud. Beneath they found only a heap of fresh flowers. The Hindus took half and cremated them at Vārānasī, the Muslims buried the other half at Maghar.

Kabīr founded a community, known as the Kabīrpanth, which exists to this day, and a dozen other sects sprang from his direct teaching. They all shunned idolatry, were open to Hindus and Muslims alike, stressed the value of the *guru*, and limited themselves to the vernacular. In the course of time, however, these sects grew more exclusive, became increasingly Hinduized, and adopted orders of *sādhus*. The most important of these sects, which was to have quite a different history, was that of the Sikhs, founded by Guru Nānak, a disciple of Kabīr.

Tulsīdās (1532–1623) was the other most famous spiritual heir of Rāmānanda. His *Rām-charit-mānas*, the *Lake of the Story of Rāma*, has been rightly called the Bible of north India. This was a new *Rāmāyana* in the vernacular, a conception so daring that it aroused the ire of the brāhmans and made the people consider Tulsīdās a reincarnation of Vālmīki. It is the favourite book of a hundred million people, for many of whom it is their main source of religious inspiration. Of Tulsīdās's life we know little for sure. He probably studied Sanskrit, then settled in Vārānasī, where he devoted himself wholly to the Rāma *bhakti*. Traditionally six minor and six major works are attributed to him. Of the latter the greatest, apart from the *Rām-charit-mānas*, are the *Vinaya-pattrikā* and the *Kavitāvalī*.

[4] *One Hundred Poems of Kabir*, trans. Rabindranath Tagore, London, 1962, poem No. XLII.

[5] Ibid., poem No. II. It is to be noted that most of the verses of Kabīr translated by Tāgore are of dubious authenticity; but they are certainly the work of his school, and reflect the doctrines of the sect he founded. [Ed.]

Attempts to ascribe to Tulsīdās a particular theology, either the Śankarite monism or the theistic monism of Rāmānuja, seem fruitless. He was not a systematic theologian, but in his own way he aspired to harmonize these different theologies. This attempt differentiates him clearly from both Rāmānanda and Kabīr. The main reason for this may be found in the *Adhyātma Rāmāyana*, a work that postdates those two and tries to combine Śankara's monism with Rāmānuja's devotion. Tulsīdās, while theoretically he may seem to lean towards Śankara, found that the solution for him lay in the very practical approach of living *bhakti* itself. In his attitude to the traditional framework of Hinduism he also moves away from his predecessors. He is not a revolutionary as they were, but upholds firmly the broad basis of traditional Hindu society and of the scriptures, and repeatedly attacks those many sects that endangered these basic structures. For him reform had to be brought about within the compass of Hinduism itself through the loving power of *bhakti*. Caste should stand, but, for a devotee as devotee, caste was of no importance, and *bhakti* was open to all.

Tulsīdās's *bhakti* is the love of the servant for his loving master. His work is totally free of even the slightest hint of sensuality, showing in fact a scrupulous concern for purity. In this his work contrasts strongly with the Krishna literature, and his enormous influence carried this over into the whole Rāma *bhakti* literature of the north. The divinity and graciousness of Rāma pervade every incident of his *Rāmāyana*; in fact, their pervasion is so great that it affects everyone in the epic, transforming eventually even the traditional villains Kaikeyī and Rāvana into devotees of Rāma. Devotion to Rāma is necessary in order to overcome the cycle of births and deaths, and the way of devotion is the simple and direct way open to all, in whatever condition of life they may find themselves.

Monkey, boatman, bear, bird or demon,
  whichever one you cared for,
Master, that very one
  at once became of service;
The afflicted, orphaned, filthy,
  wretched, whoever came for refuge,
Each one you made your own,
—such is your kindly nature;

My name was Tulsī, though
  I was ugly as the hemp-plant,
I styled myself Dās—your slave,
  and you accepted such a great impostor;
There is none other master
  so worthy—son of Daśrath,
Nor God compassionate,—you alone
  care for the shame of those who are yours.[6]

Tulsīdās's incalculable influence on Hinduism in north India was threefold. He inspired an intense devotion to Rāma that touched upon every aspect of life, and made Gāndhī cry 'Hé Rām!' as he died under the assassin's bullet.

[6] Tulsī Dās, *Kavitāvalī*, trans. with a Critical Introduction by F. R. Allchin, London, 1964, pp. 136–7.

Tulsīdās inculcated a high sense of morality, and of kindness in human relationships. And he proved a great force in strengthening the structures of the *Sanātana Dharma* at a time when both Islam and the many iconoclastic sects were threatening it seriously. In this last his stature is no smaller than that of the great Śankara himself.

The Hindī world also produced its devotees of Krishna. Mīrā Bāī (1503–73), a Rājput princess, was the first to achieve poetic fame. She was widowed at an early age, and left the Court of the Rānā to devote herself to the worship of Krishna:

> Rānā, your strange world is not to my liking,
> It has no saints, and its people are base.
> I've given up ornaments and the braiding of hair,
> I've given up collyrium and the tying of braids.
> Mīrā has found a perfect groom, Krishna the Lord.

She was no theologian, nor did she leave a great number of songs, but those that are extant have a quality all their own. There is a freshness and femininity about them, a deep pathos that expresses itself in lyrical simplicity, without the frills of conscious artistry. It is not so much the myth of Krishna that interests her as her own relationship with him. That relationship is different from most other Krishna *śāktas* in that it consists of a spiritual marriage to Krishna, her Lord.

> Friend, it's in a dream that the Lord married me,
> The doorways were festooned, and he held my hand,
> It's in a dream that he married me, happy for ever.

In their nuptials the erotic element is totally absent; there is no voluptuous imagery. It is in her poems of separation that she reaches her greatest heights, projecting her sorrow and pining for Krishna on to nature around her.

> Thunderclouds came and went, but no message from Hari,
> Frog, peacock, partridge and cuckoo started to call.
> Lightning flashed in deep darkness, but I was alone,
> Trembling in the roar of fragrant wind and pelting rain.
> Loneliness burnt and stung like a jet black cobra,
> And Mīrā's heart overflowed with love for the Lord.

Sūrdās (1483–1563) was one of the eight main disciples of Vallabha, and the most brilliant. Born in a brāhman family and blind, possibly from birth, he was a musician attached to the temples at Āgrā and Mathurā. He left a great number of songs, collected in the *Sūrsāgar*, which he himself tells us was inspired by the *Bhāgavata Purāna*. His songs have as their theme the love of Krishna, whose life he sings, taking particular delight in the child Krishna, and the lover. His verse is renowned for its exquisite melody, and the conciseness of his little tableaux reminds one of the contemporary Rājasthān Krishna miniatures, which also vividly evoke the village life of the time. As a poet he is put second only to Tulsīdās. His poetry is suffused with an essentially tender *bhakti*, sometimes passionate, yet never too explicitly physical, often full of pathos, and pervaded with a gentle affection for all that lives.

As the moth for love of the lotus loses itself in the flower
and yet is happy; so am I Thy devotee, my Lord!
As the stag for delight of a tune stands unconcernedly near the
axe of the huntsman; so am I Thy devotee.
As the pigeon for desire of the sky soars higher though only to be
dashed to the ground; so am I Thy devotee, Beloved!
As the rain-bird in its utter loneliness calls its lover continuously,
so I wait for a vision of Thee, my Lord!
For I feel forsaken and lonely and sad.[7]

SOUTH INDIA

It was in the south that the new devotional movement originally started, and we saw how it spread to the north and changed the religious panorama of north India. In general, one can say that in the south the devotional movement was much more closely wedded to the strong theological traditions and the sects than in the north, although here too the movement threw up the occasional individualistic revolutionary. Our concern is not with the theologians and sects themselves, however, but with the devotional popular movement as it expressed itself in the vernaculars.

In Tamil-land the hymns of the Ālvārs and the Nāyanārs continued to dominate the scene, and they soon gained the status of divine scripture and became part and parcel of temple worship as well as of popular devotional life. The first great poet to follow them is Kamban (twelfth century), author of the famous Tamil *Rāmāyana*, which is replete with descriptions of the country and times of the Cholas. The *Mahābhārata* and the *Bhāgavata Purāna* also found their Tamil translators. Much of the Vaishnavite effort, however, went into Sanskrit compositions, and even much of its vernacular literature derived closely from the Sanskrit, and preferred the purānic approach and style.

The Śaivites produced a new devotional literature by the hymnodists called Sittars or Siddhas. Their innumerable songs gained great popularity, and, in their fierce monotheism and equally fierce condemnation of idolatry, they arrayed themselves against the powers of orthodoxy.

When once I knew the Lord,
What were to me the host
of pagan deities,
Some fixed in temple shrines,
Or carried in the crowd;
Some made of unbaked clay,
And some burnt hard with fire?
With all the lying tales
That fill the sacred books,
They've vanished from my mind.

But yet I have a shrine—
The mind within my breast.
An image too is there—
The soul that came from God.

[7] *Temple Bells*, p. 27.

I offer ash and flowers—
The praises of my heart;
And all the God-made world
Is frankincense and myrrh.
And thus where'er I go
I ever worship God.[8]

The earliest Kannada literature was predominantly Jain, but the Hindu renaissance was inaugurated by Basava towards the end of the twelfth century. He founded the sect of the Vīraśaivas or the Lingāyats, characterized by its numerous monasteries and by the large measure of its social equality, which had a tremendous influence on the Kannada country. They invented a new kind of vernacular literature, the *vachana*, little pieces of rhythmic prose sermons, meant for the people and inculcating *bhakti* to Śiva. For over three centuries enormous numbers of these *vachanas* were composed. The Lingāyats also left collections of hymns, and a hagiographic literature in praise of their saints. Here is a sample of a *vachana*:

Oh pay your worship to God now—before the cheek turns wan, and the neck is wrinkled, and the body shrinks—before the teeth fall out and the back is bowed, and you are wholly dependent on others—before you need to lean on a staff, and to raise yourself by your hands on your thighs—before your beauty is destroyed by age and Death itself arrives. Oh *now* worship Kūdala-sangama-deva.[9]

Vaishnava literature in Kannada really started from the sixteenth century, during the Hindu kingdom of Vijayanagara, first with translations from the Sanskrit classics, the *Mahābhārata*, the *Rāmāyana*, and the *Bhāgavata Purāna*. These were then followed by popular songs composed and sung by the *dāsas*, or mendicant singers, inspired by Madhvāchārya and stimulated by the visit of Chaitanya to the south in 1510. This tradition continued for a couple of centuries, producing songs in praise of Vishnu, some venerating him in the form of the Vithobā of Pandharpur, thus linking up with the Mahārāshtrian tradition.

My stock (of sugar candy) is not packed on the backs of strong kine;
Nor pressed into bags strongly fastened with twine.
Wherever it goes it no taxes doth pay
But still is most great, and brings profit, I say.

It wastes not with time; never gives a bad smell;
You've nothing to pay, though you take it right well;
White ants cannot eat the fine sugar with me;
The city resounds as its virtue men see.

From market to market 'tis needless to run;
The shops know it not, the bazaar can have none.
My candy, you see, is the name of Vishnu,
So sweet on the tongue that gives praise as is due.[10]

Telugu literature follows closely the pattern of development of Kannada literature, starting with Jain texts, and then moving on to a Hindu renaissance

[8] L. D. Barnett, *The Heart of India*, London, 1913, pp. 91–2.
[9] E. P. Rice, *Kanarese Literature*, London, 1921, p. 57.
[10] Ibid., p. 82.

by translations from the Sanskrit. The starting-point is Nannaya (eleventh century), who translated part of the *Mahābhārata*, later continued by the great Tikkana (1220–1300), and finished by Yerrapragada (1280–1350). The *Rāmāyana* and the great *Purānas* too were soon transposed into Telugu.

The Telugu country saw a couple of figures who in many ways closely resemble some of the contemporary north Indian saints. Potana (1400–75) was a poor man without scholarship, who lived and died in the countryside. His voluminous translation of the *Bhāgavata* gained immediate popularity, because it combined a simple language of great narrative power with a deep intensity of devotion. Among Vaishnava popular devotional literature it is one of the classics. Vemana (fifteenth century) was a low-caste Śaivite, and very much an individualist and a revolutionary. His *śataka* (century) of gnomic verse is known to all Telugus, and to most south Indians. His verses bristle with sarcastic attacks on the brāhmans, on polytheism, idolatry, and pilgrimages.

> The solitariness of a dog! the meditation of a crane!
> The chanting of an ass! The bathing of a frog!
> Ah, why will ye not try to know your own hearts?
>
> What are you the better for smearing your body with ashes?
> Your thoughts should be set on God alone;
> For the rest, an ass can wallow in dirt as well as you.
>
> The books that are called the Vedas are like courtesans,
> Deluding men, and wholly unfathomable;
> But the hidden knowledge of God is like an honourable wife.
>
> He that fasts shall become (in his next birth) a village pig;
> He that embraces poverty shall become a beggar;
> And he that bows to a stone shall become like a lifeless image.[11]

The reign of Krishnadeva Rāyā (1509–29), a poet-king, brought back Sanskrit classicism, and the religious poetry of his court is ornate and more courtly than religious. The inspiration had gone out of high poetry, which became empty in content whilst seeking after new effects, but in the popular tradition the great favourites of the past continued to be treasured.

Other modern languages too like Oriyā, Assamese, Kashmīrī, Gujarātī, and Malayālam had their devotional hymnodists. In fact, devotional *bhakti* changed Hinduism profoundly over most of India, from the eleventh century onwards. Up to the seventeenth century it remained the most important single power in Hinduism, and it was only in the nineteenth century that the impact of the West was to challenge Hinduism again, and stimulate yet another renewal.

[11] L. D. Barnett, op. cit., pp. 111–12.

CHAPTER XIX

Islam in Medieval India

by S. A. A. RIZVI

ISLAM means 'submission' or 'resignation' to Allāh (God). The Qur'ān, the highest authority, calls it 'the only true religion', perfected for those whom Allāh intends to guide. The Qur'ān is revealed and not created, being the eternal word of God incarnate. It requires Muslims (the word Muhammadan is taboo among modern Muslims) to believe in God, His Angels, His Books, and His Messengers. All the prophets from Adam to Muhammad, and all the books revealed to them, are regarded as the religious heritage of Islam; but as Muhammad is the last of the prophets, Islam is the last word in the cycle of divine revelation.

Islam's strongest weapon against the scriptures of the Jews and Christians is the accusation that they are no longer authentic, having been corrupted by the sages and saints of those two faiths. Islam's condemnation of the idols of Mecca applies equally to all idol worship. According to Islam, only Allāh is to be worshipped, for he is the Creator and Lord of Judgement, with unlimited sovereignty (*rubūbiyya*) over His creation. Belief in His omnipotence and benevolence in its turn demands that Muslims treat all God's creatures with kindness, for he who loves God's creatures best, is best beloved of Him.

The oneness of God and the mission of Muhammad are recognized in the profession of faith (*shahādah*): 'There is no God except Allāh and Muhammad is Allāh's messenger'. Five times a day, their faces turned towards Mecca, Muslims are enjoined to pray in a prescribed form. The noon prayer on Friday is the only public one; but these congregational prayers have obliged Muslims, both rulers and private men, to build mosques in which to hold them. Another obligation laid on the Muslim is to give a fixed proportion of certain categories of his property as alms. Then, during the month of Ramazān, the ninth of the Muslim calendar and that in which the Qur'ān was first revealed, he must neither eat nor drink from dawn to sunset. Every Muslim who possesses the means must also make the pilgrimage to Mecca at least once in his life.

Islam has no priesthood or sacerdotal hierarchy. Heresy is a term not strictly speaking applicable to Islam, for, as Professor Holt says, it 'has been repressed only when it has been manifested as political subversion: it is also true to say that, since Islam is both a religious and a political community, the distinction between religious and political dissent is not clear cut'.

During the first century of its history, Islam split into two sects divided on political as well as religious grounds: Sunnīs and Shī'īs. The religious differences between the two arose over the interpretation of verses of the Qur'ān and over the *Hadīs*, or corpus of traditions about Muhammad's sayings and doings. Although the Qur'ān is common to both sects, their *Hadīs* differ, as do their doctrines upon the succession to Muhammad. The Sunnīs, who have always predominated in India, believe that Muhammad appointed no successor, and left this matter to the discretion of the élite of the *Umma* or community of believers. The Shī'īs assert that Muhammad's being the last of the prophets does not end men's need of intermediaries between themselves and God. They call such intermediaries Imāms, and regard 'Alī, the cousin and son-in-law of Muhammad, as their first Imām. Their jurisprudence and religious practices are based on the teachings of their Imāms.

All Shī'īs are in agreement about the legitimacy of the first six Imāms, but differ as to who succeeded the sixth Imām, Ja'far al-Sādiq, who died in 765. One group, the Ismā'īlīs, believe that the succession then continued through Ismā'īl (died 760/1), Ja'far's son. The other group, the Isnā 'Asharīs, to whom the Shī'īs of Iran belong, believe that the line was continued by Mūsa al-Kāzim, followed by five others. The Ismā'īlīs, who from the ninth to the thirteenth centuries propagated their beliefs effectively by giving inner or esoteric meaning to their religious teachings, which they explained allegorically, ruled Multān more or less continuously to 1160. Even after losing their political power there, they continued to preach their doctrines secretly in India, and one of their leaders, Nūr Turk, made a final bid for power through a *coup d'état* in Razīya's reign.

The Isnā 'Asharī faith was recognized as the state religion of Iran by Shāh Ismā'īl I (1501–24), the founder of the Safavīd Dynasty. In India the acceptance of this faith by the sultans of Ahmadnagar, Bījāpur, and Golconda, together with their patronage of Shī'ī scholars and learning in their kingdoms, sharpened the Shī'ī-Sunnī controversy in northern India, where there was a considerable influx of Shī'ī élite from both the Deccan and Iran.

The rulers of northern India were of the Sunnī faith, as were most of their subjects. Among the Sunnīs there are four principal schools of jurisprudence named after their founders: the Hanafī after Abū Hanīfa of Kūfah (*c.* 699–767); the Mālikite after Mālik ibn Anas (died 795), the leader of the Medina School; the Shāfi'īite called after ash-Shāfi'ī, who flourished in Baghdād and Cairo (767–820); and, a late-comer, the Hanbalite after Ahmad ibn Hanbal (780–855) of Baghdād. All four systems were based on the Qur'ān and *Hadīs*, in this context called the 'roots' or *usūl*. Where they failed to provide a solution, the matter was dealt with either on the basis of analogical deduction (*qiyās*) or catholic consent (*ijmā'*). Private judgement, or *ra'y*, was allowed a place of varying importance in every school. In Abū Hanīfa's system, the right of preference (*istihsān*) or departure from analogy on grounds of equity is also permissible. It was universally agreed throughout the Sunnī world to operate strictly within the existing systems and to allow no further codification. Such inflexibility provided a strong defensive position from which Sunnīs could combat schisms and other threats to their faith, both external and internal.

The greatest challenge to orthodox Sunnism came from rationalism in the form of the Mu'tazilās, who had much in common with the Shī'īs. They professed a strict monotheism, denying any resemblance between Allāh and His creatures. For them, God is just and has nothing to do with the evil deeds of man, for although He has the power to commit injustice He does not do so, and man is solely responsible for his own actions. Rejecting the orthodox view that the Qur'ān was the duplicate of a celestial original, they proclaimed that it had been created. Under the patronage of the 'Abbāsid Caliph Mā'mūn (813–33), the Mu'tazilās ruthlessly persecuted their opponents, thus setting a precedent for the relentless inquisition into free thinking later practised by the orthodox.

The Mu'tazilās made a more positive contribution to Sunnī orthodoxy, however, through Abu'l Hasan al-Ash'arī (873–935) a zealous Mu'tazilite who had learnt their techniques before deserting them, and evolved his own system of rational argument for the defence of orthodox doctrine, known as *kalām*. Parallel to the Ash'arī School developed the orthodox Māturīdī School of Abū Mansūr Māturīdī (died in 944). The differences between the two schools are listed as thirteen, but they are more serious than acknowledged.

The Ash'arī system made great progress under the leadership of its most outstanding protagonist, Abū Hāmid al-Ghazālī (1058–1111), who fought against all non-orthodox Sunnī systems, including those of the *Falāsīfa* (philosophers) such as Farābī (*c.* 870–950) and Avicenna (980–1037) who based their thinking upon Aristotelian, Platonic, or Neoplatonic works translated from Greek into Arabic between the ninth and eleventh centuries.

The influence of Ghazālī was much greater, because of the new Muslim religious leaders produced by the educational system devised by the Saljuqīd vizier, Nizāmu'l Mulk Tūsī (*c.* 1018–92). This centred on seminaries of higher Sunnite learning known as *madrasas*, designed specifically to produce scholars of the Ash'arī School qualified to run the government in accordance with orthodox Sunnī ideas. Known as '*ulamā*' (singular, '*ālim*), these scholars were mostly government officials whose religious prestige was exploited by the sultans as a counterpoise against ambitious military adventurers. But although the '*ulamā*' issued *fatwās* (legal opinions) declaring that opposition to the ruling authority was an abominable sin, not all of them were themselves loyal to their rulers. Ambitious '*ulamā*' did in fact join with military leaders in plots to replace strong monarchs by their own puppets. Many monarchs were able to overcome such situations only by drawing upon the support of the sūfīs. No sultan could wield power successfully unless he was able to balance the interests of the '*ulamā*', the sūfīs, and the military leaders—the three main pressure groups.

Contrary to the '*ulamā*', who specialized in the formal structure of Islamic law and dealt with the practical requirements of political, social, and economic life, the sūfīs claimed to penetrate to the very root and spirit of Islam. Professor Arberry describes sūfism as 'the attempt of individual Muslims to realize in their personal experience the living presence of Allāh'.

In the formative period, sūfīs generally led a retired ascetic life; but gradually they evolved a corporate system of their own, ideas and practices being borrowed from Christian and Buddhist monasticism and philosophy from Neoplatonism and Upanishadic concepts. Their originality lay in incorporating these influences within the framework of Islam, thus making them an integral part of Muslim life.

The most authentic exposition of sūfism is contained in the *Risāla* (Epistle) of Abu'l Qāsim al-Qushairī (d. 1074). What endowed sūfism with great prestige, however, and led to its being regarded as the pinnacle of religious life, was the sudden change in Abū Hāmid al-Ghazālī's life, when in 1095 he resigned from the chair of divinity in the Nizāmiyya academy of Baghdād to lead the life of a sūfī. Poetry also contributed to making sūfism a popular movement, and its organizational structure did much towards keeping it an effective one. By the twelfth century, sūfīs were divided into different *silsilas* (orders), each with its *pīr* (preceptor), also known as *Shaikh* or *Khwāja*, as an infallible guide for the neophyte. Until the fourteenth century, a *pīr* only initiated disciples into his own order, but later on distinguished preceptors were authorized to initiate disciples into other orders too.

The *khānqāh* (hospice) was the centre of the *pīrs*' activity, attracting from afar men seeking the spiritual life. Such disciples were graded into different categories, the most advanced joining the *pīr* in his prayers and meditational exercises. Some *khānqāhs* provided board and lodging for a large number of disciples and visitors. Initially the inmates of the *khānqāh* lived on the charity of the local inhabitants, but as time went by their affluence grew in step with their popularity. So much were they venerated, that their relics were sanctified and worshipped by posterity.

The earliest sūfī of eminence known to have settled in India, where the rich Hindu mystic traditions gave a new vitality to sūfism, was Hujwīrī, also known as Dātā Ganj Bakhsh (died after 1088), the author of the celebrated manual of sūfism entitled *Kashfu'l Mahjūb*.

The development of several new sūfī orders in the twelfth century led to the establishment of a network of *khānqāhs*, mainly in Iran, Central Asia, and India. In India the first leading *khānqāh* was established at Multān by Shaikh Bahā'u'd-Dīn Zakarīyya (1182–1262). He was also the founder in India of the Suhrawardī order originated by Shaikh Shihābu'd-Dīn Suhrawardī (1145–1234), the author of an Arabic manual on sūfism entitled *'Awārīfu'l-Ma'ārif*. Rulers, high government officials, and merchants lavished gifts upon these *khānqāhs*, and the hagiological literature relates how, with its overflowing granaries and general affluence, the *khānqāh* was often able to give financial assistance to the state. Shaikh Bahā'u'd-Dīn Zakarīyya openly took Iltutmish's side in his struggle against Qabācha, and received from him the title of *Shaikhu'l Islām* ('Leader of Islam'). He avoided ordinary men and associated only with the religious and political élite. His grandson, Shaikh Ruknu'd-Dīn Abu'l Fath (died 1335), in his turn was highly respected by Sultan 'Alā'u'd-Dīn and the Tughluq sultans. Another Suhrawardī sūfī, Shaikh Shihābu'd-Dīn's disciple Shaikh Jalālu'd-Dīn Tabrēzī, failed in his efforts to establish supremacy in Delhi, and retired to Bengal, where he established a *khānqāh* and a *langar* (centre for the distribution of free meals), first at Lakhnautī, and then at Devatalla near Pānduā. He is said to have converted a large number of Bengālīs to Islam.

The Panjāb, Sind, and Bengal thus became three important centres of Suhrawardī activity. It appears that the Suhrawardīs were keen to convert Hindus to Islam, and they were helped to do this by their affluence and connections with those in power. Suhrawardīs such as Makhdūm Jahāniyān (1308–84), who had travelled to various parts of the Islamic world, and his brother Rāju Qattāl were militant evangelists.

The second outstanding order to establish *khānqāhs* in the towns conquered by the Ghūrid invaders was the Chishtīyya, originating from a village near Herat called Chisht or Khwāja Chisht. It was brought to India by Khwāja Mu'īnu'd-Dīn who was born in Sijistān in *c.* 1141. Having visited the important centres of Islamic culture in the Middle East, where he came in contact with Shaikhs of all the important sūfī orders, he went to Lāhore, finally settling in Ajmer about 1206. The story that he settled there when Prithvīrāja was at the height of his power, and that his curse upon the Rājā, with whom he had quarrelled, led to his downfall, is nothing more than a pious legend. In medieval times such tales were used to prove the superiority of faith over political power; yet some modern scholars use them as evidence that the sūfīs were the great missionaries of Islam. When stricken in years, Khwāja Mu'īnu'd-Dīn married two wives. The hagiologists say this was done so that none of the Prophet Muhammad's practices should go unfollowed; but it is more probable that the Khwāja had at last decided to live a settled life. By the time he died in 1236, Chishtī *khānqāhs* were firmly established in many parts of the Delhi sultanate.

At Nāgaur an important Chishtī centre was established by Shaikh Hamīdu'd-Dīn Nāgaurī, whose parents were probably merchants who had lived in Delhi before the Ghūrid conquest. The Shaikh was certainly born there, about 1192, and he came into contact with Khwāja Mu'īnu'd-Dīn at an early age. Guided by his ascetic temperament, he decided to settle at Swalī in Nāgaur, where he lived until his death in 1274 like an ordinary Rājasthānī cultivator, dissociating himself completely from those in political power. He was an authority on Ghazālī's works, and a passionate advocate of the value of studying his *Kīmiyā' i-Sa'ādat*. He was a strict vegetarian. He adopted the local language, called in Persian Hindawī, as his own, and the Hindawī verses ascribed to him and his successors are the best extant examples of early Hindawī translations of Persian mystical poetry.

The Chishtī centre in Delhi flourished because of the towering personality of Khwāja Qutbu'd-Dīn Bakhtyār Kākī (died 1236), the successor there of Khwāja Mu'īnu'd-Dīn Chishtī. Although he took no interest in political activities, his immense spiritual prestige made his *khānqāh* a rendezvous for Muslims from all walks of life. His successor, Bābā Farīdu'd-Dīn Ganj-i-Shakar (died 1265), continued living in his own *khānqāh* in Ajōdhan (Pāk Pattan), so the Delhi centres became the charge of Khwāja Qutbu'd-Dīn's other disciples, in particular Badru'd-Dīn Ghaznavī. This did not prevent the people of Delhi, merchants, and even passing armies, from paying their respects at Bābā Farīd's *khānqāh* in the Panjāb.

Delhi became the real Chishtī centre, mainly because of Bābā Farīd's talented successor, Shaikh Nizāmu'd-Dīn Auliyā', who from 1287 until his death in 1325 was the focus for Muslims all over northern India. Muhammad bin Tughluq has been blamed by scholars for destroying the importance of Delhi as the centre of the Chishtī order, but in actual fact Nizāmu'd-Dīn's successor, Shaikh Nasīru'd-Dīn Chirāgh-i-Dihlī, died in 1356 without bequeathing the Chishtī mantle to a successor. And in any case centralization was no part of the sūfī tradition.

In Bengal, the Chishtī order was introduced by Sirāju'd-Dīn Akhī Sirāj (died 1357), who lived in Gaur. His successors, the most popular of whom was Nūr Qutb-i-'Ālam (died 1410), established their *khānqāhs* in Pānduā. In close touch with this Bengal centre was the Rudaulī centre, about fifty miles east of Lucknow. The founder of this latter group was Shaikh 'Alā'u'd-Dīn 'Alī bin Ahmad Sābir (died 1291), a disciple of Bābā Farīd. He himself retired to Kalyar, about 150 miles east of Delhi, and his two immediate successors lived in Pānipat; but Ahmad bin 'Abdu'l Haq (died 1434), third in the order of succession in this Sābiriyya-Chishtīyya branch, established his *khānqāh* at Rudaulī, then under the Sharqī rulers of Jaunpur. Another member of this branch, Shaikh 'Abdu'l Quddūs (*c.* 1455–1536/7), who established his *khānqāh* at Gangoh in the Sahāranpūr district of western Uttar Pradesh, made the Sābiriyya-Chishtīyya branch very famous in Delhi.

Another Chishtī, Saiyid Muhammad Gēsū Darāz (*c.* 1320–1422), made the first capital of the Bahmanī Dynasty, Gulbarga (in the north of the present Karnātaka State), the centre of his activities. A number of other Chishtī 'saints', compelled by Sultan Muhammad bin Tughluq to leave Delhi for Daulatābād, also became instrumental in spreading Chishtī sūfism in the Deccan. The disintegration of the central power, and the emergence of the provincial dynasties in the fifteenth century, provided more patrons, and led to the establishment of Chishtī *khānqāhs* all over India.

The Chishtī sūfīs urged their disciples to lead a life of poverty and asceticism. Their simple life devoted to Allāh, their dependence upon the charity of ordinary people, and their immediate distribution to the poor of any money they received, made a favourable impression upon all sections of the Muslim population, and even upon Hindus. Much interest was aroused by their practice of *pās-i-anfās* (control of breath), meditation, *chilla* (forty days of hard ascetic exercises in a cell or some lonely place), and *chilla'i-ma'kūs* (forty days of ascetic exercise performed with the head on the ground and the legs tied to the roof or a branch of a tree). Their most popular practice was *samā'* (the recital of holy songs), which was intended to arouse a state of ecstasy in their audience. This practice, which shocked the orthodox, was not a Chishtī innovation. Qushairī and Ghazālī had already given it their blessing and drawn up rules for it. In the thirteenth and fourteenth centuries the '*ulamā*' tried to have the government stop the practice, and several open debates were held to condemn *samā'*, but they were foiled by sūfī influence. In attempting to restore orthodoxy and forge an alliance with the '*ulamā*', Shaikh Nasīru'd-Dīn Chirāgh and some of his disciples managed to persuade the '*ulamā*' in their turn to moderate their attitude towards *samā'*, which gave it some respectability in strict circles.

By the thirteenth century, the sūfī theory of the Unity of Being, or Oneness of Existence, known as *Wahdatu'l Wujūd*, which had emerged through the works of the sūfī scholar Ibn 'Arabī (1165–1240), had made an impact on the whole ethos of Islam. It differed both from the Ash'arite conception of 'the necessary (*wājib*) existence of the Creator, Who alone exists from all eternity and alone is self-subsisting', and from the Indian monist view 'Thou Art That'. Ibn 'Arabī emphasized that, as transcendence and immanence are two fundamental aspects of Reality, God is both Transcendent and Immanent. 'He is absolute Being, and is the sole source of all existence; in Him alone

Being and Existence are one and inseparable'. 'There is no such thing as union with God in the sense of becoming one with God, but there is the realization of the already existing fact that the mystic is one with God'.

This philosophy was very compatible with the theistic philosophy of Gorakhnāth and his followers, known in sūfī literature as Nāth Yogīs, Nāth Panthīs, Kānphata (split-ear) Yogīs, or simply as Yogīs or Jogīs, who dominated the popular level of Hindu religious and ethical life from the thirteenth to the fifteenth centuries. They had even earlier counterparts in the Siddhas, who came into contact with sūfīs as early as the eleventh century. Books of sūfī discourses indicate that the Yogīs were welcome guests in Bābā Farīd's *khānqāh* and in the Chishtī *khānqāhs* in every town. Sūfīs found the Yogī definition of Ultimate Reality remarkably similar to the ideas of Unity of Being expressed in the works of their own Persian poets. On an intellectual level, sūfīs were influenced by a *hatha-yogic* treatise entitled *Amrita Kunda.* It was translated several times into Arabic and Persian, and taught the sūfīs their meditative practices, as well as imparting information about herbs and chemistry. Various anecdotes indicate that sūfīs approved of some ethical values of the Yogīs as well as of their corporate way of living.

At *samā*' gatherings in many *khānqāhs,* Persian poetry began to be relegated to the background as Hindawī poetry, with all its Śaivite and Vaishnavite imagery, came to the fore. Since Hindawī poetry was already at a highly developed stage by the time Mullā Dāūd (a nephew of Shaikh Nasīru'd-Dīn Chirāgh) wrote the *Chandā'in* in 1379–80, it would seem that there must have been a much earlier Hindawī poetry now lost. Fifteenth- and sixteenth-century sūfī Hindī poetry developed equally well in both rural and urban environments. The emergence of fifteenth-century *sants* ('saints') such as Kabīr and Nānak, and the devotional literature associated with them, which constituted a new phase in *bhakti,* were the result of two centuries of interaction between Hindu *sants* and sūfīs.

The development of *madrasas* changed the intellectual and ethical climate. In the main they followed the curriculum evolved by Nizāmu'l Mulk, and trained *'ulamā'* (scholars) to man the civil service. This training for an administrative career included the study of works of Qur'anic exegesis, *Hadīs,* and some sūfī texts, but the main emphasis was on *fiqh.* The *madrasas* and their teachers were mostly supported by state grants and stipends, but the system was free enough for *madrasas* to be established by nobles and the pious rich. This made the '*ulamā*' dependent upon the state or upon the nobility, but both kings and nobles in their turn stood in need of the '*ulamā*''s *fatwās* (legal opinions) to suppress subversive elements. The '*ulamā*' tried to influence state policy, and prevailed upon the rulers to enforce orthodoxy. The extremists among them, such as Nūru'd-Dīn Mubārak Ghaznawī (died 1234–5), even openly demanded that Hindus be either slaughtered or converted to Islam. Balban, 'Alā'u'd-Dīn Khaljī, and Muhammad bin Tughluq, however, ensured that the '*ulamā*' had as little influence as possible upon affairs of state.

Scholars have differed in their interpretation of the process of Islamization. Sir Thomas Arnold, nurtured in the liberal traditions of Europe, seeks in his *Preaching of Islam* (1895) to present the process as a purely peaceable movement led by the sūfīs. Modern Muslim scholars, particularly Indian Muslims, think that the rigidity of the caste system was responsible for the conversion of low-caste Hindus to Islam. A contemporary view, expressed by the eminent Chishtī saint, Ja'far Makkī, whose long life stretched from the close of Muhammad bin Tughluq's reign to the early years of Sultan Bahlol Lodī's, was that conversions were very complex phenomena. Fear of death or of the enslavement of families, promises of rewards and pensions, prospects of booty and, lastly, the bigotry of the Hindus, were the main factors in proselytization. He considered that Muslim preaching also contributed to Islamization, but that there was no place for such preaching in Chishtī *khānqāhs*.

Such Suhrawardī proselytizing activities as are known cannot therefore be ascribed to the moral or spiritual force of Islam, being more akin to conversion by force. The preaching was done mainly by *madrasa* teachers, official preachers, and *qāzīs*, or Muslim judges, who were the butt of attacks by both sūfīs and Hindu *sants*. By withdrawing state support for proselytizing activities and stopping forced conversion to Islam, Akbar compelled the preachers and the orthodox to rely on their own resources, thereby courting their hostility.

The fifteenth and sixteenth centuries saw the introduction of many new elements into Islam in India. One was conflict between the followers and opponents of *Wahdatu'l Wujūd*, exacerbated by the arrival of the disciples of Shaikh 'Alā'u'd-Daula Simnānī (1261–1336), the great Irani opponent of Ibn 'Arabī. In contradistinction to Ibn 'Arabī's theory, 'Alā'u'd-Daula said that Being cannot be identified with God; it is distinct from His essence although eternally inherent in Him. He believed that *Wahdatu'l-Wujūd* was the initial stage in the development of sufism, the final stage being his own theory of *Wahdatu'sh-Shuhūd* (Unity of Perception). He urged his followers to lead an active life of missionary work, and strongly denounced the quiet and passive life of the *khānqāh*. A band of his followers seem to have had some success with Gēsū Darāz of Gulbarga, who wrote a letter condemning as misguided the works of Ibn 'Arabī and sūfī poets such as Rūmī. However, the Chishtī traditions of *Wahdatu'l Wujūd* were too strong for Gēsū Darāz, and his writings opposing Ibn 'Arabī's thought did not find much popularity. Mīr Saiyid 'Alī Hamadānī (1314–85), another member of Simnānī's order, entered Kashmīr with a band of followers. Although he made little impact, and left Kashmīr in frustration, those of his sons and disciples who continued to visit and settle there introduced orthodoxy into many aspects of the religious life of Kashmīr.

Simnānī's *Shuhūdī* ideology received its main setback when the Shattārī order was established by Shaikh 'Abdu'llāh Shattārī, who reached India towards the end of his life, after visiting many sūfī centres in the Middle East. In India he travelled as far as Bengal before returning to Mālwā, where he died in 1485. He loudly challenged everyone, sūfī and yogī alike, either to teach him Unity of Being if they knew more than he, or to learn about it from him. While he himself propagated his mission in Mālwā, his disciples established strong Shattārī centres in Bengal and Jaunpur, where the writing of beautiful sūfī poetry in local dialects blossomed.

The Emperor Humāyūn's devotion to the Shattārīs made him unpopular with all other sūfī orders, particularly with the Naqshbandīs, who were the patron saints of the Turānīs or Central Asian Muslims. This order was one of the oldest sūfī orders, and flourished in Transoxiana in the midst of the still living Buddhist traditions of that region. First known as the Silsila i-Khwājgān, under the leadership of Khwāja Bahā'u'd-Dīn Muhammad Naqshband (1317–89) it became known as the Naqshbandī order. One of its most distinguished saints was Khwāja 'Ubaidu'llāh Ahrār (1404–91), who took an active part in political struggles and made strenuous efforts to save the Sunnīs from the Shī'ī onslaught on their faith. Although the Khwāja had died when Bābur was only seven, the latter drew ever-increasing inspiration from his teachings. In Humāyūn's reign the Naqshbandīs suffered temporary eclipse, but under Akbar many Naqshbandī saints occupied high government posts. Towards the end of Akbar's reign the Naqshbandī order was reorientated by Khwāja Bāqī Bi'llāh (1563–1603), who settled in Delhi in 1599. In the few years before his death, he was able, on the basis of the former reputation of the Naqshbandī order, to enrol as his disciples many eminent Mughal noblemen drawn to sūfī teachings.

In the fifteenth century the Qādirī order, started by Shaikh 'Abdu'l Qādir Jīlānī (1077–1166), established a firm hold in the Panjāb and Sind. The celebrated sūfī scholar, Shaikh 'Abdu'l Haq Muhaddis of Delhi (1551–1642), had Qādirī preceptors, but the order owed its popularity not to him but to the Sindī, Miyān Mīr (1550–1635), who advocated a broad and humane outlook on life, and urged both Jahāngīr and Shāh Jahān to be considerate to all groups of their subjects. Distinctions between believers and *kāfirs*, and heaven and hell, were frivolous; true prayer was devoted obedience to the will of God. His disciple Mullā Shāh was both a mystic and a poet. He defined a believer as one who could reach God and behold him, and a *kāfir* as one who failed to do so. Mullā Shāh had been Dārā Shukōh's preceptor, and after his execution Aurangzeb tried to harass him, but such was his popularity that the Emperor was unable to do anything more drastic than banish him from Delhi.

The *falāsifa*, or Muslim Peripatetic thinkers, came to be hated by the orthodox Sunnī world as a result of Ghazālī's denunciation. Baranī considered them as dangerous enemies of the Delhi sultanate as the Ismā'īlīs, ascribing Sultan Muhammad bin Tughluq's atrocities to his devotion to the works of these philosophers.

Although the Mongols destroyed many centres of Islamic culture in Central Asia and Iran, the religious freedom they allowed individual scholars who supported them led to the revival of the study of philosophy, mathematics, and the physical sciences at their courts. At one of them, Nasīru'd-Dīn Tūsī (1201–74) wrote commentaries on Avicenna's works. His *Akhlāq-i-Nāsirī*, a work on ethics and philosophy, became a textbook for institutions of higher learning everywhere in the Persian-speaking world.

The way of thinking cultivated by Avicenna's School was based on Peripatetic philosophy and syllogistic reasoning, but the Ishrāqī (Illuminatist) School of Iran started by Shaikh Shihābu'd-Dīn Suhrawardī Maqtūl (1153–91) emphasized that reason and intuition were necessary complements one of the other. Reason without intuition and illumination, according to Suhrawardī, is puerile and half-blind and can never reach the transcendent source of all truth and intellection. The Ishrāqīs freely borrowed ideas from the ancient Prophets, from Hermetic traditions, and even from the Zoroastrians. Their symbolism was compatible with both sūfī gnosis and Shī'ī thought, with which it is often inextricably entangled. Tīmūr's patronage of Peripatetic scholars was continued in the courts of his successors. By the fifteenth century, Multān and Gujarāt had become important centres for Ishrāqī and other Muslim Peripatetic scholars, whose strong grounding in Muslim theology enabled them to defeat the Ash'arī *kalām* on its own grounds.

Two prominent Peripatetic scholars of Sultan Sikandar's reign were Shaikh 'Azīzu'llāh and Shaikh 'Abdu'llāh; 'Abdu'llāh attracted the support of many eminent scholars in Delhi and its vicinity. The most outstanding Ishrāqī immigrant was Mīr Rafī'u'd-Dīn Safavī (died 1547) who was greatly respected by all the Delhi sultans from Sikandar to Islām Shāh Sūr.

Bābur and Humāyūn were accompanied to India by a large number of Irani scholars, poets, and philosophers, as well as by soldiers of fortune, and Akbar's patronage of the arts and sciences accelerated the immigration of the first three groups. Badā'ūnī, the orthodox Sunnī historian at Akbar's Court, gives us to understand that all of them were Shī'īs, but in fact many of them were Ishrāqīs or Tafzīliyas. Both the latter schools believe that although 'Alī should have succeeded Muhammad as the first Caliph, the matter was not of sufficient importance to let it cause bitterness so long afterwards.

Akbar's tolerant administrative laws, which deprived Sunnism of its position of dominance, upset many of the orthodox. They made common cause with elements dissatisfied for political reasons and in 1580 organized an abortive rebellion; as a result, not only the political leaders, but also their supporters from among the theologians, were punished. This made the orthodox change their tactics. Instead of opposing Akbar, they now sought to influence his policy by making a show of loyalty to him. At the same time, they misrepresented his policies and activities so as to arouse hatred against him, and also reviled the élite supporting the Emperor, blaming them for the downfall of orthodoxy. As a result of their efforts, Akbar has gone down in history as the founder of a new religion, which subsequently came to be called Dīn Ilāhī, but which was never defined by his accusers, who merely presented a distorted view of his eclecticism and new policies. The orthodox Sunnī point of view is voiced in *Najātu'r Rashīd*, written by Mulla 'Abdu'l Qādir Badā'ūnī in 1591.

Tension between the various religious groups mounted during Jahāngīr's reign. Immediately after his accession he banished Shaikh Nizāmu'd-Dīn Fārūqī Thāneswarī, an eminent Chishtī saint, for blessing his rebellious son Khusrau. The Shaikh went to Transoxiana and died in Balkh, but not before he had spread a distorted picture of the Mughals in that part of the world. Jahāngīr then imprisoned Saiyid Ahmad Afghān, a devoted supporter of 'Alā'u'd-Daulā Simnānī's *Wahdatu'sh-Shuhūd*, for he was known to have a great following among the Afghans and thus be a likely danger to the state. In 1610 Jahāngīr had a distinguished Irani Shī'ī, Qāzī Nūru'llāh Shustarī, flogged to death, although he was seventy years old. Shī'īs ascribe this to Jahāngīr's bigotry, but the evidence of contemporary Irani scholars tends to indicate that the Qāzī was the victim of a plot by certain Sunnī theologians, whose subsistence grants he had reduced in Akbar's reign. His polemical works are strongly critical of the Sunnīs, but his best-known work, *Majālis-*

u'l-Mūminīn, is a valuable contribution to Shī'ī history, in which he so extends the definition of Shī'ism as to include all the eminent sūfīs.

Striving to benefit from the accession of Jahāngīr were Shaikh 'Abdu'l Haq Muhaddis Dehlawī and Shaikh Ahmad Sarhindī. They wrote letters to distinguished nobles and imperial officials urging them to persuade the Emperor to accord dominance to the Sunnī Sharī'a. Shaikh 'Abdu'l Haq's letters are cautious, but Shaikh Ahmad Sarhindī was outspoken in his demands, which resembled Badā'ūnī's. He claimed to be himself the rebuilder of the second millennium (*Mujaddid-Alf i-Sānī*), and a great supporter of *Wahdatu'sh-Shuhūd*. The publication of Sarhindī's letters and the claims of his disciples alarmed Shaikh 'Abdu'l Haq, who wrote him a long letter of protest. Jahāngīr imprisoned Sarhindī in Gwālior fort in 1619–20. Upon his release more than twelve months later, he lived for some time in the imperial camp in order to propagate his teachings. In his autobiography Jahāngīr says that Sarhindī admitted to him that his punishment had been a valuable lesson. Naqshbandī hagiological literature has exaggerated his achievements, and modern scholars regard him as having been the saviour of Sunnism, but in fact his efforts failed to induce Jahāngīr to make any noticeable change in Akbar's policy of universal concord. The Emperor continued to admire saints of peaceable disposition, such as Miyān Mīr and Mullā Shāh. However, all those whom Jahāngīr considered a danger to the state, he punished ruthlessly. In 1627 he decided to banish Shaikh 'Abdu'l Haq, with whom he had formerly had good relations, and Shaikh Husāmu'd-Dīn, an eminent disciple of Khwāja Bāqī Bi'llāh, having already exiled to Kabul 'Abdu'l Haq's son, Shaikh Nūru'l Haq. 'Abdu'l Haq was only saved from exile by Jahāngīr's sudden death. Jahāngīr called the sūfīs *lashkar i-du'ā* (army of those who pray for the government) and he expected them to support government policy in return for state patronage.

In Shāh Jahān's reign, the Chishtīs again became prominent, although the Qādirī was the predominant sūfī order. The Chishtīs claimed that they were loyal supporters of the government and the Emperor. Shaikh Muhibbu'llāh of Allahabad (died 1648) wrote commentaries on the works of Ibn 'Arabī and popularized his teachings through short treatises on the controversial issues he raised. In his letters, Shaikh Muhibbu'llāh denounced the Sunnī emphasis on *kalām*, and urged concentration on acquiring true divine knowledge. According to him, only those ascetics and mystics who lacked a true perception of spiritual perfection followed 'Alā'u'd-Daula Simnānī. He urged his followers to acquire mystic knowledge even from the Hindus. He considered himself too old to learn from Hindu philosophy and mysticism, but deputed one of his disciples to acquire knowledge in this field.

In Akbar's reign a large number of Sanskrit works were translated into Persian under his patronage, and after his death such translations continued to be made by Muslim scholars working on their own initiative. For example, 'Abdu'r Rahmān Chishtī syncretized Hindu theories of cosmogony in his *Mir'ātu'l-Makhlūqāt*, and offered an Islamizing explanation of the *Bhagavad Gītā*. Of paramount importance was Dārā Shukōh's *Majma'u'l Bahrain*, proving that Hindu and Muslim mysticism were parallel streams which could be made to meet without much difficulty. His most valuable contribution to religious literature was a Persian translation of fifty-two *Upanishads*, which he completed within six months in 1656–7, with the collaboration of Hindu Sanskritists. His approach to Reality was Vedāntist, and differed from that of other sūfīs whose system was more compatible with that of the Nāth Yogīs.

The reign of Shāh Jahān saw the reconcilation of Avicennian philosophy with Sunnī orthodoxy. The leader of the movement which brought this about was Mullā 'Abdu'l Hakīm Siālkotī, who wrote several works on Peripatetic philosophy and the physical sciences. His contemporary, Mullā Mahmūd of Jaunpur, also wrote on these subjects. Mahmūd's best-known work, *Shams-i-Bāzīgha*, was patterned on the *Shifā* of Avicenna, and was included in the advanced courses of the traditional learning.

By Shāh Jahān's time two Naqshbandī schools had emerged. Khwāja Bāqī Bi'llāh's sons followed the general pattern of sūfism in Delhi; they indulged in *samā*', believed in *Wahdatu'l-Wujūd*, and paid little attention to the admonitions of Mujaddid, the title by which Shaikh Ahmad Sarhindī came to be known. Sarhind was the only centre of any standing to impart the teachings of Mujaddid. Its luminaries were Mujaddid's sons, Khwāja Muhammad Sa'īd and Khwāja Muhammad Ma'sūm. Another eminent disciple of Mujaddid was Shaikh Ādam Bānūrī, who wrote several works on his preceptor's teachings. His own claims that he was protecting Shāh Jahān through his spiritual power do not seem to have had much effect upon the Emperor, for in 1642–3, when his band of Afghan followers were pointed out as a potential threat to the Empire, Shāh Jahān had no hesitation in exiling him to Mecca. From a collection of his letters which has been published, it is apparent that Muhammad Ma'sūm had great expectations of Aurangzeb when a prince, although the story that Aurangzeb was his disciple cannot be proved. Both brothers went on pilgrimage in 1656, and did not return until Aurangzeb had ascended the throne. Muhammad Ma'sūm occasionally visited Aurangzeb at Court, where his own son Shaikh Saifu'd-Dīn had a position, but more often communicated by letter, thanking God that Sunnī orthodoxy had been restored. Shaikh Muhammad Ma'sūm took the credit for several puritanical administrative reforms introduced by Aurangzeb; but it is clear that, in his commitment to restore Sunnī orthodoxy, Aurangzeb relied not upon one man, but upon all the orthodox for support. No sudden change in state policy was possible, but harassment of ordinary people by his *Ihtisāb* (moral censorship) department strengthened the Emperor's orthodox image. A number of saints and scholars quite unconnected with Mujaddid's descendants were far ahead of Muhammad Ma'sūm and his successors in attempting to restore orthodoxy.

The rise of the Mujaddidīs was resented by many eminent Chishtīs, and their *khānqāhs* vied with one another in exposing them as selfish opportunists. Towards the end of Aurangzeb's reign, the Chishtīs obtained great influence through the untiring efforts of Shāh Kalīmu'llāh Jahānābādī (died 1729) who, although he himself lived in Delhi, sent his disciple, Shāh Nizāmu'd-Dīn (died 1730), to the imperial camp in the Deccan. Nizāmu'd-Dīn was advised to enrol disciples at all costs, and was even permitted to accept Hindus and Shī'īs as disciples without converting them to Sunnism; he settled in Aurangābād, and took the name of the town.

It is wrongly presumed that the influence of Shī'ism declined in Aurangzeb's reign. Following Akbar's policy of Deccan conquest, Aurangzeb did indeed seize the two Deccan Shī'ī states, but no Shī'ī is known to have lost his job or standing for religious reasons. Neither Shī'ī nor Irani participation in party politics lessened in Aurangzeb's reign; and in the cultural and religious spheres these two forces continued to assert themselves as an integral part of Indian Islam, despite Sunnī hatred.

By the beginning of the eighteenth century, although the political power of Islam had begun to disintegrate, Indian Sunnī religious and ethical values had crystallized into marked attitudes. The Mujaddidī outlook, strengthened by the officials in Aurangzeb's *Ihtisāb* department, was narrowly orthodox, legalistic, and militant, refusing to tolerate any other group. Their aim was to uproot Shī'ism, destroy Hinduism, and desecrate Hindu places of worship, if not openly then secretly. The Chishtī group belonging to Shāh Kalīmu'llāh Jahānābādī's school advocated coexistence with Hindus, Shī'īs, and even with militant Sunnī groups. Supported by them, and generally helped by the Qādirīs and the Shattārīs, were a large number of Muslims whose families had retained Hindu social practices after their ancestors' conversion, particularly in villages in Bengal and in the Deccan. The urban Muslim religious élite of Delhi and Lāhore frowned upon these syncretic practices. Nevertheless the rural classes formed the overwhelming majority of the Muslim population, and they form it to this day.

CHAPTER XX

Sikhism

by Hew McLeod

Although Sikhism is generally understood to be a simple faith, the definitions which are offered to describe it can be widely and confusingly divergent. Four such definitions are commonly encountered. All four relate primarily to the origins of the faith, each reflecting a distinctive range of predilection.

For the strictly orthodox Sikh the faith which by preference he calls *Gurmat* (in contrast to the western term 'Sikhism') can be regarded as nothing less than the product of direct revelation from God. *Gurmat* means 'the Gurū's doctrine'. God, the original Gurū, imparted his message to his chosen disciple Nānak who, having intuitively apprehended the message, thereby absorbed the divine spirit and became himself the Gurū. This same divine spirit passed at Nānak's death into the body of his successor, Gurū Angad, and in this manner dwelt successively within a series of ten personal Gurūs. At the death of the tenth Gurū, Gobind Singh, the divine spirit remained present within the sacred scripture and the community of the Gurūs' followers. He who accepts the teachings of the Gurūs as recorded in the scripture (*granth*) or expressed in the corporate will of the community (*panth*) is truly a Sikh. In its more extreme form this interpretation holds that the actual content of *Gurmat* is wholly original, owing nothing of primary significance to the environment within which it emerged.[1]

As one would expect, the three remaining definitions all dispute this claim to uniqueness, emphasizing instead the features which Sikhism so patently holds in common with other religious traditions in India. Many Hindu commentators, stressing the elements common to Sikh and Hindu tradition, have maintained that Sikhism is properly regarded merely as one of the many Hindu reform movements which have appeared from time to time in Indian history. In like manner there have been Muslim claims, based upon such doctrines as the oneness of God and the brotherhood of believers, to the effect that Sikhism is an offshoot of Islam.[2] Finally, there is the interpretation, popular in Western textbooks, that Sikhism must be understood as the pro-

[1] 'It is altogether a distinct and original faith based on the teachings of Guru Nanak in the form of Ten Gurus, and now through Guru Granth Sahib and the Khalsa Panth.' Gobind Singh Mansukhani, *The Quintessence of Sikhism*, Amritsar, 1958, p. 1.

[2] The original edition of *The Legacy of India* gives expression to both the second and the third definitions. Dr. Radhakrishnan lists Jainism, Buddhism, and Sikhism as 'creations of the Indian mind [which] represent reform movements from within the fold of Hinduism put forth to meet the special demands of the various stages of the Hindu faith' (op. cit., p. 259, supra, p. 62). In the following chapter Abdul Qadir, in direct contradiction, cites Sikhism in support of his claim that 'Islam has had a more direct influence in bringing into existence monotheistic systems of faith in India' (ibid., p. 291).

duct of a consciously eclectic intention, an attempt to fuse Hindu and Muslim belief within a single irenic system.

Two of these definitions can be summarily dismissed. Both the Muslim and the eclectic interpretations are based upon partial and superficial readings of Sikh sources. Indications of Muslim influence do appear in the recorded utterances of the Gurūs and in subsequent Sikh tradition, but in so far as they constitute significant elements of Sikh belief they normally do so in direct contradiction to the Muslim influence.[3] The eclectic interpretation depends primarily upon a misreading of certain passages which appear in the works of Nānak and of a cryptic reference recorded in the traditional narratives of his life.[4] Gurū Nānak does indeed look to a faith transcending both Hindu and Muslim notions, but for him the required pattern of belief and practice is one which spurns rather than blends.

The two remaining definitions require more careful attention. Even if one is unable to accept a doctrine of divine inspiration, there remains an obligation to consider the teachings of Nānak and his successors in terms of genuine originality. Having acknowledged this measure of originality we must also pay heed to those features of Sikhism which so obviously derive from sources within contemporary Indian society. This must be done in the light of the complete range of Sikh history, from the period of Nānak to the present day. The conclusion which will follow is that Sikhism is indeed a unique phenomenon, but that this uniqueness derives more from its later development than from its earliest forms of custom and belief.

Sikhism is generally held to derive from the teachings of the first Gurū, Nānak (1469–1539). In a sense this is true, for there can be no doubt that the doctrines which he taught survive within the community to this day. Moreover, there can be no doubt that a direct connection links the community of today with the group of disciples who first gathered around Nānak in the Panjāb during the early years of the sixteenth century. In another sense, however, the claim is open to obvious objections. An analysis of the teachings of Nānak will demonstrate that the essential components of his thought were already current in the Indian society of his period. Nānak taught a doctrine of salvation through the divine Name. Others were already preaching this doctrine, and a comparison of their beliefs with those of the early Sikh community plainly shows that Nānak taught from within a tradition which had already developed a measure of definition.

This was the *Nirguna Sampradāya*, or Sant tradition of northern India, a devotional school commonly regarded as a part of the tradition of Vaishnava *bhakti*. A connection between the Sants and the Vaishnavas does indeed exist, but there are distinctive features of Sant doctrine which distinguish it from its Vaishnava antecedents. Most of these can be traced to its other major source, Tantric Yoga. The most prominent of the Sants prior to Nānak was Kabīr, and it is no doubt due to the obvious similarities in their teachings that Nānak

[3] This aspect is briefly covered below in the discussion of eighteenth-century developments. For a more detailed discussion of this period and its results see W. H. McLeod, *The Evolution of the Sikh Community* (Oxford, forthcoming).

[4] 'There is neither Hindu nor Muslim.' See W. H. McLeod, *Gurū Nānak and the Sikh Religion*, Oxford, 1968, pp. 38 and 161.

has sometimes been represented as a disciple of his predecessor. Although there is no evidence to support this supposition, the measure of doctrinal agreement which links them is beyond dispute.[5]

This debt to the earlier Sant tradition must be acknowledged if there is to be any understanding of the antecedents of Nānak's thought. It is, however, necessary to add that, as far as can be judged from surviving Sant works, Nānak raised this inheritance to a level of beauty and coherence attained by none of his predecessors. From the quality of his Panjābī verses and the clarity of the message expressed in them it is easy to appreciate why this particular man should have gathered a following of sufficient strength to provide the nucleus of a continuing community. The evidence suggests that Nānak inherited a theory of salvation which was at best incomplete and commonly naïve in its insistence upon the adequacy of a simple repetition of a particular divine name. Kabīr, master of the pithy epigram, was certainly not naïve, nor yet does he appear to have been altogether clear and consistent. These are qualities which one cannot always expect to find in a mystic, and there can be no doubt that in Kabīr it was the mystical strain which predominated. For Nānak also salvation was to be found in mystical union with God, but Nānak evidently differed in that he recognized the need to explain in consistent terms the path to the ultimate experience. It is in the coherence and the compelling beauty of his explanation that Nānak's originality lies.

The thought of Nānak begins with two groups of basic assumptions. The first concerns the nature of God, who in an ultimate sense is unknowable. God, the One, is without form (*nirankār*), eternal (*akāl*), and ineffable (*alakh*). Considerable stress is thus laid upon divine transcendence, but this alone does not express Nānak's understanding of God. If it did there would be, for Nānak, no possibility of salvation. God is also gracious, concerned that men should possess the means of salvation and that these means should be abundantly evident to those who would diligently seek them. There is, Nānak insists, a purposeful revelation, visible to all who will but open their eyes and see. God is *sarab viāpak*, 'everywhere present', immanent in all creation, both within and without every man.

The second group of assumptions concerns the nature of man. Men are by nature wilfully blind, shutting their eyes to the divine revelation which lies about them. They commonly appreciate the need for salvation, but characteristically seek it in ways which are worse than futile because they confirm and strengthen humanity's congenital blindness. The Hindu worships at the temple and the Muslim at the mosque. Misled by their religious leaders they mistakenly believe that external exercises of this kind will provide access to salvation. Instead they bind men more firmly to the transmigratory wheel of death and rebirth, to a perpetuation of suffering rather than to the attainment of bliss.

This, for Nānak, is *māyā*. In Nānak's usage the term does not imply the ultimate unreality of the world itself, but rather the unreality of the values which it represents. The world's values are a delusion. If a man accepts them

[5] Ibid., pp. 151–8. Ch. Vaudeville, *Au cabaret de l'amour: paroles de Kabīr*, Paris, 1959, pp. 7–9

no amount of piety can save him. They must be rejected in favour of alternative values. Salvation can be obtained only through a recognition of the alternative, and through the faithful exercise of a discipline which demonstrably produces the desired result.

Nānak's teachings concerning the way of salvation are expressed in a number of key words which recur constantly in his works. God, being gracious, communicates his revelation in the form of the *śabad* (*śabda*, 'word') uttered by the *gurū* (the 'preceptor'). Any aspect of the created world which communicates a vision or glimpse of the nature of God or of his purpose is to be regarded as an expression of the *śabad*. The *gurū* who expresses, or draws attention to, this revelation is not, however, a human preceptor. It is the 'voice' of God mystically uttered within the human heart. Any means whereby spiritual perception is awakened can be regarded as the activity of the *gurū*.

Duly awakened by the *gurū*, the enlightened man looks around and within himself and there perceives the *hukam* (the divine 'order'). Like its English equivalent, the term *hukam* is used by Nānak in two senses, but it is the notion of harmony which is fundamental. Everywhere there can be perceived a divinely-bestowed harmony. Salvation consists in bringing oneself within this pattern of harmony.

This requires an explicit discipline, the practice of *nām simaran* or *nām japan*. The word *nām* ('name') signifies all that constitutes the nature and being of God; and the verb *simaranā* means 'to hold in remembrance'. The alternate verb *japanā* means, literally, 'to repeat', and for many of the Sants a simple, mechanical repetition of a chosen name of God (e.g. Rām) was believed to be a sufficient method. For Nānak much more is required. The pattern which he sets forth consists of a regular, disciplined meditation upon the *nām*. The essence of the *nām* is harmony and through this discipline the faithful devotee progressively unites himself with the divine harmony. In this manner he ascends to higher and yet higher levels of spiritual attainment, passing eventually into the condition of mystical bliss wherein all disharmony is ended and, in consequence, the round of transmigration is at last terminated. The proof of this is the experience itself. Only those who have attained it can know it.

For most people a reference to Sikhism will at once evoke an impression of beards, turbans, and martial valour. It rarely suggests doctrines of salvation through patient meditation upon the divine Name. Both, however, belong to Sikhism. In order to understand how they united it is necessary to trace the history of the Sikh community since the time of Nānak.

Concerning Nānak himself relatively little can be known with assurance, apart from the content of his teachings. Hagiographic narratives abound (the *janam-sākhīs*), but their considerable importance relates principally to the later period within which they evolved. It seems certain that Nānak was born in 1469, probably in the village of Talvandī in the central Panjāb. During his early manhood he was evidently employed in the town of Sultānpur near the confluence of the Beās and Satluj rivers. This was followed by a period visiting pilgrimage centres within and perhaps beyond India, a period which figures with particular prominence in the *janam-sākhī* narratives. Eventually he settled in the village of Kartārpur above Lāhore on the right bank of the Rāvī river and there died, probably in 1539.

The pattern of teaching through the composition and communal singing of hymns was continued by Nānak's first four successors and reached a climax in the work of Arjan, the fifth Gurū (died 1606). During the time of the third Gurū, Amar Dās (died 1574), a collection was made of the hymns of the first three Gurūs and of other writers (Sants and Sūfīs) whose works accorded with the teachings of Nānak. To this collection Gurū Arjan added his own compositions and those of his father, Gurū Rām Dās. The new compilation, recorded in a single volume in 1603–4, became the primary scripture of the community (the *Ādi Granth* later known as the *Gurū Granth Sāhib*). Notable amongst Gurū Arjan's own compositions is the lengthy hymn entitled *Sukhmanī*, an epitome of the teachings of the Gurūs.

In this respect the first four successors followed Nānak's example, faithfully reproducing his teachings in language of sustained excellence. There were, however, significant changes taking place within the community of their followers. The more important of these developments appear to have emerged during the period of the third Gurū. Whereas Gurū Nānak had laid exclusive emphasis upon the need for inner devotion, Gurū Amar Dās, faced by the problems of a growing community, introduced features which served to maintain its cohesion. Distinctively Sikh ceremonies were instituted, a rudimentary system of pastoral supervision was begun, three Hindu festival-days were appointed for assemblies of the faithful, and the Gurū's own town of Goindvāl became a recognized pilgrimage centre.

An even more significant development, one which should probably be traced right back to the period of Gurū Nānak, concerns the caste constituency of the growing community. Whereas all of the Gurūs belonged to the urban-based mercantile Khatrī caste, most of their followers were rural Jats. This preponderance of Jats, which continues to the present day, is of fundamental importance in the later development of the community. Many of the features which distinguish the modern community from that of Nānak's day can be traced, as we shall see, to the pressure of Jat ideals.

Signs of Jat influence become apparent during the period of the sixth Gurū, Hargobind (died 1644), an influence which is perhaps discernible even earlier, during the years under Gurū Arjan. It was during this period that the community first entered into overt conflict with the Mughal administration. According to tradition it was Gurū Hargobind who first decided to arm his followers, a decision which he is said to have reached following the death of his father Arjan in Mughal custody. There can be no doubt that the followers of Gurū Hargobind did bear arms (three skirmishes were fought with Mughal detachments between 1628 and 1631), yet it is difficult to accept that the martial Jats would have spurned the use of arms prior to this period.

These martial traditions received further encouragement within the community as a result of Gurū Hargobind's decision to withdraw to the Shivālik hills in 1634. During their actual tenure of the office of Gurū, all four of his successors spent most of their time in the Shivāliks. The move was significant in that it exposed the developing community to the influence of the dominant *Śakti* culture of the hills area. This did not produce a transformation, but such features as the exaltation of the sword which emerge prominently during the period of the tenth Gurū should probably be traced to Shivālik influences.

It was during the lifetime of the tenth Gurū, Gobind Singh (died 1708), that the conflict with Mughal authority assumed serious proportions. Sikh tradition ascribes to this period and to Gurū Gobind Singh the features which distinguish the later community from its precursor. It is said that Gurū Gobind Singh, confronted by the evident weaknesses of his followers, decided to transform them into a powerful force which would wage war in the cause of righteousness. This he did by inaugurating a new brotherhood, the Khālsā, in 1699.

To this decision and its fulfilment are traced almost all the distinctive features of contemporary Sikhism. All who joined the Khālsā (both men and women) were to accept baptism and swear to obey a new code of discipline. Prominent amongst the requirements of this new code were an obligation to bear the *panj kakke*, or 'Five K's', and to refrain from various *kurahit*, or 'prohibitions'. The Five K's comprised the *keś* (uncut hair), the *kanghā* (comb), *kirpān* (dagger, or short sword), *karā* (bangle), and *kachh* (a variety of breeches which must not reach below the knee). The prohibitions included abstinence from tobacco, from meat slaughtered in the Muslim fashion (*halāl*), and sexual intercourse with Muslim women. A change of name was also required of the initiate. All men who accepted baptism into the Khālsā brotherhood were thereafter to add Singh to their names, and all women were to add Kaur.

Sikh tradition also relates to the period and intention of Gurū Gobind Singh another of the distinctive features of the later Sikh community. Immediately prior to his death in 1708 Gurū Gobind Singh is said to have declared that with his demise the line of personal Gurūs would come to an end. Thereafter the function and the authority of the Gurū would vest jointly in the scripture (the *granth*, which accordingly comes to be known as the *Gurū Granth Sāhib*) and in the corporate community (the *panth*, or *Khālsā Panth*).

Tradition thus accords to the period and to the deliberate purpose of Gurū Gobind Singh almost all of the characteristic features which outwardly distinguish the modern Sikh community. It is a tradition which must in some measure be qualified. There can be no doubt that something did in fact happen in 1699 and no reason exists for questioning the claim that Gurū Gobind Singh instituted some kind of brotherhood during his lifetime. Beyond this, however, it is still difficult to proceed with assurance, for there is evidence which suggests that particular features of the Khālsā code must have emerged subsequent to the death of Gurū Gobind Singh in response to pressures independent of his intention.

Two of these pressures deserve particular emphasis. There is, first, the continuing impact of Jat ideals upon the community, which numerically the Jats dominated. During the period of the Gurūs this influence would have been minimized although, as the events of Gurū Hargobind's period indicate, it was by no means without effect. With the termination of the personal authority of the Gurū in 1708 the pressure to incorporate features derived from Jat cultural patterns evidently became much stronger. The confused political circumstances of eighteenth-century Panjāb further enhanced this Jat ascendancy, for periods of military strife would be handled with much greater success by the martial Jats than by any other group in Panjāb society. Their ascendancy was by no means complete (three of the prominent leaders of this period were not Jats), but it was nevertheless extensive and it left its imprint upon the evolving community. The militant attitude of the Sikh community must be traced to this source, together with particular features such as the Five K's.

The second of the important eighteenth-century influences also concerns the battles of that century. Because Ahmad Shāh Abdālī chose to represent his invasions as a Muslim crusade, the Sikh resistance developed a pronounced anti-Muslim aspect.[6] To this development can be traced the three examples of the Five Prohibitions cited above.

It was also during this critically important century and the early decades of its successor that the Sikh doctrine of the Gurū emerged in its modern form. For Nānak the *gurū*, the voice of God, spoke mystically within the human heart. Because Nānak was believed to give utterance to the divine message the title was conferred upon him, and upon his nine successors in the manner of a single flame successively igniting a series of torches. The death of Gurū Gobind Singh without surviving heirs created a serious crisis, for ever since the time of the fourth Gurū, Rām Dās, the office had been hereditary within his family of Sodhī Khatrīs. An attempt was made to continue the pattern of personal authority (a disciple named Bandā was widely acknowledged as leader until his execution in 1716), but disputes within the community and its dispersion during the period of persecution which followed Bandā's death eventually produced a different pattern of leadership.

During this period and the subsequent years of the Afghan invasions there emerged twelve separate guerilla bands (the *misls*). In order to preserve a measure of cohesion the leaders of the *misls* assembled on specified occasions to discuss issues of common interest. Together they constituted the Sikh community and it was as a community (*panth*) that they deliberated. Well back in the period of the personal Gurūs there had developed, in response to the increasing growth and dispersion of the community, the doctrine that the Gurū's bodily presence was not actually essential. Wherever a group of the faithful gathered to sing the songs of the Gurū, there the Gurū was himself mystically present. This doctrine was now extended to cover the periodic meetings of the *misl* leaders. Assemblies were always held in the presence of a copy of the sacred scripture and decisions reached by these assemblies were acclaimed as the will of the Gurū (*gurmattā*).

A further development in the doctrine of the Gurū came during the early nineteenth century when Mahārājā Ranjīt Singh, having established his dominance over his fellow *misaldārs*, suppressed these confederate assemblies. The doctrine of the *Gurū Panth* then lapsed into desuetude and in its place the theory of the *Gurū Granth* assumed virtually exclusive authority. The presence of the Gurū in the scriptures had long been acknowledged. All that was required was a shift in emphasis.

To this day the *Gurū Granth Sāhib* occupies the central position in all expressions of the Sikh faith. Decisions are commonly made by using it as an

[6] Ahmad Shāh Abdālī of Afghanistan invaded north India nine times between 1747 and 1769.

oracle, continuous readings are held in order to confer blessing or avert disaster, and the presence of a copy is mandatory for all important ceremonies. The scripture which is used in this manner is Gurū Arjan's collection, the *Ādi Granth*. It should be distinguished from the so-called *Dasam Granth*, a separate collection compiled during the early eighteenth century which derives from the period of Gurū Gobind Singh. Although the *Dasam Granth* also possesses canonical status it is in practice little used. The bulk of the collection consists of a retelling of legends from Hindu mythology.

Another institution which deserves special notice is the Sikh temple, or gurdwārā (*guraduārā*, literally 'the Gurū's door'). Following earlier precedents the disciples of Nānak in any particular locality would regularly gather in a room set aside for their communal hymn-singing (*kīrtan*). This room (or separate building) was called a *dharamsālā*. As the community's interests expanded beyond the narrowly devotional into areas of much wider concern the function of the *dharamsālā* expanded accordingly. In the process its name changed to *guraduārā*. The gurdwārās still remain the centre and focus of the community's activities, partly because their substantial endowments provide a considerable annual income. Contemporary Sikh political activity (expressed through the Akālī party) depends to a marked degree upon control of the wealthier of these institutions. The most famous of all gurdwārās, and still the primary centre of Sikh political power, is the celebrated Golden Temple in Amritsar.

Out of these five centuries of history there has emerged the modern Sikh community, a community which occupies in the life of India today a position of prominence considerably in excess of its actual numerical strength.[7] Sikhs today are renowned for their participation in progressive farming, the armed forces, sport, and the transport industry. In all four areas the prominence belongs principally to Jat Sikhs, the caste group which still constitutes more than half of the total strength of the community. Of the other groups which have significant representations within the community, the Khatrīs and the Arorās, both mercantile castes, are more particularly distinguished for their work in manufacturing industries, commerce, and the professions. Other substantial constituents are a group of artisan castes, jointly known as Rāmgarhīā Sikhs; and converts to Sikhism from the scheduled castes (Mazhabī and Rāmdāsiā Sikhs).

Although a measure of caste consciousness certainly persists within the community, all can join the Khālsā brotherhood and observe the common discipline. Here, however, a final qualification is required. Although Khālsā organizations normally insist that only the Khālsā Sikh is a true Sikh, there are others who lay claim to the title without observing the formal discipline. These are the so-called *sahaj-dhārī* Sikhs, noted for their adherence to the devotional patterns taught by Gurū Nānak and his successors. In a sense

[7] The total number of Sikhs living in India today is approaching 6½ million, or 1·75 per cent of the country's population. Of this total number 94 per cent live in the Panjāb, Haryānā, Delhi, and the northern district of Rājasthān. There are substantial pockets of Sikh emigrants in East Africa, Malaysia, and England. (More than 75 per cent of the recent entrants into the United Kingdom from India have been Sikhs.) Smaller groups are to be found in several other countries.

they can be regarded as the descendants of the early movement, largely unaffected by the changes which took place during the seventeenth and eighteenth centuries. Their number is impossible to determine and without the external insignia of the orthodox Khālsā Sikh they constitute a much less stable group. There can be no doubt that the Khālsā provides the community with its stability and that its success in this respect has largely derived from its insistence upon external symbols. For this reason one can readily understand the apprehension with which orthodox Sikhs of today regard any inclination to abandon the traditional code of discipline.

CHAPTER XXI

Medieval Indian Literature

by KRISHNA KRIPALANI

SINCE the beginning of the Christian era, Indian literature has had at least two major vehicles: Sanskrit with its many Indo-Āryan offshoots, Pāli, the various Prākrits and their later developments, through the stage of Apabhramśa, into the modern languages of northern India; and the four Dravidian languages of southern India. Two other distinct speech-families, the *Nishāda* or Austric (the oldest and most indigenous) and *Kirāta* or Sino-Indian, have also existed side by side for 3,000 years or more, but apart from what they have contributed, by way of vocabulary, grammar, and folk-lore, to the development of the Indo-Āryan and Dravidian languages and literatures, they have not served as literary vehicles of major significance.

To some extent the multiple character of Indian literature was always there. Even in the heydey of classical Sanskrit, there existed side by side a considerable body of non-conformist literature in other languages—in Pāli, in the Prākrits, and in Tamil. Nevertheless, there is no doubt that Sanskrit was the unifying link which has maintained the continuity of Indian civilization. While it has never wholly ceased to do this, its vitality was impaired under the onslaught of Muslim invasions beginning with the eleventh century. Then it lost its exclusive sovereign claim as the fountain-head of national culture in India, and had to share increasingly its pride of place with Persian for about eight centuries.

Persian too was Indo-Āryan in origin and a distant cousin of Sanskrit; it married into a Semitic family whose script it had adopted, along with the Islamic faith. This rich, graceful, and melodious language brought with it the refreshing breath of Sūfic thought, which served as a stimulus to the resurgence of religious consciousness in medieval India, widening the intellectual horizon of Indian poets and thinkers who felt its affinity to the spiritual insight of the *Upanishads*. Its influence on Indian thought was both healthy and liberative, a fact which is amply borne out by a considerable body of Indian literature, from Kabīr to Rām Mohan Roy. It also brought with it a tradition of secular poetry, both narrative and lyric, which was a much-needed relief from the monotony of the prevailing modes of piety.

All the modern languages of India have had substantial literatures of their own, ranging over a period of 500 to 1,000 years, and in the case of three Dravidian languages, Tamil, Kannada and Telugu, even longer. Tamil, in particular, has a literary history older than any of the European languages save classical Greek and Latin. Indeed, it may well claim a classic age of its own. Its earliest extant grammar, *Tolkāppiyam*, is placed by conservative estimate in the fifth century A.D. It is also recognized, even by the most conservative, that the extant Sangam poetry, later collected in anthologies known as the

Ettutogai, was written in the second and third centuries A.D., if not earlier; the famous *Kural*, known as the Veda of the Tamils, in the sixth century; and the *kāvyas* or epics, *Manimegalai* and *Śilāppadigāram*, in the ninth century A.D.[1] This literature is more secular than religious, a fact of almost unique significance in early Indian writing. However, from the sixth century onwards the religious consciousness began to gather strength and momentum, bursting in a remarkable flowering of *bhakti* or devotional poetry of the Śaiva and Vaishnava saints, known respectively as the Nāyanārs and the Ālvārs, and culminating in the superb classic, the *Rāmāyana* of Kamban, in the ninth century.

Of the three remaining Dravidian languages, Kannada and Telugu have a fairly old and well-established literary tradition, that of Kannada being somewhat older than that of Telugu, its earliest extant classic, *Kavirājamārga*, belonging to the ninth century. This is a treatise on poetics and refers to several earlier works, which indicates that the language had attained its distinctive literary form some centuries before, an assumption well corroborated by literary records in inscriptions of the fifth and sixth centuries. The early literatures in both these languages, as well as in Tamil, owe a good deal to Jaina inspiration, Kannada being the most indebted. Tamil, though it could not altogether avoid Sanskrit influence, has maintained a more or less independent literary tradition; Kannada and Telugu, along with Malayālam, are permeated with this Sanskrit heritage and have taken freely from its vocabulary.

While the early literature in north Indian languages was almost entirely in verse, the Dravidian languages have always had a considerable body of prose-writing, particularly in the genre known as *champū*, a mixed form of verse and prose, also familiar in Sanskrit. This form attained great distinction in Kannada during the period between the tenth and twelfth centuries in the hands of three remarkable poets, Pampa, Ponna, and Ranna, known as the Three Gems of early Kannada literature. The Telugu poets, Nannaya of the eleventh century and Tikkanna of the thirteenth, also employed this form in their famous renderings of the *Mahābhārata*. In the middle of the twelfth century a popular religious movement, known as *Vīraśaivism*, swept over Kārnātaka (the Kannada-speaking area) and later over Āndhra. The founder of the movement, Basava, and his followers embodied their teachings in a simple unadorned prose and their works, known as *vachanas*, are a landmark in medieval Kannada literature.

Two other historical phenomena which have also left a powerful impact on Kannada and Telugu literatures were the rise and consolidation in the fourteenth century of the Vijayanagara Empire, which served as a bulwark against further Muslim encroachment on the south for more than two centuries, and the spread of Vaishnava devotional movements all over India in the fifteenth and sixteenth centuries. Both of them served incidentally as powerful factors in the revival of the Hindu Sanskrit tradition. The Vijayanagara Empire achieved its highest glory in the sixteenth century under Krishnadeva Rāya,

[1] No attempt is made to harmonize the dates given here with those in Chapter IV. The wide discrepancy shows how uncertain is the chronology of many aspects of ancient Indian history and culture. There are good arguments on both sides. [Ed.]

one of the greatest rulers in Indian history and himself a poet in both Telugu and Sanskrit. Several remarkable poets flourished under his patronage, of whom the best known is Peddana. While this Sanskrit-inspired profusion of verse was mainly in narrative form, known as *kāvya* or *prabandha*, the impact of Vaishnavism resulted in a rich crop of devotional songs in Kannada composed by mendicant singers who called themselves *Dāsas* (Slaves of God), of whom Purandaradāsa is the most famous.

The destruction of the Vijayanagara Empire by the Muslim rulers of the Deccan in the latter half of the sixteenth century had its inevitable crippling consequences, and although miscellaneous literature continued to be produced it became increasingly ornate and artificial, tending not infrequently to eroticism. There were, however, two notable exceptions in Telugu, the didactic verses of Vemana in the seventeenth century or earlier, and the musical compositions of Tyāgarāja in the eighteenth, which are justly admired all over south India. But in the main, literature had lost its creative individuality and, bereft of intellectual stimulus, was becoming a preserve of pedantic learning or a vehicle of moral instruction, or was allying itself with song and dance to provide popular entertainment, as exemplified in the development of *Yakshagāna* in Kannada.

The most remarkable development of this particular form of literary composition, which aims at dramatic representation of Purānic episodes with the help of song, dance, and mime, was, however, achieved in the *Kathākalī* literature of Malayālam, particularly in the work of Kunchan Nambiar, also of the eighteenth century. Malayālam is the youngest of Dravidian languages and, although some songs and ballads of an earlier age have survived in oral tradition and some written texts are also available of the fourteenth and fifteenth centuries, the language established its full identity and distinctive quality only in the sixteenth and seventeenth centuries, mainly through translations of the Sanskrit epics by the gifted poet Ezhuttachan. Despite its Dravidian origin, the literary development of Malayālam has been mainly under Sanskrit influence, which is not surprising if one recalls that Śankarāchārya, the great Hindu philosopher of the ninth century, was a brāhman from Keralā. A modifying factor worth noting is that there are more Christians in this part of India than in any other, many of whom owe allegiance to the Syrian Church, which according to tradition came to this region in the first century A.D., long before Christianity was accepted in most parts of Europe.

As regards the languages of north India derived from the spoken dialects of Middle Indo-Āryan (of which the cultivated literary form was Sanskrit), their separate identities were not perhaps established till after the eleventh century, for their earliest extant literary classics are not older than the twelfth and thirteenth centuries. The fact that the collection of mystic songs of the tenth and eleventh centuries known as *Charyāpadas* (discovered in 1916 by the Bengālī scholar Haraprasād Shāstrī in the Nepal Darbār Library) is claimed by several of these languages as their oldest literary document is ample evidence that their identities had not yet distinctly emerged. These songs hide beneath their surface meanings esoteric doctrines, the legacy of a decadent Mahāyāna Buddhism with Tantric and Nāth-cult affiliations, which seem to have been popular religious lore all over north India. This lore is still embedded in the Hindu consciousness and has had significant literary expression in many languages, for example in the medieval narrative poetry of Bengal known as *mangala*, celebrating the worship of Dharma, Manasā, or Chandī, all non-Vedic divinities.

Among these modern Indo-Āryan languages, Hindī, with its rich and miscellaneous heritage of literary achievement in a number of widely spread dialects, may well claim the distinction of possessing one of the earliest literary records and also the earliest well-established tradition of secular writing, in the Rājasthānī classic *Prithvīrāja Rāsau* (twelfth century) by Chand Bārdāī, the court minstrel of Prithvīrāja, the last Hindu king of Delhi whose exploits it narrates. Strangely enough, one of the pioneer experimenters in Hindī is the Muslim poet Amīr Khusrau, the remarkably versatile genius of the thirteenth to the fourteenth century. Marāthī has given to north Indian languages their first great religious poet and thinker in Jnāneśvara whose commentary on the *Bhagavad Gītā*, written in the thirteenth century, still holds an unrivalled place as a literary classic. He firmly established the tradition of Marāthī literature in which *bhakti*, devotion, and *jnān*, philosophy and scholarship, are admirably blended.

The term Hindī is used loosely to denote a number of Middle Indo-Āryan dialects which had evolved, over a period of about five centuries, distinct literary forms of their own and were known by their separate names. There was (and still is) the Braj-bhāshā, the vehicle *par excellence* of medieval Vaishnava literature and of classical Hindūstānī music, the language of Sūrdās and Bihārī; the Avadhī which has given to 'Hindī' literature its greatest poet Tulsīdās, whose *Rāmāyana* is sung with devotion even today almost all over the Hindī-speaking region; Rājasthānī, in which is recorded the earliest secular literature of north India in the form of heroic ballads, and in which Mīrā Bāī wrote her exquisite songs which are today claimed by both Hindī and Gujarātī as part of their literary heritage; and Bhojpurī, Magahī, and Maithilī of modern Bihār. Bhojpurī was the mother tongue of the great poet Kabīr of the fifteenth century, although he wrote his poems in a mixed dialect and evolved a rich and vigorous vocabulary of his own which did not disdain Perso-Arabic words. Maithilī was one of the richest medieval tongues, which in the hands of Vidyāpati attained such grace and power in the fifteenth century that its influence was felt as much in Bengal and Assam as in the western zone and penetrated even into Nepal. Even today the people speaking it, who number several million, claim the status of a separate major language for Maithilī.

What is today known as Hindī has behind it this vast and varied heritage, though by itself and in its present standard literary form it is of comparatively recent origin, not earlier than the first decade of the nineteenth century. It is built on the basic structure of a western Indo-Āryan dialect spoken in Delhi and its neighbourhood known as Kharī Bolī (an epithet originally used in a derogatory sense, meaning rough, crude, or raw speech). Begun as a tentative experiment to cope with the demands of modern education and knowledge, Hindī has absorbed during the last 150 years the heritage of its illustrious predecessors and, drawing its capital from the vast reserves of Sanskrit, has established itself as the standard literary medium of the largest zone in northern India. This position has been recognized in the Constitution of India, which has conferred on it the status of the official language of the Indian Union, without prejudice to the remaining fourteen languages scheduled therein, all of which are recognized as national languages of India.

Among them Urdū is in a class by itself. Linguistically it is Indo-Āryan, born in India and built, like Hindī, on the same basic structure of Kharī Bolī. But having affiliated itself to the Persian literary tradition and adopted the Perso-Arabic script, it has evolved an individuality of its own, with the result that Hindī and Urdū in their highly standardized forms seem two different languages, scions of the same stock turned rivals by marrying into different cultural clans.

The word *Urdū* is of Turkish origin, and is a cousin of the English word *horde*. The original Turkish word *ordu* meant an army or camp. Ever since the eleventh century, when the Muslims invaded India from the north-west, the rulers, whether Afghans, Turks, or Mughals, used Persian as the language of the Imperial Court. Their army, belonging to different races, also spoke the same language, although the soldiers in course of time picked up rudiments of the local dialects so as to communicate with the common people, mainly Hindus or Muslim converts. The crude, improvised speech thus born of the confluence of Persian and a western Hindī dialect came to be known as Urdū. Its first standardized literary form, known as Dakhnī, was developed in the fifteenth century in central and south India, where Muslim adventurers had carved out powerful kingdoms for themselves. Its early writers were naturally Muslim poets who adopted for their purpose the Perso-Arabic script to which they were used and who increasingly loaded their language with a vocabulary and other literary paraphernalia, including prosody, borrowed from Persian and to a lesser extent from Arabic.

This literary medium travelled back to the north, where, under the patronage of the Mughals and later of the Lucknow Court and society, it developed a highly polished, sophisticated, and urbane form which has made it different from every other Indian language and given it an elegance and a vigour all its own. The patronage of the court and aristocracy had at one time lent it such prestige that it was freely adopted by a large number of educated Hindu families of north India, in whose hands, however, the language tended to lose its lop-sidedness and to maintain a fairer proportion of Sanskrit and Persian vocabulary. Such is, for instance, the language of families like the Nehrūs and the Saprūs. It is not without significance that the best-known of modern Hindī writers, Premchand, wrote his first stories and novels in Urdū and later turned them into Hindī.

It was, however, in the fifteenth and sixteenth centuries that the modern Indo-Āryan languages had their richest literary flowering. Its source of inspiration was twofold, a revival of interest in the Sanskrit heritage, particularly as embodied in the great epics, and the upsurge of Vaishnava *bhakti*, a widespread cult of devotion to a personal God identified with Rāma, the hero of the *Rāmāyana*, or Krishna, the hero of the *Mahābhārata* and the *Bhāgavata Purāna*; less important, but still significant, were the growth of cults of devotion to Śiva and his consort Kālī or Chandī.

This lyrical overflow of religious adoration had had an earlier literary burgeoning in Tamil, in the poetry of the Śaiva and Vaishnava saints of the sixth century onwards, referred to earlier. Its philosophy as expounded by the Tamil sage Rāmānujāchārya was carried to north India in the fourteenth century by Rāmānanda, who was traditionally the teacher of the famous poet Kabīr. Madhvāchārya from Kārnātaka carried *bhakti* to Bengal where its most ecstatic exponent was the Bengālī saint Chaitanya, whose teachings spread from Orissā in the east to Vrindāvan (near Mathurā, a district specially connected with the Krishna myth) in the west, and travelling south had a marked influence on the development of Vaishnava poetry in Kannada—a significant example of the cultural interaction of Dravidian and Indo-Āryan influences.

Almost all Indian languages, Dravidian or Indo-Āryan, count among their early classics translations or free renderings of the epics, the most famous of them being Tulsīdās's *Rām-charit-mānas* in Avadhī-Hindī (sixteenth century) and Kamban's *Rāmāyana* in Tamil (ninth century). They are creative adaptations rather than translations, and freely omit or modify incidents, scenes, and settings of the original narrative and in some cases introduce new ones. The authors have coloured the texture of their poetry with regional flavour and suffused it with their own personal devotional attitude, turning the manly hero of the epic into God Incarnate. The loss in classic dignity is, however, partially compensated by added lyrical fervour.

Along with translations or free adaptations of the epics, there was a considerable output of devotional song and verse by saint-poets whose number is legion. A few names might illustrate how widespread this upsurge was and how the same impulse worked in different languages: Śankaradeva in Assamese, Chandīdās in Bengālī, Vidyāpati in Maithilī, Narasī Mehtā in Gujarātī, Mīrā Bāī in Rājasthānī, Kabīr in a mixed form of Bhojpurī and Urdū, Sūrdās in Braj-bhāshā, Nāmdev and Eknāth in Marāthī, Saralādās in Oriyā, Guru Nānak in Panjābī. Exceptional among *bhakta* hymnodists, the Kashmīrī poetess Lāl Ded was a Śaivite mystic and belonged to the fourteenth century. The output of their successors in the sixteenth and seventeenth centuries was no less impressive. Its impact on Indian thought has been so profound that its echo can be heard even in the poetry of the twentieth century.

Besides this overflow of devotional exuberance, often wearisomely repetitive and only occasionally relieved by heroic ballad and romance, there was in most Indian languages a not inconsiderable output in other literary forms: metaphysical speculation, maxims on life, in polished and condensed verse, commentaries on aesthetics, rhetoric, and grammar, exposition of Purānic legends with not a little pseudo-scientific rigmarole, and biographical literature which was mainly hagiographical and full of an astounding *naïveté*. There was also a body of sophisticated verse analysing possibilities of erotic rapture with obvious, unashamed, and even devout delight. The famous *Sat Sāī* of the seventeenth-century Hindī poet Bihārīlāl embodies this odd Sanskrit tradition with much ingenuity and charm.

Although prose was not unknown to Sanskrit and to some Dravidian languages, its scope and range were limited. So far as the north Indian languages are concerned, what specimens there are in the Assamese *Buranjīs* (court chronicles) and in the later historical records in Marāthī and Urdū have survived as literary curiosities rather than as milestones in literary development. Poetry was the vehicle *par excellence* of literary expression, and rhyme, in the case of modern Indo-Āryan languages, its main constituent. Nor was this surprising, considering that literature itself was subservient to religious fervour and was almost entirely dependent on oral delivery for its propagation.

The Muslim contribution to medieval Indian literature was not inconsiderable. Apart from the fact that the development of Urdū language and literature is due mainly to Muslims, several modern Indian languages have been enriched by the contribution of individual Muslim writers. Although their inspiration was mainly derived from a nostalgia for the faded glory of Arabia and Iran, they also made imaginative use of purely Indian themes, e.g. the heroic tale of the Rājput Queen Padminī of Chitor which inspired Malik Muhammad Jāyasī's *Padmāvat*, an allegorical narrative in Avadhī written in the sixteenth century, as well as the Bengālī poet Alāol's poem of the same name a century later. To this may be added the general impact of Muslim thought, particularly in its nonconformist Sūfī tradition, and the gradual infiltration of Perso-Arabic vocabulary and literary lore. This influence was so profound in the case of Kashmīrī, Panjābī, and Sindhī as to be deemed predominant. The poems of Hābā Khatūn in Kashmīrī, Bulley Shāh, and Wāris Shāh in Panjābī and Shāh Latīf in Sindhī are landmarks in these literatures. These two Panjābī poets of the eighteenth century and their Sindhī contemporary wove their exquisite lyrics round popular romantic lore, the tragic love tales of Hīr and Ranjhā, Sassī and Punnū, and Sohnī-Mahiwāl. A curious fact of Kashmīrī literature is that its three greatest poets were women, Lāl Ded of the fourteenth century, Hābā Khātūn, of the sixteenth, and Arnimal of the eighteenth.

Such then, at a glance, was the general picture of Indian literature on the eve of its next revolutionary phase in the beginning of the nineteenth century. Linguistically, its two main sources were Dravidian and Indo-Āryan; culturally, it derived from the religious and literary tradition as embodied in Sanskrit, supplemented and modified by Buddhist and Jaina influences as well as by local indigenous lore. The most vital impulse that had conditioned the character of Indian literature was religious. This is true of the entire course of its development, Vedic, Buddhist, Jaina, classical, Dravidian and later Indo-Āryan, although classical Sanskrit and early Tamil literatures show ample evidence of full-blooded and secular vigour. The most passionate as well as the most characteristic expression of this religious impulse was in devotional poetry, both narrative and lyric, inspired by one or the other form of Vaishnavism or Śaivism. This impulse, clothed in Sūfistic garb and adorned with Persian finery, is also evident in the literary contribution of the Muslims, whether in Urdū or in other Indian languages.

CHAPTER XXII

Muslim Architecture in India

by MARTIN S. BRIGGS

To most people the title of this chapter would seem to be above reproach and to describe its contents accurately. Indeed, it would be difficult to find any other precise and simple description to cover the various styles of buildings produced in the vast area of India under the Muslim dominion that lasted from the year 1193 up to the eighteenth century. E. B. Havell, an enthusiastic and pugnacious champion of the Hindu genius, strongly objected to the term 'Indo-Saracenic' as 'an unscientific classification based on the fundamental error which vitiates the works of most European histories of Indian civilization'.[1] He was thinking primarily of James Fergusson's great book, the first really scholarly survey of the subject, but other and later historians came under his lash by adopting the same terminology. We may abandon the word 'Saracenic' nowadays, because it was never more than a picturesque nickname and has been discarded for many years by the learned, but it seems ridiculous to suggest that the great influence and power of Islam, implied in the words 'Muslim' or 'Muhammadan', can be neglected in considering the long series of mosques, palaces, and other buildings erected during more than five centuries. On the other hand, Muslim architecture in India does differ radically from its works in other countries. As M. Saladin has well said:

L'Inde est si éloignée du centre géographique de l'Islam que l'architecture musulmane y a subi l'influence de l'art florissant qui y était implanté depuis des siècles. Le continent indien, peuplé de races très diverses, dont les antagonismes assurèrent la servitude, constitue cependant un monde particulier. Une civilisation religieuse s'est étendue sur les races ennemies et a donné à l'art indou une vie puissante et originale.[2]

It was in 712 that the Muslim hosts first entered India and established themselves in Sind, but the colony there soon became detached from the Caliphate, eventually expired, and left no architectural remains of importance. In the tenth century, about 962, a former Turkish slave named Alptigīn entered Afghanistan from Turkīstān and established a small independent principality at Ghaznī. His successor Sabuktigīn, another ex-slave, became Amīr of Ghaznī in 977, raided the Panjāb ten years later, and founded a dynasty. His son Mahmūd, who succeeded him in 997, assumed the title of Sultan and soon began to make his power felt beyond the Indus, capturing Kanauj, the capital city of northern India, in 1019. But it was only in Ghaznī itself that he became famous as a builder, and the sack of that city by a rival chieftain in *c.* 1150 destroyed all the buildings except Mahmūd's tomb and two others.

Ghaznī lies in the modern Afghanistan, and therefore does not strictly belong to our subject. But it must be recorded here that, in the days of its

[1] E. B. Havell, *Indian Architecture*, 2nd edn., London, 1927, p. 121.
[2] H. Saladin, *Manuel d'art musulman*, Paris, 1907, Vol. 1, p. 545.

glory, it became a city of some importance. A contemporary chronicler, Firishta, wrote that 'the capital was in a short time ornamented with mosques, porches, fountains, aqueducts, reservoirs, and cisterns, beyond any city in the East.'[3] Fergusson says that:

Even the tomb of the great Mahmūd is unknown to us except by name, [but that its gates, removed to India long ago,] are of Deodar pine, and the carved ornaments on them are so similar to those found at Cairo, on the mosque of Ibn Tulun and other buildings of that age, as not only to prove that they are of the same date, but also to show how similar were the works of decoration at these two extremities of the Muslim empire at the time of their execution . . . . At the same time there is nothing . . . Hindu . . . about them.[4]

When Robert Byron visited this tomb he described it as follows:

The tomb resembles an inverted cradle of white marble, and bears a beautiful Kufic inscription whose high spots have grown translucent beneath the devotions of nine centuries. It was covered, when I entered, with a black pall, on which fresh rose-petals had been strewn, to show that the memory of the first great patron of Persian Islamic art is still revered among the people he once ruled.[5]

Byron does not mention the Jāmi' Masjid ('Friday mosque'), which Fergusson expected to provide interesting information when it came to be examined, but he saw the two remarkable towers described and illustrated by Fergusson. Apparently only the lofty six-sided bases now remain, the tapered cylindrical superstructure having vanished. Byron speaks of them as 'minarets', but Fergusson says that they were pillars of victory, adding that 'neither of them was ever attached to a mosque'. Be this as it may, the form of these towers or minarets became important in the later history of Muslim architecture in India.

After Mahmūd's death in 1030 the power of Ghaznī began to decline, and it was occupied in 1173 by the rival prince of Ghūr. Twenty years later, Muhammad, the Ghūrī ruler of Ghaznī, with his generals Qutbu'd-Dīn Aibak and Muhammad Bakhtiyār, conquered Hindūstān and established the new Muslim capital at Delhi. This date, 1193, marks the real beginning of Muslim architecture in India itself. Except for the scattered and ruined fragments at Ghaznī in Afghanistan, no earlier buildings of any note survive which are due to Muslim influence or bear its characteristic features.

Before describing the early architecture of Delhi and Ajmer it is necessary to indicate briefly the point of development to which Muslim building had attained in 1193 in Persia and the neighbouring countries whence its influence must have reached India, and then to study the nature of the existing indigenous architecture with which it became fused and on which, in spite of all statements to the contrary, it eventually impressed the unmistakable features of Islamic tradition.

The congregational mosque or 'Friday Mosque' (Jāmi' Masjid) had long attained its normal and almost standardized form, consisting of a large open rectangular court (*sahn* in Arabic) surrounded by arcades or colonnades

[3] Quoted in Fergusson's *History of Indian and Eastern Architecture*, revised edn., London, 1910, Vol. 2, p. 192. [4] Ibid., p. 193.

[5] In *The Times* for 28 Dec. 1934, article entitled 'Middle Eastern Journey'.

līwānat in Arabic) on all four sides. The *līwān* nearest to Mecca was usually made much deeper than the others and formed the sanctuary. In the centre of the back wall of the sanctuary, and on its inner side, stood the *mihrāb*, a niche with a pointed head, indicating the proper direction (*qiblah*) for prayer, i.e. the direction of Mecca. The call to worship (*adhān*) was chanted by a muezzin (*mu'adhdhin*) from a gallery near the top of a minaret (*ma'dhana*), a tall slender tower. Within the mosque the chief ritual furniture consisted of a pulpit (*mimbar*) and facilities for ceremonial ablution. A large mosque might have several minarets, their form being usually cylindrical or polygonal in Persia, though the first known example, at Qayrawān near Tunis (eighth century), is a massive square tower, slightly tapered. Arches were freely used in all parts of the mosque, their form being generally 'Persian' (i.e. somewhat depressed and struck from four centres like our 'Tudor' arch), or less frequently of ogee type. Cusping was occasionally used. Windows were often filled with plaster or stone lattices or *claire-voies* to break the force of the sun, but glazing does not appear to have been introduced before the thirteenth century. Enamelled tiles were certainly employed, also bands of decorative lettering and geometrical surface patterns ('arabesques') in profusion, while the famous 'stalactite' ornament, the hallmark of Muslim architecture in all countries, had made its appearance in the mosque of Al Aqmar at Cairo in 1125. Lastly, the masonry or brick dome had come into general use for tombs and tomb-mosques, though in ordinary congregational mosques it was normally of small size and placed over the space in front of the *mihrāb*.[6]

The buildings which the Muslim conquerors found in India in 1193 were numerous and decidedly florid in character. Indeed, it is the profuseness of the decoration in early Hindu temples that tends to obscure their structural features and thus makes them difficult for a European critic to analyse dispassionately. Havell writes that 'it may seem to the Western eye, trained in the formula of the classical schoolmaster, that the Muhammadan prescription is more pleasing, just because it is more correct according to the canons called classical',[7] but the difference seems to be more fundamental than that. However, it should be possible in this brief survey to avoid unnecessary and futile comparisons between varying styles of building, concentrating rather on matters of ascertained fact in the story of architectural development.

The story of architecture in India prior to the Muslim invasion in 1193 has already been extended backwards by 3,000 years or more since the discoveries made at Harappā and Mohenjo-dāro. Until then the prevailing belief was that the earliest surviving Indian buildings were constructed mainly of timber, but with sun-dried brick for foundations and plinths. In the prosperous reign of Aśoka (*c.* 272–232 B.C.) stone came into use, but the forms of timber members were often reproduced in stone. Aśoka, whose dominions included the whole of modern India except its southern extremity and part of Assam, became a devotee of Buddhism. Hence the monuments surviving from his day consist chiefly of great stone pillars inscribed with his religious edicts, and *stūpas*, i.e. structures or shrines enclosing relics of Buddhist saints, or marking places

[6] For a concise summary of the characteristics of Muslim architecture in general, see my chapter in *The Legacy of Islam*, Oxford, 1931, pp. 155–79.

[7] E. B. Havell, op. cit., p. 51.

where Buddha lived or worked; a few artificial caves with highly polished interiors, used as hermitages for Ājīvika monks, also go back to his day. In these buildings, which were scattered all over Aśoka's vast empire, there are many indications of foreign influence, even at this early date.

Thus the Aśoka pillars have capitals somewhat resembling the type used at Persepolis 700 years before, decorated with Persian mouldings, and crowned with lions or other beasts. Where these lions were disposed in pairs or in fours (as on the fine capital from the Sārnāth pillar, which was 50 feet high from the ground), we find the prototype of the famous 'bracket-capital' which later played so important a structural part in Hindu architecture and came to be freely used in Muslim mosques. The *stūpas* are extremely interesting monuments, but do not appear to have influenced mosque-building to any marked extent.

The Buddhist monasteries (*vihāras*), of which the earliest surviving examples date from a century or two after Aśoka, were often placed near the shrines (*chaityas*). Some of them were hewn out of the solid rock, others were free-standing structures; some had columns, others were astylar. The *chaitya* interior as a whole suggests a Christian basilica, and Fergusson pointed out that the dimensions of the temple at Kārlī are almost identical with those of the choir at Norwich Cathedral. Light was admitted through a huge sun-window in the rock façade so that it fell upon the *stūpa* or *chaitya*, the focal point of worship. The sun-window almost invariably assumed the form of a horseshoe, and Havell explained its symbolic purpose in some detail.[8] He took great pains to prove that this horseshoe-arch, which eventually became a characteristic feature of Muslim architecture in certain countries, was invented in India a thousand years or so before the first mosque was erected. It is true that this horseshoe window resembles some types of arch used in Islamic and Western architecture but the fact remains that, except for an early example at Kauśāmbī and a few small examples in a later Buddhist monastery in Orissā, which seem to have had no successors, no true arches or domes dating from before the Muslim conquest have been found in India. Thus claims such as Havell's will not stand critical examination, and the direct debt of Indian Muslim architecture to ancient Indian art appears to be limited to the use of bracket-capitals (a Persian heritage) and certain arch-forms, the latter being disputable. Other details borrowed from Persia, Greece, and perhaps Rome (e.g. the quasi-Doric capitals at Elephanta and the fluted pillars of the temple at Mārtānd in Kashmīr and elsewhere) passed out of use long before the Muslim invasion and so had no effect on Muhammadan architecture.

But it must not be inferred that nothing of importance was transmitted indirectly, and after considerable modification, from the earlier period to the later. Certain features developed during the ensuing centuries before 1193, and passed almost imperceptibly into the design of mosques after that date. Meanwhile Indian craftsmen were acquiring great skill in all decorative details. Moreover, it is quite fallacious to regard the rock-hewn *chaitya*-cave type as archaic or barbaric. As Havell says, 'in India it represents a refinement

[8] Havell, *Ancient and Medieval Architecture of India*, p. 55, etc.

of luxury for the users, an exceptional trial of skill for the craftsmen, and a special act of devotion and consecration on the part of the individual or the community for whom the work is performed';[9] and again, that 'the sculpturesque or architectonic quality which is generally lacking in pure Arab buildings, belongs pre-eminently to Hindu architectural design: the Hindu builder was a sculptor as well as a mason, having acquired his skill at Elephanta, Ellorā, and Ajantā in many generations from dealing with great masses of living rock'.[10] This last claim must be borne in mind as we come to consider the fully developed Muslim architecture of India, later in this chapter.

During the period between 650 and 1200 India was a mass of rival states. Brāhmanical Hinduism replaced Buddhism as the religion of the majority of the inhabitants, but Jainism—which was as old as Buddhism in its origin—continued to flourish abreast of it, and was responsible for the erection of many important temples. The typical Hindu temple of this period consists of two elements: a shrine-cell crowned by a curvilinear tower or steeple (*śikhara*) and an entrance porch or veranda. Havell considered that this type was directly derived from the primitive village shrine of a thousand years earlier, with its veranda giving shelter to 'the two guardians of the shrine, human or divine'.[11]

In south India, instead of the curved *śikhara*, we find a more primitive structure, a *vimāna* or pyramidal tower with stepped sides, not unlike the Babylonian *ziggurat*. Otherwise, variations from the standard plan take the form of the addition of pillared halls (*mandapam*) and enclosures (*prākāra*) round the original shrine as a nucleus, with lofty gateways (*gopurams*) at the various entrances. It is only in the pillared halls that any noteworthy structural experiments are to be seen, and there one sometimes sees primitive stone domes on an octagonal arrangement of pillars, a system which found its way into Muslim architecture.

If one can so far forget the overgrowth of ornament and the complexity of subdivision as to penetrate to the underlying structural forms and elements, it appears that the Hindu temples prior to 1193 were mainly of trabeated stone construction, based in large part on timber prototypes. Great stone lintels, beams, and purlins are freely used, and arches are almost if not entirely unknown, the tops of window openings and doorways being flat. Bracket-capitals are employed to reduce the span of openings. Pyramidal roofs are formed by successive projections of masonry courses, and domes of primitive type are constructed in the same way on an octagonal base of stone lintels, themselves supported on stone columns in late examples (after the tenth century). The top or cap of such a structure, the *āmalaka*, sometimes appears to be carried on the slightly curvilinear piers or ribs forming the skeleton of the *śikhara*, where the walls of the *śikhara* are not entirely solid, and in this system Havell finds the origin of the later ribbed dome. Columns were seldom used in the architecture of Hindu temples in north India, but are frequently found in buildings erected further south. There is no doubt that the Muslims borrowed many of these structural features, notably lintels and bracket-capitals, from Hindu tradition; and it is equally certain that the domes they built in India showed similar influence. But their architecture was not based

[9] Ibid., p. 69. [10] Ibid., *Indian Architecture*, p. 23. [11] Ibid., p. 37.

entirely on Hindu models, as extremists would have us believe. The largest group of early Hindu temples in north India is to be found in Orissā, which escaped invasion by the Muslims until 1510.

The chief Jain temples were erected between *c.* 1000 and *c.* 1300, and are distinguished by the large number of cells provided for images, as many as 236 being found in one building, but architecturally they do not differ in character very much from Hindu temples. They are usually picturesquely situated, often on hill-tops. Some of them are rock-cut, as at Ellorā and in Orissā; others are free-standing structures, such as the temples at Lakkandī in Dhārwar, at Palitānā and Girnār in Gujarāt, at Somnāth south of Girnār, and at Vindhyagiri and Chandragiri in Mysore. But the most famous examples are at Mount Ābū, about 400 miles from Bombay on the line to Delhi. Here the older temple, built in 1031, forms one of the finest architectural groups of the period. The shrine itself, with its pyramidal roof and porch, is surrounded by a closed courtyard 128 feet by 75 feet, lined with 52 cells.

When the Muslims under Muhammad of Ghūr invaded India in 1191, they at first encountered defeat from the Hindu rājā who ruled over Delhi and Ajmer. In the following year, however, they were successful, and in 1193 Delhi, Kanauj, and Vārānasī (Banāras) were captured. The surrender of Gwālior occurred three years later, the conquest of Upper India being completed in 1203. Most of the Muslim rulers were of Turkish or Arab blood, and several of the early sultans of Delhi were Turkish slaves who, like the Mamelukes of Egypt including the famous Saladīn himself, rose to the highest positions in the state from this lowly origin. The general in command of the army which conquered Delhi in 1193 was one such slave, by name Qutbu'd-Dīn Aibak, a native of Turkistān, and it was he who, even before he became the first sultan or king of Delhi on Muhammad's death in 1206, put in hand the building of two large 'congregational' or metropolitan mosques in Delhi and Ajmer. Undoubtedly this step was intended as a symbol of conquest, as an evidence of the Muslims' belief in the faith of their fathers, and possibly also as a memorial of their triumph over idolatry.

The invaders were certainly soldiers, probably marching light and without any elaborate system of administration prepared in advance for the vanquished territories. But those writers who have assumed that no architects were brought into India from Persia or Turkistān have been rather rash: even if there is no record of such an importation, it seems conceivable that it may have happened. At all events the point is unimportant, because it is obvious that somebody—perhaps Qutbu'd-Dīn himself—must have given precise instructions to craftsmen and labourers for the building of the two mosques just mentioned. It may also be assumed that these workmen were mainly if not entirely Hindus: that fact is proved by the clumsy way in which they dealt with the few non-Hindu items of construction required by the conquerors. Moreover, this was the practice in all the countries subdued by the Arabs in the early days of Islam. The plan of the mosque, utilitarian as well as symbolical in its nature, was prescribed by tradition and was insisted upon by the Muslim governor or ruler; the materials employed, and the constructional methods used to achieve the desired effects, were largely left to be determined by the local circumstances and the particular skill of the native craftsmen. As we have seen, Hindu temple architecture had reached a high level; and sculpture had become almost too easy, as it was perhaps too common.

The first mosque at Delhi, dedicated to the Quwwat-ul-Islām ('Might of Islam'), is admirably situated on a slight eminence and was completed in 1198. It originally measured externally about 210 feet from east to west (that is, from front to back) and 150 feet from north to south, the measurements inside the colonnade being 142 by 108 feet. (In India, the *mihrāb* is always at the west end.) It was erected on the site of a Hindu temple, but an Arabic inscription on the east wall states that the materials of twenty-seven 'idolatrous' temples were used in its construction. The sanctuary at the west (Mecca) end is now in ruins, only twenty-two of its numerous columns remaining, but the fine stone arcade or screen forming its frontage to the courtyard survives to show the magnificence of the original design, with a central arch of slightly ogee shape, 22 feet wide and 53 feet high. The low colonnaded sanctuary behind it, like the other colonnades surrounding the courtyard, appears to have survived from the earlier temple, so that Qutbu'd-Dīn's work was mainly confined to the erection of this huge arcaded sanctuary-façade. The Hindu craftsmen employed were unaccustomed to the construction of arches; hence, instead of proper voussoirs, they used projecting courses of masonry such as were familiar to them in building *śikharas*.

After Qutbu'd-Dīn's death, his son-in-law and successor Iltutmish proceeded in *c.* 1225 to extend this arcaded screen to treble its original width north and south, and also to erect a new east colonnade to the mosque, so that it now measured some 370 by 280 feet. Within the extended courtyard he built the great Qutb Mīnār, a detached tower or minaret 238 feet high, which may possibly have been commenced by Qutbu'd-Dīn himself. There is some doubt as to the real purpose of this remarkable monument. An inscription, and a reference by the poet Amīr Khusrau, support the theory that it was a normal minaret used by a muezzin; but many authorities hold that it was a tower of victory, perhaps inspired by the 'pillars of victory' which still stand on the plain of Ghaznī. A detached minaret is not unknown, and there are very early examples at Samarra in Mesopotamia (846–52) and at the mosque of Ibn Tulūn in Cairo (868–969). The sharply tapered cylindrical form is found at Damghān in Persia (twelfth century), and the fluting of the surface is a Persian feature (as at Rayy) derived from older Mesopotamian prototypes. The 'stalactite' cornices under the tiers of galleries round the Qutb Mīnār recall one of the earliest uses of that feature on a twelfth-century minaret at Bostam in Persia. All things considered, there is no reason to doubt the statement that the Qutb Mīnār was designed by a Muhammadan architect and built by Hindu craftsmen.[12] It is absurd to say that it is 'a Saracenic modification of the Indian type'.[13]

The tomb of Iltutmish, who died in 1235, lies near the mosque, and is a beautiful example of nearly pure Persian art, though there are certain features of its decoration—such as the design of the shafts and the cusped arches—that suggest Hindu taste, and much of the ornament betrays an inexperienced

[12] Vincent Smith, *History of Fine Art in India and Ceylon*, p. 69.
[13] Havell, *Indian Architecture*, p. 49.

hand. The mosque at Ajmer, already mentioned, was commenced *c.* 1200 and finished during the reign of Iltutmish. It originally measured 264 by 172 feet and was erected on the site of a Jain temple or college built in 1153. As at Delhi, the chief alteration to the temple consisted in erecting a great screen or arcade of Persian arches in stone, bordered with characteristic Arabic decorative lettering, and as at Delhi the arches are quite unconstructional, having horizontal joints formed by projecting courses of masonry. But only a fragment of this beautiful building now remains, including the ruins of two small fluted minarets. The legend that it was built in two and a half days, repeated by nearly all historians, may be ignored as Oriental hyperbole carried to excess.

The Mongol wars which devastated Central Asia in the thirteenth century, and the weak character of the rulers of Delhi after Iltutmish, may account for the fact that no outstanding monument was erected for nearly a hundred years by the Muslims of India. Then in 1300 'Alā'u'd-Dīn, who had succeeded to the throne of Delhi in 1296 and had previously conquered part of south India, began to enlarge the Quwwat-ul-Islām mosque and to build a *mīnār* which was intended to be more than double the height of the lofty Qutb Mīnār. 'Alā'u'd-Dīn was a megalomaniac, and his vast projects remained unfinished, but in the so-called Darwāza, a noble south gateway to the mosque enclosure (1310), he has left us a very charming and delicate little building which may be considered to mark the culmination of early Indo-Muslim art. Its general character and its ornament are Persian, but the Hindu tradition may be seen in the same features as at the tomb of Iltutmish described.

For the next period, corresponding with the duration of the Tughluq Dynasty in Delhi (1321–1421), that city continued to be virtually the capital of Muslim India, though from time to time various principalities, such as Bengal, asserted their independence. Delhi was certainly a flourishing place when the Muslims captured it in 1193. Its favourable strategical situation is considered to explain its continuance as a capital through a thousand years. The site of the old 'cities' of Delhi, reckoned at least seven in number without the pre-Muslim town, is spread over a triangular area measuring some ten or eleven miles from north to south, with the apex of the triangle at the junction of the 'Ridge' with the River Yamunā. The site of New Delhi is about in the centre of this triangle, and that of Old Delhi, the first Muslim city, founded by Qutbu'd-Dīn, at its south-west corner. The second city, Sirī, lies north-east of Old Delhi, and the third, Tughluqābād, founded in 1321, in the south-east corner of the triangle. The fourth and fifth cities, Jahānpannāh (1327) and Fīrozābād (*c.* 1354), were also established during the rule of the Tughluq Dynasty, which provided a number of interesting buildings, very different in character from the earlier architecture just described.

The tomb of Ghiyāsu'd-Dīn Tughluq (died 1325), first of the line, is a square structure of red sandstone with sharply battered walls, enormously thick, crowned with a simple white marble dome. This building, massive and severe, is surrounded by an *enceinte* of lofty stone walls with bastions. Nothing more like a warrior's tomb, and nothing less like 'Alā'u'd-Dīn's gateway, could be imagined. The other tombs of the period are no less stark in their aspect and the walls of Tughluqābād are equally impressive, while the surviving parts of the walls of Jahānpannāh and Fīrozābād show a dour disregard of architectural prettiness that seems to indicate a rigid puritanism of outlook as well as a consciousness of defensive needs. Among Delhi mosques of the fourteenth century the most important is the Kalān Masjid (finished 1387), a citadel-like building of forbidding aspect with domed bastions at its angles and acutely tapered cylindrical minarets on either side of the main entrance. It stands within Shāhjahānābād, a crowded quarter of Delhi. The remaining mosques are at Jahānpannāh and elsewhere.

Outside Delhi the chief Muslim buildings of the fourteenth century were erected in Gujarāt, Bengal, and the Jaunpur area. Gujarāt was a seat of Hindu craftsmanship, and such mosques as the Jāmi' Masjid at Cambay (1325) and the mosque of Hilāl Khān Qāzī at Kholkā near Ahmadābād (1333) contain numerous Hindu fragments as well as Hindu ideas, the columnar or trabeated effect being frequently produced. At Gaur in Bengal the enormous Ādīna Masjid near Pānduā (*c.* 1360) has a huge courtyard surrounded by five aisles of arches on the Mecca side and three aisles on the remaining sides. These arcades, constructed of brick, originally carried 378 domes of identical size and design, a most unimaginative and monotonous conception. Nothing could be less characteristic of Hindu art.

At Gulbarga in the Deccan is another large and very remarkable mosque, the only one of its kind in India, built about the middle of the century. There is a tradition or legend to the effect that it was designed by an architect from Cordova, and certainly it resembles the famous mosque in that city to the extent that the whole area is covered. There are the usual arcades on the north, south, and east, with domes at each angle and a large dome over the *mihrāb*; but the roof over the remaining area (normally occupied by the open court) and over the sanctuary consists of sixty-three small domes resting on arcades. With its stilted domes, its foliated battlements, and its fine arcades of Persian arches this striking building is essentially 'Saracenic'. One wonders why the type was not reproduced elsewhere, and it has been suggested that the innovation of having the external arcade open to the public gaze was unpopular with the mullahs, who preferred the usual type enclosed within blank walls.

Returning to north India we find two interesting mosques at Jaunpur, near Vārānasī (Banāras): the mosque of Ibrāhīm Nāib Barbak in the fort, completed in 1377, and the fine Atāla Masjid (1408). The latter has a truly impressive propylon or central feature in the Persian style, with a great Persian arch over the entrance, but the walls of the square flanking towers, which look as though they ought to carry minarets, are battered and are frankly Hindu, as are the colonnades on either hand. Yet the interior arches and domes are distinctly Muhammadan in character.

The next century, from 1421 to 1526, was interrupted by frequent wars, and Delhi ceased to occupy its predominant position of control over the semi-independent kingdoms of Bengal, Jaunpur, Gujarāt, Mālwā, the Deccan, etc. Nevertheless many notable buildings were erected in the area, most of them being tombs. The group of three, known as Tīn Burj ('Three Towers') are rough and massive square structures with blank arcading on their exteriors, the Persian arch being used. The domes are rather lower than the typical high

Saracenic dome, and thus approximate nearer to the Hindu form. The tombs of Mubārak Shāh Sayyid and Muhammad Shāh Sayyid, in or near Khairpur, are plain octagonal structures with domes, 'kiosks' surrounding the domes, and external arcading. There is another fine but nameless tomb of the same type, square on plan, in Khairpur, with Hindu brackets over the doors and blue glazed tiles used in the Persian fashion. All these are works of the Sayyid period (1421–51). Rather later is the plain but impressive tomb of Sikandar Lodī (1517) at Khairpur, surrounded by a fortified enclosure. The chief Delhi mosques of the period are the beautiful Motī-kī-Masjid, a remarkable composition with high blank walls flanked by arcaded pavilions and with effective domes, and the splendid domed mosque of Khairpur.

The two chief mosques of this century at Jaunpur are the fine Jāmiʿ Masjid (begun in 1438) and the small Lāl Darwāza mosque. Both have been frequently illustrated, and both have the characteristics already mentioned in connection with Jaunpur mosques of the preceding period.

Gaur, the capital of Bengal at this time, similarly followed and developed its fourteenth-century tradition of brick arcuated construction, a curious medley of Muslim and Hindu methods. Among its buildings may be mentioned the so-called Fīrūz Shāh Mīnār (dated 1490), a curious structure resembling an Irish 'round tower' rather than a minaret; the Eklākhī mosque and tomb, a fine domed building 80 feet square of uncertain date; and the Sonā Masjid or 'Golden Mosque', so styled because of its gilded domes, erected in 1526, and now the finest ruin in Gaur. It has no fewer than forty-four brick domes over the principal *līwān* and there are six minarets, but the courtyard has practically disappeared. The exterior is a monumental and most unusual design, combining both Hindu and Saracenic elements, yet remaining decidedly original.

Another great centre of building activity at this period was Māndū, the capital of the old kingdom of Mālwā, in the former principality of Dhār. The Jāmiʿ Masjid, finished in 1454, is a magnificent congregational mosque, of which Fergusson says that 'for simple grandeur and expression of power it may, perhaps, be taken as one of the very best specimens now to be found in India'.[14] The great courtyard is surrounded by five arcades of pointed arches on the Mecca side, two on the east, and three on the north and south. There are large domes over the *mihrāb* and the north-west and south-west corners, the remainder of the arcades being covered by an enormous number of small domes. This is an essentially Muslim building, free from Hindu trabeated construction, and is carried out in red sandstone with marble enrichments. In south India the most notable Muhammadan architecture of the period 1421–1526 is to be found in the city of Bīdar, which supplanted Gulbarga in 1428. Here there are many interesting royal tombs, and a fine *madrasa* (college) and mosque.

But the most important architectural centre of the time was Ahmadābād, the capital of the kingdom of Gujarāt. Here the mosques and other buildings erected by the Muslims are predominantly Hindu in character, in spite of the occasional use of arches for symbolical purposes. The Jāmiʿ Masjid (begun

[14] Op. cit., Vol. 2, p. 249.

c. 1411) is a huge mosque of this type, all interest being concentrated on the Mecca *līwān*, which has 260 slender pillars supporting fifteen symmetrically arranged stone domes, built up of horizontally projecting courses in the Hindu fashion. The method of lighting the *līwān* is ingenious and admirably suited to climatic needs. At Sarkhej, about five miles from the city, is another large mosque completed in 1451, which is skilfully designed and is devoid of arches. The smaller mosques of Ahmadābād include those of Muhāfiz Khān, Sīdī Sayyid, and Rānī Sipārī: all of this period and all characterized by Hindu tradition. The Jāmiʿ Masjid at Dholkā (*c.* 1485) is another interesting example, and the Jāmiʿ Masjid at Champanīr (finished in 1508) is a large mosque resembling the Ahmadābād example in general arrangement but with two graceful minarets flanking the central doorway of the *līwān*, which has eleven domes in its roof as against fifteen at Ahmadābād. This is one of the largest and finest of Indian mosques; certainly one of the most Indian. The Nāgīna Masjid at Champanīr is a small and beautiful mosque of the same period. The most notable of many fine tombs in Ahmadābād are those of Sayyid Usmān (1460), Sayyid Mubārak (1484), and Rānī Sipārī (1514); and the tomb of Ahmad Ganj Baksh at Sarhej, begun in 1446. The second of these has arches, but for the most part the tombs of Gujarāt have domes carried on an arrangement of columns in the Hindu manner.

With the year 1526, when Bābur the Mughal king of Kābul, with the aid of 700 field-guns, defeated the vast army of the Sultan of Delhi on the plain of Pānīpat, we enter on the Mughal period of architecture, which lasted nominally until 1761, but which may more conveniently end for our purpose at the death of Aurangzeb in 1707. The Muslim buildings of these two centuries form a more distinctive and homogeneous group than the architecture described hitherto, which varied greatly from province to province, and they are more familiar to foreigners, all of whom have at least heard of the Tāj Mahal. The term 'Mughal' as applied to architecture has its drawbacks, but the fact remains that the buildings erected under the Mughal emperors were more definitely Muhammadan in character than those which preceded them and need to be classified as a separate school. The chief monuments were erected by Akbar (1556–1605) and Shāh Jāhān (1628–58); during the reign of Aurangzeb (1658–1707) architecture progressively declined.

Most of the buildings of this important period are to be found in the northwestern part of India, especially in Delhi, Āgrā, Lāhore, Fatehpur-Sīkrī, and Allahābād, with an isolated group at Bījāpur. Bābur established his capital at Āgrā, but his stormy reign only lasted four years, and only two of his numerous buildings remain: the mosques at Pānīpat and at Sambal in Rohilkhand. His son Humāyūn ruled from 1530 to 1540 and again from 1555 till his death in 1556, the intervening period being occupied by the reign of an Afghan usurper, Sher Shāh. Of buildings erected between 1526 and 1556, the best-known are in Delhi. They include the Jamālī Masjid (1528–36); the mosque of 'Isā Khān (1547); and his richly decorated tomb adjoining, with 'kiosks' grouped round the central dome, altogether a bold combination of Hindu and Islamic elements. Then there is the walled 'sixth city' of Delhi known as the Purānā Qilā, in which stands the splendid mosque of Sher Shāh, a clever blending of richness and refinement. At Fathābād, in the Hissār district of the

Panjāb, is a mosque (*c.* 1540) of massive proportions, well designed and decorated with tiles in Persian fashion. Sher Shāh's tomb stands on a high platform or podium of masonry in the middle of a lake at Sasarām in the Shāhābād district. At the corners of this podium are little domed kiosks, while two tiers of still smaller kiosks are grouped round the great octagon beneath the dome. This is a picturesque and delightful group, thoroughly Indo-Muslim.

One of the first monuments erected during Akbar's reign was the tomb of his father Humāyūn at Delhi, built in 1565–9 by Humāyūn's widow, who was afterwards buried there. It is surrounded by a formal garden which still retains its original layout, though many of the trees have vanished. The base of the tomb consists of a huge podium of red sandstone 22 feet high, with arches ornamented with white marble. From this noble foundation rises the tomb itself, 156 feet square and 125 feet high to the top of the dome. But though the building forms a square on plan, in fact it consists of a central domed octagon buttressed by four octagonal towers. The facing material is red sandstone, picked out with white marble, and the dome is faced with white marble. In shape the dome is slightly bulbous, thus introducing into India for the first time a feature characteristic of late work in Persia and Turkistān, and in construction it is double, another innovation. Its summit is crowned with the Arab finial, not the Hindu water-pot finial (*kalaśa*), and indeed it is a decidedly 'Saracenic' design. The exterior of the building has Persian arches and severely flat surfaces, relieved only by the brilliant marble inlay; and the kiosks on the angle towers are the sole legacy from Hindu tradition. Everything here suggests the experienced hand of a Muslim architect from Persia, or more probably from Samarqand, where the rulers had developed tomb-building to a fine art. It is generally considered that this splendid monument was the prototype of the Tāj Mahal. Other tombs in Delhi of Akbar's reign were erected in memory of Adham Khān and Atgah Khān (1566), two deadly rivals; and at Gwālior is the large and very fine tomb of Muhammad Ghaus. It is an Indo-Muslim hybrid, with Hindu kiosks at the angles of its podium.

Akbar resided in several cities, among them Allahābād, Lāhore, where he held his court from 1585 to 1598, and Āgrā, where he remained from that date until he died in 1605. At Āgrā he began building the famous fort in 1566, and within it he laid out the first part of the palace, which was continued by his successors and has since been so much altered that the various stages of extension are difficult to trace. The courtyard of the Jahāngīrī Mahal, probably Akbar's work in spite of its name, is an Indian design with square pillars and bracket-capitals, richly carved, and rows of small arches constructed in Hindu fashion without voussoirs. Other parts of Akbar's palace are slightly more Persian in style. The hall of the palace at Allāhābād (1583), with its boldly projecting veranda roof supported on rows of Hindu pillars, is a definitely Indian design, with hardly a single 'Saracenic' feature in it.

But the chief centre of Akbar's building activity is the city of Fatehpur-Sīkrī, twenty-three miles from Āgrā, which he founded in 1569 and was the seat of his court until 1584 or 1585. It was systematically laid out by him, has hardly been altered since, and is now deserted. It originally had a circumference of nearly seven miles, with walls on three sides pierced by nine gateways and a very large artificial lake on the fourth side. The Jāmi' Masjid of the city has a quadrangle 433 feet by 366 feet, surrounded by cloisters, with a vast number of small domed cells, one behind each bay of the cloister, which accommodated the Muslim teachers and their pupils, for this mosque served as the university of Fatehpur. The Mecca *līwān* with its three domes, its rows of pillars supporting the roof, and its lofty central propylon, follows an Indo-Muslim type we have met before. Two tombs stand in the quadrangle on the north side; there is a central gateway in the east colonnade; and in the middle of the south side is the magnificent Buland Darwāza ('high gateway'), 130 feet wide, 88 feet deep, and 134 feet high. Built to commemorate Akbar's conquests, it is universally recognized as one of his greatest buildings. Though its huge recessed and vaulted portal, with a wide rectangular frame of flat ornament, is essentially Persian in character, the kiosks on its roof give it an Indian flavour. The palace of Fatehpur-Sīkrī contains a number of remarkable buildings, including Akbar's office or *Dīwān-i-'Ām*, a Hindu design with a projecting veranda roof over a colonnade; and the wonderful Hall of Private Audience (*Dīwān-i-Khās*), a masterpiece of planning, construction, and ornament, all of a distinctly Indian character. The city also contains two large houses of notable and unusual form, the palaces of Rāja Bīrbal and of Jodh Bāī.

Akbar's mausoleum (*c.* 1593–1613) is at Sikandara near Āgrā. It is a colossal structure standing on an enormous arcaded podium 30 feet high and 320 feet square. The mausoleum proper is rather more than 150 feet square and several stories high, with stepped walls of marble pierced with delicate trellis-work. The roof of this structure is flat, with a small kiosk at each corner, and it seems probable, if not certain, that a central dome was originally intended to complete the group.

Akbar was followed by Jahāngīr (1605–28), who lived mainly at Lāhore, where he carried out the charming Motī Masjid ('Pearl Mosque') and a considerable amount of extension to the palace in the fort. Jahāngīr, even more than Akbar, was a lover of gardens, some of them laid out in patterns like a Persian carpet. He built 'paradises' at Udaipur, Srīnagar, and Fatehpur-Sīkrī; but the chief examples were the Shāh-Dāra or 'Garden of Delight' near Lāhore, surrounding his own mausoleum, and the garden of the tomb of I'timādu'd-daula at Āgrā. This last monument (1621–8) is noteworthy less for its general design than for its decoration, the exterior being covered with an inlay of *pietra dura*, a fashion which may have been imported and thereafter became popular.

The reign of Shāh Jahān (1628–58) was the golden age of Mughal architecture in India and produced a series of noble buildings. By far the most magnificent of all these was the celebrated Tāj Mahal at Āgrā (1631–53), erected in memory of his favourite queen, Mumtāz-i-Mahal ('the Elect of the Palace'), after whom it is named. The frequently quoted statement that the architect was an Italian has been denied by some historians. It is not incredible, though insufficiently documented, and may be a legend invented by those who consider the design of the building so marvellous that they wish to find a non-Indian authorship for it. Admittedly it is the greatest work of the Mughals, but it is a natural growth from the tomb of Humāyūn and to a lesser extent from certain others. But it is far superior to any of them in the dignity of its grouping and disposition, in the masterly contrast between the central dome and the slender minarets, in the chaste refinement and painstaking craftmanship of its details, and above all in the splendour of its materials. The design is more Persian and less Indian than any building we have encountered hitherto, yet nothing quite like it is to be found in Persia. The mausoleum itself closely resembles the tomb of Humāyūn, being a square (of 186 feet) with canted angles rather than an octagon. The square is composed of a high central block, octagonal within, buttressed at each angle by projections, with a great Persian portal between each pair. The slightly bulbous dome rises from a circular drum. All the arches are of Persian type. On each angle of the substructure stands a small domed kiosk. The beautiful central chamber is restfully lit through marble trellis-work in the window openings, to break the glare of the sun. The mausoleum stands on a terrace 22 feet high and 313 feet square with a cylindrical minaret, divided into stages by galleries, at each angle. The whole of these buildings are in dazzling white marble and large parts of them are inlaid with coloured marbles and precious stones in delicate Persian patterns. The group is surrounded by a lovely formal garden, with avenues of cypresses and long lily-ponds leading up the mausoleum, and the river which bounds the garden on the north provides marvellous reflections. The Tāj Mahal is one of the great buildings of the world, and has inspired every serious critic who has seen it to express his admiration.

Only second in importance to the Tāj is Shāh Jahān's work in the palace at Āgrā, carried out between 1638 and 1653, and including the *Dīwān-i-ʻĀm*, the *Dīwān-i-Khās*, and the Motī Masjid. In these various buildings, though red sandstone is used to some extent, white marble with coloured inlay is the prevailing material. Opulent elegance pervades the whole scheme, and the effect is a satisfactory blending of Indo-Muslim elements. Some writers indeed profess to rate the Motī Masjid higher than the Tāj. Shāh Jahān also laid out charming gardens at Delhi and Lāhore, and in the latter city the mosque of Wazīr Khān (1634) was built in his reign. It is the chief mosque of the town, Persian in general character, and freely decorated with coloured and glazed tiles. At Ajmer are some beautiful marble pavilions on the embankment of the lake, also due to Shāh Jahān.

His work at Delhi, too, was considerable. It included the walls of the 'seventh city' of Delhi called after him 'Shāhjahānābād', and built between 1638 and 1658. Its fine walls and gates have been well preserved, as have his fort and the palace within it. Bounded on one side by the river, this vast complex of buildings, covering an area over 1,000 yards by 600 yards, is admirably laid out in an ordered sequence of courts, but it suffered severely from British military occupation in the unimaginative period before Lord Curzon came on the scene. As in the other Mughal palaces described, the two chief buildings are the *Dīwān-i-ʻĀm* and the *Dīwān-i-Khās*, and here they are of great beauty, richly decorated with marble inlay, and Indo-Muslim in character.

Shāh Jahān also built in 1644–58 the huge Jāmiʻ Masjid near the fort at Delhi, with a quadrangle 325 feet square and two fine cylindrical minarets. Its outstanding feature is its commanding position, for it is placed on a high podium, a most unusual arrangement for a Muhammadan mosque. Whereas the domes, the minarets, and certain other parts of the building are Persian, the general effect is hybrid, and the angle pavilions are definitely Indian. Marble is used here too, but in combination with red sandstone.

At Bījāpur, which was the capital of an independent kingdom from 1489 until it was taken by Aurangzeb in 1686, there was a flourishing school throughout the Mughal period, characterized by many distinctive features of design. These included the use of purely ornamental minarets—the call to prayer being chanted by the muezzin from a small platform elsewhere—rich cornices, and ingenious dome-construction in which pendentives were employed. Fergusson wrote of the architecture of Bījāpur in terms of the highest eulogy. Cousens, whose survey of the buildings of Bījāpur provides a mine of information, says that 'there is abundant evidence to show that first-class architects were induced to come south from Northern India' to Bījāpur, while there are traces of Hindu tradition in some of the buildings, proving that the Hindu craftsmen retained some of their individuality. Bījāpur at the height of its prosperity, early in the seventeenth century, is said to have contained nearly a million inhabitants and some 1,600 mosques; but during the Marāthā supremacy in the eighteenth century it fell into ruin and its buildings were freely plundered for stone and other material. They were then smothered in jungle up to 1883, when Bījāpur became a British headquarters.

Lack of space forbids more than a mention of the chief examples. The large but incomplete Jāmiʿ Masjid, commenced about 1576, is one of the finest mosques in India, severely plain but relieved by delicate *claire-voies* (pierced windows). In front of the *mihrāb* is a large dome of unusual construction, the external appearance of which would be improved by the addition of a drum. The rest of the Mecca *līwān* is covered with a number of small stone domes, supported on piers and arches but concealed externally by a flat terrace roof. The gorgeous gilt and coloured *mihrāb* is of later date (1636). The numerous halls, pavilions, and mosques in the citadel include the graceful Mihtar Mahal (*c.* 1620), a small mosque with a striking gate-tower, said by Fergusson to be 'equal if not superior to anything in Cairo'; the Sāt Manzil, a small palace of many stories; the Gegen Mahal (? 1561), an assembly hall with a noble archway; and the Jalamandir, a dainty water-pavilion. Elsewhere in the city are two large isolated monuments: the tomb of Ibrāhīm II and his family (1626–33), commonly called the 'Ibrāhīm Rauza', and the mausoleum (*Gol Gumbaz*) of Muhammad, his successor, which was finished in 1659. The former is chiefly notable for its rich decoration, the latter for the remarkable and daring construction of its enormous dome.

Shāh Jahān, whose private life was less creditable than his architecture, was deposed in 1658 by Aurangzeb, his third son. The buildings of Aurangzeb's reign are inferior in all respects to those of Shāh Jahān. Among them may be mentioned the Motī Masjid at Delhi (1659) with delicate marble decoration; and the Bādshāhī mosque at Lāhore (1674), which is almost a copy of the Jāmiʿ Masjid at Delhi, though inferior to it in several respects. From that date onwards Muslim architecture in India declined but never died. The superb standard set by the Tāj was imitated in buildings of all kinds—mosques and tombs, palaces and houses—till the British finally introduced Indo-Muslim railway-stations and hotels. Thus the well-known buildings erected by Tīpū Sultān at Srīrangapatnam in the eighteenth century are Muslim architecture of a sort, though in its most Indian form, but they are decadent in their elegance.

Undoubtedly the long occupation of the chief Muslim cities of India by British army officers with little sympathy for historical architecture led to clumsy and sometimes barbarous treatment of certain buildings, such as those royal palaces which lay inside forts. But under the administration of Lord Curzon the care of ancient monuments began to receive really serious attention. It seems that historical buildings in India may now be regarded as sacrosanct, but neither the official mind nor the intelligentsia in India appears to have any clear idea as to the proper relation between traditional architecture and modern needs in that country. Was it really desirable, as Havell so fiercely contended, that the New Delhi should be designed on old Hindu lines, with its secretarial offices and its sanitary conveniences hidden behind imitation temple facades? Is the style of the Tāj Mahal, erected by an enormously rich emperor three centuries ago, suitable in any way to the severely economical requirements of modern commerce and industry?

At a recent London exhibition of Indian architects' designs it was evident that the Indian architect of today is producing schemes and erecting buildings in every shade of fashion from the archaic Hindu temple style to the latest fad in reinforced concrete and stainless steel, while the outstanding design in the exhibition—for a mosque at Bhopāl, with a charming Cairene minaret and admirable traditional detail—bore a Muslim signature and an office-address in Baker Street, London. It will be interesting to see how India will regard her architectural heritage in the next generation: whether she will continue and revive the Indo-Muslim style of the Mughals; whether she will follow a modified European fashion, with domes and minarets added here and there; or whether she will evolve some new formula, not necessarily based on any European precedent, to meet the changed economic conditions and social habits of the day.[15]

[15] Though we have somewhat abridged the final paragraphs of this chapter, we leave them essentially as they were written forty years ago. The exhibition referred to has long been forgotten, but the author's remarks on it may still be valid, despite many impressive buildings in modern style recently erected in India and the importation of the great architect le Corbusier to plan Chandīgarh, the new capital of the Indian state of Panjāb. Typical of much modern Indian architecture is the Ashoka Hotel, New Delhi, which, further developing the hybrid styles of the government buildings of New Delhi, is an unsatisfactory mixture of Hindu, Muslim, and twentieth-century functional features. [Ed.]

CHAPTER XXIII

Medieval Indian Miniature Painting

by PRAMOD CHANDRA

THE painting of the period ushered in by the rise of Islam to political supremacy in India can be divided into two broad movements. One of these exemplifies an attempt to preserve past traditions with almost superstitious tenacity. These traditions, though often emptied of meaning, retained at least the trappings of outer form which, in more propitious times, were again to quicken with life. The second movement is rooted in new artistic forms introduced primarily from Iran in the wake of the Muslim invasion. The old and the new, the 'foreign' and the 'indigenous', had gradually to come to terms with each other; and this process, in which the individual qualities of each were enhanced and brought to a new fulfilment, resulted in some of Indian painting's greatest achievements. A mode of development in which fresh stimulus is received, reinterpreted, and transformed is hardly new to Indian art and can be seen at almost every great epoch in its history. It is true, though, that in the period with which we are dealing, this process, so natural to the Indian genius, is to a considerable extent masked and obscured by the iconoclastic zeal and religious fanaticism of the invaders, who set themselves in conscious opposition to the infidel and his traditions. But however repressive some of them may have been, the forces making for synthesis and assimilation were ever at work beneath the surface. In this context it is hardly surprising to notice the striking parallelism between the development of Maurya art in the third century B.C. and Mughal art 1,800 years later in the sixteenth century A.D., and the way in which styles of Iranian inspiration in each case were quickly and dramatically transformed under the impetus of the Indian artistic environment and taste.

That the early Muslim kings of India who ruled before the Mughal emperors patronized painting has been denied by some, mostly on grounds of their religious scruples, in spite of the rather explicit statements in contemporary literature to the contrary. But this view, like many others on the painting of this period, is proving to be quite incorrect. Patient exploration and study is constantly adding to the list of illustrated manuscripts produced between the thirteenth and sixteenth centuries, even though it must be admitted that they indicate little that is distinctive, much of the work being a somewhat impoverished imitation of the various styles of contemporary Iran. A manuscript of the *Būstān* in the National Museum of India painted at Māndū for the Sultan Nāsir Shāh Khaljī (A.D. 1500–10)[1] differs little but for colour from the sub-schools of Herāt; significantly enough, however, an illustrated manuscript of the *Ni'mat Nāma* of almost the same date (*c.* A.D.

[1] R. Ettinghausen, 'The Bustan Ms of Nasir-Shah Khalji', *Mārg*, Vol. 12, No. 3 (1959), pp. 42–3.

1500),[2] though indebted to the contemporary style of Shīrāz, shows pronounced Indian features, particularly in draughtsmanship and the rendering of female figures, and may therefore be counted as representative of a stage of artistic development when Persian influences are beginning to be assimilated by the Indian painter, a process that is of profound importance in the creation of the Mughal, and to a much lesser extent of the Rājasthānī style in the sixteenth century.

It would be well at this stage to consider the state of Indian painting aside from these works of Indo-Persian character, a term that may be appropriately applied to what amounts, in a majority of instances, to little more than another provincial Persian idiom. The national style of the period was the western Indian style, found in one version or another over almost all of India. Surviving examples indicate that the greatest concentration was in Gujarāt and that the main patronage was provided by the Jainas, though this may be accidental and occasioned by the especial care with which that community preserved its sacred books. Manuscripts with Hindu themes are known as well, and we also have illustrations done in Rājasthān, Delhi, and Jaunpur in eastern India. The favourite Jaina texts chosen for illustration were the *Kalpasūtra* and *Kālakāchārya-kathā*, large numbers of which have been preserved, though works of distinguished quality are rare, and much of the painting may be characterized fairly as mechanical workshop output. The style is emphatically linear, the forms flat, with sharp angular contours, the faces generally in profile but with both eyes shown, one of them protruding into empty space. The colours are few, red, green, blue, yellow, and black predominating, a monochrome patch of red often constituting the background.

Difficult though it may be to believe at first sight, the western Indian style is directly descended from the classic style of ancient India established around the fifth century A.D., so brilliantly represented and preserved at Ajantā, and is the result of a progressive simplification, abstraction, and linearization, the various stages of which are clearly demonstrable. Though not immune to stylistic change, the western Indian style was nevertheless remarkably conservative, adhering closely to set formulae right up to the end of the sixteenth century, around which time it gives way under the pressure of rising new schools.

Though the conservative character of the western Indian style is generally accepted, it has nevertheless to be realized that around the middle of the fifteenth century the style does begin to show signs of real change, though it is not clear whether this is due to acquaintance with paintings of Persian derivation or due to a natural development of its own inherent tendencies. Paintings illustrating this change are rare, but are clearly represented in three fine illustrated manuscripts, the *Kalpasūtra* painted at Māndū in 1439, a *Kālakāchārya-kathā* of about the same date and provenance, and the *Kalpasūtra* produced at Jaunpur in eastern Uttar Pradesh dated A.D. 1465.[3] The line

[2] R. Skelton, 'The Ni'mat Nama: a Landmark in Malwa Painting', ibid., pp. 44–50.

[3] Moti Chandra and K. Khandalavala, 'A Consideration of an Illustrated Ms from Maṇḍapadurga (Mandu) dated A.D. 1439', *Lalit Kala*, 6 (Oct. 1959), 8–29, and 'An Illustrated Kalpasūtra Painted at Jaunpur in A.D. 1465', ibid. 12 (Oct. 1962), 9–15; P. Chandra, 'A Unique Kālakacārya-kathā Ms in the Style of the Mandu Kalpasūtra of A.D. 1439', *Bulletin of the American Academy of Benares*, 1 (Nov. 1967), 1–10.

flows more smoothly, the forms are fuller, and the figures begin to lose their hieratic, effigy-like character. It should be obvious that these manuscripts herald the birth of a new style, and that this new style did come into being and was flourishing by at least the early years of the sixteenth century is confirmed by the discovery of an illustrated manuscript of the *Āranyaka Parvan* of the *Mahābhārata* dated A.D. 1516 and of a *Mahāpurāna* manuscript dated A.D. 1540.[4] The promise of this new style is carried to fulfilment in the splendid *Bhāgavata Purāna*, now unfortunately dispersed in collections all over the world, and the *Chaurapanchāśika* of Bilhana in the museum at Ahmedābād.[5] A more refined version of this style is to be found in manuscripts like the *Chandāyana* of Mullā Dāūd in the Prince of Wales Museum,[6] Bombay, which is marked by a preference for pale and cool shades of colour, of Persian inspiration, together with a delicate and fine line.

The first half of the sixteenth century, as far as painting is concerned, was a time of fervent activity. We find in existence at this time Indo-Persian styles, patronized presumably by Muslim courtly circles, a western Indian style, and new styles developing from it which have not yet been named but are represented by the group of manuscripts, including the *Mahābhārata* and the *Chaurapanchāśika*, mentioned above.

Thus the stage was set when in A.D. 1556 Akbar, a grandson of Bābur, the founder of the Mughal Empire in India, ascended the throne. The young emperor had himself received training in painting as a child and his teacher, Khwāja 'Abd us-Samad of Shīrāz together with Mīr Saiyyid 'Alī of Tabrīz had been leading artists in Iran before they came to India at the invitation of Humāyūn. Under the general supervision of these two artists and the discerning enthusiasm of Akbar, whose role as a patron was of the greatest importance, a vigorous atelier of painters drawn from all parts of the Indian Empire grew up at the imperial court. These artists brought with them elements of the various traditions to which they belonged and, in what is probably the earliest work of the Mughal School, the *Tūtī Nāma* of the Cleveland Museum of Art,[7] we can actually see the process by which their disparate idioms were welded to form something new—a style which represents a synthesis of the Persian and the Indian but is different from both. Very soon we have the fully formed Mughal style in the unusually large illustrations of the *Dāstān i-Amīr Hamza*,[8] the most ambitious undertaking of the atelier of Akbar, quite unlike Persian work in its leanings towards naturalism, and filled with sweeping movement, bright colour, and an innate sense of wonder.

The *Hamza Nāma* was certainly completed by A.D. 1575 and an undertaking of this scale was never again attempted by the Akbarī atelier. It was followed

[4] Moti Chandra and Karl Khandalavala, 'An Illustrated Ms of the Āraṇyaka Parvan in the Collection of the Asiatic Society of Bombay', *Journal of the Asiatic Society of Bombay*, 38 (1963), 116–21.

[5] K. Khandalavala and Moti Chandra, *New Documents of Indian Painting*, Bombay, 1969, pp. 83–4, 79–83.

[6] Ibid., pp. 91–8.

[7] S. E. Lee and P. Chandra, 'A Newly Discovered Tūti-nāma and the Continuity of the Indian Tradition of Ms. Painting', *Burlington Magazine*, 55 (Dec. 1963), 547–54.

[8] H. Glück, *Die indischen Miniaturen des Haemsae-Romanes*, Vienna, 1925.

by a group of profusely illustrated historical manuscripts which share several hundred paintings between them. The earliest of these now known is an incomplete history of the house of Tīmūr, once extending to the twenty-second year of Akbar's reign and now in the Khudā Bakhsh Library at Patnā;[9] and one of the most accomplished is the *Akbar Nāma* in the Victoria and Albert Museum, London.[10] The Patnā manuscript can be dated about A.D. 1584 while the *Akbar Nāma* should not be more than a decade later. The miniatures are smaller in size than those of the *Hamza Nāma* and the most notable change from the point of view of style is an ebbing of the explosive energy and movement and its gradual replacement by a studious striving for delicacy and refinement. Most of the paintings are the result of joint work by two artists, one of them the designer, generally an important painter, if not a master, and the other the artist who actually applied the colour and 'painted' the picture. To these is sometimes added a specialist in portraiture and, in rare instances, we get the name of the artist who mixes the colours, indicating the close attention paid to the manufacture and use of colour.

Stylistically belonging to the same phase as the historical manuscripts are the remarkable illustrations to the Persian adaptations of the Hindu epics, the *Mahābhārata* and the *Rāmāyana*, the imperial copies of which are now in the collection of the Mahārāja of Jaipur.[11] The Mughal painters, most of whom were Hindus, here had a subject close to their hearts, and they rose to great heights, revealing an endlessly inventive imagination and great resourcefulness in illustrating the myths.

The closing phases of the style of Akbar are marked by the growth of a very personal and intimate idiom, shown in a series of illustrations to works of classical Persian poetry, notably the *Khamsa* of Nizāmī in the British Museum, a *Khamsa* of Amīr Khusrau Dihlavī in the Walters Art Gallery, Baltimore, a *Dīwān* of Hāfiz in the Rezā Library at Rāmpur, and other poetical manuscripts.[12] The illustrations to each of these manuscripts are relatively few and each painting is executed by a single artist who lavishes upon the work all the skill of his art, filling it with exquisite detail and the most sumptuous and delicate colour.

The outstanding painters of the reign of Akbar, according to the perceptive court chronicler Abu'l Fazl 'Allāmī, were Daswant and Basāwan. Of Daswant's work the greatest part is preserved in the Jaipur *Mahābhārata*, and, though another painter is associated with him in these paintings, his genius is manifest. Basāwan's paintings are more broadly distributed and we have in him a painter of extraordinary accomplishment, who builds primarily in colour, prefers full and voluminous forms, and shows a great understanding of human emotions and psychology.

The painting of Jahāngīr's reign (A.D. 1605–27) departs markedly from the

[9] A. Muqtadir, 'Note on a Unique History of Timur', *Journal of the Bihar and Orissa Research Society*, 3 (1917), 263–75.

[10] E. Wellesz, 'An Akbar Namah Ms.', *Burlington Magazine*, 80 (1942), 135–41.

[11] T. H. Hendley, *Memorials of the Jeypore Exhibition*, Vol. 4, London, 1884.

[12] F. R. Martin, *Miniature Painting and Painters of Persia, India, and Turkey*, London, 1912, Pls. 178–81; E. Grübe, *Classical Style in Islamic Painting*, Venice, 1968; and S. C. Welch, 'Miniatures from a Ms. of the Diwan of Hafiz', *Mārg*, Vol. 11, No. 3 (1958), pp. 56–62.

style of the Akbar period, though many elements that come to the fore had been previously anticipated. The tradition of book illustration is gradually abandoned and there is a pronounced emphasis on portraiture. The great darbar pictures, thronged with courtiers and retainers, are essentially an agglomeration of a large number of portraits. The compositions of these paintings are also much more restrained, being calm and formal. The colours are subdued and harmonious, as is the movement, and the exquisitely detailed brushwork is a marvel to behold. A large number of studies of birds and animals were also produced for the Emperor, who was passionately interested in natural life, and who never ceased to observe, describe, measure, and record the things rare and curious with which the natural world abounds.

To Jahāngīr, painting is the favourite art; he prides himself on his connoisseurship, and greatly honours his favourite painters. Abu'l Hasan, the son of Āqā Rizā, who migrated to the Mughal Court from Herāt, is most admired; Ustād Mansūr is singled out for praise as a painter of animals and birds; and Bishandās is said to be unequalled in his age for taking likenesses. The works of these painters bear out the Emperor's judgement. There were other painters of exceptional quality, though they did not find their way into the Emperor's memoirs, and of these Manohar, son of Basāwan, Govardhan, and Daulat are easily as great as the Emperor's favourites.

With Shāh Jahān, whose main interest was architecture, but who was also a keen connoisseur of painting, the Jahāngīrī traditions are continued, but in a modified way. The compositions become static and symmetrical, the colour heavier, the texture and ornament more sumptuous. The freshness of drawing, the alert and sensitive observation of people and things, is overlaid by a weary maturity, resulting not in the representation of living beings but in effigies with masked countenances. The output of the imperial atelier also appears to decline so that there are far fewer works available, and of these the *Shāh Jahān Nāma* in the collection of Her Majesty Queen Elizabeth,[13] looted during the sack of Lucknow by British troops, is the finest and most representative example of the style. There are also several portraits of Shāh Jahān and the grandees of the court which again demonstrate the movement towards richness and luxury at the expense of life.

During the reign of Aurangzeb (A.D. 1658–1707) patronage seems increasingly to shift away from the court; works which can be identified as products of the imperial atelier are extremely few and continue the style of Shāh Jahān. This would at least indicate a lack of interest, though Aurangzeb's antipathy to the arts has been greatly exaggerated. The fairly large number of paintings assigned to his reign were probably executed for patrons other than the Emperor, this leading to an inevitable decline, for Mughal painting was essentially a carefully nurtured court art, and its removal from the natural habitat led to its impoverishment and debasement. There was a brief revival during the reign of Muhammad Shāh (A.D. 1719–48), but the rapid disintegration of the Mughal Empire sealed the fate of the arts which were intimately associated with it. Artists dispersed to the various provincial centres where the great nobles were establishing kingdoms of their own, and there, on occasion,

[13] L. Ashton (ed.), *Art of India and Pakistan*, London, 1949, Pl. 138.

the new environment induced a brief spasm of life. The decay, however, was irreversible, and was reinforced by the change in taste, progressively corrupted by ill-understood Western influences. Thus when the Mughal style finally passed into oblivion it was natural for it to be replaced by the so-called Company School, catering specifically to the patronage of the British ruling class in India and to the Indian gentry whose traditional tastes had been already subverted.

The Rājasthānī style of painting, spread mainly over the various states of Rājasthān and adjacent areas, came into being at approximately the same time as the Mughal School, but represents a direct and natural evolution from the western Indian style, and from painting in the style of the Bombay Asiatic Society's *Mahābhārata*, rather than a revolutionary transformation of those traditions, as was the case with the Mughal style. The subject-matter here is essentially Hindu, its primary concern the Krishna myth, which was the central element in the rapid expansion of devotional cults at this time. The style, in marked contrast to the naturalistic preferences of Mughal painting, remains abstract and hieratic, and its language, though mystical and symbolic, must have immediately evoked a sympathetic response in the heart of the Hindu viewer. Though the Mughal and the Rājasthānī styles were operating on different levels of reference, some contact between them is clearly evidenced by shared conventions and formulae; these similarities should not blind us, however, from realizing that for the most part the Rājasthānī schools were essentially unaffected by the Mughal, at least during the sixteenth and seventeenth centuries. This was true to a lesser degree in the eighteenth century, when the distance between the two styles was narrowed, but was never entirely closed.

The Rājasthānī style developed several distinct schools, their boundaries seemingly coinciding with the various states of Rājasthān, notably Mewār, Būndī, Kotah, Mārwār, Kishangarh, Jaipur (Amber), Bikāner (which is something of an exception to the rule in being quite heavily indebted to the Mughal School), and yet others whose outlines are slowly beginning to emerge. The School of Mewār is among the most important, producing pictures of considerable power and emotional intensity during the seventeenth century, the early phase between 1600 and 1650 marked by the dominance of the School of Sāhibdīn, a painter whose name has been fortunately preserved. The fervour of the early years begins to subside towards the close of the seventeenth century, and eighteenth-century paintings, though often full of charm, never capture the earlier mood. The School of Būndī, sharing slightly more with the Mughal School than does the School of Mewār, comes into being about the end of the sixteenth century and is distinguished by a more refined line and a love for vivid, rhythmic movement which survives well into the eighteenth and even the nineteenth century in the spectacular scenes of sport and hunt painted in the neighbouring state of Kotah. The vitality of many Rājasthānī schools, even in the nineteenth century, when the Mughal style had collapsed and shifting patronage under Western influence made survival difficult, is really quite remarkable.

Although the themes of Bikāner painting are the same as other Rājasthānī schools, the delicacy of line and colour are strong Mughal features which first become evident in painting of the mid-seventeenth century executed by artists imported from Delhi, and these features are retained to some extent even when the school begins to conform more closely to the neighbouring schools of Rājasthān. Of these, the School of Mārwār is of primary importance, and though its history in the seventeenth century, unlike that of Mewār, is hardly clear, it produced works of exceptional quality in the eighteenth century, all characterized by strong, almost dazzling colour, and by a direct, unhesitating statement. The School of Kishangarh, filled with lyrical mysticism, is one of great charm and finesse, owing much to Mughal technique of the eighteenth century. It is, however, much more consciously stylized, and, in its best works, quite transcends the inane secularism of the late Mughal style from which it was derived. The state of Jaipur, known as Amber in the seventeenth century, had attained a position of great wealth and influence because of its close alliance with the Mughal power. One would therefore expect a flourishing school there, but little of its early history in the seventeenth century has come to light. A rather formal and mannered style is evident during the eighteenth century, and some exceptionally fine paintings were done toward its closing years when there was a brilliant phase during the reign of Savāī Pratāp Singh (A.D. 1718–1803).

The Pahārī style is yet another important school of miniature painting, so called because of its prevalence in the former principalities of the Himālayan foot-hills, stretching roughly from Jammū to Garhwāl. Two broad phases have been distinguished. The earliest Pahārī paintings are marked by bold colour, vigorous drawing, and what can be called a primitive and intense expression, analogous to the mood of some early Rājasthānī painting of the first half of the seventeenth century, though the Pahārī examples are later in date and executed on a much more sophisticated and accomplished level. The themes are Hindu, and shared in common with Rājasthānī painting. The name most commonly used for this kind of work is the 'Basohlī' style, after a state of that name, but paintings in a similar idiom are found in other hill states also. The later phase of the Pahārī style that comes into its own about the third quarter of the eighteenth century is similarly called the 'Kāngrā' style after a state of that name, though it too is found in other hill centres. Considerable confusion thus exists with regard to the nomenclature, and an orderly classification suited to the nature of the material would considerably help understanding. What is commonly understood as the 'Kāngrā' style, however, stands in somewhat marked contrast to the 'Basohlī' School, being characterized by a sentimental and lyrical mood, smooth rhythms carried by curving lines, and cool and refreshing colour. The reasons for this dramatic change in the mood of Pahārī painting are probably to be sought in a strong incursion of the later Mughal style of the plains, but these influences were once again radically transformed in the course of assimilation, a process, it must be remembered, with which Indian art is hardly unfamiliar. The Pahārī style also lasted on into the nineteenth century, sharing in the general decline and not quite displaying the tenacity of some of the contemporary schools of Rājasthān.

More poetic in mood, though similar in technique to the Mughal School, the Deccanī style again evolves as a combination of foreign (Persian and

Turkish) and somewhat strongly indigenous elements inherited seemingly through the artistic traditions of the Vijayanagara Empire. The various kingdoms of the Deccan plateau evolved idioms with their own distinctive flavour from the middle of the sixteenth to the nineteenth century. Of these, the Bījāpur version, particularly under the patronage of the remarkable Ibrāhim 'Ādil Shāh II (1580–1627) is marked by a most poetic quality. Important work was also done in the powerful sultanates of Golconda and Ahmednagar. Contemporary with the Mughal School, the Deccanī styles were in close contact with it, and their development too follows a parallel course. In the eighteenth century, Hyderābād, the capital of the Āsāf Jāhī Dynasty, became a very vigorous centre of painting, a large volume of work similar in mood to the output of provincial Mughal centres being produced there.

The history of Indian painting from the thirteenth to the nineteenth century is filled with many riches and what has been said above provides only the faintest indications of its wealth. The Mughal School has been studied for the longest time, so that it is more or less well known, but, as far as Rājasthānī painting is concerned, most of the material has come to light only during the last twenty years or so and our knowledge of it is at best elementary. The broad currents are becoming clear but the details remain obscure, and fresh discoveries make constant reappraisal necessary. Many difficulties remain in the understanding of the Pahārī style, though its obvious beauty and charm evoke an immediate response, and the same can be said about the various schools of the Deccan. In spite of the fact that a great deal remains to be done before we can truly appreciate the achievements of Indian miniature painting, it is apparent that these were considerable. Lacking the monumentality of architecture, it is nevertheless of the greatest vitality and richness, and, on a more intimate level, as precious an expression of artistic skill.

PART THREE

CHALLENGE AND RESPONSE: THE COMING OF THE WEST

CHAPTER XXIV

The Portuguese

by J. B. HARRISON

AT the turn of the fifteenth century two invaders approached India: the Portuguese by sea, the Mughals by land. Both initiated great and lasting changes. But whereas the Mughal contribution, political, administrative, and cultural, has been justly appreciated, that of the Portuguese has been both undervalued and almost perversely misunderstood. In popular mythology the Portuguese contribution to India has often seemed narrowed down to just two personages—Vasco da Gama, dauntless navigator and to Europeans 'discoverer' of India, and Albuquerque, the creator by terror and the sword of a brief sea-borne Portuguese empire in Asia. For after 1515, by which time the work of these two was done, it is somehow assumed that a decadent obscurity set in, fitfully lit by the flash of swords at Diu or the glare of Inquisition fires, but otherwise steadily darkening under Portuguese intolerance, miscegenation, and greed.

Yet to Indian contemporaries it must have been the growing prosperity, the strength and resilience, the stability and permanence of the Portuguese power in India which was most notable until well into the seventeenth century and even beyond. Within fifty years of da Gama's arrival the Portuguese had occupied some sixty miles of coast around Goa, with territories stretching up to thirty miles inland. Northwards from Bombay to Damão, the key, with Diu across the Gulf, to the approaches to rich Gujarāt, they occupied a still larger though narrower tract with four important ports and several hundred towns and villages. Southwards they held a long loosely linked chain of sea-port fortresses and trading-posts—Onor, Barcelor, Mangalor, Cannanor, Cranganor, Cochin, and Quilon. But though their power here in Malabār was more fragmented, it was sufficient, when supplemented by judicious subsidies, to ensure influence or control over the local rulers who were masters of the pepper, ginger, and cinnamon lands. Even on the east coast at Negapatam and San Thomé further military posts and settlements were created, while, as the sixteenth century drew to a close, a wealthy settlement grew up at Huglī in Bengal and direct Portuguese rule was established over the lowlands of Ceylon.

The *Estado da India* was thus a larger element in the Indian state system than is sometimes recalled. The Portuguese early abandoned that Western attitude which had denied membership of the community of states to non-Christian powers, recognizing that the Persians, Mughals, and Deccanīs were 'most powerful nations, politic, well trained in war'. Equally, Indian governors and rulers soon gave their recognition to the *Estado* as a settled and accepted presence. Envoys and resident ambassadors were exchanged between Goa and most of the major Indian states. Treaties with Goa concluded by Deccan sultans in 1570 were regularly renewed as long as their kingdoms lasted. In the successive balances of power struck between Vijayanagara and the Deccan sultans, between the Deccanīs and the Mughals, between the Mughals and the Marāthās, the Portuguese were always one element, thrown in upon the weaker side.

The Portuguese power in India was also notably long-lasting. The number of European troops garrisoning the string of forts and manning the fleets which annually cruised against pirates and smugglers was never more than a few thousand. But behind them was the much larger body of settlers, the *casados* or married men, who from Albuquerque's day had been encouraged to take local wives. In Goa and the Province of the North they established themselves as village landlords—often improving landlords, building new roads and irrigation works, introducing new crops like tobacco and cashew nut, or superior plantation varieties of coconut. In the larger cities, Goa and Cochin especially, they settled as artisans and master-craftsmen. And everywhere they were traders. Such men, holding villages for three lives or organized in guilds, felt, and were, established. As a Dutch governor, Van Diemen, put it, 'Most of the Portuguese in India look upon this region as their fatherland, and think no more about Portugal. They drive little or no trade thither, but content themselves with the port-to-port trade of Asia, just as if they were natives thereof and had no other country.' Their permanent presence was instrumental in establishing Portuguese cultural influence. But with their families, their often considerable bodies of household slaves, and the horsemen or musketeers which as landowners they were required to maintain, they also formed the major element in the defensive strength of the *Estado*. They defeated a most determined, lengthy, conjoint attack by the sultans of Bījāpur and Ahmadnagar and the Zamorin of Calicut in 1569. It was with their aid that the loose-knit Province of the South survived for over 150 years, Malabār only falling finally to the Dutch in 1663 after a four-year siege of Cochin. And equally it was because they were fighting for their homes that the Portuguese in the Province of the North, the real settler country, held out still longer against Marāthā attack, only surrendering after a most desperate defence of Bassein in May 1739. It was almost in the fitness of things that when Goa, Damão, and Diu were overrun by the Indian army in 1961, they were the last foreign possessions in the continent.

What was the nature of this *Estado da India*, which for two and a half centuries was a considerable, and for another two still a minor element in the Indian political system? A casual reading of Barros, Couto, or Castanheda, the great Portuguese chroniclers of its rise, would suggest that it was based solely upon force, upon a policy of calculated terror ashore and piracy at sea, sustained by a combination of reckless valour and technical skill. But these historians were writing in a court tradition for a military nobility, whose vanity was best flattered by heroic descriptions of every skirmish in which they were engaged. And even from their works, or more clearly still from those of Correa and Bocarro, it is not difficult to see that the Portuguese in Asia were more concerned with trade than conquest, once the necessary minimum of coastal bases had been acquired.

The Portuguese were certainly ready to use force where it would pay. But their numbers were small, and their technical superiority much less considerable than was once supposed. In Malabār and Ceylon in the sixteenth century their use of body armour, of matchlockmen, of guns landed from the ships, might be a military innovation. But to Gujarāt, the Deccan, and the Mughal north it was the Mamelukes and Ottomans who had demonstrated the use of fire-arms and defensive works, and at a level of sophistication which the Portuguese could barely match. The Portuguese may have contributed by example to the Mughal use of field guns, the 'artillery of the stirrup', and to the more aggressive and important role given to bodies of matchlockmen by Dārā Shukōh and Aurangzeb. But it was only late in the seventeenth century that the royal arsenals at Goa and at Macao in China began to produce guns which were clearly superior in finish and lightness to Indian pieces and therefore sought after by Indian powers.[1] The one major military contribution made by the Portuguese ashore was the system of drilling bodies of infantry, grouped and disciplined upon the Spanish model, introduced in the 1630s as a counter to Dutch pressure. Taken up first by the French and English, then by the Marāthās and Sikhs, such sepoy armies became new instruments of empire in India.

At sea the Portuguese were more clearly carriers of improved techniques. The heavier construction of their multi-decked ships, designed to ride out Atlantic gales rather than run before the regular monsoons, permitted a heavier armament. Their use of castled prow and stern, an admirable device for repelling or launching boarding parties, was also new. Indian builders adapted both to their own use. But some of the Portuguese lead was organizational—as in the creation of royal arsenals and dockyards, the maintenance of a regular system of pilotage and cartography, or the pitting of organized state forces against private merchant shipping. Their legacy here was partly secured, it may be thought, by the Mughals and Marāthās, who both developed auxiliary naval forces. But the more certain heirs were other Europeans, the Dutch and English, in Asia.

The Portuguese used their real superiority at sea, limited though it always was by the very vastness of the ocean world which had opened up to them in Asia, to establish new patterns of trade. An obsession with the conquests of Albuquerque has obscured what is quite clear in the history written by Correa, for example, that the driving impulse behind the search for a sea-route to India was commercial, and that the most clear-cut orders were given and quite strenuous efforts made to secure trade without war. There occurred, it is true, an initial period of violence, sometimes provoked by the hostility of existing merchant communities, more frequently by the rashness and personal greed of Portuguese commanders on the spot. In the western Indian Ocean there was a longer-term constraint imposed by the posting of annual Portuguese fleets upon the main sea-lanes to make sure that local shipping took out Portuguese safe-conducts or *cartazes*, which prescribed what ports might be visited, what goods carried—and at which Portuguese customs-posts dues were to be paid. But, as C. R. Boxer and M. A. P. Meilink-Roelofsz have effectively demonstrated, early violence was followed by a long period of pacific trade, conducted very often in partnership with Asian merchants and upon level terms with them. It can be argued indeed that it was the peaceful pursuit of profit,

[1] Marāthā treaties of the early eighteenth century regularly provided for the purchase of guns and ammunition from the Portuguese.

whether in the unwieldy, cargo-burdened carracks of the *Estado* or the lighter craft in which handfuls of private individuals carried on their port-to-port trade, which made the Portuguese so vulnerable to early Dutch attacks. Diogo do Couto, in his *Old Soldier's Dialogue*, deplored the passionate concern which everyone displayed in trade, because it weakened the military spirit:

> In the old days, when men reached India they asked 'which is the most dangerous outpost?' or 'where are the fleets in which the most honourable service can be done?', whereas nowadays covetousness has got such a hold, that on their arrival they ask, 'who is preparing for a trading voyage to China, or Japan, or Bengal, or Pegu, or Sunda?'

However, it must be recognized that it was the profits of trade, the port-to-port trade especially, from India westwards to Africa and Arabia, and east to Malacca, the Spice Islands, China, and Japan, which sustained the whole edifice of the *Estado da India*. Trade, and the dues levied upon trade legally or corruptly, paid for the troops and administrators, made possible a missionary effort extending from Abyssinia to Peking, and made Goa, the hub of the whole system, the golden city of travellers' reports.

With their trade between Lisbon and Goa the Portuguese initiated that major commercial revolution which ended in the effective incorporation of India, indeed, of all Asia, into a single global system of exchange. The fleets returning from Goa to Lisbon and thence to the royal 'factory' at Antwerp tapped the growing markets of north Europe more thoroughly than ever before. But by way of Lisbon India was also linked with the Portuguese colony of Brazil and with their settlements in West Africa, totally new markets. Initially the use by the Portuguese of the Cape route to India was followed by some dislocation of existing routes from India to southern Europe via the Levant. However, the old pattern was soon re-established, but was now supplemented by an additional trade, of almost equal proportions, by way of the Cape. In Malabār the cultivation of pepper, the old staple of trade with Europe, and of ginger and cinnamon, was extended almost to its natural limits. Also, to meet the enlarged demand for coir rigging and cordage, there was a systematic planting of coconut groves. And in the weaving areas of Gujarāt, Coromandel, and Bengal the first ripples were felt of what was to become in the late seventeenth century a wave of demand from Europe for cotton textiles, mainly for household use still, rather than dress, but with some re-export of cloth for the Negro slaves in the colonies.

No less important was the return flow from Europe to India, not of goods but of bullion. From south Germany and Hungary one stream of silver and copper was drawn, and then, once the mines of Spanish America had been discovered, a second and much larger flow of silver and gold by way of Cadiz. In this way the gross imbalance in the supply of bullion, which caused an equally great and hampering variation in price levels between the various trading areas of the world, began to be reduced—a process further speeded up as Spanish silver began to move to the Philippines and thence to the rest of Asia. The price rise which followed, no less than the opening of new world markets, helped to stimulate Indian production and trade.

The Portuguese not only linked India with Europe, Africa, and the

Americas, they also tied India more closely and effectively to other Asian markets. Annually there set out from Goa voyages for East Africa, Bengal, Malacca, the Spice Islands, China, and Japan, which between them brought together three trading areas hitherto semi-independent in their organization. At the same time individual Portuguese merchants and ship-masters, often in conjunction with Indian partners, penetrated to all corners of the Indian Ocean and China Sea on smaller trading ventures. The Dutchman, Linschoten, in 1583 noted that in Goa one could buy the products of all Asia. It is typical that among the church vestments of Goa there are to be seen not only fine examples of local raised gold and silver embroidery, but a chasuble which in style, motifs, and composition has all the qualities of eighteenth-century Chinese porcelain, altar frontals strongly marked in their treatment of foliage by Persian influences, and capes whose decorations of flower sprigs declare a Mughal flavour.

Of such actual manufactures of the time comparatively few specimens have survived—just sufficient to trace the interchange of goods and styles which the Portuguese trade fostered. That same interchange has, however, been much more clearly and permanently recorded in the flora of India, to which the Portuguese made many notable contributions. Tobacco was one of their earliest introductions—carried to the Deccan by 1508, it reached north India in Akbar's day and was denounced by Jahāngīr as a pernicious weed. Another, less noxious gift from South America was the pineapple, brought to Europe by Cortez in 1513, carried by the Portuguese to India, and sufficiently established there in the same century for the Mughal emperor to have one on his table daily. The arrival of yet another fruit which today is fully at home in India was recorded in the 1580s by Linschoten: 'There is another fruit which came from the Spanish Indies, brought thence by way of the Philippines or Luzon to Malacca and so to India: it is called the papaya and much resembles a melon'. The Muslim name for the cashew nut—*bādām-i-farangī*—reveals that this tree, now naturalized in the Konkan and the Chittagong hills, was also a Portuguese introduction. There has been much argument about whether maize was really brought to India by the Portuguese, but that they introduced the peanut from Africa, the mandioca from which tapioca is made, and the sweet potato seems certain enough. Even the familiar Indian *lāl mirich* or red pepper turns out to have been brought by them from Pernambuco. They also did much to spread Asian plants within Asia itself—the durian and mangosteen from Malaya, *smilax glabra*, the drug 'China root', lichees, and the sweet orange among them. Since their physicians were always on the look out for new specifics, they also introduced a number of medicinal drugs, while even a number of decorative garden plants were carried with them—of which *mirabilis jalopa*, or the Marvel of Peru, may stand as an example. With such a list of introductions to their credit, the high praise given by Jean-Baptiste Tavernier, who travelled widely in seventeenth-century India, that 'the Portuguese, wherever they came, make the place better for those that come after them', may seem fully deserved.

If the Portuguese enriched the flora, they also enriched the languages of India. In the island of Goa and adjacent Bardes and Salsette the Portuguese language itself was ultimately entrenched. For a while the need to reach out to the Hindu population, and to instruct and confess converts to Christianity, led the Provincial Councils to stress the importance of Konkanī and Marāthī in missionary and pastoral work. Later, however, fear that Hindu ideas and sentiments would retain their influence, while the language in which they had been expressed survived, led to a viceregal decree in 1684 ordering parish priests and school-teachers to instruct the people in Portuguese 'so that in the course of time the Portuguese idiom will be common to one and all, to the exclusion of the mother tongue'. The Archbishop in 1812 followed this up by requiring that children in the parish schools should talk only Portuguese during school hours, while in 1831, when the first state schools were established, the Viceroy stressed the need, 'in a country like this, forming part of the Crown of Portugal, and governed by Portuguese laws', for a wide diffusion of the Portuguese language. In the main Goa territories that was achieved. In the other settler areas, too, in the Province of the North, at Mangalor and Cochin south of Goa, and even around Negapatam on the east coast, a creole Portuguese appeared.

However, Portuguese in one guise or another spread far beyond the limits of the *Estado da India*, sometimes with the missionary and priest, sometimes with the trader and skipper. At Calicut, never under Portuguese rule, private devotions were said and cathedral records maintained in Portuguese until the twentieth century, while over in eastern Bengal Augustinian converts, *Kālā Feringhīs*, preserved another pocket of corrupt Portuguese. Since the Portuguese Crown exercised the powers of patron over the Roman Catholic Church in India, the spread of Portuguese and its long survival might be expected within that community. But throughout the eighteenth century the ministers of the English East India Company were required to learn Portuguese, and in 1780 Kiernander was to be heard preaching in that language in the old Mission Church at Calcutta.

Moreover, as Lockyer noted,[2] the Portuguese merchant, too, carried his language with him: 'Thus they may justly claim that they have established a kind of *Lingua Franca* in all the Sea-Ports in *India*, of great use to other *Europeans* who would find it difficult in many places to be well-understood without it.' On first landing at Surat the English bought and sold through Portuguese-speaking Indian brokers—and two centuries later Portuguese was still the language most commonly used in business by the Company's servants in Calcutta. And, as Marshman noted, 'Clive, who was never able to give an order in any Indian language, spoke Portuguese with fluency'. Even today, when Portuguese as a language has died away in India except in Goa, loan words survive. In Laskarī, or seamen's Hindūstānī, naturally they are mainly technical nautical terms, but in the vocabulary of north Indian languages it is in such quite common words as those for room, table, bucket, or key that Portuguese lingers on.

One other Portuguese legacy to Indian linguistics sprang from that earlier-mentioned missionary need to understand and be understood by Indian people, and took the form of grammars and dictionaries of the Indian languages and of a Christian religious literature in them. In this work the

[2] 'An Account of Trade in India', p. 286.

Jesuits, those schoolmasters of Europe, proved perhaps the most active, but all the orders contributed. Thus we hear of Francis Xavier, spearhead of the Jesuit missionary thrust, busy learning the language of Malabār and coming out with a manual of grammar and a vocabulary 'to the astonishment of the natives and great benefit to our Fathers and Brothers, who ever since then by means of this and other works learn "Malabar" as easily as Latin'.[3] The English Jesuit Thomas Stephens, best known for his Christian *Purāna* or epic in Konkanī, also produced a grammar or *Arte da lingua canarim*, later enlarged by Diogo Ribeiro, author also of a vocabulary and of one of those booklets on Christian doctrine which were everywhere among the earliest vernacular works produced. All three were among the early productions of the printing press in India, which indeed owed its origin to the missionaries' needs. As the mission field expanded so did the work of the grammarians. Works were early printed in Tamil—a Christian Doctrine in 1578—and translations into Persian marked the creation of missions to the Mughal Court. The first book in Bengālī, though printed in the Roman script, was a grammar—the famous work on the Bengālī language by the Augustinian Manoel da Assumpção printed in Lisbon in 1743. His prologue sets out very clearly the driving force behind the labours of these men:

> Dear Reader and novice Missionary, since I suppose that you have come to Bengal in a spirit of Apostolic charity and zealous to convert the whole world to the law of Jesus Christ, and to bring the lost sheep into the fold of the Church, and that to that end, as foundation to your undertaking, you wish to learn the Bengali language, I here offer you this work in which you will find the grammatical rules of this language and a vocabulary in two parts, the first Bengali into Portuguese, the second Portuguese into Bengali, wherein you will find if not all, at least the major part of the words used by the people.

To the missionary or priest an ability to use the language of his flock was undoubtedly fundamental. But he called all the arts to his aid in attracting and holding the interest of his audience, and in strengthening the faith of those whom he had converted. While the Hindu songs of Goa, the *vovios*, and the *dakhinu*, or songs of the Muslim dancing girls, were put under the ban of the Inquisition, the music of Portugal was taught in the parish schools and in the seminaries of the orders. There was a powerful tradition of church schools of music in Portugal—as at Coimbra and Evora—as well as university chairs of music and enthusiastic royal patronage through the Chapel Royal. Training acquired there was thence exported first to the *Estado da India*, later to Brazil, as were particular traditions such as that of the Jesuit religious opera. At the Jesuit College at Rachol, for example, in Salsette, a school for thirty or forty poor boys was maintained in which they were taught not only Christian doctrine and the three R's, but dance, music, and the playing of instruments. This school produced clergy and chapel masters 'from whom great fruit and increase of Christianity followed throughout India'. What is more, many churches had such music schools, so that in every parish mass might be sung, accompanied by organ and instruments, to the greater glory of the Lord and edification of the new Christians.

[3] J. Lucena, *Historia da vida do padre Francisco de Xavier*, Bk. V, Ch. 25.

From such schools came the singers and musicians who performed Camões's *Filodemo* in Goa in 1555, or those who at the end of the century were summoned from Goa to celebrate a Feast in the Jesuits' little chapel at the Mughal Court, or those who somewhat later still provided the elaborate production, with Indian pupils skilfully performing on twelve different instruments, for the German traveller Mandelslo. They also taught the less elaborate skills locally required for parish services and for those in honour of the patron saint or the Holy Cross of the village or quarter, for the more elaborate nones and vespers of the Feast of the Virgin with their triple choirs and, most popular and moving, the motets sung on the Passion theme during Lent. The same skills and traditions were also put to secular use, in singing of such traditional forms as the *vilhancico* and the *loa*, sung by the women at weddings, or in the *mando*, the languid, two-part dance, sung by the Christians of Goa in Konkanī, which is the most characteristic popular musical form of Portuguese India. Such has been the strength of these traditional schools that for many years Goans have provided most of the interpreters and players of Western music in India.

The missionaries and the Church were also teachers and patrons in India of the arts of the painter, carver, and sculptor. As in music, moreover, they were the interpreters, not narrowly of Portuguese, but of European art to India. Not only was it the case that members of the religious orders came from all over Europe. Portugal itself after the establishment of the royal factory in Antwerp was strongly exposed to the influence of Flemish and thence of Italian art, while after 1580 the union of the Crowns of Spain and Portugal opened the latter country again to foreign influences. *India Portuguesa* was thus heir to many artistic traditions.

Most of the pictorial art was religious in theme and inspiration. There survives a great gallery of portraits of the governors-general and viceroys, full-length studies—though of uncertain date and attribution—covering some four and a half centuries in Goa. In the convent of Santa Monica there are patches of impressive, lively murals which record the Goan world of about 1600. Some private portrait painting survives, too. But the most influential works were certainly those which adorned churches and chapels. How they affected the great Mughal School of painting has been well explored—as, for example, in Maclagan's *Jesuits and the Great Mughal*. Portuguese, English, and Mughal records show how interested in Christianity and its art were the Emperors Akbar and Jahāngīr—and their successors in less degree. Abu'l Fazl, Akbar's biographer and minister, wrote of 'the wonderful works of European painters who have attained world-wide fame', and the presence of a Jesuit mission in north India until the eighteenth century sustained their influence.

There were important paintings in the Jesuit chapels at Āgrā and Lāhore, but many were also presented to the emperors. The Jesuits in 1595 record that Akbar possessed paintings of Christ and of the Blessed Virgin; the English envoy Hawkins, that Jahāngīr had others of the Crucifixion and of the Madonna and Child. One Jahāngīrī album of miniatures shows large European paintings as part of the audience hall decorations, while other albums introduce European subjects in their borders, or even bodily incorporate copies of imported engravings. Figures and themes from an illustrated Polyglot Bible presented to Akbar in 1580, from a calendar by Hans Sebald Behan, and from engravings, sometimes after Dürer, produced by John Wierix, all appear in the Mughal albums. And if Rembrandt used Indian themes and models, there are most delicate copies of his pen-and-ink sketches done by Mughal Court artists—one of whom, Kesho the elder, had a whole album of such copies. European art, thus presented, influenced the Mughal School at a number of points. The idea of the equestrian portrait, the use of a dark background of foliage, the rounding out of figures, new ways of handling spatial relationships are examples of such borrowings. Nor was the appreciation of European art confined to court circles. The Jesuits report great crowds of people coming to view the Borghese Madonna in 1580 or the Madonna del Populo in 1602, when displayed in their chapel. And, as Maclagan has pointed out, the modern Hindu treatment of Devakī and the infant Krishna seems to owe something to such paintings of the Madonna and Child.

Not only painting interested the Mughals—Jahāngīr had sketches made of the interior decorations of the Jesuit church at Lāhore. This was not surprising, for the church interiors of Portuguese India were notable for the richness of their decoration, particularly in elaborate gilding of woodwork, which, carved over the ceilings, produced the *igreja toda de ouro*, the church all of gold. The retable, in particular, was most sumptuously handled, with elaborate 'Mannerist' columns decorated with cherubims, festooned and swagged, starred and diamonded, with shafts, now channelled, now octagonal, twined about with vines and creepers. Such set pieces, or Solomonic columns, with polychrome sculpture, coffered and painted ceilings, and lavish use of gilding, produced the most striking effects.

Such effects, which were secured not merely in the great churches of old Goa, but also in the churches of Diu and Bassein, and even such parish churches as N.S. de Penha da Franca or that of Talegaon, were reinforced with rich church plate and vestments. Goa was a centre of the silversmith's and goldsmith's art before Albuquerque's conquest—and at least one Goan goldsmith, Raulu Chatim, early travelled to the Court at Lisbon. After the conquest there evolved a mixed style in which Portuguese forms were married to Goan exuberance in decoration. The Goan cathedral chalices, with their open, fretted foliage work and bejewelled hafts, or the reliquaries of Verná and Margão, combining Renaissance forms with the decorated, jewel-encrusted work of local artists, are fine examples of this marriage of styles to produce an appropriately telling effect. A particularly notable example is provided by the tomb of St. Francis Xavier in the Bom Jesus—a silver casket of Italianate design, worked by Goan silversmiths, with scenes from the saint's life modelled upon religious engravings, and much elaborate filigree work, the whole set upon a Florentine marble mausoleum shipped out to Goa in 1698.

Despite their wealth of woodwork and sculpture, further enlivened perhaps by painted ceilings, church interiors in Portuguese India were generally simple in their architectural plan, with square apse and usually aisleless nave. Any architectural embellishment that there was, other than the attachment of chapels, lay in such surface designs as the shell-capped niche. The exteriors, too, echo this taste for solidity and simplicity of general plan, combined with flat, linear ornamentation in façades of considerable richness and power. The earliest considerable Jesuit façade was that of their church at Bassein, now otherwise in ruins, which dates back to the mid-sixteenth century. The most famous is that of the Bom Jesus, in the dull red local *kankar*, with its strong vertical emphasis, its rectilinear treatment, and its unusual use of bulls-eye windows to form its third storey. But one of the most satisfying of all is that of the church at Diu which belonged to the order before its exclusion by Pombal. For sheer size and magnificence, however, the Augustinian church at old Goa was perhaps unrivalled—still impressive with its one surviving flanking tower, dominating the approach to the old capital. Goa, despite its narrow compass, is wonderfully endowed with religious buildings, and the Portuguese church provided the earliest introduction to European architectural ideas over the whole length of India. Portuguese domestic architecture—the long, two-storeyed house, with high-pitched roof, balconies and verandas often running the whole length of the building, and many-windowed, outward-giving façades, with inside the *sala*, or saloon, its walls lined with chairs and sofas, elaborately carved or inlaid—survives mainly in Goa itself and in the Province of the North.

The churches, with their European architecture, music, sculpture, and painting, are the aspect of Portuguese India most plainly visible today. The most substantial Portuguese contribution to India, however, is the community of Indian Roman Catholics, most numerous where Portuguese rule was longest lasting, but found all over India. Vasco da Gama, asked what brought him to India, replied 'Christians and spices'. And though, to begin with, trade was the more important, the propagation of Christianity was always an enterprise to which, throughout Asia, the Portuguese Crown devoted much thought and a considerable part of its resources. English historians, Whiteway in particular, stressed the coercive element in Portuguese missionary effort: the destruction of Hindu temples and confiscation of their lands, the ban upon heathen festivals, songs, and ceremonies, the forcible handing over of Hindu and Muslim orphans to be brought up as Christians, and the work of the persecuting Inquisition. A juster approach might note the inefficiency of many of these measures, acknowledged even at the time, or the concentration of the Inquisition upon heretics, the hapless Jewish convert in particular. It would also stress the great educational effort made by all the orders, the effort to master languages, the early use for proselytizing purposes of the press, the importance of the creation of an Indian-Christian secular clergy. (On the debit side the racial discrimination against Indian converts within the regular orders would also be noted.) The efforts of the Jesuit de Nobili, of the Madurā mission, to Indianize or Brahmanize Christianity and to understand Hinduism as a means of going beyond it, might also be given some attention, though that particular venture was an isolated one, and soon condemned as verging upon the heretical. Ultimately, perhaps, the success of the missionary enterprise under the Portuguese *Padroado* might be seen as another illustration of acclimatization. Just as the Portuguese *casado*, the married settler, made India his home, so did the Portuguese missionary. Jesuits called down from Nepal or Nāgpur, to travel by way of Āgrā and Patnā to explore a new mission field near Dāccā in 1680, moved through a countryside familiar to their colleagues for over a century, and confidently expected aid from the Mughal official Rustam Khān—an old friend from Āgrā days, 'a disciple of Father Buzco'. The missionaries were often the best interpreters of India to the Western world, notably the Jesuits with their very popular letters from the mission field. Their success was proportionate to the degree to which, like the *Estado da India* itself, they were at home in the Indian world.

CHAPTER XXV

The Mughals and the British

by PERCIVAL SPEAR

IN considering the nature of the British impact upon India it is necessary first to clear the mind on a number of points. We have to distinguish in that impact between the political, the administrative, the economic, and the social elements. Was, for example, the member-of-council, the settlement officer, the trader, the missionary, or the educationist the most important for the future of India? Or were they all so many examples of *māyā*, waves of action breaking portentously on the shores of Indian time and then vanishing like so many dreams? If the impact was in fact real, we have still to distinguish between what was the restoration of existing institutions fallen into decay, and what was the introduction of something new. We have further to consider how far the British were bringing, as it were, their own wares to India and how far they were acting as agents for European or Western culture as a whole. And, for full measure, it must be remembered that Western culture and civilization was itself undergoing rapid change and development during most of the British period.

As a first step we may consider the validity of any lasting British impact. That something occurred to India through British agency is of course certain, but it is by no means so certain that it will have a lasting effect upon the country. The Kushānas ruled large areas in north and north-west India for upwards of two centuries, not much less than the British period, yet who can say that India changed permanently because of them? What effect have all those dynasties had whose coins and copperplates tantalize numismatists and epigraphists with their hints and silences and whose chronologies tax the ingenuity of historians? In the British case, however, we have, and in spite of their nearness in time to our observation, a yardstick for measurement. This is twenty-five years of independence, during which India has been free not only politically but also mentally and morally to retain and discard as she will from the British inheritance. We are also able, with the help of modern documentation, to compare the before and after of the British impact. From a consideration of these, two points emerge as certain facts. The first is that the India of 1947 was a very different place from the India of 1757 or even of 1818. If this is thought to be an expression of the obvious, let the India of 1526 (the year of the coming of the Mughals) be compared with the India of 1761 (the Mughal collapse), or the India of 1300, with the Delhi sultanate fully established, with the India of 1526. The second emergent fact is that a mentally free India has chosen to retain a great deal of the British inheritance. Much of the British contribution has become the working capital of the new India. The administrative and judicial framework remains the same. In the educational and industrial fields there has been expansion, but not supersession. Culturally the English language has been reprieved, now that there is no political opponent to be annoyed by abolishing it. Parliamentary institutions and notions of democracy seem to be firmly based. The argument about them has been not with what to replace them, but how to make them work properly. Much of the criticism of the British in the past is on the grounds of un-British actions, behaviour, or policies.

Having accepted the British impact upon India as both real and lasting, we come to the next question. How much of the British action in India was in fact a restoration or a 'follow-up' from the wrecks of the previous regime. Though the British did not themselves overthrow the Mughals, but stepped, region by region, into their empty political shoes, they found everywhere traces of Mughal rule and unquestionably made much use of them in their reconstruction. Here we have not only to consider the question of administrative 'know-how' but also the spirit of government. The Mughal legacy to India was in fact a legacy also to the British in India. We have therefore to assess the Mughal share in the apparent British achievement before we can attempt to assess that achievement in its own right.

When Bābur descended into northern India he found a country still recovering from Tīmūr's invasion of 1398 and the collapse of the Tughluq Dynasty of the Delhi sultanate which followed it. For two centuries a series of able Turkish soldiers had ruled with such ability that they had been able both to hold the formidable Mongols at bay and to extend their rule to south India. They had devised an effective administrative machine and made Delhi one of the great cities and cultural centres of Asia. In the next 120 years this ordered imperialism vanished. Hindūstān was ruled by Afghan chiefs whose kingdoms were tumultuous confederacies of nobles rather than well-organized states. Prosperity had departed to Bengal and the Deccan and the sultans of Delhi could barely hold their own against the *rājās* of Rājasthān, whom once they had harried. The Mughals had thus very largely a free hand in reorganizing the north, and the result of this work was largely handed on to the Deccan during the seventeenth and the south in the early eighteenth centuries.

The Mughals in general were a secular-minded race. In the late Sardār Panikkar's happy phrase they were 'kings by profession', more interested in ruling than in propagating religion. Bābur set greater store on Samarqand than on Mecca, on musk melons and drinking parties than on strict religious observance. His descendants in general followed him. It is this aspect of their rule with which we are concerned.

The first contribution of their rule may be described as the imperial idea. There had of course been previous empires in India, and Hindus retained the idea of an overlord emperor or *chakravartin rājā*. But actual examples of such empires, like the Mauryan and the Gupta, lay so far in the past that they had ceased to exercise any practical influence. The ideal of unity lived on, but its actuality had ceased to be a memory. In their extension of empire from north to south India, an extension which, it is often forgotten, was still continuing while their power was collapsing in the north, the Mughals were only reviving or putting into practice a very ancient tradition. But their treatment of the idea of imperial authority was original and lasting. Briefly they removed the person and office of the emperor from the religious to the secular plane and at the same time surrounded it with a halo of mystical and religious sanctity.

The first step was the use of Persian titles and ceremonies which in themselves were neither Hindu nor Muslim. The *naurūz* ceremony, for example, was simply the Persian rite marking the solar new year in the spring. Persian also was the ceremony of weighing the emperor on his birthday against sundry grains and precious metals. These things were in themselves mere foreign importations: it was Akbar who added the element of divinity that doth hedge a king. His new or Divine Faith is usually thought of as the eccentricity of genius or a dismal political failure. In fact, while we may grant the element of whim or eccentricity, the whole episode was a calculated political risk which in the long run became a brilliant success. Akbar never dreamt of producing a new religion in whose favour both Hindu and Muslim would abandon their own tenaciously held traditions. What he wanted was to find a way of canalizing the immense reservoir of Indian devotion towards an object distinct from the traditions of both communities. His method, which seemed fantastic both at the time and later, was to create a religious cult centred round the emperor. With his death the cult disappeared, but reverence for the imperial office remained. It secured, unlike the case of the previous Muslim dynasties, the succession and recognition of Mughal emperors when they had lost all imperial power. It was a potent factor, overlooked by the British, in rallying anti-British sentiment before and during the revolt of 1857. One of the symptoms was the use of the halo for the imperial head by Mughal painters, which even the orthodox Aurangzeb allowed; another the worship or veneration of the imperial person in the style of the Hindu *darshan*; another the taking of disciples or *murīds* by the last emperors. The essence of the idea was that the emperor ruled, not only by divine permission, but with divine approval. He therefore had assumed a semi-sacred character and required not only obedience, but veneration as well.

A second Mughal gift to India was in the realm of administration. The Mughals as a race were not markedly original, but they had been 'charmed' by the Persian culture with which they had come into contact and of which they had proved apt pupils. They imported much of the Persian administrative apparatus into India and above all the idea of ordered bureaucratic authority. If it could hardly be called the rule of law it was certainly the rule of rule. There were regulations (as the *Ā'īn* testifies) for everything, whether for the emblems of royalty and court ceremonial, the assessment and collection of revenue, the payment of troops, or the branding of horses for the imperial cavalry. Much Persian terminology is in use today. Setting aside details, we may note some major contributions to India in this sphere. It is true that Sher Shāh the Afghan (1540–5) made a significant start in this direction, upon whose foundations Akbar later built. But as he only reigned for five years, most of which were spent campaigning, his measures as recorded by the chroniclers must be regarded as a blueprint for the future rather than as an actual achievement. Outstanding in this department were the revenue arrangements, which are associated with the name of Akbar's revenue minister, Rājā Todar Mal. Their essence was an assessment of the revenue according to the extent of cultivation, the nature of the soil, and the quality of the crops. There was laborious measurement, analysis of possibilities, and calculation of prospects. The actual demand was adjusted to meet seasonal, price, and cultivated area variations. The system was administered whole or partially, well or ill, at different times and places. At times it broke down altogether. But it was never altogether abandoned or forgotten and it has never been superseded by something quite novel. It is the underlying basis of the revenue system today.

In the political sphere the Mughals contributed the *mansabdār* system. This was a graded set of imperial officials who together formed an imperial military-cum-civil service. The higher grades were the 'omrah' described by European travellers like Bernier. They owed the appointment to the emperor and were paid, at first in cash and then by means of assignments on the revenue or *jāgīrs*. These grants had no resemblance to feudal tenures, for they were revocable at the imperial will and in any case lapsed at death. The *mansabdārī* service was not hereditary and in fact lacked a pension or its equivalent, since the *mansabdār*'s property was impounded at his death to offset cash advances made by the treasury during his life. This procedure amounted to a death duty of nearly 100 per cent. From this service were appointed governors of provinces (*sūbahs*), the high officers of state from the *wāzīr* downwards, administrators of districts, commanders of armies, cities, and forts. They were in fact the arteries of the Mughal system, the pulsating blood from the Mughal heart at court. They were the effective agents of the Mughal will. The titles and grades survived as aristocratic distinctions, like European titles of nobility, in the Nizām's dominions until they were absorbed by India in 1948, but the system collapsed with the empire itself in the eighteenth century. Nevertheless the system as a whole permanently influenced the Indian consciousness. During the two centuries of its effective existence it accustomed nearly the whole country to the idea of an imperial bureaucracy representing and enforcing the central government's will. It replaced in the Indian mind as the symbol of government the feudal and clan relationships of the Rājputs and the loose tribal links of the Afghans. Though the extent of government may seem slight in modern terms, there was in fact during this period and thanks to this system more regular administration than most of India had known for a thousand years. In this respect the system provided a foundation upon which the British could build far more easily than would otherwise have been the case, because India had been conditioned already to a form of bureaucracy.

The *mansabdārī* system had another characteristic which was important for the future. Its personnel was mainly foreign. An analysis of the lists given in the *Ā'īn i-Akbarī* shows that approximately 70 per cent of the officers had come to India from the north-west within fifty years; the remaining 30 per cent were Indian, roughly half of these being Muslim and half Hindu.[1] The service continued to be heavily recruited from abroad through the seventeenth century. India thus became used, not only to a regular administration, but also to a foreign one. Previous governments in north India had either been irregular or not foreign. This trait also was of value to their British successors. Indians were accustomed to rule by foreigners; the change for them was from one kind of foreigner to a stranger one.

A further feature of Mughal rule in general, remarked on by most non-

[1] W. H. Moreland, *India at the Death of Akbar*, London, 1920, pp. 69–70.

governmental sources and particularly by European travellers, merchants, and ambassadors, was the arrogance and cupidity of the average official. The latter quality, as recorded by Sir Thomas Roe during his embassy to Jahāngīr, went right up to the heir-apparent himself. It was perhaps to be accounted for by the sense of insecurity of the nobles, liable, as they were, to be superseded or dismissed at any moment without a chance of appeal, and knowing that their property would be confiscated at death. They not only took presents, held up goods to ransom and so on, but also engaged largely in trade. Here again was a feature which smoothed the transition to the early British merchant official. What was strange in the British operations to the Indian observer was not their indulgence in commerce but the extent and method of their activities. The arrogance of the Mughal *nawāb* was proverbial, so that no surprise was caused by comparable conduct on the part of their British successors. But the Mughals treated each other in the same way as they treated the Hindus. What eventually caused complaint against the British was the discovery that they had one code of behaviour amongst themselves and another for their relations with Indians.

Another characteristic of Mughal rule was tolerance. Toleration was not absolute, and was subject to considerable variations. There were times, notably in the reign of Aurangzeb, when the ruler aspired to be the head of an Islamic state rather than the Muslim head of an Indian state. But even so, though some discrimination was practised such as the imposition of the *jizya* on non-believers and the occasional demolition of temples, toleration was the general rule. Temples received grants as well as mosques, and were rarely demolished without a political motive. The emperor intermarried with Rājput families and Hindu customs were countenanced at court. It may be said that such regimes had existed before during the Islamic period, and that in any case religious toleration was an Indian tradition. But the duration and extent of the Mughal Empire, in contrast to the varying policies and briefer periods of other dynasties, served to stamp the policy afresh on the Indian mind as part of the accepted order of things.

But perhaps the most striking of the Mughal legacies were the artistic and the cultural. Both of these began with Persian importations, which were exotics to the Mughals themselves who came from Central Asia. It was as if the Scots, having adopted the French language and culture, had conquered England and then introduced French as the language of government and society, covering the country with French-style chateaux and churches. Bābur brought with him a taste for all things Persian and the Persian invasion went on through several generations of talented and artistic rulers. But it encountered the current Indian forms and its genius was to form harmonious and original combinations with them. In the field of architecture the Mughals met the existing Indo-Muslim 'Pathān' style in north India, itself an earlier synthesis of Indo-Muslim forms, as well as the surviving Hindu style. Bābur began the artistic invasion by laying out Persian gardens wherever he went. Humāyūn continued with his palace fortress in Delhi, the Purānā Qilā'. But it was Akbar who was the real parent of the Indo-Persian or Mughal school of architecture. In his palaces and mosques in Āgrā and Fatehpur-Sīkrī he employed Hindu masons under Mughal direction so extensively and skilfully as to produce a harmonious whole, neither Persian nor Hindu, but properly Indian in character. The proportion of Hindu elements was reduced without being eliminated by his successors, to produce a completer synthesis. His grandson Shāh Jahān was the director as well as the patron of Mughal building and it was in his time that the style attained its zenith with the Tāj Mahal, the palaces in Delhi and Āgrā, the Pearl Mosque of Āgrā, and the Jāmiʿ Masjid of Delhi. From Delhi and Āgrā the style spread to the far south. It became the norm of all domestic and official buildings in the north and even many small temples included the Mughal arch pattern. The style as a living tradition must now be pronounced moribund. But it is significant that when Western architects wished to draw on Indian tradition it was to this style that they primarily turned.[2] The Mughals set the pattern for gardens, palaces, mosques, and houses.

The same Persian invasion occurred with painting. Bābur brought Persian miniature painters with him and Humāyūn encouraged them. Akbar, by employing Hindu artists steeped in their own tradition along with Muslims, created the Mughal School of painting. Jahāngīr, who was the artistic director of the school as his son was of architecture, expanded the range with his passion for nature and love of animals. With Shāh Jahān came the Mughal School of portraiture. Like architecture, Mughal painting lingered on in many branches long after the fall of the empire. But unlike the architectural heritage, it can still be said to be a living influence on modern Indian painting.

The third form of Persian influence was that of literature and manners. The Mughals did not, of course, introduce the Persian language and literature into India. This had been done by the Delhi sultans, so that under the Tughluqs Delhi was a leading Persian cultural centre; the traveller Ibn Battūta, who visited the city in the time of Muhammad Tughluq, considered it one of the principal cities in Asia. But the Persian spell was broken by Tīmūr, and not restored by the Afghans who ruled north India after him. The Mughals may be said to have re-established Persian influence, not so much by bringing in something which was not there before, as by the enthusiasm with which they propagated all things Persian. Though Turkish-speakers, they were Persian-lovers, and the love remained when their descendants became Persian-speakers. They spread the use of Persian from the court and diplomacy to the whole range of administration. Their conquests extended their administration to the south of India and with it a widespread and pervading Persian influence. Indo-Persian poets and historians there had been before, though none surpassed Faizī and Abu'l Fazl of Akbar's day. What was new was the spread not only of the Persian language, but of Persian ideas, tastes, and terminology to a wide Hindu class as well as the Muslim ruling class. The Hindu managerial and secretarial classes cultivated Persian and produced a school of poets which has persisted to this day. Along with literature went Persian manners and customs. Persian modes of address, dress, etiquette, and tastes (such as the love of formal gardens) spread with the new regime all over the country. Their traces were to be found in Rājput and Marāthā courts, whatever their political or religious feelings towards the Mughals at any given time. They became the norm of social judgement and social deportment.

[2] e.g. the work of Sir Swinton Jacob of Jaipur and sundry buildings in Bombay.

In fact the Mughals went a long way towards grafting upon Indian society a new aristocratic Indo-Persian culture. Under their aegis Persian and local influences combined to produce new forms of art and literature, new canons of behaviour, and a new type of speech. Mughal architecture and painting, though compounded of Persian and Hindu elements, were fused into something distinct from either. The same was true of language. Urdū was born under the sultanate, but it was the Mughals under whom it developed as a literary language in its own right and Muhammad Shāh Rangīla who admitted it to Court. In manners the Delhi Court became the Versailles of India. Akbar's religion, followed by the exaltation of the person of the emperor, provided an emotional centre for aristocratic loyalty, and the imperial services, with their large employment of Hindus outside the *mansabdār* ranks, an administrative cement. The effort to create a new culture proved 'abortive' in the Toynbeian sense, perhaps because it was too confined to the aristocracy or perhaps because the middle class, which should have mediated it to the masses, was too small. But it left indelible marks on India in the developed Urdū language, in the arts of architecture and painting, and in manners and tastes.

We can now consider briefly how much of what is associated with the British period is really a carry-over or restoration of Mughal influences and institutions. A glance at the foregoing is enough to show that the British were by no means so original in many of their contributions to India as one has been tempted to think. The British achievement must be judged in conjunction with that of its Mughal predecessor, as the Mughals themselves must not be credited with what they took over from their past. In surveying the two periods together we can trace three processes. There is an element of restoration by one of the work of the other; there is a clothing in new forms of tendencies carried over from the past; and there is, along with a similarity of policy, an introduction of new content. Even restoration can be quietly revolutionary and revolution can be a violent form of restoration. It is the interaction of these processes which has produced the authentic British contribution. Thus while the introduction of democracy in France at the Revolution was new, it did not alter the centralizing and authoritarian tendencies of the old monarchy, while the Restoration of 1815, like the English Restoration of 1660, was itself in large measure a recognition of revolution.

The concept of the emperorship as a semi-sacred office apart from the old religions was a Mughal innovation. At first the British spurned this. One could hardly imagine a less sacred institution than the East India Company, or a less mystical person than the governor-general. This common-sense attitude strengthened with success until it received a rude shock when the Mutiny revealed the depth of sentiment still surrounding the Mughal *pādshāh* and Marāthā Peshwā. The assumption of government by the Crown and the personal attitude taken by Queen Victoria towards India were in fact leaves taken out of the Mughal book. The move was abundantly rewarded, so that it can be safely said that in the last years of her reign the Queen was more venerated in India than in Britain. The religious aura surrounding the great Mughals reattached itself to her. The assumption of the imperial title in 1876 was a corollary of the move of 1858, not in itself anything new. In idea it was a good move as appealing to the mass imagination, but this effect was largely offset by its constant use in adorning imperialist speeches. India liked being the brightest jewel, but why of someone else's crown?

There is a close relationship between the British and the Mughal revenue arrangements. From Bengal to Gujarāt, as the British spread over the country, they found either Todar Mal's *bandobast* in decline, or beheld its relics in the form of custom or what was done 'before the troubles'. After the early years of confusion and over-assessment, they felt their way towards a knowledge of the unique Indian revenue system and became more and more impressed with the range and thoroughness of the previous regime. The British in effect became pupils at the Mughal school and it was on this basis that they made their lasting contribution to the administration of rural India. They took over the Mughal system of exact measurement of the land, of distinguishing soils and crops in estimating production, and of using various kinds of agents in collection. At first they were less flexible than the Mughals in such matters as remissions on account of floods and famine and in dealing with defaulters, with much resulting hardship. The harsh dealings at the time of the Bengal famine of 1770[3] and the over-assessment in the early days of the Delhi Territory are examples. With experience they improved. Their assessments became more accurate and scientific, their revenue demand more lenient as well as more predictable than that of their predecessors. On the whole their achievement was notable, for they built up a rural administration not only stable but generally equable and equitable. There were, however, two significant departures from Mughal practice. One was the action of Cornwallis, Pitt, and Dundas in creating the Permanent Settlement of Bengal in 1793 (which extended to Bihār, Orissā, and parts of the Madras Presidency). This converted the *zamīndārs* into something like English landlords and their peasants virtually into tenants-at-will, giving them the unearned increment of land which was then far from completely cultivated. *Zamīndārī* had long been recognized as a form of property; it was the British who turned it into *landed* property.[4] The consequence was the creation of a landed class which as a whole was loyal but not progressive, tenacious but not enterprising. This work was already being undone when the British left India. The other departure was the system of selling up defaulters in the land revenue, instead of bullying them as the Mughal officials did and then leaving them in possession. This produced a displacement of classes, tending to replace old rural families by absentee city-dwellers, more interested in rents than tenants.

The Mughal *mansabdārī* system as an effective executive service was in collapse before the British began to rule. It cannot seriously be maintained that the British restored it or borrowed from it. But it is significant that they found that they could not do without an equivalent. Their administration did not settle down until they had organized a service recruited with some eye to ability, trained to some extent for the duties it had to perform, inculcated with a high sense of duty, and disciplined both financially and morally. It is

[3] See W. W. Hunter, *Annals of Rural Bengal*, London, 1897, p. 39. Thirty-five per cent of the peasantry died. Less than 5 per cent of the revenue was remitted in 1769/70: it was increased by 10 per cent in 1770/1.

[4] See Irfan Habib, *The Agrarian System of Mughal India*, London, 1962, Ch. V.

interesting to note that the Company's officials were paid for a time (till 1787) by means of percentages on the revenue, a method comparable to the later Mughal practice of assignments on the land revenue. It was Cornwallis who returned to Akbar's practice of fixed salaries as well as cash payments. Another point in common was the *foreignness* of the two services. From this point of view the British were not as bad as they have been painted, for they were only exaggerating a standing Mughal practice. The indictment, if any, is that they failed to do better. From this point the comparison fades.

The British had two separate services, the civil and military, as compared to the undivided Mughal one, and the civil had several sub-sections. The foreign ascendancy was progressively reduced until even the highest of the services, the Indian Civil Service, was half-Indian. Here indeed was a contribution of value to contemporary India. The services were handed over intact to the new administration as going concerns. They were loyal to authority and to each other. They were highly capable, they possessed a high morale, they were aloof from politics, and they possessed a degree of self-reliance and readiness to act in emergencies which was unusual in such bodies. Though shorn of their European cadres the services possessed enough Indian members who had been sufficiently integrated to shoulder the burden of independent administration. They not only did this but successfully met grave crises as well. The development of modern India could not have proceeded as it has without them. This legacy was not particularly original, since others had organized imperial services before. But it was a genuine legacy in a familiar field, since the British were responsible for the form, the tone, and the quality of the bodies they handed over.[5]

A further Mughal bequest to the British was official ostentation, arrogance, and greed. These epithets were freely applied by ambassadors, travellers, and merchants to the 'omrahs' in the Mughal heyday and to *nawābs* in general in the eighteenth century. It was not inadvisedly that the merchant officials who returned from Clive's Bengal and Benfield's Madras with fortunes were called 'Nabobs' in England. Whatever degree of envy may have entered into the jibes, the traits which called them forth were clear enough. There is no doubt that the arrogance of the British officials, and its long continuance, owed much to the Mughal example. This was the climate of authority as the British found it; not unnaturally they enjoyed and continued it. This fact should temper the criticism of British official arrogance as though it was a wholly new evil imposed on a hitherto unafflicted people. The early Company's officials, or many of them, undoubtedly shared in the Mughal ostentation and greed. But neither lasted long, the one swept away by the economies of a utilitarian age and the other by the reforms of Cornwallis and his successors. The most corrupt and colourful of services became in the nineteenth century the most dutiful and sedate; our only regret must be that in shedding their colour the services also lost some degree of imagination.

The Mughal policy of tolerance was extended and amplified by the British. But while it was more complete it was also more frigid, for the Mughals, while occasionally demolishing temples, would also endow others, give grants to

[5] For the best account of the Indian Civil Service as a living body see P. Woodruff's two volumes *The Founders*, London, 1953, and *The Guardians*, London, 1954.

Hindu as well as Muslim divines, and patronize Hindu festivals. The religious neutrality of the government, as pressured by Christian groups in Britain, forbade all this and left the people with a feeling of aloofness and disdain. On occasion indifference can be more wounding than hostility. The tradition of aloofness from religion as a complement to the policy of toleration is not one calculated to endear the idea of the secular state to the average Indian heart.

When we turn to the Mughal cultural heritage, we come to a parting of the ways with the British. Influence there was, but it was peripheral and fleeting. The British remained faithful to their own style of building, limiting their Mughal loans to the ornate marble bathroom with sunken bath (up-country) and to Bengālī style annexes for the 'zenāna'. They patronized the miniature painters to some extent and used them widely for studies of buildings, plants, and animals; they were even influenced in their own painting by Indian techniques. But this died away as European contacts increased and photography came in. The taste for Persian literature did not survive the generations of Warren Hastings, Metcalfe, and Elphinstone. The flood of books from the West overwhelmed it, and Orientalism retired to the studies of western Europe. Mughal manners never challenged the London version of Versailles, nor did their dress make an appreciable impact. The use of pyjamas can perhaps be ascribed to them, but otherwise Oriental fashions in dress came from Persia. The British needed no tutoring in wine or spirits; the taste for outdoor sport was mutual, the fashion of hookah smoking had died away by the mid-nineteenth century. Their chief loans were the game of polo and the custom of bathing.

It is now possible to consider the rest of the British contribution in its own right, as it were. The observer who visits India today will still find many visible traces of the British. Houses, public buildings, and memorials strew the land. But he will not see much of these for long. The houses were mostly brick-built and are subject to decay and change; most of the public buildings are quite undistinguished. Few of the more pretentious possess much merit and some of those that possess it are copies from England, like Barrackpore House in Calcutta. The British brought with them the classical vogue of eighteenth-century England which produced a number of graceful churches and houses in Calcutta and elsewhere. Thereafter Gothic came in, with its memorials in the Calcutta and Lāhore cathedrals and 'P.W.D.' churches. The Gothic fashion extended to bungalows, but though there was some graceful imitation of the classic style, the Gothic never took root in India. Then came Lord Curzon, who intended a British Tāj Mahal and achieved the Calcutta Victoria Memorial. In its ostentation, its obtuseness, and its solidity it was not an unfitting symbol of the current imperialism. The final British effort was New Delhi, where Lutyens and Baker disagreed in producing something of high merit and symbolic beyond their intentions. For the central complex as it now stands is an epitome, not of imperial power, but of bureaucracy. A rocky eminence, approached by a processional way, is crowned by two secretariat blocks, with the legislature dropped on one side as an apparent afterthought (as indeed it was), and the central feature of the President's (ex-Viceroy's) house pushed (unintentionally) too far back to be dominant. 'What a noble ruin it will be', exclaimed M. Clemenceau; as it stands it is the monument, not of British power but of bureaucracy; it is the mausoleum, we may say, of the British I.C.S.

Nor will the observer be much impressed by the British artistic contribution. Painters like Zoffany and the Daniells came to India but, apart from some activity in Bombay, no schools of Indo-British painting arose. The best service rendered by the British in this direction was the creation of schools of art which led Indian artists to fresh inspiration through study of their own traditions. In literature the story is different, for they have founded a living tradition, but this is connected with language, which is dealt with elsewhere. A minor contribution has been the English garden. The Mughals introduced the formal garden freshened with running water. The British, with their passion for landscaping, introduced parks wherever they had the means or opportunity and lawned flower gardens wherever flowers and grass would grow. The compensation for their cavernous and often grotesque bungalows was the profusion of their gardens.

In considering the British impact as a whole it is necessary to distinguish between the various functions which they performed. They dominated the country for a century and a half as its rulers; they acted as agents for the entry of ideas and techniques from the West, and they possessed characteristics of their own which they implanted on the country. The first impact is the more obvious, the second the more profound, and the third the most engaging. Taking the last first, we may note, as characteristics of the British as a people, marked individualism, a love of sport and games, class-consciousness, and the habit of working in groups. Some of these traits, like class-consciousness and love of sport, dovetailed into existing social habits. But in the realm of sport the British have added to the Indian stock by contributing their own games. In hockey India now leads the world, but it is three others, football in Bengal, tennis and cricket everywhere, which have attained the level of addiction and become part of the country's contemporary life. British individualism has worked by example rather than precept; it has been an impalpable influence in promoting independence in a society weighted with the restrictions of caste, the authority of parents and the joint family, and the reverence for age. The co-operative or group mode of action has taken root in the vogue of the committee, from the Congress down to the tennis club.

The British as rulers erected a system of power which had strong affinities with its predecessor. The ultimate control lay in London and it contained no trace of sanctity, but there were the same pyramid and levels of authority; the division into civil and military arms, and the means of making the government's will effective, showed marked resemblances. Up to the 1820s the system might be described as the Mughal model restored and improved, and as such it contained nothing novel. The government was a law-and-order state, concerned with preserving the social organism from attack and promoting its smooth working. Its basis was authoritarian and its concern with welfare was negative, to prevent oppression. It had, however, already made one important innovation, and from this time made several more. It will be convenient to view them together as the sum total of the British political impact.

The first of these new departures, one which has been accepted by the new India, is the judicial system and the rule of law which went with it. The judicial system began with Mayor's Courts in the settlements which were, however, only intended for the settlers themselves. Later the Supreme Court was set up in Calcutta (1774), which created confusion by applying British law to Indian cases. With the acquisition of Bengal the Company at first took over the Mughal courts; in fact in that respect they were then Mughal agents. A long period of trial and error may be said to have culminated with the completion of the Indian Penal Code. By that time India had a complete judicial system from High Courts downwards, which is functioning smoothly today. It was the first official sphere in which Indians won distinction, and perhaps for that reason is specially cherished. The law administered was Hindu and Muslim on the personal plane, and Muslim tempered with British humanism in the criminal sphere. The effect of thus bypassing the British penal system in the early years of the nineteenth century was to make it more humane than the contemporary British system. Since then a great body of commercial and public law has been added, drawing on British precedents.

But it is not so much the lawyer or the content of the law as the modes of procedure that have been significant. India had many learned *qāzīs* and pandits and her own systems were also highly developed. The whole procedure was lifted from Britain, and all proceedings were subject to record. There was therefore a steady infiltration of the principles implied by the procedure and a rapid growth of a body of case law resting on those principles. There has been much criticism of the law's delay in India and the contumely borne by the poor man, but when much of this is admitted certain broad results remain. The idea of a secular law, related to justice but apart from the great religions, has been implanted in the Indian mind. It is to the judge, not to the pandit or the *mullā*, that people look for justice. The courts stand out as a secular embodiment of the concept of right. They form in fact a pillar of the secular state.

A second characteristic of the courts has been their independence, not only from religious interference, but notably from the state executive. This independence was a British loan and it was not merely a loan on paper. From the time of Sir Elijah Impey and Warren Hastings they were often thorns in the side of the administration. Lord Ellenborough described one troublesome judge as a rogue elephant to be guarded by a tame one on either side. Canning objected to their independence in expressing their views in his Legislative Council and to the end they periodically pricked the skin of official complacency. They have continued this course in both India and Pakistan, with general approval. This independence of the judiciary on political issues, which England may claim to have won in the seventeenth century, was something new to Indian experience.

There remains the rule of law, which both emphasizes the independence of the courts and provides a safeguard against executive tyranny. The rule was declared by Cornwallis in 1793, in these words: 'The collectors of revenue and their officers, and indeed all the officers of Government, shall be amenable to the courts for acts done in their official capacities, and Government itself, in cases in which it may be a party with its subjects in matters of property shall submit its rights to be tried in these courts under the existing laws and regulations.'[6] The idea that the government could be sued as of right instead of

[6] Cornwallis Correspondence, Vol. 2, p. 588.

being petitioned as of grace or mercy, was something quite new. If the government itself could be sued with impunity, why not the big man of the district, the *zamīndār*, the princeling, the wealthy entrepreneur? The whole legal process did much to implant the idea of individual civil rights in the popular mind. A further aid in this process was the separation of the judicial and executive services. This was introduced by Cornwallis but modified later and abandoned in the north-west. Indians never ceased to argue in its favour and restored it with independence.

A further British contribution was the introduction of the idea that the positive promotion of public welfare was a normal duty of government. Classical Hindu and Muslim ideas of government made for non-interference. Society for both was a socio-religious organism which it was the government's function to protect so as to ensure its smooth working. It was not to mould or to create but to preserve. In Hindu thought for example, the *dharma* of the *rājā* was to protect the Hindu way of life. In Mughal times it was thought that Shāh Jahān had come nearest to this general ideal. 'Hail O King', said the rhapsodist, 'Thou owest a thanksgiving to God. The King is just. The ministers are able and the secretaries honest. The country is prosperous and the people contented.'[7] The Chinese attitude was similar in implication though secular in tone. Society was an organism best left to itself. The better the government the less government there would be.

The early Company's officials took over this view and maintained it into the nineteenth century. But pressures, religious, rational, and utilitarian, mounted in Britain which led the Tory Ellenborough to write in 1828 to the Governor-General Lord William Bentinck: 'We have a great moral duty to perform.' The India debates of Hastings's time and the eloquence of Burke had enforced the principle of responsibility of the government for good administration. With Bentinck the further step was taken of positive promotion of public welfare. The first steps in this direction were the negative ones of the prohibition of *satī* (suttee), the suppression of thuggee, and the discouragement of infanticide. But they were followed by the new education policy, the introduction of English, irrigation projects and the building of roads and railways, and health measures. Self-interest may have entered into some of these measures, and in many respects it may be held that they did not go nearly far enough. Nevertheless the principle was there, a principle which nationalists often used as a rod with which to beat the foreign government and cheerfully accepted afterwards. Was it not in the name of this principle that Gāndhī launched his attack on the salt tax? With Nehrū the new government accepted in principle, and to some extent realized in practice, the idea of a welfare state.

The principle of welfare can take many forms. One of these in the British case was the development of self-government. For this in itself no originality can be claimed, for it is not to be supposed that Indians in general have in the political sphere desired anything else through the centuries of foreign domination. But representative and parliamentary government was something new, and it is this which the British, in the later stages of their rule, introduced into the country and which has taken root. The British rulers in India were themselves inclined to the Mughal idea of the state; these innovations were almost

[7] Ibni-Hasan, *Central Structure of the Mughal Empire*, London, 1936, p. 360.

entirely due to pressure from outside. The first ideas of the ultimate independence of a modernized India appeared in the 1820s and 1830s with men like Mountstuart Elphinstone and Macaulay, but little was done to implement them for another eighty years. Representation of Indian opinion was introduced in a tentative way, to reach its logical development with the Morley–Minto reforms in 1909. The advent of responsible self-government on the parliamentary model was a twentieth-century development, beginning as late as 1921 with the inauguration of the Montagu–Chelmsford reforms. Nevertheless it immediately took root; this type of government became a fixed Indian demand and has been sedulously maintained since independence. But this is not surprising, because the various acts were themselves tardy responses to long-expressed Indian demands, in their turn the result of absorption of British political ideas by the Westernized classes. Parliamentary government as government by discussion and majority vote in representative assemblies seems now to be firmly rooted in the modern Indian mind. An estimate of the effectiveness of the system in practice was blurred for a time by the towering personality of Nehrū. But there seems to be a general conviction that the parliamentary is the only respectable form of democracy, as democracy is the only respectable form of government. The Indian innovations on these lines, such as universal suffrage, the revival of *panchāyats*, and the ending of autocratic princely rule, are only extensions of existing British practice and principles.

Along with parliamentary government we must link nationalism. This is perhaps one of the most remarkable examples of the British impact, for the British neither designed, nor formally introduced, nor advocated it. Nationalism was 'caught' by the new Indian intellectuals, especially in Bengal, by the joint effect of observing the habits of the British and studying their literature. Mother India, a new secular goddess, was created. The feeling was recruited on the intellectual plane by the study of Continental as well as English writers, especially Mazzini, and on the emotional by its linkage with religion. To Mahātmā Gāndhī belongs the credit of bringing it to the people at large, and presenting it as a religious but not a sectarian cult. Indian nationalism has a distinctive ethos of its own, but it is a fact of the present day and it owes its existence to the British impact.

The concept of welfare has many forms. In the 1830s it included the education and language policy of the Indian Government. Briefly, English was substituted for Persian as the language of government and the higher courts, the local languages being used in the lower. English also became the medium of instruction in the higher government educational institutions, and the content of learning included contemporary Western knowledge. Western science and history therefore came into the curriculum, and the whole range of Western ideas and attitudes was conveyed through English and European literature. Admittedly the motivation of the policy was mixed, as was that of the Indian attitude towards it. But, if a supply of English-knowing subordinates was one motive on the British side, so also was the desire to throw open Western intellectual treasures to the East. While on the Indian side many learnt English as a passport to a career, there was an active group led by the reformer Rām Mohan Roy which desired the spread of Western knowledge for its own sake.

The fact was that the decisions of 1835 gave governmental sanction and impetus to a process by which the culture and knowledge of the West were presented to India. The positive means were the government's educational institutions, reinforced by missionary educational and other activity and by the personal attitudes of the British officials and others scattered all over the country. There was no compulsion; no one was compelled to become Christian, profess utilitarianism, wear English clothes, or play cricket. Western thought and attitudes were placed side by side with Indian in an ever-widening circle of Indian minds. The significant fact is that those minds were influenced by this process to an increasing degree. An index of this fact is that whereas before the Mutiny nearly all the new educational institutions were governmental or missionary, in the twenty years from 1873 to 1893 the number of colleges, in spite of a reduction in government support, increased nearly threefold from 55 to 156.[8]

In this process the British were not merely acting for themselves; they were the agents for the whole process of the expansion of Western culture into the East, brokers, more or less honest, managing agents, more or less efficient. The failure to recognize this distinction has been the cause of much misunderstanding. While to the British bridges and railways and modern technology were all part of the 'manifold blessings of British rule', to Indians they seemed to be things which had to come anyhow. If anything, the British were to blame for not bringing them sooner or in larger quantity. In view of the rapid shrinkage of the world it must be accepted that India would have been largely Westernized anyhow; the exact nature of such a process is now a profitless speculation. None the less, the British in fact deliberately started the process with their policy decisions of the 1830s. India is the richer today because that decision, though sometimes tardily implemented, was taken as long ago as 1835, the date of Bentinck's language decisions, instead of, as in the case of Indonesia, not until the twentieth century was well advanced.

The role of the British as agents covers much of the British material achievements and also much ideological merchandise. In the former realm the British were the agents for the developing science of the West with its inductive logic and experimental methods. The first visible sign of this importation was the Calcutta Medical College established by Bentinck, where dedicated Hindu students broke caste in the name of the new knowledge and the new methods. These new principles came in their theoretical form through the colleges and in their concrete form at first through engineering and then through the new industrialism. The growth of the mechanized cotton industry in the later nineteenth century was symbolic of practical India's acceptance of Western techniques, as the growth of private arts colleges was symbolic of Indian acceptance of Western ideas. The word acceptance should not be interpreted as wholesale adoption to the exclusion of Indian ideas. It would be more accurate to say that these things were *entertained* alongside their Indian counterparts. The critical process of assimilation had still to come, but it was recognized that these things had come to stay in the country and in future had to be reckoned with as part of its heritage.

On the ideological side must be placed the whole range of ideas and values

[8] B. B. Misra, *The Indian Middle Classes*, London, 1961, p. 283.

which come from the West. Officials, non-officials, and missionaries carried them in very varied forms, but these forms were all expressions of fundamental concepts rooted in the West as a whole. None of these things were really new to India viewed in her totality; they were new to contemporary India because they had been overlaid by custom through long stretches of Indian history. Intellectually the concept of the critical reason, more particularly a product of the Enlightenment, was introduced under the cloak of criticism of Indian customs, institutions, and ideas. The cry of 'superstition' and 'abomination of heathenism' were Anglicized versions of Voltaire's 'écrasez l'infâme' and further back of Greek scepticism. When these things roused echoes in Indian minds it was the European tradition as a whole rather than the British in particular they were recording.

From the same basis of European values came the emphasis on universal human rights and duties, on the rights of the individual as a person, and his responsibility for and to society as a whole. These things came in the British forms of evangelical and radical humanism, of the radical rights of man, and of Whig contractual civil rights. But they had their root more immediately in French thought and more ultimately in the whole classical Christian tradition. To this source must be ascribed social criticism of such things as *satī*, infanticide, Hindu widowhood, caste, and popular religious cults. Equally from the same source must be derived the positive aspect of these ideas, the equality of all not only before God but also before the law, the personality and citizenship of women as well as men, the principles of democracy. The part of the British in introducing these things was very great. But in this respect they are to be judged, not so much by the things they sponsored, as by the fidelity of the sponsorship. As in the material sphere, we cannot say that these things would not have come without them; we can only say that they would have come at a different time and in a different way.

There remains the question of an Indo-British[9] culture analogous to the Indo-Persian culture of the Mughals. Will the European intrusion prove no more than a smile on the face of the elusive goddess Māyā? The Macaulayesque dream of brown Englishmen mingling the waters of the Thames with the Ganges has long since faded. But authorities like the late G. T. Garratt and Guy Wint have thought that they discerned signs of a hybrid culture more serious than the social curiosities recorded by Kipling. In so far as it existed, it was confined to a much smaller Indian circle than in the case of the Mughal 'nearly but not quite' Indo-Persian culture. The mixing of the races in the British case was far less free and less continuous. You cannot develop a hybrid culture on board ship or in the intervals between leave in Europe and retirement. The real impact of the West on India has been the steady percolation of Western ideas and values into Indian minds by all kinds of agencies and at all levels. This has produced a ferment in the corporate Indian mind itself. The symptoms first appeared with Rām Mohan Roy's activities of nearly a century and a half ago. They have since appeared in religious, social, political, and intellectual movements. But they do not add up to a new Indo-European culture. Rather these forces are working within the mind of Hinduism to

[9] This term is used in preference to the old term Anglo-Indian, which now has a different and defined connotation.

produce modifications of outlook and attitude. If the Western pressure is long and strong enough it may produce eventually a culture compounded of Eastern and Western elements but distinct from either. Previous foreign contacts could not be sustained long enough to provoke permanent large-scale change. The shrinkage of the world and the Western technological drive suggest that this condition no longer holds, in which case the prospect is exciting indeed. But the excitement is a long-term one and for the present it can only be said that a process of assimilation, of give and take, is going on. And, let it be added, the giving will not only be on the Western or the taking on the Indian side. Modern Indian influence on Europe began in the eighteenth century; it has increased in the twentieth with such figures as Gāndhī; it will steadily grow in largely impalpable but significant ways with the increase of East–West contacts. One thing is certain: the traditional brāhmanical attitude of 'neither a borrower nor a lender be' is gone for good.

CHAPTER XXVI

Hindu Religious and Social Reform in British India

by J. T. F. JORDENS

INTRODUCTION

VIEWING the millennia of Indian history, one can hardly think of a greater contrast than the one that exists between eighteenth-century and twentieth-century India. On the one hand we have a stagnating traditional culture and society at very low ebb, in fact in a state of decadence not witnessed before, a decadence condemned by most modern Indians from Rām Mohan Roy onwards. On the other hand we have a still traditional society in the throes and the creative excitement of modernizing itself, of emerging as a new nation, remaining thoroughly its own and rooted in its culture, yet taking its place in the contemporary world. The nineteenth century was the pivotal century that saw the initiation of this process, that brought about an enormous transformation in the religious, social, economic, political, and cultural spheres.

How did this transformation come about? Many interrelated factors were involved. First we have the total impact of the British Rāj. It influenced Indian life through many channels: administration, legislation, trade, the creation of a network of communications, inchoative industrialization and urbanization, all had great influence not only on the many Indians who became directly involved in them, but also on society as a whole, because every measure in some way interfered with some traditional patterns of life. In the cultural field too the British exerted pressure through the work of scholars, educators, and missionaries, orientalist, utilitarian, or evangelical. The sum total of this influence acted on the life and ideas of the people in multiple ways, forcing them to adjust their patterns of life to the new circumstances and thus effecting a continuum of social change.

Standing out as landmarks in this gradual adaptation to new conditions are the reformers. These are the Indians who consciously reacted to the new situation and advocated deliberate changes in social and religious attitudes and customs, involving a break with tradition itself. They saw change not as a slow adaptive process, but as a positive value in itself, and contrasted it with the negativity of existing patterns. As a group they had a great impact on nineteenth-century India, though they were not by far the only factor in effecting change.

Social and religious reformers were, naturally, not a new phenomenon in Hinduism; in fact in some ways the very nature of Hinduism is to be continuously adaptive and reformist. Yet the nineteenth-century reform movement was in general distinguished from previous Hindu reform by a cluster of new characteristics. It became closely wedded to a political movement, and consequently sought to influence political authority, administration, and legislation. This political movement became very soon an all-India nationalist movement, and reform acquired a nationalist flavour and an all-India extension. Whereas previously social reform was inextricably interwoven with religious motivation and religious reform, in the nineteenth century the relationship of the two oscillated, and sometimes secular and rationalistic motives were the decisive ones, though in fact the century did produce a few reformers who remained totally within the traditional pattern, and whose influence on the period remained insignificant. Among them the most noteworthy are Swāmī Nārāyana of Gujarāt, initiator of a sect bearing his name, and Mahātmā Rāmalingam of Tamilnādu.

The reformers themselves had no doubts as to the main stimulants of this new spirit. The British administration, English education, and European literature brought to India a constellation of fresh ideas which constituted a challenge to the new intellectuals. Rationalism as the basis for ethical thinking, the idea of human progress and evolution, the possibility of 'scientifically' engineering social change, the concept of natural rights connected with individualism, were all alien to traditional society. An equally strong influence was exerted by the ideas and the work of the Christian missionaries. Although some later nationalist writers tend to discount this influence, the nineteenth-century reformers themselves, starting with Rām Mohan Roy, did not hesitate to give credit where it was due, and acknowledged their indebtedness in no uncertain terms, even while vigorously opposing certain aspects of missionary activity.

I. THE FIRST STAGE: UP TO 1880

In the first decades of the nineteenth century, India had already produced a small new social group, the English-educated intelligentsia, mostly closely associated with British administration or British trade. It was amongst these people that several ideas of reform first arose. They were primarily trying to deal with a personal problem that affected their own lives very deeply: constant contact with Britishers and European ideas made them look upon some social and religious characteristics of their own society with horror and disgust. Social reform in this first stage was mostly prompted by the desire of these people to cope with the difficulties which they experienced themselves and which were experienced too by others belonging to their European-influenced group. There was not as yet any concern for the mass of the people, or any desire to transform the structure of society at large. What they wanted was to reshape their lives according to the new standards and values they were discovering. They sought to clarify their own ideas, and propagate them among their kindred intelligentsia. Thus this first stage was a time of propaganda rather than of organization, a time when the reformer was almost exclusively concerned with his own group, a time also when political concern was inchoative and when it was generally held that personal social reform needed to be based upon the solid foundation of religious reform.

Bengal

Bengal was first to undergo significant British influence and to produce the new English-educated group. By the early 1800s we notice already a crystallization of different reactions to Western influence, and there emerge three distinct groups, the radicals, the reformers, and the conservatives. Rām Mohan Roy (1772–1833) was the first great modern reformer, and has for good reason been called 'The Father of Modern India'. In his youth he studied Persian and Arabic, as well as classical Sanskrit texts. His work for the East India Company and his commercial success allowed him at the age of forty-two to retire from business and settle in Calcutta in comfortable circumstances. The twenty years left of his life were of paramount importance to Bengal and the rest of India. His studies of Islam and Hinduism and his deep acquaintance with the thought of the West equipped him more than any of his contemporaries for the role of social and religious reformer that he was to play.

In the religious sphere Rām Mohan's main target of attack was the Hindu system of idolatry, its mythology and cult. He proposed as an alternative a deistic type of theism, strongly influenced by European deism and the ideology of the Unitarians with whom he had close links. His remote, transcendent God was to be praised and adored from a distance without the quest for intercession or mystical union. His study of other religions convinced him that below their dogmas, rituals, and superstitions there lay hidden a common core of rational religion and humanitarian ethics. That is why he could write a eulogy of Christian morality in his *Precepts of Jesus* and yet attack Christian theology and engage for several years in controversy with the missionaries. He claimed that his reformed Hinduism was to be found in the ancient *Upanishads*, some of which he translated, and in the Vedānta. In fact his very schematic religious creed has, apart from the name of Brahmā, practically no specifically Hindu content.

As a social reformer, Rām Mohan's interest was mainly in the appalling condition of women in Hindu society, an interest that was to dominate the social reform movement for many decades. He is rightly famous for his long and successful campaign for the abolition of *satī*, the self-immolation of widows on the funeral pyres of their husbands, and he fought incessantly against child marriage and for female education.

Rām Mohan's method was primarily propaganda, leading on to agitation. His propaganda was carried out by streams of tracts from his pen, all related to his reforming ideas. This was reinforced by journalism: he was a pioneer in the birth of the vernacular press, mainly through his Bengālī and Persian weeklies. He also strongly promoted English-type education as the main instrument for reform. Rām Mohan's propaganda led on to agitation proper, in order to marshal public opinion by meetings and petitions and thus to influence the government. He was the first to agitate, organize, and succeed. As time went on Rām Mohan realized more and more that political agitation had to be used to influence the government, and the last years of his life spent in England were mainly directed to this work, again setting a trend for the decades to come. The crowning achievement of Rām Mohan's organizational efforts was the foundation of the Brāhmo Sabhā (later known as Brāhmo Samāj) in 1828. This was a religious body 'to teach and to practise the worship of the one God'. It had a temple of its own, where congregational worship took place, free from idolatry and superstition, modelled mostly on Unitarian worship. During Rām Mohan's lifetime and for a decade afterwards it was but a small body of men gathering regularly for religious services, but later under new leaders it became of much greater significance.

Rām Mohan never broke with Hinduism, and in his public life he was careful not to offend the orthodox: he felt reform had to be carried out from within the Hindu community. This view was repudiated by the young radicals of the time, led by the brilliant Eurasian teacher Henry Derozio (1809–31), whose movement came to be known as 'Young Bengal'. Their religion was rationalism, and they bitterly attacked orthodoxy in all its aspects. Not only was their talk revolutionary, but their actions often matched their convictions: some threw away their sacred thread, ate beef, and openly flaunted their contempt for Hinduism, and for 'half-liberals' like Rām Mohan. Orthodox society was up in arms and acted swiftly to dismiss Derozio from Hindu College and put pressure on the other young men. It was a massive campaign in which many suffered severely even from their families. Derozio's premature death in 1831 weakened Young Bengal, and by the 1840s it was dead as a movement: the youth of its members, their lack of clear ideology and leadership, their isolation from real society, were handicaps too great to allow them to survive as a group the onslaught of the orthodox. But many individuals of this group, matured by age, trained in the hard school of rational thought and fired with burning nationalism, became outstanding figures in government posts and in the hectic political and cultural life of Bengal.

The orthodox formed the extreme right in the Bengālī society of the time. Under the able leadership of Rādhākānta Deb (1794–1876), they were the defenders of the socio-religious *status quo* against both reformers and radicals, and they formed in 1830 the Dharma Sabhā. This was the most wealthy of the Hindu parties, and the largest in numbers. Through its newspaper it fought the reformers every inch of the way for the protection of orthodoxy. Yet the orthodox party in fact contributed considerably to the reform movement by its very active role in promoting English education, even among girls.

After Rām Mohan Roy's death the Brāhmo Samāj was in the doldrums for a decade, and then Debendranāth Tāgore (1817–1905) took over its leadership and gave it a new direction. He changed the Samāj from a loose society into an organization with members formally initiated by a ceremony. He drew up a declaration of faith, established a theological school, sent out the first Brāhmo missionaries, and created a new liturgy, the 'Brāhma Rites'. He himself was inclined towards the contemplative and the *bhakti* aspect of Hinduism, and averse to Rām Mohan's rationalism. With a stress on devotion, ethical duties, and the near-Vedic but non-idolatrous Brāhma rites, the Samāj moved closer to the mainstream of Hinduism, as it grew quickly in numbers. Its main preoccupation was with religious not social reform, and it avoided offending orthodoxy too much.

But with Keshub Chandra Sen (1838–84) a new wind started to blow in the Samāj. Soon after his accession to the Society, Debendranāth elevated him to leadership next to himself. Keshub was an impatient iconoclastic reformer, repudiating all Hindu cult, rejecting caste and the seclusion of women. In religion he had a new 'universalistic' tendency, with strong leanings towards Christianity. Soon the Samāj split in two; on the one hand Debendranāth and the older members, cautious in reform, Hindu in religion, formed the Ādi Brāhmo Samāj; on the other Keshub and his young men, impatient and cosmopolitan, established the new Brāhmo Samāj of India. Sen's Samāj was the most popular. Universalism was stressed by the introduction of selected texts from the great religions, and on the other hand the connection with Hinduism and with Bengal was strengthened by the adoption of modes of worship characteristic of the followers of Chaitanya, such as the public devotionalism of the *samkīrtan*. In the social sphere too Keshub forged ahead, and in 1871, after visiting England, he founded the Indian Reform Association, which organized female education, workers' education, charity, and temperance bodies. Keshub achieved a great success in the passing of the Marriage Act (1872) which legalized Brāhmo marriages. This, however, was perhaps the main factor in effectively separating the Brāhmos from the Hindu community, thus impeding greatly their effectiveness as a leaven of society.

The year 1872 constituted the peak of Keshub's career and influence: at that time he was no doubt the most vigorous, inspiring, and admired religious and social reformer in India. It was perhaps the influence of Rāmakrishna that now made Keshub become increasingly obsessed with his own religious development. He saw himself more and more as a new prophet, a new Christ, a new Chaitanya. He introduced new eclectic Hindu rites involving lights and fire and Mother-worship, while at the same time he was more and more attracted to Christianity. All this mystic preoccupation drew him away from social reform. When in 1878 he allowed his thirteen-year-old daughter to marry a prince with Hindu rites, it was the occasion for the majority of Brāhmos to break away, forming the Sādhāran Brāhmo Samāj. Keshub now formed the Church of the New Dispensation, intended to unite all creeds. It was a strange syncretism of beliefs and cults, with as its centre Keshub, the new Christ. Soon after Keshub's death it broke up into insignificant parties.

Of the three Samājes it was the Sādhāran which persisted and remained a force for reform in Bengal. Keshub somehow made it impossible for this first socio-religious reform movement in India really to become an all-India affair, and, despite his popularity, the movement proved to have no lasting effect on the masses. On the other hand, Keshub at his best did augur the next stage of the movement in his vision of an all-India reform and one that concerned the masses.

During this time Bengal also produced the scholar Īśvarachandra Vidyāsāgar (1820–91) who took up the widow remarriage movement, the first social reform cause that was taken up all over the country, and who saw it to a successful conclusion. Scholar and principal of Sanskrit College, he is venerated as the 'father of the Bengālī prose style'. The reform he advocated and saw become law, namely that a high-caste widow could legally remarry, affected few individuals and in fact was taken advantage of by very few for many years to come. Nevertheless, the widow remarriage movement was very important because it became the inspiration of other reform movements all over the country.

Mahārāshtra

From 1840 on we find in Mahārāshtra ample evidence of a growing religious and social reform awareness. There were already in many places local reform groups and societies, many of which were started by students of the Elphinstone Institution founded in 1827. In this early stage two personalities already stand out. Gopāl Hari Deshmukh (1823–92), known as Lokahitawādī, was English-educated and destined for a legal career. His writings in Marāthī contained bitter attacks against the social iniquities of traditional society, the caste system, and the condition of women. He also denounced loudly that typical feature of Mahārāshtra, the absolute intellectual and moral dominance of brāhmans over Hindu life. His friend and collaborator Jotibā Govind Phūle (1827–90), of low caste, took up this fight against brāhmanic oppression in his voluminous prose and poetic works, and gave it concrete form in his organization for the uplift of the low castes, the Satyaśodhak Samāj. Among many theoretical reformers, Phūle was a very practical man: he started girls' schools, schools for untouchables, a foundling home for widows' children. His passionate and practical concern was for the poor, the low-caste workers, the peasants. In his work we find the beginnings of the later political anti-brāhman movement of Mahārāshtra, and also of the trade unions.

In 1867 Mahārāshtra brought forth its own organization of religious and social reform, the Prārthanā Samāj. It was a visit of Keshub Chandra Sen as a Brāhmo Samāj missionary that inspired the Mahārāshtrians to found their own society. The theism of the Prārthanā Samāj was similar to that of its Bengālī counterpart, but it was consciously linked with the *bhakti* tradition of the Mahārāshtrian saints. There was the same rejection of idolatry, a negative attitude to the *Vedas* and transmigration, and a similar type of congregational worship. Social reform was also closely connected with religious reform, concerning itself mainly with the iniquities of the caste system and the condition of women.

Despite these similarities to Bengal, the movement in Mahārāshtra was also in certain aspects quite different from its Bengālī counterpart. The Mahārāshtrians saw reform as a gradual process of transformation of values and institutions. They invoked their own medieval *bhakti* tradition as another reform movement that was evolutionary, not revolutionary. Reform should not break with Hinduism nor should it break with society. Their social behaviour was guided by this caution: though iconoclastic in their pronouncements, they were careful not to offend orthodoxy and caste prejudices by rebellious action. They also had a different attitude towards the connection between religious and social reform. Whereas the Bengālīs felt the need of a close relation between the two, and were inwardly compelled either to become atheists or to form a new creed and cult in order to make the two harmonize, the Mahārāshtrians believed that social and religious reforms could go their separate, yet connected, evolutionary ways. There was no need to revolutionize the social fabric or the Hindu religion. As a result they concentrated on the propagation of their ideas through education and writing on the one hand, and they got down to the practical task of social work on the other.

The Prārthanā Samāj, as an organization, never had a great influence. But its members, like M. G. Rānade, R. G. Bhāndarkār, and K. T. Telang, were among the great leaders of nineteenth-century Mahārāshtra and they became the founders of the Social Reform Movement in later years. The special character of this movement ensured the possibility of its reaching out to the whole society, and not just to a separate sectarian group, and thus it was able to develop into a movement for general social reform, as we shall soon see.

At this early stage religious and social reform was practically non-existent in Madras. There were some Brāhmo Samāj and some Prārthanā Samāj groups, established by Bengālī and Mahārāshtrian missionaries, but Madras was very slow to get really started. The reason for this seems to have been the peculiar social structure prevalent there. It was a very rigid, ossified system, fiercely dominated by the brāhmans, who were also the few English-educated south India had so far produced. Social reform took long to break through in this region.

North India

Northern India in the meantime produced a real Hindu Luther, whose reform work was to have the deepest and most lasting effect. Dayānanda Saraswatī's (1824–83) formative years were very different from those of most other reformers, for whom English education was a major element in their development. Dayānanda, from a Gujarātī brāhman family, ran away from home in his youth to become an ascetic. For seventeen years he wandered around India, putting himself to school under different teachers, and observing Hinduism with a closeness no other reformer ever achieved. In 1863 he became a wandering preacher, and five years later he added the establishment of schools to his activities. In 1872 he met the Brāhmos in Calcutta, and he is said to have followed two suggestions of Keshub: to give up his *sannyāsī*'s near-nakedness and dress like a townsman, and to preach in the vernacular instead of in Sanskrit. By now his ideas had crystallized, and in 1875 he published his major work the *Satyārth Prakāsh* and founded his reform society, the Ārya Samāj.

This enormously impressive and powerful figure was a striking combination of the traditional ascetic and the modern reformer. The formative years of his life were spent as a wandering *sannyāsī* learning the scriptures, striving through yoga and asceticism to find his religious fulfilment, and all the time observing living Hinduism from within. Then quite suddenly he appears on the stage as a Luther, attacking the excrescences of Hinduism. But his style is still very traditional: his preaching is done orally in Sanskrit, and he challenges the great pandits to public debates where he endeavours to prove his point of view by reference to the scriptures. And finally, after his contact with the Brāhmo and Prārthanā Samāj leaders, a new approach emerges: that of the organizing reformer. And here we see him successfully adopt the modern reform techniques: the vernacular, publication, education, organization. It was the powerful combination of all these elements that made Dayānanda into a unique figure among the nineteenth-century reformers.

Dayānanda's theological vision was one that emerged neither from a personal mysticism nor from Western ideas, but from the intimate observation of the corrupt Hinduism of his day. He attacked polytheism, idolatry, and the many superstitious beliefs and rites connected with them, and the stranglehold of the brāhmans on sacred lore and religious practice. He had the vision of a primeval monotheism, above the paraphernalia and hostilities of all human creeds. This religion, he felt, was in fact the original Vedic religion, which was contained in the four *Vedas* but had become corrupted over the centuries. It was his aim to propagate the truth of that religion, to reinstate it in its purity, and thereby to reinstate the Indian people in their forgotten glory. Thus Dayānanda's religion, whilst denouncing much of contemporary Hinduism, kept close to orthodoxy in several basic ways: belief in the *Vedas*, and in *karma* and transmigration, and allegiance to the six *darshanas* and to the various Hindu names for the one God. This theology had a great attraction for many, especially because of its proud assertion of the superiority of the Vedic faith over all religions, and its offer of the possibility of being a non-idolatrous monotheist without ceasing to be a thorough Hindu.

In his reform of ritual Dayānanda was inspired by the same spirit. Though he purged them of their idolatrous and superstitious impurities, he kept the basic rites of Hinduism: the five daily sacrifices and the sixteen sacraments. To these he added the new reformist type of communal worship, including the singing of hymns, sermons, and lectures, besides the new *homa* sacrifice.

Dayānanda's social reform was founded on the basic assumption that the many sectarian or caste taboos and customs that tyrannized over every aspect of a Hindu's life had in themselves no religious meaning. Over the centuries these excrescences had accumulated and had been given religious importance by the brāhmans in order to dominate the people. The contemporary caste system was nothing but the utter degeneration of the original Vedic *varna* system: society was then divided in four classes according to the deeds and qualities of each individual person, and women had equal rights with men. That was the system, Dayānanda felt, to which India should return, and the main instruments of reform would have to be three. Schools would rear the children in the new spirit, completely isolated from contemporary society; government action would reclassify people according to qualities and merit; and a *śuddhi* campaign would bring Christians and Muslims back to the Hindu fold. This aim and programme were obviously long-range, and Dayānanda was too much of a realist to expect implementation of the perfect society in his own day: he did not launch a direct attack on caste, nor did he expect anti-caste action from his followers.

The beginnings of the Ārya Samāj were tentative. Although many aspects of Dayānanda's social platform and the iconoclastic side of his religious programme appealed to many, the intellectuals of Bombay and Calcutta, influenced as they were by their own provincial attitudes towards religious reform, found Dayānanda's Vedic creed not at all palatable. But after a few years the Samāj scored explosive success in the Panjāb, and from then on it became the most broadly based movement of all. Although Dayānanda does in a sense belong to this first period of individualistic reform, in another way he represents a transitional stage and inaugurates future developments with his vision of a complete overhaul of Hindu society and his creative amalgamation of reform and nationalism.

II. The Second Stage: 1880–1900

From 1880 two important tendencies which had been stirring in the previous decades occupied the Indian scene: nationalism and political action. From now on individuals and groups openly identified themselves with an Indian nation, a new concept in Indian history; and this élite group, consciously nationalist, conceived its function as being primarily one of political agitation and reform. This predominance of nationalism and politics now began to exert influence on the ideas of religious and social reform which had previously prevailed. Nationalism itself developed two patterns, a religious one and a secular one, and each school assigned a different place to social reform.

Two early outstanding examples of the new religious nationalism are Bankim and Tilak. It is very striking how the religious nationalism of both in fact had deep provincial roots, and may be seen as Bengālī and Mahārāshtrian nationalism respectively, only half-heartedly projected on to an all-India scale. Bankim Chandra Chatterjee (1838–94) found Bengal divided between the traditionalist orthodox and the progressive reformers, both of whom he saw as unable to create a real revival, the ones slaves to rigid tradition, the others blind admirers of the West. Bankim felt that real revival could only be achieved by changing the national character through an internal reform of Hinduism. For the last twenty years of his life Bankim wrote voluminously with that one purpose: to lay the religious foundations of the revival of a strong Bengal, virile and independent. His religion combines the humanism of Positivism with the activist interpretation of the Krishna myth and of the Bengālī cult of the Mother Goddess. His novels in particular awoke in the Bengālīs, first the middle class, and later the masses, a self-confidence and pride in their language and their religion. It was a new nationalism, profoundly Bengālī, and radically Hindu, the religious aspect of which was reinforced by a new pride in the historical heroes of Bengal as celebrated in Bankim's novels.

Bāl Gangādhar Tilak (1857–1920) was as Mahārāshtrian in his nationalism as Bankim was Bengālī. He too wanted the Indians to become strong again, proud and united in nationalism, and he too saw Hinduism as the very basis of this new spirit. To promote this spirit he published books and articles, exalting the antiquity and greatness of Hinduism, and preaching activism in his *Gītā Rahasya*. But he did more: he inaugurated new Hindu festivals, the Ganapati festival and the Śivājī festival, thus reaching the populace with his ideas of Hindu nationalistic activism, instilling in them a pride in their glorious Mahārāshtrian past. Although he was not himself against social change, he was against social reform inspired by Western ideas. He advocated the severance of social reform and political agitation. Nationalist Hindu politics should come first and extend to the masses, and this was incompatible in his mind with social reform. He relentlessly fought the reformers on this point.

It was in the 1880s that the social reform movement at last became organized on a national basis. It was a Bombay Pārsī, Behrāmjī Malabārī (1853–1912), who launched the issue that set social reform on its way to becoming consciously national: the campaign for the legal checking of infant marriage by an Age of Consent Bill. Malabārī's campaign was different from earlier ones in that it was the work of a determined and skilful journalist who was primarily intent on putting the concrete and harrowing reality before the people in such a way that it could not be ignored. And ignored it was not. No other cause excited such a storm over the whole of India for such a prolonged period. No reformer or politician could afford not to take sides. The Age of Consent Bill controversy put social reform on the national map, never to be ignored again, and achieved the indissoluble wedding of social reform with the nationalist movement. On the one hand it thus propagated effectively social reform ideas, but on the other hand it also publicized the anti-reformers, revivalists like Tilak, and made them close their ranks. This first battle between the reformers and the revivalists was won by the former, whose ideology was best expressed by Rānade and implemented in the National Social Conference.

When the Indian National Congress was founded in 1885 the question came up immediately whether or not the Congress should include social reform in its deliberations. The question was debated for a couple of years, while the Age of Consent Bill controversy was raging, and it was finally decided to exclude social questions from Congress deliberations, but to form a separate body, The National Social Conference, to meet each year immediately after the Congress meeting. M. G. Rānade (1852–1901) was the key theorist and organizer of this Conference. The first important way in which the Conference broke with the existing provincial social reform bodies, was in its affirmation of a secular ideology: thus it had the same secular roots as the Congress, emphasizing that individual conscience and humanism were the basic motives of reform. The Conference was not an active instigator of reform; its role was that of a national focus of local reform work: local work was given national recognition, and the reformers discussed their aims and methods in this forum, and passed resolutions of an all-India nature. Rānade, the guiding light, walked the tightrope in trying to keep the different approaches together, advocating reform along the lines of least resistance. But as the century drew to a close, the more radical reformers became more vocal and pressing for action. When Rānade died in 1901 and his leadership was taken over by Chandavarkār, an era of moderation ended, and a new urgency and impatience, a bolder spirit asserted itself.

While during the last two decades of the nineteenth century the evolution described above was going on on the national stage, the provincial reform groups continued their own growth. In this period the social reform movement experienced a steady growth of adherents and activities in all areas, except Bengal.

Mahārāshtra

In Mahārāshtra all major towns started their own local Reform Associations, the activity and growth of which depended much on the individual leaders. An outstanding personality was the widow Panditā Ramābāī (1858–1922) who founded in 1890 the Sharadā Sadan, a home for high class widows in Poona. She was closely assisted by Dhondu Kheshave (later Mahārshi) Kārve, who married a widow himself and revived the Widows Remarriage

Association of Poona. He too established a home for widows, and promoted female education. The Prārthanā Samāj continued its work, and sponsored reform mainly through educational work directed at women and low-caste workers, elementary schools, and orphanages. Although it was little preoccupied with religious life and reform, it retained, in an age when secularist humanism was strong, the vital connection between social and religious reform.

Madras

Madras at this time was only just beginning to interest itself in social reform. The rigidity of the caste structure and the slower political awakening in this province were certainly important causes of this delay. In 1892 the Madras Hindu Social Reform Association came into being, led mostly by radical reformers. They, however, were a small high-caste group, and their ambition was mostly turned inwards upon the members, who individually took a number of reformist pledges. Two individual reformers did make their mark in local work at the time: Vīresalingam Pantulu (1848–1919), whose efforts were concerned with the plight of widows, and R. Venkata Ratnam Naidu (1862–1939), who started a 'social purity movement' advocating temperance and combating the *devadāsī* custom.

Bengal

In Bengal, where social change had advanced rapidly, social reform went into a depression. The Sādhāran Brāhmo Samāj was very active in philanthropic work on behalf of the underprivileged and the lower classes, but it was not engaged in social reform as such. An outstanding exception was Shashīpada Banerjī, who worked valiantly for the uplift of women and widows, and married a widow himself. In this province, where the commitment by some to orthodoxy and by others to the West was more passionate and fanatical than elsewhere, the all-absorbing intensity of political commitment and the passion of cultural revival relegated social reform into the background.

Nevertheless, Bengal did produce a religious figure of immense influence: Rāmakrishna (1834–86). A simple temple priest at the temple of Kālī at Dakkhineshwarī near Calcutta, he achieved fame as a great mystic. He combined simplicity of preaching, mystical and philosophical depth, spiritual intensity, and direct earnestness, with a pure Hinduness to such a degree that even the most Westernized and sophisticated could hardly withstand his fascination. His doctrine, arrived at by experimentation with other religions, was simply that 'all religions are true', but that for everyone the religion he was born in was the best possible one. In a Śankarite way he did not condemn idolatry, as it met the religious needs of simple people. In the last years of his life he attracted around himself a group of young educated Bengālīs who were captivated by his personality and his doctrines. The leader of these was Narendranāth Datta (1862–1902), who became Vivekānanda, the founder of the Rāmakrishna Mission and of a new order of monks. His influence on Indian nationalism will be discussed later, and also the importance of the Rāmakrishna Mission as a religious and social reform organization.

North India

In northern India, the Panjāb and the North-Western Province, social reform was organized in a unique way. General bodies had little impact here: it was the Ārya Samāj and the caste organizations that dominated the scene. The Ārya Samāj, though it experienced a split between orthodox and liberals in 1893, grew as no reform body ever grew: by the end of the century its members were fast approaching 100,000. Their educational work was advancing steadily and they soon rivalled the Christian missionaries in the number of their schools. Dayānanda had certainly found the right formula for success: a combination of elements found in isolation elsewhere. The Samāj was efficiently administered and it had the cohesion and strength of a caste organization without being one; its members rivalled the Brāhmos in religious zeal; yet its social programme avoided the radicalism of the Brāhmos, but was rather inspired by the liberal approach of the Prārthanā Samāj: whilst continuing its intensive propaganda against idolatry, polytheism, and the social abuses of Hinduism, a propaganda reaching effectively an increasing percentage of the north Indian population, the Samāj did not require a break with Hindu society. The Ārya Samāj began effectively to reach out to the masses and started the process of changing Hindu society from within.

It was in the north that the first new caste organizations arose. Here the caste system had some characteristics which distinguished it from other regions and made reform through caste possible: the dominance of the brāhmans was comparatively weak, the majority of people belonged to intermediate contiguous castes, and the lowest groups were not so depressed as in other areas. Castes were traditionally well organized and held effective power over their members. What was new was that associations of related castes came into being: these were voluntary bodies to which caste leaders attached their own groups. Their prime concern was the welfare of the members, but their programme included many of the ideals and principles advocated by social reformers, so that the National Social Conference officially acknowledged them as reform societies.

In 1887 the Kāyastha Conference was formed in Lucknow, comprising the group of subcastes whose traditional occupation was that of writer. The early split of the organization into a reformist and an orthodox section testifies to the eager reformist ideas of a good number of its leaders. Another important organization was that of the Vaishyas, established in 1891. They succeeded in avoiding a split although their social reform platform was quite advanced, and their number and influence grew quickly, as can be gathered from the fact that by 1900 over 100 local *sabhās* were associated with the Conference. In this period the caste organizations kept away from politics, but in the twentieth century they assumed in several areas of India very great political importance, in fact frequently dominating the political game.

III. The Third Stage: from 1900

The first two decades of the twentieth century saw Indian politics engaged in the great debate between the moderates and the extremists, and in their struggle for control of the Congress. That story is told in another chapter. The development of the social reform movement, however, was intimately connected with that debate and that struggle. The main objections of the extremists against the moderate leadership were two: that in aims and methods the moderates were completely British-oriented and therefore slow and unpatriotic; and that they did not reach down to the mass of the people. The extremists advocated a militancy based on national and religious identification and wanted involvement of the masses. We have seen how these two essential aspects of religious nationalism and concern for the people were beginning to make themselves felt in Dayānanda, Keshub, and Bankim. Now they became the distinguishing characteristics of some of the most influential leaders of the time: Aurobindo Ghose, Lājpat Rāi, and Vivekānanda.

We saw how in the last two decades of the nineteenth century social reform was dominated by the nationalistic secularists. The revivalist extremists naturally opposed this approach vehemently, as being denationalizing and degrading because it was based on European ideas and aspired to European models. So an intense debate between the reformers and the revivalists ensued. However, most of the revivalists, except Tilak, were themselves very much committed to social reform in many spheres of life. In their interchange with the reformers it became increasingly clear that, as far as the programme of reform was concerned, there was a very large area of agreement between the two groups. The differences lay in inspiration, in motivation, and in the model of society they aspired to. The revivalists succeeded in demonstrating that a purely nationalistic motive and a Hindu model could be the inspiration for whatever reform the reformer envisaged. But they proved more than that: they showed that Hindu nationalism and an ideal Hindu society had a mass appeal that was absent in Western-type reform. These arguments were irresistible, and the reform movement as a whole changed its image and its model in the direction of revivalist Hindu nationalism, and veered towards a concern for the mass of the people. Let us now see how this revivalist Hinduism evolved in different ways in some of the outstanding personalities, and how the concern for broader-based social reform affected the evolution of reformist bodies.

Vivekānanda (1863–1902), the great disciple of Rāmakrishna, was strongly influenced by very different streams of thought. First there was his Western education, and close contact with Keshub's Brāhmo Samāj. Then followed the influence of his master Rāmakrishna, the Hindu mystic. After the master's death Vivekānanda wandered around India, and then he spent several years in America and Europe. Thus, among the nationalists of his time, his experience was perhaps the broadest. His knowledge of living Hinduism approached Dayānanda's. His knowledge of the West was not only theoretical, but he knew the West from personal experience, which allowed him to renounce all its evils and yet acknowledge its strength. He knew the reform movement at first hand, and on his wanderings through India he had verified the paltriness of its impact. The influence of Rāmakrishna on him was very great; it gave him an overriding pride in the theoretical and practical achievements of Hinduism. He saw the deficiencies of Hinduism more clearly than many, and he denounced them more vehemently: the tyranny of the brāhmans, the degeneration of caste, the stultification of ritual, the physical and moral cowardice. Yet he castigated the reformers mercilessly for their literature of abuse, their 'ornamental' reforms, their arrogance borrowed from a veneer of Western education. The reform he preached passionately was to be evolutionary, not breaking with the past, inspired by the Hindu religious conviction that man is God, reaching out to the root of all evils, the condition of the poor. Such reform would lead to the *punya bhūmi*, the holy land of India, where the nobility of man and his spirituality would both be fully developed.

His influence on his time in the short decade of his public life, on the national scale, was the influence of the powerful message of a great national saint. Having shown to the West the greatness of Hinduism, he was listened to when he spoke harshly of Hindu shortcomings, and when he proclaimed the message of national religious renaissance. This message, however, was not worked out into a programme, and he did not have a political base; therefore he did not become a national leader. However, his leadership found scope in the Rāmakrishna Mission, which in this century has become an important agency of religious reform and social service, especially in Bengal.

The long life of Aurobindo Ghose (1872–1950) was full of contrasts. His education was completely English: from the age of seven he spent fourteen years in England. On his return to India his political period began, ending in 1910 when he retired to his Pondicherry *āshram* and devoted his life to philosophy and mysticism. In an early pamphlet, *Bhavānī Mandir*, Aurobindo shows how strongly he had been influenced by Bankim's ideas. We have here the idea of a religious order devoted to the Mother, and to political and social action to regenerate India. The *Śakti*, or Mother, represents India, the motherland, which must be the focus of these modern monks. This religious basis of nationalism remained essential to Aurobindo throughout his political career; in fact to him nationalism was religion. From his very early days he also accused the Congress of failing to reach the masses, and proclaimed that it was through the religion of the Mother that the masses could be effectively reached. These ideas came to their full efflorescence during the years when he collaborated with B. C. Pāl in the editorship of *Bande Mātaram*. His term in jail in 1908, where he studied the *Gītā* and experimented in yoga and forms of mysticism, completely redirected his life. He retired to Pondicherry, where he established an *āshram*. Here he built his own original philosophy of integral non-dualism and achieved the reputation of a great mystic and a saint. He acquired a number of Indian and European followers, but the Pondicherry *āshram* was very much a circle of initiates in an esoteric gnostic religion without any significant influence on Indian life.

Lālā Lājpat Rāi (1856–1928), born in the Panjāb, was the son of a Hindu father with leanings to Islam, who was a follower of Syed Ahmad Khān, and an orthodox Sikh mother. He was brought up on Islamic teachings, but soon he rejected his upbringing and strongly identified himself with Hinduism. After a time as a member of the Brāhmo Samāj, he joined the Ārya Samāj. In 1885 he founded with Hans Rāj the Dayānanda Anglo-Vedic College at Lāhore, and became involved in Ārya leadership; at the time of the split in 1898, Lājpat became the leader of the liberal branch. In the last decade of the nineteenth century his initial interest in Congress politics faded, but he came back into the political sphere from 1900 onwards, became a very powerful extremist leader, and was accused by the non-political Āryas of drawing the Samāj into politics against the desire of Dayānanda.

Lājpat Rāi's writings and actions clearly demonstrate the man and his ideas: Ārya ideology wedded to extremist nationalist politics. During the famines of 1896–7 and 1899–1900, he was extremely active in relief operations, largely financed by his own funds, and in 'rescuing' thousands of orphans from Christian missionaries. At the 1900 Lāhore Congress he moved the resolution to devote at least half a day of each annual session to the discussion of industrial and educational problems. He was also largely responsible for the new interest of the Ārya Samāj in the low castes, and in 1920 he was elected president of the first All-India Trade Union Congress. In his opinion the moderate Congress had a beggar mentality, was smug with false hopes from the British, did not see beyond its own little circle, and was satisfied with holding an annual festival of English-educated Indians. After his visit to England he declared that the Congress was foolish to expect the British people and politicians to help India: they were not interested. Congress, he declared, should become a bold Hindu organization, building a nation from below, based on a nationalism rooted in Hinduism. He indicted the social reform leaders for basing their reform on 'rationality' instead of 'nationality', but, being a liberal Ārya, his revivalist reform ideas were tempered and he worked hard at the new nationalist direction given to the reform movement. In October 1928, although his health was failing, he led a procession against the Simon Commission and was struck in a *lāthī* charge. This aggravated his condition and he died a fortnight later.

It now remains to look at the provincial social reform organizations and see how the new spirit of the twentieth century influenced them to direct their main attention to the masses of the population and make social reform effectively a national mass-based movement.

North India

In northern India the Ārya Samāj gave the lead. Until 1900 the Samāj had preached caste reform but had not really expected anybody but ardent Āryas to act upon it, and its membership was in fact mostly restricted to the educated classes. From 1900 onwards the Samāj, the two factions collaborating, started a campaign to reform the caste system. The method was nothing short of revolutionary: the low-caste groups were recruited and their status was ceremonially raised to that of the twice-born with rights of interdining and intermarriage. The success of Christian missionaries in converting these low castes was definitely an important factor in the action of the Samāj. In fact the movement for conversion of low castes grew out of the *śuddhi* movement for conversion of Christians and Muslims, the child of Dayānanda's fierce Hindu nationalism, and gradually involved the Samāj more and more in communal agitation and in collaboration with the communal orthodoxy of the Mahāsabhā. Once the first induction of a low-caste group was achieved, the movement gained a momentum which even surprised the Ārya reformers themselves. Scores of low-caste and untouchable groups were admitted, swelling the numbers of the Samāj from about 100,000 at the turn of the century to

500,000 by 1921, and to nearly a million by 1931. The procedure of this elevation was such that it did not unduly offend orthodoxy, while yet attacking its principles. Although the new recruits were introduced to Vedic ritual, invested with the sacred thread, allowed to take water from a high-caste well, and thus moved up in the social scale, they retained their own group identity, and caste distinctions between high-caste Āryas and the purified groups were not as such abolished. Both by its successful syncretism of social reform and Hindu nationalism and by its successful reaching out to the mass of the people, the Ārya Samāj proved the most impressive and influential religious and social reform movement of the era.

Mahārāshtra

Mahārāshtra had its own approach: revivalism here did not coalesce with social reform, probably because of the hostility of Tilak and the influence of Rānade. But social reform in the twentieth century expressed its new spirit by an increased concern for the mass of the people. In Mahārāshtra a great number of societies arose, not unified like the Ārya Samāj, but in a way more practical and down to earth in their approach. Only the most important can be mentioned here. The Social Science League, started in 1911 in Bombay by Chandavārkār, active to this day, pioneered in its concern for the working classes by initiating night schools, technical schools, libraries, recreational facilities, and co-operative credit societies. The Sevā Sadan, on the other hand, established by Malabārī, specialized in the care of women of all castes, providing educational, welfare, and medical services. Mahārshi Kārve put the crown on his work for women's uplift by inaugurating a women's university.

The Servants of India Society, founded by G. K. Gokhale in 1915, was a society for an élite of dedicated individuals, who were rigorously trained and paid a subsistence salary only. Its membership remained small, its influence as an institution limited, but the work of its members in social reform was very considerable, again in the practical field of famine relief, union organization, co-operatives, and uplift of tribals and depressed classes. The Prārthanā Samāj, similarly limited in influence as a body, also entered this field by its most effective Depressed Classes Mission of India, founded in 1906. By 1913 it ran thirty educational institutions and has rightly been called 'a forerunner to Gandhian programmes for the Harijans'. The non-brāhman movement of Jotibā Phūle, mentioned previously, languished after his death, but was revived in the 1900s by the Maharāja of Kolhāpur State. In order to break the stranglehold of the brāhmans and raise the low-caste people, he trained non-brāhmans to perform the Vedic ceremonies for them and later called in the Ārya Samāj to continue this religious reform. He also reserved 50 per cent of the civil service posts in his state for non-brāhmans and organized schools for them. Later on this non-brāhman movement was to become a formidable political force in south India. The later movement in Mahārāshtra for the emancipation of the untouchables, led by Dr. Ambedkār, was primarily political in nature.

Madras

After 1900 the slow-starting movement in Madras got under way. Revivalist thought in south India had received a powerful stimulus from Vivekānanda's visit and the writings and speeches of Annie Besant, the leader of the Theosophical Society. At first Mrs. Besant was an anti-reformist religious revivalist, but around the end of the nineteenth century one of the many changes in her attitudes was on the way, and in 1904 she founded the Madras Hindu Association 'to promote Hindu social and religious advancement on national lines in harmony with the spirit of Hindu civilization'. Her great influence both in Madras and on a national scale supported the new alliance of revivalism and social reform. Madras thus became in tune with the national tendency. The great social problem of the south was the tremendous gap between the high and the low castes, and the utter degradation of the latter. Their rise in status and in power during the twentieth century was spectacular, but not as a direct result of the work of the social reform movement as such. More effective factors were first the great advance in social services for depressed classes and workers, conducted by a variety of organizations, Christian missions, the Theosophical Society, the Depressed Classes Mission, and the Rāmakrishna Mission. In fact it has been stated with good reason that before the First World War Madras may have led the rest of India in this field. The second important factor in the uplift of the lower classes, outside the scope of this survey, was the work of the political non-brāhman movements of later years.

Bengal

The situation in Bengal was very different from that in the other provinces. On the one hand Bengal possessed by far the most 'socially reformed' group: the Brāhmos and the Western-educated gravitating around them. On the other hand, the social movement as such had become practically non-existent. The Bengālī leaders themselves recognized this fact and they even analysed the causes of this decline. Essentially, the reason was the combination of the peculiar quality of Brāhmo reformism and the enormous vigour of political nationalism and cultural revivalism. Brāhmoism was the prototype of reform in Bengal, and it was intensely individualistic and Western-inspired. When cultural revivalism was set in motion by Bankim, and the intense political preoccupation was spurred to excess by the partition of Bengal, these two took complete hold of the Bengālī mind, and the appeal of the reform movement in Bengal soon dwindled to insignificance.

A good deal of practical social work was increasingly undertaken, mostly by the Sādhāran Brāhmo Samāj, but it did not grow out into social reform crusades nor did it take organizational forms. When Shashīpada Banerjī withdrew from active life just before the partition of Bengal, Bengal lost her last reformist crusader.

Conclusion

By the 1920s the Indian religious and social reform movement had lost its peculiar identity as an important and distinct phenomenon of Indian life. Many factors contributed to this. One of them was the appearance on the national stage of Gāndhī, who was to dominate and often confuse it with his new ideas on politics, religion, and society. Politics themselves developed in a different way, and from now on we see a much closer association of concern for social reform with political awareness and action, and a conviction that the state through legislation must take responsibility for the reform of society. Nehrū's concept of the Welfare State embodied this ideal at its best. Another important factor was that agitation for social reform dispersed itself more and more into the practical business of organizing social service in different special fields, such as the education and uplift of women by the All-India Women's Conference, village development projects, the organization of the depressed classes, and the foundation of labour unions. But, in the final instance, these new attitudes and approaches, while pushing 'social reform' as a specifically identifiable label into the background, owe their very existence to those leaders and organizations that, from Rām Mohan Roy to Lājpat Rāi, worked for the emergence of national identity and social reform, and for their successful integration.

CHAPTER XXVII

Islamic Reform Movements

by Aziz Ahmad

The Mughal Empire crumbled rapidly after the death of Aurangzeb (1707). Even during his rule Hindu communities like the Marāthās and Jāts, as well as the Sikhs, had become a challenge to Muslim power. After the death of Aurangzeb, as these elements, especially the Marāthās, overwhelmed the Mughal Empire, they threatened and largely destroyed the Muslim economic and political supremacy. There was no Muslim power in the subcontinent which could face this challenge or overcome it. It was at this stage that Islamic revivalism became a movement of religio-political thought rather than action in the writings of Shāh Walī-Allāh (1703–62).

He was essentially a theologian, and only in a very secondary measure concerned with political thought. At the pre-modernist stage of Islamic theological thinking in the first half of the eighteenth century the emphasis in the writings of Walī-Allāh, as of his well-known Arab contemporary Muhammad ibn 'Abd al-Wahhāb, the founder of the Wahhābī movement in Nejd, was on fundamentalism, which meant either a rejection or a symbiosis of the dogmas of various schools of jurisprudence (*fiqh*) and their replacement by a direct reference to the Qur'ān or what was generally regarded as authentic prophetic tradition (*hadīth*). In the case of both it meant a rejection of innovations or 'accretions' borrowed from other sources. Walī-Allāh especially rejected customs and beliefs borrowed from popular Hinduism, or customs and ceremonies analogically developed and thinly Islamized.

Both Walī-Allāh and Muhammad ibn 'Abd al-Wahhāb had a sense of mission and considered themselves as reformers or renovators of Muslim society. The latter was more successful in this than the former. Walī-Allāh was treated with suspicion by traditional Muslims and even his life was threatened. His political thought achieved results only after two generations; and it will be an exaggeration to say that his correspondence with the Afghan ruler Ahmad Shāh Abdālī or the Nizām al-Mulk of Hyderābād or Najīb al-Dawla of Rohilkhand played any direct part in the political history of the period, in inciting these Muslim potentates against the Marāthās.

But the impact of his religious and political thought was momentous in the second generation after him on the group of religious reformers referred to as Mujāhidīn (holy warriors) or as the followers of *Tarīqa-i Muhamadiyya*, referred to, rather confusingly, in the British records and writings as the 'Wahābīs'. In subsequent generations, especially after the Mutiny (1857–8), his religious rather than his political thought influenced every school of Islamic revivalism: the modernism of Sayyid Ahmad Khān and the Alīgarh movement, the traditionalist theologians of the Deoband School, and the neo-traditionalist *ahl-i hadīth* (followers of Muhammad's traditions).

His school in Delhi had probably, in those days of chaos and insecure communications, only a local significance. But his sons translated the Qur'ān into Urdū, as he had done into Persian. The most eminent of them, Shāh 'Abd al-'Azīz, has received wrong publicity for an anti-British ruling, in which he declared India as *dār al-harb* (enemy territory); recent research has shown his relations with the officers of East India Company were ambivalent, and at certain points friendly. His influence on Tīpū Sultān has also been suggested, but is very doubtful. Tīpū Sultān's conflict with the British and the Marāthās was much less an ideological Islamic struggle than an ambitious effort to maintain and extend an independent principality under his rule.

But when we come to the Mujāhidīn in the first two decades of the nineteenth century, there is no doubt that Walī-Allāh's movement takes the form of a social and political organization. The organizer of the movement of the Mujāhidīn was Sayyid Ahmad Barēlwī, a disciple of Shāh 'Abd al-'Azīz. Two learned scions of the family of Walī-Allāh, Shāh Ismā'īl and Shāh 'Abd al-Hayy, formed his brains trust. His was the first movement in Indian Islam to contact the masses, rural as well as urban. The party (*jamā'a*) which he built up consisted of a vast network among the Muslim population in northern India, with branches in certain major cities in the south. Propaganda was carried out by word of mouth and through tracts and poems; leaders of prayers were appointed in certain mosques to teach essentials of faith; even courts were established to administer justice among Muslims according to the Islamic law, parallel to government courts. In doctrine the movement was strictly fundamentalist and monotheistic, rejecting all associationism (*shirk*) of custom and folk-belief, and strongly opposed to syncretist trends such as visits to Hindu shrines, participation in Hindu festivals, or such social customs borrowed from Hinduism as excessive expenditure on weddings or prejudice against the remarriage of Hindus.

In the later 1820s the movement became militant, regarding *jihād* as one of the basic tenets of faith. Possibly encouraged by the British, with whom the movement did not feel powerful enough to come to grips at the outset, it chose as the venue of *jihād* the north-west frontier of the subcontinent, where it was directed against the Sikhs. Barēlwī temporarily succeeded in carving out a small theocratic principality which collapsed owing to the friction between his Pathān and north Indian followers; and he was finally defeated and slain by the Sikhs in 1831. The movement survived him for several decades, came into conflict with the British Government, and eventually petered out.

An almost independent offshoot of Barēlwī's movement was organized in West Bengal by one of his disciples, Mīr Nithār 'Alī (1782–1831), popularly known as Titū Mīr, whose organizational work among the Muslim peasants led to the opposition of Hindu landlords, powerful since the Permanent Settlement of 1793, and British indigo planters. Some Hindu landlords imposed a beard-tax on his followers and persecuted them in other ways. Titū Mīr's organization and his movement were not really as militant or revolutionary as the British records make out; only during the last year of his life was there confrontation between him and the British police. Finally he was killed in action in 1831 by a British regiment of native infantry.

About the same time, further to the east in Bengal, there spread another fundamentalist reformist movement known as the *Farā'idī* because of its emphasis on the Islamic pillars of faith (*farā'id*). Though any considerable link between Titū Mīr and the Farā'idīs is generally denied by scholars, there can be little doubt that these two Bengālī movements overlapped, in view of their proximity in time and place. They have several features in common. Both came in conflict with Hindu landlords and British indigo planters and eventually with the British administration in Bengal. Both preached a change in the mode of dress to distinguish the Muslims from the Hindus. Both preached intensively and in detail against customs and beliefs borrowed from popular Hinduism. The main difference between the two movements is that whereas the Farā'idīs suspended Friday and '*Īd* prayers, thinking of, if not proclaiming, India under the British as *dār al-harb* (enemy territory) where these prayers are not required, Titū Mīr did not do so.

But there can be little doubt that the genesis of the two movements was different. The Farā'idī movement shows the influence of Arab Wahhābism and little acquaintance with the general theological thought of Shāh Walī-Allāh. Its founder, Hājī Sharī'at-Allāh, had lived in the Hijāz from 1799 to 1818 and probably visited it once again soon after. The movement he started affirmed strongly the unity of God and aimed at the eradication of social innovations current among the Muslims of Bengal, many of them borrowed from Hinduism. These included quasi-worship at various syncretistic or pseudo-Muslim shrines, and floating of the *bherā* (ceremonial boat), a fertility rite, ceremonial dances, planting of banana trees (phallic symbols) round the house on the occasion of the first menstruation of a girl, and other such rites. Though Sharī'at-Allāh's movement clashed with the interests of the landed gentry of Bengal and he was suspected and persecuted, it remained under him religious and social rather than political. Under his son Dudū Miyān, from 1840 onwards, it became revolutionary. Dudū Miyān built it into a hierarchical organization rising from the village to the provincial level with a *khalīfa* (authorized deputy) at each level. This hierarchical organization was almost like a parallel government embracing all the Farā'idīs, their affairs and disputes. He organized a para-military force, armed only with clubs, to fight the henchmen of Hindu landlords or even the police. He was arrested and released a number of times; but the Farā'idī movement, which could once count one third of the Muslim population of Dāccā among its adherents, became weak after his arrest in 1847. After Dudū Miyān's death in 1862 it survived merely as a religious movement without any political overtones.

The main traditional Muslim opposition to the Farā'idī movement came from the Ta'ayyunī movement led by Karāmat 'Ali Jawnpurī and deriving its inspiration from the religious thought of Shāh Walī-Allāh. The direct conflict between the Farā'idīs and the Ta'ayyunīs began about 1839 and lasted for nearly two decades. Like the Farā'idīs, the Ta'ayyunīs also rejected innovations and syncretistic practices. But they rejected the Farā'idī doctrine that faith without work was insufficient. Other differences were on points of ritual. They were strongly critical of the Farā'idī suspension of Friday and '*Īd* prayers, arguing that, since there was religious freedom for the Muslims under British rule, India was not *dār al-harb*; if it was not *dār al-Islām* (Islamic territory), it was at least a land of peace (*dār al-amān*).

The Mutiny of 1857–8 is the watershed which divides the earlier pre-modernist fundamentalist movements from the modernist, the reformist, and even the traditional movements of modern times. Recent hagiographical historiography has over-emphasized the participation and role of the '*ulamā*' (Muslim theologians) in the Mutiny. While the influence of the '*ulamā*' on the course of the Mutiny can be stated as minimal, some of them at Thāna Bhawan did put up some resistance against the British, while some others in Delhi, presumably under pressure from the mutineer Bakht Khān, issued a *fatwā*' (edict) proclaiming holy war.

The Mutiny shattered the fabric of Muslim upper classes in and around Delhi, though not perhaps to the same extent in the Panjāb and Avadh. It was a Muslim of Delhi, Sayyid Ahmad Khān,[1] who first saw not merely the advisability but the necessity of a change in the religious and political outlook of the Muslim community. The prolonged Muslim confrontation with the East India Company in northern India had failed everywhere from the north-west frontier to Bengal. A change in the entire political outlook was as necessary as a recognition of the need for adjustment with the new age of Western domination and Western intellectual outlook. Sayyid Ahmad Khān's programme of reform and adjustment was threefold: educational, religious, and political.

His educational programme emphasized from the outset the advantages of the use of English as the medium of instruction. In 1864 he founded a Scientific Society for the introduction of Western sciences through translations into Urdū of works on physical sciences and through a bilingual journal. The same year he founded a modern school at Ghāzīpur. In 1868 he promoted the formation of education committees in several districts, to initiate modern education among the Muslims.

During his visit to Europe in 1869–70 he developed the plans of his life-work, a major educational institution for Indian Muslims. This institution came into being at Alīgarh, where the school classes were opened in 1875 and college classes in 1878. This Muhammedan Anglo-Oriental College was to become the Muslim University after his death. It became the nursery of Muslim political and intellectual leaders as well as of the Muslim element of the bureaucracy. Even today it is the last bastion of Muslim scholarship in the Republic of India. In 1886 Sayyid Ahmad Khān founded the Muhammedan Anglo-Oriental Educational Conference for the general promotion of Western education among Indian Muslims.

Sayyid Ahmad Khān's efforts at religious reform were more personal, though linked with, and to some extent necessitated by, his educational programme. His first major religious writing, his Commentary on the Bible, predates his educational activities, and was no doubt a genuine effort at understanding the Christian faith from a Muslim viewpoint. It was also one of the few and rare experiments in religious pluralism in the intellectual history of Islam. But his major religious writings followed his educational programme.

[1] We retain the author's spelling, which is an accurate transliteration of the Perso-Arabic script. Elsewhere in this volume the first name of this famous reformer will be found spelt *Syed*, which is the spelling he himself favoured when rendering his name in Roman script. [Ed.]

The journal *Tahdhīb al-akhlāq*, which was to revolutionize Urdū journalism, was founded to counteract the scepticism, agnosticism, and atheism which followed the study of Western sciences at Alīgarh. To counter these trends Sayyid Ahmad Khān and his two major associates, Chirāgh 'Alī and Muhsin al-Mulk, developed a new apologetics, explaining away whatever appeared to them as contrary to the conclusions of science or of 'natural law', in Islam and in the Qur'ān. Sayyid Ahmad Khān's basic religious position was that the Qur'ān was the word of God, and 'nature' was the work of God; it followed that between the 'word of God' and the 'work of God' there could be no contradiction. His apologetics took a very anti-traditional route in explaining away the Qur'ān's eschatology, angelology, demonology, and cosmology. His most characteristic religious work was his Commentary on the Qur'ān which was so 'modernistic' and anti-traditional that it was vehemently attacked by the theologians and Sayyid Ahmad Khan was dubbed a 'naturalist' (*nīcharī*). In detail the religious thought of Sayyid Ahmad Khān and his associates had no general following; but its general effect was tremendous. He liberalized Indian Islam and made it susceptible to new ideas and new interpretations.

Sayyid Ahmad Khān's political activity began with the propagation of the view that it was futile to challenge the British role in India, that it was to be accepted as a reality, and as such the Muslim community should adjust itself to a *modus vivendi* with it. This should take the form of a staunch loyalism and a support for *pax Britannica* under which the Indo-Muslim community could transform itself and come to terms with the new age. In the beginning this loyalism was in conflict with emerging Hindu nationalism. The Urdū-Hindī controversy made Sayyid Ahmad Khān doubtful of the community of Hindu and Muslim interests, in the first instance. When a Muslim, Badr al-Dīn Tayyibjī (Tyabjee), was elected the leader of the Indian National Congress in 1887, Sayyid Ahmad Khān emerged actively in opposition to it. In his view a Hindu-Muslim alliance could only be disadvantageous to the Muslim community, which was much smaller in number, educationally backward, politically immature, and economically insecure. Alliance with the Hindus against the British could only lead to the loss of the British patronage and its substitution by the exploitation and subjugation of the Muslims by the overwhelming Hindu majority. Thus began modern Muslim political separatism in India.

Another interesting, though strictly apolitical, religious movement dates from the same period. This was the Ahmadī movement founded by Mirzā Ghulām Ahmad of Qādiyān (1839–1908) who began his work as a defender of Islam against the polemics of the Ārya Samāj and the Christian missionaries. In 1889 he claimed to be Masīh (Messiah) and Mahdī, and later also to be an incarnation of the Hindu god Krishna as well as Jesus returned to earth. The movement was really a heresy well within the bounds of Islam, as Ghulām Ahmad, though he called himself a minor prophet, regarded Muhammad as the true and great prophet whom he followed. His Christology, which created a mythology of Christ's sojourn and death in Kashmīr, differs from the Christologies of both Islam and Christianity. In social morals the Ahmadī movement has been very conservative, adhering to polygamy, veiling of women, and the classical rules of divorce. The Ahmadīs have their own mosques and do not pray with other Muslims. The members of the community pay 4 per cent of their income to a religious fund and may make further contributions to it. The organization of the community is strong and centralized. Its headquarters were in the town of its origin, Qādiyān, which went to India in the partition of the subcontinent in 1947; since then their centre has been at Rabwah in West Pakistan. They total about half a million, half that number living in West Pakistan. A split occurred in the movement in 1914 and it came to be divided in two groups: the Qādiyānī which does, and the Lāhorī which does not believe in the prophethood of Mirzā Ghulām Ahmad. Both groups have produced an extensive religious literature in Urdū, English, and other languages; and the Qādiyānī Ahmadīs have been for several decades very busy in the propagation of their form of Islam in Africa with considerable success. They have also missionary centres in several cities in the West.

The later half of the nineteenth and the early twentieth centuries also saw an orthodox revival, which was as much a reaction against the 'naturalist' modernism of Sayyid Ahmad Khān and the heretical messianism of the Ahmadī movement as an assertion in its own right of the traditional Islam.

The traditional revival was spearheaded by the seminary at Deoband, founded in 1867 by theologians of the School of Walī-Allāh, the most prominent among whom was Muhammad Qāsim Nanotawī who also took a prominent part in counter-polemics against the Christian missionaries and the Āryā Samājists. The principal objectives of the seminary at Deoband were to re-establish contact between the theologians and the educated Muslim middle classes, and to revive the study of Muslim religious and scholastic sciences. As a religious university Deoband soon became an honoured institution, not only in Muslim India but also in the world of Islam at large, and had a reputation second only to that of Al-Azhar in Cairo. The later scholars of Deoband, Mahmūd al-Hasan and Husayn Ahmad Madanī, participated in the Indian nationalist movement, in alliance with the Indian National Congress, while another Deoband scholar, Shabbīr Ahmad 'Uthmanī, supported the Pakistan movement; and yet another, 'Ubayd-Allāh Sindhī, developed a theory of Islamic socialism.

A school less conservative than Deoband and more responsive to the demands of the modern age was the Nadwat al-'ulamā', founded in 1894 at Lucknow by the historian Shiblī Nu'mānī and other scholars. The school aimed to offer an enlightened interpretation of religion in order to fight the trends of agnosticism and atheism which had followed the advent of modern Western education. One of the side-growths of this school was a publishing institution at A'zamgarh which made a valuable contribution to Indo-Islamic studies from a liberal Muslim point of view.

The third famous traditional school is the much older one at Farangī Mahal in Lucknow. Its fame rests principally on evolving the 'Nizāmiyya' syllabus which was followed by most religious or communal Muslim schools all over India. Unlike the two other schools, the one at Farangī Mahal accepted Sūfism as a valid experience and a valid field of study.

Another traditionalist movement which developed in the second half of the nineteenth century and continues to the present day is that of the *ahl-i hadīth* or of the followers of the dicta of the Prophet. It was also influenced considerably by the scholarship of Walī-Allāh and earlier Indo-Muslim theologians. The *ahl-i hadīth* accepted the entire corpus of the Prophet's dicta in the six classical collections as genuine and tried to mould their faith and life in the light of these dicta. They were accused by the British of Wahhābī sympathies, a charge which was, on the whole, unfair. *Bid'a* (innovation) was, for the *ahl-i hadīth*, the antithesis of the *sunna* (the Prophet's practice) and therefore abominable. In this category they counted the modernism of Sayyid Ahmad Khān as well as the messianistic 'heresy' of the Ahmadīs. They enjoined a life of conformity, and their religious experience was sublimated by an all-embracing pessimism apprehensive of the approaching Day of Judgement. In politics they preached quietism and held *fitna* (chaos, uprising) in horror. The principal leader of the movement was Nawwāb Siddīq Hasan Khān whose works, written in Urdū, were also translated into Arabic.

Comparable and complementary to the religious revivalist movements was the political revivalist movement from the 1880's onwards. This was essentially a movement of political separatism initiated, as we have seen, by Sayyid Ahmad Khān. The political instinct of the Indo-Muslim élite was to participate in and develop this movement. In 1906, a delegation of Muslim leadership, including Sayyid Ahmad Khān's successor at Alīgarh, Muhsin al-Mulk, as well as Āghā Khān III met the viceroy, Lord Minto, and pressed the two Muslim demands; that the representation of the Muslims in various assemblies should be on the basis of a separate electorate of Muslims by Muslims; and that the percentage of the Muslim representation should be higher than their percentage in the population, in view of the special identity and interests of their community. The British Government may have encouraged this stand, though it did not 'inspire' it, as it has been accused of doing by Indian nationalists. It certainly conceded the substance of the Muslim demands. The Muslim party, called the Muslim League, was founded in the same year, and became the first platform of Muslim political interests. Bengal was partitioned in 1905 by the viceroy, Lord Curzon, a move which was advantageous economically and politically to the Muslims of East Bengal.

The partition of Bengal was annulled in 1911 under strong Hindu pressure. Muslim leaders realized the instability of British patronage and the Muslim League came to terms with the Indian National Congress in an understanding that they would face the British power jointly.

From 1919 to 1924 the Muslim League was superseded by the Khilāfat Conference as the party of the politically active Muslim élite. The Khilāfat Conference had a mass following, which the Muslim League did not have until the late 1930s. It worked in close co-operation with the Indian National Congress and accepted the over-all leadership of Gāndhī. For three or four years it seemed that Muslims would weld themselves into one nation with the Hindus. But, as Jawāharlāl Nehrū has observed: 'This nationalism was itself a composite force and behind it could be distinguished a Hindu nationalism . . . and a Muslim nationalism partly looking beyond the frontiers of India.' The real objective of the Khilāfat Conference was to prevent the dismemberment of Turkey, to preserve the independence and integrity of the Ottoman caliphate, and to prevent the subjugation of Arab lands. These objectives involved an anti-British stance, which coincided with a similar stand taken by the Indian National Congress and its non-co-operation movement against the British. The Congress-Khilāfat alliance was basically an alliance of convenience. As early as 1922 it was cracked by communal riots. It received its *coup de grace* with the abolition of the Ottoman caliphate by Kemalist Turkey in 1924, when the Khilāfat Conference lost its *raison d'être*. From 1924 to 1937 Muslim politics in India remained in its *Wanderjahre*, fighting rear-guard actions against the advances and encroachments of the Hindu-dominated Indian National Congress. It was initially concerned only with the separate electorates and safeguards for Muslims. Gradually Muslim leaders like the veteran Khilāfat leader Muhammad 'Alī began to place emphasis on the future of the provinces in the north-west and the east in which Muslims were in majority. This attitude is reflected in the proceedings of the Round Table Conferences called by the British Government from 1929 to 1931.

In 1930 the famous poet and thinker Muhammad Iqbāl suggested the idea of a separate Muslim state in the north-west. His view was that the stable political future of the Hindus and the Muslims demanded a parting of the ways. The name 'Pakistan' was given to the Muslim state thus conceived by him, by a group of Indian Muslim students, most prominent among whom was Chaudharī Rahmat Alī.

In 1937 there was a possibility of the realignment of the Indian National Congress and the Muslim League which was spurned by the leaders of the Congress. The Muslim League from then onwards became the chief forum of Muslim opposition to the Congress. In 1940 in the 'Pakistan Resolution' the League committed itself to the concept of Pakistan. This concept was conceded in various degrees by a British Cabinet delegation led by Sir Stafford Cripps in 1942, by the depressed class leader B. R. Ambedkar, and by the Congress leader C. Rājagopālāchārī. In 1944 there were even discussions between Jinnah and Gāndhī on the question of Pakistan. As late as 1946 a compromise which could have resulted in a united India was possible, when the Muslim leader Jinnah accepted the British Cabinet Mission's concept of a union of India divided into three sub-federations, of which Group A was to consist of provinces with Hindu majority, Group B of provinces in the north-west with a substantial Muslim majority, and Group C of provinces in the east with a marginal Muslim majority. Once again the ambivalence and lack of political foresight on the part of the Congress leadership led to the loss of this opportunity. Jinnah withdrew the Muslim League's acceptance of the Cabinet Mission's plan. Gradually the Indian leaders, first Sardār Patel, then Nehrū, and finally Gāndhī were convinced by Lord Mountbatten that Pakistan was the only solution of the political problems of India. In August 1947 the British power withdrew from India and the modern states of India and Pakistan came into being.

CHAPTER XXVIII

The Nationalist Movement

by H. F. OWEN

THE nationalist movement was at once a reassertion of traditional values and symbols against alien intrusions, and itself an alien, modern, untraditional phenomenon. This paradox is found embodied in the different brands of nationalism represented by such figures as Bankim Chandra Chatterjee, Dayānanda and the Ārya Samāj, Aurobindo, Tilak, Sir Syed Ahmad Khān and the Alīgarh School, Annie Besant, and above all Gāndhī and the National Congress as he influenced it. It is hardly surprising then if the paradox has continued to echo in the subcontinent since independence was won.

I

During the seventy or so years from the foundation of the first nationalist associations until the achievement of independence, the Indian nationalist movement changed its character in various ways, under the influence of the traditional past and the more recent British past, and also as a result of the new ideas and methods that marked its development. Modifying slightly the periodization which Michael Brecher has distinguished in the history of the nationalist movement,[1] one might divide the history of the movement into (1) the 1870s–1890s: the period of Moderate pre-eminence; (2) the 1890s–1914: the struggle for supremacy within the movement between the Moderates and Extremists; and (3) 1914–1947: the period of agitational politics and Gāndhī's leadership. Broadly speaking, in the first of these periods the nationalist movement was essentially British in its intellectual origins; in the second it drew both on indigenous symbols and ideas and upon Western (including British) ideologies and examples; and, in the third period, the movement drew upon widening circles of Indian and imported inspiration while becoming increasingly inventive, particularly under the impetus of Gāndhī's creative genius.

Any nationalist movement in a colonial situation is bound to have both a negative and a positive aspect. The negative aspect is the determination to expel the foreign rulers and achieve self-government; the positive aspect is the concept of the sort of nation which should emerge from the struggle for independence. In negative terms the Moderates aimed at moving slowly towards self-government for India, with the 'white' colonies of the British Empire as their model. The moderate Indian Association emerged in 1876 in Calcutta and spread across northern India with the express goal of stimulating 'the sense of nationalism amongst the people';[2] and from its earliest sessions in 1885 and 1886 the Indian National Congress pointed to Canadian and

[1] M. Brecher, *The New States of Asia: a Political Analysis*, London, 1963, p. 22.

[2] Cited in J. C. Bagal, *History of the Indian Association*, 1876–1951, Calcutta, [1953], p. 8.

Australian self-government as the models for India.[3] In terms of the sort of nation they wished to see emerge, the Moderates worked actively for a liberal, secular, democratic India through education and social and religious reform. In this they were carrying forward the social and intellectual reform movements of Rām Mohan Roy, Rānade, and others, aiming, in Gokhale's words, at the selective 'assimilation of all that is best in the life and thought and character of the West'.[4] The Moderates set up associations, such as the Poona Sarvajanik Sabhā in 1870, to work for the improvement of the whole of Indian society,[5] seeking educational and other social reforms through their membership of legislative bodies and organizations such as the National Social Conference. They hoped to achieve their ends through the introduction of representative democratic political reforms by the National Congress, and by such methods as public meetings, deputations, and the presentation of memorials—all modelled directly upon British constitutional politics.

The Extremists (who might more happily be termed 'militants', if the other term had not been sanctioned through use by the Extremists themselves and by their opponents or rivals) became increasingly assertive from the 1890s onward, and demanded self-government more rapidly than the Moderates did, and without the latter's concern for gradual preparation. The Extremists' aims in terms of the sort of India they wanted are not so clear cut as those of the Moderates, but they extolled India's pre-British past, particularly its Hindu past, as the model for the present and future, and they deplored what they regarded as the Moderates' over-hasty, subservient, and damaging acceptance of British and other Western models as suitable for reforming Indian religion, society, or polity. Aurobindo, for example, spoke rather vaguely of self-government for India as 'the fulfilment of the ancient life of India under modern conditions' and 'the final fulfilment of the Vedantic ideal in politics'.[6] In this the Extremists were the political counterpart to the Hindu revivalist movements of the last third of the nineteenth century, represented by such organizations as the Sanātana Dharma Mahāmandal, the Ārya Samāj, the Theosophical Society, and the Rāmakrishna Mission. Both Hindu revivalism and Extremist nationalism were hybrids, springing from Western and indigenous sources. Their indigenous origins were obvious enough—the conscious turning back to the Vedas, the *Gītā*, and Vedānta; the defence of Hindu ideas and worship against the criticism of missionaries and liberals; the movements to reclaim Hindu converts to Islam and Christianity initiated in the 1890s; the public festivals in honour of the Hindu god, Ganesh, and the Hindu hero-king Śivājī; and the invocation of the Mother Goddess as an embodiment of both Bengal and India, to be cherished and restored, and as witness to the oaths of patriotic conspiracy. But the very turning back to an idealized national cultural past for inspiration was in the mainstream of nine-

[3] *Proceedings of the First Indian National Congress held at Calcutta . . . 1886*, Calcutta, 1887, p. 99.

[4] Quoted in T. V. Parvate, *Gopal Krishna Gokhale: a Narrative and Interpretative Review of his Life, Career and Contemporary Events*, Ahmedabad, 1959, p. 164.

[5] See J. C. Masselos, 'Liberal Consciousness, Leadership and Political Organization in Bombay and Poona, 1867–1895' (unpublished Ph.D. thesis, Univ. of Bombay, 1964), p. 286.

[6] Cited in H. and U. Mukherjee, *Sri Aurobindo's Political Thought (1893–1908)*, Calcutta, 1957, p. 40.

teenth-century European romanticism and its offspring, nationalism. The Extremist nationalists used largely Western techniques—trying to mobilize the support of public opinion through newspapers and public meetings, employing passive resistance in its various phases,[7] and occasional terrorist tactics. The hybrid amalgam was epitomized in Tilak's famous epigram: 'Swarāj is my birthright and I will have it.' The term Swarāj ('self-rule') was hallowed by its association with the area of the Marāthā confederacy which remained self-governing longest; but the whole notion that self-government (now broadened to include the whole of India) is somehow the individual's and the nation's right has a particularly Western ring to it.

To generalize thus about the Extremists is to blur the reality of change among them with the passage of time, of individual differences, and above all of regional variations. The social groupings from which they came and to which they appealed varied from region to region, as did the traditions they invoked and the extent to which they drew upon Western and Indian sources. The Mahārāshtrian Extremists of western India were mainly from the Chitpāvan Brāhman community, which inherited traditions of political leadership and resistance to invaders. It has been argued that they shared a cultural consensus with the lower castes of the region[8] which enabled them to recruit widespread support, but they were also anxious to preserve their social dominance. In the Panjāb, on the other hand, the Ārya Samāj, which greatly influenced the character of Extremist nationalism there, shared much of the Moderates' rather Western-style concern for reform and the purification of Indian society and religion—notably by assimilating the untouchables in the higher castes. In Bengal, again, the traditions of the high-caste *bhadralok* who predominated among the Extremists were essentially élitist, making difficult the recruitment of lower-caste, not to mention Muslim, participants. The Extremist nationalists' influence was concentrated in these three regions, and it was partly because of this and their failure to unify or at least to federate these regional movements that they failed in their attempt to capture Congress. Following their ejection from Congress in 1907, nationalist activity declined markedly.

In 1914 there began a revival of nationalist activity, which led on to the triumph of agitational politics which marks the third period of the movement. Mrs. Annie Besant inaugurated this transformation, drawing on both her personal knowledge of radical methods of agitation in Britain and upon her understanding of Indian history and Hindu traditions, acquired as the head of the Theosophical Society. Under her leadership, in conjunction with Tilak, between 1914 and 1918 agitational nationalism began for the first time to spread from the cities into the countryside on a nationwide scale.[9] Under Gāndhī's leadership this process gathered momentum.

[7] See Sri Aurobindo, *The Doctrine of Passive Resistance*, Calcutta, 1948; B. G. Tilak, 'Tenets of the New Party' (1907) in *All About Lok. Tilak*, Madras, 1922, pp. 492–505; regarding Western models, see C. M. Case, *Non-Violent Coercion; a Study in Methods of Social Pressure*, New York, 1923, e.g. pp. 326–8.

[8] R. Kumar, *Western India in the Nineteenth Century: a Study in the Social History of Maharashtra*, London and Canberra, 1968, pp. 6–11, 31–2, 319–20, 332.

[9] See the writer's 'Towards Nation-wide Agitation and Organisation: the Home Rule Leagues, 1915–18' in D. A. Low (ed.), *Soundings in Modern South Asian History*, London and Berkeley, Cal., 1968.

Gāndhī himself learned much from the West—methods of civil disobedience and passive resistance from Thoreau, for instance, and the concepts of the dignity of labour and social reform—as did Jawāharlāl Nehrū and other younger leaders in their attachment to socialism and large-scale industrialization. But there was also a deliberate turning back to the indigenous and the traditional. Gāndhī advocated *swadeshī* ('one's own country'), by which he meant the use of indigenous and local institutions as well as Indian-made goods,[10] and fostered the use of the traditional Indian spinning-wheel, the *charkhā*; he invoked Hindu and Jain concepts such as *ahimsā* (non-violence) and *tapasyā* (self-inflicted suffering); and called for *hartals* or the cessation of business activity, a traditional means of persuading the authorities to modify what the protesters regard as oppression.[11] Through his celibacy (*brahmacharya*) and asceticism Gāndhī was invoking extraordinary, super-physical powers in which tens of millions of his countrymen believed deeply.[12] Much of Gāndhī's success in attracting a vast following was due to his use of concepts such as *moksha*, symbols and parables drawn from the stories of Rāma and Prahlāda, of institutions (even the Muslim Khilāfat), and of techniques like the *hartal* which were already part of the consciousness of various Indian groups.

As one of the most creative figures in modern history Gāndhī combined his own ideas and responses with influences from many sources to form a social psychology and a programme of action for remedying situations of conflict. He was probably less concerned with the 'negative' nationalist goal of evicting the British than with the positive question of the sort of India he wished to see emerge. Even so, Indian self-government was essential—the vision of India for which he was working was that of a self-reliant, fearless country obedient to its conscience and its sense of morality: as he himself said, such a country would be self-governing in reality even if foreigners remained in the administration. But he was even more concerned to inculcate his technique of *satyāgraha* as the means of solving social and political conflict in India, and eventually in the rest of the world.[13] Erik H. Erikson[14] has suggested, comparing him with Freud, that Gāndhī offered a cure for the neuroses which threaten to destroy society through the technique of *satyāgraha* (literally 'holding firmly to truth'). In this technique of non-violent resistance, or even non-violent coercion, important differences which prove unamenable to compromise or arbitration are solved by one of the opponents refusing to comply with the other's wishes and accepting the consequences, even if this involves physical injury or deprivation of liberty: such sufferings patiently endured will ultimately, possibly assisted by the non-violent pressure of public opinion, bring about a change of heart in the enemy.

[10] See 'Swadeshi' (14 Feb. 1916) in *Speeches and Writings of Mahatma Gandhi*, Madras, 1933, pp. 336–44; *Young India*, 3 Dec. 1919, p. 8.

[11] See A. L. Basham, 'Traditional Influences on the Thought of Mahatma Gandhi', in R. Kumar (ed.), *Essays on Gandhian Politics: the Rowlatt Satyagraha of 1919*, Oxford, 1971, pp. 17–42; N. K. Bose, *Studies in Gandhism*, Calcutta, 1962, esp. 'Conflict and its Resolution in Hindu Civilization', pp. 69–115.

[12] See A. L. Basham, *The Wonder that was India*, London, 1956, pp. 244–6.

[13] See the writer's 'Non-Co-operation, 1920–22' in S. N. Ray, *Gandhi, India and the World*, Philadelphia, Pa., 1970, pp. 171–2.

[14] *Gandhi's Truth: on the Origins of Militant Nonviolence*, London, 1970.

During this third period of Indian nationalism, Gāndhī led three great extended campaigns involving increasingly large numbers of people drawn from virtually all sections of society—in 1919 and, after a lull, 1920–2; in 1930 and 1931–2; and again in 1940 and 1942. He also led or guided *satyāgraha* campaigns, which were at first more localized but had widespread effects—such as those in Champāran and Gujarāt in 1917–18, which demonstrated his technique and attracted lieutenants and adherents who were to participate in the first nationwide campaign in 1919. The campaigns at Vykom in 1924–5 and Bardolī in 1928 focused national attention upon such matters as how to improve the lot of depressed social groups and how to refuse to pay taxes.

As we have seen, much of Gāndhī's success in attracting a great following in his major campaigns was due to his invocation of traditional and familiar concepts, symbols, institutions, and techniques—though, by modifying them or combining them with exotic or novel ideas, he alienated some of the most orthodox Indians. At the same time, his success was based upon concern for the material problems and deprivations of millions of his fellow-countrymen: his first campaigns were on issues of rural exactions and taxes and workers' wages. His advocacy of the *charkhā* and *khādī* (hand-spun, hand-woven cloth) was aimed at supplementing the incomes of poor people, particularly in the countryside, and forcing better-off groups to identify themselves with them; his manufacture of salt in illicit circumvention of the tax on this dietary staple was the most flamboyant example of his concern to increase material and social welfare, which included improvement in the status of women and untouchables; and even his adoption of the loin-cloth in 1921 marked his identification with the poorest Indians rather than his asceticism.[15]

Whether any of these elements in Gāndhī's programme put more than a few *paise* into any Indian's purse is doubtful, but certainly Gāndhī did bring practical benefits in terms of improved status to deprived groups, and above all he succeeded in convincing millions that their own lives and those of others would be better and nobler for following him. Recognizing that in some ways the colonial situation debased the characters of many of those who were ruled (and occasionally brought out the worst in the characters of some of the rulers and their womenfolk, as E. M. Forster and J. R. Ackerley have illustrated), Gāndhī increased his appeal by arousing the moral indignation of Indians against, for example, the repressive Rowlatt bills, the terms of the peace treaty with the Muslim Turks, the salt laws, the involvement of India in the Second World War without consulting the Indians, and generally against the imperial relationship itself, which could be seen as responsible for so many of the deprivations or weaknesses of the Indian people.

Even though Gāndhī bestrides the decades from 1919 like a colossus, other leaders with other policies also made their mark on Indian nationalism. During the 1920s, after the subsidence of the Non-Co-operation agitation, the Swarājists, under the leadership of Motīlāl Nehrū, Srīnivāsa Iyengar, Kelkār, and Vīthalbhāī Patel, contested successfully with the Moderate nationalists or Liberals for entry into the legislatures: they entered with a policy of non-co-operation with the Government from within but stayed to co-operate in parliamentary politics. In this many influences may be discerned—Gāndhīan

[15] See *Hindu*, 23 Sept. 1921, p. 5.

moral indignation at British rule; Tilak's responsive co-operation; and even Moderate appreciation of British institutions; as well as concern to protect and further the élite social and economic groups from which the Swarājist members in the various provinces were mainly drawn.[16] In the mid-1930s Congress again contested the elections, going on to form the Government in seven of the ten provinces, and in 1945–6 it stood for election, emerging as the dominant party at the centre. Already at its Karāchī session in 1931 Congress had passed its resolution on Fundamental Rights and Economic and Social Changes, which, as well as including a declaration of rights and freedoms, posited the public ownership or control of basic industries and communications. This resolution owed some elements to Gāndhī, such as total prohibition, the abolition of untouchability, and the reduction of land revenue, but its underlying socialistic tone and its passage at that time were primarily the work of Jawāharlāl Nehrū and the nascent Congress Socialists—and their inspiration was largely non-Indian, notably the American and French bills of rights, and European socialism, underscored by the example of Russian communism.

II

In terms of its negative goal of evicting the British, the history of the Indian nationalist movement is a 'success story'. To what extent, though, was the Indian nationalist movement responsible for the departure of the British? The British were apparently unmoved by early nationalist demands for progress to self-rule and by the various devices by which these demands were pressed. As early as the revision of the Partition of Bengal in 1912, however, it was revealed that a determined agitation—even though largely confined to one region of India—could make the British respond to the wishes of articulate groups of Indians organized in nationalist bodies. Again, in the memorandum which the Viceroy, Lord Hardinge, sent home in October 1915, he and at least some of the provincial executives and the members of his Council showed themselves responsive to the Indians' arguments for political reform.[17] The Home Rule agitation at the time of the First World War, reinforced by the reform proposals produced by various branches of the nationalist movement and jointly by the Congress and Muslim League, forced the Secretary of State to concede that Indian legislators' 'authority and responsibility' must be increased,[18] which led on to the Montagu–Chelmsford Reforms, and the attempts by the British governments in India to find allies among the Moderates, now comprising the Liberal Party, all of which fostered the development of parliamentary institutions in India. Gāndhī's agitation of 1920–1 seems to have prepared the Viceroy, Lord Reading, for a major concession of powers,[19] and the

[16] See D. E. U. Baker, 'The Break-down of Nationalist Unity and the Formation of the Swaraj Parties, India, 1922 to 1924', in *University Studies in History*, Vol. 5, No. 4 (1970), esp. pp. 86–7.

[17] See Memorandum by His Excellency the Viceroy, Oct. 1915, in Hardinge Papers, Cambridge University Library.

[18] Sir A. Chamberlain to the Viceroy, Lord Chelmsford, 29 Mar. 1917 and 2 May 1917, in Government of India, Home Dept. Political file A, July 1917, Nos. 299–313.

[19] See D. A. Low, 'The Government of India and the First Non-Co-operation Movement —1920–1922', *Journal of Asian Studies*, Vol. 25, No. 2 (Feb. 1966), p. 249.

agitations of the later 1920s and early 1930s encouraged the British Government to put to one side the Indian Statutory Commission's report and call the Round Table Conferences, thus reopening the whole question of the amount of power to be devolved.

Following the British Conservative Party's rejection of the 'die-hard' opposition to Indian reform, led by Churchill, at its December 1934 conference,[20] the Government of India Act of 1935 provided for provincial responsible government on the basis of greatly enlarged electorates. It was ironic that it was Churchill, under the pressure of the threatening 'Quit India' agitation in the wartime circumstances of 1942, who sent his Lord Privy Seal —significantly a Labour man—to offer the Indian nationalist leaders independence at the end of the war, recognizing wryly that Britain was defending 'India in order, if successful, to be turned out'. The ultimate timing of the departure was affected by other factors as well as Indian nationalist pressures. Britain was exhausted by the war, financially and militarily, and this weakened her determination to hold on imperially. Attlee and his Labour Party colleagues, the last and most unfettered of a line of liberal-minded politicians committed to political advance for India—in this case to the hilt—were elected to power at the critical moment. But at the same time the British were encouraged in their *exeunt* by the memory of the bitterness and extent of the wartime nationalist agitation in India, by the spectre of mutiny foreshadowed in the Indian National Army, by the disturbances surrounding the I.N.A. trials and the subsequent mutinies in Karāchī, Bombay, and elsewhere.

The effect of the nationalist movement, then, was to move the British to make specific devolutions of power at various points from 1916 onwards, even if these devolutions fell short of the 'home rule' or 'swarāj in one year' or agreement to 'quit India' which had been demanded by the nationalists; and overall it moved a sufficient number of British statesmen in positions of power and a sufficient amount of public opinion, both in Britain and elsewhere, to a readiness to grant self-determination without a war of independence.

III

India is a parliamentary democracy in the sense that the central and state governments of the day are responsible to the Parliament or state legislatures and through them to the adult population, who at election time have a true choice between candidates of various parties. The seed of Indian democracy was planted by the Western, and particularly the British, education introduced in the nineteenth century, but that India has grown into the world's largest democracy is due largely to the lengthy experience of the nationalist movement and its interaction with British governments. The demand for parliamentary democracy was also strong in other former colonial countries, but that it has taken root and lasted longer in India than in most of them is partly because Indian nationalists had formulated this demand at least sixty years

[20] See S. C. Ghosh, 'Decision-Making and Power in the British Conservative Party: a Case-Study of the Indian Problem, 1929–34', *Political Studies*, Vol. 13, No. 2 (June 1965), pp. 198–212; D. A. Low, 'Sir Tej Bahadur Sapru and the First Round-Table Conference', in D. A. Low (ed.), *Soundings in Modern South Asian History*, p. 296.

before independence was gained and had argued the case for this institution, and had heard it argued, with clarity and emotion throughout this long period.

Numbers of Congress Moderates had found their way into the legislatures in the elections on very restricted franchises (described as 'selection') under the 1892 and 1909 Councils Acts: here they learnt to operate the limited parliamentary institutions available and to press for more. Having withdrawn from Congress to form the Liberal parties in 1918, they were returned as one of the largest and certainly most articulate groups in the expanded legislatures under the Montagu–Chelmsford reforms in 1921, in the absence of Congressmen as a result of the Non-Co-operation campaign. In these councils they were able to achieve reforms and to influence the executive, which reinforced the notion of the government and the bureaucracy being answerable, and in certain areas of policy under 'dyarchy' even responsible, to elected representatives. The activities of the Liberals, along with other elected members of the councils such as the non-brāhmans in Madras and Bombay, also demonstrated that the legislatures were repositories of power, and so made numbers of Congressmen anxious to obtain election, both to further nationalist goals and to gain the fruits of power and influence for the social groups from which they came. Even when the numbers of elected Liberal members of the legislatures were reduced by Congress competitors at elections in the 1920s and 1930s, the Liberals continued to be important in Indian political and nationalist life, as nominated if not elected legislators; as members of the Viceroy's or governors' executives and as their advisers; as members of important constitutional inquiries such as the Muddiman Committee, the committees associated with the Simon Commission and the Round Table Conferences; as commissioners and investigators; and as negotiators between Congress and the British. Men such as V. S. Srīnivāsa Sāstrī, P. Sivaswāmī Iyer, R. P. Paranjpye, and M. R. Jayakār played important roles for much of this period, and a Liberal like T. B. Saprū not only seems to have played an important part in drafting Congress constitutional documents such as the Lucknow Pact of 1916 and the Nehrū Report of 1927 but also continued this role in drawing up independent India's constitution.

Those Congressmen who were elected as Swarājists in 1923 and 1926 received training in operating institutions of a parliamentary type. They found that they had to learn to operate them even in order to obstruct and protest. This constitutional tradition was reinforced in Congress when Congressmen stood successfully for election in 1937 and in 1945–6, and the experience gained in running responsible provincial governments between 1937 and 1947 stood many members of the later Congress ruling party in good stead after independence.

Under the 1935 Act the provincial governments followed the Westminster prime ministerial model rather than presidential models; it was this which Congress politicians learnt to operate and which they introduced at the centre and retained in the provinces at India's independence. An irresponsible executive was identified with foreign rule, and responsible parliamentary government was aspired to as the hallmark of self-government. In certain ways the British model was quite clearly modified or even transformed by Indian practice before independence. One of the chief examples of this is in the dominance of the system by one party, which only seemed to come into question for four years, 1967–71, out of the 25 since independence. The dominance of the particular party in question, the Congress Party, is the natural result of its role as, in a sense, the embodiment of the Indian nation during the nationalist struggle, and of the organization, prestige, leaders, and membership it inherited from that struggle.

Two factors important in maintaining the conditions in which democracy can flourish are a civil service that is impartial, intelligent, apolitical, and uncorrupt, at least in its upper levels, and an army which is independent and at the same time subordinate to the political wing. The nationalist period helped to bequeath such a bureaucracy and army to India. While Gāndhī had called for government servants to desert their imperialist masters, the nationalist movement made little attempt to undermine the position of the law, the civil service, or the army as such, and on the other hand through agitation and participation in government it contributed to their Indianization.

India's federal structure is inherited from the British, who devised it as a workable means of ruling and as a structure within which power could be devolved in the parts while retaining control at the centre, drawing on the models of the United States or the 'white' dominions. It also marks a recognition of the facts of human political geography in India. But in addition it bears influences from the nationalist period; Gāndhī reorganized Congress into linguistic provincial units in 1921, and through linguistic reorganization the Indian states have approximated increasingly towards the structure of the dominant party. The strength of the central government *vis-à-vis* the states, epitomized in the role of the President and in matters such as finance, development investment, tariffs and, imports, may be seen as the administrative reflection of the strong Working Committee or High Command in Congress.

India is a secular state—or rather, in so far as Indian governments assist all the religious groups in the county, it is more accurately described as 'pluralistic'. This owes much to the persistence of the Moderate aim of a secular state, but was modified by Gāndhī's insistence that morality and politics were one and by his appeals to the convictions of various religious groups. It was modified, too, by the Hindu communal movements of the 1920s and 1930s, such as the *sangathan* and *śuddhi* movements, the Rāshtrīya Swayamsevak Sangh, and the Hindū Mahāsābhā, in some ways the descendants of the Hindu assertiveness of Extremist nationalism; and by Congress's blunting of their appeal to Hindus by resisting the Muslim minority's demands for safeguards. The resulting dominance of the Hindu majority community inside and outside Congress was reinforced in the newly independent India by the flight of some of the best Muslim talent to Pakistan, so that there has been a continuing problem of ensuring that Muslims are treated equally with the other communities,[21] and feel themselves to be treated equally. At the same time, the Moderates' goal of secularism was pursued through the 1930s and 1940s by nationalists, such as Jawāharlāl Nehrū, attracted by the notions of social

[21] Of recruits to the Indian Administrative Service between 1948 and 1960, for example, nearly 90 per cent were Hindu and only 1·9 per cent Muslim. See R. Braibanti and J. J. Spengler (eds.), *Administration and Economic Development in India*, Durham, N.C., 1963, pp. 53–4.

egalitarianism and economic development which were gaining ground in the West.

The nationalists promoted too the other elements that are essential to Western liberal democracy—freedom of speech, freedom of association, and freedom of the press—which accord well with Indian religious notions of the relativity of truth and characterize the spirit of modern India. The modern Indian provision of special facilities to underprivileged or 'backward' groups, which include a wide range of castes and tribes, flows in a straight line from the Moderates' and Ārya Samājists' work for social reform through Gāndhīan social uplift and Nehrū's concern for greater social equality.

The nationalist movement therefore did much to form modern India, and it may be asked why its consequences were so very different for Pakistan which is not secular but Islamic, and which has experimented both with presidential democracy and military autocracy. In fact considerable areas of West Pakistan in particular had hardly been affected by British education and large parts of the population were relatively untouched by the nationalist movement, many Muslims having deliberately held aloof from it and from active or at least independent participation in the legislatures. The Muslim League, which achieved Pakistan, had only developed into a well-organized party in the seven years or so before partition, and had little experience of running parliamentary or other large-scale political institutions. Even in the principal Muslim majority regions, Bengal and the Panjāb, the Muslim League had little experience of running government. That Pakistan was a romantic and impractical solution to the Muslims' very real fears and problems—at least for many Muslims in the subcontinent—is indicated by the fact that half as many Muslims remained in post-independence India as in Pakistan before the breakaway of Bānglādesh. The abandonment of secularism and the concept of Pakistan as an Islamic state provided little guide to how the state should be ruled, as the long agony of drawing up a constitution demonstrated, and, once Pakistan had been achieved, the need for co-operation between Muslim politicians, many of them able men, disappeared. Jinnah set the country on a presidential path, but before this institution, novel to the subcontinent, could be developed he and then his successor, Liāqat Ālī Khān, died. Inheriting, like its Indian counterpart, the same traditions, the Pakistani army was at first reluctant to interfere, but on the breakdown of democratic and constitutional forms it was drawn into the process of governing.

IV

The political sociology of the independent states of the subcontinent has continued to change since independence[22]—particularly under the impact of universal franchise and economic development—but many of the social groups which have been active in politics since independence had established themselves over the preceding sixty years. Their energies had been mobilized

[22] See e.g. R. Kothari and R. Maru, 'Caste and Secularism in India: Case Study of a Caste Federation', *Journal of Asian Studies*, Vol. 25, No. 1 (Nov. 1965), pp. 33–50; L. I. and S. H. Rudolph, *The Modernity of Tradition: Political Development of India*, Chicago and London, 1967; M. Rashiduzzaman, 'The Awami League in the Political Development of Pakistan', *Asian Survey*, Vol. 10, No. 7 (July 1970), pp. 574–87.

frequently but not invariably by the nationalist movement. Research in progress on the United Provinces, for instance, shows that while the nationalist movement there was almost dormant for most of the later part of the nineteenth century, local government boards were arenas of increasing political activity, particularly along lines of rivalry between Muslims and rising Hindu groups.[23] Sooner or later, however, most groups which had stood outside the nationalist movement found that they could not afford to remain aloof from it—as in the case of the Hindus and Muslims of the United Provinces (now Uttar Pradesh), when Congress and the Muslim League sought to arrange electoral concessions on behalf of those communities in 1916.[24] Either they decided that they would benefit from joining Congress; or else the nationalist movement set out to woo and accommodate them.

The first groups to be mobilized in the nationalist associations and *sabhās* and in Congress in the 1870s and 1880s comprised Western-educated Indians, mainly men engaged in the professions or in the service of government or business firms, as well as students aspiring to such jobs. They came almost entirely from the castes and communities with traditions of administration and learning, notably brāhman castes, writer castes (Kāyasthas and Prabhus), Pārsīs, and, to a much lesser extent, Muslim groups associated with trade. Initially, they were to be found largely in the Western port-cities and Poonā.[25] During the 1890s and the early years of the twentieth century, however, the Extremists drew increasing numbers of less successful members of these Western-educated groups into political agitation, in the up-country towns in Mahārāshtra and Bengal, and in the Panjāb as well. In addition, Tilak in western India and Lājpat Ṛāī in the Panjāb succeeded in involving members of some peasant castes and urban labouring groups.

The Home Rule movement of the First World War period carried agitational politics to many new regions—to the Tamil-, Telugu-, Malayālam-, and Kannada-speaking regions of the Madras Presidency, to Gujarāt, Sind, the United Provinces, and Delhi, and to Bihār—and it caught up new social groups, notably commercial men and their caste-fellows in Bombay, Gujarāt, and Sind, and members of agricultural castes in the rural towns and villages of Gujarāt, Mahārāshtra, and northern India. At the same time, the Home Rule agitation contributed to political mobilization in ways that its leaders had not intended. Non-brāhmans in western and southern India were provoked into opposing the Home Rule movement, which they saw as likely to benefit only those high-caste groups already predominant in the nationalist movement.

[23] L. Brennan, 'Land Policy and Social Change in Rohilkhand, 1801–1911' (unpublished M.A. thesis, University of Western Australia, 1968); F. Robinson, 'Municipal Government and Muslim Separatism in the United Provinces, 1883–1916' (unpublished paper, European Conference on Modern South Asia, Copenhagen, 1970); cf. C. Bayly, 'Local Control in Indian Towns: the Case of Allahabad, 1880–1920', *Modern Asian Studies*, Vol. 5, part 4 (Oct. 1971), pp. 289–311.

[24] See the writer's 'Negotiating the Lucknow Pact, 1916', *Journal of Asian Studies*, Vol. 31, No. 3 (May 1972), pp. 561–87.

[25] See J. C. Masselos, 'Liberal Consciousness, Leadership and Political Organisation in Bombay and Poona, 1867–1895' (unpublished Ph.D. thesis, University of Bombay, 1964); B. T. McCully, *English Education and the Origins of Indian Nationalism*, New York, 1940, esp. pp. 225–9, 281–387.

These non-brāhmans were members of peasant castes in Mahārāshtra and the Kārnātak[26] and landowners and traders in the south.[27] The Home Rule movement responded to these developments in turn by setting out, with some success, to enlist the help of members of these non-brāhman groups in nationlist activities.

Gāndhī's local political movements and first all-India movements in the period 1917–22 mobilized a wide range of groups in various parts of British India. These included peasant-proprietors, notably in Āndhra and the Panjāb, as well as members of the Patidār and Anāvlā brāhman castes in Gujarāt on a much larger scale than in the Home Rule movement; and also rural tenants in parts of the United Provinces and Bihār and in the Midnāpore district of Bengal and Kāmrūp district in Assam. The response in urban areas was widespread, but varied in terms of the social groups it involved. One can point specifically to less-Westernized businessmen, such as Mārwārīs in Calcutta, central India, and towns in Madras Presidency, Baniās, Bhātiās, and Jains in western India, and local money-lending and commercial castes in Delhi and the Panjāb cities and towns; to artisans and urban proletarian groups, such as transport operatives and market labourers in the major Indian cities and in the towns of the Panjāb, Gujarāt, Sind, and the United Provinces, and increasingly in the later part of the period mill-operatives in cotton-milling centres; and to groups which had long been active in nationalist politics but now were so on a larger scale than ever before, professional men and college students. Conspicuously, too, the Khilāfat movement drew into the agitation large numbers of Muslims from virtually every socio-economic background and geographic region, though in many cases their political activity was later to be diverted into separatist channels.[28]

One should not assume that people caught up in one Gāndhīan agitation remained fully active politically thereafter. Nevertheless, once people had been involved in *hartals* or demonstrations they were linked to the network of nationalist communications and leadership, and it was easier to enlist them again later.[29] Furthermore, in the periods between his great agitational campaigns of 1919–22, 1929–32, and 1940–2, Gāndhī continued to win support through his constructive programmes which Congress took up, and through smaller-scale agitations. During the 1920s, for instance, through the Vykom and Bardolī *satyāgrahas* and through Gāndhī's campaign for women's rights and the promotion of *khādī*, he and his lieutenants drew groups of untouchables and women into the political sphere. It has been argued, too, that the ideas of social equality and justice injected into Congress by Jawāharlāl

[26] See A. T. Tansley, 'The Non-Brahman Movement in Western and Central India, 1917–23' (unpublished M.A. thesis, University of Western Australia, 1969), pp. 53–74; Maureen L. P. Patterson, 'Caste and Political Leadership in Maharashtra', *Economic Weekly* (Bombay), 6 (25 Sept. 1954), 1065–6.

[27] E. F. Irschick, *Politics and Social Conflict in South India; the Non-Brahman Movement and Tamil Separatism, 1916–1929*, Berkeley, Cal., 1969, pp. 48, 51, 61–2.

[28] This period is starting to receive close attention from scholars, see e.g. R. Kumar (ed.), *Essays on Gandhian Politics: the Rowlatt Satyagraha of 1919*, Oxford, 1971.

[29] On the importance of communications for nationalism, see K. W. Deutsch, *Nationalism and Social Communication: an Inquiry into the Foundations of Nationality*, Cambridge, Mass. 1966.

Nehrū and the Socialists from 1930 onwards helped to retain for the nationalist movement the adherence of the underprivileged, notably working-class and peasant groups.[30] Indeed it seems that the activities of the Socialists and of the Kisān Sabhās (peasants' associations) attracted such people in larger numbers as time went on.

This process was reinforced by the constitutional political activity of Congress in lengthy periods in the mid-1920s, 1930s, and 1940s, following the major Gāndhīan agitations. During these periods Congress participated, along with other parties, in the elections for the provincial and central legislatures—as it did at all times in those for local government bodies—and the mounting competition for seats, accompanying extensions of the franchise, brought increasing circles of society into the political process.

As Congress expanded its organizational machinery and achieved electoral success, it became increasingly attractive to groups which had stood aloof from the nationalist movement or opposed it. Notably the non-brāhmans of western India joined Congress in forming governments in Bombay from the 1937 elections onwards[31] and the non-brāhmans of south India likewise in the 1950s.[32] One group of whom this was not true was, of course, the Muslims. Some Muslims were attracted by the growing success and influence of Congress, and its secular ideology, but the legacy of extremist nationalism and the Hindu communal movements of the 1920s and 1930s stiffened Congress resistance to concessions and safeguards for the Muslim minority. This gave Muslims ample cause for apprehension, and enabled the Muslim League to draw Muslims into the separatist movement in the 1940s.

The nationalist movement thus helped to foster the movement for Pakistan, and by contributing to Muslim fears helped to submerge or disguise the very real conflicts of interest between the two wings of Pakistan which soon began to appear after partition. On the Indian side the political legacy of the struggle for independence was clearer, in terms of social groups which had been mobilized and the major political party through which they were to operate, though here, too, regional tensions and loyalties had developed in the course of the struggle but were somewhat disguised by the nationwide sweep of the movement for independence and were to flower later.

V

The Indian nationalist movement has had a lasting effect not only upon the successor states in the subcontinent but upon many other countries as well.

As the first great modern anti-colonial movement in the non-Western world, it encouraged nationalist movements in other Asian colonies—in Indonesia, Burma, Indo-China, and Ceylon. In the later 1920s the Indonesian nationalist movement looked explicitly to Gāndhī's ideas and the model of Gāndhīan non-co-operation, even though Sukarno came to criticize what he regarded as Gāndhī's concern with abstractions.[33]

[30] See R. Kumar, 'The Political Process in India', *South Asia*, 1 (Aug. 1971), 106.
[31] See A. Tansley, op. cit., pp. 216–17.
[32] See L. I. and S. H. Rudolph, *The Modernity of Tradition: Political Development in India*, Chicago, 1967, pp. 55–61.
[33] B. Dahm, *Sukarnos Kampf um Indonesiens Unabhängigkeit: Werdegang und Ideen eines*

Nehrū became acquainted with Mohammad Hatta, the Indonesian nationalist, at the Brussels anti-imperialist conference of 1927, and between 1947 and 1949 India assisted the Indonesian movement for independence at the United Nations and by banning Dutch flights across Indian territory.

Nationalist movements in Africa, particularly in British colonies, also looked explicitly to India, as well as to other successful nationalist movements in Asia. Uganda, Zambia, and Malawi each had its 'Congress', which sought to represent the whole nation; Africans in South Africa have their African National Congress, even though it is banned. And the Ghanaian national movement, for example, was to have its share of imprisonment before self-government was won in 1957.[34]

India's successful movement for self-determination also had a practical implication for independence movements elsewhere. Once India was independent, the *raison d'être* for much of the rest of the British Empire[35] ceased to exist. It took British statesmen some years to recognize this, but, as they did so, they became more willing to let it go, and this in turn accelerated the whole process of decolonization.

The Indian national movement has provided an inspiration to other movements for political and social reform, particularly in the democracies of the West, and these movements have turned to Gāndhī's techniques for models. In the black civil rights movement in the United States, as early as 1942 the leaders of the March on Washington Movement, aiming at equal treatment in wartime employment for both blacks and whites, considered the use of Gāndhī's methods of civil disobedience.[36] In 1950 Martin Luther King was greatly attracted by what he heard of Gāndhī, and in his campaigns for black rights, beginning with the successful Montgomery bus boycott in 1956, he deliberately modelled his strategy upon Gāndhī's methods.[37] From here, Gāndhī's methods have been extended to other movements for reform and the remedying of injustice. These methods have not always been fully understood by those who adapted them to other situations of conflict or confrontation, but they were taken over by such movements as the anti-Vietnam War campaigns in America and Australia, and in the south Asian subcontinent itself after independence by the states reorganization campaigns in India, and by

asiatischen Nationalisten, Schriften des Instituts für Asienkunde in Hamburg, Band XVIII, 1966, pp. 52, 80, 83, 125. For Indian influences on Burmese nationalism, see D. E. Smith, *Religion and Politics in Burma*, Ithaca, N.Y., 1958, pp. 193, 217–21, 300–3, 319, 412–18. For Vietnamese nationalists' invocation of Indian models, see D. G. E. Hall, *A History of South-East Asia*, London, 1964, p. 719; J. Buttinger, *Vietnam: A Dragon Embattled*, London, 1967, Vol. 2, pp. 728, 1077, n. 27. For Ceylon, see C. Jeffries, *Ceylon—the Path to Independence*, London, 1962, pp. 37, 89, 102, 110, 113–14.

[34] See T. Hodgkin, *Nationalism in Colonial Africa*, London, 1956, pp. 146–8; R. Emerson and M. Kilson (eds.), *The Political Awakening of Africa*, Englewood Cliffs, N.J., 1965, pp. 3, 8, 16, 49, 52–3, 71.

[35] See R. Robinson and J. Gallagher, with Alice Denny, *Africa and the Victorians: the Official Mind of Imperialism*, London, 1963, pp. 76, 86, 93, 114, 117–18, 123, 133, 162, 190–3, 199–202, 255, 283–91, 306, 464.

[36] H. Garfunkel, *When Negroes March: the March on Washington Movement in the Organisational Politics of the F.E.P.C.*, Glencoe, Ill., 1959, pp. 133, 135.

[37] See L. D. Reddick, *Crusader without Violence: a Biography of Martin Luther King, Jr.*, New York, 1959, esp. pp. 80–1, 133–55, 208; Coretta S. King, *My Life with Martin Luther King, Jr.*, London, 1970, pp. 176–8, 192, 202, 218, 353–4.

movements against military governments both in Pakistan and in what has become Bāngladesh.

VI

In the context of south Asia's history, the contribution of the Indian nationalist movement may prove to be long- or short-lived. The participants in the movement and their leaders were human, and as such fallible: the observer may not admire or approve of everything they did, and those who try to apply their methods to other situations of conflict or discontent may sometimes do so inadequately. But the Indian nationalist movement has earned its place in history alongside the greatest developments in human organization and men's thought, most of all because of the moral stature of its greatest leader, Gāndhī. Gāndhī was not the first Indian nationalist to appeal to the conscience of his opponents and his would-be followers, nor was he the last—Dādābhāi Nāorojī deplored the 'un-British' nature of British rule in India, and under Jawāharlāl Nehrū India for a while became a sort of conscience to the world. But there is a transcendent nobility in Gāndhī's work—in his efforts for the uplift of the depressed and for social reconciliation, in his technique of *satyāgraha*, and in his concern to love his adversaries and change their hearts through self-suffering. Above all, in his successful appeals to millions of people he called upon their better natures and noblest impulses.

CHAPTER XXIX

Modern Literature

by KRISHNA KRIPALANI

THE present linguistic position of India has been summed up in the Constitution, which has scheduled fifteen major languages of the country: the eleven Indo-Āryan languages consisting of Sanskrit with its tenfold progeny: Assamese, Bengālī, Gujarātī, Hindī, Kashmīrī, Marāthī, Oriyā, Panjābī, Sindhī, and Urdū; and the four Dravidian languages: Kannada, Malayālam, Tamil, and Telugu. To these fifteen the Sāhitya Akademī (National Academy of Letters, India) has for its own purposes added five more: Maithilī, the language of north-east Bihār, which has a rich heritage of medieval literature, Rājasthānī the language of Rājasthān, rich in ballads, Dogrī the language of the Jammū region in the State of Jammū and Kashmīr, Manipurī the language of Manipur in eastern India, and English. Sixteen of these twenty languages are the speeches of specific regions; Sanskrit and English cut across all regional boundaries, while the people speaking Urdū and Sindhī are scattered over different regions. All of them are the mother tongues of large or small communities, with the exception of Sanskrit, which is no longer a spoken tongue in India, although nearly 5,000 persons entered it as their mother tongue in the 1961 Census.

These twenty languages, including English, may be deemed the languages of major use in modern India. From the strictly philological point of view the number of languages and dialects, like the creeds and castes in the country, is indeed legion. The 1951 Census enumerated 845 languages and dialects, but whatever the interest of such meticulous analysis of minor linguistic variations for the professional philologist, it need not concern us here. Suffice it for us to note that of the four speech-families of India, over 70 per cent of the population speak one or the other of the various Indo-Āryan languages and less than one third the Dravidian languages, while a little over 1 per cent use the Austric and less than 1 per cent the Sino-Indian languages.

Although the importance of a language is not necessarily to be measured by the number of persons speaking it, the relative strength of numbers is not without its significance. From this point of view Hindī may be deemed the leading language of modern India, covering as it does the major part of north India with a population of about 150 million. This wide sweep of Hindī is, however, not without its limitations, and might be viewed more as a process than as an accomplished and uncontroverted fact.

There is, besides High Hindī and High Urdū, a large indeterminate zone where the common speech is an unpretentious middle path between the two, known as Hindūstānī. This was the speech which Mahātmā Gāndhī cherished as the *lingua franca* of modern India, hoping that it would be accepted as a common heritage by Hindus and Muslims alike. But, like many of his other dreams, the hope survives as a historical memory. Today Urdū is the official language of Pakistan and a national language of India. Despite the sharp cleavage between High Hindī and High Urdū and the ill-concealed contempt which the protagonists of both have for their common foster-child Hindūstānī, the position continues to remain so fluid that the 1961 Census was unable to compile separate statistics for it, a large number of persons describing their language as Hindī-Hindūstānī, Urdū-Hindūstānī, or some other permutation.

The relative strength of the people speaking the languages of modern India, as revealed by the 1961 Census, may be briefly summed up as follows: Assamese 6·8 million, Bengālī 33·8 million, Dogrī 2·6 million, Gujarātī 20·3 million, Hindī 133·4 million, Kannada 17·4 million, Kashmīrī 1·9 million, Maithilī 5 million, Malayālam 17 million, Manipuri 0·6 million, Marāthī 33·2 million, Oriyā 15·7 million, Panjābī 10·9 million, Rājasthānī 12·3 million, Sindhī 1·3 million, Tamil 30·5 million, Telugu 37·6 million, and Urdū 23·1 million. Panjābī and Sindhī are also languages of Pakistan and Bengālī of Bāngladesh, and it is worth noting that the number of people speaking Bengālī in Bāngladesh and Urdū in Pakistan would be as large as, if not larger than, in India; while the number of Sindhī speaking people in Pakistan would be much larger and of Panjābī speakers considerably more.

Such then is the linguistic jigsaw puzzle of modern India. Without a proper appreciation of this complex pattern one is likely to miss the significance of one of the most characteristic aspects of modern Indian literature, namely, its multiple character. It has been said that Indian literature is one, though written in many languages—a faint echo of the famous Vedic verse: 'Truth is one though sages call it by various names'. This characteristic permeates not only literature but almost every significant aspect of Indian culture. Hence the hackneyed phrase, 'Unity in diversity', which our politicians and culture-mongers are never tired of repeating, although there is at least as much diversity in our unity as there is unity in our diversity.

English had the historical advantage of coming to India at a time when Sanskrit and Persian had long played out their roles as languages of enlightenment and had become mere custodians of past glory and refuges of orthodoxy. India has had many dark ages in the long course of her history, but the latter half of the eighteenth century was perhaps the darkest. Political chaos had combined with intellectual lethargy to proliferate a wilderness of cankerous growth in which if culture survived at all it was as a few isolated oases in a vast desert.

The English language thus came at a time when all other doors to a progressive and enlightened existence seemed hopelessly closed. Patriotic Indians of the Gāndhīan era resent the harsh words with which Macaulay, with more zeal than understanding, contemptuously pooh-poohed the pretensions of Oriental learning in his famous Minute on Education in India. But it is well to recall what, more than a decade earlier, Rām Mohan Roy, himself a monument of Oriental learning, had written to the Governor-General, Lord Amherst, protesting against the Government's proposal to open a Sanskrit college in Calcutta.

If it had been intended [wrote the most enlightened Indian of his age, who is universally acclaimed as the Father of modern India] to keep the British nation in ignorance of real knowledge, the Baconian Philosophy would not have been allowed to displace the system of the Schoolmen, which was the best calculated to perpetuate ignorance. In the same manner the Sanskrit system of education would be the best calculated to keep this country in darkness, if such had been the policy of the British legislature. But as the improvement of the native population is the object of the Government, it will consequently promote a more liberal and enlightened system of instruction embracing Mathematics, Natural Philosophy, Chemistry, Anatomy, with other useful sciences . . .

The English language was thus voluntarily, and even enthusiastically, learnt by the young intelligentsia of Bengal, and later of other parts of India, fretting under the load of an inhibiting and meaningless discipline which the traditional learning had come to be. No doubt even at that time the orthodox were not lacking who denounced with righteous fervour the British Government's decision to 'impose' English on Indians, though they were no less ambitious to learn the language for themselves. This bitterness (with its anomaly of denouncing English while acquiring it) has survived and has been considerably reinforced; it has been made not a little virulent by political passions—until English has been dislodged from its position as the *official* language and has been retained on sufferance as the *associate* language, while continuing in fact to perform the same service, more or less.

This service was twofold. Politically English developed and strengthened the consciousness of national oneness more effectively and more profoundly than had ever happened before in Indian history. It also linked this consciousness with the aspiration to realize the national destiny in the context of democratic freedom. Intellectually it shook the intelligentsia out of a mental torpor which had well nigh paralysed all initiative and spirit of inquiry. The intelligentsia fostered under the new regime took to English readily, impressed by the wonderland of scientific knowledge and technique which it revealed, and charmed by a literature that seemed the more stimulating because it was so different from their own. All this would have come in any case in the course of time, as it has come to other peoples, but historical circumstances made the English language the agent of this revolutionary ferment in India and gave it a unique historical role in the development of modern India and its literatures. It would be ungracious, if not churlish, to disown this debt.

Strangely enough, knowledge of the English language and the attraction of English literature (and through it, later, of other Western literatures), instead of impeding the development of Indian languages, have proved a powerful stimulus. Perhaps this was not strange at all, but was inevitable. And this is the ultimate testimony to the creative nature of the impact. All the modern languages of India were fertilized by this contact and have yielded, some sooner, some later, rich harvests of their own. Even Sanskrit, past its age of rejuvenation, was made to reveal its treasures in a manner not hitherto exploited.

This new era of modern Indian literatures may be said to begin in 1800, when Fort William College was established in Calcutta and The Baptist Mission Press in Serampore, near Calcutta. The College was founded by the East India

Company to provide instruction to British civil servants in the laws, customs, religions, languages, and literatures of India in order to cope with the increasing demands of a fast-growing administrative machinery. The Press, the first to be set up in north India and still one of the best, was founded by the Baptist Mission mainly with the object of propagating Christian literature among the 'heathen' population. Whatever their original objects, the actual working of these two institutions produced results far beyond their scope. The credit for this must largely go to Dr. John Gilchrist, a professor of the College, his learned and indefatigable associate William Carey, and an able and devoted band of Indian scholars. Textbooks for the teaching of Bengālī, Hindī, Urdū and other Indian languages, as well as for imparting the various branches of knowledge, had to be literally manufactured, for there was little written prose available in the Indian languages, and what was available was hardly adequate for the purpose. Reading material was translated from the Sanskrit classics as well as from foreign literature, and dictionaries and grammars were compiled. William Carey, who was also one of the founders of the Baptist Mission Press, himself wrote a Bengālī grammar and compiled an English–Bengālī dictionary as well as two selections of dialogues and stories. He was also the author of *A Grammar of the Karnataka Language*.

The first printing press in India was set up by the Jesuit missionaries in Goa in 1566 and books in Tamil and other Dravidian languages began to be printed in the second half of the sixteenth century. Many foreign missionaries learnt the languages of the people. They not only translated the Bible and wrote Christian *Purānas* but also rendered considerable service to the languages by compiling the first modern grammars and dictionaries. The pioneer labour of the German missionary Ziegenbalg and his Italian successor Beschi in Tamil and of Father Leonardo Cinnoma in Kannada, as well as of many others in Telugu and Malayālam, is still recalled with gratitude in the history of these literatures. But, although the printing-press came to south India much earlier and the foreign missionary enterprise functioned much longer and more zealously than in Bengal, the impact of Western learning as such was comparatively slow and the resurgence of literary activity bore fruit in its modern form much later than in Bengal.

When, in 1800, the Fort William College was founded in Calcutta and the Baptist Mission and its Press were set up at Serampore, their primary objects were to train a more efficient civil service and to propagate Christianity among the 'heathens', but the indirect result of this two-pronged drive to hold India in thrall turned into a blessing. The textbooks written and the translations published by the Baptist Mission Press provided the much-needed incentive to the development of prose, the essential backbone of literature, which Bengālī, in common with most other north Indian languages, had so far lacked. Bengālī type was first designed and cast by Charles Wilkins, the distinguished Sanskrit scholar (and collaborator of Sir William Jones, who founded the Asiatic Society of Bengal in 1784), and was first used in Halhed's Bengālī Grammar in 1778.

The establishment of Hindu College in 1817 and the replacing of Persian by English as the language of the law and the increasing use of Bengālī were other landmarks which encouraged the introduction of modern education and the development of the language of the people. It was, however, Rājā Rām Mohan Roy (1772–1833) who laid the real foundation of modern Bengālī prose, as indeed he did of the Indian renaissance in general. Though essentially a religious and social reformer, the learning, versatility and zeal of this extraordinary man blazed new trails in almost every field of Indian life and culture. The form which he gave to Bengālī prose, necessarily somewhat crude and tentative, revealed its rich potentiality in the hands of Īśvarachandra Vidyāsāgar (1820–91) and Akshaykumār Datta (1820–86), both of whom were, like their great predecessor, primarily social reformers and educationists. Because they were men of serious purpose who had much to say, they had little use for the flamboyance and rhetoric natural to a language derived from Sanskrit, and they chiselled a prose that was both chaste and vigorous.

Path-finders rather than creative artists, they standardized the medium which their younger contemporary, Bankim Chandra Chatterjee (1838–94), turned with superb gusto and skill into a creative tool for his novels and stories. He is known as the father of the modern novel in India and his influence on his contemporaries and successors, in Bengal and other parts of India, was profound and extensive. Novels, both historical and social—the two forms in which he excelled—had been written before him in Bengālī by Bhūdev Mukherjī and Peary Chand Mitra. Mitra's *Alāler Gharer Dulāl* is in fact the first specimen of original fiction of social realism with free use of the colloquial idiom, and anticipated, however crudely, the later development of the novel. But it was Bankim Chandra who established the novel as a major literary form in India. He had his limitations, he was too romantic, effusive, and didactic, and was in no sense a peer of his great Russian contemporaries, Tolstoy and Dostoevsky. There have been better novelists in India since his day, but they all stand on his shoulders.

Though the first harvest was reaped in Bengālī prose, it was in the soil of poetry that this cross-fertilization with the West bore its richest fruit. And no wonder. The Bengālī temperament is emotional, its genius essentially lyrical; the Bengālī language is supple and musical, as though fashioned for poetry. Michael Madhusūdan Dutt (1824–73) was the pioneer who, turning his back on the native tradition, made the first conscious and successful experiment to naturalize the European forms into Bengālī poetry by his epic in blank verse, *Meghnādbadh*, based on a *Rāmāyana* episode unorthodoxly interpreted, as well as by a number of sonnets. His personal life was a tragic struggle to justify Western values in an Indian context, but the fusion he vainly sought to achieve in life he successfully accomplished in his best creative verse. He led the way but could not establish a vital tradition, for his own success was a *tour de force* of a rare genius.

It was Tāgore who naturalized the Western spirit into Indian literature and thereby made it truly modern in an adult sense. He did this not by any conscious or forced adaptation of foreign models but by his creative response to the impulse of the age, with the result that the *Upanishads* and Kālidāsa, Vaishnava lyricism, and the rustic vigour of the folk idiom, are so well blended with Western influences in his poetry that generations of critics will continue to wrangle over his specific debt to each of them. In him modern Indian literature came of age—not only in poetry but in prose as well. Novel, short story, drama, essay, and literary criticism, they all attained maturity in his hands. Though Indian literature in its latest phase has outgrown his influence, as indeed it should, Tāgore was the most vital creative force in the cultural renaissance of India and represents its finest achievement.

As poetry in Michael Madhusūdan's hands and the novel in Bankim's, the modern drama too owed its inspiration to the Western model. The tradition of classical Sanskrit drama had long been lost and had not in any case percolated into the popular pattern of culture. But there is hardly a people who do not love to watch a visual representation of their life and lore, and so there arose a kind of composite folk drama—*Kathākalī* in Kerala, *Yakshagāna* in Karnātaka, *Ankiyā Nāt* in Assam, *Tamāshā* in Mahārāshtra, *Yātra* in Bengal, *Rās-līlā* in Braj and Manipurī, etc.—in which Purānic themes were interpreted on an improvised stage with the help of declamation, mime, song, and dance, and this was popular all over India. Whatever its other virtues, it was not drama proper. It was a composite entertainment, in the sense in which the word is understood today, more melodrama than drama, which is essentially an urban growth and a cultivated and sophisticated art, requiring considerable organization and resources.

Calcutta being the first cosmopolitan city in India to grow under the new regime, it was natural that it should witness the birth of the modern drama. It has still a lively stage tradition. Curiously enough, the first stage-play in Bengālī produced in Calcutta was by a Russian adventurer-cum-Indologist, Lebedev, in 1795. It was an adaptation of a little-known English comedy, *The Disguise*, by Richard Paul Jodrell, oddly mixed with English and Hindūstānī dialogue to suit the needs of a mixed audience. The main dialogue was, however, in Bengālī and the actors and actresses were likewise Bengālī.

Many years passed before a serious attempt was made to build an authentic stage, mainly under private patronage. The first original play in Bengālī was *Kulīn Kulasarvasva,* a social satire against the practice of polygamy among *Kulīn* brāhmans, written by Pandit Rāmnārāyan. Rāmnārāyan's second play, *Ratnāvali,* based on a Sanskrit classic, provoked Madhusūdan Dutt to try his hand at this medium. His impetuous genius turned out a number of plays in quick succession, some based on old legends and some social satires. He may thus be said to have laid the foundation of modern Indian drama, as he did of poetry, although his achievement in this form did not equal his performance in poetry and he soon retired from the field.

His place was taken by Dīnabandhu Mitra (1829–74), a born dramatist whose very first play, *Nīl Darpan* (published in 1860), exposing the atrocities of the British indigo planters, created a sensation, both literary and political. The Revd. J. Long, a noble-hearted missionary who had the audacity to publish the play in English, was fined and imprisoned by the authorities. Dīnabandhu wrote many more plays and was followed by a succession of playwrights among whom were Rabīndranath Tāgore's elder brother Jyotirindranāth, Manomohan Basu, and, later, the more famous Girīschandra Ghosh and Dwijendralāl Roy. Girīschandra was actor, producer, and playwright, and it is to his indefatigable zeal that the public theatre in Calcutta is largely indebted. But though both he and Dwijendralāl achieved phenomenal popularity in their day, their popular appeal was due more to the patriotic and melodramatic elements in their plays than to any abiding literary merit. On the other hand, Rabīndranāth Tāgore's plays, though they had considerable literary merit and were marked by originality and depth of thought, were too symbolic or ethereal to catch the popular imagination. And so he too failed to create a firm tradition in this field, with the result that of all literary forms in modern Indian literature the drama remains the least developed.

Bengālī had the advantage of bearing the first impact of the introduction of English education and Western learning in India. Being a sensitive and emotional people, the Bengālīs reacted to this with whole-hearted and passionate warmth. But the general pattern of literary resurgence was more or less the same in all Indian languages, each responding in its own manner, some sooner and some later. In most of them the early spade-work was done by Christian missionaries, who helped to fashion the basic material on which the development of prose was built. Gradual fertilization by English education and literature was reinforced by the natural receptivity of the Indian mind, with its subconscious heritage of a highly refined spiritual sensibility, to the liberal-humanist tradition of Western thought. Thus stimulated and further equipped with the Western technique of research, the Indian mind discovered anew, as it were, the rich treasures of its Sanskrit legacy. The earlier renaissance in Bengal not only invited emulation in other parts of India but also generated a reformist zeal and a new faith in Indian destiny. The life and work of Rājā Rām Mohan Roy, the Mahārshi Debendranāth Tāgore, Keshub Chandra Sen, Rāmakrishna Paramahamsa, and later Swāmī Vivekānanda and Śrī Aurobindo were sources of inspiration to the whole of India. No wonder that the early pioneers in almost all Indian literatures were also active social reformers and men of outstanding moral stature.

Of the numerous languages of India perhaps Marāthī was, after Bengālī, the most vigorous in its response to the spirit of the new age, partly because of its robust intellectual tradition, reinforced by memories of the erstwhile glory of the Marāthā Empire, and partly because Bombay, like Calcutta, provided a cosmopolitan modern environment. Among the stalwarts who laid the foundation of its modern literature may be mentioned the poet Keshavsut, the novelist Hari Nārāyan Āpte, and Agarkār, Tilak, and Chiplunkār as the builders of prose. Āpte's novels stimulated the development of the novel in some other languages too, particularly in the neighbouring Kannada. Kirloskār and Deval did for the Marāthī stage what Girīschandra had done for the Bengālī.

Narmad's poetry blazed the trail in Gujarātī, while Govardhanrām's *Sarasvatīchandra* made a landmark in Gujarātī fiction. Hindī had to face the difficult task of cutting a new broad channel into which the waters of its many tributaries could flow and which could be perennially fed from the vast reservoir of Sanskrit. This feat was performed by 'Bhāratendu' Hariśchandra and Mahāvīrprasād Dwivedī.

The problem of Urdū was different. Its form, derived from the same basic structure as Hindī, the common speech known as *Kharī Bolī*, had been standardized much earlier. Flourishing under court patronage, it had made phenomenal progress and was the most important Indian language to prosper in the eighteenth century. But it luxuriated in its own affluence and remained aloof from the vital currents that were sweeping the country forward in the nineteenth century. It is not without a certain significance that its greatest poet, Ghālib, was still composing doleful—though magnificent—*ghazals* redolent of Persian rose gardens when Michael Madhusūdan, Bankim, and Dīnabandhu were cutting new paths for Indian literature.

The development of modern Assamese and Oriyā, the two eastern neighbours of Bengālī, was also late in coming and was preceded by valuable spadework done by the Christian missions. Assam was torn by civil strife in the eighteenth century and was later under Burmese occupation until the British annexed it in 1827. Orissā too had been dismembered, and recovered its homogeneous integrity in the present century. The intelligentsia in both the regions were educated in Calcutta (which was for long the main educational centre in eastern India) and carried back with them the impact of the literary resurgence in Bengal. Lakshmīkānta Bezbaruā and Padmanāth Gohāin Baruā in Assamese, and Fakīrmohan Senāpati and Rādhānāth Rāy in Oriyā were the early pioneers in their respective fields.

Kashmīrī, Panjābī, and Sindhī had an even more retarded development, partly on account of the political conditions and partly because of the cultural glamour of Urdū in regions predominantly Muslim. All the more credit to the pioneers who held aloft the banner of their mother tongue when it hardly paid to do so: Mahjūr and Master Zindā Kaul in Kashmīrī, Sardār Pūran Singh and Bhāī Vīr Singh in Panjābī, and Mīrza Kalich Beg and Dewān Kauromāl in Sindhī.

What is surprising is the rather late and tardy resurgence in the four Dravidian languages, which had had a longer and a richer literary past than the northern languages as well as an earlier and closer contact with the Christian missions. The past has weighed more heavily on the south than on the north in India and nowhere more heavily than on Tamilnādu. However, in course of time the creative spirit in these languages too responded to the impulse of the age, in as rich a flowering as in the other languages of India, led by Puttanna, 'Srī', and Kailāsham in Kannada, by Kerala Varmā and Chandu Menon in Malayālam, by Bhāratī and Kalkī in Tamil, and Vīresalingam and Guruzāda Appa Rāo in Telugu. It is worth observing that the youngest of the Dravidian languages, Malayālam, has responded to the new age more dynamically than the oldest, Tamil, which even now looks too wistfully to the past.

MAIN TRENDS

The development of modern Indian literature has been marked by certain characteristics, some of which it shares with modern literatures the world over, while others are incidental to the special circumstances attending its birth. One of the latter is a certain dichotomy in the mental attitudes of the writers, some welcoming the new impulse, some resenting it—a dichotomy no less discernible in the make-up of the individual writer, whose one eye looks wistfully backwards, the other longingly ahead. There has always been in all countries and ages a conflict between the orthodox and the unorthodox, but in India, because the new impulse was identified with an alien culture and foreign domination, the clash of loyalties has been sharper. The very impact of Western thought, with its emphasis on democracy and self-expression, stimulated a nationalist consciousness which resented the foreign imposition and searched for the roots of self-respect and pride in its own heritage. Tāgore's novel *Gorā* is a masterly interpretation of this built-in conflict in the very nature of Indian renaissance, a conflict which still persists and has coloured not only our literature but almost every aspect of our life.

The first outstanding Bengālī poet of the nineteenth century (and the last in the old tradition), Īswar Chandra Gupta (1812–59), whose remarkable journal, *Samvād Prabhākar*, was the training-ground of many distinguished writers and who wrote the first literary biographies of his predecessor poets, was a doughty champion of the native heritage and poured his biting ridicule on everything that savoured of the new, irrespective of whether it was good or bad. Even the great Bankim Chandra, himself a leading herald of the new, looked more and more wistfully to the past as he grew older. Tilak in Marāthī and Bhāratī in Tamil were even more aggressive in their native pride and had their counterparts in all Indian languages.

This pride in India's past grew more lyrical under the stress of political aspirations and provided increasing fuel to the movement for national freedom. Whilst it thus served a useful purpose, it had its unhealthy and reactionary aspect in so far as it encouraged an exaggerated self-righteousness and distorted the historical perspective. Even so chaste a spirit as Mahātmā Gāndhī could fall under its spell and uttter with passionate sincerity the dismal half-truth that the British association had ruined India not only economically but intellectually, morally, and spiritually.

On the other hand, it is well to recall the testimony of Romesh Chunder Dutt, the distinguished scholar and historian who was himself one of the builders of the nineteenth-century renaissance, as recorded in the first edition of his *The Literature of Bengal*, published in 1877.

The conquest of Bengal by the English [wrote India's first modern historian] was not only a political revolution but ushered in a greater revolution in thoughts and ideas, in religion and society. We cannot describe the great change better than by stating that English conquest and English education may be supposed to have removed Bengal from the moral atmosphere of Asia to that of Europe. All the great events which have influenced European thought within the last one hundred years have also told, however feeble their effect may be, on the formation of the intellect of modern Bengal. The independence of America, the French Revolution, the war of Italian independence, the teachings of history, the vigour and freedom of English literature and English thought, the great effort of the French intellect in the eighteenth century, the results of German labour in the field of philosophy and ancient history —Positivism, Utilitarianism, Darwinism—all these have influenced and shaped the intellect of modern Bengal. In the same degree all the great influences which told on the Bengali mind in previous centuries, the faith of Krishna, the faith of Chandi or Kali, the preachings of Chaitanya, the belief in the truth of Hinduism and the sacredness of the Shastras, the unquestioning obedience to despotic power in all its phases, the faith in the divine right of royalty and in the innate greatness of princes and princesses—all these ancient habits and creeds have exercised feebler and yet feebler influences on the modern Bengali intellect. In habits, in tastes, in feeling, freedom and vigour and patriarchal institutions, our literature therefore has undergone a corresponding change. The classical Sanskrit taste has given place to the European. From the stories of gods and goddesses, kings and queens, princes and princesses, we have learned to descend to the humble walks of life, to sympathise with a common citizen or even a common peasant. From an admiration of a symmetrical uniformity we have descended to an appreciation of the strength and freedom of individuality. From admiring the grandeur and glory of the great we now willingly turn to appreciate the liberty and resistance in the lowly.

In so far as this somewhat effusive acknowledgement of India's debt to the West contains the core of a fair analysis, it was true in 1877 of a very limited intelligentsia in the city of Calcutta. It was hardly true of the rest of Bengal and India. Nevertheless, it was this limited intelligentsia that was the main vanguard of the moral and intellectual upsurge of the nineteenth century. In any case the passage indicates the fundamental trends which are still operative, despite the contrary trends released by powerful counter-movements, led partly by the very stalwarts who were the products of this upsurge. It is also relevant to record that the author omitted this passage from the second edition of his book, published in 1895.

From the beginning of the twentieth century Indian literature was increasingly coloured by political aspirations, passionately voiced in the songs and poems of the Tamil poet Bhāratī and the Bengālī poet Kāzī Nazrul Islām. The spiritual note of Indian poetry which had attained a poignant and rapturous pitch in the medieval Vaishnava outpourings became fainter and fainter and was drowned by more earthly pains and longings. Tāgore's *Gītānjalī* is the swan song of this great tradition. Religious poetry continues to be written to this day in India, but in the main it is little better than an inane repetition of what had been much better expressed earlier. The devotional content of poetry was henceforth increasingly replaced by the political, the ethical bias by the ideological, the plaintive tone by that of challenge and mockery, until the dominant note of Indian literature today is that of protest.

Tāgore's influence, after the award of the Nobel Prize in 1913, crossed the frontiers of Bengal and was for some time a source of exhilaration, if not always of inspiration, to his contemporaries all over India, from Master Zinda Kaul in Kashmīr to Kumāran Asan in Kerala. The influence was, however, superficial, since most of them knew him only through the English translations. The influence was more fruitful in the case of Assamese, Oriyā, Gujarātī, and Hindī, where the young poets took the trouble to learn Bengālī, mainly to read him in the original. The *Chhāyāvād* or Romantic school in Hindī poetry, led by Niralā, Pant, and others, which was a potent stimulus in the development of modern Hindī literature, was directly inspired by it. Tāgore's main impact was, however, indirect, inasmuch as it gave confidence to Indian writers that they could achieve in their mother tongue what had been achieved in Sanskrit or European languages.

But Tāgore's influence, such as it was, was soon overshadowed by the impact of Gāndhī, Marx, and Freud, a strange trinity. Though none of these three was a man of letters proper, they released intellectual and moral passions and introduced new techniques of thought and behaviour which had a profound effect on young writers all over India. Gāndhī's impact, confined to India, was both widespread and deep, though it was deeper on some languages than on others, much deeper, for instance, on Gujarātī and Hindī than on Bengālī. Gāndhī transfigured the image of India and turned national idealism from its futile adulation of the past to face the reality of India as she was, poor, starving, and helpless, but with an untapped potential of unlimited possibilities.

Both Vivekānanda and Tāgore had said the same thing before, but it was Gāndhī more than anyone else who made this image vivid and real and gave a new insight to the Indian intelligentsia, enlarging their sympathies and adding a new dimension to their imagination. Indian writers learnt to discover their own country, not in ancient Banāras and Madurai but in the slums of Calcutta and Bombay, and in the innumerable 'dunghills scattered over the land', as Gāndhī described the Indian villages in their poverty and squalor. He thus provided a powerful ethical stimulus to the literary trend, which had already begun, from romanticism to realism, from the highflown and artificial 'literary' style to the vigour and raciness of the spoken idiom. The Mahātmā's insistence on non-violence and on simplicity and purity in personal life touched a responsive chord in the inherent idealism of Indian thought and thus served as an indirect inspiration to creative literature. His own employment of a simple and direct prose style, shorn of all superfluous rhetoric, was a very healthy corrective to the natural tendency to flamboyance in Indian writing. This influence was particularly fruitful in Gujarātī, in which language he wrote. In Bengālī the crispness of the colloquial speech had already achieved a literary status in the writings of Tāgore and Pramatha Chaudhury.

The eminent Hindī novelist Premchand has described in an autobiographical essay how, inspired by the Mahātmā, he resigned from government service and settled down in a village to see life in the raw and to write about it. His later career as the foremost Urdū and Hindī novelist, his imaginative insight into the life of the common folk, particularly in the villages, and his simple and direct delineation of it formed a major influence on many of his contemporaries and reflect the impact of Gāndhī on modern Indian literature. Among other writers of note who responded to this impact, each in his own fashion, may be mentioned the gifted Gupta brothers, Maithilīsharan and Sīyārāmsharan, as well as Jainendra Kumār in Hindī, Kākā Kālelkār and Umāshankar Joshī in Gujarātī, Māmā Warerkār in Marāthī, Nīlmani Phookan in Assamese, Kalindīcharan Pānigrāhī in Oriyā, Annadāshankar Rāy in Bengālī, Bhāratī in Tamil, Vallathol in Malayālam, and many more in these and other languages.

The influence of the philosophy of Śrī Aurobindo is also noticeable among some writers, like the Kannada poets, Bendre and Puttappā, and the Gujarātī poets, Sundaram and Jayant Parekh, but beyond imparting a certain mystic glow to their verse and confirming their faith in the reality of the Indian spiritual experience, it has not given any new trend or horizon to Indian literature in general.

The eruption of Marxism in the early 1930s is a phenomenon which India shares with many other countries. The infection caught by Indian literature was, however, neither virulent nor on the whole unhealthy. Gāndhī had already given a new orientation to the popular imagination by looking for God, not in the temple but in the *daridra-nārāyana*, the hungry outcaste. This moral vaccination had a twofold reaction: on the one hand, ethical sensibility moved leftwards and it became almost virtuous to be radical; on the other hand, class hatred was softened if not rendered comparatively innocuous. This would explain how a Vallathol could invoke Lenin with as much gusto as the lyrical fervour with which he sang of Mary Magdalene and Gāndhī, and why Premchand, who ended his autobiographical testament with an affirmation of the Vaishnava faith that not a blade of grass stirs but as God wills it, came to be hailed by the 'Progressives' as the Gorky of India. On the other side is the example of the works of Bengālī writers with professed Marxist leanings—Manek Bandyopādhyāy's *Putul Nācher Itikathā* is a fine illustration—who are not ashamed to delineate bourgeois types in their fiction with real sympathy and understanding. 'Progressive' writers in Urdū and Panjābī, who are a dominant influence in these literatures, are less sensitive, and indulge with naïve gusto in mockery and hatred. They make up for this lack of sensibility, however, with an added dash of virility.

The literary impact of the current explosion, in Bengal, in Keralā, and in some other parts of India, of class hatred and violence, and of an organized campaign to desecrate and destroy all vestiges of inherited cultural values in the name of a Maoist 'cultural revolution', is a phenomenon too recent for a proper assessment. To some extent this rebellious and desperate mood is part of a world-wide eruption. How far it will turn out to be a lasting or vital literary inspiration it is hard to predict. Already its excesses are causing a general revulsion.

Freud, like the Vedas, is hardly ever read by Indian writers, but as the pious justify every folly in the name of scripture, so there is no dearth of writers who imagine that they are probing the depths of the human psyche by smelling sex everywhere. Nevertheless, the impact of Freud, however naïvely interpreted, has helped to loosen many inhibitions from which the earlier writers, brought up in the climate of nineteenth-century puritanism, had suffered. The traditional Hindu attitude to sex was healthy and unashamed, as can be seen in Vātsyāyana's classic, the *Kāmasūtra.* Even medieval devotional poetry such as that of Jayadeva and Vidyāpati revelled in a voluptuous symbolism which modern orthodox scholarship would gladly slur over. But the influence of Victorian England and Brāhmo reformism, reinforced by the puritan fervour of Gāndhism, had overlaid the Indian consciousness with a complex of inhibitions which it needed the prestige of scientific psychoanalysis to break through. Having lost the honest indigenous tradition we are obliged to borrow the Western technique which, however 'scientific', is so crude that the modern gloating over sex is invariably accompanied by a sense of guilt, if it is secret, and by a sense of bravado, if it is brazen. What was a means of legitimate enjoyment to the ancients has become a source of morbid excitement to the moderns.

To these two foreign and non-literary stimuli, Marxist dialectics and Freudian probings, must be added a literary one proper, though equally an importation, namely the new formalist experiments which have achieved both popularity and prestige in the West. These experiments, known under various high-sounding names associated with such writers as Ezra Pound, T. S. Eliot,

James Joyce, Jean-Paul Sartre, and others, are mainly in form and technique and have little to do with any particular faith or ideology, although they may reflect a significant mental attitude. A writer may be very daring in form but conservative or even reactionary in religious or political faith, or vice versa. Bishnu De and Buddhadeva Bose in Bengālī, Ajneya and Shamsher Bahādur in Hindī, Mardhekār and Vinda Kārandikār in Marāthī, and a host of other parallels in Indian languages share a common iconoclastic zeal in form but are faithful to their respective orthodoxies in faith.

On the whole, the impact on Indian writing of the mixed interaction of these three imported influences has been a salutary one, despite some wild aberrations. It has given a much-needed jolt to the smugness of the traditional attitude, with its age-old tendency to sentimental piety and glorification of the past. The revolt began in Bengal, although Bengal was already the home of unorthodoxy in literary form, Tāgore and his contemporaries having long blasted 'the castle of conformism'. But the adulation of Tāgore was itself becoming an orthodoxy, which provoked in the early 1920s a group of young gifted writers known as the Kallol group to proclaim their revolt. The revolt of the new, as Tāgore pointed out, is very often its audacity only, and these writers soon discovered that Tāgore could outmodern them whenever he cared to. Nevertheless, the revolt yielded a rich harvest, in both poetry and prose, in the work of Jīvanānanda Dās, Premendra Mitra, Buddhadeva Bose, Manek Bandyopādhyāy, Subhās Mukhopādhyāy, and others. This movement has been paralleled in almost all Indian languages and has been particularly fruitful in the lyric and its counterpart in prose, the short story. While valiant champions of the older tradition have continued to hold their own, like Viswanadha Satyanārāyana in Telugu, Mahādevī Varmā in Hindī, and many more in the various languages, it is the spirit of nonconformism that gives variety and colour to much of modern writing in India. The contemporary literary output, particularly in poetry and fiction, is both lively and volum - nous, and its quality—in the work of the more mature writers—is distinguished and may well stand comparison with similar work published anywhere outside India.

But poetry hardly suits the temper of the modern industrial society and if it continues to be written in India in such profusion and with such exuberance, it is partly because the tradition of poetry being sung or chanted is very old and deep-rooted there, and partly because a certain prestige clings to poetry as 'purer' literature than any other. Even so, poetry as a form of narrative has lost its ancient vogue and has willy-nilly yielded the place of honour to the novel and the short story, which are today the most popular as well as the best cultivated forms of literature. In Bengal both these forms attained an early maturity in the hands of Tāgore and have since made phenomenal progress under his younger contemporaries and successors, among whom Sarat Chandra Chatterjee achieved a popularity, both in Bengal and outside, which equalled, if not surpassed, that of Tāgore. Though not so spectacularly popular, the novels and stories of Bibhūti Bhūshan Bannerjī (whose *Pather Panchālī* in its screen version has since received wide publicity), Tārāshankar Bannerjī, Manek Bandyopādhyāy, Satināth Bhādurī, 'Bonophūl', Achintya Sengupta, Prabodh Sanyal, and many have maintained a high standard.

Whether the treatment is romantic, realistic, or impressionist, whether the exploration is historical, regional, tribal, or psychological, the bias Marxian or Freudian, they have continued the tradition of humanism and of sympathy for the fallen bequeathed by Tāgore and Sarat Chandra.

Among notable contemporaries in other Indian languages who have handled the art of fiction with originality and skill may be mentioned Biren Bhattāchārya and Abdul Malik in Assamese, Pannalāl Patel and Darshak in Gujarātī, Jainendra Kumār and Yashpāl in Hindī, Masti and Karanth in Kannada, Akhtār Mohiuddīn and Sūfī Ghulām Mohammad in Kashmīrī, Thakāzhī (whose *Chemmīn* has been published in several foreign editions) and Bashīr in Malayālam, Khandekār and Gadgil in Marāthī, the Mohanty brothers in Oriyā, Nānak Singh and Duggal in Panjābī, Mi. Pa. Somasundaram and Ka. Na. Subramanyam in Tamil, Bāpirāju and Padmarāju in Telugu, and Kishan Chunder and Bedī in Urdū. These names are merely illustrative and can be matched by many more. They represent not only a medley of techniques and attitudes but also uneven levels of creative achievement and conflicting trends. But India is a land of contrasts, not only economically but culturally as well.

The position of Sanskrit itself is an apt illustration. Deemed a 'dead' language because it is no longer a spoken tongue, it is nevertheless not only a very vital source-language on which almost all Indian languages, except Urdū, draw for their vocabulary, but also a living fount of literary inspiration to Indian writers, an honour rivalled only by English. Perhaps there has not been a single writer of outstanding distinction in the modern period (Urdū writers excepted) who has not drawn freely on the wealth of both Sanskrit and English literatures, though some have taken more from the one than the other. Some ultra-moderns, like Sudhīn Datta in Bengālī, are indeed a curious complex of Sanskrit, Baudelaire, and Eliot, as some leftists like Rāhula Sankrityāyana are of Sanskrit, Tibetan, and Marx. But even apart from its significant role in the development of modern Indian literature Sanskrit continues to be used as a literary vehicle, both for scholarly research and for creative writing, as can be testified by a large number of books and journals published in Sanskrit annually. Not only many modern Indian writers like Bankim, Tāgore, and Sarat Chandra have been translated into Sanskrit but Shakespeare and Goethe also.

The position of English is in some respects unique in India. On the one hand it is resented by the ultra-nationalist sentiment as a relic of erstwhile foreign imposition and is allowed to continue officially on sufferance; on the other it is still the main medium of higher education in most of the universities, especially in the sciences and technology which are the backbone of modern education, and the one link among the intelligentsia all over India. The fact that Jawāharlāl Nehrū when he was the Prime Minister of India and Dr. S. Rādhākrishnan the then President of India could converse with each other in English only and employed it as their main literary vehicle, as also the fact that the collected works of Mahātmā Gāndhī are being published (under the auspices of the Government of India) in English are themselves a commentary on the current usefulness of this language in India as 'a link language', to quote Jawāharlāl Nehrū's description of it in the Indian

Parliament. It may also be noted that more books continue to be published in English than in any Indian language in India.

But apart from its utilitarian value as a language of higher education in the sciences and as a 'link language', a fair number of Indian writers, including such eminent thinkers steeped in Indian thought as Vivekānanda, Rānade, Gokhale, Aurobindo, and Rādhākrishnan, have voluntarily adopted it as their literary medium. Even the bulk of Mahātmā Gāndhī's writings are in English. This phenomenon is as old as modern Indian literature itself. There has been, from Derozio in the 1820s to R. K. Nārāyan today, an unbroken tradition of some gifted Indians choosing to write in English. Many of them, like the Dutt sisters, Toru and Aru, their versatile uncle Romesh Chunder, Manomohan Ghosh, Sarojinī Naidū, and, among contemporaries, Mulk Rāj Ānand, Rāja Rāo, Bhabānī Bhattāchārya, and many others, have achieved distinction.

Some early pioneers in the Indian languages were also tempted at the threshold of their career to adopt English for their creative writing, partly because they owed their inspiration to English literature and partly because they hoped thereby to reach a wider audience. Madhusūdan Dutt's first narrative poem, *The Captive Ladie*, and Bankim Chandra's early novel *Rajmohan's Wife*, are classic examples. Wisely they discovered in time that they could create best in their own language. Tāgore, a lover of the English language to which he owed much, was never tired of stressing that no great literature could be produced except in one's mother tongue, and he likened an exclusive reliance on English to the use of crutches which make a lot of clatter while the natural limbs become atrophied by disuse. Perhaps he overstressed the *mother* tongue aspect of it, for it is doubtful if Sanskrit was the tongue in which either Kālidāsa or Jayadeva lisped to their mothers. Many distinguished writers in Hindī and Urdū—Premchand and Iqbāl are illustrious examples—had to discard the dialects which were their mother tongues and wrote in languages which they cultivated; and even today there are a number of noted poets and writers, Mastī and Bendre in Kannada, Kākā Kālelkār in Gujarātī, Annadāshankar Rāy and Ābu Sayeed Ayyūb in Bengālī, and many others in Hindī, born to one language and successfully writing in another of their adoption.

It might be more correct to say that, if not necessarily the mother tongue proper, the language of one's cultural upbringing and environment is the best medium for one's creative expression. The names of Joseph Conrad and several American writers who (or whose parents) migrated from Germany, Italy, or Russia can be cited as relevant instances. It is therefore not only uncharitable but unreasonable to belittle Indian writers who choose to write in English. In any case a writer should be judged by the quality of his writing, irrespective of the medium he adopts. Some English novels of R. K. Nārāyan, a born story-teller with any eye for observation and the gift of gentle irony, are superior in intrinsic literary merit to a great deal of mediocre stuff that passes for literature in some Indian languages. On the other hand, it cannot be denied that, as far as creative writing is concerned, no Indian writer in English has reached anywhere near the heights attained by some of the great writers in the Indian languages.

What modern Indian literature sadly lacks is a well-proportioned and many-sided development. Against its achievement in poetry and fiction must be set its poverty in drama, in critical apparatus, and the literature of knowledge in general. Though Indian life is full of drama which is being well exploited in fiction, in scenarios for the screen, and even in plays for the radio, drama proper has failed to keep pace with the best in poetry and fiction, either in quality or output, the reason probably being that drama has little scope for growth independently of the stage and there is almost no professional stage worth the name in the cities of India, despite some brave endeavours in Calcutta and Bombay, and recently in Delhi.

There is, indeed, no dearth of books published on literary research and criticism. But much of it, unfortunately, is laborious and unimaginative pedantry, flogging the dead horse of Sanskrit aesthetics or indiscriminately applying borrowed canons and -isms from abroad, irrespective of the context of Indian life and tradition, or, worse still, unashamedly boosting regional or national claims. Happily, despite this clamour of pedantry, patriotic piety, and political bias, good literature continues to be written and, as it justifies itself, it helps to sharpen the reader's sensibility. Since the time of Tāgore a growing minority of intelligent critics well versed in the literary traditions of their own country and of the West have bravely maintained a more wholesome approach that is neither overwhelmed by the burden of the past nor overawed by the glamour of the latest fashion. This healthy trend should gain in strength with a growing realization that, in the republic of letters as in that of men, a sensitive and well-trained critical apparatus and its judicious and fearless exercise are the *sine qua non* of happy results.

THE WAR AND INDEPENDENCE

The last great war, which nearly shook the foundations of the modern world, had little impact on Indian literature beyond aggravating the popular revulsion against violence and adding to the growing disillusionment with the 'humane pretensions' of the Western world. This was eloquently voiced in Tāgore's later poems and his last testament, *Crisis in Civilization*. The Indian intelligentsia was in a state of moral dilemma. On the one hand, it could not help sympathizing with England's dogged courage in the hour of peril, with the Russians fighting with their backs to the wall against the ruthless Nazi hordes, and with China groaning under the heel of Japanese militarism; on the other hand, their own country was practically under military occupation by the very people who were resisting such occupation of their own soil, and an Indian army under Subhās Bose was trying from the opposite camp to liberate their country. No creative impulse could issue from such confusion of loyalties.

One would imagine that the achievement of Indian independence in 1947, which came in the wake of the Allies' victory and was followed by the collapse of colonialism in the neighbouring countries of South-East Asia, would have released an upsurge of creative energy. No doubt it did, but unfortunately it was soon submerged in the great agony of the partition, with its inhuman slaughter of the innocents and the uprooting of millions of people from their homeland, followed by the martyrdom of Mahātmā Gāndhī. These tragedies, along with Pakistan's invasion of Kashmīr and its more recent activities in

Bāngladesh, did indeed provoke a spate of poignant writing, particularly in the languages of the regions most affected, Bengālī, Hindī, Kashmīrī, Panjābī, Sindhī, and Urdū. But poignant or passionate writing does not by itself make great literature.

What reserves of enthusiasm and confidence survived these disasters have been mainly absorbed in the task of national reconstruction and economic development. The faith in One World, so luminous for a while, was soon overcast by suspicion and rivalry between the great powers and the menace of nuclear war. India's trust in the peaceful pursuit of a good life and in the power of non-violence have received a series of rude shocks, culminating in the tragic happenings in Bāngladesh and in Vietnam.

If no great literature has yet emerged out of this chain of convulsions, it must be recalled that half a century had to elapse after Napoleon's invasion of Russia before *War and Peace* was written. Meanwhile, Indian literature is richer today in volume, range, and variety than it ever was in the past, even if no great peaks are visible, such as once marked its landscape. The writers are exploring new fields and there is hardly a branch of literature in which experiments, some feeble, some vigorous, are not being made. Translations from one Indian language into another, as well as from many foreign languages, help to widen the writer's horizon and to stimulate his urge to experiment and to emulate. The Union and State Governments are increasingly aware of the role of literature in society and do what they can to encourage good writing, both directly and through the National and State Academies and Book Trusts. The number of writers who derive a comfortable income from their royalties, which was negligible twenty years ago, has risen rapidly. The readers' market, still poor, has nevertheless such vast potential for most languages in India that, as poverty and illiteracy are eliminated and as the publishing industry gets better organized, the Indian writer can confidently hope for opportunities such as his counterpart in the advanced countries of the West enjoys.

What produces great literature and when it will come again, it is difficult to say. What one can say with modesty is that Indian literature may look forward to a future full of possibilities. For modern Indian literature is not a mushroom growth of exotic plants in a native wilderness. It draws its sustenance from an old and rich soil to which many streams have brought their alluvial deposits. The latest stream has come from the West and its fertilizing agent has been the English language. Not that Indian literature would not have had its modern crop but for this historical accident. The spirit of the age would in any case have stirred its soil, sooner or later, and the winds were blowing fast, carrying the seeds from one part of the world to another.

PART FOUR

INDIA AND THE WORLD OUTSIDE

CHAPTER XXX

Early Contacts between India and Europe

by H. G. RAWLINSON*

NOTHING is more misleading than a half-truth, and it would be hard to find a more apposite illustration of this than the old adage about East and West never meeting. No statement could be more inaccurate. In spite of geographical, linguistic, and racial obstacles, the intercourse between India and Europe throughout the ages has been almost uninterrupted, and each has reacted upon the other in a remarkable fashion. India had never been entirely isolated. Before the dawn of history, as archaeological investigations since 1921 have shown, an extensive chalcolithic culture existed in the plains of the lower Indus, which was closely connected with contemporary cultures in Mesopotamia and Asia Minor.[1] Commerce between the mouth of the Indus and the Persian Gulf was unbroken down to Buddhist times, while we have direct evidence of early trade by sea between the Phoenicians of the Levant and western India as early as 975 B.C., when Hiram, king of Tyre, sent his fleet of 'Ships of Tarshish' from Ezion Geber, at the head of the Gulf of Akaba in the Red Sea, to fetch 'ivory, apes, and peacocks' from the port of Ophir to decorate the palaces and the Temple of King Solomon. Whether Ophir is the ancient port of Supāra, not far from Bombay, or an unidentified harbour on the south-east coast of Arabia, there is no doubt that the objects imported came from India. And with merchandise there invariably comes an exchange, not only of *motifs* in pottery, jewellery, and woven materials, but of language and ideas. The Phoenicians were the earliest connecting link between the Indian and Mediterranean cultures, and this link goes back to very early times.

We next turn to the Greeks. The language of the Āryan invaders of the Panjāb, their culture, and their social and religious traditions have sufficient similarity to those of the Indo-Germanic peoples of early Europe to warrant the conclusion that at some early period they must have been in close contact, though it is scarcely necessary to warn the modern reader that identity of language and culture do not necessarily indicate community of race. But there can be no doubt about the similarity between the societies depicted in the Homeric and Vedic poems. Both worship the gods of the 'upper air', Father Heaven (Ζεὺς πατήρ, Jupiter, Dyaus pitar), Mother Earth, the wide expanse of Heaven (Οὐρανός, Varuna), the Dawn (Aurora, Ushas), the Sun (Ἥλιος,

* The final paragraph, together with a few footnotes and small changes in the body of this chapter, have been added by Dr. Friedrich Wilhelm. [Ed.]

[1] Cf. Sir Mortimer Wheeler, *Early India and Pakistan*, London, 1959; H. Mode, *Das frühe Indien*, Stuttgart, 1959; J. M. Casal, *La civilisation de l'Indus et ses énigmes*, Paris, 1969; and W. A. Fairservis, *The Roots of Ancient India*. New York, 1971.

Sūrya). Society in both is patriarchal and tribal. It consists of a number of loosely knit clans, in each of which the king is the father of the tribe. The resemblance between the epic age as depicted in Homer and the *Mahābhārata* is very striking. In both, for instance, the warriors fight from chariots, and not, like the later Greeks or the Rājputs, on horseback. Neither the Hellenes nor the Āryans of the Panjāb, however, retained any recollection of the time when they had been united, and, when they once more met, it was as strangers.

They were brought into touch through Persia. The mighty Persian Empire, ruled over by the Iranians, stretched from the Mediterranean to the Indus, and included both Greeks and Indians among its subjects. The earliest contact between Greece and India was made about 510 B.C., when Darius the Great, having advanced as far as the head-waters of the Indus, sent a Greek mercenary named Scylax of Caryanda to sail down the river to its mouth, and make his way home by the Red Sea. Scylax took the old route followed by the Phoenicians, and, after a voyage lasting two and a half years, duly arrived at Arsinoe, the modern Suez. His account of his adventures was probably utilized by Herodotus, who was born at Halicarnassus, not far from Caryanda, in 484 B.C., about the same time as the death of Gautama Buddha. Herodotus has a good deal to tell us about India: he knows that there were two races, the dark aboriginals and the fair Āryans ('white like the Egyptians', as a later writer calls them). He talks of the crocodiles of the Indus, the extremes of heat and cold in the Panjāb, and the cotton, superior to sheep's wool, of which the Indians made their clothes. He is the first to recount the famous legend of the gigantic ants which guarded the Indian gold, and several of the stories which occur in his narrative, for instance that of the foolish Hippocleides, who 'did not care' when he danced away his wife, have been traced to the Buddhist *Jātakas* or birth stories. More important, perhaps, is his description of a religious sect which ate nothing which had life and lived on a grain like millet, for this seems to be a reference to the Jains. A later Greek traveller and writer about India who flourished about a century after this was Ctesias, who was for twenty years a resident at the Court of Susa, where he was physician to Artaxerxes Mnemon, having been taken prisoner at the battle of Cunaxa (401 B.C.). Unfortunately Ctesias has none of the sobriety of Herodotus. He is quite uncritical, and overlays a kernel of historical fact with a mass of picturesque fable. At this time India was fully aware of the existence of the Greeks or Ionians (*Yavana, Yona*), who are also mentioned in the inscriptions of Darius. During the whole of this period Persia was the link between Greece and India. Indian troops took part in the invasion of Greece in 480 B.C., while Greek officials and mercenaries served in various parts of the Empire, including India. 'At no time', it has been said, 'were means of communication by land more open, or the conditions more favourable for the interchange of ideas between India and the West.'[2]

This may account for the influence of Indian ideas upon the development of Greek philosophy. One of the most marked features of the period preceding the Persian Wars was the revolt against the simple eschatology of Homer, and the search for a deeper explanation of the meaning of life. These speculations, it must be observed, originated with the Ionian Greeks of Asia Minor, who

[2] Rapson, *Ancient India*, Cambridge, 1914, pp. 87–8.

were in touch with Persia. The father of Greek philosophy was Thales of Miletus, but the foundations of Greek metaphysics were laid by the Eleatic School, Xenophanes, Parmenides, and Zeno, who sought for the One Reality underlying material phenomena in very much the same spirit as the authors of some of the later Vedic hymns and the *Upanishads*. Then came the Orphic movement. On the ultimate origin of the complex esoteric doctrines which we may conveniently group together under the title of Orphism we are quite in the dark, but we know that its chief features were a more or less explicit pantheism, a depreciation of the body in comparison with the soul, and the belief that the soul is imprisoned in the body, from which she seeks release. Orphism appears to have originated with Pherecydes of Syros (*c.* 600 B.C.), and his disciple Pythagoras.

Pythagoras was born about 580 B.C. in the cosmopolitan island of Samos, and, according to his biographer Iamblichus, travelled widely, studying the esoteric teaching of the Egyptians, Assyrians, and even the brāhmans.

> It is not too much [says Gompertz] to assume that the curious Greek, who was a contemporary of Buddha, and it may be of Zoroaster too, would have acquired a more or less exact knowledge of the East, in that age of intellectual fermentation, through the medium of Persia. It must be remembered in this connexion, that the Asiatic Greeks, at the time when Pythagoras still dwelt in his Ionian home, were under the single sway of Cyrus, the founder of the Persian Empire.[3]

The most startling of the theories of Pythagoras was that of the transmigration of the soul from body to body. Herodotus traces this to Egypt.

> The Egyptians [he says] were the first to broach the opinion that the soul is immortal, and that, when the body dies, it enters into the form of an animal which is born at the moment, thence passing on from one animal to another, until it has circled through the forms of all the creatures which tenant the land, the water and the air, after which it enters again into a human frame, and is born anew. The whole period of the transmigration is (they say) three thousand years. There are Greek writers, some of an earlier, some of a later date, who have borrowed this doctrine from the Egyptians, and put it forward as their own.[4]

Herodotus, like Plato and others, attributes all wisdom to Egyptian sources, as was only natural. The Greeks were deeply impressed by the great antiquity of Egyptian civilization, its lofty temples, and its closely guarded religious mysteries. 'Omne ignotum pro magnifico.' Unfortunately, it is extremely doubtful whether the Egyptians did actually believe in transmigration, and it is probable that the Greeks were misled by the paintings on the tombs depicting the tribunal of Osiris, which they did not properly understand. It is more likely that Pythagoras was influenced by India than by Egypt. Almost all the theories, religious, philosophical, and mathematical, taught by the Pythagoreans, were known in India in the sixth century B.C., and the Pythagoreans, like the Jains and Buddhists, refrained from the destruction of life and eating meat, and regarded certain vegetables, such as beans, as taboo.

The theory of metempsychosis plays almost as great a part in Greek as in Indian religious thought. Both Pythagoras and Empedocles claimed to possess

[3] T. Gompertz, *Greek Thinkers*, London, 1901. Vol. 1, p. 127.
[4] Herodotus ii. 123. Compare Cicero, *Tusc. Disp.* i. 16.

the power of recollecting their past births.[5] Metempsychosis is referred to in many passages in Pindar, and, with the complementary doctrine of *karma*, it is the key-stone of the philosophy of Plato. The soul is for ever travelling through a 'cycle of necessity': the evil it does in one semicircle of its pilgrimage is expiated in the other. 'Each soul,' we are told in the *Phaedrus*, 'returning to the election of a second life, shall receive one agreeable to his desire.' But most striking of all is the famous apologue of Er the Pamphylian, with which Plato appropriately ends the *Republic*. Er sees the disembodied souls choosing their next incarnations at the hands of 'Lachesis, daughter of Necessity' (*karma* personified). Orpheus chooses the body of a swan, Thersites that of an ape, Agamemnon that of an eagle. 'In like manner, some of the animals passed into men, and into one another, the unjust passing into the wild, and the just into the tame.'[6]

It is interesting to note that India was passing through a parallel stage of development about the same time or somewhat earlier (700–500 B.C.). Men were no longer content with the pursuit of earthly happiness, to be followed by an endless life of bliss in the halls of Yama. They wanted to achieve the release of the soul by correct knowledge. Transmigration first appears in the *Brāhmanas* and *Upanishads*, the most ancient prose commentaries on the *Vedas*. The essence of their teaching is that the individual soul is an emanation of the World Soul, which, entering on a cycle of terrestrial incarnations, passes from body to body in a seemingly endless round, now as a god, now as a man, now as an animal or even a plant, finding no relief from pain and suffering until it is finally absorbed, 'as the dewdrop is absorbed in the Ocean'. This is 'deliverance' (*moksha, mukti*, λύσις). To this the Indian thinker added the doctrine of *karma* or action. He whose actions in a former life were pure will be reborn as a brāhman or kshatriya, while the evil-doer will be reborn as 'a dog, a hog, or a Chandāla'. As in Orphism, the soul during its earthly pilgrimage is regarded as a fallen angel, doing penance for her sins: only when the wheel of births and deaths comes full circle can she regain her lost inheritance. Orphism and its later developments and Indian transcendental philosophy abound in parallels. Hindu philosophy attributes rebirth to ignorance (*avidyā*): this is the Socratic doctrine that 'no one sins willingly'. The well-known simile of the Cave, with which the seventh book of Plato's *Republic* opens, reminds us of the Vedānta doctrine of *Māyā* or Illusion. The soul, imprisoned in matter, thirsts after objects of desire as the hart pants for the mirage-water of the desert. The noble prayer of the oldest *Upanishad*,

> From the Unreal lead me to the Real,
> From Darkness to the Light,
> From Death to Immortality,

finds many an echo in Plato's Dialogues. The resemblances are so numerous that it would be tedious to enumerate them, and one or two examples must suffice. The most remarkable is the Orphic legend that the Universe was

[5] Pythagoras remembered having fought, as Euphorbus, in the Trojan War. Empedocles had been, in past incarnations, 'a boy, a girl, a bush, a bird, and a scaly fish in the ocean' (Frag. 117, Diels).

[6] For the parallels between Platonism and Indian philosophy, see B. J. Urwick, *The Message of Plato*, London, 1920.

formed in the body of Zeus, after he had swallowed Phanes, the offspring of the great 'World Egg', in whom all the seeds of things are present. Thus the world is the body of God: the heavens are his head, the sun and moon his eyes, and the ether his mind. In the same way, we are told in the tenth book of the *Institutes of Manu* how the Supreme Soul produced by a thought a Golden Egg (*Brahmānda*) from which he was born as Brahmā. The resemblance between the two legends is too close to be accidental. The doctrine of Xenophanes (570 B.C.), that God is the eternal Unity, permeating the universal and governing it by His thought, occurs time after time in post-Vedic Hindu literature. Empedocles, besides believing in transmigration, holds a number of tenets which are curiously like those of Kapila, the author of the Sānkhya system. Kapila traces the evolution of the material world to primeval matter, which is acted upon by the three 'qualities' or *gunas*, i.e. *sattva*, *rajas*, and *tamas*, lightness, activity, and heaviness. Empedocles looks on matter as consisting of the four elements, earth, water, air, and fire, acted upon by the motive forces of love and hate.

Attention has been called to the resemblance between the Hindu varnas or classes, brāhmans, kshatriyas or warriors, vaiśyas or merchants, and śūdras, and the division of the ideal polity in Plato's *Republic* into Guardians, Auxiliaries, and Craftsmen.[7] The story that Socrates proposes to tell about their divine origin, in order that the system may be perpetuated, 'otherwise the state will certainly perish', is curiously like the Vedic myth about the origin of the four classes from the mouth, arms, thighs, and feet of Purusha, the Primeval Man.[8] Are these mere coincidences? Eusebius preserves a tradition, which he attributes to a contemporary, the well-known writer on harmonics Aristoxenus, that certain learned Indians actually visited Athens and conversed with Socrates. They asked him to explain the object of his philosophy, and when he replied, 'an inquiry into human affairs', one of the Indians burst out laughing. 'How', he asked, 'could a man grasp human things without first mastering the Divine?'[9] If Eusebius is to be believed, we must revise many of our preconceived notions about early intercourse between the two countries.

Greece and India, however, were destined to be brought into yet closer and more direct contact. The older Greek states were exclusive in their outlook. To them, all non-Greeks were barbarians, and it needed some great shock to break down the barriers dividing them from the outer world. This was provided by Alexander the Great, himself only half-Greek, but wholly inspired by the Greek spirit of inquiry. When he set out on his famous expedition to the East it was as an explorer as well as a conqueror: on his staff were a number of trained historians and scientists. In the spring of 326 B.C., the Macedonian hoplites, having marched half-way across Asia, entered the defiles of the Hindū Kush and found themselves in the fertile plains of the Panjāb. Alexander's first halt was at the great city of Taxila, where for the first time the civilizations of East and West found themselves directly confronted. Taxila was of special interest for the scientists in Alexander's train, as being one of the leading seats of Hindu learning, where crowds of pupils, sons of

[7] B. J. Urwick, *The Message of Plato*, London, 1920.

[8] *Republic*, Book iii; *Rig Veda*, x. 90.

[9] Eusebius, *Praep. Evang.* xi. 3.

princes and wealthy brāhmans, resorted to study 'the three Vedas and eighteen accomplishments'. After defeating the Hindu prince Porus on the banks of the Hydaspes (Jhelum), Alexander travelled down the Indus to its mouth, establishing fortified posts or 'colonies' at strategic points, and turned his face westwards in October 325 B.C. In June 323 he died of fever at Babylon.

The actual effect of Alexander's invasion of India was negligible, and no mention of the event occurs in ancient Indian literature. Alexander's Indian campaign lived on in the romance of Alexander which goes back to Pseudo-Callisthenes, and adaptations of which existed in more than thirty languages of medieval Europe and Asia Minor.[10] This Indian episode has always been subject to fantastic figuration. In Jean Racine's drama, Alexander falls in love with the Indian Princess Cléophile, for instance. After Alexander's death, the empire which he had founded quickly dissolved, and by 317 B.C. nearly all traces of Greek rule had vanished. But Alexander had broken down the wall of separation between East and West, and the contact thus made was never again totally lost.

About the time of Alexander's death, a new ruler, Chandragupta Maurya, had established himself in the Ganges valley, and he quickly extended his empire to the Panjāb. He was so successful that when, in 305 B.C., Seleucus Nicator tried to repeat his predecessor's exploits, he was defeated and glad to come to terms. An alliance was formed and cemented by a marriage between the Indian king (or a member of his family) and a Greek princess. This was the beginning of a long, intimate, and fruitful intercourse between the Greek and Indian courts, which was continued by Chandragupta's son and grandson, Bindusāra and Aśoka. Ambassadors from the Greek monarchs of the West resided at Pātaliputra, the Mauryan capital. The most important of these was Megasthenes, who wrote a detailed account of Chandragupta's empire, much of which has been preserved.[11] Megasthenes was greatly impressed by the resemblance between Greek and Indian philosophy.

> In many points [he says] their teaching agrees with that of the Greeks—for instance, that the world has a beginning and an end in time, that its shape is spherical; that the Deity, who is its Governor and Maker, interpenetrates the whole. . . . About generation and the soul their teaching shews parallels to the Greek doctrines, and on many other matters. Like Plato, too, they interweave fables about the immortality of the soul and the judgements inflicted in the other world, and so on.[12]

The account written by Megasthenes, supplementing as it did the earlier works of Alexander's companions, gave the Greek world a vivid impression of the great and opulent civilization of contemporary India. The intercourse between the Indian and Syrian courts was not confined to the interchange of occasional courtesies. Megasthenes repeatedly visited Pātaliputra. Bindusāra maintained an amusing correspondence with Antiochus I. He asked him to buy and send him samples of Greek wine, raisins, and a Sophist to teach him

[10] G. Cary, *The Medieval Alexander*, Cambridge, 1956.

[11] R. C. Majumdar has edited an English translation of the classical accounts under the title *The Classical Accounts of India*, Calcutta, 1960. Felix Jacoby edited a German edition entitled *Die Fragmente der griechischen Historiker*, Dritter Teil C, Nr. 715, Leiden, 1958.

[12] See the passages quoted in the *Cambridge History of India*, Vol. 1, pp. 419–20.

how to argue. Antiochus wrote in reply saying that he had pleasure in sending the wine and raisins as desired, but regretted that 'it is not good form among the Greeks to trade in Sophists!' Megasthenes was apparently succeeded at Pātaliputra by Daïmachus of Plataea, who went on a series of missions from Antiochus I to Bindusāra. Nor was Syria the only Greek state to depute ambassadors to the Mauryan Court: Pliny tells us of a certain Dionysius who was sent from Alexandria by Ptolemy Philadelphus (285–247 B.C.). When Aśoka became a convert to Buddhism his first thought was for the dispatch of a mission for the conversion of his neighbours, 'the King of the Greeks named Antiochus', and the four other Greek kings, Ptolemy Philadelphus of Egypt, Antigonus Gonatas of Macedonia, Magas of Cyrene, Ptolemy's half-brother, and Alexander of Epirus (or of Corinth). Whether the yellow-robed messengers of the Law of Piety ever actually reached Macedonia or Epirus may be regarded as doubtful, but there is no reason to suppose that they did not get as far as Alexandria and Antioch. Aśoka's object was not merely to promulgate Buddhism, but to establish a 'world peace', and prevent the repetition of tragedies like the Kalinga massacre, which had led to his conversion.[13]

At the same time a flourishing trade was being carried on between Syria and India. Strabo tells us that Indian goods were borne down the Oxus to Europe by way of the Caspian and the Black Sea. No doubt they travelled along the Royal Road from Pātaliputra to Taxila, and by the old route from Taxila to Balkh. This was made easier by the fact that Aśoka's empire stretched far west of Kābul, and the passage of merchandise through this wild country was comparatively safe. The evidence of the coins shows that during the period when history is silent a busy life was throbbing on both sides of the frontier, and Greek and Indian merchants were constantly coming and going, buying and selling.[14]

With the death of Aśoka in 232 B.C. the close connection with Pātaliputra appears to have been broken off, but in the meantime the Greek descendants of Alexander's colonists in Bactria, who had declared themselves independent in 250 B.C., had crossed the Hindū Kush, and established themselves in the Panjāb. The greatest of the Indo-Bactrian rulers was Menander (*c.* 150 B.C.). Menander's capital was at Sāgala (? Sialkot), and he conquered for a time a considerable portion of the Mauryan Empire. The Bactrian Greeks have been called 'the Goanese of antiquity'. By this time they had become thoroughly Indianized, and Menander was converted to the fashionable creed of Buddhism. His conversion is recorded in that famous work, the *Milinda-panha*, or *Questions of Milinda*, a kind of Platonic dialogue in Pāli, in which the sage Nāgasena plays the part of Socrates. This history of the Bactrian Greek rulers of the Panjāb has been reconstructed from their coins. The earlier issues are of great beauty, but they tend to degenerate, and the appearance of bilingual superscriptions tells its own tale. Curiously enough, the Greeks have left no other memorial in India except a column erected at Besnagar in Madhya Pradesh by Heliodorus of Taxila, an ambassador from the Mahārāja

[13] Among recent books on Aśoka cf. P. H. L. Eggermont, *The Chronology of the Reign of Asoka Moriya*, Leiden, 1956; R. Thapar, *Aśoka and the Decline of the Mauryas*, Oxford, 1961.

[14] *Cambridge History of India*, Vol. 1, pp. 432 ff.

Antialcidas to King Bhāgabhadra. This column records the fact that Heliodorus was a devotee of Vishnu, and shows how rapidly the Greeks were adopting the religions of their neighbours.[15] The Bactrian Greeks were succeeded by a number of Śaka and Parthian princes, and it was at the court of one of these that the Apostle Thomas is said to have suffered martyrdom. The *Acts of Judas Thomas*, which exists in Syriac, Greek, and Latin versions, is apparently based on a kernel of historical fact, and some of the proper names, both of persons and of places, have been identified. Gondophernes has been recognized as Gaspar, the first of the Magi.[16]

About A.D. 48 these tribes were replaced by the Yüeh-chih or Kushāna horde from Central Asia. The Kushāna Empire reached its zenith under Kanishka, who seems to have succeeded to the throne about A.D. 120, a date which is still much disputed, however. His capital was at Peshāwar, but his far-flung empire extended as far west as Kābul and as far north as Kashgar. Kanishka was a convert to Buddhism, but his coins, with their curious medley of deities, Zoroastrian, Hindu, Greek, and Buddhist, indicate the cosmopolitan nature of his territories, a veritable *colluvies gentium*, at the meeting-place of the Central Asian trade-routes. Among the deities depicted are Helios, Selene, and Buddha (*ΒΟΔΔΩ*), the latter in Greek dress. Kanishka employed Greek workmen and silversmiths, and the relic-casket discovered at the Shāhjī-kī-Dherī mound near Peshāwar bears a Kharoshthī inscription to the effect that it was the work of 'Agesilas, overseer of Kanishka's *vihāra*'. Excavations at Taxila have revealed a wealth of beautiful *objets d'art* of the Śaka and Kushāna periods, showing how strong was Greek influence there. Some of the friezes are decorated with Corinthian pillars. Under the Kushānas that curious hybrid product, the so-called Gandhāra School of sculpture, flourished. It is a mistake, perhaps, to apply the term 'school' to a number of artists of different nationalities, working in a variety of materials over a long period. Their most striking achievement, however, was the application of Hellenistic methods to the portrayal of scenes in the life of the Buddha, and, more especially, to the delineation of the Master himself. Hitherto, Buddhists had been content to represent him by conventional symbols: it was probably the Indo-Greek artists of Gandhāra who evolved the Buddha figure which is accepted as canonical all over the Buddhist world today.[17] A cosmopolitan culture, borrowed from Iranian, Hellenistic, Indian, and Chinese sources, sprang up along the Central Asian trade-route, with its centre in what is now the desert between the Tarim and Khotan rivers.

Meanwhile, the *pax Romana* was promoting the growth of a cosmopolitan culture in the Near and Middle East, where the old racial and linguistic prejudices were fast melting away. 'Videtis gentes populosque mutasse sedes', says Seneca. 'Quid sibi volunt in mediis barbarorum regionibus Graecae artes? Quid inter Indos Persasque Macedonicus sermo? . . . Atheniensis in

[15] Rapson, *Ancient India*, pp. 134, 156.

[16] A full bibliography of the Thomas and Gondophernes legend is given in the *Cambridge History of India*, Vol. 1, p. 687. See also V. A. Smith, *Early History of India*, 4th edn., p. 260, and J. F. Farquhar in *Bulletin of the John Rylands Library*, 1926–7.

[17] This is disputed. A. K. Coomaraswamy contended that the Buddha figure originated at Mathurā, quite independently of Gandhāra.

Asia turba est.'[18] In Antioch, Palmyra, and Alexandria, Indian and Greek merchants and men of letters met freely to exchange ideas. Antioch, the old Seleucid capital, was the great meeting-place of caravans (συνοδίαι) from the Gulf of Suez on the one hand and from the headwaters of the Euphrates on the other, and its bazaars and market-places were thronged with a cosmopolitan crowd, second only to that of Alexandria. Travellers from Barygaza (Broach),[19] at the mouth of the Narmadā, would probably follow the overland route up the Euphrates and then cross the desert to Antioch, while those from south India and Ceylon would preferably go via Aden and the Red Sea. Palmyra, Solomon's Tadmor in the Wilderness, on the oasis which lies midway on the desert route between the great Red Sea port of Berenice and Thapsacus on the Euphrates, enjoyed a short but brilliant period of prosperity between the time when it ousted its rival, Petra, and its destruction by the Romans (A.D. 130–273).

The Kushānas were particularly anxious to be on good terms with Rome, whose eastern boundary was the Euphrates, less than 600 miles from their western border. The closeness of their intercourse is illustrated in a striking manner by the Kushāna coinage, which imitates that of contemporary Roman emperors. The Kushāna gold coins are of the same weight and fineness as the Roman *aurei*. It appears probable from an inscription that the Kushāna King Kanishka II used the title of Caesar.

The friendly and intimate nature of the relations between Rome and India is shown by the number of embassies dispatched by various Indian *rājās* from time to time. One of these, from an Indian king whom Strabo calls Pandion (probably one of the Pāndya kings of the south), left Barygaza in 25 B.C. and encountered Augustus at Samos four years later. The time occupied by the journey seems less strange when we study the Elizabethan travellers' itineraries: people had to wait for prolonged periods at stopping-places until caravans were formed and escorts arranged for. The ambassadors brought Augustus a variety of queer presents, including tigers, a python, and an armless boy who discharged arrows from a bow with his toes. The leader of the embassy was a monk named Zarmanochegas (*Śramanāchārya*), who brought a letter, written on vellum in Greek, offering the Emperor an alliance and a free passage for Roman subjects through his dominions. Like Kalanos, the monk who accompanied Alexander the Great to Babylon, Zarmanochegas committed suicide by burning himself to death on a funeral pyre. From this it is perhaps permissible to conclude that he was a Jain, as Jainism looks upon voluntary immolation as a laudable act. According to Strabo, his epitaph was 'Here lies Zarmanochegas, an Indian from Bargosa, who rendered himself immortal according to the customs of the country.'[20] Another Indian embassy, probably from the Kushāna king Kadphises II, went to Rome in A.D. 99 to congratulate Trajan on his accession. Trajan treated his Indian visitors with distinction, giving them senators' seats at the theatre. From the time of Mark

[18] *De Cons. ad Helv.* c. vi. 'Whole tribes and peoples have changed their habitats. Why do they want Greek arts in the midst of barbarian regions? Why is the Macedonian tongue spoken among Indians and Persians? . . . There is a crowd of Athenians in Asia.' The Loeb edition of Seneca gives *urbes* (cities), in place of *artes* (arts) in the text used by Professor Rawlinson. [Ed.]

[19] Sanskrit, Bhrigukaccha.

[20] Strabo, *Geography*, xv. 73.

Antony to that of Justinian, i.e. from 30 B.C. to A.D. 550, their political importance as allies against the Parthians and Sāsānians, and their commercial importance as controllers of one of the main trade-routes between the East and the West, made the friendship of the Kushānas and other dynasties who held the Indus valley and Gandhāra of the highest value to Rome.

Meanwhile, a brisk trade was springing up between the great mart at Alexandria and the coast of Malabar. The products of southern India had, as we have seen, been in demand in the Mediterranean from time immemorial, and Alexandria had replaced the old Phoenician ports of Tyre and Sidon as the clearing-house for Oriental goods. Owing to the discovery about A.D. 50 of the existence of the monsoon winds, it was now possible for vessels to run directly across the Indian Ocean, from Aden to the great Malabar port of Muziris (Cranganore), instead of hugging the coast. This so shortened the distance that the journey from Italy to India could be accomplished in sixteen weeks.[21] The importance of this fact will be realized when we recollect that, up to the opening of the overland route in 1838, it took travellers from five to eight months to reach India. India was nearer to Europe in the first century A.D. than at any time up to the middle of the nineteenth.

An interesting little book, called *The Periplus of the Erythraean Sea*, written by an Alexandrian sea-captain about the time of Nero, gives an account of a voyage down the Red Sea and round the Indian coast from the mouth of the Indus to that of the Ganges. Pliny, who complains of the 'drain' of Eastern luxuries upon Rome, which he estimates at over a million pounds sterling,[21a] deplores the fact that the two countries had been 'brought nearer by lust for gain'; and, from the enormous number of Roman coins found in southern India and references in Tamil writers, it is highly probable that there were actually Roman colonies at Cranganore or Muziris (where there is said to have been a Roman temple), Madurai, Pugar at the mouth of the Kāviri, and other places. A small seaport containing numerous sherds of Arretine pottery and other evidence of contact with the Roman West has been discovered at Arikamedu south of Pondicherry on the Indian east coast.[22] A Tamil poet sings of 'the thriving town of Muśiri, where the beautiful large ships of the Yavanas, bringing gold, come splashing the waters of the Periyār, and return laden with pepper'. These colonies doubtless resembled the European factories at Surat and other places along the Indian coast in the seventeenth and eighteenth centuries. The colonists were probably natives of Syria and Egypt. It also appears that Roman mercenaries, 'dumb *mlecchas*' or barbarians, were employed by some of the Tamil kings. The *Periplus* mentions the import of

[21] Pliny (*Natural History*, vi. 22) tells us of a revenue-ship of Annius Plocamus, in the reign of Claudius, which was caught in the monsoon and covered the distance between Aden and Ceylon in fifteen days. The usual time was about forty days.

[21a] The author was writing in the 1930s. The source (*Nat. Hist.* xii, 41) reads: 'By the lowest reckoning India, China, and the [Arabian] Peninsula take from our empire 100 million sesterces every year—this is the sum which our luxuries and our women cost us.' It is not clear how much of this sum Pliny believed was absorbed by India. The sestertius was a large bronze coin. [Ed.]

[22] Sir Mortimer Wheeler, 'Roman Contact with India, Pakistan and Afghanistan in Aspects of Archaeology: *Essays Presented to R. G. S. Crawford*, ed. W. F. Grimes, London, 1951.

Greek girls for the Indian harems, and Chandragupta's guard of Amazons may well have been Greeks. It was not unusual for Indian sovereigns to employ a foreign bodyguard as a protection from assassination.

Alexandria, in the first century A.D., was the second city in the Empire. In the height of her glory she must have resembled Venice in the full tide of her prosperity. The mercantile shipping of half of the ancient world tied up at her quay-sides, and scholars from the four quarters of the earth met and disputed in the Museum, and made use of the vast stores of literature in her great libraries. The Alexandrians were essentially cosmopolitan. They had none of the contempt for the 'barbarian' of the old Greek city-states, and a large proportion of the population, like the Athenians, 'spent their life in nothing else, but either to tell or hear some new thing'. A Buddhist monk from Barygaza would receive the same attentive hearing as did Saint Paul at the hands of the Areopagus, and the medium was Hellenistic Greek, the lingua franca (κοινή) from the Levant to the Indus. The *Milinda-panha* mentions Alexandria as one of the places to which Indian merchants regularly resorted, and Dio Chrysostom, lecturing to an Alexandrian audience in the reign of Trajan, says: 'I see among you, not only Greeks and Italians, Syrians, Libyans, and Cilicians, and men who dwell more remotely, Ethiopians and Arabs, but also Bactrians, Scythians, Persians, and some of the Indians, who are among the spectators, and are always residing there.'[23]

These Indian residents must have come to Alexandria from one of the numerous seaports on the western coast, probably Barygaza or Muziris. Barygaza was the chief port of call for vessels from the Persian Gulf. A road ran from Barygaza to Ujjain, a place where several routes converged, and from Ujjain through Vidiśā, Bhārhut, Kauśāmbī, and Prayāga to Pātaliputra. Pātaliputra was linked up with Champā, the port on the Gangā for trading-vessels going to Ceylon, the Golden Chersonese, and the Far East. The traders who settled at Alexandria were probably mostly Jains or Buddhists, as caste-rules discouraged, and later forbade, orthodox Hindus from crossing the black water. The *Jātakas* are full of references to Buddhist merchants and their adventures on voyages to distant countries. For this reason Alexandrian writers are generally better acquainted with the Buddhists than with any other Indian sect.

Indian philosophy was acquiring a growing reputation in the Hellenistic schools of Asia Minor and Egypt. That famous miracle-monger, Apollonius of Tyana (*c.* A.D. 50), went to Taxila to study under brāhman preceptors. Bardesanes the Babylonian, the well-known Gnostic teacher, learnt many curious facts about India from an Indian embassy which came to Syria in the reign of Elagabalus (A.D. 218–22). The lost work of Bardesanes is freely quoted by later writers, and was evidently held in great esteem. Bardesanes knew a great deal about the brāhmans and Buddhists and their discipline and mode of life. He describes, in accurate detail, life in a Buddhist monastery, and a visit to a cave-temple in western India, containing an androgynous image of the god Śiva.[24] Plotinus, the founder of the Neoplatonic School, was so anxious to be instructed in Indian philosophy that he accompanied the

[23] *Oratio* xxii. McCrindle, *Ancient India*, p. 177.

[24] Stobaeus, *Physica*, i. 56. McCrindle, op. cit., pp. 172–3.

expedition of Gordian against Sapor (Shāhpuhr, Shāpur), king of Persia, in A.D. 242, in the hope that this might bring him into personal contact with some one who could help him. The resemblances between Neoplatonism and the Vedānta and Yoga systems are very close. The absorption of the individual into the World Soul is described by Plotinus in words which have a typically Indian ring: 'Souls which are pure and have lost their attraction to the corporal will cease to be dependent on the body. So detached they will pass into the world of Being and Reality.' Neoplatonism also has many points of contact with Buddhism, especially in enjoining the abstention from sacrifices and animal food.

Buddhism was well known to Clement of Alexandria (A.D. 150–218). He repeatedly refers to the presence of Buddhists in Alexandria, and declares that 'the Greeks stole their philosophy from the barbarians'. He is the first Greek writer to mention Buddha by name. 'There are', he says, 'some Indians who follow the precepts of Boutta, whom by an excessive reverence they have exalted into a god.'[25] He knows that Buddhists believe in transmigration (παλιγγενεσία) and 'worship a kind of pyramid (*stūpa*) beneath which they think the bones of some divinity lie buried'. Perhaps these facts throw some light on the curious resemblances between the Gospel story and the life of Buddha as told in late Buddhist works like the *Lalita Vistara*. Some of these are the Buddha's miraculous conception and birth; the star over his birthplace; the prophecy of the aged Asita, the Buddhist Simeon; the temptation by Māra; the twelve disciples with the 'beloved disciple', Ānanda; and the miracles, coupled with the Buddha's disapproval of these as proofs of his Buddhahood.

More startling still are the points of similarity between the Buddhist and Christian parables and miracles. Thus in *Jātaka* 190 we read of the pious disciple who walks on the water while he is full of faith in the Buddha, but begins to sink when his ecstasy subsides. On his arrival the Master inquires how he has fared. 'Oh, Sir,' he replies, 'I was so absorbed in thoughts of the Buddha, that I walked over the water of the river as though it had been dry ground!' As Max Müller remarks,[26] mere walking upon the water is not an uncommon story; but walking by faith, and sinking for want of it, can only be accounted for by some historical contact and transference, and the *Jātakas* are centuries older than the Gospels. In *Jātaka* 78 the Buddha feeds his 500 brethren with a single cake which has been put into his begging-bowl, and there is so much over that what is left has to be thrown away. In a late Buddhist work, the *Saddharma Pundarīka*, there is a parable which bears a close resemblance to that of the Prodigal Son.

During this period,

> nascent Christianity met full-grown Buddhism in the Academies and markets of Asia and Egypt, while both religions were exposed to the influences of surrounding Paganism in many forms, and of the countless works of art which gave expression to

[25] *Stromata*, i. 15. McCrindle quotes other passages from other Alexandrian divines referring to Buddha, which show that Alexandrians must have been well acquainted with him and his teaching by the third century A.D. (*Ancient India*, pp. 184 ff.). They were greatly impressed with the story of the Immaculate Conception of Queen Māyā.

[26] 'Coincidences', in *Last Essays*, 1st Ser. (1901), p. 250. Gifford Lectures (1890), ii. 390.

the forms of polytheism. The ancient religion of Persia contributed to the ferment of human thought, excited by improved facilities for international communication, and by the incessant clash of rival civilizations.[27]

It is possible that the rosary, the veneration of relics, and the exaggerated forms of asceticism which were such a striking feature of Alexandrian Christianity, may be traced to Indian sources. When the French missionary travellers, Huc and Gabet, visited Lhasa in 1842, they were deeply shocked at the close resemblance between Catholic and Lamaistic ritual.

The crozier, the mitre, and chasuble, the cardinal's robe, . . . the double choir at the Divine Office, the chants, the exorcism, the censer with five chains, the blessing which the Lamas impart by extending the right hand over the heads of the faithful, the rosary, the celibacy of the clergy, their separation from the world, the worship of saints, the fasts, processions, litanies, holy water—these are the points of contact which the Buddhists have with us.

Max Müller traces these to the contact between Tibetan and Nestorian monks in China between A.D. 635 and 841, when both were suppressed. At the famous monastery of Hsian-Fu they actually collaborated.

Gnosticism was a deliberate effort to fuse Christian, Platonic, and Oriental ideas at a time when syncretism was particularly fashionable at Alexandria. Gnosticism has been described as 'Orientalism in a Hellenic mask'. The great Gnostic teacher Basilides, a Hellenized Egyptian who was a contemporary of Hadrian (A.D. 117–38), definitely borrowed his philosophy from the wisdom of the East, which he interwove in an ingenious fashion into the framework of Christianity. Like Buddha, he was a pessimist. 'Pain and fear are inherent in human affairs.' He had a remarkable explanation of the reason why God permitted His saints to suffer martyrdom, which is evidently based on the Buddhist doctrine of *karma*. 'The theory of Basilides', says Clement, 'is that the soul has previously sinned in another life (πρὸ τῆσδε τῆς ἐνσωματώσεως), and endures its punishment here, the elect with the honour of martyrdom, and the rest purified by appropriate punishment.' Basilides was a firm believer in transmigration, and cited texts such as John 9:2 and Romans 7:9 in support. Basilides' theory of personality has strong Buddhist affinities. The soul is without qualities, but the passions, like the Buddhist *skandhas*, attach themselves to it as appendages or 'parasites' (προσαρτήματα). God is unpredicable, almost non-existent (οὐκ ὢν θεός), and the divine entity of Jesus at death alone passed into Nirvāna (ὑπερκοσμία).[28]

After many vicissitudes Alexandria as a centre of learning came to an end in A.D. 642. But the Arabs were far from being mere vandals, and schools arose in Baghdād, Cairo, and Cordova, which rivalled the glories of the civilization which they superseded. Baghdād, founded in A.D. 762, occupied a commanding position on the overland route between India and Europe. It was frequented by Greek and Hindu merchants. The 'Abbāsids, like the Sāsānians, were great patrons of literature, and had foreign works translated into Arabic. Baghdād remained the great clearing-house for Eastern and Western culture until its destruction by the Mongols in A.D. 1258. During the Dark Ages it

[27] V. A. Smith, *Oxford History of India*, p. 134.
[28] 'Buddhist Gnosticism', by J. Kennedy, *J.R.A.S.*, 1902.

was the Arabs who kept the torch of learning alight, when Rome had perished and Europe was still plunged in barbarism. The Arabs had little indigenous culture, and much of their learning was borrowed from Hindu or Greek sources. The widespread diffusion of the Arabic language, however, made it an excellent medium for the transmission of ideas from Asia to Europe. Arabic travellers and scholars like Albīrūnī were strongly attracted by Hindu civilization, and transmitted it to the West. Albīrūnī is particularly important in this respect. Born in A.D. 973, he accompanied Sultan Mahmūd of Ghaznī to India, learnt Sanskrit, and read the Hindu classics, the *Purānas*, and the *Bhagavad Gītā*. He was acquainted, we are told, with 'astronomy, mathematics, chronology, mathematical geography, physics, chemistry, and mineralogy'.

One curious result was that many ideas, which were originally borrowed by India from the West, found their way back to Europe in an Arabic guise. Three typical examples are provided by Arabian astronomy, mathematics, and medicine.[29] Hindu astronomers freely acknowledge their indebtedness to Alexandria. One of the principal Sanskrit astronomical treatises was the *Romaka Siddhānta* or Roman manual. Another, the *Pauliśa Siddhānta*, was based on the works of Paul of Alexandria (A.D. 378). The Sanskrit names for the signs of the Zodiac, and other astronomical terms, are of Greek origin. These Sanskrit treatises were later translated into Arabic, and from Arabic into Latin. Much the same happened in the case of Hindu mathematics, though the question is too technical to be discussed here. The medical works of Charaka and Suśruta may have been somewhat influenced by Hippocrates and Galen, and if, as is usually stated, Charaka was court physician to Kanishka, this is easily explicable. They had a marked influence on Arabic medical writers like Avicenna, whose works, in Latin translations, were the standard authorities in medieval Europe. The game of chess found its way from India to Europe through the Arabs, perhaps at the time of the Crusaders. It is first mentioned by the Sanskrit novelist Bāna, about A.D. 625: its Sanskrit name is *chaturanga*, the 'four arms' of the Hindu army. In Persian this becomes *shatranj*. Many of its terms, such as 'checkmate' (*shāh māt*, the king is dead), and 'rook' (*rukh*) are of Persian origin.

The East is the home of fables, and some of the oldest folk-stories, which are woven into the very web of European literature, may be traced to those great Indian collections of tales, the Buddhist *Jātakas* or Birth-stories, the *Panchatantra*, and the *Hitopadeśa* or Book of Useful Counsels.[30] Some of these tales reached the West at a very early date. The story of the Judgement of Solomon is an excellent example. In the Buddhist version the two women are ordered to try to pull the child away from one another by main force. The child cries out, and one of the women at once lets go, whereupon the wise judge awards him to her, as the true mother.[31] It is impossible not to wonder whether this story may not have reached Judaea along with the ivory, apes, and peacocks from Ophir. Many of these folk-stories are tales of talking beasts, and appear

[29] See Macdonell, *India's Past*, pp. 175–93.

[30] See Max Müller, 'On the Migration of Fables', in *Chips from a German Workshop*, iv. 412. *Selected Essays*, i. 500.

[31] Rhys Davids, *Buddhist Birth Stories*, i, xiii, xliv.

on Buddhist sculpture at Bhārhut and Sānchī, and later in Gandhāra. They began to find their way to Asia Minor as far back as the sixth century B.C., and the earliest Greek version was attributed to Aesop, who was said to have lived at the Court of Croesus of Lydia. Some of them, as we have seen, appear in Herodotus. There is a reference to the fable of the ass in the lion's skin in Plato's *Cratylus* (411 A). A collection of 'Aesop's' fables was made in Latin by Phaedrus in the time of Tiberius, and by Babrius in Greek at Alexandria about A.D. 200.

One of the most famous of all the old Indian story-books is the 'Seventy Tales of a Parrot' (*Śukasaptati*). This was several times translated into Persian under the name of *Tūtīnāmeh*, and through it many Indian stories found their way into Europe, the best-known, perhaps, being the tale of the fraudulent ordeal, made famous in Gottfried von Strassburg's *Tristan and Isolde*.[32] Another source through which many Indian *motifs* reached medieval Europe was the *Arabian Nights*. Mas'ūdī, the 'Arabian Herodotus', writing at Basra about A.D. 950, says that this great collection contains Persian, Greek, and Hindu tales, and it was no doubt put together in the first instance at Baghdād, perhaps shortly after the reign of Hārūn al-Rashīd, to whom so many of the tales allude. The best-known of the stories, that of Sindbad the Sailor, is of Hindu origin, and contains may Indian references.[33] One of the best-known of the stories which found its way from the *Arabian Nights* to Europe is that of the Ebony Horse, which appears in Chaucer's *Squire's Tale*.[34] Another collection of Indian fables, the *Panchatantra*, was made and rendered into Pehlevī in the sixth century A.D., by order of the Sāsānian King Anushīrvān, and from Pehlevī into Arabic by the Caliph al-Mansūr (A.D. 753–84). Their Arabic and Syriac title, *Kalīlah wa Dimnah*, is apparently derived from the two jackals, Karataka and Damanaka, who play a leading part in them. These stories were translated into Persian, Syriac, Latin, Hebrew, and Spanish. A German version, made in 1481, was one of the earliest printed books. In the next century they were turned into Italian, and from Italian into English by Sir Thomas North, the translator of Plutarch, and in this guise were probably known to Shakespeare. In Europe they were known as the Fables of Pilpay, Pilpay being probably a corruption of Bidyāpat or Vidyāpati, 'Master of Wisdom', a wise brāhman who plays a leading part in them. La Fontaine made use of the fables of the 'Indian sage Pilpay'.

That the migration of fables was originally from East to West, and not vice versa, is shown by the fact that the animals and birds who play the leading parts, the lion, the jackal, the elephant, and the peacock, are mostly Indian ones. In the European versions the jackal becomes the fox: the relation between the lion and the jackal is a natural one, whereas that between the lion and fox is not. This change in the species of the animals in the course of the wandering of the fables is very instructive. Take, for instance, the well-known

[32] Macdonell, *India's Past*, p. 128.

[33] Ibid., p. 129. Macdonell is confident that the *Arabian Nights* was originally composed by a Persian poet imitating Indian originals. The framework, as well as a large number of the stories, is of Indian origin.

[34] Burton says that the story of the Ebony Horse originated in a Hindu story of a wooden *Garuda*. It came from India via Persia, Egypt, and Spain to France (*Le Cheval de Fust*) and thence to Chaucer's ears.

Welsh story of Llewellyn and Gelert. The father comes home and is greeted by his hound, which he had left to guard his infant daughter. Its jaws are covered with blood and, thinking it has killed the child, he slays it. Then he finds the child asleep in her cradle, safe and sound, a dead wolf by her side. In the original tale in the *Panchatantra*, a mongoose and a cobra play the part of the dog and wolf. Again, in La Fontaine's fable, a girl carrying a pail of milk (in some versions, a basket of eggs) on her head, builds 'castles in the air' about what she is going to do with the proceeds of selling it. She becomes so absorbed that she drops her burden. In the original, a brāhman whose begging-bowl has been filled with boiled rice dreams of the profits he will make when a famine breaks out and he sells it. In his sleep he kicks the bowl over and the contents are spilt. The 'beast-story' has been revived in a delightful manner in Rudyard Kipling's *Jungle Books*.

Numerous European fairy-stories, to be found in Grimm or Hans Andersen, about the magic mirror, the seven-leagued boots, Jack and the beanstalk, and the purse of Fortunatus, have been traced to Indian sources. Many of them are found in the *Gesta Romanorum*, the *Decameron*, and Chaucer's *Canterbury Tales*. The *Pardoner's Tale* is derived ultimately from a story in the *Vedabbha Jātaka*. One of the most interesting examples of the migration of a tale is provided by the famous story of Barlaam and Josaphat.[35] This is the edifying history of the young Christian prince Josaphat, who is so moved by various distressing sights which he encounters, that he renounces the world and becomes an ascetic. It was written in Greek by John of Damascus in the eighth century A.D. From Greek it was translated into Arabic at the Court of the Caliph al-Mansūr, and from Arabic into a number of European languages. In the Middle Ages it was immensely popular, and in the sixteenth century Josaphat actually became a Christian saint! This is extremely interesting, as it is now evident that Josaphat is the Bodhisat or Bodhisattva, and the story is nothing more or less than that of the Great Renunciation of Gautama Buddha, as narrated in the *Lalita Vistara*. It is adorned with numerous apologues. One of them is the story of the Three Caskets, which was utilized by Shakespeare in the *Merchant of Venice*. Another story in the *Merchant of Venice*, that of the Pound of Flesh, is also of Buddhist origin, though it does not appear to be clear by what channel it came to Shakespeare's knowledge.

The classical accounts remained the main source on India, and it is through them that references to India came into medieval epics like the *Divina Commedia* and *Parzival*. In the latter, India is called 'Tribalibot', which is a play on the Latin word *Palibothri* (the inhabitants of Pātaliputra).[36] New contacts with the Orient were established through the Crusades and Arabic rule in Spain, but they only led to fantastic exaggerations such as can be seen in romances like *Herzog Ernst*. India lies at the end of the world, and to have been to India becomes, *pars pro toto*, to have seen the whole world. Thomas

[35] The text and translation are in the Loeb Classics. See Max Müller, *Selected Essays*, i. 500; F. Jacobs, *Barlaam and Josaphat* (1896); E. Kuhn, *Barlaam und Josaphat*, Abhandlungen der Bayerischen Akademie der Wissenschaften, Munich, 1894. An extensive bibliography on this subject is given by H. Peri (Pflaum) in *Acta Salamanticensia*, Vol. 14, No. 3, Salamanca, 1959.

[36] F. Wilhelm, 'Die Entdeckung der indischen Geschichte', *Saeculum*, xv/1, Freiburg, 1964, p. 30 ff.

More obviously made use of Indian motifs in his *Utopia*.[37] There are striking coincidences in medieval thought between Śankara's Vedānta and the mysticism of Meister Eckart; and parallels in the field of fine arts: Indian *mandalas* and the symbolism of the knot have their Western counterparts.[38] However, as long as we have no conclusive proof of Indian influence we should always keep in mind that such convergences can be the result of similar spiritual attitudes.

[37] J. Duncan M. Derrett, 'Thomas More and Joseph the Indian', *Journal of the Royal Asiatic Society*, Apr. 1962, pp. 18 ff.

[38] A. K. Coomaraswamy, 'Iconography of Dürer's Knots and Leonardo's Concatenation', *Art Quarterly*, Detroit, 1944.

CHAPTER XXXI

Indian Influence in Ancient South-East Asia*

by ALASTAIR LAMB

BY the opening of the Christian era the civilization of India had begun to spread across the Bay of Bengal into both island and mainland South-East Asia; and by the fifth century A.D. Indianized states, that is to say states organized along the traditional lines of Indian political theory and following the Buddhist or Hindu religions, had established themselves in many regions of Burma, Thailand, Indo-China, Malaysia, and Indonesia. Some of these states were in time to grow into great empires dominating the zone between metropolitan India and the Chinese southern border, which has sometimes been described as 'Further India' or 'Greater India'. Once rooted in South-East Asian soil, Indian civilization evolved in part through the action of forces of South-East Asian origin, and in part through the influence of cultural and political changes in the Indian subcontinent. Many scholars have described the eastward spread of Indian civilization in terms of a series of 'waves'; and there are good reasons for considering that such 'waves' are still breaking on South-East Asian beaches today.

The cultures of modern South-East Asia all provide evidence of a long period of contact with India. Many South-East Asian languages (Malay and Javanese are good examples) contain an important proportion of words of Sanskrit or Dravidian origin. Some of these languages, like Thai, are still written in scripts which are clearly derived from Indian models. South-East Asian concepts of kingship and authority, even in regions which are now dominated by Islam, owe much to ancient Hindu political theory. The Thai monarchy, though following Hīnayāna Buddhism of the Sinhalese type, still requires the presence of Court brāhmans (who by now have become Thai in all but name) for the proper performance of its ceremonials. The traditional dance and shadow-puppet theatres in many South-East Asian regions, in Thailand, Malaya, and Java for example, continue to fascinate their audiences with the adventures of Rāma and Sītā and Hanumān. In Bali an elaborate indigenous Hindu culture still flourishes, and preserves intact many Indian ideas and practices which have long passed out of use in the subcontinent; and here we have a fossil record, as it were, which can be exploited to throw much light on the early cultural history of India itself. The fact of Indian impact on South-East Asian civilization, past and present, is, indeed, in no doubt. Much

* As South-East Asian archaeology is one of the most rapidly developing fields of study at present, and as Professor Lamb has not for the last few years been directly involved in that field, Professor Lamb has agreed that Dr. H. H. E. Loofs should add a brief appendix to his contribution to cover the latest evidence of Indian contacts with the region. [Ed.]

controversy, however, has arisen over the precise way in which this impact took place.

There has long been a temptation for Indian scholars, and those brought up in an environment of Indian studies, to see in early Indianized South-East Asia an exact reflection of the various periods and schools of the civilization of metropolitan India. Much scholarly writing, for example, has been devoted to attempts to determine the precise Indian prototypes for such great South-East Asian monuments as the Borobodur *stūpa* in Java and the Khmer temples of Cambodia. These structures are obviously in the Indian tradition. Their ground-plans, for example, and the subject-matter of their sculptural decoration, can easily be related to Indian religious texts. Yet a careful study of monuments such as these suggests that the Indian aspect is only one part of the story. While beyond doubt showing signs of Indian influence, yet Borobodur and Angkor Wat are not *copies* of Indian structures. There exists nothing quite like them in the Indian archaeological record. The vast majority of the Hindu and Buddhist monuments of South-East Asia which were constructed in the pre-European period, that is to say before the opening of the sixteenth century, possess, as it were, a definite South-East Asian flavour. It is reasonable to consider the styles of art and architecture of the Khmers, Chams, and Javanese as styles in their own right and something much more than the imitation of Indian prototypes. These styles, as Coedès and other scholars have expressed it, are *Indianized* rather than *Indian*. The Indian inheritance in South-East Asia is not to be found in the unthinking repetition of Indian forms; rather, it is to be seen in the inspiration which India gave to South-East Asia to adapt its own cultures so as to absorb and develop Indian concepts. The resulting syntheses are peculiar to South-East Asia.

The concept of Indianization, which is one of the keys to the understanding of South-East Asian cultural history, raises a number of questions which are not at present easy to answer. Why, and when, did India begin to extend her influence eastwards? What kind of people did the early missionaries of Indian civilization meet across the Bay of Bengal? Were they naked savages following a food-gathering economy in the jungles, or were they settled populations with ways of life which might be described as civilizations of their own? How exactly did the forms of Indian civilization enter into the fabric of South-East Asian cultural life? Inevitably, suggested solutions to these problems of the first phases of Indianization must be rather tentative and expressed in general terms. Neither the indigenous South-East Asian texts and inscriptions, nor the narratives of foreign visitors to the region, take us back with any degree of certainty beyond the third century of the Christian era. The record of South-East Asian protohistoric archaeology is as yet far from fully elucidated. The term South-East Asia, moreover, covers a very extensive area within which there exists a considerable range of environments and ethnic types, and throughout which there cannot possibly have been a uniform operation of any one of the several likely processes of Indianization. Some populations, like the Khmers, the Chams, and the Javanese, became heavily Indianized. Others, like some of the tribes in Sulawesi (the Celebes), were indeed subject to Indian influence, but lightly and, most probably, indirectly. Yet others, like the Negritos of the Malay Peninsula, cannot be said to have been Indianized at all.

The evidence at present available, which is far less abundant than might be desired, suggests that there must have been a measure of contact between India and South-East Asia for several centuries before the opening of the Christian era. While it is extremely unlikely that there was at this early period any extensive migration eastwards of Indian populations—the theory of the Indian origin of the Malays, for example, is no longer taken very seriously, and most authorities are inclined to agree with Heine-Geldern in seeing a Chinese origin for the prehistoric migrations into South-East Asia which have left an archaeological or anthropological trace capable of detection—yet sufficient Indian trade across the Bay of Bengal there must have been to explain the presence in early Indian epics like the *Rāmāyana* of references to such South-East Asian regions as *Suvarnadvīpa* (the Golden Island or Peninsula, usually identified with Sumatra or the Malay Peninsula). Significant cultural influence, however, can hardly have begun before the Aśokan period; and we have no real archaeological or literary evidence for it until well on into the Christian era. It seems most probable, on the present available information, that Indianization started in earnest in the period from the first century B.C. to the first century A.D. There can be no doubt, at all events, that by the fifth century A.D. Indian culture was widely known in South-East Asia, and that Indianized states had appeared not only in regions with relatively large populations practising a settled agriculture, like Cambodia, Vietnam, and Java, but also in remote and sparsely peopled districts like Kalimantan (Indonesian Borneo) and Sulawesi (Celebes).

If this chronology is correct, then it is unlikely that, as has sometimes been suggested, the initial impetus to Indianization in South-East Asia was provided by the migration overseas of the people of Kalinga following Aśoka's devastating invasion in about 261 B.C. There is certainly no archaeological record of an extensive Indian population movement into South-East Asia at this period, or, indeed, at any period until fairly recently. Indian colonization of South-East Asia, on the pattern of European colonization of North America or Australia and New Zealand, is no longer regarded by the majority of scholars as a major factor in the initiation of the Indianization process, which now tends to be interpreted in the light of an expansion of international maritime trade.

The links by land trade-routes between the major centres of population on the Eurasian continent date back to at least the days of the Persian Empire of the Achaemenians. No doubt by the time of Alexander the Great there also existed a measure of maritime trade in the Indian Ocean, following coastal routes, particularly between the Persian Gulf and the Indus. In the first century B.C. the major Eurasian land routes were supplemented to an important degree by sea lanes across the Indian Ocean which exploited the convenient seasonal alternations in direction of the monsoon winds. The discovery of the monsoons was unlikely to have been, as the story has it, the feat of a single Greek sea captain, Hippalus by name. It was rather the employment on a wider scale of a phenomenon, no doubt well known to the inhabitants of many an Indian Ocean coast, under the powerful stimulus of economic and political factors, of which the creation of the great consumer market of the Roman world was probably the most important. The demand in the Mediterranean for Chinese silks and for the spices and medicinal plants of the Indies, combined with the rapacity of the powers straddling the main land routes, certainly stimulated the quest for new and unobstructed channels of trade. Just before the opening of the Christian era the sea routes to the east, with termini in the Red Sea and the Persian Gulf, had become important to the commerce of the Roman world, as is made clear in the writings of such authorities as the Elder Pliny and Strabo. By the second century A.D. these routes had brought Mediterranean (if not Roman) merchants to the shores of India and Ceylon, to parts of mainland South-East Asia, and to China. In the process, South-East Asia was joined to India by bonds which have never since been entirely severed.

Whether Mediterranean and Middle Eastern trade brought Indians into South-East Asia, or the West was exploiting routes which India had already pioneered, is an issue which it is now impossible to resolve. Archaeology in mainland South-East Asia has revealed objects of Western origin (Mediterranean and Iranian) which appear to antedate the first undoubted Indianized artifacts. The bronze lamp of Mediterranean provenance from P'ong Tük in central Thailand and the Roman medal dated A.D. 152 from Oc-Eo in South Vietnam near the Mekong Delta are examples of a trade which helps explain how South-East Asia may have entered into the 'known world' and have found its place in the *Geography* of Claudius Ptolemy, writing in the second century A.D. Oc-Eo, it is probable, was an entrepôt of considerable importance in the East–West trade in the first centuries of the Christian era; and research at this site has yielded a wealth of small finds, such as glass and metal beads and intaglio seals, of Mediterranean and Iranian (Parthian and Sāsānian) origin which invite reference to the site of the ancient trading port at Arikamedu near Pondicherry on the south-east coast of India, which was certainly an entrepôt used by Mediterranean merchants at this period. There is archaeological evidence from both India and South-East Asia to suggest that it was the stimulus of demand in the West which set Indians sailing in significant numbers across the Bay of Bengal; but positive proof is lacking. It is certain, however, that once the economic importance of the routes from India eastwards through South-East Asia was established, they were extensively exploited by Indians who, unlike the Westerners of this time, left a lasting impression upon the South-East Asian cultural landscape.

We possess very little direct evidence as to the manner in which the Indians, once they began to trade and travel widely in South-East Asia, actually proceeded to Indianize the indigenous peoples with whom they came into contact. It is clear, however, that more than one mechanism must have operated and that there can have been no question of a single pattern of events holding good for the whole region. In some places it is reasonable to suppose that there grew up actual settlements of Indian merchants, just as European merchants later established themselves in the modern entrepôt cities like Penang and Singapore. We have no positive evidence for such early Indian mercantile colonies; but we know from inscriptions that settlements of this type existed at Baros in western Sumatra and Takuapa on the Isthmus of Kra by the tenth or eleventh centuries A.D. Such communities would no doubt provide an example for the techniques of urban life along Indian lines and the practical advantages of the major Indian religions, which could be copied by neighbouring indigenous populations.

Another mechanism can perhaps be detected in the deliberate borrowing by indigenous South-East Asian rulers of the techniques of Indian political organization, of which they learned either from merchants visiting their territories or from themselves visiting the early entrepôts. More recently we have examples of this kind of mechanism at work in Asia in the efforts towards self-Westernization made by Japan and Thailand in the latter part of the nineteenth century. Here there was no blind swallowing in its entirety of an alien culture: rather, specific aspects of Western civilization, mainly technical and political, were married into the indigenous way of life. The finer points of art, philosophy, and literature tended to be ignored. Since ancient Indian political life was so inextricably bound up with the religious cosmology, one would expect that self-Indianization, as it were, would result in the establishment, at an official level, of an Indian-type religion in the charge of a brāhmanical priestly caste, whose role would be comparable to that filled today by Western advisers in an under-developed nation.

For a third mechanism of Indianization the narratives of Chinese travellers, which, preserved in the Chinese histories, are an invaluable source for the early history of South-East Asia, give us some indications. This was Indianization through the activities of adventurers, Indians who sought fame and fortune overseas, and who either became advisers to the indigenous rulers of South-East Asian states (as did that remarkable Greek, Phaulkon, at the Court of the Siamese King Narai in the seventeenth century), or actually carved out kingdoms for themselves (as did Raja Sir James Brooke in Sarawak in the nineteenth century). The Chinese texts, confirmed by epigraphy, describe the founding of the Indianized kingdom of Funan in Indo-China in terms which could well suggest the career of the Indian equivalent of Brooke. Kaundinya, so the story goes, guided by a dream, set out in search of a kingdom which he won by kidnapping and marrying Willow Leaf, Queen of Funan. This tale was later phrased in more orthodox Indian terms, with the brāhman Kaundinya marrying Nāgī Somā, the daughter of the King of the Nāgas, or serpent spirits, a legend strikingly similar to that accounting for the origin of the Pallava Dynasty of south India. The Khmers, whose empire was a successor state to Funan, later adopted this story as their official myth, and the Nāga motif came to dominate their decorative art.

There can be little doubt that the fusion of brāhman and Nāga, of Indian and indigenous South-East Asian, took place during the early stages of Indianization mainly at the official level and had relatively little impact upon the popular cultures of the regions concerned. Most of the archaeological remains of this early period, images of Buddha and Vishnu, *lingas* and other Hindu cult objects, are far more 'Indian' and far less characteristic of any regional culture than was to be the case later on. Almost ubiquitous in South-East Asia, for example, is a category of Buddha image showing very clear signs of Gupta or Amarāvatī influence; and some examples of this can, on the established principles of Indian iconography, be dated to very early in the Christian era. Specimens have been found in Indo-China, Thailand, Burma, Malaysia, Indonesia, and the Philippines. The earliest South-East Asian inscriptions, some of which may perhaps date to the fourth century A.D., show the use of a script generally considered to be of a south Indian type, with little if any sign of evolution in a South-East Asian environment. All this rather suggests the deliberate acquisition by the first South-East Asian Indianized rulers of the signs and symbols of Indian political organization, the language and script of the brāhmans, and the cult objects of the major Indian religions. (The distinction between Hindu and Buddhist sometimes tends to become blurred in early South-East Asia.) It is difficult, however, to use this archaeological record to prove that Indian influence came from any one Indian region, as many scholars have attempted, but with little success, to do. There is evidence pointing to influence from north India; there is also evidence indicating Dravidian origins: but much of this evidence consists of cult objects which may well have been either imports or local copies of imports, and of which the significance should be interpreted with extreme caution.

In time of process of regional evolution, the interaction of Indian and indigenous ideas began to produce a number of distinctive styles of Indianized South-East Asian art and architecture. The Mon art of Burma and of the so-called kingdom of Dvāravatī in what is now Thailand, while retaining much that might be called Gupta, had by the sixth century A.D. begun to show a number of distinctive features of its own, some of them easy to detect by eye but very hard to define verbally. Perhaps the most obvious departure from the Indian norm is to be seen in the representation of the human face, which comes to show physical features characteristic of a non-Indian ethnic group. The Khmers, Chams, and Javanese had all likewise by the end of the eighth century evolved styles so individual as to have become something much more than a reflection of one or more Indian prototypes.

There is much evidence to suggest that Indian ideas, as well as Indian art, were modified in 'Further India' through the influence of indigenous cultures. The cult of the *Devarāja*, the God King, though certainly expressed in Indian terminology, developed, so many scholars believe, into a distinctive corpus of political and cosmological ideas which lies behind the proliferation of Khmer temples built in the form of mystic mountains and the Javanese *chandis* which were not only places of worship but also royal tombs and mechanisms, as it were, designed to link the dynasty on earth with the spirit world. No more extreme examples of this cult, with its identification of ruler with god, be it Śiva, Vishnu, or Buddha, can be found than in Angkor Thom, the city of the late twelfth- and early thirteenth-century Khmer ruler Jayavarman VII. Here, on the gateway towers of the city, and on its central monument, the Bayon, the face of the king himself becomes the dominant architectural motif. From all four sides of every tower of the Bayon, Jayavarman VII looks out over his capital, his lips and eyes suggesting an enigmatic and slightly malevolent smile. This is something which the Roman emperors, who deified themselves in their own lifetimes, would have understood, but which would have been beyond the comprehension of the great Hindu and Buddhist dynasties of India. The *Devarāja* cult of the Khmers, Chams, and Javanese Indianized kings has survived to the present day in Thailand, where it explains many features of the modern Thai monarchy.

The individuality of the major art styles of Indianized South-East Asia is, as we have already noted, to a great extent the result of interaction between Indian and pre-Indian indigenous South-East Asian concepts and traditions. The South-East Asian component in this cultural equation, however, is far more difficult to define than the Indian. Archaeological, anthropological, and linguistic research has indicated two categories to which many elements of the pre-Indian cultural substratum may be assigned, the Dong-son and the 'Megalithic'. Neither of these terms can be used with particular precision, and they must be regarded as being on the whole no more than convenient labels for features which it would otherwise be extremely hard to classify.

Dong-son refers to a site in what is now North Vietnam which revealed, between the two World Wars, a wealth of objects in iron and bronze of which a number of bronze kettle-drums are perhaps the best-known. The Dong-son drums, like many other artifacts from this site, show strong signs of Chinese influence. Dong-son geometrical decoration is closely related to the art of Han Dynasty China. Since the Second World War a number of important Dong-son sites have been found in Yunnan Province of China. The typical Dong-son drum, however, is not quite Chinese; and in its decoration, especially in the bands of highly stylized human and animal figures on its tympanum and around its barrel, have been detected features relating Dong-son to many of the surviving folk-arts of both island and mainland South-East Asia. This discovery, coupled with the wide distribution outside Indo-China of bronzes identical to those found at Dong-son, has given rise to the concept of the existence of a definite Dong-son culture among many of the peoples whom the first missionaries of Indianization encountered. The significance of Dong-son has perhaps been exaggerated; but it does provide a useful term under which to group many elements of similarity between the arts of, for example, the heavily Indianized Javanese and peoples like the Borneo Dyaks, who show very little trace of Indian influence.

The term 'Megalithic' is even less precise than Dong-son. It refers to a wide range of the discoveries of South-East Asian archaeology, including alignments of standing stones (menhirs) from Malaya and Sumatra which would not look out of place in Brittany, carved boulders from Sumatra, Borneo, Laos, and Sulawesi (Celebes), cyst burials from Sumatra, Malaya, and Java, large cylindrical stone burial urns from Burma, Laos, and Sulawesi, and extensive fields of burials in ceramic jars from many parts of Indonesia, the Philippines, Vietnam, and Burma. There is no reason to believe that all these manifestations of indigenous South-East Asian cultures, to which the term 'Megalithic' has been applied, are of necessity closely related to each other. Nor have attempts to add precision to the 'Megalithic' concept by subdividing it into two or more chronological phases been particularly convincing. Like Dong-son, 'Megalithic' is a very useful term, but one into which too much significance should not be read. There is some evidence that a number of 'Megalithic' remains have Dong-son affinities: a boulder from south Sumatra with a Dong-son kettle-drum carved on it is perhaps the best example. 'Megalithic', whatever its validity as a category for indigenous South-East Asian cultures, does not of necessity mean very old; and many 'megaliths' are still used by modern South-East Asian peoples.

In some Indianized South-East Asian styles there was a marked tendency in the course of time for features of Dong-son and 'Megalithic' type to all but swamp the obvious Indian elements. In the last stages of Hindu and Buddhist art and architecture in Java, for example, from the fourteenth century onwards when Islam was actively establishing itself in the archipelago, temples both in plan and in decoration became increasingly hard to compare with any known Indian style. They tended, in the Majapahit period, to become open altars, situated on hill terraces or on masonry platforms representing mystic mountains; and in the process they acquired striking similarities to certain 'Megalithic' and definitely non-Indian structures of which good examples are to be seen in south Sumatra. The decoration of these monuments departed widely from those Indian canons so obvious in the earlier Javanese structures of the Śailendra period (*c.* ninth century A.D.); and it can easily be related to Javanese folk-art, in which has been detected many Dong-son elements. The evolution of later Javanese Indianized art has often been interpreted, and convincingly so, as the wearing thin, as it were, of the Indianized veneer and the resurgence of an indigenous pre-Indian civilization to which are applicable the terms Dong-son and 'Megalithic'. A similar process, though generally not quite so dramatic in its results, has been observed in the other major Indianized South-East Asian styles of the mainland, those of the Khmers, Chams, and Burmans.

The revival of the indigenous was not, of course, the only factor leading to Indianized South-East Asian cultural evolution. Indianization, once initiated, did not come abruptly to a halt. Contacts between India and South-East Asia along the trade-routes, once established, persisted; and cultural changes in the Indian subcontinent had their effect across the Bay of Bengal. During the late Gupta and the Pāla-Sena periods many South-East Asian regions were greatly influenced by developments in Indian religious ideas, especially in the Buddhist field. The pilgrimages to Indian religious centres like Nālandā, of which devout Chinese like Hsüan Tsang and I Ching have left celebrated accounts, were also made by South-East Asians, sometimes with much encouragement on the part of their rulers. The Indonesian King Bāladeva, for example, so an inscription records, made in A.D. 860 a benefaction to the Buddhist university at Nālandā. It should cause no surprise, therefore, to find a strong late Gupta and Pāla influence in many manifestations of Mahāyāna Buddhism in South-East Asia. The art of the Śailendra Dynasty in Java, the builders during the eighth and ninth centuries A.D. of Borobodur and many of the other architectural glories of central Java, shows abundant evidence of this particular influence, as also does the art of Śrīvijaya, a state which dominated the Malayan and Sumatran shores of the Malacca Straits from the seventh to the thirteenth centuries A.D.; and Pāla influence can also be seen to a varying degree in the major styles of the South-East Asian mainland. Thus the great temple at Pahārpur in Bengal, dating perhaps from the seventh or eighth century, of which excavation has revealed the ground-plan, may well be representative of an inspiration shared in common by such widely separated monuments as Borobodur and Prambanan in central Java, Angkor Wat in Cambodia, and the Ānanda temple at Pagan in Burma.

Inscriptions show that there was also a very close contact between many South-East Asian regions and the Tamil kingdoms, particularly during the period of the Chola Dynasty (ninth to thirteenth centuries A.D.). There were Tamil trading settlements at this time at Baros in western Sumatra and at Takuapa on the Kra Isthmus. Indonesian rulers endowed shrines in Chola territory in India. This connection between both sides of the Bay of Bengal was so important that, in the eleventh century A.D., it induced the Chola kings Rājarāja and Rājendra to undertake demonstrations of their sea power in the direction of Sumatra and the Malay Peninsula, with the probable objective of securing a commercial monopoly rather than the acquisition of territory. It is not difficult, therefore, to find explanations for the presence of a Chola element in many South-East Asian arts and architectures.

In the thirteenth century two closely related people, the Shans and the Thais, migrating from the Chinese province of Yunnan, began to dominate much of Burma and Thailand. At about the same time another group from the Chinese borderlands, the Vietnamese, were advancing southwards down the Annamese coastal strip into Cham territory. These movements of peoples had a profound effect upon the subsequent shape of the cultural history of mainland South-East Asia. The Shans, following in the wake of a series of attacks by the Mongol (Yüan) Dynasty in China, had by A.D. 1300 brought about the abandonment of the great Burman city of Pagan with its thousands of Buddhist temples. The Thais, entering what is now Thailand, brought Mon and Khmer peoples under their rule; and their pressure, by the end of the fourteenth century, had proved too much for the Khmer kingdom with its centre at Angkor in Cambodia. The Vietnamese, by the end of the fifteenth century, were well on the way to bringing all of what is now Vietnam under their sway, and, in the process, creating a major South-East Asian population which, unlike the Indianized Chams, looked for its example to China.

The Thais, once established in the Menam basin, underwent a process of Indianization which, because it is well documented, provides an invaluable example of the mechanics of cultural fusion in South-East Asia. On the one hand, Thai rulers set out deliberately to Indianize themselves. They sent, for example, agents to Bengal, at that time suffering from the disruption of Islamic conquest, to bring back models upon which to base an official sculpture and architecture. Hence Thai architects began to build replicas of the Bodh-Gayā *stūpa* (Wat Chet Yot in Chiengmai is a good example) and Thai artists made Buddha images according to the Pāla canon as they saw it. On the other hand, the Thais absorbed much from their Khmer and Mon subjects; and the influence of Angkor and Dvāravatī is obvious in Thai art. Thai kings embraced the Indian religions, and they based their principles of government upon Hindu practice as it had been understood by their Khmer predecessors. Hence the Khmer version of the *Devarāja* cult was absorbed by the Thai monarchy; and traces of it survive to this day.

The thirteenth century, which saw the conquests of the Thais, also witnessed two major developments in South-East Asian religious life, both, if sometimes rather indirectly, the product of Indian influence. Theravāda Buddhism established itself as the dominant form of religious expression on the South-East Asian mainland; and the saffron-robed monk became ubiquitous in Burma, Thailand, Laos, and Cambodia. This movement appears to have originated in Ceylon and is unconnected, except in the most remote way, with the Buddhism which came to South-East Asia in the first centuries of Indianization. At the same time, in the archipelago, the Malay Peninsula, and Champā (all inhabited by peoples speaking languages of the Malayo-Polynesian group), Islam began to spread. Muslim traders had been in contact with South-East Asia at least since the days of the early 'Abbāsid Caliphate. Archaeological sites like Takuapa on the Isthmus of Kra have yielded Islamic glazed wares, almost certainly brought by Persian traders, which date to the ninth or tenth centuries; and in both Java and Vietnam Islamic inscriptions of the eleventh century have been found. But it seems that the actual conversion of South-East Asian populations to Islam on a significant scale did not begin until the thirteenth century, when Indian Muslim merchants from Gujarāt or Bengal brought the faith with them as their ancestors had brought the Hindu and Buddhist religions. When Marco Polo passed through the Malacca Straits in the late thirteenth century there were thriving Muslim communities in Sumatra. With the conversion to Islam in the middle of the fifteenth century of the Malacca kingdom, which was an heir to Śrīvijaya in the domination of commerce through the Straits, Islam began to penetrate deep into the Malay Peninsula; and at the same period it extended its influence eastwards through Java and the rest of the archipelago, continuing a rapid expansion up to the middle of the sixteenth century.

The conversion to Islam of much of island South-East Asia was the last phase of Indianization which we can treat in the same terms as our discussion of the earlier establishment of Hindu and Buddhist influence; for in the sixteenth century the South-East Asian cultural scene was greatly complicated both by the coming of the European empire-builders and by the great increase in Chinese settlement. Indian influence, of course, has continued up to the present; but it has done so in competition with the influences of Europe and China, to which, in recent years, have been added those of America and Japan. The Islamic conversion in South-East Asia took place along lines very similar to those which marked the coming of Buddhism and Hinduism in earlier years. It was established by influence and example, not by force; and there is no South-East Asian parallel to the Islamic Turkish invasions of India. Once established on South-East Asian soil, Islam began to acquire peculiarly South-East Asian features, the product of its intermarriage with earlier cultural strata, both Indianized and pre-Indian. Thus women in Malaysia, Indonesia, and the Philippines have not, as they have in India and the Middle East, taken to veiling their faces in public. The first South-East Asian mosques were not replicas of Indo-Saracenic art: they were based on the forms of existing Buddhist and Hindu temple architecture; and the dome is a late, and rather exotic, development in this region. Many old pre-Islamic customs and ceremonies survived. Islamic peasants continued to be entertained by stories from the *Rāmayāna*. Much of Malay and Indonesian court ceremonial, marriage customs, and the like can be traced without difficulty back to the days of Buddhist and Hindu dominance. Perhaps no better symbol of the way in which South-East Asia absorbed Islam can be found than in the 'Megalithic' menhir from Pengkalan Kempas in the Malaysian State of Negri Sembilan, which has carved upon it in high relief in Kufic letters the Muslim name of God.

The Indianization of South-East Asia was a slow and gradual process. With a few exceptions like the Chola attacks of the eleventh century, it was carried out by peaceful means; and in consequence, as it developed, it did not build up a resistance to its further progress. Though its initial impact was probably at the level of the ruling classes, Indian influences had no difficulty in merging with indigenous cultures to create a series of distinct South-East Asian amalgams in which it is now virtually impossible to disentangle all the Indian from the non-Indian. The result may not have simplified the task of the cultural historian; but it has without doubt guaranteed the Indian heritage a place in South-East Asian civilization from which it cannot possibly be dislodged without the total destruction of that civilization.

APPENDIX BY H. H. E. LOOFS

Possibly no other area in the world has recently experienced such an astonishing development in archaeological research as South-East Asia. Once a backwater in this respect, it has become in the past few years one of the centres of attention of world archaeology, as this area's importance for the understanding of the early cultural history of other parts of Asia is slowly being recognized.

These new developments can be put under three headings. First (because most striking), those leading to the reappraisal of the cultural level of populations at the receiving end of Indianization at the time when the latter began. Here mention must be made in particular of discoveries made in Thailand which, although still somewhat controversial, point to the possibility that South-East Asia, far from having constantly been an area culturally less developed than its neighbours, was on the contrary often one from which powerful cultural impulses radiated to both east and south Asia, not to speak of the Pacific. It now seems that not only the cultivation of plants but also the development of sophisticated (though not literate) metal-using civilizations started here considerably earlier than hitherto thought; some even maintain that they began earlier than in China and India. The notion of a 'Neolithic South-East Asia' as the receiver of influences from an India culturally vastly superior in all aspects has to be abandoned: it was rather as equals that the two met. This would also explain the surprisingly rapid and willing acceptance and assimilation of Indian cultural elements, which is difficult to account for if the gap between Indian and South-East Asian civilizations was a wide one.

Secondly, there are new theories about the reasons for the coming of Indian influence to ancient South-East Asia and the way this influence spread. These show a clear tendency away from a predominantly commercial or economic interpretation of the process of Indianization (i.e. traders seen as the main agents of the spread of Indian influence), let alone one based on the assumption of large-scale migrations, abandoned long ago. Emphasis is now put on brāhmans or missionaries, or even on the initiative of South-East Asians themselves, a development foreshadowed by Professor Lamb's adoption of the term 'self-Indianization' to describe one possible mechanism of the process. The frequent use of the words 'Sanskritization' or 'brāhmanization' in recent publications underlines this tendency. Archaeological evidence now available also points to a slightly earlier date than that suggested by Professor

Lamb for the effective results of this Sanskritization in some parts of South-East Asia, if not for its beginning.

One theory (published in 1969 by Eveline Porée-Maspero) even has it that the Sanskritization of Indo-China took place far earlier than usually thought, and also that it was the work not of Indians coming by sea, but of *Man* peoples from southern China; South-East Asian seafarers then established the first direct contact with India by maritime routes. In view of the extremely scholarly work on which this theory is based, it cannot be dismissed off-hand. As regards the extension of Sanskritization, which until recently was thought not to have reached the eastern parts of South-East Asia, it has now been shown that even the Philippines got a fair share of it, although it did not result there in the establishment of Indian-inspired kingdoms as in the more western and southern parts of the region.

Thirdly, discoveries made during the last decade have added to our knowledge both of the growth of some Indianized kingdoms themselves, and of the role non- or pre-Indian indigenous cultural elements played in the development of these civilizations, leading to several quite drastic reappraisals. Thus the formerly rather nebulous concept of 'the Megalithic' and the latter's relation to art styles in South-East Asia, China, and the Pacific have been considerably clarified by the last works of Heine-Geldern, whose earlier theories on the South-East Asian Neolithic are now, however, far less generally accepted than they were ten years ago. A number of other publications have also helped to elucidate the matter, to which several international symposia have been devoted in recent years.

With regard to the earliest phase of development of Indianized kingdoms in South-East Asia, the most recent research—again mainly in Thailand—also paints a different picture from that we are used to. Older archaeologists saw Funan developing in the southernmost part of the Indo-Chinese peninsula, whence it extended its domination westwards over large parts of what is now Thailand, where the kingdom of Dvāravatī emerged in the sixth century A.D. as a result of the breaking up of Funan. Now some archaeologists propose to see in the Lower Menam basin itself the heartland of Funan. From there, Funanese civilization expanded on all sides, possibly even into Lower Burma, where recent excavations have yielded objects astonishingly similar to those found not only in central Thailand but even in Oc-Eo, usually considered the main site of Funan and dated to the same time. Dvāravatī would thus be the successor state of Funan, and would have expanded into northern Thailand.

The related problem of the origin and migration of the Thai has also been dealt with at length during the last decade, and various alternative theories to that of their migration from Yunnan into northern Thailand just prior to the thirteenth century have been put forward; however, no agreement has yet been reached on this matter. The same is true for the question of the origin of the Śailendras, the date of the Borobudur, etc., where much of what has been written recently has only added to the mystery surrounding these issues, which looked so beautifully clear and simple only ten years ago.

The stages of the development of Thai art (in particular of the Buddha figure and of religious architecture), on the other hand, with its alternating urge to affirm its own identity and to copy Indian, Khmer, or Mon models, are now too well known to need to be couched in the generalizing terms used in the preceding chapter.

Finally, the results of recent research in the spread of Islam into mainland South-East Asia indicate that it may have arrived there even earlier than in the archipelago—an intriguing possibility which, again, could lead to a drastic reappraisal of developments, this time not at the beginning but towards the end of the period of the Indianization of South-East Asia.

CHAPTER XXXII

Indian Influences on China

by J. LeRoy Davidson

Buddhism was India's contribution to China. Moreover, it was a contribution that had such shocking and seminal effects on the religion, philosophy, and arts of the adoptive country that it penetrated the entire fabric of Chinese culture.

We know that Buddhism had been brought to China by the year A.D. 69, for it was then that the White Horse Monastery was founded in the city of Loyang. Any contacts that might have been made earlier cannot have been influential. During the first and second centuries, however, China was torn by numerous rebellions and economic disasters and it was then, evidently, that the Middle Kingdom was ready to receive the unfamiliar religio-philosophical tenets of its neighbour to the west. China's own traditions, supported for centuries by Confucianism, had reached a state of flux, having been weakened by one component of the population masquerading as Confucianists and by another openly favouring the totalitarian philosophy of the Legalists. Philosophical Taoism had degenerated to such a degree that it had become a vehicle for practitioners of alchemy and magic. Rationalist thought was promulgated chiefly by Wang Ch'ung (A.D. 27–*c.* 97), but scepticism such as his added an even greater force to the disruption of Han society. Neither Wang Ch'ung nor any other individual could direct the future of Chinese thought at a time when traditions, ideals, and the social structure were disintegrating simultaneously. But Buddhism could—and did.

In times of national security and well-being the introduction of a foreign religion such as Buddhism would have had little chance of success in a country as traditional and xenophobic as China. But conditions in the last centuries of the Han Dynasty were propitious for the Buddhist missionary, whether he came directly from India or from Central Asia, where Buddhism had already been firmly implanted.

Buddhism had many facets and consequently could appeal to different segments of Chinese society. Proselytizing monks, masters of the expedient, had no scruples in choosing tactics for their campaigns. In order to impress a people with a long tradition of reverence for the written word, what was most essential, however, was a Buddhist literary canon and in due course this was established. The earliest known text, *The Sūtra in Forty-two Sections* (*Ssŭ-shih-erh-chang-ching*), was composed in the first century. This sūtra is a simplified statement of Hīnayāna doctrine.

By the end of the third century great strides had been made both quantitatively and qualitatively in translations of Indian sūtras. This was accomplished under the direction of Dharmaraksha (260–313), a monk, and himself a distinguished translator. But it was Kumārajīva, a brilliant missionizing monk from Central Asia, who, together with a large secretariat of assistants, produced numerous translations in excellent Chinese. By the beginning of the fifth century they had completed a corpus that was acceptable to a nation in which the literati enjoyed both power and prestige. Kumārajīva's heroic output provided the proponents of Buddhism with a literary arsenal.

The most basic doctrines of Buddhism had to be taught to a people who had never been exposed to such philosophical concepts as *karma*, *samsāra*, and *nirvāna*. The dispossessed were attracted less to the ideal of a vague, distant, and incomprehensible *nirvāna* than to the possible attainment of immediate rebirth in the delightful paradise of the Buddha Amitābha or Maitreya. Cults focusing on the paradises of different Buddhas developed rapidly; they required no abstruse philosophical knowledge on the part of the believer. The way to salvation from the unpredictable Wheel of Life was easy, merely requiring faith in the Buddha, a bodhisattva, or even a few words from a sūtra such as the *Saddharmapundarīka*, the *Sukhāvatī Vyūha*, or any Maitreya sūtra. In effect, this religion of faith ultimately derived from the Indian concept of *bhakti*.

If Buddhism attracted the masses because of future rewards in heaven, or even for more immediate advantages in this world, it also had an appeal on a higher level to many of the Chinese intelligentsia. Anarchical warfare had divided their country into various contending kingdoms; they were disillusioned and alienated. But they were fascinated by the elaborate metaphysics and hair-splitting philosophy of the Buddhist commentators.

Other segments of the population were attracted by the extraordinary powers of those missionaries who demonstrated the potency of their religion through acts of magic. A case in point is the career of Fo T'u-teng, the subject of a study by Professor Arthur F. Wright. Fo T'u-teng, a fourth-century religious, attached himself to a warlord named Shih Lo whom he had impressed initially by the performance of a simple magical trick. The missionary subsequently rose to power because of what was believed to be an ability to induce rain, cure the sick, and, perhaps most of all, to advise successfully in matters of warfare, a function inherently non-Buddhist.

The numbers of Chinese won over to Buddhism increased alarmingly during the fifth century. Monks, nuns, clergy, and monasteries multiplied so rapidly that, in the years 444 and 446, repressive measures were imposed on them by the court. The charges levelled against the clergy were on moral and political rather than religious grounds, not always without reason. Certainly many had become monks in order to evade military conscription. Furthermore, laxities in the monasteries gave the government additional cause for punitive measures.

Despite occasional setbacks, a good percentage of the population was persuaded for one reason or another to espouse the new faith. Converts, temples, and monastic establishments continued to proliferate throughout the land. In time, the concepts pervading Buddhist thought found their way into Confucian philosophy. Occasional persecutions and attacks by the Confucian gentry failed to halt the growing power of the Buddhists. Indeed, when China, after centuries of fragmentation, was unified under the Sui Dynasty (589–618), the religion adopted from abroad became a stabilizing force within the empire.

The Sui ruler, in order to gain support from his numerous subjects, compared himself to a *chakravartin* and, like a latter-day Aśoka, noted that, after having been victorious in many battles, he, too, promoted the ten Buddhist virtues. Royal and governmental support of Buddhism became, in fact, a matter of state policy under the Sui. Further, in 591 the last of the Sui emperors, Yang Kuang, convened an assembly of monks under the auspices of Chih-i, founder of the T'ien-t'ai sect. There the Emperor himself took the 'bodhisattva vows' of a lay Buddhist.

During the early part of the T'ang Dynasty (618–906) Buddhism commanded considerable prestige in the royal court and was even manipulated for political control. The usurping Empress Wu (684–710) went to such lengths as to have a sūtra written in which it was prophesied that the future Buddha, Maitreya, would be reborn as a woman destined to rule China. To maintain that deceit the Empress occasionally dressed herself as a bodhisattva.

The worldly success of Buddhism, however, led to its eventual downfall. Just as Buddhism had insinuated itself into China during a period of anarchy, it lost much of its vitality and power during a similar period of disruption that occurred in the ninth century. The foreign religion was a convenient scapegoat, and in 845 severe persecutions drastically reduced the influence of orthodox Buddhism. While it survived as a popular religion, Buddhism changed as it fused with Taoism and incorporated beliefs and superstitions of indigenous cults. The concept of *karma*, however, was engraved permanently on Chinese thought, as were the Indian visions of the heavens and hells in the hereafter. The creative impulse of Buddhism was to come from the Ch'an or Dhyāna sect which, according to legend, had its roots in the sixth century. This eminently unconventional form of Buddhism has been characterized by Dr. Hu Shih as the Chinese 'rejection' of Buddhism. It should be noted, however, that some aspects of Ch'an philosophy are closely akin to Tantricism, another offshoot of traditional Buddhism, and one that was prevalent in India during the ninth-century persecutions in China.

With the decline of orthodox Buddhism, Confucianism triumphed, but it was a Confucianism so permeated with Buddhist thought that, as Professor Arthur F. Wright has said, it would have been incomprehensible to a Confucianist living in Han times. Even the definition of *li*, a term that encompassed the basic Confucian ideal of an empirical natural order, was transformed to mean the transcendental absolute, a principle of the Mahāyānists. Throughout the Sung Dynasty (960–1279) Neo-Confucianism remained dependent on Buddhist philosophy. Even as late as the Ming Dynasty (1368–1644) the most prominent Neo-Confucianist, Wang Yang-ming (1472–1529), was criticized by his opponents for being a crypto-Buddhist. Actually, his inspiration came specifically from Ch'an Buddhism.

Under the Manchus, who established the Ch'ing Dynasty (1644–1912), Buddhism once again achieved royal approval. But this time Tibetan influence prevailed and Indian ideals were obfuscated by elaborate rituals. Europe rather than Asia was to become the revitalizing force in China.

We have said that India's contribution to China was Buddhism. To this we should also add trade, which followed the same long and difficult routes ploughed by the missionaries. As China expanded territorially under the T'ang, silks flowed westward in exchange for an abundance of exotica transported eastward along those same routes. India sent incense, fruits, flowers, and spices. More, it sent music, which had a vogue in the T'ang capital, and information about discoveries in astronomy. It is even said that, during the eighth century, three Indian families had a monopoly as calculators for the official calendar. A century later, Gautama Siddhārtha, an Indian who was director of the Royal Observatory under Emperor Hsüan Tsang (847–60), tried to introduce the zero and table of sine functions, but these Indian inventions were not acceptable to the Chinese.

While most of the influences from abroad were ephemeral, the effect of Indian art was more lasting. The acceptance of Buddhism by the Chinese created a profound change in the art of China, not only because of the nature of the religion but also because of the nature of the art forms that had evolved in India and Central Asia. The Chinese craftsman had to absorb a totally new roster of subjects and styles as well as a totally new religion.

Before the advent of Buddhism, anthropomorphic sculptures in monumental scale were rare. There was no need for them in daily worship. The skill of the sculptor was employed mostly for the elaborate burial requirements connected with ancestor worship. Large sculptures, usually in animal form, were designed specifically for ceremonial approaches, or spirit paths, to the tombs. Within the tomb chambers didactic reliefs represented either historical events or subjects relating to Taoist or Confucian traditions. There were also enormous quantities of tomb figurines, modest in scale, made to accompany the deceased in their future existence.

Probably the earliest example of Buddhist art extant in China is a small Buddha that was carved in relief on a lintel over the entrance of a cave tomb in Chiating, Szechwan, *c.* A.D. 200. The Buddha is seated and has his right hand raised in *abhaya mudra*, signifying 'have no fear'. This figure, while small and in relief, may be regarded as a model for countless numbers of Buddhas that were to embody the religious and aesthetic attitudes of later centuries. Stylistically, however, it is almost a direct copy of the type of Buddha image prevalent in the Gandhāran region at the same time.

The concentric folds of the heavy drapery on the Szechwan Buddha leave no doubt as to the source. The same is true of the earliest dated Buddha, cast in A.D. 338, about a century later. This figure, now in the Brundage Collection (San Francisco), still maintains the Gandhāran tradition, but the Chinese artist has left his imprint by slightly levelling the folds of the drapery and abstracting the facial features of the Buddha. These two objects are particularly important because they are the chance survivors of what must have been a prodigious output during the initial impact of Indian iconography. Records tell of many huge and magical images, some of which, it was believed, had been transported miraculously from India. Some were even said to have been associated with Aśoka, which would have endowed them with an antiquity even greater than any anthropomorphic image of the Buddha in India. The extraordinary prestige of such icons persisted for centuries. For example, a temple possessing a sculpture that had been found in the sixth century and subsequently installed in that building, was visited by the great T'ang Emperor, T'ai Tsung, who was so impressed by the history of the image that he provided for the adornment of the shrine. We have another echo of the prestige of Indian icons in fragments of a painting (found at Tun-huang and now in London and New Delhi) in which some Chinese devotee made careful renderings of various sculptures of Buddhas and bodhisattvas. While all of his models were apparently Indian, one is actually identifiable as an Udayana Buddha, a type of image mentioned in many reports as having come miraculously to China.

The art of India was more than a reservoir of images from which copies could be made. It was an inspiration. By the third quarter of the fifth century, Chinese sculptors at Yun Kang were transforming the Indian idiom (already adapted in Central Asia) into a purely Chinese statement. Planimetric and linear stylizations of drapery and archaic modelling produced a Buddha image that reflected the most profound teachings of the Enlightened One. These icons are recognized as being human and iconographically identifiable as deities. But the stylistic abstraction removes them from the immediacy of humanness while the simple purity of the line emphasizes the concepts they embody.

We have already noted that as Buddhism was adapted to China during the sixth century, pragmatic Chinese attitudes led to the dominance of the Paradise cults or Pure Land sects. We can infer from many inscriptions that the goal of an after life in a paradise, if not the ultimate one, became an acceptable substitute for an abstract, indefinable *nirvāna*. This compromise, probably a subconscious one, was reflected in the iconography and style of Buddhist sculpture. Avalokiteśvara, known in China as Kuan Yin, became the most popular Bodhisattva. At this time the quintessential linearity of Chinese art was evolving toward three-dimensional naturalism. Sculptors were modelling the human figure with greater subtlety and drapery with more freedom; painters were reaching beyond the picture plane into deeper space. The move toward naturalism seems to have been in response to the materialism inherent in the Paradise cults. It seems obvious that the Chinese devotee, his goals focused on the Sukhāvatī Paradise of Amitābha, wanted to find in his icons the richness he could visualize through the magnificent imagery of the sūtras describing the Land of Bliss.

In the seventh century, when Buddhism was virtually the state religion, Indian art had its last great impact on China. Earlier, while the Chinese Buddhist was in the throes of conversion, a peak of idealism and passionate orthodoxy, his art failed to register any interest in emulating the sensuousness so characteristic of the full-bodied images from India. But around the year 700, when the arts burgeoned under the worldly T'ang rulers, Chinese sculpture became thoroughly imbued with the warm, human, and sensuous quality of Gupta and post-Gupta Indian forms.

Major persecutions of Buddhism in 845 greatly weakened the religion, which, however, continued to be a creative force under the Ch'an (Zen) sect. Chinese painting was the major vehicle for Ch'an art and India ceased to be a significant influence on the culture of China. Yet the tenacity of Buddhism, despite hostility and change, has been demonstrated even in recent years and by none other, surprisingly, than the People's Republic of China. In 1959 'official sources' described China as the Pure Land of Amitābha and Mao Tse-tung as the Buddha. The paradise which was originally the goal of the dispossessed in the Middle Kingdom was thus equated with present-day China. Evidently the traditional appeal of Buddhism is still viable.

CHAPTER XXXIII

India and the Medieval Islamic World

by S. A. A. RIZVI

BY the eleventh century the 'Abbāsid Caliphate of Baghdād had started to disintegrate, and the '*ulamā*' and ministers in the service of the Iranian Saljūq Dynasty (1038–1157) had come to regard the sultanate as an institution apart from the caliphate, and the sultans as the 'shadows of God upon earth'. Many sultans who had acquired their own independent kingdoms nevertheless found recognition by the Khalīfa a valuable asset in dealing with pressure groups and internal rebellions.

Amongst these was Iltutmish, who celebrated in splendid style the arrival of the envoys sent to Delhi by Caliph Mustansir B'illāh to invest him, and who went to the extent of having the Caliph's name inscribed in the local Devanāgarī script on his billon currency. Even after Hulāgū's conquest of Baghdād in 1258 the last caliph's name, or his titles, continued to be inscribed on Indian coins until 1296, when Ruknu'd-Dīn Ibrāhīm and then 'Alā'u'd-Dīn replaced it by general titles such as 'The Right Hand of the Caliphate'. Amīr Khusrau in his time made no distinction between the caliph and the sultan, and Qutbu'd-Dīn Mubārak Shāh (1316–20) proclaimed himself Khalīfa on his coins. In fact, from the fourteenth century on, 'caliph' and 'sultan' were interchangeable designations.

When Muhammad bin Tughluq found himself unable to crush incessant rebellions, and wished to justify his rule as legitimate, he sought and eventually found in Egypt an alleged successor to the 'Abbāsid caliph, whom he recognized as his overlord and in whose name he commenced striking coins in 1340. Four years later he received formal investiture, but, in spite of the dramatic expressions of humility he uttered to the caliph's envoy, and the celebrations to mark the occasion, he did not manage to stave off disaster. However, a precedent had been established, and when Fīrūz received his investiture it was with genuine respect for the caliph.

Of more real concern to the Delhi sultans were their efforts to establish peaceful relations with the Mongols, who played havoc on the north-west frontier of the sultanate and tried their utmost to seize Delhi. In 1260 Balban gave a magnificent reception to Hulāgū's envoy, parading his forces in their full splendour to impress the latter with his military power. Later the Ilkhānīd Mongol ruler, Ghāzān Mahmūd (1295–1304), sent the celebrated scholar Rashīdu'd-Dīn as an envoy to 'Alā'u'd-Dīn Khaljī, mainly to gain his friendship and submission, but incidentally to procure useful drugs. Rashīdu'd-Dīn had gifts showered upon him and the revenue of four villages allotted to him in perpetuity, to be remitted through merchants.

Such friendly overtures on the part of the Delhi sultans to the Mongols, both heathen and Islamized, did not, however, stem the tide of their invasions.

The country remained vulnerable to the cataclysm of Tīmūr's invasion, which prostrated Delhi for a long time afterwards.

In the sixteenth century Turkey and Iran began to emerge as great monarchies in the eastern Islamic world, the former being Sunnī and the latter Shī'ī. The conversion of the sultans of Bījāpur, Ahmadnagar, and Golconda to Shī'ism increased Irani influence in the Deccan. Diplomatic relations between Iran and the sultans of the Deccan had commenced in the reign of Shāh Ismā'īl (1501–24), the founder of the Shī'ī Safavī Dynasty, and the Mughal designs upon the Deccan, swelling steadily from Akbar's reign, further strengthened the friendship between them. Shāh 'Abbās II (1642–66) made persistent efforts to dissuade Shāh Jahān from depriving the Deccan sultans of their independence; but Shāh Jahān's aggressive policy towards the sultans of Bījāpur and Gōlconda was primarily designed to force them to give up their special relationship with Iran; and Qutb Shāh, the ruler of Golconda, was compelled to abandon his practice of naming the Shāh of Iran in the *khutba* (the exordium of the Friday and 'Īd sermons in the mosque).

The belief that the last 'Abbāsid caliph of Egypt transferred his office to Sultan Selīm I (1512–20) of Turkey, who conquered Egypt in 1517, is a late eighteenth-century fiction, exaggerated for political purposes by twentieth-century Indian advocates of Pan-Islamism. What Sultan Selīm in fact prided himself on was that his conquests had given him control of Mecca and Medīna, and that the Sherīf of Mecca was obliged to admit his suzerainty.

This must have strengthened Shēr Shāh in his resolve to annihilate Iran and to establish diplomatic relations with Turkey, with the specific purpose of 'knitting the bonds of religious brotherhood' and obtaining from the sultan the guardianship of either Mecca or Medīna.

Akbar's relations with the contemporary Islamic world were ruled by a new political realism. No longer was the main aim to strengthen the bonds between the Mughals and other powers of the same religious and sectarian persuasion; it was to achieve a balance of power between countries such as Shī'ī Iran, Sunnī Transoxiana, and Turkey, which might not only have different religious beliefs, but also be suspicious of Akbar's political motives.

Direct confrontation with Transoxiana was narrowly avoided. When its ruler, 'Abdullāh Khān Uzbeg, acquired Farghāna in the east and Balkh and Badakhshān in the south, the former ruling princes and chiefs of these regions took refuge in India under Akbar's protection. In order to save Kābul, hitherto independent, from 'Abdullāh Khān Uzbeg, Akbar annexed it to the Mughal Empire in 1585, upon the death of its ruler, his cousin Mirza Hakīm. 'Abdullāh Khān Uzbeg, his ambitions thwarted in this area, then turned his attention to Khurāsān. Backed by Turkey, which shared his aggressive designs on Iran, he endeavoured to extinguish the Shī'ī dynasty of Iran, thus arousing sectarian hatred, with each side condemning the other as heretics. Qandahār, cut off from the Iranian Government by the Uzbeg conquest of Herāt, was now itself in danger. Akbar faced this crisis with decision and himself seized Qandahār in 1590, and soon afterwards Sind and Balūchistān. He had already annexed Kashmīr (in 1586) to prevent the Khān turning his attention in that direction, and to strengthen his own frontiers. It was not until Transoxiana was weakened by civil strife following the death of 'Abdullāh

Khān Uzbeg in 1598 that Akbar felt free to return to Āgrā from the Panjāb, where he had remained since 1585, except for occasional tours to Kashmīr and Kābul.

But throughout this period Akbar had kept up diplomatic correspondence with 'Abdullāh Khān Uzbeg, trying to dissuade him from aggrandizement at the expense of Iran, and pointing out that even if the Iranian Dynasty were Shī'ī, they were still descendants of the Prophet Muhammad. At one stage he even went to the length of suggesting to the Khān that the Indian and Turānī armies might combine to save Iran from Turkey; an impracticable scheme, but serving to remind 'Abdullāh Khān Uzbeg that were he to favour Turkey too much, Akbar could retaliate by supporting Iran. In order to wield some influence in Turkish-occupied Mecca and Medīna, where the image of the Mughal Government needed better presentation, Akbar showered upon the Sherīf and the religious and other élite of these two centres a regular supply of money and gifts.

Jahāngīr at first followed his father's foreign policy where Iran was concerned, his respect for Shāh 'Abbās increasing until he retook Qandahār. Jahāngīr thereupon began to consider an alliance with the Uzbegs and the Ottomans against Iran, one of fellow Sunnīs against Shī'īs; but this did not eventuate. Shāh Jahān in his turn made a bid for a Turkish alliance in 1638, when Murād IV was preparing to reconquer Baghdād from Iran, but Murād captured Baghdād without his help and the proposal lapsed. Shāh Jahān then invaded Balkh and Badakhshān, inviting mutual suspicion between the Ottomans and the Mughals and precluding any thought of a Sunnī alliance against the hated Shī'īs. Nevertheless the diplomatic contact, once made, continued more or less uninterruptedly throughout Shāh Jahān's reign.

When Aurangzeb succeeded, Balkh and Bukhārā promptly sent envoys to welcome his accession, but the Sherīf of Mecca and the Turkish governors of Yemen and Basra waited seven years before recognizing him, while the Ottomans sent no envoy at all until 1690, when they needed his help as a result of their defeat at Vienna in 1683, and loss of Hungary in 1686. They did not know that he was now having great difficulty in keeping his own empire intact.

Long before that, in February 1661, a Persian envoy had arrived in Delhi, to be given a royal welcome. But it seems that his report of the circumstances of Aurangzeb's accession, together with an exaggerated account of rebellions by the *zamīndārs*, convinced Shāh 'Abbās II that India retained only the shadow of its past glory. No doubt he was already disgusted by the behaviour of Aurangzeb as related by envoys from Shāh Jahān and Dāra Shukōh. At all events, although in 1663 he graciously received the return embassy led by Tarbiyat Khān, Governor of Multān, he did not forbear from condemning Aurangzeb for the unscrupulous manner in which he had ascended the throne, and for his presumption in taking the title of 'Alamgīr ('World Conqueror'). On his return, Tarbiyat Khān was temporarily disgraced by Aurangzeb for not having won over the Shāh, and relations between Iran and the Mughals deteriorated; but the mutual military build-up on the borders was an idle threat in both cases, for neither power was strong enough to attack the other. Beset by domestic problems, India was diplomatically isolated under

Aurangzeb, although the fugitive Prince Akbar tried in the 1680s to persuade the Shāh to help him overthrow his father.

The position was different where trade and cultural relations were concerned. The fact that the Arabs dominated seaborne trade before the discovery of the Cape route and the coming of the Portuguese meant that Indian Muslims were easily able to develop commercial links with the Muslim world at large, and at the same time maintain their cultural contacts. Thus, when diplomatic relations with other Muslim countries failed, trade, commerce, visits by scholars, and the exchange of ideas made for a certain unity.

The Malabār coast was a key area in the pattern of trade at this time, with such ports as Calicut the entrepôt for trade between Pegu and Malacca in the east and the Persian Gulf and Red Sea in the west. Although not itself under Muslim rule, as the centre of this medieval commercial activity Malabār was the point from which the message of Islam radiated peacefully to the Far East and other non-Islamic regions.

From the Red Sea and the Persian Gulf there were two overland trade-routes to Europe, one through Egypt and the other through Syria. The contact made through the Egyptian route in particular is responsible for India's figuring so prominently in fourteenth-century Arabic books on geography, travel, and adventure, although there are also numerous accounts of India dating from the ninth and tenth centuries. Shihābu'd-Dīn al-'Umarī of Damascus (1297–1348), for instance, based the account of India in his encyclopedic *Masālik al-Absār fī Mamālik al-Amsār* mainly on information supplied by merchants. But, even though his information on the political, religious, social, and economic life of India was obtained at second hand, it has been largely corroborated by the Indian political histories of the period and by the monumental *Reḥla* of the Moorish traveller Ibn Battūta (1304–77).

There was also an overland trade-route, with Ghaznī and Multān as entrepôts, from the ninth to the twelfth centuries. The importance of Ghaznī declined in the thirteenth century, but the Multān route continued to be used. In the sixteenth century the route through Lāhore and Kābul became more popular.

During the twelfth and thirteenth centuries many merchants, sūfīs, and scholars came to Multān and Uch through the Khurram, Tochī, and Gomal passes. These areas were as heavily studded with flourishing centres of sūfism as with trade centres. By this time a close connection had developed between the Muslim craft and trade guilds and the sūfī saints; in fact many eminent sūfīs had originally been merchants or artisans. Some Chishtī sūfīs of India had close links of this kind, and depended for their subsistence on cash gifts from merchants rather than on permanent revenue grants from official sources, which would have made them dependent upon fluctuating political power.

The Muslim merchants of India often maintained cordial relations of their own with the outside world. For example when the Mongol chief Tayir attacked Lāhore in 1241, the Lāhore merchant community, who constantly travelled to Khurāsān and Turkistān, took no part in defending Lāhore or resisting the Mongols, from whom they had passes to travel in the countries under Mongol control. Nor did the Indian rulers interfere with the merchants, who were valuable as intermediaries between themselves and the Mongol rulers, and who invariably remained neutral in any political struggle.

By the reign of Muhammad bin Tughluq there were also Iranian merchants in India. Khurāsānī merchants owned great mansions in Delhi, and were engaged in exporting slaves, gold, silver, paper, and books to Khurāsān, and also elephants to the Iranian courts.

Slaves were imported too, from Egypt, Aden, and Turkistān; and horses were bought from Turkistān, Iraq, and Bahrain, the horse trade being monopolized by the Afghans from the fifteenth century onwards. It is well known that luxury goods were imported for the Court at Delhi; but there was also, from the sixteenth century, an extensive export trade in silk and linen from Bengal and Cambay to Iran, Tartary, Syria, Africa, Arabia, and Ethiopia. Indian herbs, too, were in great demand at the Iranian Court, and their influence on medicine is reflected in contemporary medical works.

An important factor in the trade of the medieval Muslim world was the role of Hindu merchants, bankers, and money-lenders. Documents from the thirteenth to the fifteenth centuries are lacking, but there is no reason to believe that the situation then was radically different from that prevailing in the sixteenth and seventeenth centuries, for which there is ample evidence.

The Arabic *Fatāwa* literature and trade documents of the period do not distinguish between Hindus and Jains, and the appellation *Baniyān al-Kuffār* ('Heretic Merchants') was given to Indian merchants living on the south Arabian coast irrespective of which community they belonged to. Their clerks were called *karrānīs*, a term which was thus in use long before it became popular because of its usage by the East India Company. The baniyāns mainly handled the cloth trade and money-lending. The best-recorded aspects of their life amongst a predominantly Muslim population are the accounts of their disputes with Muslims over such matters as non-payment of loans by Muslim debtors or the conditions of employment of Muslim menials such as sweepers. In the latter case, where employees gave religious reasons as grounds for insubordination, it was ruled that such service should not be regarded as degrading the status of a Muslim (*Ihānah lī'l-Muslimīn*), and Hindu employers, like Hindu creditors, were protected by the government in return for the taxes they paid.

Pietro della Valle and Thomas Herbert found Hindu merchants in both Isfahān and Bandar 'Abbās when they visited Iran in the reign of Shāh 'Abbās I (1581–1629); and another traveller, Chardin, noted that they charged exorbitant rates of interest, remitting their profits to India in the form of precious metal, and exerting a decisive influence on the money market. The Shāh generally favoured them in disputes. Another visitor, giving their number as 12,000, describes them as mostly good-natured and friendly, occasionally short-tempered, vegetarian, and of poor physique. They were closely in touch with the Mughal Court and were authorized to make advances to Mughal envoys and Iranian scholars invited to visit India, their Delhi agents being reimbursed for these by the Mughal administration.

A great number of outstanding poets, scholars, sūfīs, and theologians emigrated to India from the twelfth century on, but the number of Indian Muslim scholars who made their mark in the medieval Islamic world at large was also by no means small, and many Indian ideas had a significant impact on contemporary thinking outside India. For example, Maulāna Razīu'd-Dīn Hasan Sāghānī, born and educated in Badāūn (about 170 miles east of Delhi), wrote a celebrated work on the traditions of the Prophet Muhammad entitled *Mashāriqu'l Anwār*. This text was copied, read, and studied throughout the Islamic world.

There was the legendary figure, Ratan al-Hindī or Bābā Ratan, said to have been converted to Islam by the Prophet himself. This legend was obviously concocted to prove the cosmopolitanism of Islam. Together with other unauthentic traditions, it was criticized by Sāghānī in the *Mashāriqu'l Anwār*. The gullible pious paid little attention to such critical scholars, however, and popular Islamic literature continued to draw upon unauthentic traditions. Those concerning Bābā Ratan were defended even by the celebrated Irani sūfī and scholar, Shaikh 'Alā'u'd-Daula Simnānī (1261–1336); and another Irani sūfī scholar, Mīr Saiyid 'Alī Hamadānī (1314–85), and his disciples propagated Islamic orthodoxy in Kashmīr, popularizing traditions relating to Bābā Ratan through their writings.

Another Indian scholar who left an indelible mark on the world of Arabic learning was Shaikh 'Alī Muttaqī (1480–1567), who completed his higher education in Mecca. A prolific writer, his main contribution to learning was his edition of the *Hadīs* entitled *Kanzu'l 'Ummāl*, in which he rearranged more systematically the traditions given in Abu'l Fazl 'Abdu'r Rahmān Suyūtī's (1445–1505) monumental edition.

The recognition accorded to Shaikh 'Alī Muttaqī by leading Arabic scholars enhanced the reputation of Indian scholarship as a whole, and many Indian scholars, such as Shaikh 'Alī's disciple Shaikh 'Abdu'l Wahhāb Muttaqī, settled in Mecca as teachers and preachers and became celebrated for their encyclopedic knowledge of all branches of Islamic theology.

These Indian teachers in Mecca and Medīna attracted other Indian scholars who wished to specialize in *Hadīs*. Although pilgrims from many other places settled there, Indians in the seventeenth century enjoyed a special status, thanks to the temporary or permanent residence of Indian sūfīs. The disciples of one eminent *'ālim* and sūfī, Shaikh Wajīhu'd-Dīn Gujarātī (died 1589/90), propagated the teaching of the Shattārī order in Mecca and Medīna, whence it spread to other parts of the Islamic world, in particular to the Malay archipelago.

The spread of knowledge about Indian Islam to Acheh and Fansur in north Sumatra would seem to have been the work of merchants. Abu'l Fazl's *Āīn-i-Akbarī* shows that Fansur camphor, for instance, was greatly in demand at Akbar's Court, and it is not unlikely therefore that merchants from Acheh and Fansur visited Delhi and Āgrā, and returned home via the western Indian ports and Mecca, where they acquired information about Indian sūfīs.

The main link in the spread of the Shattārī order to the Malay archipelago was Safī-u'd-Dīn Ahmad, known as Qushāshī, who had been initiated into the Shattārī order before he left India to conduct schools in Mecca and Medīna. He was fortunate to have among his disciples 'Abdu'r Raūf of Singkel. This famous scholar, who is said to have been born in Acheh in 1615, left for Mecca in 1643. There he studied under Qushāshī for nineteen years before returning to Acheh, writing important sūfī works in both Arabic and Malay.

Some of the Indian sūfīs who visited Mecca would appear to have been so impressed with what they heard there of Acheh, then known as the 'Forecourt of the Holy Land', that they wished to visit the Court of the Acheh rulers themselves. One such was Nūru'd-Dīn al-Rānīrī of Rander, Gujarāt, who visited Mecca in 1620. In 1637 he went to Acheh and did not return home until 1644, dying in 1658. He wrote several works in Arabic and Malay, the most significant being his sūfic work, *Asrār-al-Insān* (*Secrets of Human Beings*), and his *Būstān al Salātin* (*Garden of Kings*), a history of the kings of Acheh on the lines of those of the regional sultans of India.

In the seventeenth century the Naqshbandī order became a channel through which sūfī works, and Indian ones in particular, were popularized throughout the Arabic- and Turkish-speaking world. A prominent member of this order was Shaikh Tāju'd-Dīn. After the death in 1603 of his preceptor, Khwāja Bāqī Bi'llāh, he tried in vain to gain supremacy over Shaikh Ahmad Sarhindī in spiritual matters; he then left for Mecca. He translated from Persian into Arabic Kāshifī's *Rashahāt 'Ain ul-Hayāt* (*Distillations of the Spring of Life*), a leading work on Naqshbandī history and doctrines, and wrote in Arabic himself on the Naqshbandī order. Many of the important disciples he initiated came from Java and Sumatra, where they in turn spread Naqshbandī influence. Tāju'd-Dīn is much quoted, for instance, in the Arabic treatises of Shaikh Yūsuf of Macassar (Borneo). Shaikh Yūsuf, who flourished in the second half of the seventeenth century, was a very influential figure at the Court of Sultan Hajjī (1682–7) of Bantam, the last of the independent sultans in this region.

In 1656–7 Shaikh Ahmad Sarhindī's sons, Khwāja Muhammad Sa'īd and Khwāja Muhammad Ma'sūm, went to Mecca. Their two-year visit seems to have increased the involvement there in the controversy then raging in India between the supporters and opponents of *Wahdatu'l Wujūd*, and consequently led to its being reflected in the works of Sumatran scholars. Towards the end of the seventeenth or early in the eighteenth century, compilations of the letters of Shaikh Ahmad Sarhindī and Shaikh Muhammad Ma'sūm were translated into Turkish, and the existence of many copies, both manuscript and printed, in the libraries of Turkey indicates that the subject was of considerable interest in that country too. In response to the inquiries of a Turkish correspondent, Shāh Walī-Allāh (1703–62) wrote a treatise suggesting a compromise between the two opposing views.

Arabic translation of Sanskrit works had been going on since the end of the eighth century, when philosophical, astronomical, and mathematical texts were translated for the 'Abbāsid Court, leading to the development of the decimal system and the numerals now adopted throughout most of the world. The works of scholars such as Shahrastānī (1076–1153), the author of *Kitāb al Milal wa'l Nahl*, a treatise in Arabic on various religions and sects, show the influence of Gardezī's *Zainu'l Akhbār*, written in about 1041, and of Al-bīrūnī's Arabic translations of several Sanskrit works and his own contribution to the knowledge of India, *Kitāb fi Tahqīq mā Li'l Hind*.

The depth of the impact made by theistic Upanishadic concepts such as *Brahmāsmi* (I am Brahma) or *Tat tvam asi* (Thou art that) is illustrated in such utterances by Bāyazīd Bistāmī (died 874) as 'Glory be to me. How Great is My Majesty!', and in his assertion that he had finally shed his ego in *fanā* (passing away) as a snake sheds its skin; and also in the celebrated declaration of the great sūfī martyr Hallāj (executed in 922): *Ana'l Haq* (I am Truth). It is not known whether Bāyazīd had any contact with Indians (the story of his learning the doctrine of *fanā* from a Sindī teacher is a myth), but Hallāj was definitely in personal contact with Buddhist scholars. The Indian system of breath control, *prānāyāma*, became an integral and increasingly important part of sūfism in Iran and Ghaznī as early as the tenth century.

Hujwirī (died after 1088) speaks of the Hashwīyya and Mujassima (anthropomorphist) sūfī orders in Khurāsān, whose ideas on Unification were influenced by brahmanical concepts. Although they said they were Muslims, they denied that the Prophets were specially privileged. Annihilation or *fanā* does not involve among the sūfīs the loss of essence and destruction of personality, but according to Hujwirī some sūfīs did regard the soul in a brahmanical light. The following verse by Maulānā Jalālu'd-Dīn Rūmī (1207–73) presents man in microcosmic terms similar to Brahmanical terminology concerning the transmigration of the soul:

I died as mineral and became a plant
I died as plant and rose to animal
I died as animal and I was a Man.
Why should I fear? When was I less by dying?
Yet once more I shall die as Man, to soar
With angels blest; but even from angelhood
I must pass on: all except God doth perish.
When I have sacrificed my angel-soul,
I shall become what no mind e'er conceived.
Oh, let me not exist! for Non-existence
Proclaims in organ tones: 'To Him shall we return!'

Another Islamic movement which gained a new dimension because of the teachings of an Indian, in this case Saiyid Muhammad of Jaunpur (1443–1505) and his Indian disciples, was the Mahdawī movement based on the expectation of the appearance of a Mahdī or Islamic messiah. After examining all the traditions on the subject, Ibn Khaldūn sums it up 'It has been well known... by Muslims in every epoch, that at the end of time a man from the family [of the Prophet] will without fail make his appearance, one who will strengthen religion and make justice triumph. The Muslims will follow him, and he will gain domination over the Muslim realm. He will be called the Mahdī.' This belief has been responsible for the appearance in Islamic countries of various adventurers who sought political power by claiming to be the Mahdī, each causing the traditions to be distorted or reinterpreted in such a way as to support his own claims. Saiyid Muhammad of Jaunpur, according to Mahdawī sources, declared himself Mahdī at Mecca in 1495–6, and again at Ahmadābād in 1497–8. His significance lies in his reorientation of the Mahdī traditions, stressing that when these allude to the Mahdī ruling the whole world, they refer not to political domination, but to spiritual domination through an Islam restored by the Mahdī to its pristine state. Hounded from Gujarāt and Sind by the local '*ulamā*', who branded him a heretic and a danger to the state, he started for Khurāsān but died on the way, at Farāh in Afghanistan, where he seems to have made a deep impression. Some of his disciples who remained there tried to prove, by lives led in poverty and service to God and mankind, that Mahdīism was the real Islam.

As far as the influence of India on Persian literature is concerned, the most indelible mark was left by Amīr Khusrau (1253–1325). Born at Patiālī about 150 miles east of Delhi, he was as popular at Court as he was at the Chishtī hospice of Shaikh Nizāmu'd-Dīn Auliyā'. Although his *masnawīs* (long poems) and panegyrics on sultans and nobles have historical importance, his most important contributions to literature are his *ghazals*, which are models of simplicity, harmony, inner coherence, and wealth of feeling, and were recognized as outstanding by the leading Irani poets.

Further lustre was added to Persian poetry by Faizī (1547–95), the poet laureate of Akbar's Court. Having absorbed all he could learn from Amīr Khusrau and the Iranian poets, he strengthened the *Sabk i-Hindī* (Indian style) which was to dominate sixteenth- and seventeenth-century Persian poetry. Later, under the Safavids, this style spread rapidly in Khurāsān, Turkistān, and Iraq, but in the second half of the eighteenth century it was strongly discouraged by official circles in Persia, and so it virtually disappeared.

The second outstanding contribution made by India in the realm of Persian literature was *Inshā* or letter-writing. The pioneer in this field was Shaikh Abu'l Fazl, Faizī's younger brother, who freed epistolography from conventional rhetoric and theological idiom and developed a powerful style of his own to express broadly based humanitarian and philosophical grounds for his opinions. In Iran the main reason for the popularity of this style was its profuse use of concepts borrowed from Ishrāqī theosophy of illumination (p. 289). Abu'l Fazl was successfully imitated by Chandrabhān Brāhman (*c.* 1600–60), a secretary at the Court of Shāh Jahān; Muslim scholars lost their predominance in the art of epistolography as the merits of Hindu writers in Persian were given full recognition by scholars of the contemporary Persian-speaking world.

CHAPTER XXXIV

India and the Modern West

by FRIEDRICH WILHELM and H. G. RAWLINSON*

DURING the Middle Ages there was little or no direct intercourse between India and the West. Direct contact was established for the first time since the fall of the Roman Empire on the eventful day, 20 May 1498, when Vasco da Gama sailed into the harbour of Calicut. A poetical description of his landing is contained in *Os Lusiadas* by the Portuguese poet Camoëns (1525–80). The English appeared on the field much later. The first Englishman (if we except the rather mythical Sighelmus, sent in the reign of Alfred on a pilgrimage to the shrine of St. Thomas at Mailāpur) to visit India was Father Thomas Stevens, a Jesuit who went out to Goa in 1579. He was one of the earliest Europeans to take an interest in Oriental languages; he published a grammar of the Konkanī dialect, and in 1615 he wrote a remarkable poem, entitled the *Kristana Purāna*, in Konkanī. This covers the whole Bible story from the Creation to the Resurrection, and was intended to be used by Indian converts in the place of the Hindu *Purānas*, or popular poems about the gods. It contains many beautiful passages, and from its wealth of classical allusions and the polish of the style and metre it appears probable that Father Stevens knew Sanskrit. For the Marāthī language he has the highest admiration. 'Like a jewel among pebbles, like a sapphire among jewels, is the excellence of the Marāthī tongue. Like the jasmine among blossoms, the musk among perfumes, the peacock among birds, the Zodiac among the stars, is Marāthī among languages.' Another distinguished visitor to Goa at the same time was Jan Huyghen van Linschoten, who was the guest of the Archbishop of Goa from 1583 to 1589. His *Itineratio*, published in 1595–6, is one of the earliest and best European books of its day on India, and was translated into English and other languages. One of the most interesting reports on India, that of the fifteenth-century Russian merchant Afanasiy Nikitin, entitled *Khozheniye za tri morya* (*Voyage beyond Three Seas*), 1466–72, has been neglected by historians of India.[1]

In 1583 a party of English merchants, armed with a letter from Queen Elizabeth to the Emperor Akbar, set out to India by the overland route through Asia Minor. They went to Tripolis in the *Tyger*, a fact which is alluded to in *Macbeth*, when the witch says:

> Her husband's to Aleppo gone, master o' the Tyger.

From Aleppo they followed the old caravan route to the Euphrates, and made their way downstream to Basra. From here they went to Ormuz, where they

* The paragraphs on music, pp. 485–86, are contributed by Dr. N. Jairazbhoy.

[1] Ed. Moscow, 1960. On the Russian–Indian relations in the seventeenth and eighteenth centuries a collection of documents in two volumes was published in Moscow in 1958 and 1965.

were arrested by the Portuguese and sent to Goa. Eventually, however, they escaped and, after many adventures, three of them, Ralph Fitch, John Newbery, and William Leedes, reached the Imperial Court at Āgrā in 1585, but only the first-named returned alive to England. Fitch describes Āgrā as 'a very great city and populous, built with stone, having fair and large streets, with a fair river running by it, which falleth into the gulf of Bengala. It hath a fair castle and a strong, with a very fair ditch.' In 1608 the East India Company received permission from the Emperor Jahāngīr to hire a house to serve as a factory on the banks of the Tāptī at Surat, and this was the cradle of the British Empire in India.

But the English came to India as merchants, not as antiquarians or explorers, and were little interested in the religion or culture of the country. An exception may be made in the case of the two chaplains, Lord and Ovington. Henry Lord's *Display of Two Forraigne Sects in the East Indies* (1630) is the first English account of the Hindus and Pārsīs of Surat, and Ovington's *Voyage to Surat in the Year 1689* also contains a number of lively and interesting observations. There was, however, a steady stream of travel literature relating to India in the seventeenth century, and upon one great poet the magic of the 'Silken East' reacted powerfully. John Milton, sitting in blind solitude, 'by darkness and by dangers compassed round', must have been deeply impressed by the accounts of the Mughal Empire given by travellers like Sir Thomas Roe, and it is probable that he heard more than one of them first-hand. When we read how

> High on a throne of royal state, which far
> Outshone the wealth of Ormuz or of Ind,
> Or where the gorgeous East with richest hand
> Showers on her kings barbaric pearl and gold
> Satan exalted sat

our minds instinctively go back, as Milton's must have gone back, to Roe's dramatic first interview with the Emperor Jahāngīr, when 'high on a gallery, with a canopy over him and a carpet before him, sat in great barbarous state the Great Mogul'. References to India in Milton's epic are almost too numerous to be quoted, but few can forget the wonderful description of the fig-tree, beneath the branches of which Adam and Eve take refuge after eating the forbidden fruit:

> They chose
> The figtree, not that kind for fruit renowned,
> But such as, at this day to Indians known,
> In Malabar or Deccan spreads her arms,
> Branching so broad and long, that in the ground
> The bended twigs take root, and daughters grow
> About the mother tree, a pillared shade,
> High over-arched, with echoing walks between;
> There oft the Indian herdsman, shunning heat,
> Shelters in cool, and tends his pasturing herds
> At loop-holes, cut through thickest shade.[2]

[2] For other references to the Indian fig-tree in English literature see the article on 'Banyan Tree' in Yule's *Hobson-Jobson*.

The flying Fiend, winging his way through the air, suggests to him a fleet of East Indiamen under full sail,

> By equinoctial winds
> Close sailing from Bengala, or the isles
> Of Ternate and Tidore, whence merchants bring
> Their spicy drugs.

Asiatic proper names had a peculiar attraction for Milton, and he uses them with magnificent effect in the Vision of Adam, where he beholds

> the destined walls
> Of Cambalu, seat of Cathaian Can,
> And Samarchand by Oxus, Temir's throne,
> To Paquin of Sinaean kings, and thence,
> To Agra and Lahore of Great Mogul . . .
> Mombaza and Quiloa and Melind
> And Sofala thought Ophir.

Nor, lastly, can we omit the beautiful and arresting little pen-picture of

> The utmost Indian isle, Taprobane,
> Dusk faces with white silken turbants wreathed.

To seventeenth-century England, India was the land of the Great Mogul, whose Court was so dramatically, if fantastically, portrayed in Dryden's popular drama *Aurengzebe* in 1675. This impression was strengthened by the narratives of the two famous French travellers, Tavernier and Bernier, which were translated into English in 1684, and give a vivid picture of the Mughal Empire. European travellers in India in the seventeenth and eighteenth centuries usually took the Muhammadan point of view about the Hindus. They looked upon them as degraded and superstitious, and this attitude was strengthened by the publication of works by missionaries like the Abbé Dubois,[3] who saw only the darker side of Hinduism. If Europeans studied any Oriental language, it was Persian. The poetry of Persia has certain affinities with classical literature, and the rendering of the stanzas of Sa'dī or Hāfiz into English verse was an elegant exercise almost as diverting as making versions of Horace. Curiously enough, it was through Persian sources that the West first became acquainted with the language and literature of the Hindus. In the eighteenth century a few missionaries like Hanxleden had managed to gather materials for a Sanskrit grammar, and a Dutchman named Abraham Roger had made a translation of the Hindu poet Bhartrihari, but these had excited little attention. The Saxon missionary Ziegenbalg became famous for his *Grammatica Damulica* (1716). Voltaire's praise of the lore of the *Ezour Vedam* created some interest, though it was proved afterwards to be founded on a worthless forgery. But the great Emperor Akbar, and after him that brilliant but ill-fated prince, Dārā Shukōh, were both keenly interested in Hinduism, and the traveller Bernier brought home to France a manuscript translation into Persian of those ancient Sanskrit works, the *Upanishads*, made by order

[3] *Hindu Manners, Customs, and Ceremonies*, 1817. The Abbé wandered about south India from 1792 to 1823, and had unique opportunities for observation, which he utilized to the full.

of Dārā. This fell into the hands of another famous French traveller and scholar, Anquetil Duperron, who in 1771 had discovered the *Avesta*. Duperron translated it into a strange mixture of Latin, Greek, and Persian in 1801, and this caught the attention of the German philosopher Schopenhauer.

Meanwhile, in British India, Warren Hastings was encouraging the study of Sanskrit for purely utilitarian reasons. He was engaged in drawing up a code of laws for the Company's Hindu subjects, and for this purpose it was necessary to obtain an accurate knowledge of the ancient Sanskrit law-books. In 1785 Charles Wilkins published a translation of the *Bhagavad Gītā*, the first rendering of a Sanskrit work into English, and a few years later Sir William Jones (1746–94), the real pioneer of Sanskrit studies and the founder of the Asiatic Society of Bengal, produced his famous version of the Code of Manu, the greatest of the Hindu law-books. In 1789 a brāhman pandit told him of the existence of the Sanskrit drama, and in that year he astonished the Western world by a translation of Kālidāsa's famous masterpiece *Śakuntalā*. Scholars now prosecuted the search for Sanskrit manuscripts with the avidity of explorers seeking for Australian goldfields, and the study of Sanskrit was put upon a scientific footing by H. T. Colebrooke (1765–1837), the greatest of all the early Sanskrit scholars.

Here[4] mention should be made of what is probably the earliest European novel about India, written from first-hand experience. This is *Hartly House Calcutta*, the work of an anonymous author, apparently a lady, published in London in 1789. Evidently the writer had had first-hand experience of the Calcutta of Hastings's day, and her work combines the characteristics of a novel and a travel book. Like many of the novels of the period it is in the form of a series of letters written by the heroine, Sophia Goldborne, to a close lady friend in England. It is of small literary merit, but a pirated edition appeared in Dublin in the year of publication and a German translation two years later.[5]

The novel gives an interesting picture of the luxurious life of the Calcutta nabobs, as seen by their ladies. Its most significant feature, from the historian's point of view, is its very sympathetic attitude to Hinduism. Sophia, who admires their music and dancing, writes thus about 'the Gentoos':[6] 'They live... the most inoffensively and happily of all created beings—their Pythagorean tenets teaching them, from their earliest infancy, the lesson of kindness and benevolence'. (Letter XII.) She meets a young brāhman, a student of 'the Gentoo university at Benares', with whom she falls platonically in love. She understands the broad principles of the Hindu class system, which she approves of, and she admires the brāhmans who have 'countenances such as Guido would have bestowed on a heavenly saint'. She seems to have no objection to Hindu idolatry and she even admires the devoted self-sacrifice of the *satī*. She is half-inclined to believe the doctrine of transmigration. She is taught the principles of Hinduism by her brāhman student, and in one letter she even states that she has become a Hindu. 'Ashamed of the manners of modern Christianity . . . I am become a convert to the Gentoo faith, and have

[4] This and the following paragraph are inserted by the Editor.

[5] A reprint, annotated by John Macfarlane, was published by Thacker, Spink and Co., Calcutta, 1908.

[6] i.e. the Hindus; from the Portuguese *gentio*, 'gentile'.

my Bramin [*sic*] to instruct me *per diem*.' (Letter XXVI.) The convenient death of the brāhman ('O! he was all that heaven has ever condescended to make human nature—and I will raise a pagoda to his memory in my heart, that shall endure till that heart beats no more') makes it possible for Sophia to marry without misgivings the young East India Company officer who has been paying her court ('for much did he honour and prize my Bramin') (Letter XXXII), and return to England. The novel is a striking comment on the effects of self-confident nineteenth-century imperialism and of the rise of the Evangelical movement on the attitudes of the British in India.

Sanskrit was introduced into Europe by a curious accident. One of the East India Company's servants, Alexander Hamilton, was detained in Paris during the Napoleonic Wars. He spent his time in cataloguing the Indian manuscripts in the Bibliothèque Nationale and in teaching Sanskrit, and among his pupils was the German poet and philosopher Friedrich von Schlegel. Schlegel, on his return to Germany, published his work *On the Language and Wisdom of the Indians* (1808). This sudden discovery of a vast literature, which had remained unknown for so many centuries to the Western world, was the most important event of its kind since the rediscovery of the treasures of classical Greek literature at the Renaissance, and luckily it coincided with the German Romantic revival. The *Upanishads* came to Schopenhauer as a new *Gnosis* or revelation.

That incomparable book [he says] stirs the spirit to the very depths of the soul. From every sentence deep, original, and sublime thoughts arise, and the whole is pervaded by a high and holy and earnest spirit. Indian air surrounds us, and original thoughts of kindred spirits. And oh, how thoroughly is the mind here washed clean of all early engrafted Jewish superstitions! In the whole world there is no study, except that of the originals, so beneficial and so elevating as that of the *Oupnekhat*. It has been the solace of my life, it will be the solace of my death.[7]

Through Schopenhauer and von Hartmann, Sanskrit philosophy profoundly affected German transcendentalism. Kant's great central doctrine, that things of experience are only phenomena of the thing-in-itself, is essentially that of the *Upanishads*. This may be a coincidence. However, Kant was indeed deeply concerned with Indian culture, and lectured on India on the basis of the knowledge available at that period. Thus his judgement of the Hindus was that 'They are gentle, that is why all nations are tolerated amongst them and why they are easily subdued by the Tartars. . . . They are industrious and upright in their business and much more honest than the Chinese.' Kālidāsa's *Meghadūta* (*The Cloud Messenger*), that beautiful lyric in which the banished *yaksha* sends a message by the monsoon-clouds, hurrying northwards, to his wife in the distant Himālayas, has an accidental parallel in the passage in Schiller's *Maria Stuart* where the exiled queen calls on the clouds, as they fly southwards, to greet the land of her youth. The poem in honour of Luke Howard, the English meteorologist, written by Goethe in 1821 is, on the other

[7] *Welt als Wille und Vorstellung*, 1st edn., p. xiii; *Parerga*, 3rd edn. i. 59, ii. 425–6. Schopenhauer, curiously enough, preferred Duperron's barbarous translation to later and more readable versions. Paul Deussen spoke of the Vedānta as 'the strongest support of pure morality, the greatest consolation in the sufferings of life and death'. *Elements of Metaphysics*, p. 337.

hand, full of conscious allusions to the *Meghadūta*, which Goethe had read and admired in Wilson's translation (1813).

Śakuntalā was translated into German by Forster in 1791, and was welcomed by Herder and Goethe with the same enthusiasm that Schopenhauer had shown for the *Upanishads*. Goethe's epigram on the drama is well known:

> Willst Du die Blüte des frühen, die Früchte des späteren Jahres,
> Willst Du was reizt und entzückt, willst du was sättigt und nährt,
> Willst Du den Himmel, die Erde, mit Einem Namen begreifen;
> Nenn' ich Sakontala, Dich, und so ist Alles gesagt.
>
> Wouldst thou the young year's blossoms and the fruits of its decline,
> And all by which the soul is charmed, enraptured, feasted, fed,
> Wouldst thou the earth and Heaven itself in one sole name combine?
> I name thee, O Sakontala! and all at once is said.

The Prologue of *Faust*, where the author, stage-manager, and Merry-Andrew converse, is modelled on the prologue of the Sanskrit drama, which consists of a dialogue between the stage-manager and one or two of the actors, including the Jester or Fool (*vidūshaka*). Goethe had at one time formed a plan for adapting *Śakuntalā* for the German stage. He toyed with the idea of metempsychosis, and used to explain his attachment to Frau von Stein by the hypothesis that they had been man and wife in a previous existence. Goethe's poems *Der Gott und die Bayadere* and the *Pariah* trilogy were based on Indian legends which he had found in the German translation of Sonnerat's *Voyages aux Indes*. The first part of the trilogy contains the pariah's prayer to God Brahmā. The second part tells of the brāhman wife who has faithless thoughts and is beheaded by her husband. Her son wishes to bring her back to life, but joins her head to the body of an executed woman. The new being so made becomes the patron goddess of all pariahs. The third part contains 'The Pariah's Thanks':

> Mighty Brahma, now I'll bless thee!
> 'Tis from thee that worlds proceed!
> As my ruler I confess thee,
> For of all thou takest heed.
>
> All thy thousand ears thou keepest
> Open to each child of earth;
> We 'mongst mortals sunk the deepest,
> Have from thee received new birth.
>
> Bear in mind, the woman's story,
> Who through grief, divine became;
> Now I'll wait to view His glory,
> Who omnipotence can claim. (Trans. A. Bowring.)

A drama, *The Pariah*, was written by Michael Beer (1800–33), a brother of the composer Meyerbeer. Actually it was a camouflaged advocacy of Jewish emancipation, and Heine commented ironically that the Pariah is a 'disguised Jew'.

Heinrich Heine (1795–1856)[8] attended the lectures of August Wilhelm von Schlegel (the first German Professor of Sanskrit, appointed in 1818) in Bonn, and of Franz Bopp in Berlin. In his prose writings Heine again and again

[8] F. Wilhelm, 'Das Indienbild Heinrich Heines', *Saeculum*, x/2 Freiburg, 1959, pp. 208

makes critical comments about the first achievements of Western Indology, and opposes biased interpretations of Indian culture. In his poetry (*Book of Songs*, etc.) we find ironical references to Indian myths such as that about Viśvāmitra who makes efforts to win the cow of plenty. However, the romantic approach is predominant:

On the wings of song, my dearest,
  I will carry you off, and go
To where the Ganges is clearest,
  There is a haven I know . . .

And lightly, trespassing slowly,
  Come the placid, timid gazelles;
Far in the distance, the holy
  River rises and swells.

O, that we two were by it!
  Beneath a palm by the stream,
To drink in love and quiet,
  And dream a peaceful dream.

Heine's *Lotus-blossom* became known as a song set to music by Schumann:

The lotus-blossom cowers
  Under the sun's bright beams;
Her forehead drooping for hours,
  She waits for the night among dreams.

The Moon, he is her lover,
  He wakes her with his gaze;
To him alone she uncovers
  The fair flower of her face.

She glows and grows more radiant,
  And gazes mutely above;
Breathing and weeping and trembling
  With love and the pain of love.

We remember the Indian poet Bhartrihari:

yāṃ cintayāmi satataṃ mayi sā viraktā
sāpy anyam icchati janaṃ sa jano 'nyasaktaḥ.

when we read Heine's poem:

A young man loves a maiden
  Whose heart for another has yearned
This other loves another
  By whom his love is returned . . .

(Translations of Heine's poems by L. Untermeyer.)

It is interesting to speculate to what extent Indian philosophy influenced Coleridge, Carlyle, and the pioneers of the English Romantic movement through the medium of Germany. Shelley and Wordsworth looked to France rather than Germany for inspiration, but their pantheism seems full of reminiscences of Hindu thought. There is no evidence, however, that either of these poets had any special interest in India, or had read much Indian literature in translation. We must attribute their mystical ideas chiefly to Neoplatonism, which itself may have been influenced by Hinduism and Buddhism. Attempts to show that William Blake's poetry was directly influenced by India are equally unconvincing and the theory that some of the names of his mythological beings are Indian-inspired is equally so. His art, however, shows that he had seen images or pictures of the Hindu gods, and that he had read Wilkins's translation of the *Bhagavad Gītā*.

Hindu philosophy played an important part in the American Transcendentalist movement, which was a strange compound of Plato and Swedenborg, German idealism, Coleridge, Carlyle, and Wordsworth. Emerson, one of the leading spirits in the movement, though he was no Orientalist, had read Sanskrit, Pāli, and Persian literature in translations. Ideas which he had imbibed in this way emerge from time to time in his essays, especially those on the Oversoul and Circles, and in his poetry. Human personality presented itself to him as a passing phase of universal Being. Born of the Infinite, to the Infinite it returns. Nowhere does Emerson's Transcendentalism find more complete expression than in his remarkable poem *Brahma*:

> If the red slayer think he slays,
> Or if the slain think he is slain,
> They know not well the subtle ways
> I keep, and pass, and turn again.
>
> Far or forgot to me is near;
> Shadow and sunlight are the same;
> The vanished gods to me appear;
> And one to me are shame and fame.
>
> They reckon ill who leave me out;
> When me they fly, I am the wings;
> I am the doubter and the doubt,
> And I the hymn the Brahmin sings.

The Western response to Indian culture, which manifested itself in the ways just mentioned among others, came to its first culmination at the end of the eighteenth and the beginning of the nineteenth century.[9] However, a great number of Western poets, essayists, novelists, and philosophers continued to be indebted to the cultural heritage of the south Asian subcontinent.

We must thank the great scholars of Indology for providing the Western approach to India with a scientific foundation. Indology started with Sir William Jones, who declared in his presidential address to the Asiatic Society of Bengal in 1786, that Sanskrit, Greek, Latin, and probably the Celtic and Teutonic languages, sprang from a common source, no longer existing; and this led to the foundation of the science of Comparative Philology by Franz Bopp in 1816. 'If I were asked', says Max Müller, 'what I considered the most important discovery of the nineteenth century with respect to the ancient history of mankind, I should answer by the following short line: Sanskrit *Dyaus Pitar* = Greek *Ζεὺς Πατήρ* = Latin Jupiter = Old Norse Tyr.'

At first, scholars had been mainly confined to classical Sanskrit, though Jones and Colebrooke had both seen some *Vedas*. Gradually, however, manuscripts were obtained, and in 1838 Rosen published the first edition of some of

[9] See R. Schwab, *La Renaissance orientale*, Paris, 1950.

the hymns of the *Rig Veda*. Milestones in Indology were the Sanskrit dictionaries of Böhtlingk (*Petersburger Wörterbuch*) and Monier-Williams, Aufrecht's *Catalogus Catalogorum*, and editions of famous Sanskrit texts. Rosen's work was carried on by Burnouf, Roth, and Max Müller, and from their patient researches sprang the study of Comparative Religion, which has had an effect upon modern thought only comparable to that of Darwin's *Origin of Species*. Max Müller said that the two great formative influences in his life were the *Rig Veda* and the *Critique of Pure Reason*. The publication, in 1875, of the first of the great series of the Sacred Books of the East, under the editorship of Max Müller, made the Hindu scriptures available for the first time to the ordinary reader; and here, perhaps, is the proper place to pay homage to the great scholar who did so much not only to popularize Sanskrit learning, but also to break down the barriers of prejudice and misconception between East and West. Sanskrit led to Pāli, and the study of the Buddhist scriptures revealed for the first time to the West the life and teachings of the greatest of all Indian religious reformers, Gautama Buddha. Pioneers in Buddhist studies were Burnouf, Lassen, Rhys Davids, Stcherbatsky and Trenckner. Standard works appeared on Indian history, literature, religion, and linguistics. Scholars from nearly all Western countries took part in this research, not only from England, France, and Germany (still the majority), but from Poland and Norway, from Switzerland and Denmark, etc. Western research led to a new orientation in India itself, and collaboration between Indian and Western scholars has always proved most fruitful since the days of Sir William Jones and even long before, in the days of the first travellers and missionaries.

It would be out of place here to make more than a passing reference to the work of archaeologists. Generations of devoted scholars, including Horace Hayman Wilson, Alexander Cunningham, Sir John Marshall, and Sir Mortimer Wheeler, have wrested from oblivion, brick by brick and stone by stone, the long-buried secrets of India's glorious past. In 1834 James Prinsep, by discovering the clue to the Kharoshthī alphabet from the bilingual Bactrian coins, enabled scholars for the first time to read the early inscriptions, the contents of which had hitherto baffled interpretation, and so to reconstruct the pre-Muhammadan history of the country. In the present century, the excavation of the remains of the Indus civilization, carried out by British and Indian archaeologists, has fundamentally altered our approach to south Asian history.

In addition to the scientific exploration of Indian civilization, a great number of popular books, such as Sir Edwin Arnold's famous poem on the Buddha, *The Light of Asia* (1879), have increased our knowledge of Indian religion and philosophy. It is even more through the medium of such books than through the works of specialists that Western poets and thinkers have become acquainted with India.

In France, Lamartine, Victor Hugo, and Alfred de Vigny bear witness to the fascination of India in the course of the nineteenth century. One of Hugo's poems is modelled on a passage from the *Kena Upanishad*.[10] Exoticism and

[10] L. Renou, *The Influence of Indian Thought on French Literature*, The Adyar Library, 1948, p. 9.

symbolism were among the new literary movements in which Indian culture evoked a response, in the form of Mallarmé's *Contes indiens* or Pierre Loti's picturesque travel book *L'Inde sans les anglais*, for instance. In Poland, the representatives of Młoda Polska (the Young Poland party) were inspired by Indian religiosity, as is shown by K. Przerwa-Tetmajer's *Hymn do Nirwany* (1894), for instance. Not seldom, however, do we find references which show little more than a taste for the exotic and exaggerated. One example amongst many is found in Apollinaire's *La Chanson du Mal-Aimé*:

L'époux royal de Sacontale
Las de vaincre se réjouit
Quand il la retrouva plus pâle
D'attente et d'amour yeux pâlis
Caressant sa gazelle mâle . . .

The technical achievements of the nineteenth century, exemplified in the completion of the Suez Canal, which 'welded together' the world and brought far India near, may have been the initial inspiration for the American Walt Whitman's enthusiastic poem *Passage to India* (1871):[11]

Passage O soul to India!
Eclaircise the myths Asiatic, the primitive fables . . .
Lo soul, the retrospect brought forward,
The old, most populous, wealthiest of earth's lands,
The flowing literatures, tremendous epics, religions, castes,
Old occult Brahma interminably far back, the tender and junior Buddha,
Central and southern empires and all their belongings, possessors,
The wars of Tamerlane, the reign of Aurungzebe,
The traders, rulers, explorers, Moslems, Venetians, Byzantium the
Arabs, Portuguese,
The first travelers famous yet, Marco Polo, Batouta the Moor,
Doubts to be solv'd, the map incognita, blanks to be filled . . .

Yet it is more than 'the retrospect brought forward', it is the truly romantic appeal which attracts him to India:

Passage indeed O soul to primal thought . . .
To reason's early paradise,
Back, back to wisdom's birth, to innocent intuitions,
Again with fair creation.

Among the exponents of neo-Romanticism affected by India was Hermann Hesse (1877–1962),[12] who was particularly attracted by Indian thought. The conflict between spirituality and sensuality revealed in the poems of Bhartrihari led him to regard the Indian poet as his 'ancestor and brother':

Wie du, Vorfahr und Bruder, geh auch ich
im Zickzack zwischen Trieb und Geist durchs Leben,
Heut Weiser, morgen Narr, heut inniglich
Dem Gotte, morgen heiss dem Fleisch ergeben . . .[13]

[11] G. W. Allen and C. T. Davis, *Walt Whitman's Poems*, New York, 1955, pp. 233 ff., Critical Note, pp. 242 ff.

[12] F. Wilhelm, 'The German Response to Indian Culture', *Journal of the American Oriental Society*, Vol. 81, No. 4 (1961), p. 402.

Yoga and Māyā are interwoven in Hesse's *Glasperlenspiel* (1943) to which he attaches an imaginary Indian *curriculum vitae*. In his *Siddhartha* the way to redemption is based on the story of the Buddha. It is because of such adaptations from Indian thought, as well as novels such as *Steppenwolf*, that Hesse has posthumously become one of the prophets of the 'psychedelic generation'. Hugo von Hofmannsthal also had an awareness of India, and in one of his poems reflects on *samsāra:*

> Jede Seele, sie durchwandelt der Geschöpfe Stufenleiter . . .[14]

He envisages manifold rebirths:

> . . . Aber wissend seines Werdens, hat er werdend auch erschaffen:
> Hat Gestalten nachgebildet der durchlaufnen Wesensleiter:
> Den Vampir, den niedern Sklaven, Gaukler, Trunkenbold und Streiter.[15]

A psychological approach tempered the romanticism of Stefan Zweig, whose story *Die Augen des ewigen Bruders* (*The Eyes of the Eternal Brother*) was written in 1922 some time after he had visited India. It tells of an Indian warrior who wins a great victory, but who kills his own brother, whose eyes he sees again and again until he renounces the world. Ultimately, however, he must experience the fact that even inactivity is entangled with guilt. Thomas Mann's short story *Die vertauschten Köpfe* (*The Transposed Heads*, 1940), which treats of the interaction between body and mind in a sophisticated, ironic way, also using a psychological approach, was suggested to him by a story from the *Vetālapanchavimśati* made known to him by the Indologist Heinrich Zimmer.[16]

India also had its effect on the Danish writer Karl Gjellerup (1857–1919), whose novel *Pilgrimen Kamanita* (*The Pilgrim Kamanita*), which won him the Nobel Prize, tells of a pair of lovers forcibly separated on earth and brought together with the help of the Buddha in the paradise of the west, both finally attaining *nirvāna*. In *Den Fuldentes Hustru* (*The Perfect Wife*), the Buddha's wife tries to make him abandon his renunciation, but is converted by him and becomes the leader of a religious order. Gjellerup's *Verdensvandrerne* (*The Wanderers in the World*) is based on the Indian conception of rebirth.

Leo Tolstoy (1828–1910) came in contact with Oriental literature at the University of Kazan. Gradually his intellectual interest in Indian culture led to a profound understanding of Indian thought. He amalgamated Buddhist and Hindu ideas with corresponding Christian conceptions. Tolstoy's principle of non-violence, while applicable to Christian pacifism also, was mainly modelled on Buddhist *ahimsā*, and it was largely through Tolstoy that this principle became an effective part of the life and work of Mahātmā Gāndhī.[17] Tolstoy, as author of the *Letter to a Hindu*, had a strong influence on Gāndhī,

[13] 'Like you, forerunner and brother, I too go through life zigzagging between natural ways and spirit, today a wise man, tomorrow a fool, today intimate with God, tomorrow intensely devoted to the flesh.'

[14] 'Every soul passes along the step-ladder of creation.'

[15] 'But knowing of his becoming, in becoming he has also created, has copied the forms of the ladder of being which he has climbed: the vampire, the base slave, buffoon, drunkard, and fighter.'

[16] F. Wilhelm, 'Thomas Mann über seine indische Legende', *Euphorion* Vol. 64, nos. 3–4, 1970, pp. 399 ff.

[17] Milan I. Markovitch, *Tolstoi et Gandhi*, Paris, 1928.

who regarded himself as a disciple of the Russian writer. Tolstoy congratulated him on his successful struggle in South Africa, where he founded a 'Tolstoy Farm' which was to be a faithful copy of an Indian *āshram*. Adherence to the principles of non-violence, service to mankind, and simplicity of life were as characteristic of Tolstoy in his later phase as of Gāndhī, who advocated that social and political progress should be based on moral and religious principles.

It was also through Tolstoy's influence that a famous French writer gained a deep understanding of Indian thought. This was Romain Rolland (1866–1944), called the 'Leo Tolstoy of France' by Gorky, and the 'Conscience of Europe' by Stefan Zweig. He wrote a monograph on Gāndhī, and his *Essai sur la mystique et l'action de l'Inde* treats of the Indian saint Rāmakrishna and his student Vivekānanda, on both of whom he wrote biographies. Rolland fully appreciates the combination of mystic insight and moral policy in the work of these Indian teachers and emphasizes its universal appeal. His diary (published as *Inde* in 1952) bears witness to his role of mediator between India and the West.

British rule in India resulted in the appearance of a body of Anglo-Indian literature.[18] Among the most successful of its writers was Rudyard Kipling (1865–1936), whose verdict that 'East is East, and West is West, and never the twain shall meet', out of its context,[19] has been as often taken for granted as it has been disputed. His Indian novels and short stories, such as the *Jungle Books* (1894 and 1895) and *Kim* (1901), both of which were later made into films, are adventurous blends of elements from the Indian scene. Very different was E. M. Forster's famous novel, *A Passage to India* (1924), which throws a critical light on British rule and, in the romantic symbolism of its three sections 'Mosque', 'Caves', and 'Temple', reveals a deep understanding of Indian psychology. Rumer Godden gives a fascinating description of Kashmīr in *Kingfishers Catch Fire*, which explores the effects of alien surroundings on isolated Europeans, as does her *Black Narcissus*, in which the five members of an English religious sisterhood are confronted with conditions of life in a Himālayan state which constitute a challenge they are unable to meet. In *Elephant Hill*, Robin White has written an Indian version of the chalk circle theme, in which an Indian boy is torn between his foster-father, an American missionary, and his real father—a conflict which is resolved by the missionary's sister-in-law who loves the boy's father. Two American novelists who wrote of India are Pearl Buck and Louis Bromfield. The former, better known for her books about China, wrote *Come, My Beloved*, which can be regarded as an attempt at reconciling Christian and Hindu beliefs. The novel for which Louis Bromfield became world-famous was *The Rains Came* (1937), in which the bursting of a dam constructed by Europeans in an Indian state reveals the true characters of the people concerned. James Hilton has perhaps a more symbolic intent in giving his novel *Lost Horizon* (1933) a Himalāyan setting

[18] For details, see *The Cambridge History of English Literature*, Vol. 14, Cambridge, 1961, Part 3, Ch. X.

[19] The ballad, written in 1889, goes on:

Till Earth and Sky stand presently at God's great Judgement Seat;
But there is neither East nor West, border, nor breed, nor birth,
When two strong men stand face to face, though they come from the ends of the earth.

with a Lamasery called Shangri-La preserving the spiritual treasures of mankind, a modern utopia in a world threatened by technology.

The number of travel books on India is tremendous. Ever since the Age of Discoveries, travellers, merchants, missionaries, and diplomats have written about the south Asian subcontinent, and since the end of the nineteenth century this type of literature has greatly increased. Many such books merely aim at catering for a certain European taste for Oriental glamour. Others give realistic descriptions and are of true literary worth, for example Alberto Moravia's *Un idea dell' India* (1962) and Allen Ginsberg's *Indian Journals* (1970). Some, such as *Indiabrand* (*Conflagration in India*) by Arthur Lunquist and *Indiya bez chudes* (*India without Miracles*, 1948) by O. Tshetshetkina, emphasize the economic and social aspects of modern India. The contrast between Gāndhī and Lenin is reflected in Arthur Koestler's book *The Yogi and the Commissar* (1945), but his *The Lotus and the Robot*, written after a rationalistic pilgrimage to India and Japan in 1958–9, scintillates with biting comments on Hindu Yoga.

Since the days of Friedrich Rückert (1788–1866), Western writers have made literary adaptations into their own languages of Indian works. We find several poetical versions of *Nala and Damayantī*, by Mallarmé for instance. Sanskrit poems have even been translated into such unfamiliar languages as Albanian, by Anton Zako (1866–1930), which demonstrates more clearly than do long enumerations the wide response to Indian poetry in the West. Kālidāsa's dramas, especially his *Abhijñānaśakuntala*, have been translated into nearly every European language, including Czech (by H. Hrubin) and Rumanian (by the poet Gheorghe Cosbuc, 1866–1918). *Śakuntalā* and *The Little Clay Cart*, and from modern times the plays of Rabīndranāth Tāgore (*Post Office*, etc.), have been staged in many European theatres. André Gide, who translated various works of Tāgore, voiced the then-prevalent enthusiasm for this poet: 'It seemed to me that no thinker of modern times deserved more respect, I might almost say devotion, than Tagore. I took pleasure in humbling myself before him as he had humbled himself to sing before God.'[20]

Since the second half of the nineteenth century an increasing number of Europeans have declared their faith in Indian religions. A Theosophical Society was founded by H. P. Blavatsky in 1875, and a number of neo-Buddhist sects have also come into being. Nowadays the interest in Yoga and Tantra is stronger than ever before. Madame Blavatsky had a remarkable influence on the Irish poet William Butler Yeats, who himself had founded a 'Hermetic Society'. His interest in the occult attracted him also to Indian religiosity. Three Indians played an influential role in this respect: Tāgore, Śrī Purohit Swāmī (with whom Yeats translated *The Ten Principal Upanishads*, in 1937), and Mohinī Chatterjī, who brought about his belief in rebirth. In the poem he called after the latter, Yeats writes:

> I asked if I should pray,
> But the Brahmin said,
> 'Pray for nothing, say
> Every night in bed

[20] L. Renou, *The Influence of Indian Thought on French Literature*, Adyar Library, 1948, p. 25.

"I have been a king,
I have been a slave,
Nor is there anything,
Fool, rascal, knave,
That I have not been ..."'

Attempts to spread the teaching of Rāmakrishna in the West have proved very successful. Vedāntic in its theology, it has been combined with social aims. Universal in its appeal, it regarded each religion as a 'ghāt' to the spring-water of godhead. Rāmakrishna's disciple Swāmī Vivekānanda established the Rāmakrishna Mission in 1897, three years after he had founded the Vedānta Society in New York. This mission had great influence in the United States, especially in California. Two prominent writers engaged in furthering the mission's aims were Aldous Huxley and Christopher Isherwood. The latter, together with Swāmī Prabhavānanda, translated the *Bhagavad Gītā* and Śankara's *Crest-Jewel of Discrimination.* A volume entitled *Vedanta for the Western World* was edited in 1948 by Huxley, Isherwood, G. Heard, J. van Druten, and various Indian monks. For those 'not congenitally members of an organised church', Aldous Huxley advocated the line taken by Rāmakrishna and Vivekānanda as 'the minimum working hypothesis':

> That there is a Godhead, Brahman, Clear Light of the Void, which is the unmanifested principle of all manifestation.
> That the ground is at once transcendent and immanent.
> That it is possible for human beings ... to become actually identical with the divine ground.
> That to achieve this unitive knowledge of the Godhead is the final end and purpose of human existence.

Not only Indian religion, but also Indian philosophy has occupied the minds of Western thinkers from Kant and Schopenhauer onwards. Henri Bergson compared Indian and Christian mysticism in his *Deux sources*, and recognized that the ultimate aim of the Hindu was 's'évader de la vie'; and in *Die Weltanschauung der indischen Denker* (1935),[21] Albert Schweitzer emphasized the 'life-negation' of Indian thought in contradistinction to Western beliefs as well as to those of Zarathuštra and of Chinese philosophers.

In the twentieth century science and learning are replacing a biased Western approach with a universalist attitude. The imaginary 'glass curtain' between East and West should, it is felt, be removed; and a new humanism is being postulated in place of the parochial limitations of the recent past.[22] Whereas formerly 'world histories' were confined to Europe and Asia Minor, with the writer's own country of central importance within this framework, today it stands to reason that equal rights (if not always equal space) should be conceded to other continents, as is evident from the historical works of Arnold Toynbee. Such a change in emphasis is equally valid for other sciences, for the fine arts, and for the production of modern encyclopedias.

In the field of sociology, Max Weber included Hinduism and Buddhism in his *Die Wirtschaftsethik der Weltreligionen* (1916–17). But as early as 1853 Karl Marx had started presenting his views on India's social problems in the

[21] English translation: *Indian Thought and its Development*, London and New York, 1936.
[22] R. Iyer (ed.), *The Glass Curtain between Asia and Europe*, London, 1965, pp. 329 ff.

New York Daily Tribune. While Marx restricted himself to the assumption of an 'Asiatic mode of production', Lenin imposed the Marxist theory of the five stages of historical development on the interpretation of the history of India and other Asian countries.

In works such as *Yoga und der Westen* (1936) and *Über Mandalasymbolik* (1938), the psychologist C. G. Jung showed how modern psychology could elucidate Yoga and Tantrism, and even profit by a confrontation with these systems. According to Jung, the 'psychology of the unconscious' has its counterpart in the *kleśas* (afflictions) of Indian mystical psychology, although with the basic difference that Yoga knows no moral conflict. Jung's psychology of the 'collective unconscious' was applied by Heinrich Zimmer to the interpretation of Indian myths and symbols.

As far as the fine arts are concerned, Indian influence has been restricted to occasional adaptations. John Nash was commissioned by George IV when Prince of Wales to construct the Royal Pavilion at Brighton, for example, and this became the most extravagant specimen of Mughal architecture in the West, demonstrating the nineteenth-century 'Indian taste'. In Great Britain there were even country-houses built in Indian style. Nowadays the Indian word 'bungalow' has become a widespread term in the West for the modern one-storey villa.

In India itself, colonial rule led to strange but fascinating amalgamations of European and Oriental styles of architecture. After Independence, Albert Mayer and Le Corbusier designed the new capital of the Indian state of Panjāb at Chandīgarh, which developed into a remarkable mixture of Western functionalism and Indian town-planning. Since 1968 a new cosmopolis has been under construction near Pondicherry: Auroville, named after Śrī Aurobindo. In accordance with his philosophy it is to become a city of human unity with the Temple of Truth (Mātrimandir) in the centre—a virtual *mandala* in the form of a town constructed by all nations and open to all mankind.

While East Asian, Polynesian, and African art has had a remarkable influence on modern Western painting, the appeal of India has been less evident, although there are cases in which it is apparent, such as in E. L. Kirchner's style in a picture like *Frauen im Bade*, which owes something to the representation of women in the Ajantā frescoes as depicted by Griffith. A. Kubin was devoted to Buddhism, but the inspiration for his 'Sansara' collection is to be found in the Japanese colour prints of Hokusai rather than in Indian Buddhist works. And several of Gauguin's sculptures (*Idole à la perle*, *Idole à la coquille*) are iconographically indebted to Borobudur rather than to any Indian model. The sculptor Brancusi was attracted by Indian and Tibetan mysticism (*Milaraspa*) and he designed a *Temple of Liberation* for the Mahārāja of Indore. His sculptures represent abstract conceptions, however; his wooden figure, the *Spirit of Buddha* (in the Guggenheim Museum), using the spiral as a symbol of transcendence, for example. Although there is no hint in ancient Indian literture of religious experience being induced by the use of drugs, modern psychedelic art, as exemplified in the work of A. Atwell for one, shows a predilection for *mandalas*, and names pictures after Indian concepts, for example I. Abrams's *All Things are Part of One Thing*.

In the early 1950s, Indian classical music was introduced into western Europe and North America, mainly through the pioneering efforts of Pandit Ravi Shankar and, a few years later, Ustād Alī Akbar Khān. These two eminent musicians gave concerts in many cities of the world, sometimes to small audiences and for insignificant remuneration, but their incredible technique and musicianship did not pass unnoticed, and by the beginning of the 1960s they were already performing to full concert-halls, at least in the larger cities. Admittedly the audiences often consisted mostly of Indians, but more and more Westerners were gradually being brought into the fold. As news of their success reached India, other famous musicians, such as Ustād Vilāyat Khān, Ustād Imrat Khān, Ustād Bismillah Khān, and Pandit Nikhil Bannerjee, were persuaded to visit the West and were received by groups of enthusiastic followers. Perhaps Indian music might never have reached much beyond a select audience if it were not for the fact that Yehudi Menuhin and the 'Beatles' became interested in it. Menuhin's interest was an important factor in conveying to the 'serious' musicians of the West that Indian music was a complex and sophisticated musical form which had retained a feeling of spontaneity and audience communication in spite of being a system of classical music.

Apart from the fact that there is a growing awareness of Indian music, and that a few modern composers such as Alan Hovhaness, Peter Feuchtwanger, John Barham, and Olivier Messiaen have tried to utilize elements of Indian music in their compositions, there does not appear to have been much impact on 'serious' music in the West.

The 'Beatle' involvement with Indian music and with Ravi Shankar did, however, result in a short period of hysteria when numerous 'pop' and jazz groups, and films, as well as radio and television advertisements, incorporated the sound of the *sitār* and *tablā*, largely to be in with the 'craze'. The *sitār* became fashionable, as did Ravi Shankar; Indian music was swept along on a wave of popularity, but it was clear from the outset that it was the sound of the instruments which was the focal point of the craze, not Indian music in itself. Some of the "Beatles" songs do, of course, show the influence of Indian culture, but their achievement lies rather in broadening the horizon of 'pop' music than in channelling it in any one direction. By using Indian instruments and some Indian philosophical ideas, they showed how foreign elements could be incorporated into the mainstream of Western 'pop' culture. Purely from the musical point of view, those of their compositions which are said to been influenced by Indian music are not particularly Indian, nor do they have the spirit of Indian music. One recognizes the occasional Indian motif, the *tambūrā* drone and the modal basis, but this appears to be the full extent of the influence. The unique properties of the *sitār*, for instance, the technique of producing sliding tones by deflecting the melody string sideways, have not been utilized by these 'pop' musicians. On the rare occasions when this technique has been used it has sounded like a parody, for accurate intonation by this method requires a long period of training. Perhaps the influence of Indian music on popular music in the West can be seen in the gradually increasing use of drone-like effects, the greater use of modes, and the more frequent use of melisma in the songs.

The moment of hysteria is now over, but a few more non-Indians have become seriously involved with Indian classical music. Conscious attempts at fusing Indian and Western music have not been particularly successful as yet. It would appear that most of these attempts were premature and based on an incomplete understanding of one or the other system. Ethnomusicology programmes in many universities, especially in North America, have been developing over the last decade. Some of these are focused on the music of Asia, and a better understanding of Indian music could well lead to new developments and more realistic attempts at fusion.

Apart from the large number of scholars in Europe and America who are engaged on research work in all fields of Indology, people in all walks of life in the West are once more fascinated by India. Incense sticks and *sitār*-playing, Indian hemp and the Indian look, are accessories in the life of the 'psychedelic generation'. Indian influence is apparent in 'pop' art and 'pop' music. Many young people strive for esoteric initiation. Mahāgurus from India or from the West teach the experience of unity with the universe. The use of drugs is given a religious motivation, and Vārānasī and Kāthmandu have become hippy Meccas. 'Flower power' is advocated against aggressiveness.

Never before have the achievements of technology been so conspicuous as today when man has set his foot on the moon. Despite, or in consequence of, these efforts, the influence of India, where the accent has always been on spirituality, is having a second renaissance.

CHAPTER XXXV

Conclusion

by A. L. BASHAM

This book was originally intended as a second edition of *The Legacy of India*, published in 1937. It contained fifteen chapters, written by fourteen contributors who included some of the ablest scholars of the day. Yet only four of those chapters have been retained in this volume, and that after considerable editing. The interval between the two volumes is less than forty years. Perhaps the time for writing yet a third volume on the lines of this one will come even sooner, with the rapid growth of our knowledge of the past and the even more rapid change in the world's attitudes. No book like this, even in those chapters dealing with remote antiquity, can be more than provisional. Whatever we may write about India, past, present and future, will be open to correction in coming years, and we can only draw up an interim balance-sheet. India's history, like that of many other lands, teaches the lesson of her most famous son, Gautama the Buddha, that nothing is permanent, that the most solid rocks may crumble, slowly or suddenly, that the values and institutions seemingly so securely established may gradually weaken until they become mere vestigial traces of their former selves, or may even vanish almost overnight.

Though even in the nineteenth century a few far-sighted people in Britain realized that sooner or later their imperial regime in India would come to an end, and the conviction spread during the first decades of the twentieth century, the comparative ease and speed with which the British withdrew surprised many nationalist Indians themselves. The orderly replacement of British rulers by local ones, however, was offset by immense movements of people across the borders of the two succession states of the old Indian Empire, with much bloodshed, pillage, and human suffering. The situation was worsened by actual hostilities in Kashmīr and the assassination of Mahātmā Gāndhī by a Hindu fanatic, an event which flung practically the whole of India into a mood of extreme grief. Many Western observers (especially some of the old British governing class) forecast indefinite anarchy—the return of India to the condition she was in at the end of the Mughal Empire, broken into several states with fluctuating boundaries, dominated by warlords constantly harassing and raiding one another.

That such conditions did not return was perhaps chiefly due to three factors. The first of these was the spirit of Mahātmā Gāndhī, which had for nearly thirty years inspired and disciplined the Indian National Congress and its supporters to service and self-sacrifice, and continued to do so after his death; the average Indian responded to the challenge of the times with remarkable self-discipline. Another factor was the army, police, and civil service inherited by both India and Pakistan from their former rulers. These maintained law and order and kept the machinery of government in motion in very difficult circumstances. A third factor making for stability was the very sense of freedom, the faith in the democratic process which most of the more politically minded Indians and Pakistanis had learnt, chiefly from the West. Now that their lands were free parliamentary democracies, there was reasonable hope that regional and sectional wrongs would be righted without bloodshed.

Whatever strains may have been imposed upon it, democracy has survived in India. Unlike most former colonial countries, India is a land where the critic can still freely express his dislike of the government, in the press, in the public meeting, and in the polling booth. Political consciousness, if sometimes of a rather naïve kind, has permeated every section of the population, and even the small peasant in the outlying village is aware of his power as an elector. It is this, perhaps more than any other factor, which has held India together. In Pakistan, on the other hand, democracy did not take root so firmly. With the imposition of military dictatorship the two sections of the state lost their cohesion, for the government was one of West Pakistan. Thus the Bengālī inhabitants of the Eastern wing saw no prospect of legitimately redressing their grievances, and soon their loyalty to the very idea of Pakistan began to waver, ultimately resulting in repression, carnage, and the birth of the state of Bānglādesh. Had Pakistan continued to be governed by a stable democratic system, her two wings might yet have held together. In India, on the other hand, incipient separatist movements in some parts of the country were contained and pacified because the people as a whole had faith in the ballot box.

Industrially South Asia has made much progress in the past twenty-five years. The Gāndhīan policy of local self-sufficiency based on cottage industries and small-scale production is virtually forgotten, and large-scale industry, much of it state-owned or state-controlled, is the order of the day throughout the sub-continent. Striking industrial progress has been made, though, allowing for differences of size and population, this is not as impressive as the economic progress made by certain other formerly backward countries with more uncompromisingly capitalist regimes, such as Taiwan, South Korea, and Iran—not to speak of communist China.

The material, and to some extent the cultural, progress of both India and Pakistan has been set back by the armed confrontation of the two states, occasionally boiling over into brief hostilities. The loss, both human and material, incurred by the two countries as a result of this confrontation has been very considerable, and stable peace and co-operation between India and Pakistan are absolutely essential before real prosperity can be achieved. India's efforts to raise her standards have also been set back by another factor. Following on the occupation of Tibet, China laid claim to certain frontier areas of India and proceeded to occupy them. Thus India was forced to divert a greater proportion of her national income to military expenditure, without being able to dislodge the Chinese.

Meanwhile all the nations of the sub-continent have had to face a terrible problem which at the time of partition seemed to most observers a cloud no bigger than a man's hand—the 'population explosion'. We have no clear evidence of the population of India before the nineteenth century, but there is no doubt that it was kept more or less stable by the natural factors of plague, drought, flood, and warfare. Whatever its shortcomings, the British regime produced a situation in which these factors became progressively less operative. Rudimentary health precautions, attempts at flood control and famine relief, inadequate though they might be, and the absence of enormous predatory armies overrunning large areas of the countryside all tended to lower the death-rate, especially that of small children, without raising the standard of living of the masses. The process has operated approximately by geometrical progression, and has been accelerated since independence by increased efforts at epidemic control, child welfare, and famine relief. The phenomenal growth of the population has robbed the average south Asian of most of the benefits of a greatly increased gross national product. Valiant attempts are now being made to lower the birth-rate, by methods which would have horrified earlier reformers such as Mahātmā Gāndhī. Ultimately the situation will be brought under control, whether by human effort or natural forces or, more probably, by a combination of both. But meanwhile India and her neighbours are faced with a tremendous problem unique in their history, for which no easy solution presents itself.

Nevertheless India, for all her unsolved problems, for all the shortcomings of her rulers, has cause for sober satisfaction, when she compares herself with many other former colonies. Communal, social, and regional tensions have been contained, and the country remains a single political unit. Great advances have been made in popular education and the literacy rate has risen considerably, though the standards of higher education may have declined somewhat. Industrialization has advanced so far that India has even exported the products of her heavy industry to the United States. New strains of seed, the increased use of fertilizer, and the spread of technical knowledge have greatly raised agricultural output. How is this affecting the legacy of India from her own past?

The social system based on the joint family and the caste is slowly breaking up. From the days of the Buddha, if not before, reformers had attacked the caste system, but to little real effect. It resisted the Muslim '*ulamā*' and the Christian missionaries. But now, at least in the cities, it is beginning to crumble. Though one can imagine a caste system permitting miscegenation, which in fact seems to have been possible in very early times, the Hindu lawgivers realized that the hierarchical social structure of India depended on arranged marriages. These are still the rule in India, but inter-caste marriages freely contracted between the parties concerned are becoming increasingly common, and the presence of more and more people of good social status, claiming to be Hindus but in fact having strictly no caste at all, must ultimately destroy the old social system. Steadily, moreover, the taboos associated with caste are disappearing. When the young Mohandās Gāndhī first travelled abroad, almost every respectable Hindu who crossed the seas was compelled, under penalty of complete social ostracism for himself and his family, to perform an expensive purificatory ritual on his return. Now hardly anybody bothers to do this, even among the more conservative sections of the community.

The institution of the joint family, graded heirarchically according to age and sex, is also beginning to lose its grip on India, at least among many of the educated folk in the towns, though the sense of kinship in India is still in general much stronger than in the Western world. Younger members of the family are no longer so inclined to contribute to the upkeep of impoverished relations or to carry out the wishes of their elders implicitly, especially when they have reached maturity. Industrial society and the influence of Western social ideas are chiefly responsible for these developments, and such ideas are carried to a wide range of ordinary people through the film and the popular novel, both of which, though in theory respecting traditional values, exploit the Romeo-and-Juliet theme with telling effect, with the variation that the star-crossed lovers are often members of different castes. Though one cannot foretell with confidence, it seems that, if modern trends continue, in fifty years' time the social and family system of India will be little different from that of the contemporary West. This forecast is not necessarily made in a spirit of hope or optimism, for the caste and the family have in earlier times been potent sources of material and psychological security for the individual, and they cannot be satisfactorily replaced by the state on the one hand and the small nuclear family on the other. But already the old Hindu family law has been abrogated, replaced by a new code, modelled largely on that of the West. Divorce is now possible both for wives and husbands, monogamy is enforced, and women are entitled to possess property of their own.

In politics there have been conscious attempts to revive the past in a new form, and to fit traditional Indian conceptions into the framework of twentieth-century democracy. The process began early in the present century, when able historians like R. K. Mookerjee showed with some justification that certain villages in ancient and medieval India had local semi-democratic ruling bodies, and when K. P. Jayaswāl, a competent Sanskritist, proved to his own and his readers' satisfaction that ancient India had republics and constitutional monarchies, with popular assemblies and cabinet government. Jayaswāl's handling of his sources verged on the unscrupulous, like the clever barrister, who by taking a crucial phrase out of its context and interpreting its words in a forced, unnatural manner, succeeds in persuading judge and jury that it means something completely different from what its author obviously intended. But Jayaswāl succeeded in convincing a wide audience of educated Indians that constitutional democracy and limited monarchy were well known to their remoter ancestors, and there was some truth in his arguments, though his claims were greatly exaggerated.

Thus the ancient texts on polity have been ransacked for apophthegms on statecraft appropriate to contemporary progressive democracy, socialism, and the welfare state. Even Indian communists have utilized their country's ancient literature to further their ends. But this is hardly evidence of the survival of India's political legacy, but rather the use of that legacy, otherwise almost forgotten except in academic circles, to support political concepts which are in fact modern imports.

The hereditary is still strong in many aspects of Indian life, but the Indian tradition of monarchy has been undermined by contemporary values. The Hindu of earlier centuries was used to obeying a charismatic hereditary ruler who lived in great luxury and pomp and was thought by many of his subjects to be in some sense divine. The Muslim sultans, *bādshāhs*, and *nawābs* did not claim divinity but the justification of hereditary principles was made by their apologists. They too lived in luxury and pomp, far above the heads of their subjects. The British rulers of India, especially after the Sepoy Revolt, recognized this tradition in Indian political life and preserved the mahārājas as tributary kings, while their viceroys enjoyed a pomp and circumstance hardly equalled by that of the British monarchs whom they represented.

The events of 1947 changed all this. Gāndhīan ethics on the one hand and progressive Western political ideas on the other were not particularly favourable even to limited monarchy, far less to that of a king hedged about with charismatic splendour. In this Hindu India was definitely untrue to her traditions, and one wonders whether she did not make a mistake in this respect. Shortly before independence, when the Cabinet Mission of 1946 was vainly attempting to bring Hindus and Muslims together in a last effort to avoid partition, a number of fairly important Indians put forward a suggestion that received very little publicity and no support whatever. This was to the effect that, when the British withdrew from India, power should lawfully rest with the Mughal Empire, in the person of the closest surviving relative of the last emperor, Bahādur Shāh II, who died in exile in 1862. This man, it was suggested, should become the constitutional emperor of a free India.

Such a suggestion had no hope of acceptance by the political leaders in the atmosphere of the times. It was, however, in keeping with India's traditions, and it had the advantage that it would have effectively prevented the partition of the country, for a restored Mughal emperor, ruling from Delhi, would surely have won enough Muslim support to undermine the movement for Pakistan. From the point of view of strict legality, it may have been the right thing to do. One wonders how India would have fared if this suggestion had been adopted. As it is, even the tributary mahārājas have lost all their powers and privileges and much of their wealth, so strongly has the twentieth century affected the thought of India's rulers. Possibly in many of the former princely states the common man still feels respect, and in some cases affection also, for his former ruler and his family, but it seems that the tradition of monarchy has gone for ever in India, as it has in most other parts of the world. India is certainly less colourful as a result.

In one respect, however, the Indian government has consciously tried to revive past political traditions. This is in the establishment of elected village councils, continuing the tradition of the *panchāyats*. These committees of about five village elders, generally the most substantial peasants of the community, usually holding office by heredity or appointed by co-option, were most vigorous when the central government was weak. They declined in influence in British days, but they are now again active, as small democratic units of the governmental system.

In the field of the arts the fate of India's ancient heritage has varied. The classical tradition of music, once reserved for the rich, is now available to much larger audiences through the radio and the electronically amplified performance in a large hall. A unique genre of popular music, a hybrid of Indian and Western conventions, commonly known as *filmī gīt* ('film song') is immensely popular. Decried by conservatives and purists, it is nevertheless (in the opinion of one observer at least) among the finest music of its kind composed anywhere in the world. The wonderful traditions of the Indian dance (an aspect of the legacy of India which we have not been able to cover in this book), once mainly exploited by *devadāsīs* (temple prostitutes) and courtesans, have been made respectable, and classical dances are performed before large audiences. On the other hand Western dancing, whether ballet or ballroom, has not 'caught on', and few Indians are interested in it.

In the field of the visual arts the ancient traditions, whether Hindu or Muslim, have virtually disappeared. Modern buildings, often in hybrid Hindu-Muslim styles with a few twentieth-century functional features added for good measure, have appeared in all the great cities, alongside others which have nothing distinctively Indian about them at all. Architecturally the latter are usually the more pleasing. The wonderful traditions of Hindu classical sculpture have been dead for many centuries. Now sculpture is perhaps the weakest of the arts in India, and few traces of the Indian tradition are to be seen in the products of post-independence ateliers. The tradition of Indian painting seems also to be lost. In the closing years of the last century a group of able Bengālī artists, led by Abanīndranāth Tāgore, brother of the great poet, tried to develop a typically Indian style of painting, based on the murals of Ajantā and the Rājput and Pahārī miniature schools, but this school, its productions always rather effeminate, survives only in the humbler fields of applied painting, such as book illustration and the designing of greeting cards. Later the greatest of modern Indian painters, Jāminī Roy, developed a very personal style based on the folk art of his native Bengal. His followers, like those of Abanīndranāth Tāgore, are now mainly concerned with the production of advertisements and greeting cards. The woman painter Amritā Sher Gil, half-Sikh and half-Hungarian, developed a beautiful and individual style, but it was more European than Indian in inspiration, though she painted Indian subjects. Now there is probably no good Indian painting, though there is plenty of good painting in India. The work of the best painters of modern India is not true Indian painting—it is international painting which happens to be produced by Indians.

Literature flourishes. Probably more poems are composed in India, in proportion to the population, than in any part of Europe or America, though the Far East and Iran may rival India in this. Poems are still composed according to strict conventions and traditions, especially in Urdū, but here too the influence of the West is apparent, and all the major trends in Western poetry writing have had their impact on India. The novel and short story also flourish, in all the languages of India including English. Here too the influence of the West is felt, but of course the tradition is also in evidence. The stories of the epics and *Purānas* provide most Indian writers with material for metaphors and similes, as, until recently, the Bible and the classical world provided an easily available stock of allusions to writers of Europe and America.

Nowadays the most popular form of aesthetic entertainment, for the average Indian, is the film. The Western observer, who has seen only a few Indian films of the very highest quality, such as those made by Satyajit Ray, may obtain a very false impression of the character of the more popular cinema. The 'highbrow' Indian film may give a vivid, accurate, and moving picture of one or other aspect of Indian life, but its style and technique are essentially international. The legacy of the past survives better (some would say in a degenerate and perverted form) in the popular films made by the big commercial film companies of Bombay and Madras. These films of epic length, immensely popular with the masses, were once divided into two broad classess, according to the terminology of their distributors, 'mythological' and 'social', with a third, smaller category 'historical', giving thoroughly inaccurate pictures of the great men and women of India from Chandragupta Maurya to the Rānī of Jhānsī. Nowadays 'mythological' films, telling very freely adapted stories of the gods and heroes, with many interludes of song and dance and wonderful effects produced by trick photography, are becoming progressively less popular, and few are made. The emphasis of Indian production is on the 'social' film, dealing with contemporary and near-contemporary life. Here the influence of Hollywood is clearly in evidence, but nevertheless these films have a distinctively Indian flavour which commercialism cannot suppress, for the public will not have it otherwise. Intense melodrama, tear-jerking partings and reunions, the hero or heroine (or both) saved from a dreadful fate at the last minute, the conventional exaggerated over-acting, much reinforced by carefully controlled gestures, the regular interpolation of songs and dances, without which the average film-goer would demand the return of his admission fee—all these features show a striking continuity with the ancient Indian dramatic tradition, particularly as exemplified by such plays as Śūdraka's *Little Clay Cart* and Bhavabhūti's *Mālatī and Mādhava*. It is very doubtful if there has been any conscious transmission of the dramatic tradition from the Sanskrit play to the film—rather the taste of the Indian audience has remained stable over the centuries, and still demands the same strong simple melodrama as it did in the past. It is fashionable among educated Indians to decry the popular film (though many of them are its secret devotees); but it is in a class by itself, and in its techniques, though not always in its content, it is thoroughly in line with the Indian dramatic tradition. Moreover its pleasant songs and delightful dances provide evidence of how Indian culture can still absorb foreign elements and make them distinctively its own.

Only two of the ancient sciences of India continue as effective elements in the life of the country. The traditional Indian systems of medicine, the Hindu *āyurveda* and the Perso-Islamic *yūnānī*, are still very active. Both these systems, though based in their classical forms on false premisses, are pragmatically effective in curing and relieving many diseases, and their drugs and therapy are less expensive than those of modern Western medicine. Thus *āyurveda* in India and *yūnānī* medicine in both India and Pakistan still have an important part to play in maintaining the health of the people, especially of the poorer people. In India āyurvedic practitioners are trained at special schools, some of them attached to universities, where they learn the elements of scientific physiology and biology as well as traditional medical lore. Whether traditional medicine will survive once India becomes rich enough to establish free and comprehensive medical services on the Western model is not certain, but meanwhile it is very important in contributing to the well-being of the poorer folk. In this connection notice should be taken of a medical system, imported from the West, where it is now almost forgotten, though in India it still flourishes. This is homoeopathy. Every city of India has many homoeopathic pharmacies, which still do a lively trade, and often claim spectacular cures.

The other traditional science of India which appears to be as thriving as ever is astrology. The highly reputed practitioners of this art seem to find as many wealthy patrons as ever, and the roadside astrologer, who will cast a horoscope for a rupee, still flourishes in town and village. Probably almost every ordinary Hindu even now believes in the power of the astrologer to forecast his future, and most educated Hindus, even those who claim to be rationalists with no faith in the gods, still look on his art with a degree of grudging respect. This pseudo-science, incidentally, is a comparative late-comer on the Indian scene. No Indian astrological text is earlier than the Gupta period, before which time prognostication was carried out mainly by the study of physiognomy, birth-marks, and portents. Astrology came to India from the West, probably in the wake of the trade with the Roman Empire.

Though the orthodox, both Hindu and Muslim, complain of the decline of faith, it seems that it is in her religious life that India's ancient heritage is best preserved. On the other hand the number of worshippers attending the great festivals or the more famous temples is said to be decreasing, and the priests, feeling that there is no future in their profession, are said to be training their sons in other trades and crafts. In South India the long-standing anti-brāhman movement has a lively anti-religious wing, which stages demonstrations near famous temples, and displays posters bearing crudely vigorous cartoons which pour scorn on the gods.

Nevertheless the traveller is far more likely to be impressed by the vitality of India's religious life than by its decline. Hindu reform movements, such as the Rāmakrishna Mission, expand their activities. The temples are thronged on festival days. As in the days of the Buddha, young men still abandon their homes and become penniless mendicants in search of the divine, and the old men, feeling that the world is too much with them, still give up their professional and family affairs in order to prepare for the next life. New *swāmīs* and *gurus* appear every year, and draw large followings, often including well-educated people and followers from the Western world. Even the myth-making capacity of Hinduism, so vigorous in earlier centuries, is still alive. This is proved by the appearance of a wholly new divinity, the goddess Santoshī Mātā, who was unheard of in 1960, but is now worshipped widely throughout the Gangā plain as a bringer of good luck and material advantage, and has been equipped with a mythology and legend of her own. Another divinity, of somewhat earlier origin, whose creator was the nineteenth-century Bengali novelist Bankim Chandra Chatterjee, is Bhārat Mātā, Mother India, who has shrines here and there, and in Vārānasī is worshipped in a special temple where a large map of India replaces the sacred image. But though evidence of patriotic fervour is not lacking in modern India, Bhārat Mātā has never achieved the popularity of Santoshī.

The most vigorous features of modern Hinduism are to be found in popular manifestations of simple faith (*bhakti*), rather than in the intellectual religion of the philosopical schools. In the great religious centres such as Vārānasī and Mathurā the traditional pandits' training colleges are still there, and attract many students, but their principals complain that the annual intake is diminishing, as is the intellectual standard of the students. Similarly, as with the classics in Western universities, the number of university students taking Sanskrit or the Muslim classical languages, Arabic and Persian, has diminished considerably since independence. Thus it is the grass roots of Hinduism that seem to show the strongest persistence, rather than the fine flowers of mystical philosophy.

One significant feature of the Indian religious scene, especially in Mahārāshtra, is the revival of Buddhism. After the coming of the Muslims Buddhism virtually disappeared from most parts of India, surviving only in the hills of the North. It began to return early in this century, when the Mahābodhi Society, based on Ceylon, established new monasteries at the sacred sites of Buddhism and increasingly attracted the attention of intelligent young Indians. In recent years it has received a great accession of strength as a result of the conversion of the great untouchable leader, the late Dr B. R. Ambedkar, who, mainly no doubt out of inner conviction but also in order to raise the status of his followers in their own eyes and in the eyes of the world, proclaimed himself a Buddhist and was imitated by large numbers of his followers. At first it appeared that this was merely a political gesture, and their profession of a new faith had very little effect on the lives of the converts. But Theravāda missionary monks from Ceylon and South-East Asia began to take an interest in these humble people, and the neo-Buddhists now have an active religious life. They number over a million.

Islam maintains its hold on its followers in India and Pakistan. Of all the great world religions this one is perhaps least affected by contemporary tendencies to doubt and unbelief. In Pakistan, founded by Muslims and for Muslims, everything is done to further the faith. India is officially a secular state, but understandably it has a certain leaning towards Hinduism. Yet the Muslim citizens of India do not appear to suffer any legal disadvantages, and their personal law regarding marriage, inheritance, and the administration of endowments remains secure and guaranteed.

Of the lesser Indian religious communities the Sikhs hold their own and claim to be gaining converts. Some of their younger members are restless under the restrictions of the faith, and, when removed from parental control, cut their hair, shave their beards, and smoke tobacco, but they rarely renounce their religion altogether. The same is true of the Indian Christians, who also claim to be gaining converts, although foreign missionary propaganda is now forbidden in India.

Though India's religious life is thus still very vigorous, much of the earnest ethical quality implanted in the social life of India by Mahātmā Gāndhī has been lost. Many religious bodies still work for the welfare of the masses, but the *Sarvodaya* movement is little heard of nowadays. This movement was founded by Vinobā Bhāve on Gāndhīan principles to bring about village uplift, and especially the improvement of the lot of landless and near-landless peasants by the voluntary gift of land on the part of richer villagers. *Sarvodaya* was very active immediately after independence, and many sympathetic observers believed that it might ultimately change the face of rural India. But it has had little effect. In fact in present-day India the most important work for the uplift of the underprivileged is done by state agencies.

And what of the world's legacy from India? In fields of literature, music, and the arts this has been far from negligible, but it can be overestimated. Some of India's religious literature has made a considerable impression on the Western world, but this has been in respect of its spiritual content rather than its literary form. No classical Indian author is so well known in the English-speaking world as the Persian Omar Khayyám, thanks to Fitzgerald, or the Chinese Li Po, thanks to Arthur Waley. Germany has done better in producing literary translations of classical Indian literature, but even in German one would hardly claim that classical Indian literature had had a major impact. An exception, for a while, was Tāgore, who in the twenty years following his winning the Nobel Prize was widely read and admired, and was translated into many languages. Since then his writings have lost ground in the West, though they are still much loved and respected in India.

In music the influence of India has been even less significant, until very recently, when the *sitār* has been introduced into popular music. Nevertheless, as pointed out in the previous chapter, the influence of India on Western popular music is more apparent than real. The same is true of Western art, though Indian classical sculpture has been increasingly admired in the present century, and had some influence on Rodin and Epstein.

The influence of India on the rest of the world has always been most strongly felt in the fields of religion and philosophy, and this is still the case. It is easy to overemphasize the religious content of traditional Indian culture —at all times, but especially at the present time, the land has known a vigorous secular life. But from the time when Charles Wilkins first translated the *Bhagavad Gītā* into a European language, and Anquetil Duperron the *Upanishads*, it has been the 'spirituality' of India that has made the greatest impression on the Western observer. The previous chapter has shown how, over the last two centuries, the life of the West has been subtly affected by Indian religious ideas, even though it may not be fully conscious of this.

Since Keshub Chandra Sen lectured with great success in Victorian England, a series of Indian sages, *swāmīs*, mystics, thaumaturges and yoga practitioners have followed his footsteps to Europe and America, with varying success. Already before the original *Legacy of India* was published, the percipient philosopher Dr C. E. M. Joad, with his eye mainly on Professor Rādhākrishnan, could write about a cultural 'counter-attack from the East'. Since those days the counter-attack has intensified, especially after the Second World War, when many people in the Western world have lost faith in their traditional religious values. The widespread psychological insecurity of an age without belief, the lonely inner agony of individuals who feel isolated in a cold and unfriendly cosmos immeasurable in its vacuities, have led many to turn to India in search of solace and strength. The 'counter-attack from the East' has generally been inspired by intellectual Vedānta and has had most impact upon the well educated. It appealed to philosophers and literary men, such as

Schopenhauer, Emerson, and Aldous Huxley. Some of the most impressive recent developments, however, are making a wider appeal, and are affecting other classes and categories of the people of the West.

Thus the streamlined Vedānta of neo-Hindu propagandists has found a wider response than ever before. Some have turned to the sexual mysticism of the *Tantras*, in an age when widespread knowledge of simple and secure contraceptive techniques has so much altered the sexual life of the world. Modern India is now filled with young men and women of all nationalities from Europe, America, and Australia, most of them living very simply and some suffering real hunger, who have come in search of what to them will be the truth, of a deep wisdom beyond words which they hope will bring them peace of mind and a stable bliss transcending any of the fugitive and inadequate substitutes provided by sex, wine, or drugs. Few really find what they were seeking, but many return happier and wiser than when they set out on their pilgrimage.

Yoga has become popular in many circles in the Western world, and regular yoga classes are held in almost every city of Western Europe, America, and Australia. Usually the form of yoga taught by Western practitioners is based on the Indian *hatha-yoga*, ranging from simple breathing exercises to complicated and difficult acrobatics, and most of those who attend yoga classes seem primarily interested in promoting their health and longevity rather than their spiritual welfare. Among such forms of mystical and psychic training the 'Transcendental Meditation' of Mahesh Mahārishi has achieved fame since it was taken up some years ago by a number of popular entertainers, who gave it considerable publicity. The methods of the Mahārishi in inducing a state of meditation, with a minimum of preliminary training and metaphysical presuppositions, are followed by a growing number of people, and their pragmatic effectiveness in relieving tension has been proved by controlled physiological and psychological tests.

A new aspect of the counter-attack from the East is the importation not only of the mystical gnosis of India, but also of her simple faith. This is chiefly the work of what is generally called the Hare Krishna movement, founded by Swāmī Prabhupāda. This society now has branches in many of the larger cities of the West and its adherents follow the rituals of the devotional Vaishnavism of the Chaitanya Sect of Bengal, wearing orthodox Hindu dress and dancing and singing in the streets. The movement is looked on by most of the Western public with some amusement, and its members are thought of as harmless cranks, but, whatever the public reaction to the Hare Krishna cult, it is historically very significant, for now, for the first time since the days of the Roman Empire, an Asian religion is being openly practised by people of Western origin in the streets of Western cities.

Throughout the world the speed of change grows faster, and two opposed trends make themselves felt with increasing force. The first is the tendency for culture to become one and the same, with slight regional variations according to climate. This can be seen already in architecture, art, and music, and to a lesser extent in the general values of civilization. The other tendency is a reaction against this, an attempt to preserve the traditions of national and regional cultures against the pressure of twentieth-century technology, which makes for greater uniformity, and against other pressures, often of a political type, which tend in the same direction. Both trends are to be seen in contemporary India.

Many qualified observers at the present time would say that the first tendency, the tendency towards international uniformity, is bound to triumph, in India as elsewhere, within another generation or two. But certain cultural traditions seem to have considerable power of survival, and we cannot be sure. Indian art and architecture, as distinct from international art and architecture practised by Indians, may be dead or dying. The future literature of India may only differ from that of the rest of the world in respect of its languages and subject-matter. Yet there are some aspects of life and thought which go deeper than aesthetics, or than artistic and literary fashions and styles. The Indian tradition of a hierarchically graded society may yet survive, but in a form rather different from the traditional caste system. The intense feeling of kinship which seems common to almost all Indians, whatever their religion, may persist even after the break up of the joint family.

Throughout the history of India for more than 2,500 years many men and women have been striving for *moksha*, release from the bonds of transmigration in a state of bliss believed to be permanent and unchanging. Different sects interpret this in different ways. For the Buddhist it is the impersonal, ineffable state of *nirvāna*. For the Jain it is the complete isolation of the soul in *kaivalya*. For the Vedāntic Hindu it is the full realization of the identity of *ātmā*, the individual soul, and *brahman*, the impersonal world-spirit. For the Hindu who practises *bhakti* it is union with God. This quest has not been by any means the only driving force in the life of India—the myth of India as a land wholly devoted to religious values and aims is absolutely false of any period of Indian history, perhaps most of all of the present day. But it is a fact that in the past this aim, *moksha*, has been looked on by almost every Indian (the Muslims having their own terminology for it) as in theory the final goal of all men, for which they should strive at least indirectly. The theoretical purpose of the whole social and political structure of classical India was to promote *moksha*—to help as many individuals as possible to achieve it. The complex social order of Hinduism existed primarily to serve this end, and the state was there to promote the well-being of society. Prior to the state was the social order, and prior to the social order was the individual, striving in the best way he could for salvation. We emphasize the word 'individual' here, because despite all appearances to the contrary the thought of India is essentially individualist. The ancient Indian seer, unlike the Chinese sage or the Hebrew prophet, thought not in terms of the salvation of the whole people, an aim which he believed to be impossible in an age of decline, but of the salvation of individual men and women. This fundamental individualism is perhaps the reason why India, unlike most other former colonial countries, has taken so enthusiastically to parliamentary democracy, where ultimate political power is in the hands of an enormous number of individuals, each casting his vote alone and in secret.

The Indian quest for *moksha* goes on, and there is no reason why it should not remain the aim of the India of the future. It may express itself in new, non-religious terms, but this concept, which has been the desire of India for so long, and the search for which has given direction and point to many of her best minds through all her vicissitudes, will not, we believe, disappear, whatever the technological or political forces which affect India in the latter part of the twentieth century. The highest common factor of the various legacies of India is simply the message that there are values more important than material ones, that prosperity and political power are not the ultimate tests of a nation's greatness or of the greatness of an individual, that there are aims and purposes in man's existence which override even the claims of society and the state. Alone, as best he can, whether by acceptance or detachment, the wise man strives for a harmony transcending the temporal, a peace passing all understanding. Few reach that goal—but the secret of the good life is to travel hopefully towards it.

BOOKS FOR FURTHER READING

(Except where mentioned the titles are provided by the authors of the chapters concerned)

CHAPTER I

Introduction

(Some general books on South Asia)

Basham, A. L. *The wonder that was India.* 3rd ed., London, 1967.

De Bary, W. Th. (ed.). *Sources of Indian tradition.* New York, 1958.

Dodwell, H. H. (ed.). *The Cambridge history of India.* 6 vols. and supplement (vol. ii has not appeared), Cambridge, 1922–53.

Mahar, J. Michael. *India: A critical bibliography.* Tucson, Arizona, 1964.

Majumdar, D. N. *Races and cultures of India.* 4th ed., Bombay, 1961.

Majumdar, R. C. (ed.). *History and culture of the Indian people.* 11 vols. London, Bombay, 1952–65.

Singhal, D. P. *India and world civilization.* 2 vols. Michigan State University, 1969.

Smith, V. A., ed. Spear, T. G. P. *The Oxford history of India.* Revised ed., Oxford, 1958.

Spate, O. H. K. *India and Pakistan: a general and regional geography.* 3rd ed., London, 1967.

CHAPTER II

The Indus Civilization

(compiled by the Editor)

Allchin, Bridget and Raymond. *The birth of Indian civilization.* Harmondsworth, 1968.

Fairservis, Walter A., Jr. *The roots of Ancient India.* New York, 1971.

Gordon, D. H. *The prehistoric background of Indian culture.* Bombay, 1958.

Lal, B. B. *Indian archaeology since Independence.* Delhi, 1964.

Marshall, Sir John. *Mohenjo-Daro and the Indus civilization.* 3 vols., London, 1931.

Piggott, Stuart. *Prehistoric India.* Harmondsworth, 1950 (and reprints).

Sankalia, H. D. *Prehistory and protohistory in India and Pakistan.* Bombay, 1962.

Sankalia, H. D. *Indian archaeology today.* Bombay, 1962.

Subbarao, B. *The Personality of India.* 2nd ed., Baroda, 1958.

Wheeler, Sir R. E. Mortimer. *Early India and Pakistan.* London, 1959.

Wheeler, Sir R. E. Mortimer. *The Indus civilization.* 3rd ed., Cambridge, 1968.

CHAPTER III

The Early Aryans

Childe, V. G. *The Aryans: a study of Indo-European origins*. London, 1926.

Crossland, R. A. 'Immigrants from the North', *Cambridge Ancient History*, Vol. I, Chapter XXVII. Cambridge, 1967.

Geiger, W. 'La Civilisation des Aryas', *Le Museon*, III, pp. 430–438, and IV, pp. 11–36.

La Vallée Poussin, L. de. *Indo-Européens et Indo-Iraniens: l'Inde jusque vers 300 av. J.C.* Paris, 1924.

Mayrhofer, M. *Die Indo-Arier im alten Vorderasien*. Wiesbaden, 1966.

Piggott, S. *Prehistoric India to 1000 B.C.* London, 1962.

Thieme, P. 'The "Aryan" gods of the Mitanni treaties', *Journal of the American Oriental Society*, Vol. 80 (1960), pp. 301 ff.

CHAPTER IV

The Early Dravidians

Asher, R. E. (ed.). *Proceedings of the second international conference-seminar of Tamil studies, Madras, 1968*. Vol. I. Madras, 1971.

Caldwell, R. *A comparative grammar of the Dravidian or South-Indian family of languages*. 3rd ed., London, 1913.

Daniélou, Alain (tr.). *Shilappadikaram* (*The Ankle Bracelet*). London, 1967.

Kailasapathy, K. *Tamil heroic poetry*. Oxford, 1968.

Lahovary, N. *Dravidian origins and the West*. Bombay, 1963.

Mahadevan, I. 'Corpus of the Tamil Brahmi inscriptions', in *Seminar on inscriptions*, pp. 57–73. Madras, 1966.

Marr, John R. 'Letterature dravidiche', in *Storia delle letterature d'Oriente*, Vol. IV, pp. 559–626. Milano, 1969.

McCrindle, J. W. *Ancient India*. Vol. IV. Bombay, 1885.

Nilakanta Sastri, K. A. *The culture and history of the Tamils*. Calcutta, 1964.

Nilakanta Sastri, K. A. *Foreign notices of South India*. Madras, 1939.

Nilakanta Sastri, K. A. *A history of South India*. 3rd ed., Madras, 1966.

Parpola, Asko, and others. *Decipherment of the Proto-Dravidian inscriptions of the Indus civilization*. Scandinavian Institute of Asian Studies Special Publications Nos. 1 to 3. Copenhagen, 1969–70.

Schoff, W. H. (tr.). *Periplus of the Erythraean Sea*, with translation and annotation. Philadelphia, 1912.

Thani Nayagam, X. S. (ed.). *Proceedings of the first international conference-seminar of Tamil studies. Kuala Lumpur, 1966*. Vol. I. Kuala Lumpur, 1968.

CHAPTER V

Aśokan India and the Gupta Age

Kosambi, D. D. *The culture and civilisation of Ancient India*. London, 1965.

Majumdar, R. C. (ed.). *The Gupta-Vakataka age*. Lahore, 1946.

Majumdar, R. C. (ed.). *History and culture of the Indian people*. Vol. III. *The classical age*. Bombay, 1954.
Narain, A. K. *The Indo-Greeks*. Oxford, 1957.
Nilakanta Sastri, K. A. (ed.). *A comprehensive history of India*. Vol. II. Calcutta, 1957.
Subrahmanian, N. *Sangam Polity*. Bombay, 1966.
Thapar, R. *Aśoka and the decline of the Mauryas*. Oxford, 1961.
Warmington, E. H. *Commerce between the Roman Empire and India*. Cambridge, 1928.
Wheeler, R. E. M. *Rome beyond the Imperial frontiers*. London, 1957.
Yazdani, G. (ed.). *The early history of the Deccan*. London, 1960.

CHAPTER VI

Medieval Hindu India

Devahuti, D. *Harsha, a political study*. Oxford, 1970.
Gopal, Lallanji. *The economic life of northern India* (*c. A.D. 700–1200*). Delhi, 1965.
Nazim, Muhammad. *Sultan Mahmud of Ghazna*. Cambridge, 1931.
Nilakanta Sastri, K. A. *The Colas*. 2nd ed., Madras, 1955.
Ray, H. C. *The dynastic history of northern India*. 2 vols., Calcutta, 1931–36.
Sewell, Robert. *A forgotten empire* (*Vijayanagar*). London, 1924. (First ed. 1900).
Sharma, Brij Narain. *Social life in northern India* (*A.D. 600–1000*). Delhi, 1966.
Sharma, R. S. *Indian feudalism c. 300–1200*. Calcutta, 1965.
Tod, James. *Annals and antiquities of Rajasthan*. Rev. ed., 2 vols., London, 1957–60 (first published, 1829).
Tripathi, R. S. *History of Kanauj*. Benares, 1937 (reprints).

CHAPTER VII

Hinduism

(compiled by the Editor)

Carpenter, J. Estlin. *Theism in medieval India*. London, 1921.
Crooke, W. *Religion and folklore of northern India*. 2 vols., Oxford, 1926.
Eliade, M., tr. Trask, W. R. *Yoga, immortality and freedom*. (Bollingen series No. 56), New York, 1958.
Farquhar, J. N. *An outline of the religious literature of India*. 2nd ed., Oxford, 1920 (Indian reprint, 1967).
Farquhar, J. N. *A primer of Hinduism*. 2nd ed., Oxford, 1912.
Gonda, J. *Aspects of early Viṣṇuism*. 2nd ed., Delhi, 1969.
Gonda, J. *Viṣṇuism and Śivaism. A comparison*. London, 1970.
Jaiswal, Suvira. *The origin and development of Vaiṣṇavism*. Delhi, 1967.

Kane, P. V. *History of Dharmaśāstra.* 5 vols., Poona, 1930–62. (For reference.)

Mahadevan, T. M. P. *Outlines of Hinduism.* 2nd ed., Bombay, 1960.

Radhakrishnan, S. *Eastern religions and western thought.* 2nd ed., Oxford, 1940.

Radhakrishnan, S. *The Hindu view of life.* 10th impression, London, 1957.

Singer, Milton (ed.). *Krishna: myths, rites, and attitudes.* Honolulu, 1966.

Walker, Benjamin. *Hindu World.* 2 vols, London, 1969. (For reference.)

Zaehner, R. C. *Hinduism.* Oxford, 1962.

CHAPTER VIII

Buddhism

(compiled by the Editor)

Bareau, A. *Les sectes bouddhiques du Petit Véhicule.* Paris, 1955.

Conze, E. *Buddhism, its essence and development.* Oxford, 1951.

Conze, E. *Buddhist thought in India.* London, 1962.

Dasgupta, S. B. *Introduction to Tantric Buddhism.* 2nd ed., Calcutta, 1958.

Keith, A. B. *Buddhist philosophy in India and Ceylon.* Oxford, 1923.

Lamotte, É. *Histoire du Bouddhisme indien.* Vol. I. Louvain, 1958.

Murti, T. R. V. *The central philosophy of Buddhism.* London, 1955.

Robinson, R. H. *The Buddhist religion.* Calcutta, 1970.

Stcherbatsky, T. *Conception of Buddhist Nirvana.* Leningrad, 1927 (reprint, The Hague, 1965).

Thomas, E. J. *History of Buddhist thought.* London, 1933 (reprint, 1958).

Thomas, E. J. *The life of the Buddha as legend and history.* London, 1927 (revised ed., 1951).

Warder, A. K. *Indian Buddhism.* Varanasi, 1970.

CHAPTER IX

Jainism

Basham, A. L. *History and doctrines of the Ājīvikas.* London, 1951. (For the historical background of early Jainism.)

Glasenapp, H. von. *Der Jainismus.* Berlin, 1925 (photographic reproduction, 1964).

Handiqui, K. K. *Yaśastilaka and Indian culture.* Sholapur, 1949.

Jaini, J. L. *Outlines of Jainism.* Oxford, 1916 (revised ed., 1940).

Kalaghatgi, T. G. *Some problems in Jaina psychology.* Dharwar, 1961.

Mehta, M. L. *Jaina psychology.* Amritsar, 1956.

Padmarajiah, Y. J. *Jaina theories of reality and knowledge.* Bombay, 1963.

Renou, L. *Religions of ancient India.* London, 1953.

Schubring, W. *Die Lehre der Jainas nach den alten Quellen dargestellt.* (*Grundriss,* III, 7). Berlin, 1935 (English translation, Delhi, 1962).

Tatia, N. *Studies in Jaina philosophy*. Banaras, 1951.
Williams, R. *Jaina yoga*. London, 1963.

CHAPTER X

Philosophy

(compiled by the Editor)

Chatterjee, S. and Datta, D. M. *An Introduction to Indian philosophy*. 5th ed., Calcutta, 1954.
Dasgupta, S. N. *A history of Indian philosophy*. 5 vols., Cambridge, 1922–55.
Dasgupta, S. N. *Yoga philosophy in relation to other systems of Indian thought*. Calcutta, 1930.
Datta, D. M. *Six ways of knowing*. 2nd ed., Calcutta, 1960.
Hiriyanna, M. *The essentials of Indian philosophy*. London, 1949.
Keith, A. B. *Indian logic and atomism*. Oxford, 1921.
Müller, F. Max. *The six systems of Indian philosophy*. London, 1919 (reprint).
Potter, Karl H. *Presuppositions of India's philosophies*. Englewood Cliffs, N.J., 1963.
Radhakrishnan, S. *Indian philosophy*. Revised ed., 2 vols., London, 1958.
Radhakrishnan, S. and Moore, C. A. *A source book of Indian philosophy*. Princeton, 1957.
Srinivasachari, P. N. *Advaita and Viśiṣṭādvaita*. Bombay, 1961.

CHAPTER XI

Social and Political Thought and Institutions

Aiyangar, K. V. Rangaswami. *Aspects of ancient Indian economic thought*. Banares, 1934.
Aiyangar, K. V. Rangaswami. *Aspects of the social and political system of Manusmṛti*. Lucknow, 1949.
Altekar, A. S. *State and government in ancient India*. 4th ed., Delhi, 1962.
Chatterjee, Heramba. *Law of debt in ancient India*. Calcutta, 1971.
Derrett, J. D. M. *Religion, law and the state in India*. London, 1968.
Ghoshal, U. N. *History of Indian political ideas*. Bombay, 1959.
Gonda, J. 'Ancient Indian kingship from the religious point of view.' *Numen*, Leiden, Vols. III–IV, 1956–57. Reprinted, Leiden, 1966.
Heesterman, J. C. *The ancient Indian royal consecration*. The Hague, 1957.
Kane, P. V. 'Rājadharma.' *History of Dharmaśāstra*, Vol. III, pp. 1–241. Poona, 1946.
Lingat, Robert. *The classical law of India*. Berkeley, 1972.
Losch, Hans. *Rājadharma*. Bonn, 1959.
Spellman, John, W. *Political theory of ancient India*. Oxford, 1964.
Sharma, R. S. *Śūdras in ancient India*. Delhi, 1958.

Sharma, R. S. *Aspects of political ideas and institutions in ancient India*. Delhi, 1959.

Varma, V. P. *Studies in Hindu political thought and its metaphysical foundations*. 2nd ed., Delhi, 1959.

CHAPTER XII

Science

Bhishagācārya, G. M. *History of Indian medicine*. 2 vols. Calcutta, 1923–26.

Datta, B. and Singh, A. N. *History of Hindu mathematics*. 2 parts in 1 vol., Bombay and London, 1962. (Has excellent bibliography at the end of Part I.)

Filliozat, J. 'L'Inde et les échanges scientifiques dans l'antiquité.' *Journal of World History* (UNESCO), Vol. I, p. 353, 1953.

Filliozat, J. and others. 'Transmission of scientific ideas and techniques.' *Indian Journal of the History of Science*, Vol. V, No. 2, Section XIII, New Delhi, 1970.

Gurjar, L. V. *Ancient Indian mathematics and Vedha*. Poona, 1947.

Menon, C. P. S. *Ancient astronomy and cosmology*. London, 1931.

Neugebauer, O. *The exact sciences in antiquity*. Copenhagen, 1951; Princeton, 1952.

Quaritch Wales, H. G. *The making of Greater India*. London, 1951.

Ray, P. *History of chemistry in ancient and mediaeval India*. Indian Chemical Society, Calcutta, 1956.

Sachau, E. C. *Alberuni's India*. 2 vols, London, 1910.

Sanyal, P. K. *A story of medicine and pharmacy in India*. Calcutta, 1964.

Sengupta, P. C. *Ancient Indian chronology*. Calcutta, 1947.

Sigerist, H. E. *History of medicine*. Vol. II, *Early Greek, Hindu and Persian medicine*. Oxford, 1962.

Winter, H. J. J. *Eastern science* (Wisdom of the East series). London, 1952.

CHAPTER XIII

Ancient and Modern Languages

Andronov, M. S. *Dravidian languages*. Moscow, 1970.

Bloch, J. *La developpement de la langue marathe*. Paris, 1915.

Bloch, J. *L'Indo-aryen du Veda aux temps modernes*. Paris, 1934.

Bloch, J. *Morphologie comparative des langues dravidiennes*. Paris, 1946.

Burrow, T. *The Sanskrit language*. 2nd ed., London, 1959.

Chatterjee, S. K. *The origin and development of the Bengali language*. Calcutta, 1926.

Chatterjee, S. K. *Indo-Aryan and Hindi*. 2nd ed., Calcutta, 1960.

Geiger, W. *Pali Literatur und Sprache*. Strassburg, 1916.

Macdonnell, A. A. *Vedic grammar*. Strassburg, 1910.

Pischel, R. *Grammatik der Prakrit-Sprachen*. Strassburg, 1900.

Renou, L. *Histoire de la langue sanskrite*. Paris, 1956.

Zvelebil, K. *Comparative Dravidian phonology*. The Hague, 1970.

CHAPTER XIV

Classical Literature

Aśvaghoṣa. *Buddhacarita*, translated by E. H. Johnston, Panjab University, Calcutta, 1936, and *Acta Orientalia*, 1937; first part reprinted Motilal Banarsidass, Delhi, 1973.

Bāṇa. *Harṣacarita*, translated by Cowell and Thomas, Royal Asiatic Society, London, 1897.

Bāṇa. *Kādambarī*, translated by C. M. Ridding, Royal Asiatic Society, London, 1896.

Bhāsa. Translated by Woolner and Sarup as *Thirteen Trivandrum Plays attributed to Bhāsa*, Panjab University Oriental Publications, Oxford University Press, London, 1930–1.

Bhavabhūti. *Mālatīmādhava*, translated (French) by G. Strehly, Leroux, Paris, 1885.

Bhavabhūti. *Uttararāmacarita*, translated (French) by N. Stchoupak, Institut de Civilisation Indienne, Collection Émile Senart, Paris, 1935.

Guṇāḍhya. *Bṛhatkathā*; the *Ślokasaṃgraha* by Budhasvāmin has been translated into French by Lacôte, Leroux, Paris, 1908–29.

Harṣa. *Naiṣadhacarita*, translated by K. K. Handiqui, Deccan College Monograph Series, Poona, 1956.

Kālidāsa. *Abhijñānaśākuntala* and 'Śūdraka': *Mṛcchakaṭika*, translated by Monier Williams and Ryder in *The Genius of the Oriental Theater*, Mentor Books, New York, 1966.

Krishnamachariar, M. *History of Classical Sanskrit Literature*, Oriental Book Agency, Poona, 1937, reprinted Motilal Banarsidass, Delhi, 1970.

Sātavāhana or 'Hāla'. *Gāhāsattasaī* (*Saptaśatī*), translated (German) by Weber in *Abhandlungen für die Kunde des Morgenlandes*, Leipzig, 1870 and 1881, reprinted Kraus, Liechtenstein, 1966.

Vidyākara. *Subhāṣitaratnakoṣa*, translated by D. H. H. Ingalls, Harvard Oriental Series, Cambridge, Mass., 1965, is an excellent anthology of Sanskrit lyrics from about 250 classical poets, readably translated with good introductions.

Viśākhadatta. *Mudrārākṣasa*, translated by K. H. Dhruva, Oriental Book Agency, Poona, 3rd ed. 1930.

Viṣṇuśarman. *Pañcatantra*, reconstructed and translated by F. Edgerton, American Oriental Series, New Haven, Conn., 1924.

Warder, A. K. *Indian Kāvya Literature*, Motilal Banarsidass, Delhi, Vol. I, 1972, Vol. II, 1973, Vol. III, in press.

CHAPTER XV

Early Art and Architecture

Auboyer, J. in *Eliky Zinniş, Khajurāho.* 's-Gravenhage, 1960.

Auboyer, J. in *The Oriental World.* London, etc., 1967.

Barrett, D. and Gray, B. *The Painting of India.* Cleveland, 1963.

Brown, P. *Indian Architecture Buddhist and Hindu.* 3rd ed. Bombay, 1956.

Coomaraswamy, A. K. *History of Indian and Indonesian Art.* London, 1927.

Frederic, L. *Indian Temples and Sculpture.* London, 1959.

Goetz, H. *India: Five Thousand Years of Indian Art.* London, 1959.

Piggott, S. *Prehistoric India.* Harmondsworth, 1950.

Rawson, P. S. *Indian Painting.* London etc., 1961.

Rowland, B. *The Art and Architecture of India.* Revised edition. London, 1967.

Singh, M. *The Cave Paintings of Ajanta.* London, 1965.

Wheeler, M. *Early India and Pakistan.* London, 1959.

Zimmer, H. *The Art of Indian Asia.* New York, 1955.

Zimmer, H. *Myths and Symbols in Indian Art and Civilization.* New York, 1946.

CHAPTER XVI

Music

Bake, A. A. 'The music of India', in *The new Oxford history of music*, Vol. I. London, 1957.

Bhatkhande, V. N. *A short historical survey of the music of Upper India.* Bombay, 1934.

Bhattacharya, S. *Ethnomusicology and India.* Calcutta, 1968.

Deva, B. C. *Psychoacoustics of music and speech.* Madras, 1967.

Fox Strangways, A. H. *The music of Hindostan.* Oxford, 1914.

Gangoly, O. C. *Rāgas and Rāginīs.* Bombay, 1958.

Grosset, J. 'Inde: histoire de la musique . . .', in A. Lavignac, *Encyclopédie de la musique*, Vol. I. Paris, 1921.

Jairazbhoy, N. A. *The Rāgs of North Indian music.* London, 1971.

Joshi, B. and Lobo, A. *Introducing Indian music.* Bombay, n.d. (A series of four records, with spoken text, musical examples and booklet.)

Kaufmann, W. *The rāgas of North India.* Bloomington, 1968.

Popley, H. A. *The music of India.* Calcutta, 1950.

Powers, H. S. 'An historical and comparative approach to the classification of ragas (with an appendix on ancient Indian tunings)', in *Selected reports.* Los Angeles, 1970.

Prajnananda, Swami. *A history of Indian music*, Vol. I. Calcutta, 1963.

Sambamoorthy, P. *South Indian music.* 6 vols., Madras, 1958–69.

Shankar, R. *My music, my life.* New York, 1968.

Staal, J. F. *Nambudiri Veda recitation.* The Hague, 1961.

te Nijenhuis, E. *Dattilam, a compendium of ancient Indian music.* Leiden, 1970.

CHAPTER XVII

The Muslim Ruling Dynasties

Ashraf, K. M. *Life and conditions of the people of Hindustan* (*under the Sultans before Akbar*). 2nd ed., Delhi, 1959.

Athar Alī, M. *The Mughal nobility under Aurangzeb.* Aligarh, 1966.

Ahmad Aziz. *Studies in Islamic culture in the Indian environment.* Reprint, Oxford, 1966.

Bosworth, C. E. *The Ghaznavids.* Edinburgh, 1963.

Frykenberg, R. E. (ed.). *Land control and social structure in Indian history.* Wisconsin, 1969.

Habīb, I. *The agrarian system of Mughal India.* London, 1963.

Habīb, M. and Nizāmī, K. *A comprehensive history of India.* Vol. V, Bombay, 1970.

Hardy, P. *Historians of Medieval India.* London, 1960.

Hasan, I. *The central structure of the Mughal Empire.* Reprint, Karachi, 1967.

Ikram, S. M. *Muslim civilization*, edited by T. Embree Ainslie. New York, London, 1969.

Irvine, W. *The army of the Indian Moghuls.* 2nd ed., New Delhi, 1962.

Moreland, W. H. *The agrarian system of Moslem India.* Cambridge, 1929.

Moreland, W. H. *India at the death of Akbar.* London, 1920.

Moreland, W. H. *From Akbar to Aurangzeb.* London, 1923.

Nigam, S. B. P. *Nobility under the Sultans of Delhi.* Delhi, 1960.

Qureshi, I. H. *The Muslim community of the Indo-Pakistan subcontinent (610–1947).* The Hague, 1962.

Rizvi, S. A. A. *Religious and intellectual history of Akbar's reign.* Delhi, in press.

Saran, P. *Provincial government of the Mughals.* Allahabad, 1941.

Tripathi, R. P. *Some aspects of Muslim administration.* 2nd rev. ed., Allahabad, 1959.

Tripathi, R. P. *Rise and fall of the Mughal Empire.* 3rd ed., Allahabad, 1963.

CHAPTER XVIII

Medieval Hindu Devotionalism

Appasamy, A. J. *Temple bells: readings from Hindu religious literature.* Calcutta, 1930.

Barnett, L. D. *The heart of India.* Wisdom of the East series. London, 1908.

Deleury, G. A. *The cult of Viṭhobā.* Poona, 1960.

Farquhar, J. N. *An outline of the religious literature of India.* London, 1920.

Jnānadeva. *Jnāṇeshvarī* (*Bhāvārthadīpikā*), trans. by V. G. Pradhān, ed. by H. M. Lambert, 2 vols., London, 1967, 1969.

Kabīr. *One hundred poems of Kabir*, trans. by Rabindranath Tagore, assisted by Evelyn Underhill. London, 1915.

Kennedy, M. T. *The Chaitanya Movement.* Calcutta, 1925.

Kingsbury, F. and Philips, G. E. (trans.). *Hymns of the Tamil Śaivite Saints.* Calcutta, 1921.

Macnicol, N. *Psalms of the Maratha Saints.* The Heritage of India series. Calcutta, 1919.

Nilakanta Sastri, K. A. *Development of religion in South India.* Bombay, 1963.

Ranade, R. D. *Indian mysticism: mysticism in Maharashtra.* Poona, 1933.

Rice, E. P. *Kanarese literature.* The Heritage of India series. Calcutta, 1921.

Tulsīdās. *Kavitāvalī*, trans. with critical introduction by F. R. Allchin. London, 1964.

Westcott, G. H. *Kabir and the Kabir Panth.* Cawnpore, 1907.

CHAPTER XIX

Islam in Medieval India

Arnold, T. W. *The preaching of Islam.* Reprint, Lahore, 1961.

Carpenter, J. E. *Theism in medieval India.* London, 1926.

de Bary, W. T. *Sources of Indian tradition.* New York, 1958.

Hasrat, B. J. *Dārā Shikūh.* Visvabharti, 1953.

Hollister, J. N. *The Shī'a of India.* London, 1936.

Ja'far Sharīf. *Islam in India* (*Qānūn-i Islām*), trans. by G. A. Herklots. Oxford, 1921.

Nizāmī, K. A. *Some aspects of religion and politics in India during the thirteenth century.* Aligarh, 1961.

Qanungo, K. R. *Dārā Shukōh.* Lucknow, 1953.

Rizvī, S. A. A. *Muslim revivalist movements in northern India in the sixteenth and seventeenth centuries.* Agra, 1965.

Sharma, S. R. *The religious policy of the Mughal emperors.* 2nd ed., London, 1962.

Tara Chand. *Influence of Islam on Indian culture.* 2nd ed., Allahabad, 1963.

Yusuf Husain. *Medieval Indian culture.* Bombay, 1959.

Zaehner, R. C. *Hindu and Muslim mysticism.* London, 1960.

CHAPTER XX

Sikhism

Banerjee, Indubhusan. *Evolution of the Khalsa.* 2 vols., Calcutta, 1936.

Ganda Singh (ed.). *Sources on the life and teachings of Guru Nanak.* Patiala, 1969.

Grewal, J. S. *Guru Nanak in history.* Chandigarh, 1969.

Gupta, Hari Ram. *A history of the Sikhs.* 3 vols., Vol. I, Simla, 1952, Vol. II, Lahore, 1944.

Harbans Singh. *The heritage of the Sikhs.* Bombay, 1964.

Kapur Singh. *Parasharprasna or the Baisakhi of Guru Gobind Singh.* Jullundur, 1959.

Khushwant Singh. *A history of the Sikhs*. 2 vols., London/Princeton, 1963, 1966.

Macauliffe, M. A. *The Sikh religion*. 6 vols., Oxford, 1909.

McLeod, W. H. *Gurū Nānak and the Sikh religion*. Oxford, 1968.

Sinha, Narendra Krishna. *Rise of the Sikh power*. Calcutta, 1946.

Teja Singh. *Sikhism: its ideals and institutions*. Calcutta, 1951.

Trilochan Singh, *et al. The sacred writings of the Sikhs*. London, 1960.

CHAPTER XXI

Medieval Indian Literature

Ajwani, L. H. *History of Sindhi literature*. New Delhi, 1970.

Barua, Birinchi Kumar. *History of Assamese literature*. New Delhi, 1964.

Chatterji, Suniti Kumar. *Languages and literatures of Modern India*. Calcutta, 1963.

Contemporary Indian literature: a symposium. 2nd ed., New Delhi, 1959.

Iyengar, K. R. Srinivasa. *Indian writing in English*. Bombay, 1962.

Jesudasan, C. and H. *A history of Tamil literature*. Calcutta, 1961.

Jhaveri, K. M. *Milestones in Gujarati literature*. Bombay, 1914.

Jindal, K. B. *A history of Hindi literature*. Allahabad, 1955.

Mansinha, Mayadhar. *History of Oriya literature*. New Delhi, 1962.

Mugali, R. S. *History of Kannada literature*. New Delhi, English ed. in preparation.

Parameswaran, P. K. *History of Malayalam literature*. New Delhi, 1967.

Sen, Sukumar. *History of Bengali literature*. New Delhi, 1960.

CHAPTER XXII

Muslim Architecture in India

(compiled by S. A. A. Rizvi)

Batley, C. *The design development of Indian architecture*. Bombay, 1965.

Briggs, M. S. *Muhammedan architecture in Egypt and Palestine*. Oxford, 1924.

Brown, P. *Indian architecture: the Islamic period*. 2nd ed., Bombay, n.d.

Cresswell, K. A. C. *Early Muslim architecture*. 2 parts, Oxford, 1932, 1940.

Cresswell, K. A. C. *A provisional bibliography of the Muhammadan architecture of India*. Bombay, 1922.

Fergusson, J. *A history of Indian and Eastern architecture*. 2 vols., London, 1910.

Havell, E. B. *Indian architecture*. London, 1914.

Havell, E. B. *A handbook of Indian art*. London, 1920.

Hürliman, M. *Delhi, Agra, Fathpur-Sikri*. London, 1965.

Pope, A. U. *Persian architecture*. London, 1965.

Rizvi, S. A. A. *Fatehpūr-Sīkri*. Delhi, 1972. (A brief guide)

Rizvi, S. A. A. and Flynn, V. J. A. *Fatḥpūr Sīkrī*. Bombay, 1974. (Detailed study.)

Saladin, H. *Manuel d'art musalman*. Paris, 1907.

Smith, V. A. *History of fine art in India and Ceylon*, revised by K. de B. Codrington, Oxford, 1930.

Unsal, Behset. *Turkish Islamic architecture*. London, 1959.

CHAPTER XXIII

Medieval Indian Miniature Painting

Archer, W. G. *Central Indian painting*. London, 1958.

Archer, W. G. *Indian painting in the Punjab hills*. London, 1952.

Arnold, T. W. and Wilkinson, J. V. S. *The Library of A. Chester Beatty*. 3 vols., Oxford, 1936.

Barrett, D. E. *Painting of the Deccan XVI–XVIII century*. London, 1958.

Barrett, D. E. and Gray, Basil. *Painting of India*. Geneva, 1963.

Brown, Percy. *Indian painting under the Mughals*. Oxford, 1924.

Chandra, Moti. *Jaina miniature paintings from western India*. Ahmedabad, 1949.

Chandra, Moti. *Mewar painting*. New Delhi, 1958.

Chandra, P. *Bundi painting*. New Delhi, 1959.

Coomaraswamy, A. K. *Rajput painting*. Oxford, 1916.

Dickinson, E. and Khandalavala, K. *Kishangadh painting*. New Delhi, 1959.

Khandalavala, K. *Pahari miniature painting*. Bombay, 1958.

Khandalavala, K. and Chandra, Moti. *New documents of Indian painting*. Bombay, 1969.

Skelton, R. *Indian miniatures from the XVth–XIXth centuries*. Venice, 1961.

Stchoukine, I. *La peinture indienne*. Paris, 1929.

Welch, S. C. *Arts of Mughal India*. New York, 1964.

CHAPTER XXIV

The Portuguese

Boxer, C. R. *Portuguese society in the tropics*. Madison, Wis., 1965.

Boxer, C. R. *Race relations in the Portuguese colonial empire, 1415–1825*. Oxford, 1963.

Boxer, C. R. *The Portuguese sea-borne empire*. London, 1969.

Potter, G. R. *et al.* (eds.). *The new Cambridge modern history*. Vols. II, III, IV and V, Cambridge, 1958–1970.

Campos, J. J. A. *History of the Portuguese in Bengal*. Calcutta, 1919.

Chatterji, S. K. and Sen, P. *Manoel da Assumpçam's Bengali grammar*. Calcutta, 1931.

Correia-Afonso, J. *Jesuit letters and Indian history*. Bombay, 1955.

Lach, Donald F. *India in the eyes of Europe: the sixteenth century*. Chicago, 1968.

Livermore, H. V. *Portugal and Brazil*. Oxford, 1953.

Maclagan, Sir E. D. *The Jesuits and the Great Mogul*. London, 1932.

Priolkar, A. K. *The printing press in India*. Bombay, 1951.

CHAPTER XXV

The Mughals and the British

I. *The Mughals*

Bernier, F. *Travels in the Mogol empire*, edited by V. A. Smith and A. Constable. 2nd ed., Oxford, 1934.

Brown, P. *Indian painting under the Mughals*. Oxford, 1924.

Edwardes, S. M. and Garrett, H. L. O. *Mughal rule in India*. London, 1930.

Moreland, W. E. *India at the death of Akbar*. London, 1920.

Qureshi, I. H. *Administration of the Mughal empire*. Karachi, 1966.

Sarkar, J. A. *History of Aurangzeb*. 5 vols., Calcutta, 1916–25; 3rd single-volume ed., Calcutta, 1962.

Smith, V. A. *Akbar, the Great Mogul*. Oxford, 1917.

Smith, V. A. *History of fine art in India and Ceylon*, revised by K. de B. Codrington. Oxford, 1930.

Spear, T. G. P. *The twilight of the Mughuls*. Cambridge, 1951.

Villiers-Stuart, C. M. *Gardens of the Great Mughals*. London, 1913.

II. *The British*

Archer, W. G. *Indian painting for the British*. London, 1955.

Mayhew, A. *The education of India*. London, 1926.

Misra, B. B. *The Indian middle class*. London, 1961.

O'Malley, L. S. S. (ed.). *Modern India and the West*, London, 1941.

Spear, T. G. P. *History of India*, Vol. 2, *The Mughals and the British*. 4th impression, London, 1970.

Spear, T. G. P. *The Oxford history of modern India*. Oxford, 1965.

Thompson, E. and Garratt, G. T. *Rise and fulfilment of British rule in India*. London, 1934.

Wint, G. *The British in Asia*. 2nd ed., London, 1955.

Woodruffe, P. *The Men who ruled India*, Vol. I, *The founders*; Vol. II, *The guardians*. London, 1953, 1954.

CHAPTER XXVI

Religious and social reform in British India

Ahmed, A. F. Salahuddin. *Social ideas and social change in Bengal 1818–1835*. Leiden, 1968.

Chintamani, C. Y. *Indian social reform*. Madras, 1901.

Farquhar, J. N. *Modern religious movements in India*. London, 1924.

Heimsath, C. H. *Indian nationalism and Hindu social reform*. Princeton, 1964.

Irschick, E. F. *Politics and social conflict in South India: the non-brahman movement and Tamil separatism, 1916–1924*. Berkeley, 1969.

Kumar, R. *Western India in the nineteenth century*. Canberra, 1968.

Lajpat Rai, Lala. *The Arya Samaj. An account of its origins, doctrines, and activities, with a biographical sketch of the founder, Swami Dayananda Saraswati*. London, 1915.

Natarajan, S. *A century of social reform*. Bombay, 1959.

Ranade, M. G. *Religious and social reform. A collection of essays and speeches*, edited by M. B. Kolaskar. Bombay, 1902.

Saradananda, Swami. *Sri Ramakrishna, the great master*, trans. from the Bengali by Swami Gagadananda. Madras, 1965.

Sen, P. K. *Biography of a new faith*. 2 vols., Calcutta, 1950, 1954.

Sivanath Shastri. *History of the Brahmo Samaj*. 2 vols., Calcutta, 1911, 1912.

Wolpert, S. A. *Tilak and Gokhale*. Berkeley and Los Angeles, 1962.

CHAPTER XXVII

Islamic Reform Movements

Ahmad, Aziz. *Islamic modernism in India and Pakistan*. London, 1967.

Ahmad, Aziz and von Grunebaum, G. E. *Muslim self-statement in India and Pakistan*. Wiesbaden, 1970.

Ahmad, Qeyamuddin. *The Wahabi Movement in India*. Patna, 1966.

Aziz, K. K. (ed.). *Ameer Ali: his life and work*. Lahore, 1968.

Baljon, J. M. S. *The reforms and religious ideas of Sir Sayyid Ahmad Khan*. Leiden, 1949.

Ikram, S. M. *Modern Muslim India and the birth of Pakistan*. Lahore 1965.

Jalbani, G. N. *Teachings of Shah Waliyullah*. Lahore, 1967.

Khan, M. A. *History of the Fara'idi Movement in Bengal*. Karachi, 1965.

Malik, Hafeez. *Moslem nationalism in India and Pakistan*. Washington, 1963.

Philips, C. H. (ed.). *The evolution of India and Pakistan, 1858–1947*. London, 1962.

Qureshi, I. H. *The struggle for Pakistan*. Karachi, 1965.

Rizvi, S. A. A. *Muslim revivalist movements in Northern India in the sixteenth and seventeenth centuries*. Agra, 1965.

CHAPTER XXVIII

The Nationalist Movement

Bondurant, Joan. *Conquest of violence: the Gandhian philosophy of conflict*. Princeton, 1958.

Bose, Nirmal K. *Studies in Gandhism*. Calcutta, 1962.

Brecher, Michael. *Nehru: a political biography*. London, 1959.

Gandhi, Mohandas K. *An autobiography, or the story of my experiments with truth*. Ahmedabad, 1940; London, 1966.

Heimsath, Charles H. *Indian nationalism and Hindu social reform*. Princeton, 1964.

Kumar, Ravinder (ed.). *Essays on Gandhian politics: the Rowlatt Satyagraha of 1919*. Oxford, 1971.

Lewis, Martin D. (ed.). *Gandhi: maker of modern India*. Problems in Asian Civilizations series. Boston, 1965.

Low, D. Anthony (ed.). *Soundings in modern South Asian history*. London, Berkeley, Canberra, 1968.

McLane, John R. (ed.). *The political awakening in India*. Englewood Cliffs, 1970.

Park, Richard L. and Tinker, Irene (eds.). *Leadership and political institutions in India*. Princeton, 1959.

Rudolph, Lloyd I. and Susanne H. *The modernity of tradition: political development of India*. Chicago, London, 1967.

Smith, Donald E. (ed.). *South Asian politics and religion*. Princeton, 1966.

Wolpert, Stanley A. *Tilak and Gokhale: revolution and reform in the making of modern India*. Berkeley, 1962.

CHAPTER XXIX

Modern Literature

See bibliography to Chapter XXI.

CHAPTER XXX

Early Contacts between India and Europe

(compiled by Dr. F. Wilhelm)

Basham, A. L. (ed.). *Papers on the date of Kaniṣka*. Leiden, 1968.

Cary, M. and Warmington, E. H. *The Ancient explorers*. Harmondsworth, 1963.

Derrett, J. D. M. 'Greece and India: the Milindapanha, the Alexander-romance and the Gospels', *Zeitschrift für Religions- und Geistesgeschichte*, Vol. XIX, pp. 33 ff. Cologne, 1967.

Gary, G. *The medieval Alexander*. Cambridge, 1956.

Majumdar, R. C. *Classical accounts of India* (compiles the translations of J. W. McCrindle). Calcutta, 1960.

Narain, A. K. *The Indo-Greeks*. Oxford, 1957.

Rawlinson, H. G. *Intercourse between India and the Western World*. Cambridge, 1916 and later editions.

Warmington, E. H. *Commerce between the Roman Empire and India*. Cambridge, 1928.

Wheeler, Sir Mortimer. *Rome beyond the Imperial frontiers*. London, New York, 1955.

CHAPTER XXXI

Indian Influence in Ancient South-east Asia

Briggs, L. P. *The ancient Khmer Empire*. Philadelphia, 1951.
Coedès, G. *The Indianized states of Southeast Asia*. Hawaii, Canberra, 1968.
Groslier, B. P. *Indochina: art in the melting-pot of races*. London, 1962.
Groslier, B. P. *Indochina*. Archaeologia Mundi series. London, 1966.
Hall, D. G. E. *A history of South-East Asia*. 3rd ed., London, 1968.
Kempers, B. *Ancient Indonesian art*. London, 1960.
Le May, R. *The culture of South-East Asia*. London, 1954.
Maspero, G. *Le Royaume de Champa*. Paris, 1928.
Quaritch Wales, H. G. *The making of Greater India*. London, 1951.
van Heekeren, H. R. *The Bronze-Iron Age of Indonesia*. The Hague, 1958.
Wagner, F. A. *Indonesia: the art of an island group*. London, 1959.
Winstedt, Sir Richard. *The Malays, a cultural history*. London, 1953.

CHAPTER XXXII

Indian Influences on China

Davidson, J. Leroy. *The Lotus Sutra in Chinese art*. New Haven, 1954.
Edwards, Richard. 'The cave reliefs at Ma Hao', *Artibus Asiae*, Vol. XVII, 1954, 1, pp. 4–28; 2, pp. 103–129.
Miller, Roy Andrew (tr.). *Accounts of western nations in the history of the Northern Chou dynasty*. Berkeley, 1959.
Needham, Joseph. *Science and civilisation in China*, Vol. I. Cambridge, 1954.
Schafer, Edward H. *The golden peaches of Samarkand*. Berkeley, 1963
Soper, Alexander Coburn. *Literary evidence for early Buddhist art in China*. Ascona, 1959.
Wright, Arthur F. *Buddhism in Chinese history*. Stanford, 1959.
Wright, Arthur F. *The Confucian persuasion*. Stanford, 1960.

CHAPTER XXXIII

India and the Medieval Islamic World

See relevant chapters in books recommended for Chapter XVII.
'Abdu'r Rahīm. 'Mughal relations with Central Asia', *Islamic Culture* (Hyderabad), Vol. II, 1937, pp. 81–94, 188–99.
'Abdu'r Rahīm. 'Mughal Relations with Persia', *Islamic Culture*, Vol. VIII, 1934, pp. 457–73, 649-64; Vol. IX, 1935, pp. 113–30.
Riazul Islam. *Indo-Persian relations*. Teheran, Lahore, 1970.

CHAPTER XXXIV

India and the Modern West

Aronson, A. *Europe looks at India: a study in cultural relations*. Bombay, 1946.

Bartold, V. V. *La Découverte de l'Asie*, traduit du Russe et annoté par B. Nikitine. Paris, 1947.

Bissoondoyal, B. *India in French literature*. London, 1967.

Brown, W. N. *The United States and India and Pakistan*. Cambridge, Mass., 1963.

Chatterjee, A. and Burn, R. *British contributions to Indian studies*. London, 1943.

Glasenapp, H. von. *Das Indienbild deutscher Denker*. Stuttgart, 1960.

Greenberger, A. J. *The British image of India*. London, 1969.

Iyer, Raghavan. *The glass curtain between India and Asia*. London, 1965.

Leifer, W. *India and the Germans*. Bombay, 1971.

Marshall, P. J. (ed.). *The British discovery of Hinduism in the eighteenth century*. The European Understanding of India series. Cambridge, 1970.

Radhakrishnan, S. *East and West*. London, 1954.

Rawlinson, G. G. 'Indian influences on the West', in L. S. S. O'Malley (ed.), *Modern India and the West*, London, 1941.

Schwab, R. *La Renaissance orientale*. Paris, 1950.

Sencourt, R. *India in English literature*. London, 1923.

Ward, B. *India and the West*. London, 1961.

Wilhelm, F. 'The German response to Indian culture', *Journal of the American Oriental Society*, Vol. 81, 4, 1961.

Windisch, E. *Geschichte der Sanskrit-Philologie und indischen Altertumskunde*. 2 vols., Strassbourg 1917; Berlin, 1920.

INDEX

Abbreviations

arch.—archaeological
c.—city
dyn.—dynasty
k.—king
leg.—legendary
M.P.—Madhya Pradesh
n.—proper name
pl.—place name
reg.—region
U.P.—Uttar Pradesh

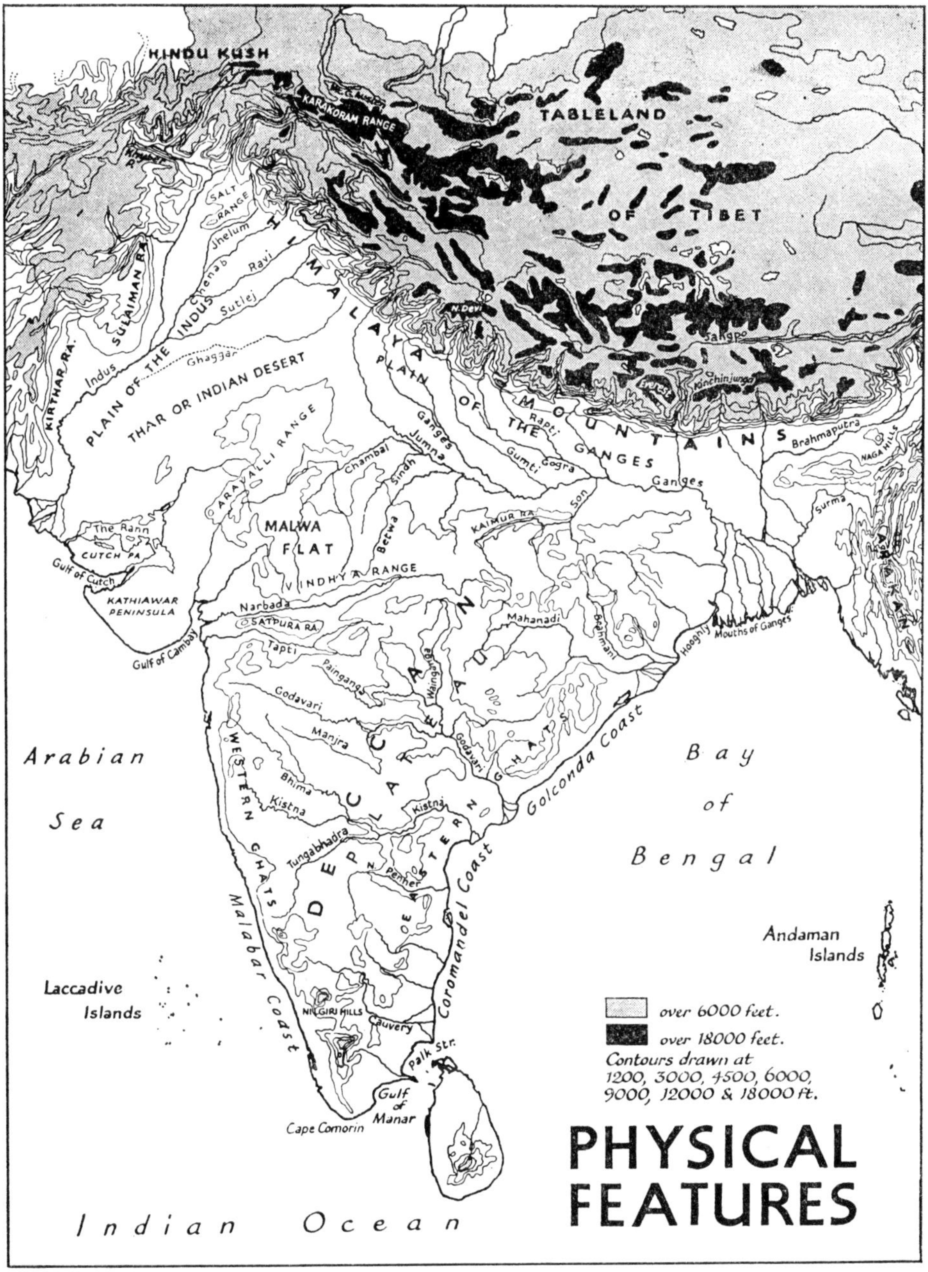

HINDU KUSH
KARAKORAM RANGE
TABLELAND
OF TIBET
SALT RANGE
HIMALAYA
MOUNTAINS
SULAIMAN RA.
KIRTHAR RA.
Indus
Jhelum
Chenab
Ravi
Sutlej
Ghaggar
PLAIN OF THE INDUS
THAR OR INDIAN DESERT
ARAVALLI RANGE
PLAIN OF THE GANGES
N. Devi
Everest
Kinchinjunga
Sangpo
Brahmaputra
NAGA HILLS
Ganges
Jumna
Chambal
Sindh
Rapti
Gumti
Gogra
Son
Surma
ARAKAN
The Rann
CUTCH RA.
Gulf of Cutch
KATHIAWAR PENINSULA
MALWA FLAT
Betwa
KAIMUR RA.
VINDHYA RANGE
Narbada
SATPURA RA.
Gulf of Cambay
Tapti
Mahanadi
Brahmani
Hooghly
Mouths of Ganges
Painganga
Wainganga
Godavari
Manjra
Bhima
Kistna
Tungabhadra
N. Penner
DECCAN PLATEAU
WESTERN GHATS
EASTERN GHATS
Golconda Coast
Coromandel Coast
Malabar Coast
Arabian Sea
Bay of Bengal
Andaman Islands
Laccadive Islands
NILGIRI HILLS
Cauvery
Palk Str.
Gulf of Manar
Cape Comorin
Indian Ocean
over 6000 feet.
over 18000 feet.
Contours drawn at 1200, 3000, 4500, 6000, 9000, 12000 & 18000 ft.
PHYSICAL FEATURES

MAP I

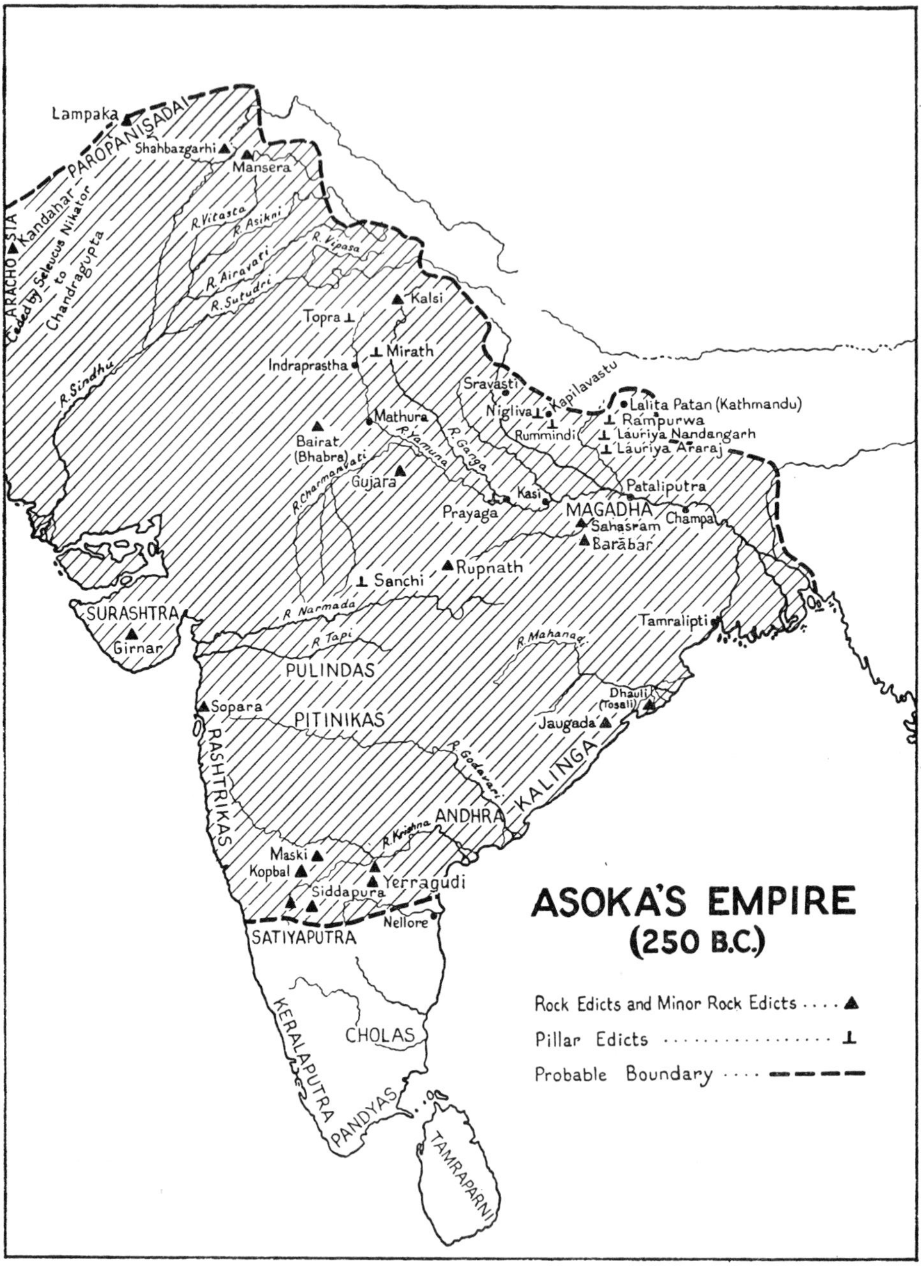
ASOKA'S EMPIRE
(250 B.C.)
Rock Edicts and Minor Rock Edicts
Pillar Edicts
Probable Boundary
Lampaka
PAROPANISADAI
Shahbazgarhi
Mansera
Kandahar
ARACHOSIA
Ceded by Seleucus Nikator to Chandragupta
R. Vitasta
R. Asikni
R. Vipasa
R. Airavati
R. Sutudri
R. Sindhu
Kalsi
Topra
Mirath
Indraprastha
Sravasti
Kapilavastu
Nigliva
Rummindi
Lalita Patan (Kathmandu)
Rampurwa
Lauriya Nandangarh
Lauriya Araraj
Mathura
R. Yamuna
R. Ganga
Bairat (Bhabra)
R. Charmanvati
Gujara
Kasi
Prayaga
Pataliputra
MAGADHA
Champa
Sahasram
Barabar
Rupnath
Sanchi
R. Narmada
SURASHTRA
Girnar
R. Tapi
Tamralipti
R. Mahanadi
PULINDAS
Sopara
PITINIKAS
Dhauli (Tosali)
Jaugada
R. Godavari
KALINGA
RASHTRIKAS
ANDHRA
R. Krishna
Maski
Kopbal
Yerragudi
Siddapura
Nellore
SATIYAPUTRA
KERALAPUTRA
CHOLAS
PANDYAS
TAMRAPARNI

MAP II

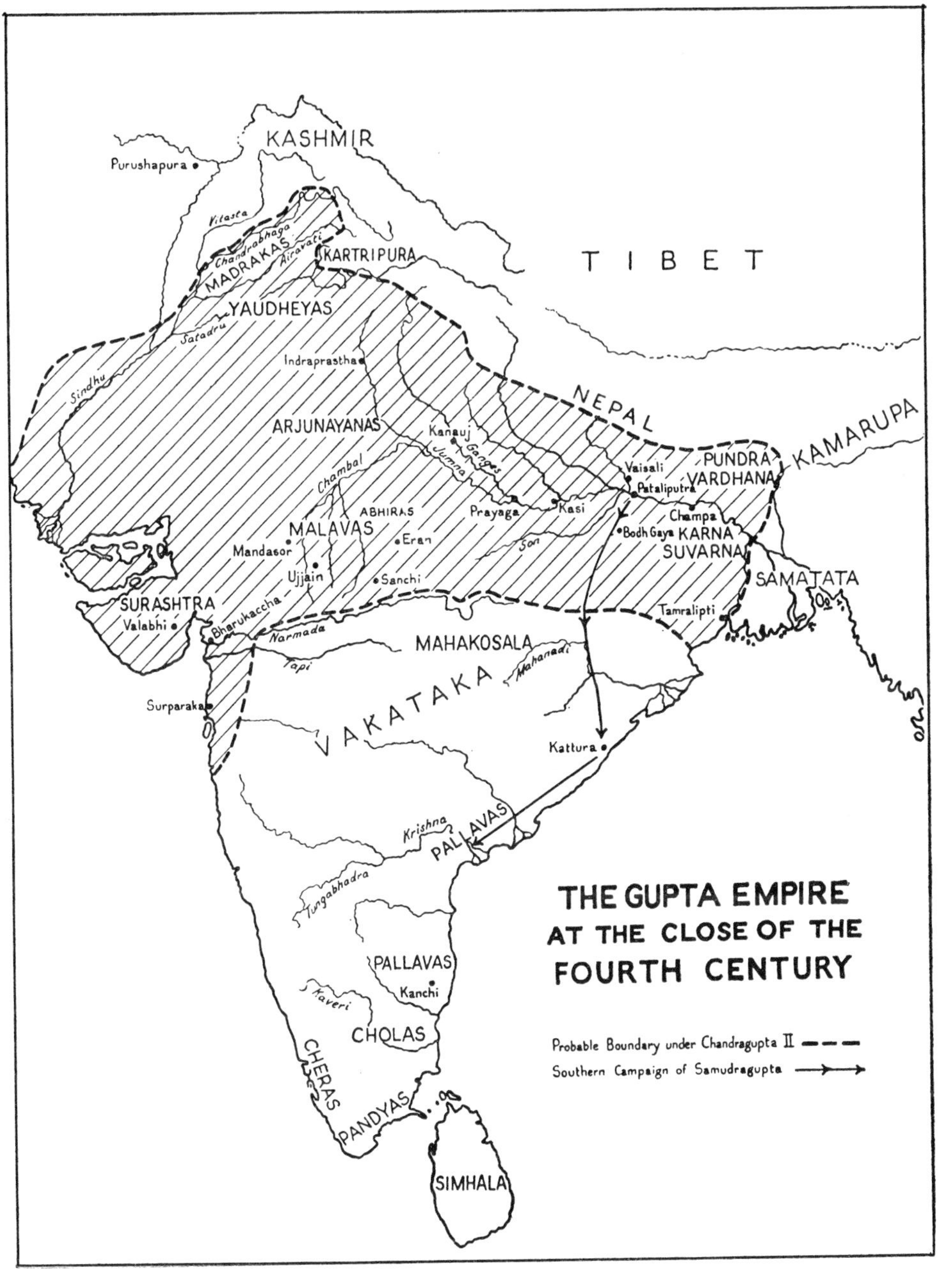
KASHMIR
Purushapura
TIBET
Vitasta
Chandrabhaga
MADRAKAS
Airavati
KARTRIPURA
YAUDHEYAS
Satadru
Indraprastha
Sindhu
NEPAL
KAMARUPA
ARJUNAYANAS
Kanauj
Ganges
Jumna
Chambal
Vaisali
Pataliputra
PUNDRA
VARDHANA
ABHIRAS
Prayaga
Kasi
Champa
MALAVAS
Eran
Bodh Gaya
KARNA
SUVARNA
Mandasor
Son
Ujjain
Sanchi
SAMATATA
SURASHTRA
Valabhi
Bharukaccha
Tamralipti
Narmada
MAHAKOSALA
Tapi
Mahanadi
VAKATAKA
Surparaka
Kattura
Krishna
PALLAVAS
Tungabhadra
THE GUPTA EMPIRE
AT THE CLOSE OF THE
FOURTH CENTURY
PALLAVAS
Kanchi
Kaveri
CHOLAS
CHERAS
Probable Boundary under Chandragupta II
Southern Campaign of Samudragupta
PANDYAS
SIMHALA

MAP III

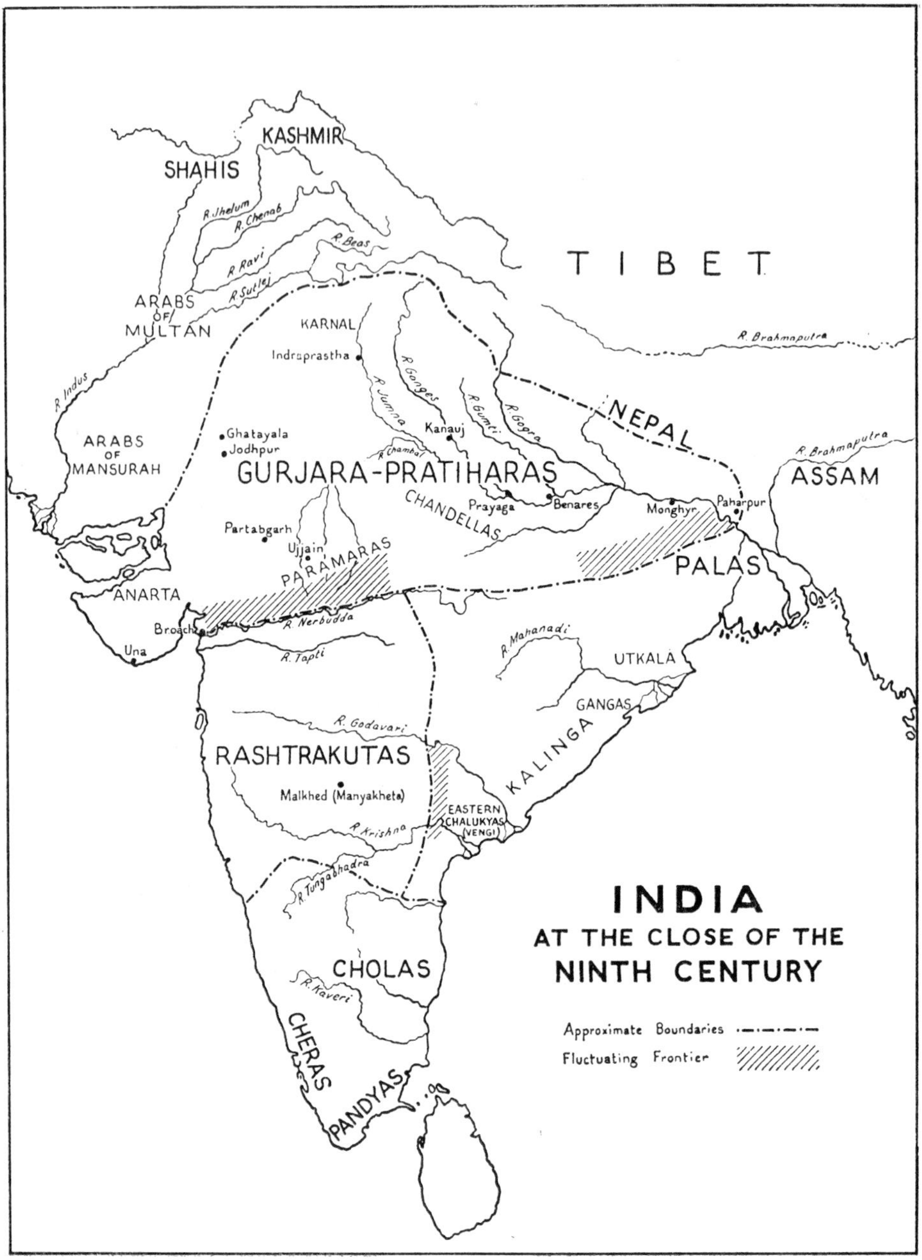
KASHMIR
SHAHIS
R. Jhelum
R. Chenab
R. Beas
R. Ravi
R. Sutlej
TIBET
ARABS OF MULTAN
KARNAL
Indraprastha
R. Brahmaputra
R. Indus
R. Ganges
R. Jumna
R. Gumti
R. Gogra
NEPAL
Kanauj
ARABS OF MANSURAH
Ghatayala
Jodhpur
R. Chambal
GURJARA-PRATIHARAS
ASSAM
CHANDELLAS
Prayaga
Benares
Monghyr
Paharpur
Partabgarh
Ujjain
PARAMARAS
PALAS
ANARTA
Broach
R. Nerbudda
Una
R. Tapti
R. Mahanadi
UTKALA
GANGAS
R. Godavari
KALINGA
RASHTRAKUTAS
Malkhed (Manyakheta)
EASTERN CHALUKYAS (VENGI)
R. Krishna
R. Tungabhadra
INDIA
AT THE CLOSE OF THE
NINTH CENTURY
CHOLAS
R. Kaveri
Approximate Boundaries
Fluctuating Frontier
CHERAS
PANDYAS

Map IV

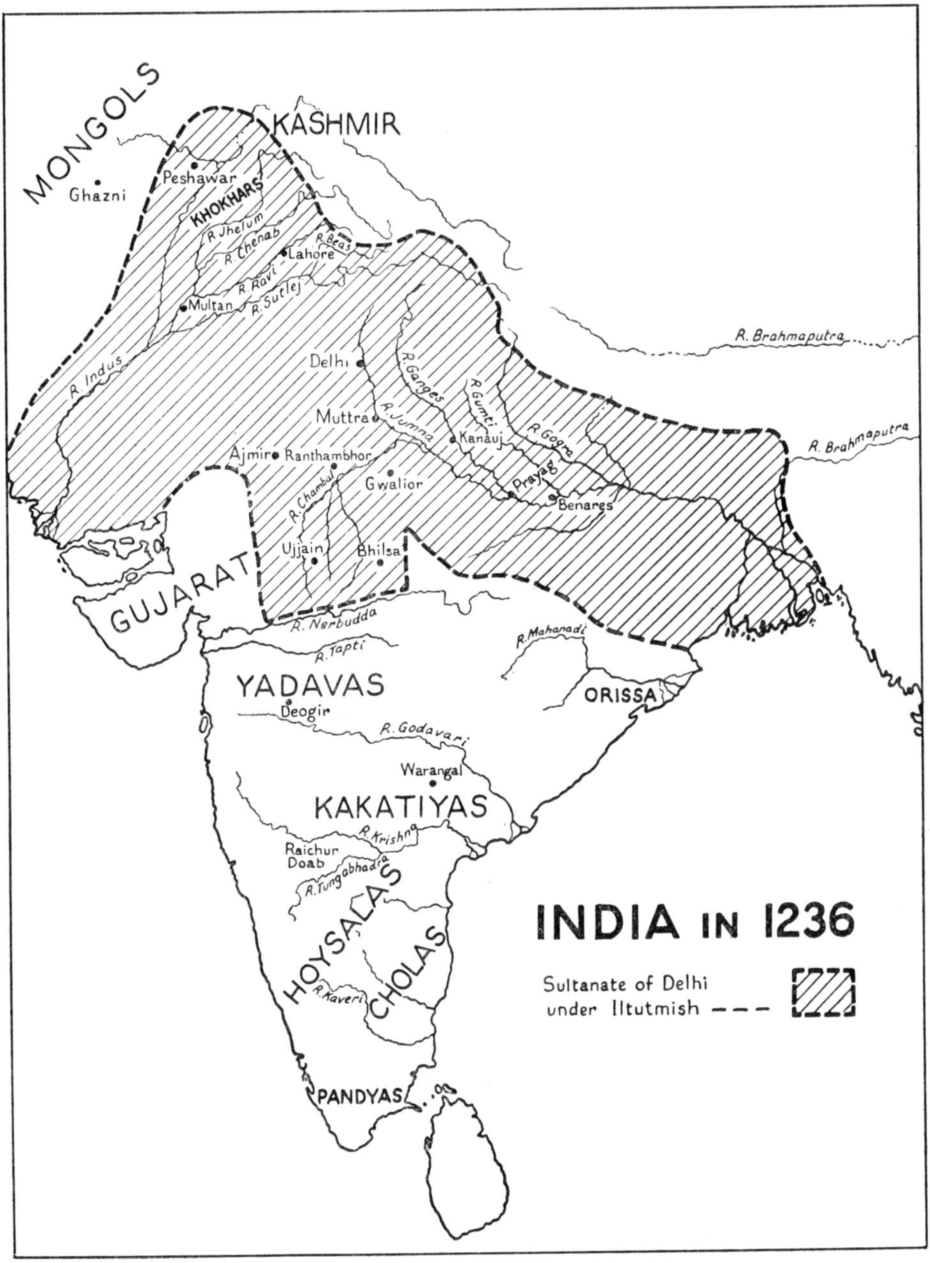
MONGOLS
KASHMIR
Ghazni
Peshawar
KHOKHARS
R. Jhelum
R. Chenab
Lahore
R. Beas
R. Ravi
R. Sutlej
Multan
R. Indus
R. Brahmaputra
Delhi
R. Ganges
R. Gumti
Muttra
R. Jumna
Kanauj
R. Gogra
R. Brahmaputra
Ajmir
Ranthambhor
Gwalior
R. Chambal
Prayag
Benares
Ujjain
Bhilsa
GUJARAT
R. Nerbudda
R. Tapti
R. Mahanadi
YADAVAS
Deogir
ORISSA
R. Godavari
Warangal
KAKATIYAS
R. Krishna
Raichur Doab
R. Tungabhadra
HOYSALAS
CHOLAS
R. Kaveri
PANDYAS
INDIA IN 1236
Sultanate of Delhi under Iltutmish

Map V

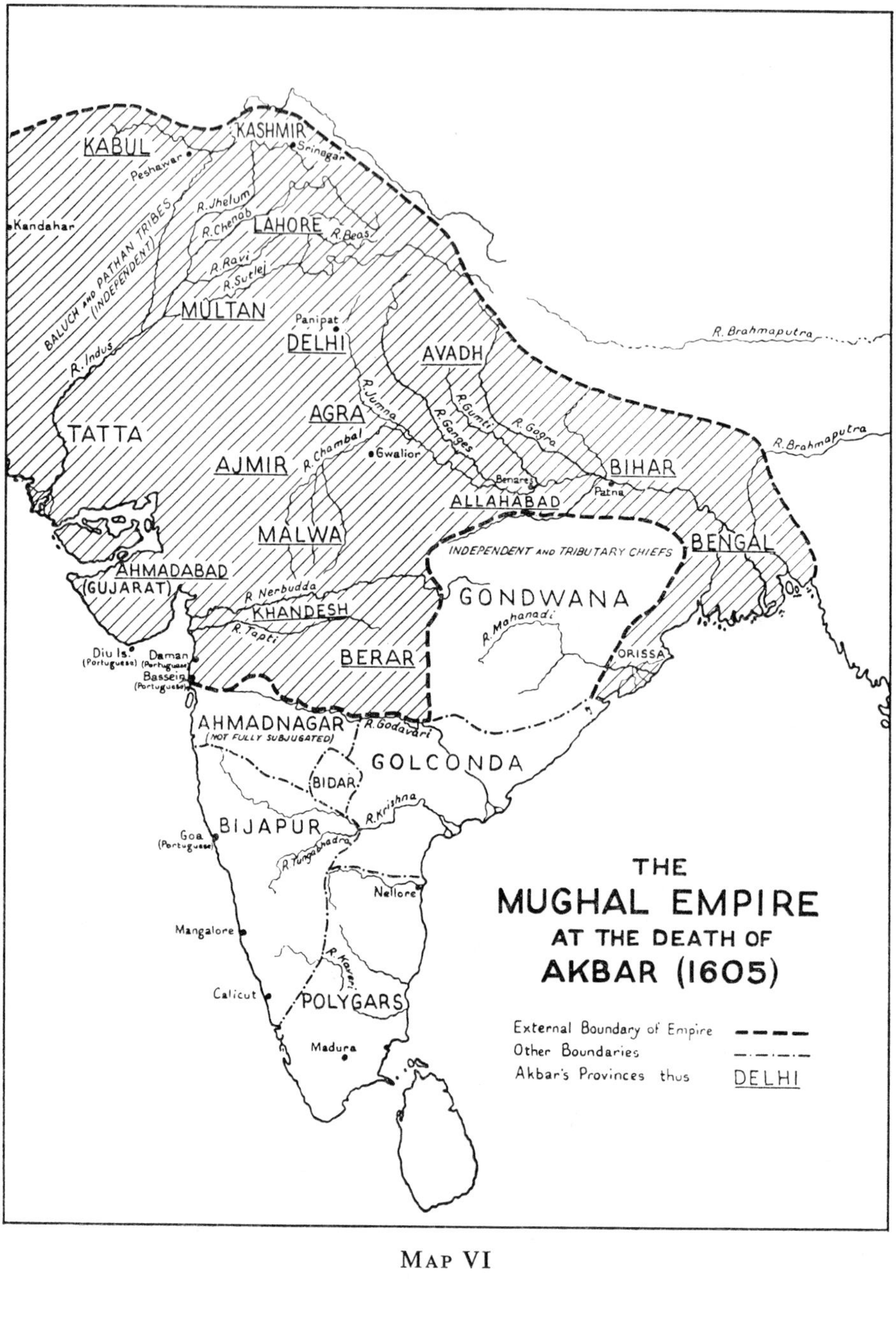
THE MUGHAL EMPIRE AT THE DEATH OF AKBAR (1605)
External Boundary of Empire
Other Boundaries
Akbar's Provinces thus DELHI
KABUL
KASHMIR
Srinagar
Peshawar
Kandahar
BALUCH AND PATHAN TRIBES (INDEPENDENT)
R. Jhelum
R. Chenab
LAHORE
R. Beas
R. Ravi
R. Sutlej
MULTAN
Panipat
DELHI
R. Indus
AVADH
R. Brahmaputra
R. Jumna
R. Gumti
R. Gogra
R. Ganges
AGRA
TATTA
AJMIR
R. Chambal
Gwalior
Benares
Patna
BIHAR
ALLAHABAD
MALWA
INDEPENDENT AND TRIBUTARY CHIEFS
BENGAL
AHMADABAD (GUJARAT)
R. Nerbudda
KHANDESH
GONDWANA
R. Mahanadi
R. Tapti
Diu Is. (Portuguese)
Daman (Portuguese)
Basseín (Portuguese)
BERAR
ORISSA
AHMADNAGAR (NOT FULLY SUBJUGATED)
R. Godavari
GOLCONDA
BIDAR
R. Krishna
BIJAPUR
Goa (Portuguese)
R. Tungabhadra
Nellore
Mangalore
R. Kaveri
Calicut
POLYGARS
Madura

Map VI

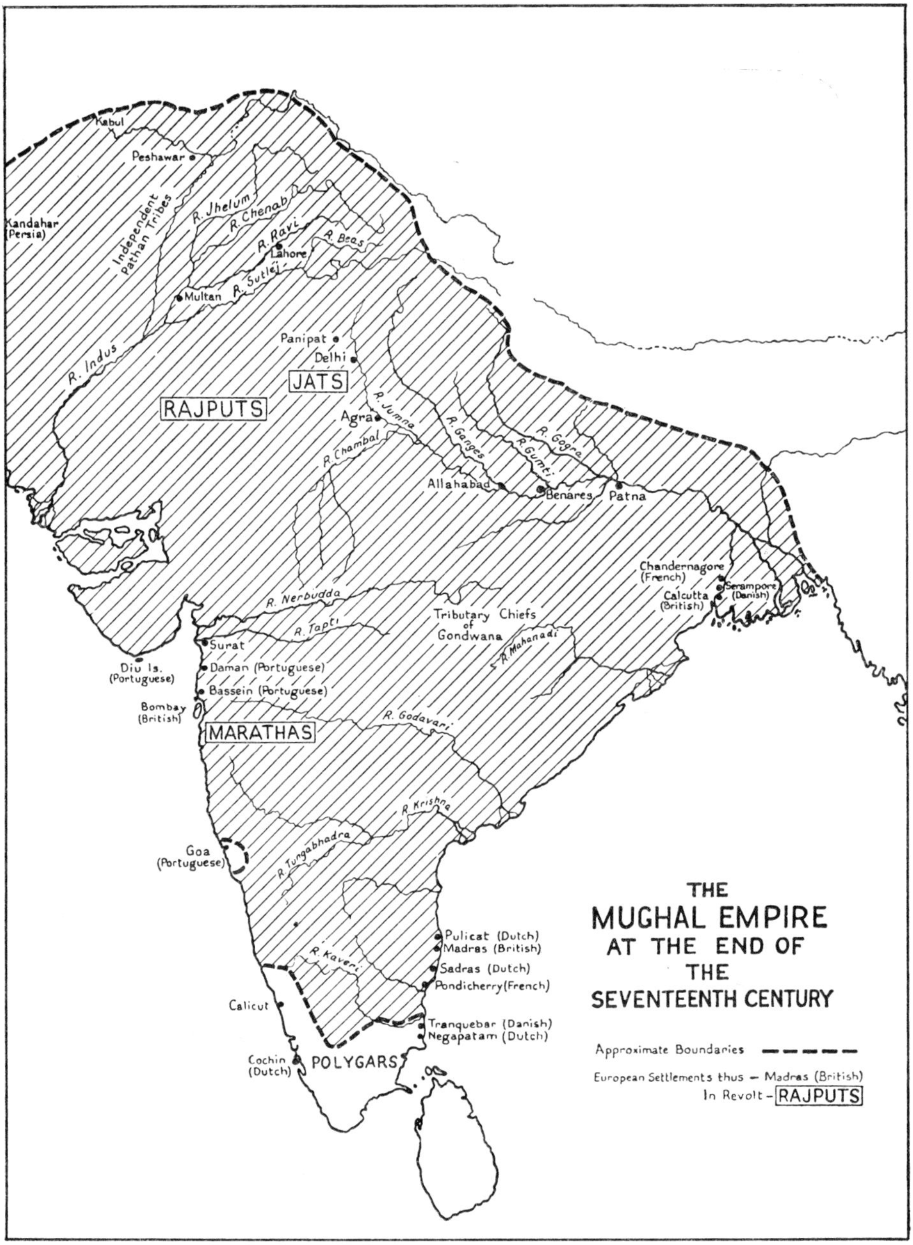
THE
MUGHAL EMPIRE
AT THE END OF
THE
SEVENTEENTH CENTURY
Approximate Boundaries
European Settlements thus – Madras (British)
In Revolt – RAJPUTS
Kabul
Peshawar
Kandahar (Persia)
Independent Pathan Tribes
R. Jhelum
R. Chenab
R. Ravi
R. Beas
Lahore
R. Sutlej
Multan
R. Indus
Panipat
Delhi
JATS
RAJPUTS
Agra
R. Jumna
R. Chambal
R. Ganges
R. Gumti
R. Gogra
Allahabad
Benares
Patna
Chandernagore (French)
Serampore (Danish)
Calcutta (British)
R. Nerbudda
R. Tapti
Tributary Chiefs of Gondwana
R. Mahanadi
Surat
Diu Is. (Portuguese)
Daman (Portuguese)
Bassein (Portuguese)
Bombay (British)
MARATHAS
R. Godavari
R. Krishna
R. Tungabhadra
Goa (Portuguese)
R. Kaveri
Pulicat (Dutch)
Madras (British)
Sadras (Dutch)
Pondicherry (French)
Calicut
Tranquebar (Danish)
Negapatam (Dutch)
Cochin (Dutch)
POLYGARS

MAP VII

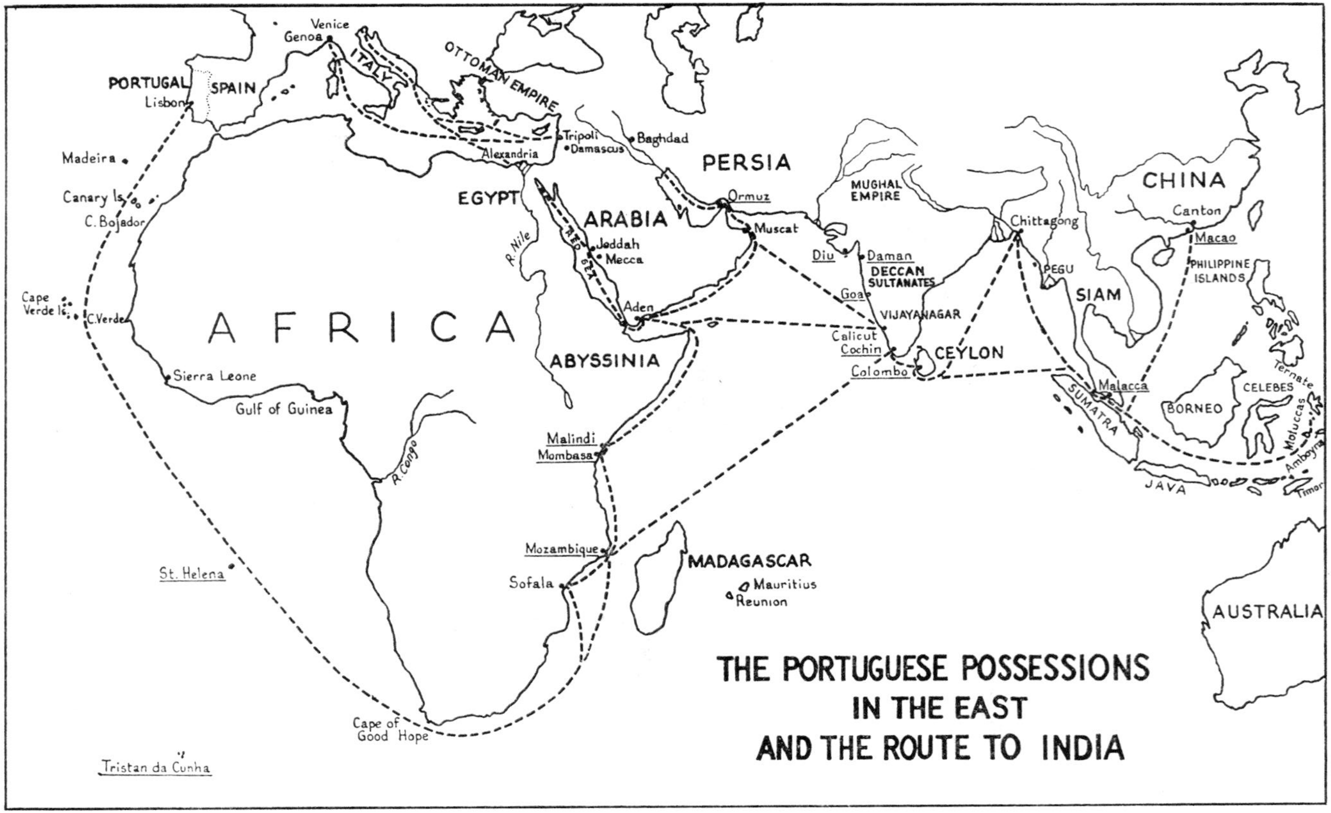
THE PORTUGUESE POSSESSIONS
IN THE EAST
AND THE ROUTE TO INDIA
PORTUGAL
SPAIN
Lisbon
Venice
Genoa
ITALY
OTTOMAN EMPIRE
Tripoli
Damascus
Baghdad
Alexandria
PERSIA
Madeira
Canary Is.
C. Bojador
EGYPT
ARABIA
Ormuz
Muscat
MUGHAL EMPIRE
CHINA
Canton
Macao
Chittagong
Jeddah
Mecca
RED SEA
R. Nile
Diu
Daman
DECCAN SULTANATES
PEGU
SIAM
PHILIPPINE ISLANDS
Cape Verde Is.
C. Verde
AFRICA
Aden
Goa
VIJAYANAGAR
Calicut
Cochin
CEYLON
Colombo
ABYSSINIA
Sierra Leone
Gulf of Guinea
Malacca
SUMATRA
BORNEO
CELEBES
Ternate
Moluccas
Amboyna
Timor
JAVA
Malindi
Mombasa
R. Congo
Mozambique
Sofala
MADAGASCAR
Mauritius
Reunion
St. Helena
AUSTRALIA
Cape of Good Hope
Tristan da Cunha

MAP VIII

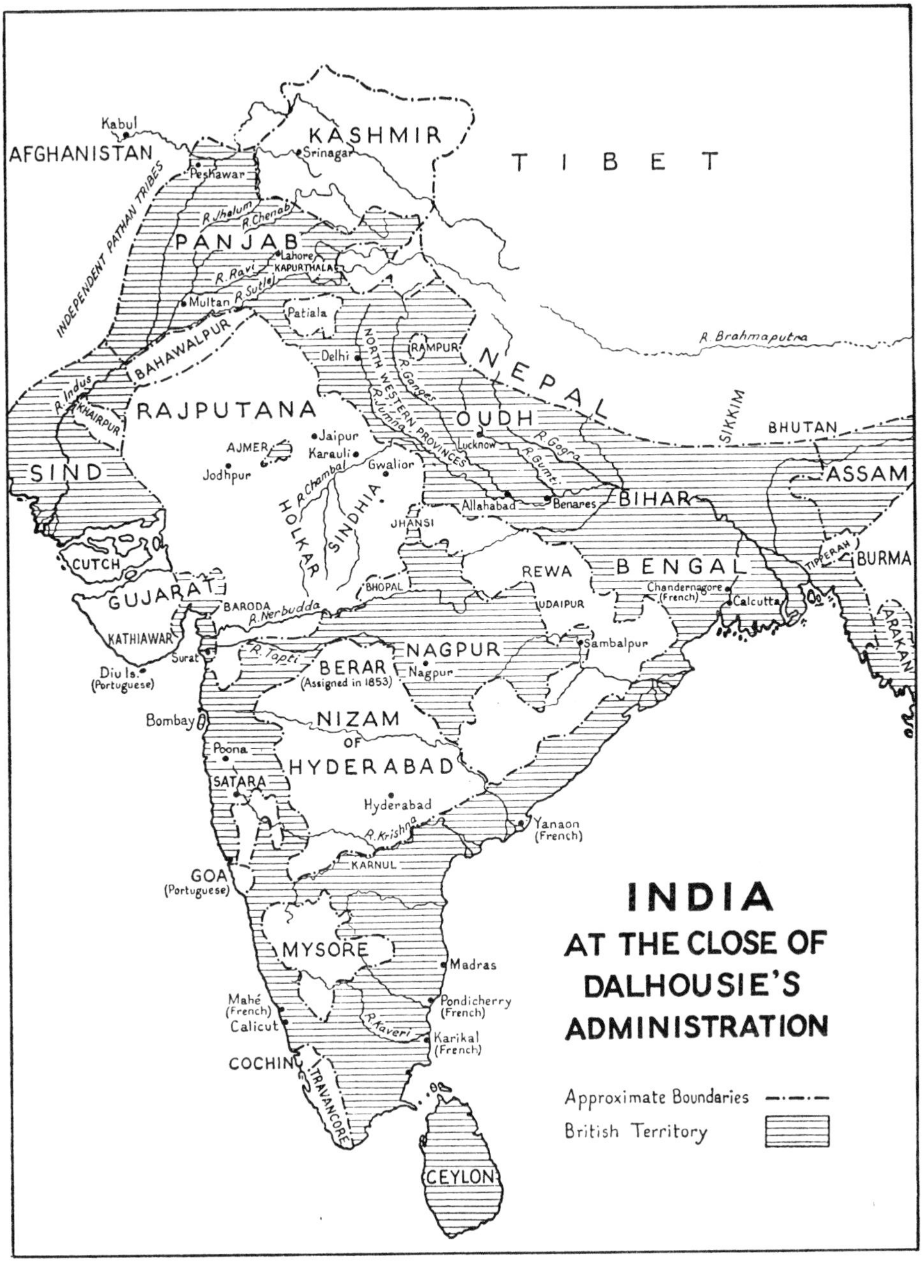
INDIA
AT THE CLOSE OF
DALHOUSIE'S
ADMINISTRATION
Approximate Boundaries
British Territory
Kabul
AFGHANISTAN
KASHMIR
Srinagar
TIBET
Peshawar
INDEPENDENT PATHAN TRIBES
R. Jhelum
R. Chenab
PANJAB
Lahore
KAPURTHALA
R. Ravi
R. Sutlej
Multan
Patiala
BAHAWALPUR
R. Indus
Delhi
RAMPUR
NORTH WESTERN PROVINCES
R. Jumna
R. Ganges
NEPAL
R. Brahmaputra
SIKKIM
BHUTAN
KHAIRPUR
RAJPUTANA
OUDH
Lucknow
R. Gogra
R. Gumti
AJMER
Jaipur
Karauli
Jodhpur
SIND
R. Chambal
Gwalior
ASSAM
HOLKAR
SINDHIA
Allahabad
Benares
BIHAR
JHANSI
CUTCH
TIPPERAH
BURMA
REWA
BENGAL
BHOPAL
Chandernagore
(French)
Calcutta
GUJARAT
BARODA
R. Nerbudda
UDAIPUR
ARAKAN
KATHIAWAR
Surat
R. Tapti
NAGPUR
Sambalpur
BERAR
(Assigned in 1853)
Nagpur
Diu Is.
(Portuguese)
Bombay
NIZAM
OF
HYDERABAD
Poona
SATARA
Hyderabad
R. Krishna
Yanaon
(French)
KARNUL
GOA
(Portuguese)
MYSORE
Madras
Mahé
(French)
Calicut
Pondicherry
(French)
R. Kaveri
Karikal
(French)
COCHIN
TRAVANCORE
CEYLON

MAP IX

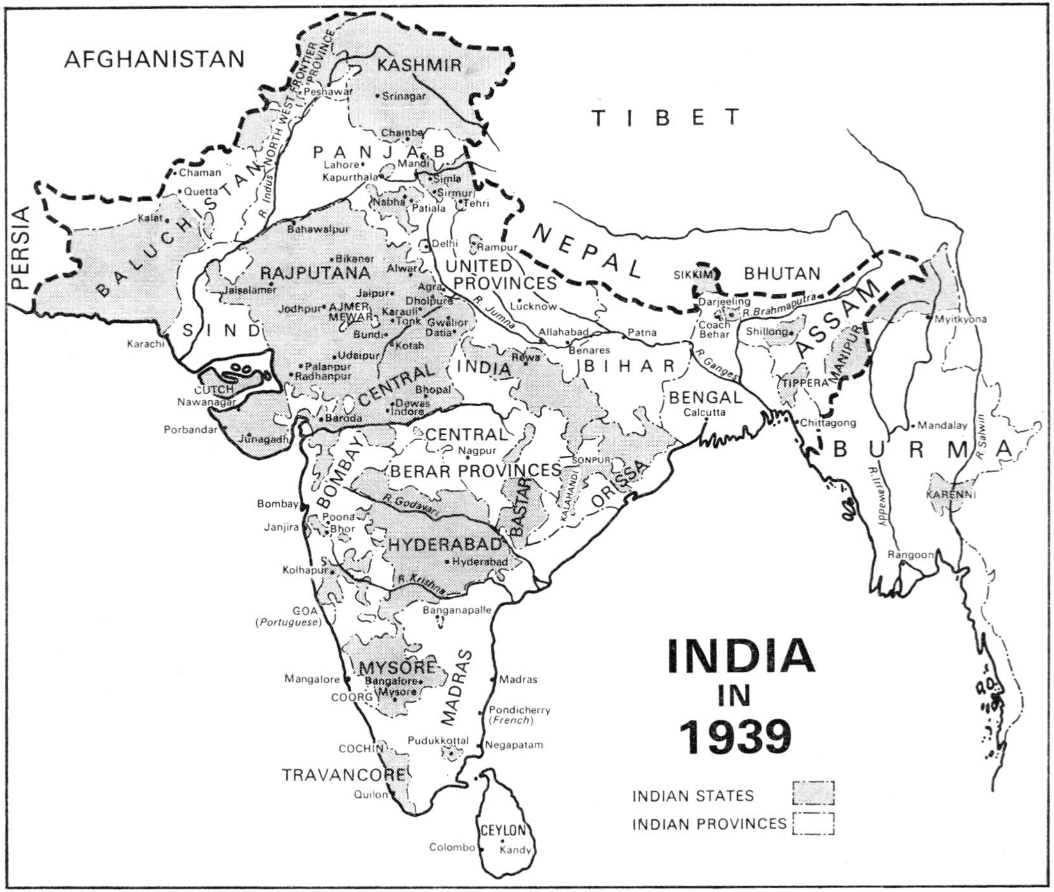
INDIA IN 1939
INDIAN STATES
INDIAN PROVINCES
AFGHANISTAN
PERSIA
TIBET
KASHMIR
NORTH WEST FRONTIER PROVINCE
Peshawar
Srinagar
Chamba
PANJAB
Lahore
Kapurthala
Mandi
Simla
Sirmur
Tehri
Nabha
Patiala
BALUCHISTAN
Chaman
Quetta
Kalat
R. Indus
Bahawalpur
Bikaner
RAJPUTANA
Jaisalmer
Jodhpur
AJMER MEWAR
Alwar
Jaipur
Agra
Dholpur
Karauli
Tonk
Gwalior
Datia
Bundi
Kotah
Udaipur
Palanpur
Radhanpur
SIND
Karachi
CUTCH
Nawanagar
Porbandar
Junagadh
Baroda
CENTRAL INDIA
Bhopal
Dewas
Indore
Rewa
Delhi
Rampur
UNITED PROVINCES
R. Jumna
Lucknow
Allahabad
Benares
NEPAL
SIKKIM
BHUTAN
Darjeeling
Coach Behar
R. Brahmaputra
Patna
BIHAR
R. Ganges
BENGAL
Calcutta
Shillong
ASSAM
TIPPERA
MANIPUR
Chittagong
Myitkyona
Mandalay
BURMA
R. Salwin
R. Irrawaddy
KARENNI
Rangoon
CENTRAL
Nagpur
BERAR PROVINCES
SONPUR
KALAHANDI
ORISSA
BASTAR
BOMBAY
Bombay
Poona
Bhor
Janjira
R. Godavari
HYDERABAD
Hyderabad
Kolhapur
R. Krishna
GOA
(Portuguese)
Banganapalle
MYSORE
Bangalore
Mysore
Mangalore
COORG
MADRAS
Madras
Pondicherry
(French)
Pudukkottai
Negapatam
COCHIN
TRAVANCORE
Quilon
CEYLON
Colombo
Kandy

Map X

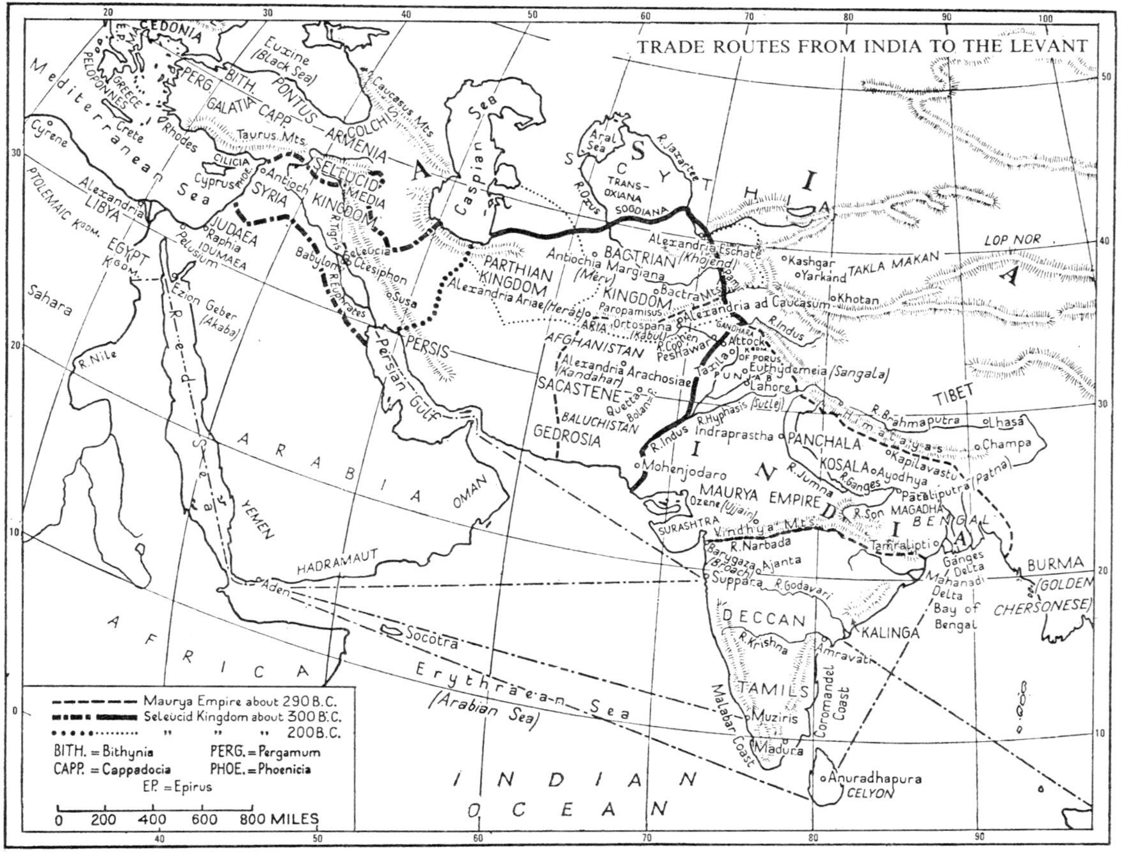

TRADE ROUTES FROM INDIA TO THE LEVANT
Maurya Empire about 290 B.C.
Seleucid Kingdom about 300 B.C.
" " 200 B.C.
BITH. = Bithynia
PERG. = Pergamum
CAPP. = Cappadocia
PHOE. = Phoenicia
EP. = Epirus
0 200 400 600 800 MILES
Mediterranean Sea
Euxine (Black Sea)
Caspian Sea
Aral Sea
Persian Gulf
Red Sea
Erythraean Sea (Arabian Sea)
INDIAN OCEAN
Bay of Bengal
ARABIA
AFRICA
ASIA
SCYTHIA
INDIA
PARTHIAN KINGDOM
BACTRIAN KINGDOM
SELEUCID KINGDOM
MAURYA EMPIRE
TAKLA MAKAN
LOP NOR
TIBET
BURMA
(GOLDEN CHERSONESE)
DECCAN
TAMILS
KALINGA

Map XI

PLATES

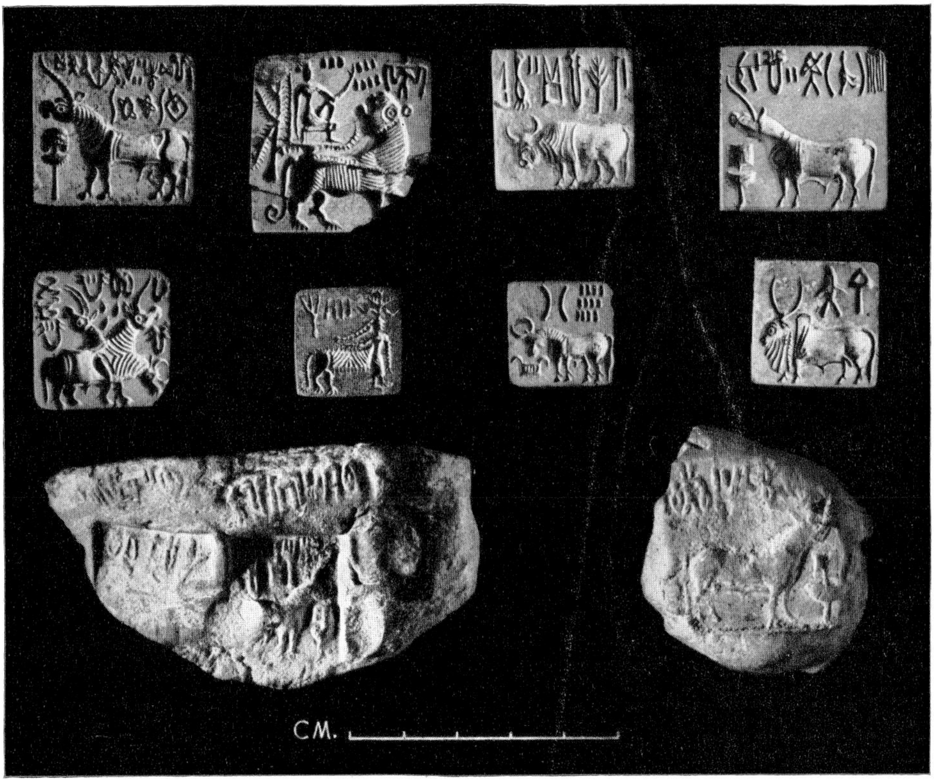

1. Kalibangan: steatite seals (two upper rows) and clay sealings (bottom row)

2. Lothal: cast of obverse and reverse of a seal of 'Persian-Gulf' style

3. Surkotada: general view of the citadel, with entrance-ramp in the middle distance on the right

4. Surkotada: entrance to the citadel, with ramp, staircase, and guardrooms(?)

5. Indo-Greek and Persian coins

1. Persian daric struck in India, *c.* 337 B.C.
2. Athenian *owl*, struck in India.
3. Coin of Sophytes, king of the Salt Range, *c.* 327 B.C.
4. Coin of Eucratides, king of Bactria, *c.* 175 B.C.
5. Coin of Demetrius, king of Bactria, *c.* 190 B.C.
6. Coin of Menander, Greek king of the Punjab, *c.* 165 B.C.

6a. Bronze statuette of Harpocrates from Taxila

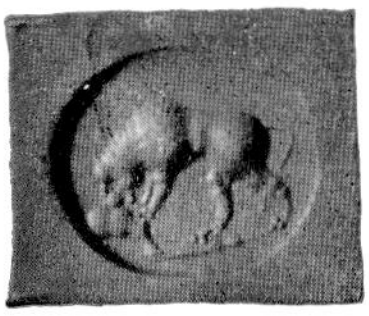

6b. Greek intaglio gems from north-west India

7. North Indian Astrolabe, brass. ? 18th century. Obverse

8. North Indian Astrolabe, brass. ? 18th century. Reverse

9. Samrāṭ yantra: Delhi

10. Mother Goddess, moulded terracotta plaque. Tamluk (near Calcutta). *c.* 1st century B.C. Ht. 20 cm

11. Yakṣa, stone. Besnagar, now in Vidiśā Museum. *c.* 1st century B.C.

12. Seated Buddha, sandstone. Sarnāth. Late 5th century A.D. 1·61 × 0·79m

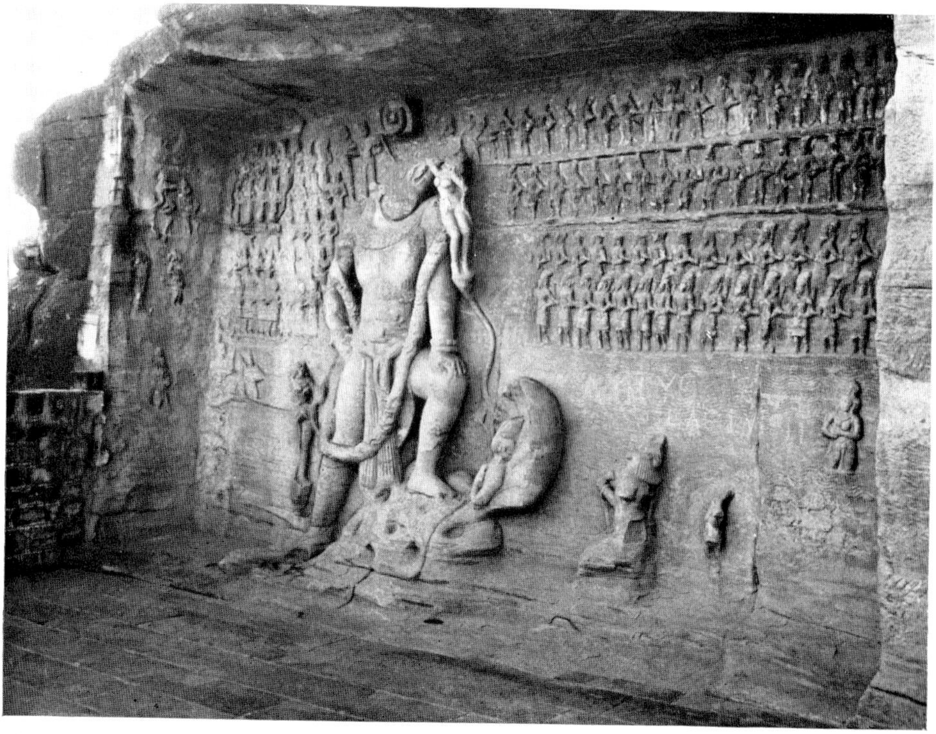

13. Viṣṇu in his Boar incarnation, sandstone. Udayagiri (Madhya Pradesh). Early 5th century A.D.

14. Śivālaya-Malegitti (a Śiva temple). Badami (Mysore State). First half of 7th century A.D.

15. Head of Śiva from an Ekamukhalingam, spotted red sandstone. Mathura. 4th–5th century A.D.

16. Śiva Naṭarāja (Śiva as Lord of the Dance), bronze. From Tamilnadu, probably Pudukottai, Tanjore region. Chola Dynasty. 10th century A.D. Ht. 68·6 cm

17. Bodhisattva. Gandhāra (Graeco-Buddhist). 2nd–5th century A.D.

18. Karli: interior of chaitya cave. *c.* 150 B.C.

19. Nasik: sun-window and horseshoe-arch. *c.* 150 B.C.

20. Bow-harps and flutes, Amarāvatī. *c.* A.D. 200

21. Vīnā in the hands of Sarasvatī. *c.* A.D. 900

22. Ajmer: Great Mosque. *c.* A.D. 1200

23. Delhi: Qutb Mīnār. A.D. 1232

24. Delhi: Tomb of Humāyūn

25. Fatehpur-Sīkrī: the Buland Darwāza. A.D. 1575

26. Agra: the Tāj Mahal. A.D. 1632

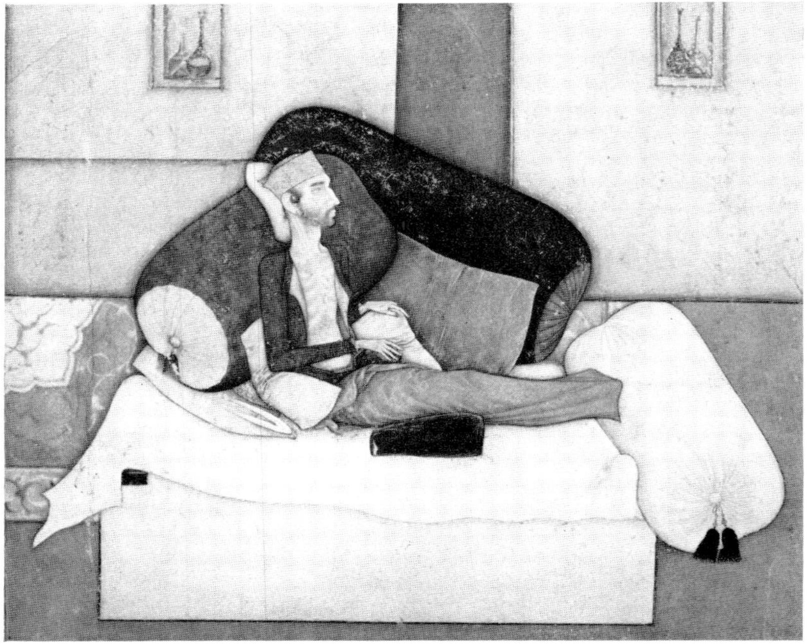

27. The Dying Inayat Kahn, miniature painting. Early 17th century.
12·5 × 15·5 cm

28. *Asvārī Rāginī* (a musical mode personified). Early 17th century.
14·5 × 10 cm